Educational
Innovator's
Guide

AREA OF SCHOOL OPERATIONS	TRENDS TOWARDS	CURRENT EMPHASIS
Instruction	⟶	Individualization
School-Community Relations	⟶	Accountability
Organization	⟶	Flexibility
Climate	⟶	Humaneness
Management	⟶	Participatory Decision-Making
Staffing	⟶	Differentiation And Teaming
Student Goals	⟶	Self-Actualization
Processing	⟶	Systems Approach
Materials	⟶	Broad Variety

Concepts Underlying Present-Day Educational Innovations

Educational

Innovator's

Guide

Herbert I. Von Haden
Miami University

Jean Marie King
Alachua County, Florida, Schools

Charles A. Jones Publishing Company
Worthington, Ohio

Cover adaptation and photo on page 1 courtesy of the Fairfax County, Virginia, Public Schools

Photo on page 65 courtesy of the Gesu Elementary School, University Heights, Ohio

Photo on page 137 courtesy of the Alachua County, Florida, Schools

Photos on pages 251 and 338 courtesy of Highline School District 401, Seattle, Washington

Photo on page 341 courtesy of the Tulsa, Oklahoma, Public Schools

Photo on page 421 courtesy of the Spokane, Washington, Public Schools

1 2 3 4 5 6 7 8 9 10 / 78 77 76 75 74

Library of Congress Catalog Card Number: 72-93897
International Standard Book Number: 0-8396-0034-8

Printed in the United States of America

Preface

Educational Innovator's Guide was written for all those who want to improve education. The material will be beneficial to school board members, administrators, and supervisory personnel who carry special responsibility for charting educational improvement. We hope citizens' groups and other school supporters will find ready information to help them understand proposed innovations and weigh the pros and cons. The material should be valuable to young people preparing to be teachers and teachers in service.

Forty innovations are treated here. Some of them might more properly be called *revivals* rather than *innovations,* but all of them are having an impact on education today and promise to exert increasing influence in the years ahead.

The section for each of the innovations includes:

- A definition of the practice together with background and illustrative material.

- Significant components consisting of conditions that are necessary to make the innovation effective.

- Proposed advantages and claims made by the proponents.

- Opponents' criticisms and difficulties to be anticipated.

- A summary assessment of the present status of the innovation.

- A list of a few leaders and their affiliations and places associated with the movement.

- A complete annotated reference list for that innovation.

At the end of many chapters is a section listing audiovisual and other resources for that innovation. And the index has been developed to be of maximum use in locating educational terms, concepts, leaders, and information within the volume.

The lists of proposed advantages and criticisms have been compiled from presentations at conferences, readings, informal conversations, class discussions, and reflections of the authors— who are appreciative of those listed in the acknowledgments, and to many more, for their valuable assistance.

The arguments for or against an innovative practice may or may not possess validity. Some of them may be quite significant; others may be totally indefensible. All of them, real or perceived, should warrant consideration. They should serve to stimulate further study and help in thoughtful decision-making. Even false impressions and irresponsible objections must be considered and answered if broad support for new practices is to be generated.

Educational Innovator's Guide is designed to help all those who are sincerely interested in weighing the potentials of innovative practices in educational content, organization, and methodology for upgrading programs or making good ones even better. It is our hope that schools may be able to demonstrate their accountability more clearly, to justify continued public confidence and support, and to move forward to serve youth and the nation even more effectively than they have in the past.

Herbert I. Von Haden
Jean Marie King

Acknowledgments

Educational Innovator's Guide takes into account valuable suggestions that have come from many sources—particularly from persons involved in the preservice preparation of school personnel, from those who plan educational change, and from those who bear the everyday responsibilities of working with boys and girls in the classrooms.

The authors are grateful to the graduate students who supplied valuable ideas and assisted in the preparation of the material. Appreciation is expressed to the colleagues and professional friends who reviewed various parts of the manuscript.

Readers' reactions have reenforced our belief, as expressed in the volume *Innovations in Education: Their Pros and Cons,* that ". . . change may be either good or bad." Readers have clearly indicated the need for careful evaluation of innovations before they are substituted for practices that have served well for many years, although these practices may not have completely fulfilled all the diversified needs of children or satisfied all the varied desires of society.

Reactions to the first book also show that some teachers and administrators continue to resist change. Their aversion to adopting new approaches has been most evident in such areas as behavioral objectives, programed learning, and performance contracting. Similarly, public controversy appears to have increased regarding such practices as public aid for parochial and private schools, busing for the purpose of desegregation, and the voucher system. Individualization of instruction, humaneness in education, accountability, environmental improvement and drug education have gained increased support during the past several years.

Alphabetical List of Topics Included

Contents

The Charles A. Jones Publishing Company
International Series in Education

Adams, *Simulation Games: An Approach to Learning*
Allen/Adair, *Violence and Riots in Urban America*
Allen/Barnes/Reece/Roberson, *Teacher Self-Appraisal: A Way of Looking Over Your Own Shoulder*
Anderson, *Education in Anticipation of Tomorrow*
Anderson, *Sex Differences and Discrimination in Education*
Armstrong/Cornell/Kraner/Roberson, *Development and Evaluation of Behavioral Objectives*
Braun/Edwards, *History and Theory of Early Childhood Education*
Brieve/Johnston/Young, *Educational Planning*
Carlton/Goodwin, *The Collective Dilemma: Negotiations in Education*
Congreve/Rinehart, *Flexibility in School Programs*
Criscuolo, *Improving Classroom Reading Instruction*
Crosswhite/Higgins/Osborne/Shumway, *Teaching Mathematics: Psychological Foundations*
Denues, *Career Perspective: Your Choice of Work*
DeStefano, *Language, Society, and Education: A Profile of Black English*
Doll, *Leadership to Improve Schools*
Drier, *K-12 Guide for Integrating Career Development Into Local Curriculum*
Drier, *Career Development Resources*
Elashoff/Snow, *"Pygmalion" Reconsidered*
Epps, *Black Students in White Schools*
Frymier/Hawn, *Curriculum Improvement for Better Schools*
Goodlad/Klein, *Looking Behind the Classroom Door*
Gysbers/Drier/Moore, *Career Guidance: Practice and Perspectives*
Hauenstein, *Curriculum Planning for Behavioral Development*
Higgins, *Mathematics Teaching and Learning*
Hitt, *Education as a Human Enterprise*
Lessinger/Tyler, *Accountability in Education*
Levine, *Models for Integrated Education*
Levine/Havighurst, *Farewell to Schools???*

Lutz, *Toward Improved Urban Education*

Marien/Ziegler, *Potential of Educational Futures*

Mecklenburger, *Performance Contracting*

Nerbovig, *Unit Planning: A Model for Curriculum Development*

Overly/Kinghorn/Preston, *The Middle School: Humanizing Education for Youth*

Passow, *Reactions to Silberman's "Crisis in the Classroom"*

Perry/Wildman, *The Impact of Negotiations in Education: The Evidence from the Schools*

Pula/Goff, *Technology in Education*

Ressler, *Career Education: The New Frontier*

Rich, *Humanistic Foundations of Education*

Shane/Shane/Gibson/Munger, *Guiding Human Development: The Counselor and the Teacher in the Elementary School*

Stevenson, *Introduction to Career Education*

Thiagarajan, *The Programing Process*

Tyler/Williams, *Educational Communication in a Revolutionary Age*

Von Haden/King, *Educational Innovator's Guide*

Von Haden/King, *Innovations in Education: Their Pros and Cons*

Weber, *Early Childhood Education: Perspectives on Change*

Wernick, *Teaching for Career Development in the Elementary School*

Wiles, *Changing Perspectives in Educational Research*

Wiman, *Instructional Materials*

Worthen/Sanders, *Educational Evaluation: Theory and Practice*

Part One
Individualizing Learning

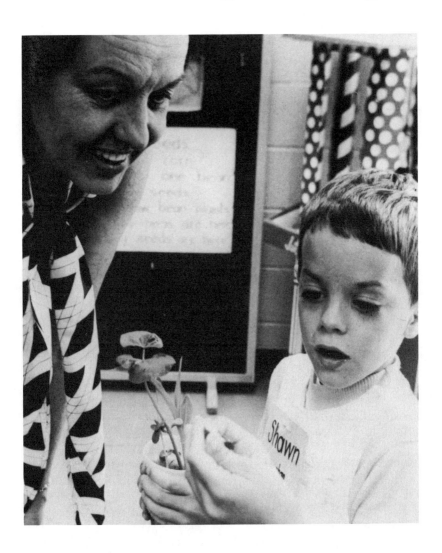

Individualized Instruction

1

Definition

Individualized instruction is the use of a unique learning program for each child. It seeks to identify the social, physical, emotional, and intellectual needs of the learner and to involve him in learning experiences that will fulfill those needs. Precise and clear objectives must be written for each pupil's program so that instruction can be aimed at correcting the identified disabilities and assessment can be made of the extent to which the individual's needs have been satisfied. Because of practical limitations in resources, in the teacher's time and ability, and in the child himself, the ideal of complete individualization will perhaps never be realized. Hence individualization becomes a compromise in the form of differentiation or diversification. Even if a teacher had only one pupil, he would be unable to identify and diagnose all the child's difficulties and make adequate provisions for them.

During recent years the growing concern of many people about the quality of education and the attitude of young people toward their school experience stimulated a reexamination of instructional practices. The appraisal revealed that too often instruction was geared to the average of widely divergent students. Some were uninvolved and labeled as failures, and many gifted pupils were unchallenged and bored. Too often the school failed to look within itself for the cause of poor results. Gradually teachers and lay citizens have come to the realization that mass education has left millions of youth unmotivated and badly equipped for self-actualization and constructive involvement in the affairs of life.

In searching for a solution to the problem, educators have become convinced that the traditional practice of using the same methods and materials to instruct classes of 30 does not work. This approach can neither meet the needs of the children nor produce the results that their parents want and demand. Repeatedly, critics of the schools seeking a better way to promote learning refer to practices of the medical profession. They point out that days and sometimes weeks are spent in analyzing a patient's condition. The diagnosis is always made for each individual. Doctors do not herd 30 patients into a single room and attempt to treat them as one average patient. Like the teacher, the doctor is often unsuccessful in his efforts, but he constantly tries to "doctor the patient where he is sick."

John Goodlad and others have forcefully called attention to the unavoidable need for diagnosing the deficiencies of each individual learner; for determining the root causes of the child's disabilities; and for prescribing materials, methods, and learning activities appropriate for meeting his specific needs. The process of "diagnosis" and "prescription" has become a recurring, almost trite, theme in the professional literature. Putting the concept into classroom practice has, however, been quite a different matter.

The objective of individualization is to take into account all the differences that exist in body chemistry, experiential background, specific interests, purposes, personal needs, and learning skills and styles among children. Having identified these differences, the teacher can offer unique learning experiences to accommodate this perplexing diversification. This approach calls into play the teacher's total philosophy of education, of children, and of teaching and learning. In reality a teacher cannot be an "individualized" teacher; he can only try to provide optimum conditions for an "individualized" learner. He can guide the student toward the realization of his own ability. The pupil must become involved, experience the excitement, and respond to the involvement. He is a unique and individual learner.

A number of teaching-learning systems have been constructed specifically to individualize instruction. The American Institute for Research, for example, and the Westinghouse Learning Corporation have their project, called Program of Learning According to Needs (PLAN), which structures objectives, individualized programs, learning materials and activities, and evaluation procedures. The computer is used extensively. Individually Guided Education (IGE), developed by the Institute for Development of Education Activities (/I/D/E/A/), separates the learning process into four steps. These include the diagnosis of the learner's needs, establishment of objectives consistent with these needs, the learning program, and assessment of outcomes. The Institute is field-testing its system in a large number of schools and is using intermediate agencies—universities, state departments of education, large school systems, and other educational agencies—to facilitate the adoption of the program through inservice training of teachers. Research for Better Schools has its Individually Prescribed Instruction (IPI). It emphasizes independent work, teacher assistance rather than domination, careful diagnosis, and evaluation of results in terms of individually developed objectives.

Significant Components   *Which ones are essential?*

1. Patterns of instruction should change the primary focus of the classroom from teaching to learning.
2. Student-centered teachers should perceive themselves as diagnosticians and facilitators of learning.
3. Creative and imaginative teachers are quick to diagnose problems and see ways in which they can provide appropriate help.
4. Materials, including texts, must be plentiful and varied to accommodate a multi-sensory approach.
5. Effective individualization requires small classes, not only for instruction but perhaps even more significantly for identifying needs and diagnosing deficiencies.
6. Precise, detailed, and clear objectives must be worked out with the learner to guide him in his work.
7. The long-range goals must be understood by teachers, parents, and administrators.
8. Flexible schedules provide for necessary variation in activities and facilitate in-depth independent study.
9. Methods of reporting pupil progress must be individualized rather than based on comparisons among students.

10. It is necessary to make a careful preliminary assessment of each pupil's competence in order to choose the appropriate activities and materials.

11. A variety of space to accommodate large and small group instruction and provide for individual work is important.

12. Lecturing and presentations to the whole group must be kept at a minimum.

13. The learning style of each student must be given careful consideration.

14. Teacher aides and clerical help enable the teacher to give more special attention to the students.

15. Students should be allowed to engage in learning activities of their own choosing and to advance at their own rate.

16. Rigid standards, such as the expectation that children must read in the first grade or spell certain words in the second, must be discarded.

17. Intimate and frequent interaction between student and teacher is essential if the teacher is to know the student well enough to develop an individualized program for him.

18. The student must be allowed to work alone when the need for it is indicated.

19. Provisions must be made for retraining teachers and for maintaining communication with the community.

20. More responsibility for setting the direction of his learning, selecting appropriate procedures, initiating change, and evaluating his results must be placed upon the student.

Proposed Advantages   *With which ones do you agree?*

1. Provision for enrichment and remedial work is a natural part of the program.

2. Individualization reduces the tendency to stereotype students according to intelligence, socioeconomic status, or other factors.

3. Incentives are provided for self-direction, self-motivation, and self-activity.

4. Individualization takes into account variations in learning styles as well as ability and background.

5. Deep involvement of the teacher with the individual student humanizes the learning process.

6. Assuming more responsibility for planning his own learning and achieving results makes the student and his parents more accountable.

7. Pupils may go as far as they can at rates compatible with their capabilities.

8. Greater enjoyment of work results in a decrease in disciplinary problems.

9. Parents who see that the needs of their children are being carefully considered and met are more supportive of the schools.

10. Variable time for completing tasks makes mastery possible and encourages in-depth study.

11. Initiative and creativity are developed.

12. Seeing his students succeed in overcoming deficiencies increases the teacher's satisfaction with his job.

13. Students are given the opportunity to discover new interests and talents that uniform learning activities for the entire class would not uncover.

14. Minimizing failure improves the pupil's self-concept and stimulates him to greater effort.

15. Individualized instruction is conducive to the introduction of new materials and other innovative practices.

Criticisms and Difficulties to Be Anticipated   *Do you agree?*

1. No teacher can devote the time and energy necessary to provide a special program for each child.

2. Students are too immature to participate in planning their programs, to work alone, and to evaluate their own progress.

3. Teachers, as a rule, are not genuinely interested in students as isolated individuals, do not understand them, and do not have special ability in diagnosing difficulties and devising ways of overcoming them.

4. The danger exists that the methodology of individualization will be applied to the study of the same old content, objectives, and materials.

5. Teachers resent the fact that additional burdens are constantly being placed upon them.

6. It is impossible to persuade an entire faculty to change its basic approach to instruction sufficiently to insure success with a program of individualized learning.

7. Retraining supervisors, administrators, and specialists is more difficult than retraining teachers.

8. Common learnings, unity of purpose, and conformity to standards are likely to be neglected.

9. Pupils need more direction and specific assignments than most people realize.

10. Students left to pursue their interests rather than their needs overlook many gaps in learning that will cause them great difficulty in the years ahead.

11. Teachers in succeeding grades cannot assume a common background of knowledge on which to build.

12. Parents, confused and unhappy with unstructured programs, will withhold their support of education.

13. Students who are accustomed to traditional practices find it difficult to adjust to the new approach.

14. It is impossible for a teacher to discover how a student really perceives himself, a basic consideration for diagnosis.

15. Lack of finances makes it impossible to provide the materials and personnel needed to individualize instruction.

Summary Assessment

During the past century and a half, America has struggled with the problems of providing free public education for all its youth. Attention has often been directed primarily to quantitative considerations. Currently, the chief concern is to assure appropriate education for each youth. Qualitative factors are coming into their own.

The behavioral sciences have demonstrated the broad range of differences in intelligence, special talents, interests, backgrounds, frustrations, and satisfactions that children bring to school. Teachers, too, have recognized the many problems that these multifold variations present in the classroom. Rapid growth in school enrollments and shortage of qualified teachers have, in many quarters, resulted in excessive class size and focused attention on group instruction. However, during the last few years the nation's birth rate has declined, and the supply of teachers has increased.

Now the hope grows stronger that, as attention shifts to quality of learning, individualization of instruction may finally come into its own. Many of its advantages have been demonstrated; new materials and a broad range of teaching aids have recently been developed to facilitate its adoption. Although the idea seems definitely to have taken hold, especially among the younger teachers and administrators, its implementation has been slow.

One of the advantages of individualization is that it can be implemented in self-contained classrooms, departmentalized programs, and open-space or team-teaching situations. Large and small schools and all subject areas can find it beneficial. Individualization does not mean a child will always be working by himself on his own special program. He may be part of a large or small group, but something in the experience is intended to meet a personal need that has been identified.

Although individualized instruction is likely to cost more than conventional programs, it can be begun with judicious use of present personnel and other available resources. Teachers usually report that they work harder, but they also report increased personal and professional satisfaction from their success in reaching their students. Pride in greater accomplishment more than offsets the uneasiness that teachers express when they contemplate the changes in philosophy and practice demanded by individualized instruction. Grade standards and group methods must be replaced by different objectives and learning activities for individuals. Concern shifts from whether a child is ready for a particular grade or subject to whether the school and teacher are ready for him. They must be equipped to take the child where he is and help him move forward.

The concerns that teachers have and the difficulty that they experience in changing their roles are natural and should not be ignored. Individualizing instruction requires a teacher who is committed to its philosophy, has faith that children can and really want to learn, and is professionally secure enough to let the child explore and experiment with his own learning. Even those who possess these characteristics are likely to find the change quite difficult in the beginning. The focus must be on learning rather than on teaching. This new emphasis is particularly beneficial in providing compensatory education for the disadvantaged in that it tends to create an atmosphere of humaneness, to discard unrealistic standards and expectations, and hence improve the self-concept of the child. In individualized instruction a close teacher-child relationship is essential so that the teacher can assess the affective as well as the cognitive area and prescribe successfully.

In the classroom, confronting a wide range of talents, disabilities, and differences in needs is inescapable. It is imperative that the successful teacher take advantage of these differences to develop individuality and creativity in his students. Individualization fosters curiosity, discovery, and a desire for continuous learning. It is perhaps the most significant concept with which educators have wrestled during recent years. It suggests promising approaches to the solution of such pressing problems as dropouts, disadvantaged children, education of the gifted, alienated youth, and public reluctance to support education. It should add new dimensions to educational accountability. Research workers will be stimulated to find out more about the different ways in which people learn.

The record of the past decade indicates that individualization is on the move. Grants from governmental and private agencies have provided for experimenting with and installing new programs. Many new teaching materials have been developed. Parents are discussing new approaches to improving learning and demanding that they be considered. Increasingly colleges and universities are stressing individualized instruction in their teacher-education courses.

Reports of improvement in pupil attitudes and behavior as well as in knowledge and skills are encouraging. Students seem to exhibit greater enthusiasm, self-motivation, and ability to evaluate their own progress. They indicate that perceiving different elements of learning in their own ways and developing their own relationships among them add meaning to the educational process. When education is pupil-oriented and humanized, greater interest in learning results. Flexibility in content and process fosters in the student the flexibility in thought and behavior essential for being a productive member of his society.

Nongrading, team teaching, the middle school, programed learning, use of paraprofessionals, audiovisual aids, cybernetics, computers, and better-trained teachers all stand ready to provide unique programs for unique learners. Diagnosis and prescription, the true prerequisites for individualized instruction, may become a reality in the classroom.

A Few Leaders in the Movement

John M. Bahner
  Institute for Development of
  Educational Activities
David W. Beggs
  Indiana Univ.
B. Frank Brown
  Institute for Development
  of Educational Activities

Edward G. Buffie
  Indiana Univ.
John V. Edling
  Oregon State System of
  Higher Education
Alexander Frazier
  Ohio State Univ.

John I. Goodlad
   Univ. of California
   at Los Angeles
Madeline Hunter
   Univ. Elementary School,
   Los Angeles
William Kesson
   Yale Univ.
David Killian
   Miami Univ.
Herbert Klausmeier
   Univ. of Wisconsin

William Olsen
   Pasadena City College
Edwin Reid
   Univ. of Utah
Samuel G. Sava
   Institute for Development of
   Educational Activities
J. Lloyd Trump
   Nat'l. Association of Secondary
   School Principals

A Few Places Where the Innovation Is Used

Baltimore, Md.	Harrisburg, Pa.	Racine, Wis.
Cypress, Texas	Haxtun, Colo.	Salt Lake City, Utah
Dayton, Ohio	Janesville, Wis.	San Francisco, Calif.
Decatur, Ga.	Los Angeles, Calif.	Springfield, Ohio
Denver, Colo.	Melbourne, Fla.	Temple City, Calif.
Duluth, Minn.	Palo Alto, Calif.	Valhalla, N. Y.
Evanston, Ill.	Pendleton, Oreg.	Washington, D. C.
Fort Lauderdale, Fla.	Philadelphia, Pa.	Webster Groves, Mo.
Hagerman, Idaho	Phoenix, Ariz.	West Dover, Del.

Annotated References

Allen, Dwight W., "How You Can Individualize—Right Now," *Nation's Schools,* LXXXI, No. 4 (1968), 43-46. Describes one method of developing individualized instruction. The individually prescribed instruction program, one of the most notable plans in operation today, is used as a model.

Arena, John E., "An Instrument for Individualizing Instruction," *Educational Leadership,* XXVII, No. 8 (1970), 784-787. Explains the IMS (Interrelated Mathematics Science) project which was started at Nova High School. Learning Activity Packages (LAPS) are described. Ten excellent suggestions are made for consideration before a school initiates a program of individual instruction.

Aukerman, Robert C., *Approaches to Beginning Reading.* New York: Wiley, 1971. Presents the significant features of over 100 approaches to beginning reading. Individualized reading approach is described as one which utilizes the interests of children and permits the pupils to select their own reading materials in keeping with those interests.

Baker, Gail L. and Isadore Goldberg, "The Individualized Learning System," *Educational Leadership,* XXVII, No. 8 (1970), 775-780. Makes a distinction between independent study and individualized learning and stresses the necessity of teacher-pupil interaction, behavioral objectives, and a variety of activities. A number of currently used systems are mentioned.

Bergeson, John B. and Charles Roettger, "We Had a Smooth Road," *Instructor,* LXXX, No. 6 (1971), 70-72. Reports success as a result of support from library-media center and building administrator and of careful preplanning of philosophy and procedures as spelled out in five underlying principles. Problems and help to getting started are discussed, and results are explained.

Blake, Howard E. and Ann W. McPherson, "Individualized Instruction—Where Are We?" *Educational Technology,* IX, No. 12 (1969), 63-65. Concludes that we have arrived at the point where individualized instruction programs have proved successful. However, there has been too great a lag throughout the country in installing them in schools.

Bolvin, John O. and Robert Glaser, "Developmental Aspects of Individually Prescribed Instruction," *Audiovisual Instruction,* XIII, No. 8 (1968), 828-831. Describes the current progress that individualized instruction is making. Some of the more successful programs are explained, and their eminent success is reported.

Botts, Robert E., "The Climate for Individualized Instruction in the Classroom," *Journal of Secondary Education,* XLIV, No. 7 (1969), 309-314. Points up the need for having a good individualized program in a continuation high school, where it is necessary to improve self-concepts. Evaluation based on behavioral goals is a necessary part of continuous, individual progress.

DeMarko, Sharon K., "A Place Where Learning Happens," *American Education,* VII, No. 4 (1971), 21-23. Describes a program which treats the learner as a creative person who really wants to learn. The student's motto states his freedom to choose and set goals and his responsibility for the choices that govern his life.

Duker, Sam, *Individualized Reading: Readings.* Metuchen, N. J.: Scarecrow Press, 1969. A compilation of articles about individualized reading. The volume includes specific approaches at various grade levels and contains numerous charts and graphs.

Edling, John V., *Individualized Instruction: A Manual for Administrators.* Corvallis, Oreg.: Oregon State University, 1971. Presents the results of a study of individualized instruction based on visits to 46 key schools in 24 states. Reports of interviews with teachers and administrators, pictures, and other materials illustrate objectives, diagnostic procedures, instructional activities, evaluation, and reporting. Evidence of effects of individualized instruction is discussed.

_____, "Individualized Instruction, The Way It Is—1970," *Audiovisual Instruction,* XV, No. 2 (1970), 13-16. Shows where we are with this innovation and its impact for teachers. Reviews trends in individualized instruction in the last 10 years, the advantages of individualized instruction, and the teacher's role in such a program.

Fantini, Mario D., "Schools for the Seventies: Institutional Reform," *Today's Education,* LIX, No. 4 (1970), 43-44, 60-61. Points out the need for a new conception of education tied to the needs of groups and individuals. Presently education is unequipped and unprepared to provide the required diversity of program. Ten factors are listed that should characterize the reform of the 70's.

Flanagan, John D., "Individualizing Education," *Education,* XC, No. 3 (1970), 191-206. Distinguishes between individualizing instruction and independent study and indicates specific essentials of individualizing education. Details are given about Project PLAN (Program for Learning in Accordance with Needs).

Foster, Walter and Norman Jacobs, *The Beginning Elementary School Teacher, Problems and Issues.* Minneapolis, Minn.: Burgess Co., 1970. Offers the beginning teacher practical helps in procedures and techniques, quite specific yet general enough to be adapted to the various situations encountered.

Frazier, Alexander, "Individualized Instruction," *Educational Leadership,* XXV, No. 7 (1968), 616-624. Deals with the way in which one individualized instruction program (IPI) is already expanding its practices. The staff needs retraining for its new role in organization, communication, and analysis of data for individualization.

Goodlad, John I., *School, Curriculum, and the Individual.* Waltham, Mass.: Blaisdell, 1966. A compilation of papers previously written by the author concerning the function of the school in relation to the individual and society. Reorganization is considered in the light of present and future needs.

Guggenheim, Fred and Corrine L. Guggenheim, eds., *New Frontiers in Education,* pp. 91-103. New York: Grune and Stratton, 1966. Considers free choice of reading material and one-to-one conferences between pupil and teacher to be salient characteristics of individualized reading. The quality and quantity of material, procedures, group teaching, evaluation, and conferences are explained.

Hawk, Richard L., "Individualized Instruction in the School Setting," *Educational Horizons,* XLIX, No. 3 (1970), 73-80. Depicts the school of tomorrow as one characterized by a new level of humanistic emphasis. To discharge its responsibility, balanced adaptation must occur between learner and teacher.

Henry, Nelson B., ed., "Individualizing Instruction," Part I, *The Sixty-first Yearbook of the National Society for the Study of Education.* Chicago: The National Society for the Study of Education, 1962. Contains four sections: Conditions to Encourage or Suppress Individual Differences—Theoretic Issues; Illustrations of Individual Differences; Current School Practices for Individualizing Instruction—Values and Limitations; and Implications of Attempts to Individualize Instruction.

Hensley, Charles, "Individualized Instruction," *School and Community,* LVIII, No. 2 (1971), 32-33, 46. Points out that individualized instruction does mean many things but does not mean other things. Four essential ingredients are suggested: 1) individual pupils work independently and interact with programed material, 2) individual pupils receive counseling, 3) small groups work together, 4) large groups engage in some activities.

Hillson, Maurie and Ronald Hyman, *Change and Innovation In Elementary and Secondary Organization.* New York: Holt, 1971. Offers a collection of readings selected to provide insight into the whole range of innovations that presently mark the educational scene.

Innovation In Education: New Directions For the American School, pp. 38-41. New York: Research and Policy Committee of the Committee for Economic Development, 1968. Stresses the need for instruction that is designed for the individual rather than for the class. Diversified grouping and scheduling, differentiated staffing, and variety of materials and media are promising approaches.

Kinghorn, Jon Rye and Donald E. Overly, "Individualized Instruction," *Ohio Schools*, XLVI, No. 7 (1968), 35. Touches briefly on the philosophy of adapting innovations in education to meet the needs of the local situation. Haxtun High School in Colorado is used to illustrate the points under discussion.

Lewis, James, *Administering the Individualized Instruction Program*. West Nyack, N. Y.: Parker, 1971. Describes the particular atmosphere of the ghetto which tends to "miseducate" children. The author's personal experiences with individualized learning through Individual Study Units are explained.

Lindvall, C. M. and John O. Bolvin, "The Role of the Teacher in Individually Prescribed Instruction," *Educational Technology*, X, No. 2 (1970), 37-41. Stresses the need of a system to help the teacher individualize instruction. Freed from being a continuing dispenser of information, the teacher is able to diagnose, counsel, and prescribe.

McBurney, Wendell, "Individualized Instruction: A Case for the Independent Student Investigation in Science," *School Science and Mathematics*, LXIX, No. 9 (1969), 827-830. Recognizes positive student reaction as a major contributor to the success of individualized science programs in which students define problems and work toward solutions. Twenty-one benefits of individualization are listed.

McNamara, Helen, Margaret Carrol, and Marvin Powell, *Individual Progression*. New York: Bobbs-Merrill, 1970. Presents the theoretical and applied aspects of individual progression. Includes the results of two research studies of individualized instruction programs.

Meizel, Stephen and Gerald G. Glass, "Voluntary Reading Interests and the Interest Content of Basal Readers," *The Reading Teacher*, XXIII, No. 7 (1970), 655-659. Concludes that basal readers must be supplemented even in first grade, since neither primers nor pre-primers corresponded to the actual reading interest of the child.

Mitzel, Harold E., "The Impending Instruction Revolution," *Phi Delta Kappan*, LI, No. 8 (1970), 434-439. Forecasts a thoroughgoing revolution in classroom instruction by the turn of the century. Tailoring material to each learner, new methods of appraisal, and greater heterogeneity among students will characterize the change to individualization.

Ogston, Thomas J., "Individualized Instruction: Changing Role of the Teacher," *Audiovisual Instruction*, XIII, No. 3 (1968), 243-248. Describes a highly individualized program in the Chester Park School, Duluth, Minnesota. Teachers require a great deal of training, and a vast amount of material is needed to carry out a truly individualized program.

Olson, Miles C., "A School for the 70's: An Immodest Proposal," *Clearing House*, XLV, No. 8 (1971), 488-492. Proposes a new high school program to overcome the shortcomings of schools geared to mass education. Personalized programs for individual students are proposed. The financial model is explained which provides stipends for teachers based on the services demanded of them and provided by them.

Renzelman, Al, "Why Not?" *Audiovisual Instruction,* XV, No. 2 (1970), 27. Shows where we are at present in individualized instruction and discusses the new role of the teacher.

Sanders, William B., "Our Road Was Rougher," *Instructor,* LXXX, No. 6 (1971), 70-71, 73. Discusses problems and successes in one room of children who needed special help. The program aimed at developing better people through improving attitudes, expanding interests, and fostering cooperative effort. Positive results are reported in these areas and also in skills.

Saylor, J. Galen and William M. Alexander, *Curriculum Planning for Modern Schools,* pp. 369-401. New York: Holt, 1966. Contains four sections: the dilemma of the individual in mass education, categorizing learners for curriculum differentiation, a continuum of differentiation, and differentiation through the individualization of instruction.

Scanlon, Robert G., "The Expansion of an Innovation," *Audiovisual Instruction,* XIII, No. 9 (1968), 946-948. Offers alternatives or short cuts for instituting a program. In the main, the suggestions are administrative short cuts to individualized instruction and flexibility. Some of the more obvious problems are analyzed.

Shipley, Blanche, "Take the Plunge—I Did!" *Instructor,* LXXX, No. 1 (1970), 82. Suggests strongly that today's teachers better get on the wagon and individualize instruction. Presents the author as a product of the old school of straight rows of chairs and quiet pupils. She prefers the busy and exciting atmosphere of her present classroom.

Stahl, Dona Kofod and Patricia Murphy Anzalone, *Individualized Teaching in Elementary Schools.* West Nyack, N. Y.: Parker, 1970. Contains practical suggestions for putting the idea of individualization to work in the classroom. Individual chapters are devoted to such aspects as pupil teams, homework, questioning techniques, and multimedia.

Taylor, Gary, "The Lone Learner," *Audiovisual Instruction,* VI, No. 4 (1971), 54-55. Presents the argument that the trend toward the individualization of instruction may be undercutting what relevance current curricula do have.

Thomas, George I. and Joseph Crescimbeni, *Individualizing Instruction in the Elementary School.* New York: Random House, 1967. Addresses itself to new concepts in providing for individual differences. Motivation, evaluation, and improving instruction in six subject areas of the elementary school are treated in detail.

Thompson, Scott D., "Beyond Modular Scheduling," *Phi Delta Kappan,* LII, No. 8 (1971), 484-487. Modular scheduling benefits only a minority of students. A client-oriented approach to individualization seems to be a more promising way of providing for student needs.

Turnbull, William D., "The Uses of Measurement in Individualized Education," *Bulletin of the National Association of Secondary School Principals,* LIV, No. 346 (1970), 80-87. Expresses confidence that individualization of instruction is finally becoming a reality. Accurate data of many types are needed for selection, placement, and guidance that will enable learning to fit the student's peculiar needs.

Wang, Margaret C. and John L. Yeager, "Evaluation under Individualized Instruction," *Elementary School Journal,* LXXI, No. 8 (1971), 448-452.

Stresses the need for revising methods of assessing pupil progress in light of the increasing emphasis on individualization of instruction and differences in rate of learning among pupils. The necessity for examining the learning objectives and types of skills to be learned together with the learning opportunities that prevail is emphasized.

Zabawski, Irene, "As Long as My Child Reads," *The Reading Teacher*, XXIII, No. 7 (1970), 631-632. Proposes that it doesn't matter what medium is used to teach a child to read as long as ideas are appreciated, words are readily identified, and speed and fluency are attained.

Audiovisual and Other Resources

Adapting to Student Differences (audiotape, $10). Robert Glaser, chief architect of Individually Prescribed Instruction and former president of the American Educational Research Association, presents his views. Vimcet Associates, P. O. Box 24714, Los Angeles, Calif. 90024.

Elementary School Media Programs: An Approach to Individualizing Instruction (booklet, 32 pp., $1). Study and action publication planned in cooperation with the American Association of School Librarians and the Association for Educational Communications and Technology. American Association of Elementary-Kindergarten-Nursery Educators, NEA, 1201 16th St., N. W., Washington, D. C. 20036.

How to Provide Personalized Education in a Public School (5-film series, 35 to 49 min., complete series $600, rental $180). John I. Goodlad and Madeline Hunter explain theory and show how individualization techniques work. Special Purpose Films, 26740 Latigo Shore Dr., Malibu, Calif. 90265.

Individualization of Instruction (guide, programed workbooks, individualization profiles, evaluation workbooks, transparencies and miscellaneous workshop materials, $125). Programed approach to inservice training in individualizing instruction. Paul S. Amidon & Associates, Inc., 5408 Chicago Ave., S., Minneapolis, Minn. 55417.

Individualized Instruction in Continuous Progress Programs (series of 5 cassette tapes, $39.95). Sidney P. Rollins, dean of graduate studies, Rhode Island College, discusses individualized instruction. Instructional Dynamics Inc., 166 E. Superior St., Chicago, Ill. 60611.

Individualized Instruction Kit (6 filmstrips and audiotape sets, 46 case study brochures and administrator's manual, $87.50; sets may be ordered separately at $12 each). Titles include: Nature and Effects; Objectives and Evaluation Procedures; Diagnostic and Instructional Procedures; Materials and Their Use; Problems and Some Solutions; Recommendations for Implementation. NEA, 1201 16th St., N. W., Washington, D. C. 20036.

Individuals (16mm film, sound, color, 18 min., 1973, $74, rental $10). Shows teacher who allows students to plan and set goals. Also *Learning Strategies* (16mm film, sound, color, 11 min., 1973, $50.50, rental $7.50). Documents Cleveland, Ohio, school which helps students guide their own development. Distribution Branch, National Audiovisual Center, Washington, D. C. 20409.

Multimedia Centers

2

Definition

A multimedia center is a vast treasure house, a creative workshop, a busy learning laboratory. In the treasure house are exciting materials ranging from books, pictures, slides, filmstrips, models, and transparencies to television broadcasting equipment and computers. In the workshop are production areas with materials and equipment from paint brushes to television cameras for the use of media specialists, teachers, and pupils. In the busy laboratory are children surrounded by all learning opportunities and aids that the financial resources of the school district and the imagination of the teachers can discover, produce, and mobilize to assist pupils with their learning. The complete media concept combines the resources of the library, audiovisual department, workroom, and electronic learning center. The terms *multimedia center, instructional materials center,* and *learning resources center* are commonly used interchangeably.

Books, libraries, chalkboards, and other learning aids have been used in schools for centuries; but the years since World War II have been characterized by an expanding technology leading to an explosion of materials, equipment, and concurrent strategies for their effective utilization. As multimedia aids grow in popularity and availability, their presence increases the challenge and opportunities for administrators, teachers, and students.

There are two kinds of multimedia centers. Individual building centers include space, materials, and equipment for the use of teachers and pupils in the learning process. Central, system-wide centers are for curriculum development, inservice improvement of staff, and preparation and distribution of materials and equipment that cannot be provided economically or expeditiously in the individual buildings. In a sense, both are depositories since they keep materials and coordinate use; but their purposes are different, and their personnel perform different functions.

In individual building centers, printed materials and audiovisual resources are readily accessible to teachers and students, both on a group and individual basis. Individual multimedia carrels equipped with screens and other appropriate facilities enable students to pursue independent, often individualized, tasks. Slide trays, audiotape cartridges, filmstrips, transparencies, and film loops lend themselves well to individualized study. Where computer-assisted instruction is used, the learning resources center also contains remote terminals.

But printed materials must not be neglected. Many students and teachers find them to be the most versatile and useful of all materials. Under competent leadership, maintaining a balance between printed and audiovisual resources should not be a serious problem except in very small school districts.

Even in small districts where funds are limited, much progress can be made toward developing a reasonably adequate instructional materials center if the teachers and their principal are committed to the philosophy of such a center. Starting with what they have, they will discover that enthusiastic leadership, sharing of ideas and materials, and careful selection and purchasing of materials and equipment will overcome many handicaps.

Many factors have contributed to the rapid growth of instructional materials centers. During World War II the armed forces developed and used many previously untried devices and methods to accelerate the training of inductees. They had to be prepared quickly for a multitude of jobs for which there were no effective programs for training large numbers. After the war, glowing reports of the effectiveness of the new techniques came from returning veterans and those who had trained them. The urgency of the situation, commitment of the entire nation, and massive defense funding had launched the electronic age.

As demand for the new products of research and development declined, producers naturally tried to generate interest in the civilian economy, including the schools. The sound motion picture, television, and tape recorder rapidly became common media equipment in homes, schools, offices, and factories. Schools were compelled to search for better ways of educating the tidal waves of pupils that descended upon them. Additional impetus was given to the movement toward utilization of the products of technology by government matching funds for development of multimedia centers.

The introduction of media into schools created new situations —housing had to be found, personnel had to be assigned responsibility for media management, and policies and procedures for utilization had to be developed. Although librarians had little experience and in many cases little interest in audiovisual materials and methods, the library seemed to be a logical place in which to establish and conduct a multimedia program. As a result the new instructional materials center combined its functions with those of the library, extended its goals and operations, increased financial support, added personnel competent in the field of multimedia instruction, and moved ahead. The new learning centers are dynamic laboratories and service headquarters for imaginative thinking, creative production, and thoughtful utilization of every conceivable aid to learning.

Significant Components   *Which ones are essential?*

1. It is necessary to prepare the staff in the philosophy of multimedia resources and in skills for effective utilization.
2. To effect full utilization, school systems should devote funds and planning to workshops and other means of media instruction for teachers, supervisors, and administrators.
3. System-wide and individual-building centers are needed, both serving distinctly different and yet overlapping and interrelated functions.
4. Easy access to materials prevents their becoming merely "pretty showpieces."
5. Professionals should not waste time charging out materials; children can assume many routine responsibilities.
6. Evaluation must include assessment of pupil growth, the materials, and the total media program.
7. Pre-purchase consultation, pre-use examination, viewing, and other experiences with materials and equipment enhance the likelihood of effective use.

8. In the individual building centers, space should be provided to facilitate the work of large groups, small groups, and individual students.

9. The budget should be large enough to employ competent personnel and to purchase materials and equipment in sufficient quantity and variety to justify their employment.

10. Long-range planning is essential to avoid duplication of services and equipment and to insure effective utilization of materials.

11. Space, equipment, and supplies should be available and accessible in each building for students and teachers to produce their own unique materials.

12. The district-wide center should stay in close contact with all building personnel, keeping them informed of new acquisitions and improved processes.

13. Wherever possible services of the multimedia center should be available to citizens and groups outside the school.

14. Teachers should have time to experiment with the multimedia center equipment so that they will feel comfortable in using it.

15. Use of aids should be a justifiable part of the instructional program and should be coordinated with it.

16. Special effort should be made to introduce children to materials and their potentials, to show them how to find materials, and to teach them how to use aids for different purposes.

17. Teachers should start where they are and with what materials they have and move forward from there.

18. Continuous experimentation is necessary to determine how to use different aids more effectively and to identify those that are of little value.

19. Attention should be given to such matters as size and adequacy of space, light control, ventilation, size and shape of screens, and freedom from competing interferences.

20. In school construction, the media center should be planned as the instructional nerve center of the building.

21. The media center should provide a climate which encourages constant use of well-selected learning aids.

22. Such facilities as workrooms for teachers, space for viewing and listening, and carrels should not be overlooked.

23. Wherever possible, students should be involved in preparing and presenting materials and in other related experiences.

24. Special attention must be given to the appropriateness of media for specific instructional purposes and for the various maturity levels of the learners.

25. Obsolete and unused materials should be weeded out.

26. Efficiency should be assured in such matters as management, specifications, purchasing, maintenance, distribution, and designing of facilities.

27. Competent technical, production, and clerical assistants are needed for optimum benefits.

28. The director should have a deep commitment to service.

29. Specialists should work together with the teachers as a team in planning the entire program, in selecting materials, and in carrying out the instruction.

30. Provision should be made for rental or lease of materials and equipment not available or too expensive to maintain in a school district.

Proposed Advantages   *With which ones do you agree?*

1. A variety of media provides vital material for learners of different capacities, interests, and learning styles.

2. Student production of materials promotes involvement, motivation, and pupil-team learning.

3. The activities of the learning center can assist teachers in pupil diagnosis and remediation.

4. Learning center activities can add vividness to learning, thus increasing retention.

5. A variety of media lends itself well to instructional systems.

6. Instructional material centers facilitate grouping and individualization.

7. Students are encouraged to assume a greater share of responsibility for their own learning.

8. Exploration, discovery, and decision-making are promoted.

9. Students are helped to avoid overemphasis on verbalism and abstraction by reality of experiences.

10. The availability of new media stimulates curriculum development by opening up new possibilities and a search to realize them.

11. By presenting greater choice to the teacher, media centers make his work more exciting and satisfying.

12. A variety of activities clarifies and demonstrates the relationship between thinking and doing.

13. Media of many kinds conserve time in developing insight and understanding.

14. Multimedia materials assist in showing the sequential steps in a developmental process.

15. By presenting new dimensions, the learner is helped to assimilate old information and reinforce concept development.
16. Tactile and other senses are brought into play.
17. "Learning by doing" becomes a reality.
18. Multimedia materials lend themselves well to the inductive method of developing principles.

Criticisms and Difficulties to Be Anticipated   *Do you agree?*

1. The facilities of the multimedia center are too costly.
2. Establishing a center usually prevents materials from remaining in the classroom, where they should be.
3. Some teachers resent the interference of specialists.
4. Competent media personnel usually cannot be found and cost too much.
5. Multimedia centers are better for training than for educating in its best sense.
6. Media emphasize devices to the neglect of intellectual processes and promote activity for activity's sake.
7. When media people move into instruction, they are out of their field.
8. Failure of materials to arrive when scheduled or difficulty in getting equipment to function properly causes many disruptions.
9. Ineffective leadership can ruin a multimedia center.
10. Some teachers expect machines to do their work.
11. More teachers than like to admit it do not use the materials and equipment.
12. Many materials are inappropriate for the purposes for which they are used.
13. Learners are encouraged to stay too long with the concrete.
14. Transfer is obstructed since the specificity of direct experiences gets in the way of abstraction and generalization.
15. An assumption is likely to be made that sensory experience is equally important to learners at all ages and intellectual levels.
16. Abstractions are necessary for creativity and adaptability to change.
17. Civilization has made more progress through ideas and verbal communication than through manipulation of things.
18. In many instances presentations through the use of media distort reality and mislead the learner.

19. The use of many materials and pieces of equipment often wastes much time in getting to the point of a lesson.
20. Many films, tapes, filmstrips, and other materials are quite mediocre.

Summary Assessment

The past quarter century has brought phenomenal growth in multimedia materials and equipment, particularly electronic devices. The extension has been both in quantity and sophistication. In education, the multimedia center has begun to tear down the walls of the traditional classroom. The diversity of the materials, their increased accessibility, and their growing appeal have begun to revolutionize teaching methods. Well-organized multimedia centers have added new dimensions to teaching and learning and new meaning to individualization of instruction. Few teachers question the value of well-equipped learning centers for stimulating children and individualizing their learning. Relevance and meaning are added to the verbalism of traditional schooling.

It is commonly accepted that accessibility of a variety of materials provides all students with greater motivation, but that it is particularly beneficial for children who, because of limited abilities or unique learning styles, find it difficult to learn from hearing and reading. Pupils become involved in a greater variety of experiences, share them, learn from them, and apparently retain longer what they have learned. Being able to choose from several approaches fosters creativity, initiative, and self-reliance.

Learning centers appear to provide students with greater opportunity to gather data for developing generalizations and attitudes and for testing hypotheses. They appear to improve learning by bringing more of the student's senses to bear upon the learning process. Teachers find the instructional materials center particularly helpful in motivating children and for allowing them to work on problems of particular interest to them. They see new hope for being accountable for the successes and failures of their students.

For some teachers their satisfaction and hopes for even greater benefits are dampened by having many of their plans delayed because of insufficient funds to develop the learning centers as rapidly and as fully as they would like.

Many teachers still have reservations about the real value of some audiovisual aids. They question the appropriateness of these materials for all students and all types of learning. Some believe the audiovisual approach is better suited to training than to education in its broader sense. Others still fear that the computer and other sophisticated devices may destroy the humanizing value of education. A few are apprehensive lest multimedia developments forestall the expansion of study trips, outdoor education, community projects, and other direct experiences with the resources and problems of the community. They believe that much of the feeling and personal interaction of the real world is lost in the representations of the multimedia center.

Whatever the truth regarding these concerns may be, it appears that the expansion of multimedia centers and services will move forward at an accelerated rate as soon as sufficient funds are available. Technology will develop more sophisticated and more versatile devices and systems. Although all schools will not be in a position to take advantage of these improvements, enough districts will have adequate financial resources to encourage their development and examine their effectiveness.

Television has been available to schools for more than twenty years, but many educators feel that they have made too little progress in using its potential as an instructional tool. Experience has verified its power to capture and hold the interest of children and its value for producing many kinds of learning.

Just around the corner, poised with power and potential, stands the computer. Its possibilities are just beginning to be realized. The retrieval of information should in itself be a significant help to teachers and learners. Dial-access systems are gaining in popularity. Educational technology will continue to develop auxiliary display devices to coordinate the use of audiovisual aids with computerized programs. Like other learning aids the computer can be combined with human resources and experiences in the real world to enhance learning, but it is not the answer to all educational problems. Educators must not be misled by its awesome intricacies. Neither should they ignore its untapped potentialities.

Schools can be exciting places in which the needs of individual students are met more adequately than ever before if educators can address themselves with enthusiasm to developing, servicing, and using multimedia centers that even approach excellence. Printed materials, real objects, and representations of objects, which can be read, seen, heard, felt, and manipulated, will continue to provide increasingly richer opportunities for learning. Good centers, however, cost money; and it appears that for the immediate future there will continue to be keen competition for the tax dollar.

A Few Leaders in the Movement

Lucius Butler
  Univ. of Hawaii
Edgar Dale
  Ohio State Univ.
Ralph Ellsworth
  Univ. of Colorado
Carlton Erickson
  Univ. of Connecticut
Ruth Erstad
  Univ. of Chicago
Frank Haley
  Pacific Lutheran Univ.
John B. Haney
  Univ. of Illinois
Marie McMahan
  Kent (Ohio) State Univ.

James Page
  Michigan State Univ.
Neville Pearson
  Univ. of Minnesota
M. G. Phillips
  State Univ. of New York at Albany
G. Donald Smith
  Washington State Univ.
C. Spearman
  Univ. of London
J. Lloyd Trump
  Nat'l. Association of Secondary School Principals
Paul Witt
  Michigan State Univ.

A Few Places Where the Innovation Is Used

Arlington Heights, Ill.
Athens, Tenn.
Ball State Univ.
Baton Rouge, La.
Bibb County, Ga.
Buffalo, N. Y.
Eugene, Oreg.
Farmington, Utah
Grand Island, Nebr.

Grand View, Idaho
Grosse Pointe, Mich.
Hattiesburg, Miss.
Indianapolis, Ind.
Lakewood, Ohio
Madison, Wis.
Mechanicsburg, Pa.
Munster, Ind.
Muskegon, Mich.

Owatonna, Minn.
Pacific Lutheran College
Penfield, N. Y.
Rockville, Md.
San Diego, Calif.
Summit, N. J.
Univ. of Cincinnati
Univ. of Colorado
Washington State Univ.

Annotated References

Anderson, Vernon, "Service is the Center," *Educational Leadership,* XXIII, No. 6 (1966), 447-450. Suggests that learning centers may be spread throughout large school buildings, but that a good system of central cataloging must be maintained. Examples of the variety of learning centers used at the University of Maryland are described.

Bonner, D., "Media Units Grow Into Service Centers," *Audiovisual Instructor,* XVI, No. 5 (1971), 81-82. Explains the regional educational service centers in Texas, which provide materials, technology and consultants, each one adapted to the needs of its own area.

Church, John G., "Creating a Curriculum Laboratory," *California Education,* I, No. 6 (1964), 21-22. Makes suggestions for planning, financing, and establishing a curriculum laboratory. Its functions include curriculum construction and revision, acquisition and dissemination of materials, and assistance to teachers in effective utilization of its resources.

Clark, Patricia, "The Magic of the Learning Center," *California Teachers Association Journal*, LXV, No. 2 (1969), 16-20. Describes the value of the learning center for diagnosis and prescription. The teaching team includes master teachers, specialists, and aides all helping to utilize the facilities for individualization.

Cole, Georgia Rankin, "System-Wide Instructional Materials Centers," *Contemporary Education*, XLI, No. 2 (1969), 74-76. Lists and explains the services which should be performed by the staff of the central media center. Most materials should be kept in the schools, but the central materials center should keep materials that are used infrequently and equipment which is too expensive to have in each school.

Culclasure, David, *Effective Use of Audiovisual Media*. Englewood Cliffs, N. J.: Prentice-Hall, 1969. Gives special attention to the procurement and utilization of hardware and materials necessary for individualized and group instruction. The advantages of different types of equipment and their evaluation are discussed. Practical suggestions are made for planning, budgeting, equipping, and maintaining a functional center.

Dale, Edgar, *Audiovisual Methods in Teaching*. New York: Holt, 1969. Provides a comprehensive coverage of the theoretical considerations of learning, their psychological foundations, materials, and strategies. The "cone of experience" ascends from direct experiences to verbal symbols. Many audiovisual approaches are illustrated with meaningful pictures and diagrams.

Daniels, Paul R., "Learning Centers and Stations: A Different Concept," *Audiovisual Instruction*, XV, No. 9 (1970), 29. Calls attention to some of the problems that have developed with the use of some media, and makes suggestions for improving the learning center.

Darling, Richard L., et al., "IMC—Library Services," *The Instructor*, LXXVII, No. 3 (1967), 83-94. Presents the services of the instructional materials centers in the elementary school of Montgomery County, Maryland. All members of the Department of Instructional Materials participate in planning and developing units for the classrooms.

Davis, Harold, *Organizing a Learning Center*. Cleveland, Ohio: Educational Research Council of America, 1968. Discusses the different types of instructional materials centers, their design, and personnel. Several examples of efficient and well-planned media centers are given, and their special strong points are indicated.

Drummond, T. Darrell, "The Learning Center—A Chance For Every Child," *National Elementary Principal*, L, No. 1 (1970), 30-39. Advocates a variety of assignments for each learning center. Centers should be readily available so the child can proceed at his own pace, be multilevel in expectation, and offer a challenge and success to every child.

Erickson, Carlton W. H., *Administering Instructional Media Programs*. New York: Macmillan, 1968. Reviews the whole range of media administration and use. Individual chapters deal with many aspects such as organization, staffing, physical facilities, implementation, and budgeting.

Fite, R., "In-Service Training on Long Island," *Educational Screen and Audiovisual Guide,* XLII, No. 1 (1963), 26. Discusses a practical preparation and utilization plan of audiovisual material in Central High School, Merrick, Long Island. Resource people were used and an aggressive inservice teacher training program was coupled to a good audiovisual center.

Foley, Margaret, "Instructional Materials Center in the Elementary School," *American Library Association Journal,* April 15, 1962, 18-20. Listing of what belongs in an elementary instructional materials center. The ways in which this center can service the needs of teachers and students are discussed.

Hall, Sedley D., "The Instructional Materials Center," *Elementary School Journal,* LXIV, No. 4 (1964), 210-213. Contrasts the centralized center with the centers in the individual school buildings. In the future both types will be essential in a good school system, with the centralized center supporting the others.

Haney, John B. and Eldon J. Ullmer, *Educational Media and the Teacher.* Dubuque, Iowa: Wm. C. Brown, 1970. Discusses in detail the relationship between media resources and the 1) establishment of goals and objectives, 2) development of strategies, 3) implementation of instruction, and 4) evaluation of outcomes. Valuable references are provided for a media bookshelf, periodicals in educational media, guides for media materials and equipment, and media materials on media.

Hatfield, Frances, "Using Media in Our Teaching," *The Instructor,* LXXX, No. 3 (1970), 58-60. Expresses the enthusiastic support of three teachers from Palmview School in Pompano Beach, Florida, of their open-plan school, designed around a multimedia center, and their rewarding experiences as teachers there.

Herman, Jerry J., "The Instructional Service Center: A New Concept?" *The American School Board Journal,* CXLVIII, No. 2 (1964), 17-19. Defines the Instructional Service Center and its purposes. The operation is seen as primarily central. A chart depicts the scope of operation by material type to show where Dr. Herman believes various materials should be—central location or individual building.

Knight, Hattie and Elsie Dee Adams, "The IMC Concept," *Peabody Journal of Education,* XLV, No. 5 (1968), 303-305. Discusses the contents and functions of media centers and contrasts the functions of the traditional librarian with the responsibilities of a modern media coordinator. Use is the criterion of quality.

Krohn, Mildred L., "Learning and the Learning Center," *Educational Leadership,* XXI, No. 4 (1964), 217-222. Describes a project with the Ford Foundation in Shaker Heights, Ohio. Two elementary schools have been remodeled to include extensive learning centers. These allow and encourage teachers and pupils to work on projects of specific and real interest to them.

Lewis, Philip and John V. Deal, "Coming Attractions in Technology," *Nation's Schools,* LXXXVI, No. 4 (1970), 70-77. Points out some of the recent developments in educational technology. The electron video recording is discussed along with improvements in the media.

Lister, A. J., "Feedback and the Audiovisual System," *The Times Educational Supplement,* 2878, July 17, 1970, 39. Explains how painted wooden cubes, electronic switchboards, and closed circuit televisions can provide immediate feedback for evaluation to instructors and learners.

Mead, Melvin, "Planning Media Centers: Prescription vs. Communication," *Educational Screen and Audiovisual Guide,* XLVIII, No. 10 (1969), 8. Presents the idea that students should be more involved in planning media centers and in selecting materials. Teachers, administrators, and media specialists should seek suggestions and advice from students.

Medlicott, Paul, "Escape Through Machines," *The Times Educational Supplement,* 2886, September 11, 1970, 20-21. Describes how some educational machines are helping the director of a school for the severely retarded. He attempts to overcome feelings of inadequacy and to teach coping with the simple daily necessities.

Neagley, Ross L., N. Dean Evans, and Clarence A. Lynn, Jr., *The School Administrator and Learning Resources.* Englewood Cliffs, N. J.: Prentice-Hall, 1969. Develops the team concept of administrative leadership in curriculum development and in relating learning resources to instruction. Plant planning, organization of resources, financial guidelines, and evaluation are discussed.

Pastoret, Gertrude, "Classroom Centers for Independent Learning," *Audiovisual Instruction,* VIII, No. 8 (1963), 574-577. Explains three types of classroom centers: viewing, listening, and exploring. The ways in which each may be used is described and illustrated.

Pate, G. B., "Beginning An Instructional Materials Center," *Michigan Educational Journal,* XLI, No. 11 (1964), 30-31. Explains how the goals of the materials center at Livonia Junior High School call for a center for student work and study, planning center for teachers, and a program that would carry learning materials into every teacher's classroom. These goals have been attained through the involvement of teachers.

Pearson, Neville P. and Lucius Butler, *Instructional Materials Centers Selected Readings.* Minneapolis, Minn.: Burgess, 1969. A compilation of articles written in various periodicals from 1959-1969. The readings are organized into the following sections: The Philosophy of the IMC, The Elementary School, The Secondary School, The College and University, Operation of an IMC, Personnel of an IMC, and Evaluation of an IMC.

Pfeil, M. P., "Off the Shelf and Into the Classroom: Mobile Educational Technology Unit," *American Education,* VI, No. 7 (1970), 13-16. Advocates the training of teachers in the use of audiovisual equipment. After receiving training from a county mobile unit, teachers in one school were able to make their classrooms come alive with interest.

Ray, Henry W., "Designing Tomorrow's School Today: The Multi-Sensory Experience Center," *Childhood Education,* XLVII, No. 5 (1971), 254-258. Describes a circular multisensory experience laboratory in a Warminster, Pennsylvania, elementary school which produces various geographical environments incorporating vision, sound, odor, and temperature, and which converts to a planetarium, a theatre, a dance studio, or a light and shadow experience.

Simmons, Marilyn, "Learning Centers in a Self-Contained Classroom," Annapolis, Md., 1970. 15 p. available from ERIC Document Reproduction

Service, 4936 Fairmont Ave., Bethesda, Md. 20014; microfiche, $.65; hardcopy, $3.29; order number ED 046 647. Describes a learning center in a classroom where activities in concept development and skill reinforcement are self-selected, self-motivated, self-paced, and self-corrected.

Squyres, Weldon, "Four A-V Wonders Boards Will Buy in the Seventies," *American School Board Journal*, CLVIII, No. 5 (1970), 45-48. Enumerates the advantages of four of the media in use today—the cassette audio tape recording, simplified video tape recording, random access audio-video system, and the computer.

Sylwester, Robert, Jack Middendorf, and Darrel Meinke, "Four Steps to a Learning Center," *The Instructor*, LXXVI, No. 10 (1967), 73-84. Describes four maxims—learn how, put to use, buy wisely, and arrange well. Many suggestions are made in each section, with references to obtaining specific kinds of media.

Tanzman, Jack, "Cost of Audiovisual Instruction," *School Management*, XIV, No. 10 (1970), 25-29. Reports on the amount of money spent for audiovisual material during the school year 1969-70. Charts show expenditures by school districts and for the more popular equipment items.

————, "What You Need to Build an Instructional Media Center," *School Management*, XV, No. 1 (1971), 62-63. Describes the specific qualifications needed by both a flexible librarian and an audiovisual coordinator in a media center to accomplish planning, teacher training, evaluation, and storage and care of equipment.

Tozier, Virginia, "The Child and the Library Center," *Educational Leadership*, XXI, No. 4 (1964), 223-226. Views the IMC as a place where pupils go to choose books and use educational media of interest. Educational TV is utilized to keep pupils in touch with the center and to teach them to utilize the library and its many contents. Teachers meet as teams to make best use of the center—much joint planning.

Turk, Beatrice, "Blueprint for Media Centers," *Catholic School Journal*, LXX, No. 2 (1970), 11. Gives helpful suggestions for setting up a good multimedia center. Having up-to-date materials which are well catalogued and easily accessible to all students is basic.

VanderMeer, Abram W., "The Impact of New Materials and Media on Curricular Design," *Educational Technology*, X, No. 4 (1970), 53-57. Suggests that a variety of media provides for achieving a wider range of goals. Appropriateness of content and method in relation to the needs and learning styles of teachers and students is important.

Van Wyck, W. F., "Reducing Teacher Resistance to Innovation," *Audiovisual Instructor*, XVI, No. 3 (1971), 90-91. Proposes some conditions which are necessary for any innovation to succeed. Opposition feels that media mechanize instruction and lose feedback, and that they should be reliable, easily obtained, and simple to operate.

Washington Office of State Superintendent of Public Instruction, "Program for the Learning Resources Center; Standards for Integrating School Library and Media Services," 1968. Available from ERIC Document Reproduction Service, order number ED 048 883. Delineates the quantitative standards for the learning resources for the schools in the state of Washington, with the purpose of setting a basis for the evaluation of their programs.

Wey, Herbert W., *Handbook for Principals,* pp. 55-60. New York: Schaum, 1966. Provides a concise, but comprehensive, outline of the principal's responsibilities in supervising an audiovisual program; in producing, selecting and using materials; and in evaluating the program. Numerous suggestions are made for effective performance in each of the four areas.

Wiman, Raymond and Wesley Meierhenry, eds., *Educational Media: Theory into Practice.* Columbus, Ohio: Merrill, 1969. Considers the importance of the effect of mass media on society and particularly on education. Communication theory and process are developed in the context of their significance for learning. Learning-systems concept and media centers enhance opportunities for rich experiences.

Audiovisual and Other Resources

And Something More (film, color, 28 min.). Shows a Charlotte, North Carolina, elementary school library which is a center for all instructional materials. Audio-Visual Utilization Center, 5448 Cass Avenue, Wayne State University, Detroit, Michigan 48202.

Educational Media (filmstrip, record, script, 16 min., $10). Surveys media available. NEA, 1201 16th St., N. W., Washington, D. C. 20036.

IMC Bibliography (booklet, $1.20). Information about staffing and operating an instructional materials center. Educational Research Council of America, Rockefeller Bldg., Cleveland, Ohio 44113.

Making a Library a Learning Center (filmstrip). Essential Education, Box 968, Huntsville, Tex. 77340.

The Media Center (filmstrip, record). Library Filmstrip Center, 3033 Alama, Wichita, Kan. 67211.

The Media Center in Action (16mm film, 13½ min., $150). Coronet Instructional Materials, 65 E. South Water St., Chicago, Ill. 60601.

Media Programs for Individual Schools (filmstrip, tape, 15 min., $10). NEA, 1201 16th St., N. W., Washington, D. C. 20036.

New Arrangement for Learning—The Media Facilities Story (filmstrip, record). University of Washington, Seattle, Wash. 98105.

New Dimensions Through Teaching Films (16mm film, color, 27 min., $100). Set in an instructional materials center, the film shows the role of film as an educational tool. Coronet Instructional Materials, 65 E. South Water Street, Chicago, Ill. 60601.

Teaching the One and the Many (16mm film, color, 28 min., 1968, $175, rental $10). Reviews technology, hardware and software available to schools. NEA, 1201 16th St., N. W., Washington, D. C. 20036.

The Nongraded School 3

Definition

Nongrading is a philosophy of teaching and learning which recognizes that children learn at different rates and in different ways and allows them to progress as individuals rather than as classes. Such designations as grade one or grade three are eliminated. Flexible groupings allow the pupil to proceed from one level of work to another whenever he is ready. Thus the child's progress is not dependent upon that of others in the room. His own readiness, interest, and capacity set the pace for each pupil. He learns that he actually controls his own learning and is expected to assume increased responsibility for its management.

In theory, an ideal nongraded school would discover all the needs, interests, abilities, and deficiencies of each child and provide a unique program for him. However, the constraints of time, money, and energy make this impossible. Actual practice, then, strikes a compromise between a completely individualized approach and conventional instruction by grades.

Flexible grouping permits each child to move ahead with other children of approximately the same level of ability. Groupings are different for each subject area and can be changed at any time. Failure, retention, and skipping of grades are replaced by continuous progress as the pupil proceeds at his own rate. Slower children are not forced to go on with the class group before they are ready. Faster workers are not compelled to wait for the others. Individualization and continuous progress are the key elements of nongrading.

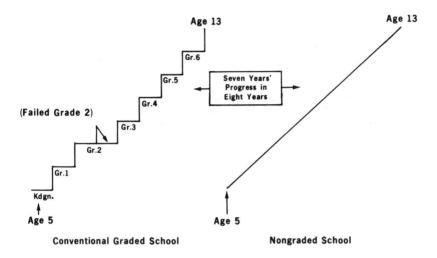

The Nongraded School: Replacing Irregular, Disrupted Advancement with Smooth, Continuous Progress.

Those who look upon the nongraded school as a radical departure from standard practice are often surprised to learn that the history of the graded school is really quite short. The Quincy Grammar School, generally considered to be the first American school established as a graded school, was built in Boston in 1848. Separate rooms were provided for groups of children of one age. Economy of time and effort was effected by having the teacher conduct recitations for the entire class and by using the same texts for all children in the room.

The one-room schools in rural areas, including pupils from age five to 15, continued to operate on an ungraded basis well into the twentieth century. Here the teacher gave the children books and assigned lessons which he considered appropriate for each maturity and educational level.

William Holmes McGuffey, whose readers dominated the elementary schools for almost a century, wrote his *First Eclectic Reader* to help teachers help children begin to learn to read. To him it was not important whether the pupil was five or 12 years old. His was not a "first-grade reader." It was the "first" in a series of increasing difficulty. When the child had mastered the first reader, he moved to the second in a program of continuous progress. *McGuffey's Alternate Readers* were "intended to furnish additional reading in those schools where it is felt that such fresh reading-matter is necessary or desirable." In McGuffey's thinking a child might complete half of the first reader, or he might master four readers in one term depending upon his capabilities, the number of days that he attended school in a given term, or any other pertinent factors. When the pupil was ready, he was encouraged to proceed to reading the Bible or *Pilgrim's Progress.*

Publishers provided vital help to teachers in advancing learning, but unknowingly they contributed to the establishment of a rigid graded system. Within a few years after the opening of the Quincy Grammar School, texts shifted their emphasis to mass instruction. In Noah Webster's *Elementary Spelling Book* the publishers announced to "teachers and school officers" that they could secure "standard books in every department of study and for every grade of schools."

Ray's Mathematical Series, published in 1877, included 14 volumes ranging from primary arithmetic to differential and integral calculus. *Ray's New Primary Arithmetic* began with counting objects and writing numbers and, in the 94 pages with 89 short lessons, moved to "liquid or wine measure," "apothecaries weight," "fathoms," "farthings," "quires," "circular measure," "pounds Troy," "quartos," and "octavo." The book did not specify what should be taught in a particular grade.

In the course of a half century the innovative graded school had become the traditional elementary school. The new philosophy had become commonly accepted. Grade standards and norms were definitely established. The pupil was expected to fit the curriculum. Children should not be admitted to first grade until they were mature enough to do first-grade work. They should not be passed to fifth grade until they had met the standards for completing fourth grade. Instead, they should be failed or "retained" to begin again in September with the first lesson in every subject and every text.

In the autumn the teacher who discovered children with learning disabilities in his room was comforted by the conviction that the previous teacher had made a mistake. He was sure these students should have been failed. To maintain professional respect among their colleagues, teachers often felt constrained to fail children who did not meet grade standards although they knew full well that the repeaters would do no better the secor or third time around. Whether the pupils had special handicap or had been in school only part of the term was considered irrele vant. Grade standards were the deciding factor. Teachers faile children, and children failed grades to the dismay and frustratio of both. The nonmotivated child and the defeated teacher wer being spawned.

About the time the graded school became firmly entrenched thoughtful teachers began to question the basic assumptions of which it rested. Should all students be expected to progress a the same rate? Should slower learners be humiliated because they cannot keep up with their faster classmates? Should bright pupils mark time while the teacher drills and re-explains to some of the others? Should graded materials and mass in-struction be geared to the average of the class, those who possess leadership potential, or those who need help most? Is mass education in graded classrooms really working? What can be done to improve the situation? Teachers read such disturbing statements as, "If a child fails, it is really the teacher who has failed."

The seeds of individualization of learning were sown in the minds of conscientious teachers who were searching for a better way of helping children. Interest turned to exploring the pos-sibilities of breaking the lock step by returning to a nongraded program characterized by continuous progress. The beginnings appeared in such school districts as Western Springs, Illinois, 1934; Richmond, Virginia, 1936; Athens, Georgia, 1938; and Youngstown, Ohio, 1938. In the 1940's Florence C. Kelley of Milwaukee, Wisconsin, was using the term nongraded in plan-ning changes in the primary school, and a decade later John I. Goodlad and Robert H. Anderson began to assert their leader-ship.

In a sense, the nongraded school represents a return to many principles and organizational patterns of a former era. Advances in knowledge of young people and how they learn, better trained personnel, and improved facilities of many kinds should insure that the strengths of the old and the new are blended to the advantage of children.

Presently the nongraded concept is most common in the primary unit, is frequently incorporated in the program of the middle school, and is slowly gaining acceptance at the secondary level. It requires flexibility in time schedules, in grouping, and in diagnosis and evaluation. An abundance of material of varying interest and difficulty is essential. Rate of progress of each pupil varies from one subject to another. Many modifications exist under the name of nongradedness. No common pattern has yet emerged, and it appears that no such pattern could serve all situations with equal effectiveness.

Significant Components   *Which ones are essential?*

1. Grade levels, grade labels, and grade expectations are discarded.
2. Allowance must be made for varying maturity levels, developmental tasks, and learning rates within a group of pupils and within an individual pupil.
3. Only teachers who possess a philosophy of, and commitment to, nongrading and individualization can succeed in the program.
4. Teachers must be willing to function as facilitators of learning rather than as dispensers of information.
5. Sound principles of the philosophy of education, psychology of learning, and mental and physical development must be dominant in the program.
6. The support of the entire school system, as well as that of the pupils and parents, is necessary.
7. Continuous program revision should be an integral part of the process.
8. A wide variety of materials, both in regard to difficulty and interest, must be available.
9. Flexibility in staff utilization, program scheduling, and grouping of pupils must be provided.
10. It must be recognized that instituting a nongraded program demands additional time and energy and is likely to require some additional money.
11. Moving pupils from one level or one group to another must be flexible.
12. Dynamic and imaginative supervisory leadership is a prerequisite to success.
13. Sufficient time should be allowed to prepare teachers and administrators, orient the community, secure materials, and plan the organization and sequence of the program in order to insure its success.
14. Opportunity in terms of space and personnel should exist for working with pupils in small groups and on a one-to-one basis.

15. Appropriate procedures must be developed for evaluating progress and reporting it to the children and their parents.
16. It should be recognized that some pupils may learn better than others in a more structured program.
17. Unless the principal is vitally interested in nongrading and gives it strong support and dynamic leadership, it is not likely to succeed.

Proposed Advantages   *With which ones do you agree?*

1. A sense of success, confidence, and self-reliance enhances positive development of the student's self-concept.
2. The elimination of pressures due to boredom and excessive competition reduces many forms of undesirable behavior.
3. The dilemma of whether to promote or retain a pupil at the end of the year is avoided.
4. Because teaching and learning become matters related to a specific child, teachers are likely to work more closely with parents.
5. By progressing at his own rate, the pupil may avoid the damaging effects of failure and repetition.
6. The philosophy moves in the direction of individual diagnosis and prescription.
7. Children who are absent from school for extended periods may resume their work more smoothly and more effectively.
8. The program provides a stimulus for experimentation and the introduction of new and different practices.
9. Improved mental and emotional health is a likely result.
10. Since it is an inherent part of the total operation, special help is no longer a special consideration.
11. Seeing each child make progress gives teachers a great deal of joy and satisfaction.
12. Continuous progress eliminates the gaps that occur when pupils miss certain aspects of instruction because of double promotion.
13. The program provides for more careful diagnosis and more adequate counseling in regard to personal as well as academic problems.
14. Pupils develop better attitudes toward school, learning, and their teachers.
15. The problem of different rates of forgetting, particularly during vacation periods, is minimized.

16. There are many social advantages in having children of differing ages and diverse abilities working together.
17. Pupil learning, rather than years spent in school, becomes the basis for assessing progress.
18. The greatest advantage of nongradedness is individualization of teaching and learning with resultant increased achievement.

Criticisms and Difficulties to Be Anticipated   *Do you agree?*

1. Too much time and planning are needed to establish and carry out an effective nongraded program.
2. Children may be unhappy if the changes from group to group are not made smoothly.
3. Because nongrading requires a flexible personality, teacher turnover may increase because of requests for transfer or resignations.
4. Some competent older teachers find it difficult to change their thinking and procedures.
5. Most textbooks are designed for graded programs.
6. Misunderstanding often occurs about philosophy, purposes, procedures, and evaluation.
7. Excessive time may be spent with parents because they have no way to understand the progress of their children.
8. Failure to prepare and involve the community will result in confusion and dissatisfaction.
9. The nongraded concept is not feasible at the high school or junior high level, particularly if the elementary levels are not ungraded first.
10. There may be a tendency on the part of teachers to persist in reverting to uniform expectations and standards.
11. It is not certain that improved learning will result.
12. The wide range of needed instructional materials makes the program expensive.
13. Colleges are not training teachers for the program, and experienced personnel is scarce.
14. Transition to a graded system at the end of the nongraded experience may cause difficulty.
15. Serious problems may arise when pupils transfer into or out of the school.
16. Parents may exert pressure to move children to higher levels before they are ready.

17. Teaching teams may break off communication with other teams and become isolated.
18. Pupils will not put forth effort to achieve grade standards because nongrading has no fixed standards.
19. Whether a pupil passes or fails is left entirely to the teacher's judgment.
20. Most nongraded programs merely substitute levels for grades.
21. Increased time will be devoted to diagnosis, record keeping, and reporting.

Summary Assessment

Recent concern about problems of education in the large cities and recognition of the shattered self-image of many nonmotivated children have spurred educators to seek new approaches. Currently nongraded programs appear to hold promise for enhancing the self-concept of pupils by eliminating continual failure. Some pupils benefit from having the additional time needed for mastering certain elements, and others are spared the boredom brought about by wasting time waiting for their slower classmates.

The need for careful planning to develop agreement on purposes and procedures cannot be overemphasized. A poorly conceived program is likely to fail. Undue difficulty in implementing a nongraded program may discourage teachers and force them to abandon the program, making it impossible to generate interest in trying again after an unsuccessful first attempt.

Somewhat surprisingly, many teachers report that parents who understand the principles, purposes, and practices involved see great promise of enhanced learning opportunities for their children. Teachers are aware of the additional time they must devote to their work, but appear to receive increased satisfaction from their efforts. Because of the demands of time and effort, the nongraded program requires teachers of great skill and commitment. However, the new approach proposes to raise the self-image of children beaten down by repeated failure, motivate them to greater effort, and increase their feeling of responsibility for their own learning. The concept of nongrading could very well usher in an era of schools without failure. If it can contribute to these ends, the price of additional time and effort is indeed low.

A Few Leaders in the Movement

Robert H. Anderson
  Harvard Univ.
B. Frank Brown
  Institute for Development
  of Educational Activities
Jerome Bruner
  Harvard Univ.
Edward G. Buffie
  Indiana Univ.
Ruth Chadwick
  Horace Mann School
Robert DeLozier
  Univ. of Tennessee
Lillian Glogau
  Plainfield, N. Y.
John I. Goodlad
  Univ. of California at Los Angeles

Maurie Hillson
  Rutgers Univ.
James Lewis, Jr.
  Davenport College
Jimmy Nations
  Montgomery County, Md.
Daniel Purdom
  Univ. of South Florida
Lee L. Smith
  South Frederick, N. J., Schools
John L. Tewksbury
  Ohio State Univ.
J. Lloyd Trump
  Nat'l. Association of
  Secondary School Principals

A Few Places Where the Innovation Is Used

Amherst, Ohio
Appleton, Wis.
Beavercreek, Ohio
Bellevue, Wash.
Boston, Mass.
Brunswick, Md.
Cedar Falls, Iowa
Cincinnati, Ohio
Covington, Ky.
Des Plaines, Ill.

Essexville, Mich.
Franklin, Ohio
Greeneville, Tenn.
Joplin, Mo.
Lexington, Ky.
Milwaukee, Wis.
Miranda, Calif.
Newton, Mass.
Newton Falls, Ohio
Park Forest, Ill.

Philadelphia, Pa.
Plainview, N. Y.
Richmond, Va.
Tampa, Fla.
Tipp City, Ohio
Titusville, Fla.
Tooele, Utah
Torrence, Calif.
Tuscon, Ariz.
Wilmington, Del.

Annotated References

Anderson, Robert H., "The Nongraded School: An Overview," *The National Elementary Principal*, XLVII, No. 2 (1967), 4-10. Deals with many facets of nongradedness pointing out what constitutes a strong program and what makes for a weak one. Problems encountered in developing an effective program are discussed.

————, *Teaching In a World of Change*, pp. 45-70. New York: Harcourt, 1966. Points out that the graded school developed during the mid-nineteenth century, when teachers were afraid of precocious children. The unique nature of each child and the consequent need for unique, flexible programs are stressed.

Beggs, David W. and Edward G. Buffie, *Nongraded Schools in Action.* Bloomington: Indiana University Press, 1967. Discusses the philosophy and purposes of nongradedness. Programs in representative schools at both the elementary and secondary levels are discussed to illustrate different approaches and varying degrees of individual progress.

Berlak, Harold, "Values, Goals, Public Policy and Educational Evaluation," *Review of Educational Research,* XL, No. 2 (1970), 261-278. Goes into racial segregation, federal aid, sex education, public aid to parochial schools, and the conflict of rich and poor school districts.

Brown, B. Frank, *The Appropriate Placement School: A Sophisticated Nongraded Curriculum.* New York: Parker, 1965. A critical account of some of the traditional practices with helpful suggestions for implementing change. Special sections are devoted to specific ways nongraded schools can be most beneficial to disadvantaged youngsters.

_____, *The Nongraded High School.* Englewood Cliffs, N. J.: Prentice-Hall, 1963. Describes the program of one of the pioneer nongraded high schools, Melbourne High School in Florida. The principal explains independent study, course offerings, registration, scheduling, student placement, and progress reports.

Budde, Ray, "Jump On the Nongraded Bandwagon? Stop! Think!" *The National Elementary Principal,* XLVII, No. 2 (1967), 21-23. Explains that nongraded schools often started as an attempt to handle larger numbers of students. Cautions are expressed against trying to institute nongradedness without other innovations such as team teaching, flexible scheduling, variations in grouping, and resource centers. The article presents a good overview for those contemplating a nongraded program.

Carswell, Evelyn M., "The Nongraded School: Planning for It, Establishing It, Maintaining It," *The National Elementary Principal,* XLVII, No. 2 (1967), 11-15. Stresses the importance of careful planning. Time and thoughtful effort must be devoted to developing philosophy, orienting staff, building commitment, and securing facilities. Community understanding and support are essential.

Chadwick, Ruth E., Rose Durham, and Marion Morse, "The Report Card in a Nongraded School," *The National Elementary Principal,* XLVII, No. 3 (1968), 22-28. Presents three bases used in evaluation of a child's progress: in terms of his own ability, in terms of his immediate peers, and in terms of a national sampling of children. Individual progress demands elimination of traditional A, B, C, D, F grades.

Dufay, Frank, *Ungrading the Elementary School.* Englewood Cliffs, N. J.: Prentice-Hall, 1966. Describes the process of changing from a conventional to a nongraded program. The program of the Parkway Elementary School on Long Island is explained to illustrate problems to be overcome and advantages to be achieved.

Glogau, Lillian and Murray Fessel, *The Nongraded Primary School.* West Nyack, N. Y.: Parker, 1967. Relates the story of Old Bethpage School,

New York, during the year of its transition to nongradedness. Successes and problems with grouping, movement, differentiation of instruction, teachers, and parents are reported with equal frankness.

Goodlad, John I., "The Nongraded School," *The National Elementary Principal,* XLVII, No. 2 (1967), 2-4. Relates the new teaching methods now being used in various parts of the United States.

Goodlad, John I. and Robert H. Anderson, *The Nongraded Elementary School,* rev. ed. New York: Harcourt, 1963. Presents a rationale for nongradedness in light of realities of child development and of modern curriculum theory. The establishment and operation of the nongraded school are described, with a look to the future.

Guggenheim, Fred and Corinne L. Guggenheim, eds., *New Frontiers In Education,* pp. 206-223. New York: Grune and Stratton, 1966. Explains premises from which nongrading proceeds, the goals of the program, and procedures for setting it up. A 10-step, primary levels program of reading progress is presented together with an example of skills to be attained at one level.

Hoover, William F., "Patterns of Organization for Learning," *Audiovisual Instruction,* XIII, No. 6 (1968), 588-590. Reports discussion by a panel of various organizational patterns and the importance of media in these innovations. An instructional materials center is very important.

Houts, Paul L., "Profile of the Nongraded Child," *The National Elementary Principal,* XLVII, No. 3 (1968), 4-9. An interview with a young man for whom Goodlad and Anderson recommended early admittance to the local university because he was extremely advanced. Having achieved success, he now gives lectures about the nongraded school.

Howard, Eugene, Roger W. Bordwell, and Calvin E. Gross, *How to Organize A Nongraded School.* Englewood Cliffs, N. J.: Prentice-Hall, 1966. Discusses nongradedness at elementary and secondary levels. The program is built on the idea that flexibility in assignment to classes, time schedules, and learning experiences further individualization. Steps in development are illustrated through examples.

Lewin, David, "Go Slow on Non-grading," *Elementary School Journal,* LXVII, No. 3 (1966), 131-134. Discusses teacher problems, economic value, and curriculum decisions. Time is devoted to materials and the importance of philosophy.

Lewis, James, Jr., *A Contemporary Approach to Nongraded Education.* West Nyack, N. Y.: Parker, 1969. Traces the development of a nongraded program from initial planning through evaluation. Three curriculum plans are presented in detail. Examples of reporting forms and materials for parent orientation are included.

McCarthy, Robert J., *How to Organize and Operate an Ungraded Middle School.* Englewood Cliffs, N. J.: Prentice-Hall, 1967. Points out to teachers, administrators, and the public the pros and cons of nongraded schools. The appendix contains several forms used in assigning, evaluating, and carrying out independent study programs.

McLaughlin, William P., *Evaluation of the Nongraded Primary.* Jamaica, N. Y.: St. John's University, 1969. Reports results of a research study comparing graded and nongraded schools. Pupil progress, teacher differences, and programs are analyzed in light of the various factors that affect them.

———, "The Phantom Nongraded School," *Education Digest,* XXXIII, No. 7 (1968), 11-13. The opening sentence summarizes the article, "Preached more than practiced, practiced more than appraised—this appears to be the present status of the nongraded school."

Miller, Richard I., ed., *The Nongraded School.* New York: Harper, 1967. Explains the importance of the administrator in leading the development of a nongraded school. Methods of preparing for nongradedness and carrying it on, its values, and criteria for evaluation are presented.

Models for Nongrading Schools, An /I/D/E/A Occasional Paper. Dayton, Ohio: Institute for Development of Educational Activities, 1970. Stresses the point that nongradedness means many different things to different people. Programs in practice deviate greatly from conceptual models in regard to function, curriculum, instruction, evaluation, organization, and role of the learner. Examples of schools employing different degrees of nongradedness are included.

The Nongraded School, Department of Elementary School Principals, National Education Association. Washington, D. C., 1968. A reprint of articles dealing with nongradedness that were printed in the November 1967 and January 1968 issues of *The National Elementary Principal.* Nineteen leaders in the field discuss many facets of the program.

Otto, Henry J., *Nongradedness: An Elementary School Evaluation.* Austin: The University of Texas at Austin, 1969. Reports research conducted in two elementary schools relating to instructional and grouping practices. Representative samples of programs written by teachers are presented. No effects of nongradedness on anxiety are reported.

Purdom, Daniel M., *Exploring the Nongraded School.* Dayton, Ohio: Institute for Development of Educational Activities, 1970. Explains the philosophy of nongrading and approaches to its implementation. Purposes, organization, and evaluation are considered.

Shuster, Albert H., "Principals and Teachers for Nongraded Schools: Preservice and Inservice Education," *The National Elementary Principal,* XLVII, No. 3 (1968), 10-14. Deals with suggested improvements in preservice education and suggests that trainees for positions in schools should work in modern schools as part of their training. Seminars, workshops, and other inservice experiences are needed to keep programs up to date.

Smith, Lee L., *A Practical Approach to the Nongraded Elementary School.* West Nyack, N. Y.: Parker, 1968. An account by the principal of the programs at Brunswick Elementary School and South Frederick Elementary School in Frederick County, Maryland. Those initiating a nongraded program will find this book helpful.

Street, David, ed., *Innovations in Mass Education,* pp. 52-90. New York: Wiley, 1969. Discusses nongrading in depressed urban areas. An experimental study reveals a slight advantage in achievement for the nongraded structure and little difference in attitudes of either pupils or teachers.

Tewksbury, John L., *Nongrading in the Elementary School.* Columbus, Ohio: Merrill, 1967. Examines the transition from graded to nongraded schools. The book deals with the problems which may arise with grouping procedures and with the effectiveness of various plans.

Trump, J. Lloyd and Delmos F. Miller, *Secondary Curriculum Improvement*, pp. 297-306. Boston: Allyn and Bacon, 1968. Presents two models for developing the content of materials for a nongraded school, one in social studies and another in home economics. Plans for nongrading vary, but all must provide for team teaching, flexible schedules, and great variety of materials.

Wolfson, Bernice, "The Promise of Multiage Grouping for Individualizing Instruction," *The Elementary School Journal*, LXVII, No. 7 (1967), pp. 354-362. Points up the challenges and rewards of multiage grouping. The teacher is forced to give up thinking in terms of a group and begins to plan work for each of the individuals. When the teacher plans with individual students, he can encourage each child to assume increasing amounts of responsibility in selecting materials and carrying on activities.

Audiovisual and Other Resources

Charlie and the Golden Hamster—The Nongraded Elementary School (16mm film, color, sound, 13 min., $125, rental $7.50). Designed for inservice training or community discussion of the concept. /I/D/E/A/, P. O. Box 628, Far Hills Branch, Dayton, Ohio 45419.

Continuous Progress—Cooperative Teaching (booklet, $2). Outlines K-6 nongraded continuous-progress program with attention to roles, evaluation, and bibliography. Educational Research Council of America, Rockefeller Bldg., Cleveland, Ohio 44113.

Continuous Progress Learning (16mm film, color, sound, 22 min., $200, rental $11). Shows the transition of a graded program into a continuous progress system. /I/D/E/A/, P. O. Box 628, Far Hills Branch, Dayton, Ohio 45419.

The Improbable Form of Master Sturm—The Nongraded High School (16mm film, color, sound, 13 min., $125, rental $7.50). Inside view of a high school that has been nongraded for more than 10 years. /I/D/E/A/, P. O. Box 628, Far Hills Branch, Dayton, Ohio 45419.

Models for Nongrading Schools (report, $1.50). Examination of the concept and guidelines for improving. /I/D/E/A/, P. O. Box 628, Far Hills Branch, Dayton, Ohio 45419.

Nongraded Education for the Modern Elementary School (4 color filmstrips, cassette tapes, $37). Discusses various theories of nongraded education. Eye Gate House, 146-01 Archer Ave., Jamaica, N. Y. 11435.

Nongradedness—How It Looks in the Real World (5 cassette tapes, $39.95). By Curtis Van Alfen, assistant dean, college of education, Brigham Young Univ., to stimulate discussion and serve as a guide in development of nongraded programs. Instructional Dynamics Inc., 166 E. Superior St., Chicago, Ill. 60611.

Programed Learning: Particularly Computer-Assisted Instruction 4

Programed learning is change in response or behavior brought about through the use of materials and experiences built into a carefully organized sequential system. In the present context, it refers specifically to the utilization of teaching machines, programed texts, and computers.

Perhaps the most promising educational advance of recent years has been the serious concern for individualizing instruction. Revived by S. L. Pressey in the 1920's, the idea of teaching machines moved forward at an accelerated rate in the 1950's under the leadership of B. F. Skinner. Skinner's small, inexpensive teaching machines involved learners in active response as they moved through successive frames of small steps proceeding from the known to the unknown in a straight-line sequence.

The programs were based on the theory that learning is aided by knowledge of progress and by keeping errors at a minimum. Following the linear sequences, Norman Crowder and others developed branching programs, which provide for alternate paths through a course. If the student responds incorrectly, he is shown his error and is returned to the original or an alternate frame to correct his answer.

In a few years, programed texts, incorporating the principles of the original machines, virtually replaced teaching machines.

43

Like branching programs, scrambled texts provide the learner with alternative paths. Slides, films, pictures, diagrams, and tape recordings complement the printed material. Small cumulative frames direct the learning sequence. Feedback is provided to guide and motivate pupil response. Both programed texts and teaching machines require student responses, follow a planned sequence, frequently allow learners to move at their own rate, provide feedback, and promote reinforcement of learning through successful response. Programed texts have gained acceptance over teaching machines because of their financial economy and greater flexibility.

It now appears that much of the programed learning of tomorrow will emanate from computer-assisted instruction. Use of the computer has been on the increase in the Census Bureau and business and industry for more than a decade. In recent years Stanford and other universities have led the way in exploring its use for instructional purposes. As in other developing practices, the keynote for using computers for instructional purposes is individualization. The goal is to take the backgrounds, deficiencies, and needs of students into account and to provide instruction appropriate to each individual. The objectives are established, materials are written, and programs are developed for the computer.

In present operations, learners are in direct or on-line communication with the computer for short periods of time, usually not more than 15 minutes per day. The terminal used by the student commonly consists of a teletype machine or electric typewriter connected with the computer by means of a telephone wire. The computer is complex; however, the student's terminal is relatively simple and inexpensive. Visual and auditory dimensions are frequently added through the use of slides, filmstrips, and tapes. Among recent improvements are cathode ray tubes, similar in appearance to small television screens, and a light pen, with which the student points to appropriate responses on a screen. More sophisticated equipment is constantly being developed.

To a degree, branching is automatically taken care of by the computer, and feedback can be immediate. Computer-assisted instruction makes greater provision than programed texts for taking into account the background and experiential level of the learner. Many of the routine functions of the classroom and drill exercises are being provided for with a high degree of effectiveness. Tutorial systems approximate the interaction of student and teacher. Dialogue systems, providing for rapid-fire exchange between student and computer on many potential subjects, confront problems in utilizing the full computational capacity of the system. Nevertheless, rapid-fire dialogue for instruction is not beyond the possibilities of future development.

Significant Components   *Which ones are essential?*

1. It must be recognized that even the computer, the most advanced of the devices for programed learning, is only in its early stages of development.
2. In programing, the description of process must avoid ambiguity and be exact and precise enough to be carried out by a machine.
3. Feedback, immediate or delayed, about the correctness or incorrectness of responses is essential.
4. Provision should be made for following correct responses with positive reinforcement.
5. The programer must understand that his primary responsibility is to serve the learners rather than the computer.
6. Teachers must resist authoritarianism and intolerance on the part of the programer.
7. Every effort should be made to safeguard the worth of the individual.
8. The program should guide the student carefully, but not oppressively.
9. Carefully developed behavioral objectives, including specific skills and performance levels, must be the basis for programs.
10. Pre-planning should determine the scope of the material to be learned and the depth to which it will be pursued.
11. Feedback should be provided to teachers and administrators for improving the total operation as well as the learning of pupils.
12. The time that students are permitted to use their terminals must be carefully scheduled, and they should be able to operate the terminals easily and efficiently.
13. Expectations must not exceed available machine capability.
14. Classroom teachers using computer-assisted instruction must be deeply involved in planning and revising programs and must have extensive inservice training in using programed materials effectively.

15. Provisions should be developed for closed prescription loops, followed by opportunities for practice on the part of students and continuous updating of data in the information retrieval system.

16. It should be possible for students to check their results against standards established in the retrieval system.

17. The materials specialist, curriculum expert, subject specialist, technologist, writer, programer, and teacher must work as a team.

18. In writing programs, teachers should usually start with very simple exercises involving primarily drill and practice and move forward in a gradual progression.

19. Students should be allowed to proceed at their own rate.

20. Special effort should be made to relieve teachers of feelings of being threatened.

21. Programed learning experiences must be closely integrated with the total course of study.

22. It is important to develop systems personnel with strong interest and competence in the instructional aspects of programing.

23. Long and careful study, including orientation of the public, should precede the adoption of programs and the purchase of equipment.

24. Educators must be aware that programed learning can cause a heavy dependence on programed materials and stifle human efforts.

Proposed Advantages   *With which ones do you agree?*

1. Programed instruction is the key to a significant breakthrough in improving learning by providing experiences appropriate to the needs of each child.

2. Programed learning is particularly valuable in coping with problems resulting from acceleration and retardation—categories most often neglected in conventional classrooms.

3. Programed learning takes a big step toward having one teacher for one student.

4. Diagnosis of learning deficiencies is provided and serves as a basis for remediation by guiding the student to new material and improved responses.

5. The amount of direction and help can be varied for each individual.

6. Programed learning, particularly computer-assisted instruction, offers high motivation.

7. Revisions in programs can be made with comparative ease.
8. Programed instruction is well adapted to the utilization of a broad range of new instructional tools.
9. Children's questions and problems are addressed promptly and patiently by computers.
10. In the mind of the child, the computer is fair and free from the threat of personal dislikes and vindictiveness.
11. The student is allowed to use his own style in solving problems, thereby being encouraged to engage in inquiry and discovery learning.
12. The computer fosters creativity as well as objectivity in that it invites search for solutions to all problems presented.
13. Learners are involved in active response.
14. Learning can be directed toward attaining specific, preplanned outcomes.
15. Scrambled texts are especially well adapted to the instruction of brighter students.
16. The talents of outstanding teachers who develop programs are brought into many classrooms.

Criticisms and Difficulties to Be Anticipated   *Do you agree?*

1. If machines take over instruction, people will be dehumanized and human values killed.
2. Programed learning distorts the purpose of true education by its neglect of attitudes and values.
3. The results of programed learning may be extraneous because of errors in programing, which cannot be avoided.
4. Programed learning is insensitive to the delicate individual differences in personality and temperament.
5. Programing is effective only as learning can be made a matter of logic and science, devoid of emotional intensity.
6. Course content may fall under the control of people with vicious biases, who use programing to brainwash children.
7. Few people are available who possess technical knowledge of programing and can develop significant educational objectives and understand principles of child growth and development.
8. The cost of equipment for computer-assisted instruction is too great for most schools.
9. Computers cannot care for children or be their good friend.
10. The time, money, and energy needed for planning, writing, and programing is long, arduous, and out of proportion to the value of the process.

11. Models are too discrete to capture the real world, thus losing essential subtleties of reality.
12. Computer-assisted instruction could contribute to making pupils sedentary.
13. The glamor of computer-assisted instruction may leave the impression with pupils that other forms of instruction are unimportant.
14. Limited access to the computer's computational capacity makes its use limited.
15. The computer may be effective in transmitting information, but it is likely to be ineffective in processing it.
16. Programing proceeds on the false assumption that a machine can learn for the child. He alone can respond internally and thus learn.

Summary Assessment

Programed texts are recognized as valuable aids to many aspects of teaching and learning. Computer-assisted instruction has advanced to the point that major breakthroughs are expected to make it a significant help to schools in the near future. Upward of 1,500 courses or parts of courses that are already developed form a basis for further growth and improvement. As has been the case in business and industry, new installations are expected to increase at an accelerated rate.

Dramatic reductions in production costs of equipment and in operating expense indicate that the cost for classroom use will decrease substantially. More sophisticated technology and teaching strategies will be developed. The potential of the computer seems to be limited primarily by the creativity of those planning its use and by available financial resources to utilize its full capacity. Teachers who learn its capabilities and how to use them will be masters of a helpful new servant.

The teacher will not be replaced, but his role will change significantly. He will be able to do many of the things for children which he knows he should be doing, but which he cannot now do because of the demands of less productive tasks on his time and energy. He will cease to be primarily a dispenser of information, a drill master, a checker of papers, and a clerk. He will be able to direct increased attention to instilling the humaneness into education so desperately needed in our impersonal, urbanized society.

New impetus will be given to increasing professional competence, curriculum development, discovery of new strategies, and better evaluation as the computer delivers and presents material, conducts drills, grades papers, and performs a multitude of routine chores. Those who complain that communication between teacher and student will be impaired might keep in mind that it is not as good now as many teachers would like to believe.

Being publicly replicable, computer-assisted instruction is likely to increase productive research in many areas of teaching and learning and, as a result, effect significant and valuable innovation in education. For the immediate future, teachers may look forward to most help in factual areas such as foreign language, mathematics, spelling, punctuation, and some aspects of science. For the long haul, programed learning inspires renewed hope for educational programs tailored for each individual learner.

However, it may be important to warn against undeliverable expectations. Progress will be slow. Computer-assisted instruction will never be magic. It will leave many problems unsolved. It will not make the work of the teacher easier, but it will provide him with a tool to make his instruction more effective and to make his new professional role more satisfying. As a tool, it will be effective or ineffective to the extent to which the imagination of educators can harness its potential and the degree to which they use it wisely or carelessly.

The chairman of the board of International Business Machines (IBM) warns the master and defends the defenseless computer:

> A computer has no conscience. It feels no passion. It has no life of its own, nor any sense of values. It is neither poet nor philosopher. A computer, in short, is a machine, not a man; a tool, not a tyrant.*

A Few Leaders in the Movement

Don L. Bushnell
  Brooks Foundation
John Caffrey
  Education Systems
  Research Group

Donald R. Cruickshank
  Ohio State Univ.
Robert Gagné
  Florida State Univ.

---

*William D. Patterson and Thomas J. Watson, Jr., "Man Over the Machine in League with the Future," *Saturday Review*, L, No. 3 (1967), 74.

Robert Glaser
  Learning Research and
  Development Center
Edward J. Green
  Michigan State Univ.
Albert Hickey
  Enteleck, Inc.
Phil C. Lange
  Columbia Univ.

S. L. Pressey
  Ohio State Univ.
William A. Rodgers
  Kent (Ohio) State Univ.
B. F. Skinner
  Cambridge, Mass.
Patrick Suppes
  Stanford Univ.

A Few Places Where the Innovation Is Used

Altoona, Pa.	Morehead Univ.	Saginaw, Mich.
Beverly Hills, Calif.	New Orleans, La.	St. Louis, Mo.
Dartmouth College	New York, N. Y.	Scotia, N. Y.
Deerfield, Ill.	Oak Park, Ill.	Stanford Univ.
Florida State Univ.	Palo Alto, Calif.	Traverse City, Mich.
Harvard College	Philadelphia, Pa.	Univ. of Illinois
Kansas City, Mo.	Pittsburgh, Pa.	Waterford, Mich.
Maywood, Ill.	Rome, N. Y.	Wilmington, Del.

Annotated References

Anderson, Richard C., Raymond W. Kulhay, and Thomas Andre, "Feedback Procedures in Programmed Instruction," *Journal of Educational Psychology,* LXII, No. 2 (1971), 148-156. Reports an experiment with computer tests that showed that students who received the correct answer to a question (i.e., "knowledge of correct response, KCR") only after they had attempted an answer to a question learned more (determined from subsequent testing) than those who either received no KCR immediately after they responded or had an opportunity to look at the correct answer before responding.

Apter, Michael I., *The New Technology of Education.* Toronto: Macmillan, 1968. Refutes criticisms that programed instruction dehumanizes people and produces deadly uniformity. Computers are most effective for processing and transmitting information and for teaching skills.

Boblick, John M., "The Use of Computer Simulations in the Teaching of High School Physics," *Science Education,* LIV, No. 1 (1970), 77-81. Outlines the following CAI categories: tutorial dialogue, drill and review, testing, remote computing, and simulation. Emphasizes use of simulation with an example of how students could "operate" a nuclear reactor, synchrocyclotron, or a laser. Actual lab work by the student himself must not be abandoned.

Bushnell, Don L. and Dwight W. Allen, *The Computer in American Education.* New York: Wiley, 1967. Contributions by outstanding authorities consider individualization of instruction through the use of computers, research, teaching the computer sciences, and information processing for education systems. Problems are analyzed, and approaches to solutions are suggested.

Calvin, Allen D., ed., *Programmed Instruction—Bold New Venture.* Bloomington: Indiana University Press, 1969. Practitioners discuss and illustrate practical considerations of programed instruction, including advantages and pitfalls. Programing in spelling, reading, social sciences, foreign languages, mathematics, and adult education is treated in depth.

Cohodes, Aaron, ed., "How Schools Use Computers in the Classroom," *Nation's Schools,* LXXVII, No. 4 (1966), 58-60. Cites four examples of computers in use for various age levels in school systems across the nation. Positive results are reported for spelling, mathematics, and business education.

Computer in Education, The Bulletin of the National Association of Secondary School Principals, LIV, No. 343 (1970). The issue is devoted to the use of computers for instruction, testing, grading, and record keeping. Advantages and problems encountered in making the computer the servant of the teacher and the pupil are discussed.

DeCecco, John P., ed., *Educational Technology Readings in Programmed Instruction.* New York: Holt, 1964. Book of readings on educational technology and its relationship to theory of learning and various methods of instruction. Approaches to evaluating materials and procedures are described. A glossary of terms is included.

Deep, Donald, "The Computer Can Help Individualize Instruction," *The Elementary School Journal,* LXX, No. 7 (1970), 351-358. Points up the differences between computer-assisted instruction, where the child is actually instructed by the machine, and computer-managed instruction, where the computer aids the teacher.

Ginther, John R., "Let's Challenge Technology," *Educational Leadership,* XXV, No. 8 (1968), 716-721. Recognizes the advantages of programed learning for freeing the teacher, improving the educational environment of the student, creating simulations and games, and retrieving information.

Glaser, Robert, ed., *Teaching Machines and Programed Learning,* II. Washington, D. C.: National Education Association, 1965. A comprehensive volume covering the utilization of teaching machines and computer-based systems. Programed instruction in five subject areas is explained. Effectiveness is promised.

Gleason, Gerald T., "Computer Assisted Instruction," *Education Digest,* XXXIII, No. 7 (1968), 14-17. Surveys the status of CAI and indicates significant problems and issues that must be considered openly. Underlying principles, capabilities, costs, and results are presented as persistent problems. Encouraging developmental activities are reported.

Goodlad, John I., "Learning and Teaching in the Future," *Today's Education,* LVII, No. 2 (1968), 49-51. Reports positive reaction of students, parents, and teachers to computer-assisted instruction. Students are motivated, and teachers are freed for lesson planning and diagnosis of learning difficulties.

Goodlad, John I., John F. O'Toole, Jr., and Louise L. Tyler, *Computers and Information Systems in Education.* New York: Harcourt, 1966. Discusses computer technology in relation to the changing American school. Scope of developments and factors hampering and promoting computer technology in education are considered.

Green, Edward J., *The Learning Process and Programmed Instruction.* New York: Holt, 1963. Attempts to bridge the gap between findings of psychology relating to learning and the classroom practices of teachers. The concept of programed instruction is applied to teaching machines and programed texts.

Hicks, Bruce L., "Will the Computer Kill Education?" *The Educational Forum*, XXXIV, No. 3 (1970), 307-312. Whether the computer will serve or kill education depends upon the programer, not the machine. He may work for the computer or for the learners. Bigots and demagogues could control course content, but this must and can be avoided.

Hullfish, William R., "Use of Drill Programs to Teach Abstract Concepts by Computer Assisted Instruction," *Audiovisual Instruction*, XVI, No. 2, (1971), 35-60. Describes specific programs that drill students on word meaning and word association. Success in teaching abstract concepts is reported.

Inlow, Gail M., *The Emergent in Curriculum*, pp. 163-183. New York: Wiley, 1966. Explains and illustrates the difference between linear patterns and branching or scrambled programs. Machines and electronic aids will not replace the teacher. He can devote his time to more intricate aspects of teaching.

Jamison, D., P. Suppes, and C. Butler, "Estimated Costs of Computer Assisted Instruction for Compensating Education in Urban Areas," *Educational Technology*, X, No. 9 (1970), 49-57. Focuses on drill and practice programs developed for grades K-6 in areas of reading and arithmetic. Statistics and tables indicate the effectiveness of CAI.

Lange, Phil C., ed., "Programmed Instruction," *The Sixty-Sixth Yearbook of the National Society for the Study of Education*. Chicago: The National Society for the Study of Education, 1967. Covers foundations for instructional programing, program development, and issues and problems. Ten chapters direct attention to the administration, development, and evaluation of programs of instruction.

Lee, Beatrice C., publications ed., "The Use of Computers for Instruction," *National Education Association Research Bulletin*, XLIX, No. 1 (1971), 3-4. Reports statistics reviewing how little computers are used at the present in school systems. Although the frequency of use is increasing, progress is slow.

Littledale, Harold, ed., "Tell It To The Computer!" *Grade Teacher*, LXXXVII, No. 7 (1970), 108-114. Reports that, after three years of testing, commercial programs for computer-assisted instruction are effective, and that classroom teachers can play a role in designing and revising programs. The computer is the friend of these teachers.

Lunnetta, Vincent N. and O. E. Dyrli, "Computers in the Science Curriculum: Some Concrete Applications in the Physical Sciences," *Science Education*, LIV, No. 2 (1970), 147-154. Reviews the present state of the art of computers in education, explains roles which computers may be expected to fill in education, and assesses what science education should do to take advantage of computer potential most effectively. Examples are given of computer use in physics, particularly through the use of simulation.

Margolin, Joseph B. and Marion R. Misch, *Computers in the Classroom*. New York: Spartan, 1970. Considers the place of computers in the context of rapid changes that are affecting elementary and secondary education.

The volume presents alternatives for advancing teaching and learning through computer-assisted instruction. The information was gathered through on-site visits to many schools.

Nelson, James H. and N. Thomas Hoskins, "Computer as a Teaching Aid," *Science Teacher,* XXXVIII, No. 3 (1971), 61-62. Describes the use of the computer to do the calculations for high school chemistry experiments. The program was used only as a check. The students did their own calculations and submitted these calculations to the computer to be checked. Advantage: enables instructor to check the student's work step by step, not just his final answer.

Oettinger, Anthony G. and Sema Marks, *Run, Computer, Run.* Cambridge: Harvard University Press, 1969. Exposure of myths surrounding educational technology and a confident reassurance of its great promise. Failure to avoid pitfalls and abuses will lead to reversals and disillusionment; caution and thoughtful planning will result in real progress.

O'Neal, Fred, "The Role of Public Schools in Computer Assisted Instruction," *Educational Technology,* X, No. 3 (1970), 5-10. Describes a three-year program of planning, preparing, implementing, and testing a program of computer-assisted instruction in junior high school mathematics and science. An encouraging outcome is predicted.

Patterson, William D. and Thomas J. Watson, Jr., "Man Over the Machine in League with the Future," *Saturday Review,* L, No. 3 (1967), 74. IBM's chairman of the board points out the potential of computers for helping teachers, but warns against expecting too much from them.

Pula, Fred John and Robert J. Goff, *Technology in Education: Challenge and Change.* Worthington, Ohio: Charles A. Jones, 1972. Presents 22 articles by leading thinkers in the field of technological change and its effects on education. The areas covered include foundations of education and educational technology, tools of instruction, and organization.

Roberts, A. D. and P. A. Zirkel, "Computer Applications to Instruction," *Journal of Secondary Education,* XLVI, No. 3 (1971), 99-105. Presents an overview of computer applications to instruction, what they are, and where and how they are used. The use of a computer is explained in the areas of drill and practice, inquiry, problem solving, testing, storage and retrieval of information, and counseling. Several projects are discussed.

Rothbart, Andrea and Esther Steinberg, "Some Observations of Children's Reaction to Computer-Assisted Instruction," *Arithmetic Teacher,* XVIII, No. 1 (1971), 19-21. Describes the overall enthusiastic response of children to the PLATO (Programmed Loger for Automatic Teaching Operations) Project set up by the University of Illinois in the Washington Elementary School, Champaign, Illinois.

Stansfield, David, "The Computer and Education," *Educational Technology,* VIII, No. 10 (1968), 3-8. Expresses the viewpoint that reinforcing the present system of education is a misuse of the computer. To serve individualization of learning, computer-assisted instruction must decrease standardization, schools must be reorganized, and flexibility must be maintained.

Strain, John P., "Educational Technology and the Hidden Realities," *Educational Leadership,* XXV, No. 8 (1968), 722-724. Points out some of the

54   *Individualizing Learning*

pitfalls of educational technology and proposes solutions for alleviating these problems. Among them are the students' feeling of dehumanization, the expectation that instruction must be entertaining, and the growing absence of teacher control.

Suchek, Arthur M., "A Remote-Access Instructional Systems Model for a Regional Occupation Center," *Audiovisual Instruction,* XV, No. 4 (1970), 47-50. Reports the development of a dial access information retrieval system in a regional occupational center. A student's total occupational curriculum will be programed on a plastic card. Provision is made for dialogue with a master teacher.

Suppes, Patrick and Barbara Searle, "The Computer Teaches Arithmetic," *School Review,* LXXIX, No. 2 (1971), 213-225. Describes CAI programs in operation and explains two types: "block program" and "strand program." Evaluates programs and reactions from parents, students, and others. Presents plans for design of an individualized curriculum.

Suppes, Patrick and Max Jerman, "Computer-Assisted Instruction," *The Bulletin of the National Association of Secondary School Principals,* LIV, No. 343 (1970), 27-40. Gives a source of current activities in computer-assisted instruction and projects some of the future directions in improving effectiveness and overcoming current difficulties.

Thiagarajan, Sivasailam, *The Programing Process.* Worthington, Ohio: Charles A. Jones, 1971. A workbook for the training of student-programmers. The five areas of the instructional process include task analysis, design, editing, developmental testing, and validation testing.

Van Til, William, "Supervising Computerized Instruction," *Educational Leadership,* XXVI, No. 1 (1968), 41-45. Emphasizes the role of the supervisor in relation to programed learning: 1) determine what is to be taught, 2) hold teachers to tasks, 3) evaluate results, and 4) rate teachers on performance.

Whalley, Noel, *A Guide to the Preparation of Teaching Programs.* Bristol, England: Mark Lane, 1966. A handbook designed to assist the program writer in a practical way with linear and branching programs. Planning, frame writing, editing, routing, program analysis, and validation are explained.

Audiovisual and Other Resources

Learning and Behavior—The Teaching Machine (16mm film, sound, b&w, 26 min., $135). A CBS "Conquest" Production. B. F. Skinner and R. J. Hernstein show how science can measure the learning process. Carousel Films, Inc., 1501 Broadway, Suite 1503, New York, N. Y. 10036.

Programmed Instruction—The Development Process (16 mm film, color, 19 min., $65, rental $10). Introduction to the major stages in development of programed instructional materials. National Audiovisual Center, Washington, D. C. 20409.

Programmed Instruction—The Teacher's Role (series of 16mm films, b&w). Designed to stimulate teacher discussion of programed instruction in reading, science, vocabulary, geography, and mathematics. National Audiovisual Center, Washington, D. C. 20409.

The Teacher and Technology (16mm film, b&w, 49 min., $87.50, rental $15). The impact of technology on education—its beginnings and history—is traced and modern day uses of technology are illustrated. National Audiovisual Center, Washington, D. C. 20409.

Parent-Teacher Conferences   5

Definition

A parent-teacher conference is a face-to-face meeting of one or more teachers with one or both of a pupil's parents. It is arranged for the purpose of exchanging information about a child so that the teacher, parents, and school as a whole can work together more effectively in furthering the pupil's educational development. This common goal of improvement should provide a basis for free and helpful consideration of any pertinent factors and relationships which might assist in motivating and guiding the child. His home and school life, habits and interests, likes and dislikes, strengths and limitations, frustrations and hopes, should be discussed openly and in a professional atmosphere. His self-concept and his attitude toward and relationship with his parents, other members of the family, teacher, and classmates are vital matters for discussion. His proficiencies and shortcomings, both in and out of school, are important considerations.

Although the conference is frequently looked upon as a means for the teacher to report progress or lack of it to the parents, it should really be a mutually beneficial exchange. At the conclusion, the teacher should have learned as much from the parents as they have learned from him about the pupil's progress. The conference should provide valuable information about the effectiveness or ineffectiveness of the school's attitudes and program. To be most beneficial, the total development of the child, including his personal as well as his academic growth, should be of concern to teachers and parents.

As instruction increasingly moves toward individualization, it is more essential than ever that teachers understand as much as possible about each child. Every means of securing vital information should be used so that teachers can be of maximum help to pupils. Because of their deep interest in their children and their long and intimate association with them, parents can supply invaluable information to help teachers identify the child's interests, needs, strengths, and weaknesses. They can provide significant data that cannot be secured from diagnostic tests, personality inventories, or anecdotal records. When special problems arise, conferences with parents are often as beneficial as conferences with the pupil. In the case of students new to the school, a face-to-face exchange is particularly beneficial for providing teachers with vital information and for helping parents understand the expectations and services of the school.

Individual conferences between parents and teachers are essential when the school is planning program changes such as nongrading, team teaching, or differentiated staffing. Parents often make valuable suggestions. Their concerns and anxieties can be identified and relieved more easily and effectively than through the use of written bulletins or mass meetings. Teachers who appreciate a part in policy development and decision-making are likely to find that parents respond positively to similar opportunities to exchange ideas relative to the education of their children. It is a distinct mistake to assume that many parents are not interested in their children's progress in school.

School conferences give parents an opportunity to see the environment in which the pupil spends a significant portion of his time and to discuss the extent to which the child is profiting from his opportunities. Understanding of the problems of teachers, parents, and pupils are often enhanced. Misunderstandings and false impressions left by inadequate or inaccurate reports from students and teachers can be clarified. Unity of purpose, mutual confidence, and productive approaches to joint effort are developed. Working together, parents and teachers can recognize opportunities for discharging their common responsibilities and reinforce each other's efforts.

Many teachers find home visitation a very effective way of communicating with parents. Getting into the home allows the teacher to see the personal environment and assess the climate which determines to a great extent what the child brings to the learning situation in the classroom. It enables the teacher to discover family interests and other learning resources that can be related to classroom activities. Parents are often encouraged to take a greater interest in the school life of the child if teachers exhibit a real interest in home life. When parents go to the school or the teacher comes to the home to consider ways of making education more productive, the pupil senses their sincere interest in him and realizes more fully the importance of education.

Too often parents come to school and teachers go to the home only when some special problem has arisen. Almost automatically one or the other is prepared to defend himself against an accusation. Recent change in the purposes of parent-teacher conferences and growing realization of the help that they can provide for both teacher and parent should continue to relieve the defensiveness and anxiety that too often arise when one or the other asks for a conference. When both appreciate the value of each other's insights, a request for a conference will be viewed as an indication of sincere interest and willingness to help in whatever way each party can. Parent-teacher conferences should be genuinely enjoyable and mutually beneficial encounters between those most vitally concerned about the education of children.

Significant Components   *Which are essential?*

1. To achieve maximum results, teachers should engage in in-service training for conducting conferences.
2. In preparation for the conference the teacher should study the cumulative record of the pupil, gather examples of his work, and review information about the parents and home.
3. A brief list of points to discuss will help move the discussion forward.
4. If the conference is scheduled in advance, the pupil should know about it.
5. The conference should be held in a quiet, private, comfortable place.
6. Some teachers find it effective to hold the meeting in a lounge or conference room, where the teacher is less an authority figure than in his own office or classroom.
7. The conference should open on a friendly, positive note.

8. The prevailing attitude should be that of being of help to each other in contributing to the child's maximum development.

9. Information should be exchanged honestly and confidentially.

10. The teacher should make a special effort not to place parents on the defensive.

11. Sincere interest in the child, courtesy, patience, and kindness should be illustrative of a genuinely professional attitude on the part of the teacher.

12. Teachers must be good listeners, avoiding the supposition that the conference is principally an opportunity to tell the parents about the child and his progress.

13. Arrangements should be made for the parents to see other members of the staff if they so desire.

14. Desirable follow-up action that has been agreed upon should be reviewed and clearly understood.

15. Teachers should be prepared for unanticipated reactions of parents, even for personal attacks and insults.

16. Whenever possible, the teacher should pursue suggestions of parents and not make promises that cannot be fulfilled.

17. A subsequent meeting at the school or at the home, letters, or telephone conversations may be agreed upon.

18. The teacher should summarize the discussion before the conference is closed.

19. The conference should end as it began, on a friendly, positive note.

20. A record of the conference should be prepared for the cumulative folder.

Proposed Advantages   *With which ones do you agree?*

1. The teacher learns about the child's family and community life, and the parents learn about his school life.

2. Comparison can be made between apparent inconsistencies in attitude or behavior in the child's role as a member of the family and of the class.

3. Goodwill that has been established is likely to generate broader and stronger support for the total school program.

4. Mutual responsibilities of teacher and parents are highlighted.

5. Teachers who visit the home see the child in a setting different from that of the school.

6. Insights gained from home visits will assist teachers in analyzing and interpreting problems and information.

7. The parent-teacher conference, if properly conducted, is one of the most vital and effective tools for diagnosing educational and personal problems.

8. Parents are provided with the opportunity to understand better the role of the school and its philosophy.

9. Often interests and activities of the child at home and in school are uncovered that can serve as bases for subsequent conversation between parents and child and teacher and pupil.

10. Frequently parents and teachers learn things about the strengths and weaknesses of the child that they would not discover otherwise.

11. Teachers who are skillful in conferences enhance the status of the teaching profession in the eyes of the public.

12. Through discussions with teachers, parents gain useful knowledge, attitudes, and skills to help them in bringing up their children more effectively.

13. Conferences between parents and teachers often are the beginning of lasting personal friendships.

Criticisms and Difficulties to Be Anticipated   *Do you agree?*

1. Parents are often uncomfortable when they come to the school to discuss their children.

2. Teachers lack personal qualities and skill for carrying on an effective exchange.

3. Work schedules, small children at home, and other factors present problems in scheduling conferences.

4. Teachers may be poor listeners or tend to be overcritical.

5. Parents may come to the conference with a generally negative attitude toward education, schools, and teachers.

6. Inadequate preparation is likely to prevent the attainment of positive outcomes.

7. Teachers are particularly challenged when preparing for conferences with parents of children who are not doing well in school.

8. The focus of attention may shift from the child to the shortcomings of the teacher, the inadequacies of the school, or the failures of the parents.

9. Parents may take the attitude that teachers are interested only in academic achievement.

10. "Talking down" to the parents or excessive use of negative comments may render the conference ineffective.

11. Many parents refuse to respond to an invitation to a conference.
12. Teachers may proceed on the assumption that parents know little about children and their development, or they may assume that parents understand more than they actually do.
13. Failure to respect confidences may prevent success.
14. A pedantic approach or the use of educational jargon by the teacher is likely to bewilder and antagonize parents.
15. If differences in viewpoints arise, the teacher and the parent may not realize that both need to make adjustments.
16. Sometimes parents will try to discuss siblings, other children, or other teachers' treatment of the child.
17. Arguments may result from misunderstanding of the purpose of the meeting or the proper roles of parents and teachers.

Summary Assessment

During recent years, parent-teacher conferences have become a common and widely acclaimed method of reporting to parents and communicating with them. Generally the conferences are held at the school, but many teachers feel that conferences held in the home provide a significant advantage by permitting the teacher to gain deeper insights into the surroundings and social climate in which the child spends most of his time.

Although parent-teacher conferences at the high school level are different from those in the elementary school, similar problems and potential benefits exist. In many high schools, the guidance counselor is the chief liaison between the school and the home. In others, the homeroom teacher performs this function. Since he commonly does not have his homeroom student in class, his perspective is somewhat different. General adjustment to school and home, program planning, social relations, and consideration of education beyond the high school take on increased significance. High school students, too, look upon conferences between their parents and teachers differently from elementary pupils.

Some teachers find it effective to have students present at the conferences. The student's participation in the discussion relieves his concerns about what is being considered and adds significance to the meeting. The learner becomes involved in the planning and frequently assumes greater responsibility for the success of agreed-upon procedures. His views are important in analyzing past failures and successes, in resolving problems, and in charting new courses. Conferences with his parents and teachers help him to discharge his important responsibility for self-evaluation. His cooperation and commitment are crucial for successful achievement.

When conferences are used to replace or supplement conventional report cards, they offer distinct advantages. Samples of pupil work and school records are available for meaningful review. Audio and video tapes are being used with increasing frequency for observing pupil performance and participation in class activities. Face-to-face reporting provides an opportunity to question, explore reasons for the child's lack of success, and suggest approaches to extending his conspicuous successes. If managed adeptly, teachers' reporting to parents may take on a new dimension of parents' reporting to teachers and students' reporting to both of them.

"How well have we done since we last sat down together?" may be an appropriate question for parents, teachers, and students to consider as they address themselves to accountability for educational progress. Emphasis may be shifted from blaming one another to what each one can do to help the other achieve the goals which they have set for themselves. Responsibility for optimum results in learning cannot rest entirely upon the school. The learner, his parents, and school personnel must plan together, work together, and evaluate together. What have we done well? Where have we been unsuccessful? Why have we been ineffective? How can we overcome our shortcomings? How can we use available facilities to best advantage? What additional resources are needed to get the job done? These and many other related questions need to be studied thoughtfully and cooperatively if the tax dollar is to produce optimum results. If all those involved in the development of youth hold themselves as well as others responsible for a reasonable share of the joint enterprise, accountability in education can be a strong force for improving learning.

To promote these exciting outcomes and to help relieve many of the acute problems of youth, continued systematic effort toward conference improvement should be encouraged. Recordings, films, simulation techniques, readings, and discussions are being used extensively to assist teachers in developing an interest in parent-teacher conferences and in improving their skills in conducting them.

Planning for a parent-teacher conference demands time comparable to that required for planning an effective classroom lesson. Parents should also recognize the importance of devoting time and effort to planning in order to make the conference productive. Providing released time for teachers to confer with parents is justifiable, but growing flexibility in time schedules and in personnel utilization often make it unnecessary to dismiss school to provide for conferences. Many teachers think that spending some additional time after school hours conferring with parents at the school or in the home is a reasonable part of their professional responsibilities.

Most teachers report gratifying results from the time they spend with parents. The interest, concern, and positive response of the parents are frequently sources of encouragement. Equally significant is the help that teachers receive from parental information, which enables them to attack many baffling problems with greater understanding.

After a conference, the development of the "whole child" often takes on new meaning. The understanding and sympathy of the teacher increases; the regard of the parents for the school and teachers is often improved. Continued systematic effort directed toward the inservice improvement of teachers should assure that this regard is more often enhanced.

A Few Leaders in the Movement

Virginia Bailard
  Long Beach (Calif.) Schools
E. H. Brady
  American Council on Education
Hollis Caswell
  Columbia Univ.
Elliott D. Landau
  Univ. of Utah
Grace Langdon
  Southern Illinois Univ.

Carol LeFevre
  Univ. of Chicago
Irving W. Stout
  Arizona State Univ.
M. Ruth Strand
  San Diego State College
Herbert W. Wey
  Univ. of Miami

A Few Places Where the Innovation Is Used

Burkburnett, Texas
Gilford, N. H.
Greece, N. Y.
Hamilton, Ohio

Hooker, Okla.
Indianapolis, Ind.
McMinville, Oreg.
New Haven, Conn.

Oxford, Ohio
Racine, Wis.
Seminole, Texas
Tampa, Fla.

Annotated References

Anderson, Linda G., "My Sweet Caroline: A Failure in Second Grade," *Redbook*, CXXXVII, No. 1 (1971), 24-30. Describes teacher behavior in school conferences. Armed with half-truths and hazy descriptive phrases, many teachers protect themselves and their system. Parents should investigate the system to find its faults and make others aware of them.

Bailard, Virginia and Ruth Strang, *Parent Teacher Conferences.* New York: McGraw-Hill, 1964. An informative book covering many phases of a conference. It also includes discussions of parent education, group meetings, and special counseling for special children.

Barda, David, "Parent Conferences: Guidelines for the Counselor," *The Clearing House,* IV, No. 9 (1971), 520-523. Emphasizes eight major topics of behavior for school counselors in parent conferences. Overt counselor behavior in discussions should maximize benefits of communication between the home and the school.

Bell, Joseph N., "A Fond Farewell to Back-to-School Night," *Today's Health,* XLVIII, No. 9 (1970), 16-17, 68, 70. Describes travesty of parent-teacher conferences. Everyone involved would like to do away with them, but can't. Nobody really listens. Most parents come late, and few are really interested.

Caswell, Hollis and Arthur Foshay, *Education in the Elementary Schools,* pp. 404-407. New York: American, 1968. Considers the school as a positive force for social betterment. There are benefits for the community from the school, and for the school from the community. Communication must be established and channels kept open at all times.

Cheyney, Frazier, "Tape Recorder and Parent Conferences," *Audiovisual Instructor,* XIV, No. 5 (1969), 82. Explains the value of using the tape recorder in a conference to illustrate a problem the teacher has with a child.

Cholden, Harriett, "Making the Most of a Parent Conference," *The Instructor,* LXXVII, No. 3 (1968), 87-88. Outlines specific areas to cover in a conference. Teachers must use tact in approaching problems and plan for keeping the conference moving forward toward improved understanding.

Graves, Dorothy, "Getting Ready for a Teacher-Parent Conference," *PTA Magazine,* LXIII, No. 1 (1968), 26-28. Presents many suggestions for parents and teachers to make conferences more effective. Those involved must assume the attitude that they are working toward common goals. A PTA meeting in which members act out situations is helpful.

Herman, Barry E., "The Parent-Teacher Conference," *Catholic School Journal,* LXVIII, No. 9 (1968), 43-44. Emphasizes planning for the parent-teacher conference, establishing rapport, and providing for follow-up. Sincerity on the part of the teachers is the key to success. The gratitude and response of parents are mentioned as some of the real satisfactions of teaching.

Horn, Gunnar, "Home Visits," *Today's Education,* LIX, No. 6 (1970), 44-46. Suggests that the chief purposes are to enable school personnel to see the child in his home environment and to allow the family to become acquainted with members of the staff and with school procedures. Fewer than 10 per cent of schools have established programs of home visitation.

LeFevre, Carol, "Face to Face in the Parent-Teacher Conference," *The Elementary School Journal,* LXVIII, No. 8 (1967), 1-8. Discusses the "subterranean" feelings a teacher brings to a conference and how to avoid transmitting a negative attitude to the parent. Gives suggestions for building a positive attitude through the art of listening and praising.

Looney, Douglas, "When You Go To See the Teacher," *Better Homes and Gardens*, XLVIII, No. 10 (1970), 118. Discusses the proper attitude for parents in parent-school communications. Sample questions and topics of discussion are suggested centering on the child to develop a clearer picture of his educational achievement.

McCracken, Samuel, "Schools in Trouble," *Parent's*, XLVI, No. 2 (1971), 57-59, 78. Beckons parents as "voters and customers" to scrutinize, criticize, pressurize, and thereby maximize the effectiveness of their educational system. The education monolith (present standards of certification, the bureaucracy school environment, curriculum) can only be modified by energetic parental action.

Sunley, Robert, *How to Help Your Child in School.* New York: Public Affairs Pamphlet, 1965. A booklet suggesting ways that parents can help their children to learn better by conveying to them a positive attitude toward school. Parent-teacher conferences provide an opportunity for fostering positive parental attitudes.

Weaver, Charles, "Parent-Teacher Communication," *Childhood Education,* XLIV, No. 6 (1968), 420-423. Presents guidelines for more effective communication to help in making parent-teacher conferences successful.

Wey, Herbert W., *Handbook for Principals,* chapter 3, "Conducting Parent-Teacher Conferences." New York: Schaum, 1966. Presents a concise account of aids to successful conferences. The book presents ideas for starting a new program and gives hints for helping teachers conduct more effective conferences.

Audiovisual and Other Resources

But He's Not An Ordinary Child. (16mm film, 21 min., $115). Special Purpose Film, 26740 Latigo Shore Dr., Malibu, Calif. 90265.

Conference Time Multimedia Kit (2 color filmstrips, $25). Includes *Conference Time for Teachers and Parents,* 12 min., $15 if bought separately, and *How to Confer Successfully,* 8 min., $12 if bought separately. NEA, 1201 16th St., N. W., Washington, D. C. 20036.

I Don't Want to Question Your Program, But . . . (16mm film, 14 min., $77). Special Purpose Film, 26740 Latigo Shore Dr., Malibu, Calif. 90265.

I Want To Talk Right Now (16mm film, 22 min., $121). Special Purpose Film, 26740 Latigo Shore Dr., Malibu, Calif. 90265.

Parent-Teacher Conferences (2 records, $2 each). Dramatizations show techniques for successful, productive conferences. Audio-Visual Utilization Center, 5448 Cass Avenue, Wayne State University, Detroit, Michigan 48202.

Trends and Techniques in Parent Education (pamphlet, 95¢). Child Study Press, 50 Madison Ave., New York, N. Y. 10010.

Part Two
Accountability

Accountability

6

Definition

Accountability is the extent to which an individual or institution is willing and able to stand behind its work or its product and to correct a demonstrated or perceived fault. In public education, it refers to the commitment of teachers, administrators, and board members to being responsible for their performance and answerable for the results of their instructional programs.

Education, public and private, has not escaped the dissatisfaction and public criticism that is currently being leveled against almost all institutions. These include government, law-enforcement agencies, the military, business, industry, colleges, courts, churches, the young, the old, employers, employees, and the home itself. The public clamors for holding presidents, legislators, educators, police, industrial leaders, and army privates accountable. In the minds of many, accountability is not a commitment or deep feeling of responsibility which exists within the individual and directs his behavior. To them it is a prerogative of a consumer or taxpayer to demand proof of effective performance or excellence of a product.

When applied to education, accountability attempts to determine whether the schools have produced the promised results. It tries to relate input into the educational enterprise to output as revealed by what students know, how they think, what they can do, what they value, and how they act. Educators are held accountable for the appropriateness of goals and objectives which they select as well as for success in producing satisfactory results. This point is too often overlooked.

Immediately many questions present themselves. Who should be held accountable, and who should properly hold them accountable? What are the schools supposed to be doing? What system and criteria of evaluation can be used? How can long-range results be assessed? Who should establish the objectives and determine what evidence will be acceptable to indicate satisfactory results? What will be done if the assessment reveals unsatisfactory accomplishment? What will happen if an individual or school has produced outstanding results?

Equally baffling are the problems of determining the extent to which and how parents, taxpayers without children in school, boards of education, the student's peers, and governmental officials at all levels should be held accountable for the success or failure of an enterprise that serves a third of the total population.

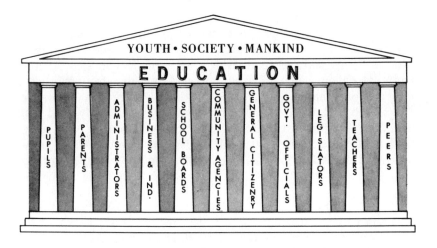

Accountability to Humanity Rests on Many Pillars

Restless, often disillusioned, youth are challenging the relevance of education. Disadvantaged pupils find it impossible to compete with many of their classmates. Citizens in general are deeply concerned about the rapid increase in delinquency, drug addiction, and crime. Many parents are unable to communicate with their children; many people without children are disturbed by the rapid change in values, dress, and conduct of young people. All these phenomena are directly or indirectly associated with education and blamed on the schools.

Beleaguered by a multitude of disruptions, many of them beyond their control, many teachers, administrators, and school board members have lost much of their zest for the challenges of educating youth. They appear to be waiting for the storm of dissent and militancy to pass. To many citizens, the bewilderment and disillusionment of school personnel appear as indifference and lack of concern and responsibility.

Since early 1970, accountability has become one of the most discussed topics in education. Perhaps the attention currently being directed to it is long overdue. Certainly those entrusted with a responsibility as costly, vital, and far-reaching as education must possess an abiding sense of responsibility and should welcome all fair and sincere approaches to holding them accountable for their trusteeship, their performance, and the performance of their students. Without education civilization cannot move forward, and without accountability education will wither.

It is encouraging, then, that teacher organizations are holding conferences on accountability, that school board members choose "On Being Accountable" as their convention theme, and that colleges of education are conducting seminars on the subject. Fortunately, many recent developments in education are closely related to the concept of accountability and will facilitate its implementation. Most obvious among these are behavioral objectives, national assessment, collective negotiations, performance contracting, PPBS, and the voucher system.

Significant Components   *Which ones are essential?*

1. Accountability must be directed toward better education for children rather than toward assessing blame.
2. To keep the focus of accountability on improving education, openness, confidence, and mutual respect must prevail among pupils, teachers, administrators, boards of education, and the public.
3. Parents, pupils, and board members, as well as teachers and administrators, should be held accountable for discharging their respective responsibilities.
4. The objectives of the schools must be significant, capable of achievement, and clearly understood so that their attainment

can be recognized and assessed to the joint satisfaction of teachers, administrators, board members, and school patrons.

5. Fear, anxiety, defensiveness, and unjustified assessment of blame must be minimized.

6. Schools should not be held accountable for outcomes that are beyond their control or for which they do not have adequate funds and other resources.

7. Deficiencies in performance of students, teachers, and administrators should be looked upon as opportunities for diagnosing problems, determining needs, and planning appropriate, positive action.

8. The discovery and analysis of successes or failures should be followed up with appropriate action.

9. Employees who are incompetent or unwilling to perform effectively should be dealt with kindly, but firmly.

10. Time, patience, and hard work must be devoted to developing a workable system of accountability that will accentuate the positive and avoid undue emphasis on the negative.

11. Careful attention should be given to assessing the long-range objectives and outcomes of education.

12. A variety of approaches and criteria are needed to insure the significance and objectivity of the accountability standards.

13. Resources must be allocated for developing effective procedures and preparing valid and objective instruments and other devices for assessing pupil progress.

14. Emphasis on readily measurable skills such as reading and mathematical computation must not be allowed to preempt careful attention to the development of values, attitudes, and other humane qualities.

15. Since the schools are the principal educational agency in all communities, teachers, administrators, and board members should be willing to accept primary responsibility for the quality of education and the progress of pupils.

16. It must be recognized that learning and learning styles vary greatly, but it must also be conceded that they are not effective unless positive outcomes result.

17. In order to keep accountability in reasonable perspective, all those involved must recognize the importance of learning, responsibility for commitment on the part of educators, willingness or reluctance of taxpayers, the complexity of forces that affect the development of children, and the intricate nature of teaching and learning.

18. The accountability system itself must be continuously evaluated and revised.

Proposed Advantages   *With which ones do you agree?*

1. Accountability will enhance educational opportunities for students and improve their learning.
2. Careful assessment will assist in diagnosing deficiencies and needs and give direction to planning for educational improvement.
3. Areas that need additional financial and other resources will be identified, and securing of funds will be facilitated.
4. The teacher's role will change from that of a performer to that of a developer of performance—from presenting material to seeing to it that it is learned.
5. Administrative leadership will be evaluated in terms of its contribution to better learning.
6. Parents and pupils will be brought to realize that they too are responsible for the outcomes of education.
7. All those who want better education will be forced to sit down together to establish significant, understandable goals and agree upon mutually acceptable criteria that assess effort in terms of results.
8. Accountability will stimulate a search for better ways of promoting learning, including differentiated staffing, individualized learning, and use of technological aids.
9. Existing procedures and proposed innovative practices will be evaluated in terms of their actual or potential contribution to learning, and materials and equipment will be purchased upon the basis of their value for producing results.
10. Teachers will place productive effort above filling the class periods with busywork, and students will distinguish between being busy and achieving results.
11. Salaries of teachers and administrators who meet the challenge for improved performance will be enhanced.
12. Because the scope of assessment will extend beyond measurement by paper-and-pencil tests, the demand for evaluative evidence of many kinds, from many sources, will foster realism and relevance in the curriculum.
13. Accountability will benefit the children of the poor, whose parents often do not know how to protect their children's interests.

Criticisms and Difficulties to Be Anticipated   *Do you agree?*

1. Trying to measure the outcomes of education objectively will further neglect those educational outcomes that are at the root

of society's trials by focusing instruction on measurable, often meaningless, minutiae.

2. Faithful teachers and administrators, already discouraged by the failure of the home to discharge its responsibility for bringing up children, will be completely disheartened by being brought to task for deficiencies beyond their control.

3. Meddlers, from the proponents of basic education to social do-gooders, have created a public climate in which sound education is all but impossible and are now trying to blame the schools for their own failures.

4. Many educators are convinced that homes, boards of education, law-enforcement agencies, legislatures, and courts have not given schools the backing needed to do an effective job.

5. Teachers should be responsible to their pupils, not to squabbling power groups, whose demands are often short-term and personal.

6. It is impossible to get the public and educators to sit down together long enough to agree on sound, identifiable, and measurable objectives and outcomes.

7. Many of the most valuable outcomes of education cannot be adequately assessed until the student has been out of school for many years.

8. Insistence upon assigning definite responsibility to individuals will retard innovations that stress teamwork and cooperative effort.

9. Schools already know what many of the deficiencies are and how they could be corrected, but sufficient funds are not available to do the job.

10. The attempt to hold board members, administrators, and teachers strictly accountable will cause conflict and strife among people who should work in harmony for better education for all children.

11. The whole accountability movement is being promoted by disgruntled people who are unwilling to support an adequate educational program for children.

Summary Assessment

It is unfortunate that those who saw the need for accountability in education felt it necessary to emphasize this need by insisting that the schools have failed miserably in discharging their responsibility. Even deeply committed people when bluntly confronted with blame have a natural tendency to assume a defensive posture and become resistant to well-meant suggestion.

Although it is difficult for educators openly to oppose a concept as reasonable as accountability for educating children, the emotional reaction of many school people has been that they are being unjustly put upon. This feeling of injustice is particularly offensive and destructive to those who have, through the years, been most responsible and conscientious. To thousands of administrators, board members, and teachers, the failure of pupils to achieve in the affective as well as in the cognitive and skill areas has been a matter of deep concern.

Hundreds of thousands of school people may be justified in their view that the unrest and changing values of a society that seems to lack direction, unity of purpose, and commitment to identifiable goals have made it impossible for teachers to achieve as they know they should, and what most citizens expect of them. Thousands of others have contributed to the problem rather than to its solution.

But before teachers and school leaders can set a course for improving the schools, the American people must discharge one of their responsibilities that they have thus far failed to discharge. If citizens want to participate in determining the direction and quality of education, if they want to hold schools accountable, teachers and administrators should expect and welcome their sincere interest and needed help. Surely education belongs to all the people. All the people should be interested in knowing the facts about their educational system; and all of them should participate in an orderly, workable, democratic process for making decisions relating to public education.

Society should answer several questions before it presumes to hold its educators accountable. What do we as a society hold dear? What values and attitudes should be taught in the schools? For which areas of the development of youth should the school be responsible? What is the proper relationship of the home, the school, and other agencies to the various other components of the total education of youth? What are the most important and immediate concerns? What long-term objectives can be developed and agreed upon? What level of excellence are we willing to support?

How to isolate the influence of the many variables that affect the development of young people will continue to plague those who would like to hold individuals responsible for certain results. Even when more sophisticated techniques are developed, it may be necessary to shift attention from the individual teacher or administrator to the faculties as a whole in a particular school building or even to the entire school system.

Such an approach might well have the advantage of fostering unity of purpose, teamwork, and a climate of helping relationships among all those charged with improving pupil performance. It might contribute significantly to bridging the ever-increasing differences between teachers and administrators as they seek to make one another successful.

It has been pointed out that a system of accountability cannot be meaningful without incorporating opportunity for redress for the consumer and incentive for the producer. Alternative schools might appear to be a remedy for the dissatisfied and distressed parent, and incentive pay might seem to be a reasonable reward for the teacher or administrator whose accountability profile reveals a high degree of effectiveness.

Good faith and cooperative effort of all those concerned about better education are needed to answer the many persistent questions that must be answered before a workable system of accountability can be developed.

If goals can be agreed upon, adequate resources made available, and reasonable and objective performance criteria developed, the schools should welcome accountability. It could help the public and teachers be more responsive to the needs of youth, for it promises not only opportunity for learning but the assurance that every child will actually learn.

A Few Leaders in the Movement

Charles L. Blaschke
  Education Turnkey Systems, Inc.
Stanley Elam
  Phi Delta Kappan
Robert J. Garvue
  Florida State Univ.
Calvin Grieder
  Univ. of Colorado
Anna L. Heyer
  Hudson Valley Community College
Leon Lessinger
  Univ. of South Carolina

Myron Lieberman
  City Univ. of New York
J. D. McComas
  Univ. of Tennessee
Sidney P. Marland, Jr.
  U. S. Office of Education
James Mecklenburger
  Nat'l. Association of School Boards
Ralph W. Tyler
  Univ. of Chicago
Kenneth E. Underwood
  Fargo (N. D.) Schools

A Few Places Where the Innovation Is Used

California State Board
  of Education
Dallas, Texas
Fargo, N. D.

Guernsey Co., Ohio
Louisville, Ky.
New York, N. Y.

Oregon State Department of Education
Virginia State Department of Education
Yale Univ.

Annotated References

Austin, Gilbert, "Accountability—Hallmark of 1970's," *Science Teacher,* XXXVIII, No. 5 (1971), 26-28. Surveys historical antecedents of accountability. Are children "more intelligent" than they were at the same age three decades ago? Why have levies failed? Do we need performance contracting?

Banton, Lee, "Public Accountability!" *Virginia Journal of Education,* LXIV, No. 8 (1971), 20-21. Emphasizes the accountability of the pocketbook. Parents should be held accountable, in part, for the performance of their offspring. Teacher salaries should become commensurate with responsibilities.

Bowens, C. A., "Accountability from a Humanist View," *Educational Forum,* XXXV, No. 4 (1971), 479-486. Takes the position that accountability is a mask for rampant behaviorism. Who or what does the accounting? Does accountability, in its present state, constitute a threat to academic freedom?

Burgett, Russell E., "Accountability: Just the Teacher?" *School and Community,* LVIII, No. 4 (1971), 30-31. Suggests that learners can be held accountable for many aspects of their progress or lack of it. This implies greater involvement of students in planning and evaluating. Six areas are mentioned for which children can justifiably be held accountable.

Caney, Albert R. and Donald L. Garris, "Accountability for School Counselors," *The School Counselor,* XVIII, No. 5 (1971), 321-322. Suggests that counseling is on the brink of accountability. Subscribes to the view that if there is a quick tumble in this direction, counseling will become mechanistic in search of premature justification.

Cleary, Robert, "Responsibility and Accountability in the American System of Education," *Teachers College Record,* LXVII, No. 6 (1967), 466-470. Stresses the need for public interest and assistance if government is to be held accountable. The limited influence of citizens can be extended through broader participation.

Davies, Don, "Come out from under the Ivy," *American Education,* VI, No. 2 (1970), 29-31. Challenges teacher education to adopt clinical and case-study approaches to preparing teachers. Making teachers accountable will individualize, equalize, and humanize education.

Durost, Walter N., "Accountability: The Task, the Tools, and the Pitfalls," *The Reading Teacher,* XXIV, No. 4 (1971), 291-304, 367. Explores the problems raised by accountability under Title I. Criterion for success in Title I reading is a gain of one grade for seven months to nine months instruction. The schools are currently overcommitted. Tests lack validity.

Elam, Stanley, "The Age of Accountability Dawns in Texarkana," *Phi Delta Kappan,* LI, No. 10 (1970), 509, 511-514. Describes a visit to the Rapid Learning Centers and reports some favorable results in reading and mathematics with some deficiencies. Vandalism and dropout problem show positive trend, and community support is strong. Further exploration is warranted.

Elliott, Osborn, ed., "Accountability," *Newsweek,* LXXV, No. 24 (1970), 72. Discusses accountability of universities to students as presented by Yale's President Brewster. The general public and legislatures are demanding an accounting of returns for expenditures.

Fox, Willard, "How 'In' Is Accountable?" *Ohio School Board Journal,* XIV, No. 6 (1970), 5-6. Explains the concept of accountability. Attention will shift from sanctimonious administrative arrangements and methods to pupils' learning. Tasks given to teachers must be attainable if teachers are to be held accountable.

Gallup, George, "The Public Attitudes toward the Public Schools," *Phi Delta Kappan,* LII, No. 2 (1970), 99-112. Reports 67 per cent of those polled favored holding teachers and administrators accountable and 21 per cent opposed. National tests are favored 75 to 16 and pay for quality performance 58 to 36.

Gooler, Dennis D. and Arden D. Grotelueschen, "Curriculum Development Accountability," *Educational Leadership,* XXIX, No. 2 (1971), 165-169. Suggests that the "curriculum developer" has responsibility with the "curriculum distributor" and the "curriculum consumer" for failure and success. The developer needs to identify different audiences and the questions they are likely to ask.

Grieder, Calvin, "Educators Should Welcome Pressure for Accountability," *Nation's Schools,* LXXXV, No. 5 (1970), 14. Takes the position that accountability for professional activities and expenditure of funds will eventually lead to better teaching. Determining objectives and outcomes the schools should achieve will be difficult.

Johnson, Rita B., "Objectives—Based Accountability Procedures for Classroom Use," *Educational Technology,* XI, No. 6 (1971), 49-51. Explores the use of objectives in demanding accountability. Assumes 95 per cent of students can learn, hence teachers ought to be held accountable. Procedures are outlined for developing an accountability plan which is built on objectives.

Lessinger, Leon, "Focus on the Learner: Central Concern of Accountability in Education," *Audiovisual Instruction,* XV, No. 6 (1970), 42-44. Concludes that independent evaluation from evidence of many kinds will add realism and relevance. Resources for development are necessary to hold schools accountable for quality. Educators' pride in humanistic successes has been a false pride.

Lessinger, Leon M. and R. W. Tyler, *Accountability in Education.* Worthington, Ohio: Charles A. Jones, 1971. Clarifies many of the issues connected with accountability. Attempts at implementation, shifts in criteria, objectives, and limitations are reviewed. The possible effects on instructional programs are discussed.

McNeil, John D., *Toward Accountable Teachers.* New York: Holt, 1971. Points out the need for assessing accountability in terms of pupil progress. A four-phase program of supervision by objectives is projected for student teachers and teachers in service. The focus is on appraisal for improvement in results.

Meade, Edward J., Jr., "Accountability and Governance in Public Education," *Education Canada,* IX, No. 1 (1969), 48-51. Emphasizes the shift of accountability from the individual class and teacher to the particular school. The principal now becomes more important. The school must know its goals and the direction of the change it is to produce.

Nottingham, Marvin A. and Louis D. Zeyen, "Commitment to Accountability— A Case Study," *Journal of Secondary Education,* XLVI, No. 1 (1971), 3-8.

Describes implementation of accountability. The article goes into detail on how to establish goals and behavioral objectives. It suggests ways to assign priorities among broad goals and to analyze data relating to achievement.

Raths, Louis E., *Teaching for Learning.* Columbus, Ohio: Merrill, 1969. Urges schools to find out just what is happening in the classrooms, especially in regard to quality. The time and effort devoted to each of the 10 listed elements of teaching should be determined.

Rothstein, Arnold M., "Start Measuring Your School's Effort or Your Public Will Do It for You," *The American School Board Journal,* CLVII, No. 11 (1970), 2, 6. Reviews Louis Rath's *Teaching for Learning.* The teacher should do something that is identifiable and recognizable. Ten components of teaching are listed that might serve to measure teacher performance.

Schaefer, Carl J., "Accountability: A Sobering Thought," *American Vocational Journal,* XLIV, No. 4 (1969), 21-23. Stresses the responsibility for vocational-technical education to be answerable for prudent spending of the funds provided by the 1968 amendments. Goals and measurement need refinement.

Stock, Joseph and Donald F. Wilson, "Accountability and the Classroom Teacher," *Today's Education,* LX, No. 3 (1971), 41-56. Presents the demand for accountability as a reflection of public concern about the results of education. Eight areas are listed for which the classroom teacher reasonably can be held accountable to eight different groups. Numerous conditions must exist if teachers are to be held fully accountable. Members of local associations are charged with 18 things to do about accountability.

Underwood, Kenneth E., "Before You Decide to Be 'Accountable,' Make Sure You Know for What," *The American School Board Journal,* CLVIII, No. 3 (1970), 32-33. Warns against introducing innovations without providing for objective evaluation of their effectiveness or failure. Behavioral objectives tell boards what benefits they are receiving, and what weaknesses need to be resolved.

Von Haden, H. I. and K. M. Glass, *Accountability for Results in Education.* Swarthmore, Pa.: A. C. Croft, Inc., 1972. Explains the meaning of accountability and the forces that brought about interest in it. The relationship between accountability and PPBS, behavioral objectives, national assessment, performance contracting, and the voucher system are treated in detail.

Audiovisual and Other Resources

Alternative Avenues to Educational Accountability (filmstrip, tape, instructor's manual, $17). Examines personal, professional and public accountability. By James Popham and Eva Baker. Vimcet Associates, P. O. Box 24714, Los Angeles, Calif. 90024.

The Teacher and Accountability (audiotape, $10). Robert Stake of Univ. of Illinois on the teacher's role in educational accountability. Vimcet Associates, P. O. Box 24714, Los Angeles, Calif. 90024.

Planning, Programming, Budgeting System (PPBS)

7

Definition

PPBS is an integrated system for providing public administrators and legislative bodies with reliable information for analyzing the quality and quantity of ongoing and proposed programs and for making decisions relating to these programs and their financial support. It is budgeting for program and performance. Costs are analyzed in terms of the achievement of objectives. Recently the term *Planning, Programming, Budgeting, Evaluating System* has become widely used.

Among the questions which PPBS assists educational planners in answering are: What objectives should the schools achieve? How effectively are existing programs achieving them? What are the long-term plans? What resources are needed, and how can they be allocated to best advantage? Are there promising alternative approaches to securing better results? What priorities should be established among the goals and programs? Should some activities be eliminated? Which ones should be given greater support? Should taxes be increased? How will additional revenue be spent? What specific benefits will result? Should some of the current responsibility of the schools be turned over to other agencies? Should the schools assume additional functions to fulfill unmet needs? What are they?

In planning for the educational program, an accountable board of education and its superintendent must be constantly concerned about the results that are achieved with the resources that they commit to the various programs. It is difficult to determine what contribution each component of the total school program makes to the education of boys and girls. PPBS is an approach to costing out, in terms of results achieved, the clusters of activities that make up various programs. Money, which is converted into buildings, equipment, personnel, and other facilities, constitutes the input. Desirable learning on the part of students is the output. School boards and administrators are accountable to the extent that their commitments of resources have produced the desired results. They are also responsible for not having overlooked more economical alternates which could produce comparable or even superior learning outcomes. Obligations to parents and pupils demand that those charged with assessing the needs of the schools and making provision for resolving them have at their disposal the best possible data in order to make sound decisions.

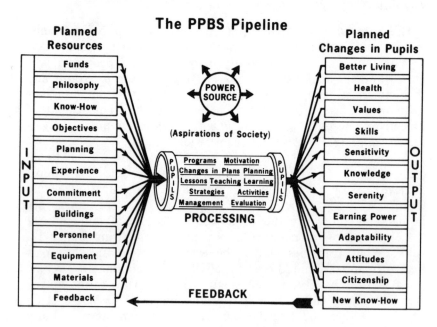

The PPBS Pipeline

Planned Resources	Planned Changes in Pupils
Funds	Better Living
Philosophy	Health
Know-How	Values
Objectives	Skills
Planning	Sensitivity
Experience	Knowledge
Commitment	Serenity
Buildings	Earning Power
Personnel	Adaptability
Equipment	Attitudes
Materials	Citizenship
Feedback	New Know-How

INPUT — OUTPUT

POWER SOURCE

(Aspirations of Society)

PUPILS — PUPILS

Programs   Motivation
Changes in Plans   Planning
Lessons   Teaching   Learning
Strategies   Activities
Management   Evaluation

PROCESSING

FEEDBACK

PPBS: Planned Output Determining Planned Input

For a number of years business and several agencies of the federal government have used a systems approach in securing information relating to the failures, successes, and needs of many of their programs. In industry it is often much easier to identify and evaluate a distinguishable product than in education in which great differences prevail regarding the goals and desirable outcomes. What one parent applauds as high-level teaching of values and conduct, another condemns as intolerable indoctrination. What one citizen commends as independent thinking on the part of a high school graduate, another decries as revolutionary heresy. Under these circumstances, educational accounting becomes a far more challenging process than testing an appliance or an automobile. Realizing the predicament in which a systems approach to assessing educational production may place them, many teachers and administrators continue to look with apprehension upon the idea of relating input to output.

The first step in a PPB system is listing what the school system expects to do. The objectives must be stated in clear, precise, and, as far as possible, measurable terms so that they can be used as bases for evaluating the effectiveness of educational activities. The school then *explores* alternatives for achieving its objectives, *chooses* the most promising and feasible approaches, *analyzes* its program needs, and *allocates resources* necessary to carry out learning activities needed to achieve the goals it has set. Evaluation, inherent in PPBS, reveals the extent to which the objectives supported by the allocated resources have been achieved.

The effectiveness of alternative approaches to instruction can be compared and used as bases for subsequent decisions. Components of the various programs are identified and analyzed to provide data on the amount of time, money, and personnel used for them. The system, then, seeks to determine where the school is going, how it will get there, what financial and other resources are needed, and whether or not the objectives have been achieved. Through the consideration of alternatives, the process encourages innovation, personnel involvement, and program improvement. The total educational endeavor must be integrated. The line-item concept of budgeting according to common categories of anticipated expenditures must be replaced by a new way of thinking and of allocating funds according to results to be achieved. If $15,000 is budgeted for technical assistants, the budget must show precisely the purpose the expenditure will accomplish. Input is determined as it is needed to produce desired output.

Significant Components   *Which ones are essential?*

1. Most important in PPBS is a commitment to the approach.
2. A clear, precise statement of measurable objectives is basic to initial planning.
3. PPBS assesses the total program, what ought to be, and the contributions of the individual segments.
4. Program analysis and cost analysis must proceed together, and costs must be grouped according to the job to be done.
5. Projections of programs, resources, needs, and costs should be long-term, perhaps for a five-year period.
6. Alternative ways of accomplishing various goals more effectively and efficiently must be explored.
7. Three years might be considered as the minimum time required to restructure thinking, gain acceptance of the idea, develop forms and procedures, and launch a PPB system.
8. Administration must understand the importance of gaining the support of staff and public.
9. The desired services must be grouped and determination made of the contributions that each of the various programs will make in providing these services.
10. To the extent that it can reasonably be done, the individual activities of a program should be identified and isolated so that the contribution of each to learning results obtained can be assessed.
11. The model must provide for producing and delivering the necessary information in such a form that it can be readily used for intelligent decision-making.
12. The line-item approach to budgeting must be discarded, and a whole new concept of accounting must be accepted.
13. If $10,000, as an illustration, is to be spent for mimeograph paper, the system should reveal the objectives that the expenditure is expected to accomplish.
14. A five-year plan should be flexible so that it can be updated annually to modify action in the light of actual experience.
15. Teachers and curriculum specialists must participate in setting objectives, assessing needs, and planning outcomes.
16. Flexibility must be provided so that the system can be adapted to the peculiar needs of an individual district.

17. Provision should be made for an educational as well as a financial audit.
18. Everybody involved must realize that measuring inputs and outputs in education is more complex and difficult than in industry.
19. More productive use of resources, rather than reduction in cost, should be the primary goal of PPBS.
20. Inservice training of staff is necessary to increase competence in dealing with the hardware and software of the program.

Proposed Advantages   *With which ones do you agree?*

1. PPBS provides administrators and boards of education with data for making decisions, establishing priorities, and allocating resources.
2. The system fosters accountability for assessing the role of the schools, the expenditure of funds, and program performance.
3. Legislative and administrative groups have a basis for choosing from among alternatives.
4. Integrated planning among agencies and among various programs within one agency is facilitated.
5. PPBS provides for conducting public business more economically, effectively, and expeditiously.
6. The system offers a basis for deciding whether a change in output is worth the required change in input.
7. PPBS reduces unnecessary and undesirable pressure on public officials because justification for requests and recommendations is an inherent part of the system from the outset.
8. Inherent in the system are suggestions for program improvement through elimination, revision, expansion, or addition.
9. Educators are forced to avoid broad, meaningless generalizations.
10. PPBS promotes better education because it requires that a budget request or expenditure is made only for the attainment of a worthwhile educational goal.
11. The objectivity of the system builds confidence in administrative and legislative leaders, thereby generating greater public support for education.
12. By tying instructional and business planning together in unity of purpose and function, PPBS permits comparisons among various agencies and services, as to their effectiveness and their cost.
13. Planning of needs and funds is placed on a multiyear basis.

14. PPBS gives direction to the entire educational enterprise by indicating what demands it must be prepared to meet and what resources it will need to achieve its goals.

15. Complex programs are broken down into manageable components.

16. Knowledge of progress promotes professional growth and satisfaction among school personnel.

17. Ineffective programs are identified so that they can be eliminated, thus releasing physical facilities and human resources for redeployment to more fruitful pursuits.

Criticisms and Difficulties to Be Anticipated   *Do you agree?*

1. PPBS oversimplifies the complex nature of teaching and learning and the intricacy of the mind and emotional system.

2. Establishing objectives may fall into the hands of demagogues with a distorted view of what education really is.

3. Costing various alternatives implies that the value of these options can be assessed before they are tested.

4. The whole idea of PPBS is built on the premise that the value of education should eventually be measured, as in business, in terms of monetary output as a return for financial input.

5. Although PPBS is designed to reduce costs, it actually increases them substantially because most schools do not have the trained personnel and equipment necessary to implement an effective systems approach.

6. The system discourages experimentation, which by its very nature cannot be expected to yield immediate returns.

7. The most significant decisions of man are based on judgment; and for developing judgment, thoughtful experience is the best teacher.

8. It is ridiculous, for example, to attempt to determine to what objectives the cost of the multimedia center should be charged.

9. Since budgeting takes place in a political environment, many administrators and boards may resist public scrutiny of all their operations, and conflict with political pressures of vested interests must be expected.

10. Assuming that PPBS can be established simply by putting new categories into the traditional budget is a serious pitfall.

11. It is impossible to determine which school activities are responsible for which outcomes.

12. In too many instances, those who institute innovations are the same people who supply data for evaluating them.

Summary Assessment

Currently, next to national defense, public education claims the largest share of total tax revenue. Because of the benefits that accrue to a society from the development of its human resources, the massive funding for education has appeared to be a good investment. However, in recent years, taxpayers have exhibited growing resistance to what seems to be an endless increase in demands and costs of education. They have begun to question the programs and practices of the schools. They have talked more and more about the school's accountability for performance.

As budgeting practices have been examined, many questions have arisen. What are the purposes and goals of public education? Is education taking on too much? How much of the various services do we want and can we afford? Are the schools performing as well as they should? Will the demand for more money ever stop? Would smaller appropriations show any decline in educational achievement? What proportion of public expenditures should be allotted to education? How much of this expenditure are we willing to devote to the education of one age group—those between the ages of five and 22?

Computing costs and other inputs in relation to quantity and quality of production has, in varying degrees, been part of business and industrial practice for a half century. Only during the past 10 years, however, has PPBS been introduced into public agencies. Beginning in the Department of Defense, its use has spread throughout the departments and bureaus of the federal government. The 5-5-5 project, involving five states, five counties, and five cities, focused attention of educators on the possibilities of PPBS for educational planning and budgeting.

At the present time, thousands of school systems throughout the country use some aspects of PPBS, although full utilization of the program is growing slowly and resistance to it continues among many educators. It is a valuable tool for improving decision-making. The system facilitates better choices and decisions by providing factual data about plans, programs, needs, resources, and performance. It requires long-term planning, encourages accountability, and generates public support. As ways of determining the relationship between input and output are refined, PPBS will become more pertinent and valuable. It may not reduce costs, but it should increase the effectiveness of educational programs.

As utilization of the program has moved forward, it appears that school administrators have placed more emphasis upon the analysis of financial input than of education output. Budget preparation has continued to be looked upon as the responsibility primarily of the school's business management. Although the figures in the budget have been rearranged, the line-item continues to influence the thinking of those who do the financial planning.

Educational auditing lags behind financial accounting because learning objectives and their achievement are less suited to being perceived and appraised at an actual or approximate value than are dollar amounts. Then too, instructional personnel are often satisfied to think in rather elusive terms of general goals and are reluctant to try to reduce them to manageable specifics. To them teaching is such an intricate art that attempting to determine definite cause-and-effect relationships between financial resources committed and results obtained threatens to destroy teaching for genuinely worthwhile long-term values.

Gradually, however, teachers, administrators, and school boards are being challenged to rethink their objectives critically, to redirect their efforts toward greater productivity, and to evaluate their results in terms of pre-established goals. Reason demands that educators give serious attention to the promising possibilities of PPBS for integrating efficient operation with effective performance.

A Few Leaders in the Movement

Robert F. Alioto
  Yonkers, N. Y.
William H. Curtis
  American Association
  of School Administrators
Harry J. Hartley
  New York Univ.
H. Thomas James
  Spencer Foundation
Richard A. Johnson
  Poiter School District
  Tampa, Fla.
Anton Jungherr
  Pearl River (N. Y.) School Dist.

Fremont E. Kast
  Univ. of Washington
Edgar Morphet
  Univ. of California at Berkeley
David Novick
  Rand Corp.
John Pagen
  Waterford (Conn.) Public Schools
Charles Ryan
  Utah State Univ.
Allen Schick
  Tufts College

A Few Places Where the Innovation Is Used

Clark County, Nev.
Dade County, Fla.

Darien, Conn.
Davidson County, Tenn.

Douglas County, Colo.
Greenwich, Conn.

Long Island, N. Y.	Milwaukee, Wis.	Peoria, Ill.
Los Angeles, Calif.	Montgomery Co., Md.	Portland, Me.
Memphis, Tenn.	Parma, Ohio	Skokie, Ill.
Milford, N. H.	Pearl River, N. Y.	Westport, Conn.

Annotated References

Alioto, Robert F. and J. A. Jungherr, "Using PPBS to Overcome Taxpayers' Resistance," *Phi Delta Kappan,* LI, No. 3 (1969), 138-141. Cites the example of the author's school district in which there was a turmoil created by budget defeats. PPBS was used to organize and display data to overcome taxpayers' resistance.

Baynham, Dorsey, "PPBS and Several Good Reasons It Shouldn't Scare You Off," *American School Board Journal,* CLVIII, No. 2 (1970), 27-29. Warns against hasty implementation and attempting to secure good results from input of bad data. However, reason demands that educators study thoughtfully the possibilities for good that lie in systems analysis.

Buskin, Martin, "PPBS Means Better Money Management," *School Management,* XIII, No. 11 (1969), 64-68, 80-82. Explains advantages, difficulties, and roadblocks encountered in five school districts. Public understanding of rising costs is a common benefit, but establishing the program areas to be budgeted and allocating certain costs to them present knotty problems.

Carter, Vernon, "PPBS in a Small High School—It Can Be Done," *Journal of Secondary Education,* XLV, No. 7 (1970), 313-319. Reports on case study of PPBS in Sierra, California, Joint Union High School. Board support, planning and implementation, resources, and procedures are discussed in relationship to effective operation.

Curtis, William H., "Program Budgeting Design For Schools Unveiled, With Much Work Still to Go," *Nation's Schools,* LXXIV, No. 5 (1969), 40-42. Addresses itself to eight pilot projects, giving reactions of educators, business officials, and teacher organizations. Flexibility of design and time for development are essential. Planning and evaluation are likely to cause difficulty for schools.

Drew, Elizabeth B., "HEW Grapple With PPBS," *The Public Interest,* I, No. 8 (1967), 9-27. Looks at PPBS in Washington and calls it primitive. The study stresses the point that it may take a number of years for benefits to become apparent. Ten questions reflect the increasing sophistication of newer studies.

Furno, Orlando F., "Planning Programming Budgeting Systems: Boon or Bane?" *Phi Delta Kappan,* LI, No. 3 (1969), 142-144. Outlines a number of problems that may be encountered by school administrations as they accept PPBS. PPBS yields some benefits but not as many as some of the proponents believe. The article points out that other proposals may fit the situations better.

Gibbs, Wesley, Gustave Rath, and Arthur Kent, "PPBS: What We've Learned in One Year," *Nation's Schools,* LXXXIV, No. 5 (1969), 43. Suggests modifications which can be used and were used in Skokie, Illinois, after a rocky year of trying to apply PPBS. The biggest difficulty was the development of specific technical skills within the existing school staff in order to make the transition.

Greenhouse, Samuel M., "The Planning - Programming - Budgeting System: Rationale, Language, and Idea-Relationships," *Public Administration Review,* XXV, No. 4 (1966), 271-277. Bases PPBS on the premise that public agencies should be accountable to the public. Planning includes identification of objectives and mobilization of resources needed to secure the desired output. The merits of alternate approaches for securing results are considered.

Grieder, Calvin, "Program Budgeting May Not Solve Your Planning Problems," *Nation's Schools,* LXXXI, No. 6 (1968), 8. Ascribes apparent tardiness of introducing systems into educational operations to the fact that identifying and measuring input and output in learning is more complex than in industrial or business production.

Hartley, Harry J., *Educational Planning - Programming - Budgeting: A Systems Approach.* Englewood Cliffs, N. J.: Prentice Hall, 1968. Advocates a need for budgeting reform and outlines a system approach. Also discussed are administrative issues, recent projects, limitations of PPBS and future research needs. Many selected references are included for the reader.

———, "Limitations of Systems Analysis," *Phi Delta Kappan,* L, No. 9 (1969), 515-519. An authority in the field identifies 25 shortcomings and pitfalls of systems approaches to the analysis of educational processes. He concludes, however, that the potential advantages far outweigh the deficiencies and limitations.

———, "Twelve Hurdles To Clear Before You Take on Systems Analysis," *American School Board Journal,* CLVI, No. 1 (1968), 17-18. Urges careful study before plunging into any innovation involving a systems approach. Twelve problem areas are identified that require thoughtful reflection and advance planning to assure success.

Hereford, Karl, "New Management Information Systems Due By End of 1972," *Nation's Schools,* LXXXV, No. 5 (1970), 63-64. Explains four guides for reporting to the United States Office of Education. They include a Program Information Report, an Evaluation Survey, a Guide for Preparing Narrative Reports, and a Management Review.

Horton, Roger L. and Kent W. Bishop, "Keeping Up with the Budget Crunch," *Audiovisual Instruction,* XV, No. 10 (1970), 49-51. Describes some of what PPBS is all about and how one can use the technique. Steps are outlined to follow and tables are included which show functions for the staff to perform.

Jones, D. M., "PPBS—A Tool for Improving Instruction," *Educational Leadership,* XXVIII, No. 4 (1971), 405-409. Addresses itself to PPBS as used in the Pearl River, New York, School System, why it is needed, and the benefits derived from it.

Livingston, James A., "Educational Goals and Program Planning and Budgeting Systems (PPBS)," *Journal of Secondary Education,* XLV, No. 7 (1970), 305-312. Lists well-defined goals needed to implement a sound PPBS program to provide greater accountability. Goal categories and program grids are presented for developing goals and objectives.

Lyden, Fremont J. and Ernest G. Miller, eds., *Planning Programming Budgeting: A Systems Approach to Management.* Chicago: Markham, 1967. A book of readings explaining why and how the PPBS system developed in the federal government, together with some of its limitations. It seeks to supply a basis for further development and for public understanding of this approach to changing governmental management.

Manning, William R., "Cost Analysis and Curriculum Decisions," *Educational Leadership,* XXVII, No. 2 (1969), 179-183. Advocates PPBS for maximum effectiveness in educational spending. Discusses cost-effectiveness analysis which is an important element in PPBS. It is proposed that the utilization of cost-effectiveness analysis will result in greater educational benefits.

Morphet, Edgar L. and Charles O. Ryan, eds., *A Report of Designing Education for the Future: An Eight-State Project,* pp. 266-290. New York: Citation, 1967. Predicts great benefits for increasing support and results from education; but acknowledges difficulties in recognizing importance of judgment, evaluating instruction in values, specificity, and the uniqueness of the learning of individual children.

Parker, Stephenson, "PPBS," *California Teachers Association Journal,* LXV, No. 3 (1969), 9-11. Explains the design of the program developed by a commission of the California legislature in 1967. Expediency often requires acceptance of conflicting goals such as unity of purpose and independent thought. Present evaluation procedures have difficulty in assessing many significant outcomes of education.

Peterson, M. W., "Potential Impact of PPBS on Colleges and Universities," *Journal of Higher Education,* XLII, No. 1 (1971), 1-20. Presents a clear and concise definition of what PPBS is and how it will affect the various elements of our universities.

Planning for Educational Development in a Planning, Programming, Budgeting System. National Education Association Committee on Finance. Washington, D. C., 1968. Indicates the value of PPBS for supplying factual data with which public administrators and legislative bodies can make better decisions. These judgments involve kinds, quantity, and quality of services; allocating of responsibility to particular agencies; and deployment of resources.

Poindexter, Charles C., "Planning-Programming-Budgeting Systems for Education," *High School Journal,* LII, No. 4 (1969), 206-217. Describes the purposes and processes involved in establishing a PPB system. The attempt to establish PPBS is beneficial to a school even if full implementation is never realized.

Schick, Allen, "Planning-Programming-Budgeting System: A Symposium," *Public Administration Review,* XXV, No. 4 (1966), 243-258. Outlines three stages of development in budgetary reform. The initial stage sought central control over spending, the second stage addresses itself to efficient performance of work and management. The present stage is directed toward planning and decision-making.

Szuberla, Charles A., "How to Ease into PPBS," *The American School Board Journal,* CLVI, No. 11 (1969), 20. Relates the experience of Niles Township Community High School District, a Chicago suburb, as it moved into PPBS. The article outlines the figures in use and the total aspects of PPBS implemented in this school district.

What Is A Programming, Planning, Budgeting System? National Education Association, Research Bulletin 46. Washington, D. C., 1968. Indicates improvement in educational process as a result of focusing school activities on specific objectives and evaluating them in terms of results produced. Integration into a total system, not specific technique, is the significant feature.

Wilsey, Carl E., "Program Budgeting: An Easy Guide With Confusion Removed," *The American School Board Journal,* CLVI, No. 11 (1969), 16-19. Presents a simplified explanation of PPBS and the good and bad points. It is advocated that PPBS is so promising every school system should look at its possibilities. The article explains the components and the interrelationships so that the overall picture can be grasped.

Audiovisual and Other Resources

Management by Objectives (kit of 5 filmstrips, cassette tapes, manuals, $95). Describes steps a school district may take in organizing for management by objectives. By Robert Boston and David Spencer, Bloomfield Hills, Mich. Paul S. Amidon & Associates, 5408 Chicago Ave. S., Minneapolis, Minn. 55417.

Behavioral Objectives

8

Definition

A behavioral objective is an observable criterion of performance. It is a clear, precise statement of the student's behavior that will be accepted as evidence of his having achieved what he and the teacher set out to accomplish. It is a goal indicating a task which the student is expected to perform, a way in which he should respond, or a skill which he can demonstrate after certain learning experiences. The statement of the proposed outcomes is precise and describes in unambiguous terms the kind of behavior and level of proficiency that is expected.

In a sense, the term *behavioral objective* is unfortunate. For many teachers it carries the implication that all desirable outcomes of instruction must result in demonstrable overt behavior and be subject to precise quantitative measurement. Hence many teachers consider behavioral objectives quite appropriate for psychomotor learning but less applicable to the cognitive area and inappropriate for affective learning. Learning should be looked upon as the process of achieving changed ways of responding in cognitive and affective as well as in psychomotor behavior.

These objectives, requiring outcomes that demonstrate observably improved performance, replace such general terms as *knows, enjoys, understands,* and *appreciates* with such terms as *lists, constructs, correctly names,* and *selects.* Because they frequently proceed from the general to the specific, a distinction is made between goals, general objectives, and precise behavioral objectives.

A goal might be: To foster interest in good literature. A general objective might be: To develop deeper understanding and appreciation of the thought and style of William Wordsworth. Stated in behavioral terms, the objective might be: Given 16 two-line selections of poetry—four from Shakespeare, four from Tennyson, four from Milton, and four from Wordsworth—and asked to select the four passages written by Wordsworth, the student should correctly identify at least three of the four selections from Wordsworth and misidentify not more than one passage. Sometimes a time limit for completion of the exercise and other conditions are specified. If the student is able to present this evidence, both he and the teacher will know that he has achieved the acceptable level of performance to demonstrate his understanding and appreciation of the thought and style of Wordsworth.

During the late 1960's educators and the public sensed discrepancies between high-sounding educational goals and student performance. Upon closer examination, the objectives appeared so vague and elusive that educators and critics of schools lacked common ground for assessing the effectiveness of education and for planning what many considered an urgently needed revitalization. It is perhaps fair to say that the publication of Robert F. Mager's book in 1962 spearheaded the emphasis of recent years on behavioral objectives.

The absence of clear objectives has handicapped evaluation of innovative practices, novel school organization, and new materials and equipment. The inability to measure recognizable performance in relation to commonly accepted goals has continued to puzzle researchers and taxpayers. Rapid change in values and attitudes has raised questions concerning the proper affective role of the school, the responsibility of the home and church, education versus indoctrination, the effectiveness of various approaches to teaching values, and many other perplexing problems.

As a result, the need has become clear for objectives stated in precise behavioral terms, for instructional programs designed to achieve the objectives, and for evaluation procedures that provide observable evidence that the desired ends have been attained. Behavioral objectives have potential for giving increased direction and focus to instruction, shaping the learning experiences, and providing for meaningful evaluation by specifying the performance and its minimal level that indicate success.

Significant Components   *Which ones are essential?*

1. Behavioral objectives must be precise statements of specific goals.
2. In order to give substance and direction to teaching and learning, the objectives should state what the student will do after completing the learning activities.
3. Objectives must be based on the needs of the pupils and society and consistent with a sound philosophy of education.
4. Establishment of objectives must be followed with appropriate methods, materials and learning activities to achieve the specified performance.
5. The significance of concomitant learning should not be overlooked.
6. A logical and natural sequence involves setting objectives, engaging in relevant learning activities, and assessing results in terms of the planned behavioral outcomes.
7. Teachers and other staff members of each school must develop their own objectives.
8. Pretesting performance is highly desirable so that the teacher can adjust his original objectives.
9. If pretests show that a student can already perform at the level stated in the objective, the goal should be revised upward. If certain originally assumed behavior is absent, the standard should be lowered.
10. The teacher must develop proficiency in applying sound principles of learning.
11. The established objectives must be worthwhile in the eyes of the learner and attainable for him, and he must find satisfaction in having achieved them.
12. The learner must see a relationship between assigned exercises and the attainment of the behavioral objective.
13. The objectives must be stated clearly and precisely enough to be meaningful and readily understood and communicated.
14. The lowest level of acceptable performance must be indicated.
15. When appropriate, time limits and other conditions should be stated.

Proposed Advantages   *With which ones do you agree?*

1. Behavioral objectives serve as the basis for justifying and establishing a relevant program of measurable quality.

2. Curriculum planning, program revision, and meaningful evaluation are facilitated.

3. Behavioral objectives may be written for all levels of the affective, psychomotor, and cognitive domains.

4. When learning is expressed in behavioral terms, it takes on meaning and clarity and can be communicated to all those involved in the educational process.

5. By telling the learner how he is expected to behave, behavioral objectives suggest to him what to do, how to go about doing it, and what to use to accomplish his ends.

6. Objective research is aided by clear, precise objectives.

7. Teachers are given feedback as to whether or not certain strategies and activities are leading in the right direction.

8. Assignments have significance, and knowledge of progress provides motivation for the learner.

9. Appropriate objectives insure success; observable success stimulates interest and builds confidence; interest and confidence generate increased effort and learning.

10. The teacher is enabled to evaluate and report with greater certainty and assurance.

11. Behavioral objectives help the students in diagnosing deficiencies and in planning further study.

12. Specific, clearly stated objectives are more easily and meaningfully revised than vague, general ones.

13. Aid is provided for the selection of appropriate subject matter, materials, methods, and equipment.

14. The teacher is assisted in self-evaluation and discussion with supervisors.

15. Behavioral objectives point out that the cognitive is often overemphasized to the neglect of the affective and psychomotor.

16. Behavioral objectives demonstrate that the attainment of knowledge is defensible as a goal; but that it is only a base on which to build higher levels of analysis, synthesis, and understanding.

Criticisms and Difficulties to Be Anticipated   *Do you agree?*

1. It may be difficult, and indeed awkward and frustrating, to express certain desired outcomes in precise behavioral terms.

2. Outcomes that are easily described and measured are often unimportant.

3. Undue emphasis on behavioral objectives may lead to neglect of broad concepts, principles, and the understandings that give meaning to behavior.

4. Behavioral objectives may focus attention on parts of wholes, minutiae, and trivia to the detriment of integration and unity.

5. Insistence on defining objectives in behavioral terms may invite neglect of affective teaching and learning.

6. Emphasis on behavior may overlook the reasons underlying it.

7. Overemphasis on behavioral outcomes may neglect the development of improved thinking processes and stress the quantitative to the neglect of the qualitative.

8. Behavioral objectives are appropriate for typing or machine shop, but not for history or literature.

9. The concept of behavioral objectives and performance is sometimes misinterpreted as implying that no outcomes of learning are important except overt behavior.

10. Stating in advance precisely what should happen in a class precludes much significant and valuable incidental learning.

11. Precise objectives tend to preclude readjustments as the learning activities proceed.

Summary Assessment

National assessment is moving forward. Collective negotiations in education is rapidly becoming common practice. PPBS (Planning, Programming, Budgeting System), performance contracting, and the voucher method all propose to relate input to output. Goals must be determined, and results must be measured. Accountability requires clearly stated objectives with valid means of assessing performance.

All of these recent developments relate directly or indirectly to accountability and a systems approach to educational auditing. Most of these approaches seek to assess the results of instruction and relate outcomes in some way to the resources that have been committed to achieving them. In this evaluation, vague, ambiguous statements of objectives and sweeping generalizations about outcomes no longer satisfy those who are raising serious questions about the goals of education and the results that are actually being achieved.

Since promoting learning in its broadest sense is the basic reason for the existence of schools, it seems incongruous that educational auditing has fallen behind auditing practices in other areas of school operations. During the past half century educators have, for example, insisted on increasingly specific and detailed building specifications and have held the contractors accountable for their performance. Similarly, financial accounting has become more sophisticated and precise.

Yet teachers and administrators have been slow to devote commensurate concern and effort to developing a system of precise educational specifications that would assist in instructional planning, contribute to establishing priorities, aid teachers and learners in directing their efforts, and more readily demonstrate accountability. Without exact building specifications endless conflict would result between boards of education and contractors. Perhaps the absence of more exact performance criteria contributes significantly to many of the misunderstandings and dissatisfactions, warranted or unwarranted, that exist relative to the results that schools are achieving.

People are no longer content to purchase "good" packaged food or "good" garden seed or "good" vitamins. They are demanding to know more and more about the quantity and quality of the product or service for which they are spending their money. It appears that schools cannot escape this relentless pressure for accountability.

Those who are impatient with what appears to them to be slow progress on the part of school people must face the indisputable fact that assessing short- and long-term results in many really significant areas is not a simple matter. Evaluating progress in thinking, development and application of principles, social sensitivity, responsibility, aspirations, and judgment is delicate and intricate. To neglect these qualities and take refuge in the measurement of easily recognizable skills and factual information would pervert some of the most fundamental responsibilities of quality education.

Educators, on the other hand, must not hide behind the difficulty and complexity of the problem in an attempt to avoid the challenging and arduous task of converting vague generalities into more precise and understandable statements. Broad goals continue to have an important place in education, but professional educators must not tolerate undeterminable or insignificant results.

In recent years, professional meetings at all levels, inservice workshops, college classes, and publications have been devoted to furthering understanding and skill in developing behavioral objectives. These activities bear evidence to the fact that teachers, administrators, and college professors are seriously concerned and determined to improve the learning of children by establishing sound objectives and carefully evaluating results.

Behavioral objectives have already accomplished much by giving meaning and validity to many aspects of teaching, learning, and evaluation. Continued study, practice, and research will improve the process and increase the benefits. Progress will continue toward further developing materials and learning activities that are actually related to the attainment of desired outcomes. Meaningless results, neglect of the affective areas of learning, and irrelevant assignments will come under close scrutiny. Effective development of understandable objectives promises to facilitate growth in self-direction both on the part of the teacher and the student. It should be an invaluable aid to independent study for out-of-school adults as well as for children by enabling them to set their goals, focus their learning, and assess their progress.

A Few Leaders in the Movement

Robert Armstrong
  Univ. of Arizona
Eva L. Baker
  Univ. of California at Los Angeles
Larry L. Barker
  Florida State Univ.
Benjamin S. Bloom
  Univ. of Chicago
Lee Cronbach
  Stanford Univ.
Thorwald Esbensen
  Duluth (Minn.) Schools
John B. Gilpin
  Earlham College
H. M. Harmes
  Florida Atlantic Univ.
John B. Hough
  Syracuse Univ.

Darwin Keye
  Mt. Healthy (Ohio) Schools
Robert Kibler
  Purdue Univ.
D. R. Krathwohl
  Syracuse Univ.
H. H. McAshan
  Univ. of Florida
Robert Mager
  Stanford Univ.
B. B. Masia
  University of Chicago
Forrest Moran
  Miami Univ.
Ralph Ojemann
  Educational Research Council
  of Greater Cleveland
W. J. Popham
  Univ. of California at Los Angeles

A Few Places Where the Innovation Is Used

Alachua Co., Fla.
Bloomfield Hills, Mich

Carlisle, Pa.
Carson City, Nev.

Centerville, Ohio
Edina, Minn.

Hillsborough Co., Fla.   Portland, Oreg.   Univ. of Illinois
Mt. Healthy, Ohio   Sioux Falls, S. D.   Univ. of Nebraska
Norwalk, Conn.   Temple City, Calif.   Westerly, R. I.

Annotated References

Armstrong, Robert, Terry Cornell, Robert Kraner, and E. Wayne Roberson, *The Development and Evaluation of Behavioral Objectives.* Worthington, Ohio: Charles A. Jones, 1970. Explains the purposes of objectives and their relationship to a philosophy of education. The need for clear, precise objectives is stressed. Provision is made for developing skill in writing behavioral objectives. A list of distributors of evaluation instruments is provided.

Atkin, J. Myron, "Behavioral Objectives in Curriculum Design: A Cautionary Note," *The Science Teacher,* XXXV, No. 5 (1968), 27-30. Raises pertinent questions about the limiting effects which the use of behavioral objectives has on teaching and learning. So much of what we want children to learn is extremely difficult, or perhaps impossible, to state in precise, objective terms.

Baker, Eva L., "Project For Research on Objective-Based Evaluation," *Educational Technology,* X, No. 8 (1970), 56-59. Explains research that PROBE is setting up to study the effectiveness of using behavioral objectives.

Broudy, Harry S., "Can Research Escape the Dogma of Behavioral Objectives?" *School Review,* LXXIX, No. 1 (1970), 43-56. Argues that due to the dominance of behavioral objectives in educational research, we ignore the possibility of learning and knowing from some trivial or irrelevant item.

Caffyn, Lois, "Behavioral Objectives: English Style," *Elementary English,* XLV, No. 8 (1968), 1073-1074. Takes the position that stating objectives in such terms as "enjoy," "know," and "appreciate" leaves teacher and student confused. Little relationship is evident between objectives and classroom activities. The student cannot assess his progress.

Cohen, Ed, "If You're Not Sure Where You're Going, You're Liable to End up Someplace Else," *Media and Methods,* VI, No. 7 (1970), 39-41, 70-75. Stresses the importance of establishing sound behavioral objectives. The teacher must recognize the importance of an effective learning climate and its relationship to established goals in order to achieve desired behavioral change in pupils.

Cronbach, Lee J., *Educational Psychology.* New York: Harcourt, 1963. Describes how knowledge and skills, confidence, and a set goal will affect behavior. Objectives must be stated concerning the situations that the person is expected to encounter as well as the proper ways of responding.

Dessler, Norman, "Behavioral Objectives . . . Something for Student and Teacher," *Journal of Secondary Education,* XLV, No. 4 (1970), 174-176. Advocates behavioral objectives as a way of helping the student know where he is going, what he is doing, and how he is progressing. They also help the teacher evaluate his effort and provide a basis for dialogue between administrator and teacher.

Ebel, R. L., "Behavioral Objectives: A Close Look," *Phi Delta Kappan,* LII, No. 3 (1970), 171-173. Describes the origin, history, justifications, problems, and limitations of behavioral objectives.

Esbensen, Thorwald, *Using Performance Objectives*. Tallahassee, Fla.: State of Florida, Department of Education, 1970. Indicates the inadequacy of vague, broad goals and suggests the use of performance objectives that "we can see or measure." A friend and a critic of performance objectives present arguments for and against them. Suggestions are made for writing indirect and direct objectives.

Flanagan, John C., William M. Shanner, and Robert F. Mager, *Language Arts Behavioral Objectives*. Palo Alto, Calif.: Westinghouse Learning Press, 1971. Presents illustrative behavioral objectives covering 11 areas of language arts study in the primary, intermediate, and secondary schools. In addition to the conventional areas of language arts, listening skills, study skills, original writing, and oral and dramatic interpretation are examined in terms of behavioral objectives.

————, *Mathematics Behavioral Objectives*. Palo Alto, Calif.: Westinghouse Learning Press, 1971. Includes upward of a thousand behavioral objectives for the mathematics program at the primary, intermediate, and secondary levels. Objectives are listed for seven aspects of mathematics instruction.

————, *Science Behavioral Objectives*. Palo Alto, Calif.: Westinghouse Learning Press, 1971. Provides hundreds of objectives for primary, intermediate, and secondary instruction covering life science, physical science, earth science, and science inquiry skills. Broader objectives are broken down into smaller ones, more limited in scope.

————, *Social Studies Behavioral Objectives*. Palo Alto, Calif.: Westinghouse Learning Press, 1971. The entire volume is devoted to objectives in seven areas of the social studies for primary, intermediate, and secondary programs. Inquiry skills for social studies are included, and the appendix supplies terminal objectives for each area.

Haberman, Martin W., *Readings in Curriculum, Behavior Objectives, Breakthrough or Bandwagon*. Boston: Allyn and Bacon, 1970. Presents both sides of the issue without attempting to defend either. A number of problems must be clarified before behavioral objectives can achieve maximum effectiveness.

Hardner, R. J., and D. L. Pratton, "Curriculum Reform Through Behavioral Objectives," *Junior College Journal*, XLI, No. 2 (1970), 12-16. Reports the results of an inservice project at a community college. Behavioral objectives are defined, and a program for developing a curriculum using them is outlined.

Harmes, H. M., "Specifying Objectives for Performance Contracts," *Educational Technology*, XI, No. 1 (1971), 52-56. Discusses four elements which are considered critical to good performance contracts. The article also points up the necessity of good behavioral objectives to determine specific output.

Hernandez, David E., *Writing Behavioral Objectives*. New York: Barnes and Noble, 1971. Uses programed exercises to teach an understanding of behavioral objectives and skill in writing them. The purpose of the booklet is to help teachers learn to write clear, precise objectives stated in behavioral terms.

Huenecke, D., "Knowledge of Curriculum Works: Its Relation to Teaching Practice," *Journal of Teacher Education*, XXI, No. 4 (1970), 478-483. Describes a study of 21 teachers to show the relationship between familiarity with several outstanding curriculum works and teacher's instructional objectives. Tables are used to show the difference between those who knew the various taxonomic levels and those who did not.

Jenkins, Joseph and Stanley L. Deno, "Influence of Knowledge And Type of Objectives on Subject Matter Learning," *Journal of Educational Psychology,* LXII, No. 1 (1971), 67-70. Describes a study which looks at the influence of specific objectives. The results show no conclusive proof that behavioral objectives help make learning easier.

————, "A Model For Instructional Objectives," *Educational Technology,* X, No. 12 (1970), 11-16. Offers three answers to the behavioral objective controversy. First, different kinds of educational objectives should and do exist. Second, different individuals make different kinds of objectives. Finally, objectives do have an effect on teacher and student.

Johnson, Stuart R., "When Should You Lie To Students?" *Educational Technology,* X, No. 11 (1970), 51-53. Suggests that teachers define objectives clearly to their students so that the students understand teacher's "instructional" intentions. The article further explains ways of stating objectives without giving test answers to pupils.

Kibler, Robert J., Larry L. Barker, and David T. Miles, *Behavioral Objectives and Instruction.* Boston: Allyn and Bacon, 1970. Presents a general model of instruction and discusses controversial issues regarding behavioral objectives. The behavioral approach is appropriate to all three domains. Examples are included, and exercises in writing objectives are provided.

Kimball, Roland B., "Educational Philosophy and Behavioral Objectives," *The Clearing House,* XLV, No. 8 (1971), 496-500. Emphasizes the need for behavioral objectives to cover the whole system's educational objectives for one area so that the teacher can see how each discipline fits into the educational objectives for the system.

Kirkton, C. M., "Reference Shelf for Curriculum Planning, Part III: Behavioral Objectives," *English Journal,* LX, No. 1 (1971), 142-150. Gives many valid arguments for and against the use of performance objectives. The article points up the frustration many teachers feel when trying to create behavioral objectives for courses such as literature. The article concludes with summaries of several books and pamphlets on these objectives.

Klausmeier, Herbert J., "Individually Guided Motivation," *Elementary School Journal,* LXXI, No. 6 (1971), 339-350. Explores the procedure for developing individually guided education in the elementary school. Behavioral objectives are defined, methods of achieving these objectives are listed, and a method for assessing progress toward the goals is developed.

Krathwohl, David R., Benjamin S. Bloom, and Bertram B. Masia, *Taxonomy of Educational Objectives.* New York: D. McKay, 1956. A study of directing educational objectives toward behavior and actual situations. The three areas which educational objectives should cover are explained, and ways of developing behavioral outcomes in the affective domain are clarified.

McAshan, H. H., *Writing Behavioral Objectives.* New York: Harper and Row, 1970. Develops skills in recognizing the components of precise objectives and developing clear goal statements. Detailed instruction is given in writing the objectives. The objectives of each chapter are stated in behavioral terms.

MacDonald, James B. and Bernice J. Wolfson, "A Case Against Behavioral Objectives," *Elementary School Journal,* LXXI, No. 3 (1970), 119-128. Argues that behavioral objectives are inadequate and restrictive to the educational purpose of school. The authors suggest the solution is planned activity from which individuals select their own learning experiences.

Mager, Robert F., *Preparing Instructional Objectives.* Palo Alto: Fearon, 1962. Defines behavioral objectives as statements of what the learner will be doing when he completes the prescribed learning activities. Identifying, naming, and describing the behavioral act clearly and objectively are real challenges.

Montague, Earl J. and David P. Butts, "Behavioral Objectives," *The Science Teacher,* XXXV, No. 3 (1968), 33-35. Gives a clear definition of what behavioral objectives are and explains how to write them in unambiguous terms. Teachers must make a greater effort to include affective as well as cognitive learning.

Newport, J. F., "Behavioral Objectives," *School and Community,* LVII, No. 9 (1971), 22, 29. Discusses the trauma of forcing the use of behavioral objectives on teachers who are not prepared to use them. The article stresses the fact that teachers must learn how to write behavioral objectives and use them effectively.

Ojemann, Ralph H., "Should Educational Objectives be Stated in Behavioral Terms?" *Elementary School Journal,* LXIX, No. 5 (1969), 229-235. Cites misuses of stating objectives in behavioral terms. The purpose of stating them in this way is to make them clear to all those involved and to provide agreement as to the degree of their attainment.

Okey, J. R., "Tasks of Instruction," *Educational Leadership,* XXVIII, No. 4 (1971), 381-384. Considers basic changes which the author feels must come about in education if students are to be guided in proper learning. The changes discussed are changes in attitude, in specific educational objectives, in curriculum development and in teacher training.

Plowman, Paul D., *Behavioral Objectives.* Chicago: Science Research Associates, 1971. Offers help for developing behavioral objectives in eight curricular fields. Procedures and examples of objectives are provided for classes from the primary school through the high school. The material includes cognitive, kinesthetic, creative, and social aspects of learning.

Popham, W. J., "The Instructional Objectives Exchange: New Support for Criterion Referenced Instruction," *Phi Delta Kappan,* LII, No. 2 (1970), 174-175. Explains the Instructional Objectives Exchange in Los Angeles. The exchange gathered over 20,000 objective collections during the first year and a half of its operation. Schools may purchase sets of objectives and have the teachers select those which seem most appropriate for their students.

Popham, W. J. and E. L. Baker, "Measuring Teachers' Attitudes Toward Behavioral Objectives," *Journal of Educational Research,* LX, No. 10 (1967), 453-455. Describes the development of the Instructional Objectives Preference List, which is used to determine which prospective teachers would use behavioral objectives. The 20 items used in the IOPL are listed and an explanation of each is given.

Raths, J. D., "Teaching Without Specific Objectives," *Educational Leadership,* XXVIII, No. 7 (1971), 714-720. Suggests that activities should be included in the curriculum that have no specific objectives leading to immediate changes in behavior. Criteria for such worthwhile activities are discussed in considerable detail. Twelve principles of worthwhileness of activities are stated.

Rothstein, Herbert M., "A Humanistic Approach to Behavioral Objectives," *English Journal,* LX, No. 6 (1971), 760-762. Refers to the 1969 caution by the National Council of Teachers of English against indiscriminate use of behavioral objectives for English curricula and its appeal for a humanistic approach. A compromise is outlined suggesting clear objectives that allow for humanism.

Webster, W. J. and G. K. McLeod, "An Empirical Approach To Curriculum Design," *Education,* XC, No. 3 (1970), 252-260. Describes the use of learning objectives in the Program of Learning in Accordance with Needs (PLAN). Examples of specific objectives are given along with ideas on how to use them most effectively.

Audiovisual and Other Resources

Behavioral Objectives Debate (audiotape, 47 min., $10). Debate on the value of measurable instructional objectives featuring W. James Popham, George F. Kneller, and John I. Goodlad of the Univ. of California, Los Angeles. Vimcet Associates, P. O. Box 24714, Los Angeles, Calif. 90024.

Making Behavioral Objectives Meaningful (3-film series, 30 mins. each, $400, rental $120). Three filmed lectures by Dr. Madeline Hunter on objectives and accountability, and objectives in the cognitive and affective domains. Special Purpose Films, 26740 Latigo Shore Dr., Malibu, Calif. 90265.

Planning Instruction by Defining Behavioral Objectives (planning booklet, 75¢, exercise booklet, 50¢). Written in programed style, booklets are designed for self-instruction, teacher education, or inservice workshops. Paul S. Amidon & Associates, 5408 Chicago Ave., S., Minneapolis, Minn. 55417.

Target for Tomorrow (16mm film, color, 12 min., 1969, $115, rental $4.20). Steps in composing instructional objectives. Audio Visual Center, The University of Iowa, Iowa City, Iowa 52240.

Performance Contracting 9

Definition

Performance contracting is a procedure by which a school system enters into a contract with an outside agency to carry out a specific instructional task such as teaching reading or mathematics. For a stipulated amount of money, the firm guarantees to produce specific results within a specified period of time. The private contractor may be a research laboratory or learning corporation, a university, or a group from the professional staff within the district or from another school system. Contracting for guaranteed results is part of the widespread movement toward accountability. Some look upon it as an alternative system of education.

The demand for accountability and the appeal of guaranteed performance are perhaps the result of rising costs of education, student dissatisfaction with their curricula, the apparently decreasing value of their education, and the poor performance of nonmotivated youth, particularly in urban centers. Many citizens have begun to lose faith in their public schools and colleges. Parents want to hold educators accountable for their stewardship of public funds. How did the present crisis come about? Why have the schools failed to achieve their goals? Who is responsible? What can be done to remedy the situation? These and other related questions are being raised.

101

Many of the problems which schools face today are the inevitable result of inability to keep abreast of change. Throughout the years, very few school budgets have included a single dollar specifically allocated to research and development. Blame that is often placed on the lack of imagination and foresight of educators might more properly be attributed to the basic conservatism of teachers and administrators, general satisfaction of board members with their schools, and reluctance of taxpayers to suggest new programs that might cost more. When additional funds were appropriated, they had to be used to take care of increased or rising costs of existing services. In recent years, increases in the cost of living have forced teacher organizations to demand the lion's share of new moneys. In the meantime, private industry has sensed a vast market for educational programs. The federal government has encouraged private research agencies to explore new approaches to solving knotty social and educational problems. These agencies have examined the possibility of applying new technology to some of these problems and of assuring accountability for their solution.

Performance Contracting: Private Enterprise Guarantees Precise Levels of Specific Achievement

Sensing a need for their services as well as an opportunity for profit, scores of research bureaus and educational development centers have sprung up throughout the country during the past few years. The widely publicized contract of the Texarkana schools with a private firm is an example of one of the early experiments with guaranteed performance. The objective was to reduce dropouts by improving reading and mathematic skills of low-achieving students. The nationwide publicity given to the project and some of the irregularities that occurred stimulated broad public interest and caused schools and contractors to seek ways of improving the practices of private firms operating in the schools.

The number of districts actually involved in performance contracts or contemplating or negotiating them changes so rapidly that it is difficult even to estimate, but it runs into the thousands. The number of firms, most of them small companies, prepared or preparing to bid for contracts is definitely in excess of a hundred and continues to grow.

Experience gained from the early projects has produced desirable changes. Both parties in contracts have come to insist on independent audits of results and are giving more attention to those learning outcomes not specifically designated in the contracts. These and other improvements are now being incorporated in second-generation contracts. Increasingly, teachers and other staff members within the district are looked upon as potential bidders, and the value for inservice training of staff in innovative practices is receiving greater recognition. The goal of many contracts is to introduce new programs with minimal political and financial risk and to train the staff of the local district to incorporate the new ideas into ongoing programs after the contract has been fulfilled and the private initiators have withdrawn. This practice is referred to as the "turnkey" feature.

In 1970 the Office of Economic Opportunity launched an experiment, involving approximately 28,000 students, to test efficacy of performance contracting. The study was designed to test the effect of technological aids, incentives, and other instructional devices on learning mathematics and reading skills. The focus was on children in grades 1-3 and 7-9 selected from low-income families who lacked motivation and interest because of repeated failure in competition with their peers. Experiments in three school districts studied only the effects of incentives. In all instances, control, comparison, and special programs were carried on. Provision was made for assessment by independent evaluators. Twenty-one school systems, six contracting firms, and $6.5 million dollars were involved. The United States Office of Education funded six similar programs.

Contracts between the schools and business firms are for the attainment of specific objectives. Most frequently they are limited to reading and mathematics, but other areas such as vocational information are beginning to appear. Instruction is characterized by extensive use of rewards, pleasant surroundings, teaching machines, multimedia aids, reorganized tests, teacher aides, small classes, and individualized instruction.

Significant Components   *Which ones are essential?*

1. Entering into a contract to bring an outside firm into the school to conduct all or part of the instruction must be looked upon as a very important decision, which may have far-reaching effects.
2. No contract can produce valuable results without careful pre-planning and orientation of the staff of the school to the objectives of the program.
3. Improved learning, rather than financial savings, must be the basic consideration.
4. Care must be exercised to distinguish between desirable educational outcomes and unintentional or undesirable byproducts.
5. Public and private enterprise must exercise care in order to avoid destructive competition and conflict between the schools and industry.
6. Understanding and support from parents, community, and professional organizations of teachers are vital.
7. Consideration should be given to developing a contract with a group of employees from the school district.
8. Competitive bidding among firms is important, but bids should be solicited only from those contractors whose philosophy of education and personnel policies are consistent with those of the district.
9. The district must select a director for the project who can devote as much time as is necessary to assure effective operation of the program and is qualified to direct the continuation of those elements of the experiment that have proved successful.
10. Early consideration should be given to the turnkey potential of the contracted program—the possibilities for the district to carry on after the contractor has left.
11. The obligations of the district as well as those of the outside performer must be clearly specified.
12. Provision should be made for incentives and penalties.
13. The materials which the contractor proposes to use should be carefully examined to insure their acceptability.
14. Results of instruction and compliance with other stipulations of the contract must be assessed by an independent agency, and adequate funds must be provided for the evaluation.
15. Proposals and bids should be studied with extreme care.

16. The school system should be prepared to make necessary changes such as flexible schedules and programed learning, including computer-assisted instruction.

17. Tacit understandings and oral commitments have no place in performance contracting.

18. The roles which employees of the district will be expected to perform, proposed incentives, and other conditions of employment must be clearly understood in advance.

19. The relationship between administrators and supervisors who are not directly involved and the contractor must be clearly understood.

20. The objectives must be clear and specific, the instruction sound and significant.

21. The contracting firm's capability to perform should be carefully investigated.

22. The needs of the school system, current programs, and prevailing levels of accomplishment must be thoroughly analyzed.

23. The evaluation should test for process as well as for knowledge and skill.

24. Legal constraints relating to such things as finance, personnel policies, and certification must be resolved.

25. The permanence of learning and its transferability to solving related problems must be given special consideration.

26. To assure maximum benefit for inservice development, local teachers and administrators must be deeply involved so that they can carry on after the contractor has left the scene.

27. Assessment must be specific enough to evaluate the attainment of the contracted objectives, yet broad enough to avoid overemphasis on minutiae.

28. The improvement of staff through the demonstration of new aids to teaching and learning must be recognized as a valuable outcome and pursued systematically.

29. Commitment to broad or long-term utilization of innovative practices should be made only after rigorous evaluation of the entire program—its concomitant effects as well as the results for achieving specific outcomes.

30. Safeguards must be established to prevent teaching only those areas included in the contract to the neglect of other important outcomes.

Proposed Advantages   *With which ones do you agree?*

1. Contracting is based on sound principles of productivity and accountability and develops a procedure for applying them to teaching.

2. Efficiency provides better education for the same money.

3. Performance contracting avoids fuzzy thinking by insisting on precise, clearly stated, and significant objectives whose achievement can be identified and measured.

4. Unlike education, industry understands the value of research, and industrial budgets demonstrate commitment to searching for better methods and products.

5. Industry approaches challenges with a positive attitude which assumes that no problem is too difficult or too costly to solve, while schools constantly complain that they could do many things better if they had the money.

6. Opportunity for further refinement and expansion into the affective areas of learning is limited only to the extent of the imagination of educational and industrial leaders, their determination to meet the challenge, and their willingness to work together.

7. Performance contracting lends itself well to differentiated staffing.

8. Since private enterprise is close to the realities of life, its ideas project an educational program more relevant to the needs of society.

9. The public is shown that it takes real effort and support to secure results.

10. Industry has had long and successful experience with analyzing all factors of input as they contribute to output.

11. The profit incentive places at the disposal of education the expertise and other vast capabilities of corporations.

12. Competition stimulates interest, increases effort, and demands continuous search for better ways of achieving goals.

13. Performance contracting proposes to supplement, not replace, conventional programs and to assist schools in installing new programs.

14. Accounting for learning as well as for costs is emphasized.

15. Private enterprise is not shackled by the bonds of educational tradition and resignation to defeat resulting from repeated failure.

16. Opportunity is provided to employ more teachers and auxiliary personnel for the benefit of children.

17. Accountability forces schools to give higher priority to achieving results than to custodial care of children.

18. For the first time boards of education have a basis from which to discharge their responsibility for evaluating the effectiveness of their programs.

Criticisms and Difficulties to Be Anticipated   *Do you agree?*

1. Because its objectives must be readily agreed upon and measured, performance contracting emphasizes the cognitive areas of learning and neglects the affective and other areas.

2. Control of education is moved away from the local community to national corporations and the federal government.

3. The whole philosophy and most of the methods are geared to machines and mechanistic learning.

4. The threat of being eliminated or reassigned to nonprofessional functions destroys the morale of teachers.

5. Performance contracting sounds the knell of public education as we have known it in America.

6. There is a danger of prostituting good teaching to achieve immediately observable results.

7. A democratic society cannot afford to promote an educational program that sows the seeds of its destruction through the neglect of societal needs.

8. A real danger exists of developing a generation of programed people.

9. Mutual understanding, interdependence, respect of man for man, and cohesiveness are given only casual attention.

10. Results of performance contracting cannot be compared with those of the conventional classroom because they are secured in small classes with an abundance of expensive equipment.

11. The Hawthorne Effect, which may produce improved outcomes simply because of involvement in an experimental program, contaminates the results of experimental programs like contracted performance.

12. Profit-making firms will exploit education; nobody should be allowed to profit from the education of children.

13. A generation of resistance to merit pay demonstrates the likelihood of teacher resistance to accountability.

14. Performance contractors oversimplify the purposes and problems of education and overemphasize minutiae and highly organized routines for developing skills.

15. Many of the conflicts between citizens, students, and schools have sprung from the impersonal nature of our urban-industrial society. Now the agencies that created the problem propose to solve it by greater impersonalization.

16. Performance contracting is excessively expensive.

17. Teaching to the test can be controlled, but teaching to the narrow specifications of the contract will become established practice.

18. Great teachers spend much time in guiding and inspiring students in invaluable ways that are not reflected in test results.

19. The pressure of accountability as conceived in performance contracting will force great teachers to become drill masters, dispensers of information, and developers of fads and mechanistic skills.

Summary Assessment

The proponents of performance contracting stress the point that public education is in dire trouble because of its failure to experiment with new approaches to meeting the needs of disadvantaged youth, lack of incentives for students and teachers, and resistance to technological advances. They believe private enterprise will bring the stimulation of competition, new perspective, and vast human and material resources to a floundering educational system that has lost public confidence.

Some educators point out that industry too is in dire trouble. Young people express serious dissatisfaction with the schools; but these same youngsters are perhaps more deeply disturbed about what they conceive of as selfish and materialistic interests of private enterprise. They blame industry for contributing to making war possible, for polluting the environment, for exploiting minority groups, and for disregarding the interests of the consumer. Both industry and education are victims of demands for accountability, rapidly changing values, confrontation politics, and waning faith in endless and limitless progress.

Producers of instructional programs and electronic equipment, publishers, and research and development firms are convinced that they can demonstrate better ways of effecting learning. They say that, in contrast to the average taxpayer, business is willing to commit the resources to do what needs to be done to produce results. The claims of private enterprise must not be dismissed lightly or ignored completely.

Performance contracting has already yielded some valuable results. Many teachers and school administrators have begun to re-examine their objectives and practices. Preliminary study of the needs and difficulties involved has convinced many segments of industry that education of children is more complicated than they once thought. Public concern has been aroused about the danger of emphasizing readily measurable results to the neglect of broader, less tangible, but perhaps more important outcomes of education. New energy and hope have been added to the search for ways of making sure that all children not only have the opportunity to learn, but that they actually do learn. The ability of private capital to make the initial outlay for experimentation and their help in installing innovative practices increasingly have become recognized.

Gradually some educators have come to accept the proposal that they should be held accountable for developing behavioral objectives and experimenting with alternatives for achieving better results. They are beginning to see new possibilities for discharging these responsibilities through use of the developmental capital, expertise, and turnkey opportunities of performance contracts. But school people still view with apprehension the entrance of business firms into the actual instruction of pupils and are suspicious that entrepreneurs will in some way exploit children for profit.

Many of the positive effects of the programs for guaranteed results are likely to spread far beyond the districts that actually enter into contracts. The wide publicity given to the contracting movement has stimulated reflection and speculation among educators and parents. Teachers often stress the importance of developing humane qualities through sympathetic understanding, time-consuming patience, and delicate manipulation of concomitant learnings. Performance contracting helps them to see that even in these areas changing times demand and invite a continuous search for new and better ways of attaining improved performance on the part of teachers and pupils.

A large-city superintendent, confused by performance contracting, raises a few challenging questions that still bother him. "Where have all these experts been all these years," he asks, "while the board, staff, and citizens in our city have been searching for better ways of coping with our perplexing problems? Why didn't they come forth with some of their simple answers to help us before things got to the point of bankruptcy? Now that I am ready to retire, they say they have gadgets and tricks that will guarantee results or your money back. What about all our blood, sweat, and tears?"

The new manager of learning replies, "The trouble with your superintendent is that he retired at the dawn of the electronic age, and the public forgot to take him off the payroll. We were ready to help him, but he and his teachers were always suspicious and defensive. They thought experience was the mother of invention, and that we had gimmicks to sell."

Perhaps the proponents and opponents of performance contracting do not have the same idea of what a good education is, or what accountability means. Perhaps some of them do not want to understand one another; but the movement will move forward, at least in the immediate future. As time goes on, many of the principles and practices of contracting for results may become part of standard operations in ongoing school programs. Educators and industrial leaders must, at this point, join hands to prevent the education of children from becoming a football in a competitive struggle. Unless they do, there's a stormy road ahead for performance contracting.

A Few Leaders in the Movement

Charles L. Blaschke
 Education Turnkey Systems, Inc.
B. J. Chandler
 Northwestern Univ.
Stanley Elam
 Phi Delta Kappan
Martin Filogamo
 Texarkana (Ark.) Schools
Lloyd Homme
 Independent Learning Systems
Donald Johnson
 Jacksonville, Fla.

Howard Johnson
 Denver (Colo.) Schools
Leon Lessinger
 Univ. of South Carolina
Albert V. Mayshofer
 Atlanta, Ga.
Edward C. Pino
 Cherry Creek (Colo.) Schools
Ronald Schwartz
 McGraw-Hill World News Bureau
Joan Webster
 Grand Rapids, Mich.

A Few Places Where the Innovation Is Used

Anchorage, Alaska
Cherry Creek, Colo.
Clarke County, Ga.
Dallas, Texas
Dayton, Ohio
Detroit, Mich.
Duluth, Minn.
Fresno, Calif.
Gary, Ind.
Grand Rapids, Mich.

Greenville, S. C.
Hammond, Ind.
Jacksonville, Fla.
Las Vegas, Nev.
Little Rock, Ark.
McComb, Miss.
Mesa, Ariz.
New Orleans, La.
Oakland, Calif.
Philadelphia, Pa.

Portland, Oreg.
Providence, R. I.
Rockland, Me.
San Diego, Calif.
San Francisco, Calif.
Savannah, Ga.
Stockton, Calif.
Texarkana, Ark.
State of Virginia
Wichita, Kans.

Annotated References

Beaven, Keith, "Rewarded With Transistors, Sweaters, Stamps and Stock," *The Times Educational Supplement,* No. 2857 (1970), 16. Cites Texarkana as the first place that a performance contract has been negotiated between a public school system and a corporation for instruction. The number of districts that want to try performance contracting-accountability programs is estimated at 250.

Blaschke, Charles, *Performance Contracting in Education: The Guaranteed Student Performance Approach to Public School System Reform.* Champaign, Ill.: Research Press, 1970. Accepts performance contracting in the schools as a reality. The Texarkana experience is treated in some detail. Attention is given to the contracting process, turnkey, and implications for education. Valuable illustrative materials are included in the appendices.

Blaschke, Charles, Peter Briggs, and Reed Martin, "The Performance Contract-Turnkey Approach to Urban School System Reform," *Educational Technology,* X, No. 9 (1970), 45-48. Emphasizes the turnkey value of performance contracting for introducing new practices into a school system. School leaders, normally handicapped by lack of funds and public and staff resistance, have the advantage of a demonstration period with guaranteed performance.

Carlson, Elliot, "Education and Industry: Troubled Partnership," *Saturday Review,* LIII, No. 33 (1970), 45-47, 58-60. Indicates traditional partnership between industry and schools. Recently big corporations have entered the knowledge field with frustrating results. Concentrating on disadvantaged areas, the corporate giants have found profits slow and success with students varied.

Cass, James, "Profit and Loss in Education," *Saturday Review,* LIII, No. 33 (1970), 39-40. Credits the stimulus for new approaches to education's failure to deal adequately with the problems of the disadvantaged. Contracts of the OEO, Texarkana, and Gary test the competing demands of business pragmatism and professional dedication.

Davis, Jeanne L., "The Texarkana Project," *Audiovisual Instruction,* XV, No. 6 (1970), 97. Suggests that a government-industry-education troika introduced the guaranteed performance concept. The article credits Dorsett with glowing reports of pupil achievement.

Donovan, Hedley, ed., "Free Enterprise for Schools," *Time,* XCVIII, No. 8 (1970), 58, 60. Reports turning over the Benneker School in Gary, Indiana, enrollment 800, to Behavioral Research Laboratories for full management and instruction. An experiment of the OEO in 21 school systems is announced.

Dropout Prevention Program Request for Proposal #2, Texarkana School District 7, Arkansas, June 30, 1970. Provides the instruction and forms necessary for submission of a performance contract proposal as part of a four-year dropout prevention program.

Elam, Stanley, "The Age of Accountability Dawns in Texarkana," *Phi Delta Kappan,* LI, No. 10 (1970), 509, 511-514. Describes a visit to the Rapid Learning Centers and reports some favorable results in reading and mathematics with some deficiencies. Vandalism and dropout problem show positive trend, and community support is strong. Further exploration is warranted.

————, "Where the Action is in Performance Contracting," *Phi Delta Kappan,* LI, No. 10 (1970), 510. Describes contracts negotiated in five city systems with various firms involving thousands of K-12 students. Most common areas are reading and mathematics. Occupational training is appearing. Number of competing firms is growing.

Elliott, Lloyd H., "Education at a Profit?" *Educational Record,* LI, No. 1 (1970), 53-56. Insists that education lost its effectiveness because of bureaucracy and loss of parental involvement. The profit motive would increase efficiency, effect economies, and guarantee greater accountability to parents. Students and parents would be given greater choice.

Elliott, Osborn, ed., "Teaching for Profit," *Newsweek*, LXXXVI, No. 7 (1970), 58. Reviews the stir for performance contracting around the country. Gary, San Francisco, and Texarkana are highlighted among the 170 districts that are experimenting with programs conducted by private business.

Filogamo, Martin J., "Texarkana Battles 'Dropout Dilema,'" *Elementary English*, XLVII, No. 2 (1970), 305-308. Explains that the Texarkana project seeks to reduce the dropout rate by relieving deficiencies in reading and mathematics. New electronic devices, improved environment, varied materials, and rewards characterize the approach.

Gillis, James C., Jr., "Performance Contracting for Public Schools," *Educational Technology*, IX, No. 5 (1969), 17-20. Presents three models: limited subcontracting, total prime contracting, and individual contracting. More effective use of technology through the cooperation of industry, government, and education may further individualized instruction.

Grayboff, Marilyn N., "Tool for Building Accountability: The Performance Contract," *Journal of Secondary Education*, XLV, No. 8 (1970), 355-368. Explains the groundwork necessary to consider and implement a performance contract situation. Presents 12 of the essential elements of a Request for a Design Solution which lays the foundation for the program.

Green, Norman S., "Whither Performance Contracting?" Paper presented at Pennsylvania School Boards Association annual conference, Pittsburgh, Pa., October 14, 1970. Briefly describes performance contracting and discusses its shortcomings and disadvantages. Speaks of the future of this concept. Two shortcomings are highlighted: 1) teaching to the test, and 2) school board abdication of responsibility.

Hickman, L. C., ed., "Performance Contracting," *Nation's Schools*, LXXXVI, No. 4 (1970), 85-86, 88. Reports that an independent audit of the Texarkana program found student achievement invalid because of contaminated test results. The superintendent, however, minimizes this and is continuing with a new contract with another firm.

_____, ed., "How Education Groups View Contracting," *Nation's Schools*, LXXXVI, No. 4 (1970), 86-87. Reports reactions of leaders in the country's education associations. The AFT expresses much stronger opposition than the NEA, which opposed it at Senate hearings. The American Association of School Administrators, National Association of Secondary School Principals, and Council of Chief State School Officers have reservations, but see some possibilities.

Holliday, Alfonso D. II, "Performance Contracting: Why the Gary School Board Bought It and How," *American School Board Journal*, CLVIII, No. 7 (1971), 19-21. Explains that failure of Gary students to achieve prompted the board of education to turn over operation of the Banneker Elementary School to Behavioral Research Laboratories. Attack from the teacher union, guaranteed results, and positive parental reaction are factors. AFT has set up a "monitoring post" in Gary to alert the community to apparent dangers of performance contracting.

Lessinger, Leon M., "Four Key Ideas to Strengthen Public Education," *Journal of Secondary Education,* XLV, No. 4 (1970), 147-151. Questions school's capability to meet its continually increasing burden. Seven ways are suggested for improving productivity in education. Performance contracts are an approach to accountability and to securing results, particularly for disadvantaged youth.

Lipsitz, Lawrence, ed., "Performance Contracting as Catalyst For Reform," *Educational Technology,* IX, No. 8 (1969), 5-9. Presents in detail the Request for Proposal that was sent out by the Texarkana schools to over 100 firms. General conditions, performance requirements, methods of measuring, personnel, and costs and pricing are explained.

Mecklenburger, James A., *Performance Contracting.* Worthington, Ohio: Charles A. Jones, 1972. Explores the emotion and criticism generated by performance contracting. Banneker and Texarkana are analyzed in detail. Evaluations are made, and conclusions are drawn.

Mecklenburger, James A. and John A. Wilson, "Learning C.O.D.: Can the Schools Buy Success?" *Saturday Review,* LIV, No. 38 (1971), 62-65, 76-79. Explores four areas of performance contracting. Offers a definition. Tells where performance contracting is being used. Recognizes the related problems, and suggests that performance contracting may be more widely used in the future.

Morton, John, "Contract Learning in Texarkana," *Educational Screen and Audiovisual Guide,* XLIX, No. 2 (1970), 12-13. Indicates that Dorsett was chosen from among 17 bidders because its equipment was inexpensive enough to use after federal funding ceases. The purpose is to discover better ways to teach. Time spent by students and teachers is now precious.

————, "Performance Contracting: Clouds and Controversy Over Texarkana," *Nation's Schools,* LXXXVI, No. 4 (1970), 85-86, 88. Explains the problem of contamination of test results in the Texarkana experiment. Explores the reaction of the contractor and the superintendent. Reports that Philadelphia will try performance contracting for reading improvement in grades 1-8.

Porter, John W., *An Introduction to Guaranteed Performance Contracting.* Lansing, Mich.: Michigan Department of Education, 1971. Provides practical guidelines for boards of education and their administrators who are considering performance contracting. Step-by-step phases of planning are outlined in the context of accountability. Essential elements of contract preparation, implementation, monitoring, and evaluation are explained.

Schiller, Jeffry, "Performance Contracting: Some Questions and Answers," *American Education,* VII, No. 4 (1971), 3-5. Provides a sketchy history and reaction to performance contracting. Addresses itself to many of the most frequently asked questions about this topic. Does not take a stance, but offers guarded optimism.

Schwartz, Ronald, "Performance Contracting," *Nation's Schools,* LXXXVI, No. 3 (1970), 53-55. Reports growth in the number of companies, but some of the larger ones are holding back from competitive bidding. Smaller, more aggressive contractors consider contracting the wave of the future; others think it may be a passing fad.

———, "Performance Contracts Catch On," *Nation's Schools,* LXXXVI, No. 2 (1970), 31-33. Lists and describes six programs to be funded by USOE, three directed by states and three by cities. OEO announces 21 contracts in districts from Georgia to Alaska amounting to $6.5 million.

Stenner, Jack and Michael H. Kean, "Four Approaches to Education Performance Contracting," *Educational Leadership,* XXXIII, No. 7 (1971), 721-725. Presents the advantages and disadvantages of entering into performance contracts using for selection purposes the following four models: Competitive Performance Contracting Model, Sole Source Performance Contracting Model, Modified Sole Source Model, and the Comparative Performance Contracting Model.

"Texarkana: The Second Year Around," *Nation's Schools,* LXXXVII, No. 3 (1971), 32-33, 36. Relates the following problems that Texarkana had in utilizing performance contracting: management support, requests for proposals, selection of company, staffing, and attitude. The greatest problem was attitude.

Audiovisual and Other Resources

Performance Contracting—The Grand Rapids Experience (film, b&w, 27 min., $165, rental $7.25). Documentary on three contracts in Grand Rapids, Michigan, viewed from the perspective of a child, a teacher, and a principal with statements from company representatives, school officials, and children. Indiana University A-V center, Bloomington, Indiana 47401.

National Assessment   **10**

Definition

National assessment is a nationwide program for evaluating the outcomes of education by means of written tests, interviews, observation of performance, and other techniques. Its purpose is to find out what large groups of students have and have not learned so that intelligent decision-making regarding improvement of education may be based on reliable information.

The sample of those being tested is made up of four cross-sectional age groups: 9-year-olds representing those who have completed primary instruction, 13-year-olds who have finished elementary school, 17-year-olds at the end of their secondary programs, and adults between the ages of 26 and 35. Ten areas of learning are being studied: (1) science, (2) writing, (3) citizenship, (4) literature, (5) mathematics, (6) social studies, (7) music, (8) reading, (9) art, and (10) occupational knowledge.

The findings are being reported for the northeastern, southeastern, central, and western regions of the country. The four types of sample communities are large city, urban fringe, small city, and rural town. Socioeconomic status is divided into two groups—those above and those below the poverty level. Provision is made for distinguishing between the performance of boys and girls.

Three or four subject areas are studied each calendar year following a cycle which comes back to each subject every three to five years. Science, writing, and citizenship were selected for the year 1969, when the program began by assessing the progress of 17-year-olds in March of that year. The evaluation turned to adults during the summer and to elementary pupils during the autumn. Reading and literature were the two areas studied in 1970, music and mathematics in 1971, and social studies, art, and occupational knowledge in 1972. With tests having been given in the 10 areas of learning originally selected, the first round of assessment was completed. Funds for the initial effort were supplied by the Carnegie Corporation, the Ford Foundation Fund for the Advancement of Education, and the U. S. Office of Education. The annual cost of the assessment approximated five million dollars.

The program is not one of individual testing. Each student takes only one-twelfth of the total test items, and a score is not derived for any individual. Group results are not being compiled for states or school districts. Each item stands by itself, and results of the large group are reported for each item. Hence the program constitutes an assessment of our total national educational effort, not that of a child, teacher, or school system. The questions including knowledge, skills, and attitudes are based upon objectives of education as determined through long and careful study by professional and lay groups.

The care exercised in arriving at the objectives of the 10 subject areas should contribute significantly to the validity of the program and to making it more acceptable to teachers and administrators. The objectives included were only those considered important by scholars, thought to be legitimate responsibilities of schools, and accepted by lay citizens as being significant to individuals and society. The evaluation seeks to determine the extent to which the objectives have been achieved. Tests, interviews, and observation of performance are techniques used in the assessment.

The program plan, objectives, and assessment procedures were developed by the Exploratory Committee on Assessing the Progress of Education established by the Carnegie Corporation in July 1964. In 1969 the Education Commission of States assumed responsibility for managing the project. Reporting conferences for public discussion are being held.

The results of the assessments are reported in percentages of correct responses for each group and for each question and are consequently easily understood. Those conducting the program suggest that the "census-like" data are intended to supply reliable information for maintaining schools and planning their improvement. The information is also important for evaluating the validity of claims made by educators or criticisms of those who attack the schools. Making comparisons between age groups provides material for analyzing the progress of learning as children mature. Keeping precise and comparable records as the cycle is repeated allows for reviewing the progress of education over a period of years. Comparisons by regions, within various settings, between boys and girls, and between respondents from different socioeconomic levels provide important information for program planning. Introduction of new courses and materials, revisions in policies and practices, and shifts in emphases may be suggested. Comparison between input and output on a national basis is facilitated.

Significant Components   *Which ones are essential?*

1. The promised and established procedure of assessing large groups, rather than individual students or schools, must be zealously guarded lest the bitter battle of the middle-1960's between the proponents and opponents of national assessment be renewed with even greater intensity.

2. The program must continue to be controlled by a responsible agency.

3. Long-term, stable financial support is necessary.

4. Provision must be made for modifying objectives and assessment procedures to keep abreast of rapid societal changes.

5. The program must be free from political interference and governmental dictation.

6. Continuous attention must be given to improving the validity of the objectives and to broadening the scope of the assessment to include additional subject fields, out-of-class learning experiences, the affective areas of learning, and learning processes.

7. Objectives and evaluations should include only matters that are worth learning in the eyes of lay citizens as well as educators.

8. Teachers, lay citizens, subject area specialists, and those skilled in test construction and other evaluation procedures must work together in establishing objectives and planning the assessment.

9. Provision must be made to develop among professional educators and the public the understanding necessary for avoiding misinterpretation of assessment results and for effective use of the information.

10. The examinations and other techniques of evaluation must be carefully pretested.

11. Uniformity and optimum conditions for administering evaluation instruments must be assured.

12. New approaches to evaluation that go beyond paper-and-pencil tests and continuous refinement of present devices must be pursued.

13. Professional organizations of public school teachers, administrators, and college personnel must be involved in evaluating the program of national assessment and in promoting utilization of its findings.

14. Continuous effort should be directed toward assuring wide dissemination of the assessment results.

15. The national assessment program should refrain from setting standards or drawing implications from the reported findings.

16. Excessive emphasis on cognitive skills, isolated facts, and rote learning must be avoided.

17. Separate tests should be used for each age level.

18. The national effort should be coordinated with a total program that will encourage local districts to establish local norms and assess their own programs critically.

19. To be of value, the information secured must be analyzed and followed up with improvement programs in local districts.

Proposed Advantages   *With which ones do you agree?*

1. National assessment supplies significant information for making decisions to revise content and processes.

2. Teachers are provided guidelines in establishing objectives, developing strategies, and assessing outcomes.

3. The public has a basis for deciding whether or not it is getting its money's worth.

4. Legislatures and school boards can use the information to establish direction and priorities and for basing actions on facts rather than on personal bias.

5. The program provides information relating to differences among various regions, socioeconomic groups, types of communities, sex, and age groups.

6. The program supplies data to defend the schools against irresponsible attacks.

7. A basis is provided for developing a commonality of experiences needed in a highly mobile society.

8. The focus of national reports is shifted from emphasis on enrollment, dollars, number of teachers, and other quantitative matters to the more significant consideration of quality of instruction and learning.

9. The assessment program stimulates an examination of the relationship between goals and results.

10. A national effort brings together financial support and personnel that can demonstrate to local districts effective procedures and instruments for assessment.

11. Reporting the percentage of a group that can perform a given task provides data that can be readily understood and interpreted by educators and laymen and used by teachers in their daily work.

12. Traditional programs of evaluation provide information on how well individuals or groups have learned. National assessment reveals what they have or have not learned.

13. National assessment provides information for comparing progress in education over a period of years.

14. The program is a boon to research in every area of teaching and learning.

Criticisms and Difficulties to Be Anticipated   *Do you agree?*

1. National assessment is the first big step that the federal government is taking to assume control of the school curriculum. It is only a small step from national assessment to national testing and another small step to a national curriculum.

2. Federal control will destroy local interest, initiative, and support and remove from local communities and local schools the privilege of deciding what they want their children to learn.

3. Because attitudes and values are difficult to measure, they will be omitted from the assessment and, as a result, neglected by the schools.

4. Those subjects included in the assessment will be stressed to the neglect of other subjects, and teachers will teach for the assessment techniques and instruments.

5. National assessment does not supply information for making decisions for local schools; it makes the decisions.
6. Despite good intentions at present, the program will move toward making comparisons among individuals and districts.
7. Many valuable outcomes of education cannot be measured until the student is out of school for many years.
8. The program provides no help for diagnosing learning deficiencies.
9. Misunderstanding, division, and conflict among parents, teachers, administrators, legislatures, and boards of education develop.
10. Eventually national assessment will establish monolithic standards that disregard unique community needs and inhibit experimentation and search for better approaches to learning.
11. Laymen and administrators are likely to consider success on the items of a national assessment test a complete measure of effective teaching and learning.
12. Since many outside influences that cannot be controlled by the school are included in the assessment, schools will be blamed for all deficiencies of youth.
13. The program is diametrically opposed to individualization of learning.
14. Publishers of textbooks and other materials will focus upon the narrow concepts of the national assessment program.

Summary Assessment

National assessment must be ranked with integration and busing, religion in the classroom, aid to parochial schools, professional negotiations, and teacher strikes as one of the stormy educational issues of recent years. Today the climate is quite different from that of the middle and late 1960's. For this the Exploratory Committee on Assessing the Progress of Education deserves great credit. It was the patience, caution, and wisdom with which the committee proceeded in a persistent forward movement that cooled tempers and allayed suspicions. In 1969 the selection of the Education Commission of the States to manage the program also did much to establish confidence and advance the cause. But a degree of mistrust, suspicion, and fear still continues in some quarters.

In the light of the strong opposition to the program during the years of its planning and development, the cooperation of local schools since the actual assessment has gotten under way is surprising and indeed gratifying to those who want to see the program succeed. The observation that national assessment establishes the machinery for moving toward national testing, national curriculum, and national control cannot be ignored. However, those who have managed since 1964 to avoid making comparisons between schools and classrooms realize the dangers ahead. Any movement in the direction of making comparisons among schools would surely revive the conflict.

Changes in educational technology and continuous pressures for shifting greater responsibility for school support to state and national government make national assessment appear more reasonable than it did a decade ago. Problems of school integration, resistance of taxpayers to approving levies, and the increasing mobility of the population make assessment only at the local level appear to be inadequate.

Those who guided the course of national assessment during its formative years have demonstrated the importance of caution and patience in initiating and implementing programs that educators perceive as accusations and threats. By carefully guarding against misuse of data, they built confidence in the integrity of those who were promoting the program, and in the value of the results. Another important outcome of the program has been the increasing realization that assessments of any kind are genuinely valuable only to the extent that they assist in analyzing existing practices and point to better teaching and learning.

Those who may appear to be too hasty in their demands for accountability of teachers, administrators, and boards of education should profit from these experiences. Careful planning, sincere exchange of ideas, sound objectives, and valid and reliable procedures for evaluating results are important for all assessment. The growing demand for accountability has made it clear that, regardless of the apprehensions of school people, the schools are being continuously evaluated or misevaluated. Behavioral objectives, PPBS, performance contracting, and the voucher system are among the movements that call attention to the urgent need for more dependable information about the effectiveness of our schools. The experiences of national assessment in developing its program, implementing its operation, and using its results should be carefully studied by those who look to accountability as a way of helping education achieve its potential for benefiting those who attend schools and those who support them.

Under good leadership both national assessment and the development of a system for appraising accountability may well improve understanding and cooperation between a restless public and defensive educators. There are few who think that national assessment will cure many of our educational ills, but there are many who believe that it will be a valuable tool to help education chart a better course for improving the quality of the nation's schools.

A Few Leaders in the Movement

J. Stanley Ahmann
  Colorado State Univ.
Frances S. Berdie
  St. Paul, Minn.
George Brain
  Washington State Univ.
Carmen J. Finley
  Nat'l. Assessment of
  Educational Progress
James Hazlett
  Univ. of Chicago
Thomas R. Knapp
  Univ. of Rochester

William A. Mehrens
  Michigan State Univ.
Jack C. Merwin
  Univ. of Minnesota
Wendell Pierce
  Education Commission
  of the States
James Tukey
  Princeton Univ.
Ralph Tyler
  Univ. of Chicago
Frank Womer
  Univ. of Michigan

Information about national assessment may be secured from Wendell Pierce, Education Commission of the States, 1860 Lincoln Street, Denver, Colorado.

Annotated References

Beavan, K., "National Standards Agreed; United States," *London Times Educational Supplement,* No. 2890 (1970), 12. Reports in newspaper fashion of the events in the United States concerning the progress of the National Assessment of Educational Progress.

Brain, George, "National Assessment Moves Ahead," *Today's Education,* LX, No. 2 (1971), 45. Presents some significant trends found in the first published results of the National Assessment of Educational Progress program; editorial in nature; advocating the program.

———, "What's The Score On National Assessment?" *Today's Education,* LVIII, No. 7 (1969), 18-21. Describes the nature and purposes of national assessment. The examination of about 35,000 seventeen-year-olds in the spring of 1969 received positive response from 90 per cent of the schools asked to participate.

Donovan, Hedley, ed., "Report Card for Americans," *Time,* XCVI, No. 3 (1970), 38. Reports the summer meeting of the Education Commission of the States, which released the results of the first round of testing. Sample questions are presented with a few percentage figures for each of the age groups.

Elam, Stanley M., ed., "The Assessment Debate at the White House Conference," *Phi Delta Kappan,* XLVII, No. 1 (1965), 17-18. A panel discusses points favoring and questioning national assessment. The difference between testing an individual child and testing the national educational effort is brought out.

————, "Who Should Do The Assessing?" *Phi Delta Kappan,* XLVIII, No. 8 (1967), 377. Refutes some of the objections to national assessment including odious comparisons, conformity, and federal control. An agency to assume responsibility for the program is being sought.

Ferris, Manfred, "Sequel to 'A Parable on National Assessment,'" *Phi Delta Kappan,* LII, No. 4 (1970), back cover. In parable and humorous form, defends the national assessment program solely on the grounds that it has just begun and therefore it is still too early to evaluate the program.

Finley, Carmen, "National Assessment: Reports and Implications for School Districts," *National Elementary Principal,* L, No. 3 (1971), 25-32. Reviews methodology and results of the 1969 National Assessment of Educational Progress report. Explains that the growth in educational abilities will be reported in 1972-73.

————, "National Assessment—Spring 1968," *California Journal of Educational Research,* XX, No. 2 (1969), 69-74. Explains the goals of National Assessment and the development of the objectives of instruction and preparation of items. National assessment is contrasted with the California statewide testing program.

Finley, Carmen J. and Frances S. Berdie, *The National Assessment Approach to Exercise Development.* Ann Arbor, Mich.: Education Commission of the States, 1970. Presents the history of the development of assessment exercises from the outset of planning in 1964. Objectives, validity, and simplicity and clarity of wording were significant considerations. Rationale, criteria, writing, and review of test exercises are explained in detail.

Hand, Harold C., "National Assessment Viewed as the Camel's Nose," *Phi Delta Kappan,* XLVII, No. 1 (1965), 8-13. Presents six arguments against national assessment including perpetuation in inequalities of opportunity, centrally controlled curriculum, and stifling of innovative practices. The author suspects private bribery in the proposal.

Higgins, Martin J. and Jack C. Merwin, "Assessing the Progress of Education," *Phi Delta Kappan,* XLVIII, No. 8 (1967), 378-380. Reviews development of objectives and other progress from 1965 to 1967. The major objectives in 10 fields are listed together with exercises proposed to sample achievement in each area that can be demonstrated by about half of a given age group.

Iona, Mario, "Physics Teaching and the National Assessment of Educational Progress," *Physics Teacher,* VIII, No. 8 (1970), 445-448. After giving a brief background of the national assessment program, investigates the potential implications of results as related to teaching, curriculum designing, and testing of physics.

Kock, Reino, "National Assessment of Education Progress—A Diffusion Study," *School and Society,* XCVII, No. 2315 (1969), 95-97. Blames failure to involve leading professional groups in the initial deliberations of the "elite" Exploratory Committee on Assessing the Progress of Education for much of the opposition to the program of national assessment.

Lansner, Kermit, ed., "The National Educational Assessment," *Newsweek,* LXXVI, No. 3 (1970), 40. Comments on the first report of the Education Commission of the States. Although national assessment holds promise for improving education, immediate reactions indicate that techniques need refinement.

McMorris, Robert F., "National Assessment: Coming in 1968-69?" *Phi Delta Kappan,* XLIX, No. 10 (1968), 599-600. Describes progress made by the Exploratory Committee and the search for a project sponsor. The criteria established for assessing the 10 areas are explained.

Mehrens, William A., "National Assessment Through September, 1969," *Phi Delta Kappan,* LI, No. 4 (1969), 215-217. Presents in concise form the development, organization, and progress of national assessment. Early unfounded criticisms of the program are mentioned and the assessment program through 1970, including literature, mathematics, and music, is outlined.

Mollenberg, Wayne P., "National Assessment: Are We Ready?" *The Clearing House,* XLIII, No. 8 (1969), 451-454. Emphasizes the need for establishing local norms to accompany the national program of assessment. Despite the inadequacy of tests to measure many significant aspects of education, the program promises to be a boon if educators and the public are instructed in the proper use of results.

National Assessment of Educational Progress, A Project of the Education Commission of the States, Report 1, Science National Results 1970. Denver: Education Commission of the States, 1970. Makes comparisons of ages 9 and 13, 13 and 17, 17 and adults, and 9 or 13 and adults. The results for the four age groups are presented for 449 test exercises covering four general objectives. Group comparisons are made according to geographical regions, size of community, types of community, sex, color, and education of parents.

National Assessment of Educational Progress, A Project of the Education Commission of the States, Report 2, Citizenship National Results 1970. Denver: Education Commission of the States, 1970. Presents and analyzes results of the first assessment of citizenship for four age groups, 9, 13, 17, and adults. Percentage figures are given for the individual test exercises, and summaries are provided for each of the nine goals.

Prakken, Lawrence W., "The National Assessment: Initial Report, Reactions, and Benefits," *The Education Digest,* XXXVI, No. 1 (1970), 1-5. Reviews the results of the first round of national assessment. Reports some examples of percentage figures for the four age groups, immediate benefits, and favorable reactions to the initial effort.

Robinson, D., "General Optimism but Doubts Linger On," *Phi Delta Kappan,* LII, No. 1 (1970), 67-68. States that the first results released in Denver can serve only as a baseline for future comparisons. Raises theoretical questions as to the use and construction of national assessment revolving around the difference between understanding and performance and whether or not it is desirable for students to possess the material measured by this program.

"Science Area Results Reported by National Assessment of Educational Progress," *Science Teacher,* XXXVII, No. 7 (1970), 65-67. Basically summarizes the design of the national assessment program and describes the four objectives surveyed in the area of science.

Shafer, Robert E., "What Can We Expect from a National Assessment in Reading?" *Journal of Reading,* XIII, No. 1 (1969), 3-8. Expresses the view that the assessment of reading will be of more than usual interest because of broad public concern about this field. Several considerations relating to the selection of objectives and test items are discussed.

Turney, David and Burton E. Altman, "National Assessment—Why All The Fuss?" *Educational Leadership,* XXIII, No. 6 (1966), 442-446. Stresses the importance of planning ways for utilizing information secured from national assessment for improving education. Four ways are suggested in which the program can serve educational needs.

Tyler, Ralph W., "Assessing the Progress of Education," *Phi Delta Kappan,* XLVII, No. 1 (1965), 13-16. Stresses the need for reliable and comprehensive data for intelligent planning and decision-making. National assessment differs from achievement testing in that no scores for individuals are computed. What the superior and average students learn is reported.

_____, "First Reports from the National Assessment," *Educational Leadership,* XXVIII, No. 6 (1971), 577-580. Gives a report of the status of national assessment and describes its purposes. Several charts are used to illustrate results of assessment in citizenship and science.

_____, "Let's Clear the Air on Assessing Education," *Nation's Schools,* LXXVII, No. 2 (1966), 68-70. Explains the program and clarifies common misunderstandings relative to its purposes, danger of federal control of curriculum, and comparisons among individuals and states. Providing dependable information is its goal.

_____, "National Assessment—Some Valuable By-Products For Schools," *National Elementary Principal,* XLVIII, No. 6 (1969), 42-48. Indicates seven valuable by-products that have come out of assessment. These benefits were not built in as part of the initial planning, but are among the significant outcomes.

Walker, Jerry, "National Assessment of Reading," *Reading Teacher,* XXIV, No. 8 (1971), 711-714. Advocates the national assessment program and cites the experts involved in selecting valid criteria for reading skill. Also presents basic design of the program.

Willson, Thomas E., "In Rebuttal," *Ohio Schools,* XLIV, No. 2 (1966), 15. Responds to five charges frequently leveled against national assessment. Current plans avoid the dangers feared by many educators. The inadequacy of paper and pencil tests is conceded.

Wilson, Brent, "Status of National Assessment in Art," *Art Education,* XXIII, No. 9 (1970), 2-6. Describes how the objectives of national assessment in art have changed from 1965-69, resulting in postponing the assessment from 1970-71 until 1974-75.

Womer, Frank B., *What Is National Assessment?* Ann Arbor, Mich.: National Assessment of Educational Progress, 1970. Describes in detail the significant considerations underlying the assessment program—its purposes, procedures, and scope. The 10 areas are explained together with plans for administering the exercises and reporting the results. The changing nature of the program is stressed.

Voucher System 11

Definition

The voucher system is a plan for financing elementary and secondary education through the use of certificates which the government gives to parents who have school-age children. The parent selects a school of his choice and presents the certificate as payment for the instruction of the child. The school presents the voucher to the government and receives a check for its services. A family receives a voucher for each child, which can be used at a public school, parochial or private school, or at one operated by a corporation. The value of the voucher and the payment by the government is in the amount established by a formula. The basic value might be the average expenditure per child in a given district or area. Some proposals suggest additional amounts for disadvantaged children, going as high as double the basic value of the voucher.

The idea goes back two hundred years to Adam Smith, the Scottish economist, who proposed that the government finance schools by giving parents money to buy education for their children. In 1969 the Office of Economic Opportunity initiated study of this alternative to existing practice and proposed to conduct a five-year demonstration project in an urban community. Among the suggestions that came out of the preliminary study was one for setting up an agency for establishing standards

126

and regulations. One suggestion would prevent parents from supplementing the value of the voucher. This procedure was offered as one of several safeguards to prevent discrimination against minority groups and children of the poor.

In the spring parents would indicate to the voucher agency which school each child wants to attend in the autumn. A lottery system might be employed to prevent discrimination by schools which have more applicants than openings. Different plans include provisions for parents' supplementing the amount of the voucher, adjusting the value of the certificate upward for disadvantaged children, charging parents additional money for schools that set higher tuition rates, prohibiting schools from accepting supplementary funds, and other arrangements.

The premises upon which the system is based seem to be that public education has failed, and that alternative schools should be provided to give parents free choice in deciding what kind of education is most appropriate for their children. The probability has been pointed out that parents, particularly those of disadvantaged children, may be unwilling or unable to choose wisely among a variety of schools. Implicit in the suggestion for a voucher system is the assumption that parochial and private schools can achieve what public schools have failed to accomplish, and that competition will break up the monopoly now held by public education and spur it on to greater concern and effort.

It is possible that those who strongly advocate public financial support of alternative schools have misinterpreted the public's resistance to paying higher taxes and its criticism of some of the things that are going on in the schools. Parents may be unhappy about the inability of education to achieve all that needs to be done, particularly for children of the poor, but there is ample evidence to indicate that the vast majority of parents do not believe that their schools are educationally bankrupt. There is likewise little evidence to insure that alternative schools would solve many of the knotty problems that plague public education. On the other hand, it can hardly be denied that, in some areas, too many teachers and administrators have accepted many problems as insoluble, resigned themselves to defeat, and therefore definitely need rejuvenation. Challenge from other adequately supported schools might cause them to give greater attention to the needs and desires of parents and children, re-examine their objectives, revise their procedures, and be more concerned about the results achieved.

Significant Components   *Which ones are essential?*

1. Time, patience, experimentation, and careful testing are necessary to allay suspicions and fears of the system.

2. Some kind of regulatory agency will have to be developed for establishing and maintaining standards of quality.

3. The needs of disadvantaged children must be provided for without destroying maximum opportunities for the advantaged.

4. Using vouchers to promote segregation and provincialism should be prevented.

5. The agency administering the voucher system should be an arm of government.

6. The focus of the program should be on improvement of opportunities for learning rather than on convenience of financial support.

7. Compensatory payments are likely to be necessary to induce schools to accept pupils who are difficult to educate.

8. Safeguards should be established to prevent the whims of children or the pressures of parental desires from having adverse effects upon the curriculum and how teachers deal with their pupils.

9. From the outset, a broad base for planning must be developed and include public officials, school people, and citizen groups.

10. Provisions of the constitution and state and federal laws relating to church-state relations must be observed.

11. Caution must be exercised to avoid providing public funds for constructing buildings for schools that may close after a brief period of experimentation.

12. Plans need to be made to anticipate changes in the local school organization and facilities that will be necessitated by shifts in student enrollment.

13. It is important that all information about the various schools be made available to the public, including detailed financial reports.

14. Parents should be helped to become more competent in making decisions about the education of their children and in assessing their learning.

15. The needed approval of local, state, and federal officials, legislative groups, and departments must be secured.

16. Justification of need for the establishment of a new school should be paramount for granting a charter.

17. Safeguards should be established to prevent established regulations from taking away a school's incentive to upgrade its program.

18. Equal opportunity for all children should be assured regardless of their social, economic, or intellectual status.
19. Misleading claims and fraud must be dealt with promptly and decisively.
20. Cooperation and support of boards of education, administrators, and teachers are essential.
21. The feasibility of the program and its effect on existing schools should be carefully tested before it is given broad support.
22. Provision should be made for objective evaluation of the voucher system and for its discontinuation if it fails.

Proposed Advantages   *With which ones do you agree?*

1. The voucher system would make schools more responsive to the needs of children and the desires of parents.

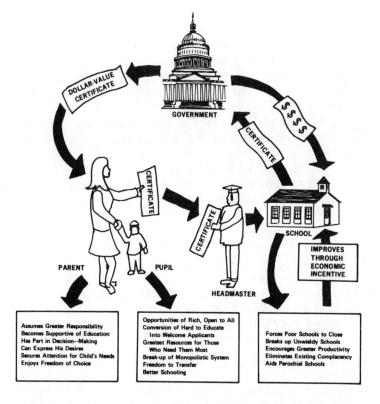

Proposed Advantages of a Voucher System: A Plan to Finance Schools with Government Certificates Given to Parents to Purchase Education of Their Choice

2. Parents would be encouraged to assume greater responsibility for planning the education of their children and would become supportive of education.

3. The plan would provide the same freedom of choice for the poor that is now open only to the wealthy.

4. The poor would have a part in educational planning, improvement, and decision-making.

5. The plan would tend to break up large, cumbersome, and ineffective schools.

6. The voucher system follows the principle of consumer sovereignty and would improve existing public and private schools by the addition of economic incentive.

7. The plan provides incentives that would make children who are hard to educate welcome applicants for admission.

8. Compensatory models follow the principle, long observed in hospitals, of devoting greater resources and providing the best services to those who need them most.

9. Administrators and teachers would be urged to consider innovative strategies and to experiment with improved approaches to teaching and learning.

10. Good schools would become better because of increased moral and financial support, and poor schools would improve or go out of business.

11. If, because of excessive personal conflict, a child developed an emotional block against one school, he could transfer to another.

12. Eventually schools would make better provision for all children, but particularly for the talented and the disadvantaged. The common tendency of teachers to teach to the middle of the population would be reduced.

13. Competition would shake present complacency of the public schools and stimulate more concern and greater effort.

14. The system would be a welcome aid to thousands of deserving parochial schools.

15. Parents who seek highly academic programs or those who want to emphasize moral and spiritual values could find schools to meet their desires.

Criticisms and Difficulties to Be Anticipated   *Do you agree?*

1. Parents would be confused and frustrated because they would be required to exercise more responsibility than they are capable of or willing to accept.

2. The system is an invitation for hucksters to make money by deceiving parents, particularly parents of disadvantaged children.

3. The government would be called upon for massive funding of plant and equipment for fly-by-night speculators who might leave the building within a short time.

4. Instability of future enrollment and support would make long-term planning of facilities impossible for the public schools.

5. The public schools would gradually become the dumping ground for children rejected by other schools.

6. Problems of transportation would be multiplied as children shuttle back and forth, to and from the schools of their choice.

7. Duplication of expensive buildings and equipment would be tremendously wasteful.

8. The advances made through school consolidation would be wiped out.

9. The idea of free choice in selecting schools is built on the premise that educators do not know any more about educating children than the man on the street.

10. Although the public school has always been the poor man's school, advocates of the voucher plan want to replace it with private schools.

11. Competing schools would stress personal gain for the individual and neglect the welfare of society.

12. The voucher system would result in segregation along many lines—racial, social, intellectual, political, economic.

13. The proponents advocate a free, competitive market with strict controls to prevent segregation.

14. Forbidding parents to supplement the value of the voucher is tantamount to making it illegal to provide for developing talented youth to the maximum.

15. Strict regulations to enforce freedom of choice and variations in the value of vouchers would result in personal strife and legal conflict yet undreamed of.

16. The plan destroys the finest system of education ever developed for the children of the common man.

17. Sensationalism, gadgets, gimmicks, and extreme emphasis on meaningless test scores are likely to be used to attract and retain students.

18. The plan is being promoted by people who are bitter because of some unfortunate experience with the public schools.

19. An unregulated voucher system would discriminate unmercifully against disadvantaged children.

20. Very small schools taught in recreation rooms in teachers' homes would spring up everywhere.
21. Under an unregulated plan, affluent citizens would vote against public support and provide the quality of education that they desire by supplementing the worth of the vouchers; and public schools would deteriorate rapidly.
22. The system would create greater cleavage between economic and social groups since affluent people would have to band together to protect their own interests.
23. Children would move to a different school whenever their teachers tried to discipline them.
24. Elaborate and costly machinery will have to be established to combat abuses and fraud.
25. If the government provides funds for the construction of new schools, new equipment, administration of new schools, elaborate transportation systems, and some profit for the private enterprise operating the schools, little money will be left for educating children.
26. Although the voucher system may be advocated by well-meaning theorists, the chief argument against it is that it simply will not work.

Summary Assessment

The educational voucher system faces a long, hard struggle. Many people are deeply concerned about inequality in our public schools, particularly the lack of opportunity for disadvantaged and poor children. Public education, they believe, has become a bankrupt monopolistic bureaucracy. But the opponents of the voucher system are even more passionate in their condemnation of what they conceive of as a sinister and vicious scheme to destroy an educational system that has progressed steadily for three centuries.

Now that it falters under tensions and pressures that are affecting the entire world, the supporters of public education think that impatient people with little perspective or vision are willing to abandon the course of steady progress. They believe that a small number of individuals who are bitter because of unfortunate personal experiences with the schools are exaggerating the imperfections of education and trying to wrest control of it from the establishment.

However, offhand rejection of proposals like the voucher system does not appear to be proper or becoming to educators who profess to be genuinely dedicated to experimentation, discovery, and improvement. It might be more appropriate for them to proceed on the assumption that suggestions for change, no matter how unworkable they may appear to be at first glance, are sincere, well-intended, and deserving of penetrating examination. New approaches to school support and organization are worthy of the same thoughtful consideration that educators must give to suggestions for innovations in school buildings, curriculum, and instructional practices. An institution whose very purpose is to prepare youth for change must itself face change realistically and with confidence and composure.

As one begins to examine the proposals for a voucher system, obvious problems appear. Children and parents may better know what they want than what children need. Opportunists could move in to exploit education. It may not be in the long-range interest of the nation to devote more resources to those who do not learn well and are difficult to teach than to those who learn easily and should be looked to for leadership in the years ahead. The voucher system may make long-range planning difficult. But it is possible that reasonable safeguards against abuses could be established, many of the dangers avoided, and perhaps most of the problems overcome. Those who bitterly oppose the voucher system appear to have forgotten that state scholarship programs and the G. I. Bill give money directly to individuals with which they can purchase education. It is not beyond the realm of possibility that alternative programs of education would, as the proponents suggest, revitalize a tired system of public education and actually stimulate better teaching and learning.

Even the most sincere critics of public education may be overlooking the serious concerns and dedicated efforts of hundreds of thousands of competent educators. Nevertheless, some of their feelings of urgent need for changing many aspects of school programs may be well grounded. On the other hand, the thought of splintering the American system of free public education, which has served the nation well, arouses fear and anxiety among many educators and laymen alike. They will resist what they consider a breakdown of the bulwark of educational opportunity to repair some of its defects.

The report of the Office of Economic Opportunity puts the problem this way:

> Indeed, an unregulated voucher system could be the most serious setback for the education of disadvantaged children in the history of the United States. A properly regulated system,

on the other hand, could inaugurate a new era of innovation and reform in American schools.*

Harold Spears, distinguished educator, replies that if the voucher plan is broadly accepted,

> The hand of tradition in American education would be scorched by the fire of criticism, and new ideas would spring up all over the place. You might even find a completely automated school with personnel limited to repairmen; education as well as food dispensed by machines.†

At the present time a number of states are exploring the possibility of using some form of voucher system to relieve the financial burdens of parochial and private schools. These plans propose to make grants to parents rather than directly to the school.

If the voucher system is to make a positive contribution to American education, it must be nurtured by a thoughtful blending of innovation and tradition, impulse and reflection, action and caution, energy and patience, theory and practice.

A Few Leaders in the Movement

Helen Bain
  National Education Association
Medill Bair
  Hartford (Conn.) Schools
Kenneth B. Clark
  Metropolitan Applied Research
  Center

Frederick W. Hill
  Univ. of California at Davis
Christopher Jencks
  Harvard Univ.
Theodore Sizer
  Harvard Univ.

A Few Places Studying the Voucher System

Alum Rock, Calif.
Gary, Ind.
Hartford, Conn.

Oakland, Calif.
State of Ohio
Philadelphia, Pa.

San Diego, Calif.
San Jose, Calif.
Seattle, Wash.

Annotated References

Berube, M. R., "Trouble with Vouchers," *Commonweal*, XCIII, No. 17 (1971), 414-417. Opposes the system listing its failures by citing that it doesn't touch key problems and gives arguments for and against with a discussion of how the voucher plan works.

---

*Christopher Jencks, et al., *Education Vouchers* (Cambridge, Mass.: Center for the Study of Public Policy, 1970), p. 17.
†Harold Spears, "Please Get in Line for Your Voucher," *The School Administrator*, The American Association of School Administrators, summer 1970, p. 12.

Betchkal, James, "Boardmen Can't Think of One Good Thing to Say About Voucher Plans," *The American School Board Journal,* CLVIII, No. 4 (1970), 33-37. States negative views of eight school board members such as causing prejudices, fragmenting public effort to educate young, creating imbalance, diluting finances, and lessening educational opportunity.

Branan, Karen, "Vouchers—Schools in the Marketplace," *Scholastic Teacher,* Junior/Senior High Teacher's Edition, January 11, 1971, 6-8. Warns against many dangers inherent in a voucher system. Laws would have to be rewritten. A scramble for competent teachers would result. Parents are unable to make wise choices, and children of the poor would suffer most. Schools would spring up to promote particular philosophies of special groups. Nine principles for guiding a voucher system are presented.

Cohodes, Aaron, "Voucher System Gets Chance to Show How it Would Work," *Nation's Schools,* LXXXVI, No. 3 (1970), 20. Credits Milton Friedman with the idea of the voucher system, which can provide new options or create more confusing bureaucracy. The proposal warrants trying it out.

Coyne, J. R., "Slates and Hamsters," *National Review,* XXIII, No. 11 (1971), 309-311. Presents the history of the voucher system, its workability, areas trying the plan, pros and cons, and alternatives. "Given the condition of the schools that serve poor youngsters, it takes a depressing amount of paranoia to suggest that we should not even give the voucher plan a reasonable trial."

Donovan, Hedley, ed., "Free Enterprise For Schools," *Time,* XCVIII, No. 8 (1970), 58, 60. Explains the voucher system proposed by Christopher Jencks to allow parents to choose schools for their children. Reference is made to suggested safeguards to insure educational opportunity for children of the poor.

Elliott, Osborn, ed., "Pay-As-You-Go-Schooling," *Newsweek,* LXXVI, No. 6 (1970), 49. Presents Jencks' arguments for the voucher system. Benefits for disadvantaged children, concern of parents, freedom of choice are advantages. The AFT, NEA, and NAACP fear it.

Hickman, L. C., ed., "OEO Launches It's Voucher Experiment," *Nation's Schools,* LXXXVII, No. 3 (1971), 30-31. Cites Gary, Indiana, and Alum Rock, California, as examples of preplanning voucher grants for fall 1971 by the OEO and gives purposes and charges against the system.

———, ed., "OEO Releases Voucher Timetable," *Nation's Schools,* LXXXVII, No. 4 (1970), 29. Considers Educational Voucher Agency organization, OEO requirements, future plans of preliminary schools, and oppositions to the plan.

Hill, Frederick W., "Voucher System—Bane or Boon?" *American School and University,* XLII, No. 11 (1970), 16-17. Discusses dangers inherent in the voucher system, but suggests a trial run. New ideas for facing financial crisis of the schools should not be feared. Public schools will survive if they merit public support.

Janssen, P. A., "Education Vouchers," *American Education,* VI, No. 10 (1970), 9-11. Recognizes that low-income children should have an equal educational opportunity and shows why NAACP and NEA warn against the voucher system while OEO advocates it with certain safeguards. "The success of the program," Christopher Jencks says, "depends on the effectiveness of the effort to give parents some idea of what constitutes a bad school." (p. 10)

Jencks, Christopher, et al., *Education Vouchers,* A Preliminary Report on Financing Education by Payments to Parents. Cambridge, Mass.: Center for the Study of Public Policy, 1970. Proposes a voucher system to provide freedom of choice for parents and their children and to make schools more responsive to public needs and desires. Special concern is expressed about the special needs of poor children.

Jencks, Christopher, "Education Vouchers," *The New Republic,* CLXI, No. 1 (1970), 19-21. Explains role of the Educational Voucher Agency as one of issuing vouchers, approving schools for receiving vouchers, and disseminating information about schools. Responds to several arguments against the system. Sectarian schools may be ineligible.

Lambert, S. M., "After All," *Today's Education,* LX, No. 5 (1971), 64. Argues that an experimental plan weakens confidence in public schools and adds financial obstacles as illustrated by the Holland educational incident.

Lawrence, D., ed., "A Constitutional Way to Avoid Discrimination in Aiding Schools; Tuition Grants to Parents-Schools," *U. S. News and World Report,* LXXI, No. 3 (1971), 88. Stresses that the government shouldn't tell the parent which schools his child must be sent to; suggests that parochial schools should receive help from the voucher certificates.

————, "A Student-Aid Plan Runs into a Fight," *U. S. News and World Report,* LXXI, No. 6 (1971), 20-21. Summarizes what advocates and opponents of the voucher idea believe, discusses the plan and its restrictions, and gives six views by various people.

Rogers, C., "Jencks's Education Plan: Sure to Backfire; National Education Voucher Plan," *Christian Century,* LXXXVII, No. 40 (1970), 1176. Opposes Jencks and the system because the plan underestimates the possibilities of the present educational system; describes the plan and its intentions.

Sizer, Theodore and Phillip Whitten, "A Proposal For a Poor Children's Bill of Rights," *Psychology Today,* II, No. 3 (1968), 59-63. Proposes to give money directly to the parents of poor children to help them finance the education of their children. Two financial assistance plans are submitted that discriminate in favor of poor children.

Spears, Harold, "Please Get in Line for Your Voucher," *The School Administrator,* The American Association of School Administrators, Summer 1970. Cites the G. I. Bill, Head Start, and Job Corps as examples of federal action to serve the "general welfare." The voucher system is based upon tenuous assumptions that may do serious harm without positive results.

Part Three

Reorganization for Better Learning

Community School   12

Definition

A community school is a school whose educational program grows out of the life of the community and serves to improve that life. Through mobilizing all available human and other resources, it becomes a center of vital learning and of many varied opportunities. It is a unifying force for community services directed toward improving the living of individuals and groups, as well as a life-centered educational institution designed to develop mature, productive citizens.

Two closely related, yet somewhat different, approaches are included within the school-community partnership. The one focuses upon the regular school program for youth and advocates a school where learning and living join hands. The school program moves out into the community for its learning experiences, establishes relevance of learning exercises, and pursues the principle of purposeful learning by doing. Community resources and action projects provide rich opportunities for education and at the same time assist in solving individual and group problems. The community serves as a learning laboratory for school youth, and the school offers leadership for improving the life of the citizenry.

The advantages of going into the community to motivate learning and to provide significant experiences for students in vocational and technical education, nature study, and social problems are quite obvious. Less frequently recognized, however, are the benefits that active involvement in the community can offer for such subjects as mathematics, literature, physics, or foreign language. Effective utilization of the community as a learning laboratory for students goes far beyond an occasional study trip to active and continuous involvement, not only in the study but also in the solution of community problems. Human as well as material resources are regularly brought into the classroom, and the talent of teachers and students is taken out into the community.

The other concept of community education emphasizes building an education-centered community by opening the schools to people of all ages from early morning until late at night on an all-week, year-round schedule. The offerings, determined by the needs and interests of the people, include everything from literacy programs and creative writing to sports and weight-watching. Multimedia centers, swimming pools, laboratories, health facilities, art rooms, and centers for the aging are open to all who want to use them.

The schools are centers of neighborhood and community life. Participation in self-government, health services, social and recreational activities, continuous study, and community improvement is stressed. Frequently, special attention is directed toward strengthening the ability of lower socioeconomic groups to improve their living. Opportunities are provided for upgrading vocational competencies, attacking problems of crime and drugs, securing personal and legal counseling, improving home management, building better social relations, and expanding recreational interests.

The community school concept is based upon the idea of helping people help themselves and recognizes the value of education in improving the quality of life. Schools become life-centered, and communities become learning-centered. Social and economic problems often spawn an interest in utilizing the buildings and other resources of the schools to assist in their solution. During the great depression, for example, many schools were thrown open to meet the educational, social, and recreational needs of the unemployed and to fill idle hours with constructive activities. During recent years attention again turned to the possibilities that lie in uniting the efforts of the community and its schools to cope with increasing delinquency, crime, unrest in urban centers, changes in job requirements, and other problems.

The community school contributes significantly to developing well-informed, competent people who can more readily solve their own problems and contribute to relieving those of society as a whole. By involving youth in learning and working in the community and by bringing all citizens into the schools, people of all ages and of divergent social and economic backgrounds learn to work together for the improvement of themselves, their families, and their communities. New life is injected into the school program, citizens' interest in their schools is increased, and a learning community becomes a better place in which its people can work, live, and rear their children with security and satisfaction.

Significant Components   *Which ones are essential?*

1. The community school must have concern for and provide services for all socioeconomic levels and all ages.
2. The curriculum and services of the school must evolve out of the interests, problems, and needs of the community.
3. Planners must recognize that the purpose of the program is to strengthen living in the community through studying and serving the problems of that community.
4. All segments of the community must be involved in identifying needs and desires and in planning, carrying out, and evaluating the activities.
5. The community must learn and be served in the school, and children and teachers must learn and serve in the community.
6. Educational opportunities and services must be available from early morning until late evening, all week throughout the year.
7. The school must be a center of community life, and its program must be life-centered.
8. Services must be available at the neighborhood level.
9. The community school should be under a single board of education and a single administrative staff and be well financed.
10. It must proceed on the philosophy that there is a great deal more to education than intellectualism.

11. It must operate as a service center to meet the health, recreational, social, economic, and other needs of the people.

12. The community school must have a well-trained, competent community services director, who understands the community in which he is working, and a lay as well as a professional staff that is thoroughly committed to the philosophy of the community school and has competence in developing a life-centered program.

13. The community school must be flexible enough to accommodate an infinite variety of changing interests and demands.

14. Support from all segments of the community is needed: clubs, social agencies, governmental divisions, churches, board of education, and political leadership.

15. New buildings should be designed so that certain parts can be used independently of the rest of the building, and the cost of maintenance and supervision can be minimized.

16. Effective programs of public relations and communications must be established and maintained.

17. An in-depth survey of the thinking, problems, interests, and resources of all segments of the community is essential.

18. The school must have established machinery for co-operating with all other agencies in the community.

19. Special attention should be given to the problems and needs of the inner city.

20. Careful evaluation should frequently be made to determine whether or not the program is achieving its objectives, and whether alternative approaches might be more effective.

Proposed Advantages   *With which ones do you agree?*

1. The community school stresses the concept that a person's education depends upon the totality of his life, and the quality of his life depends upon education.

2. Low-income people and others develop self-respect, self-confidence, and self-reliance through the practice of political and social skills and participation in decision-making.

3. A feeling of attachment to and pride in the community is developed in people from all economic levels.

4. Participation in school planning fosters a feeling of responsibility for assisting with such problems as student strikes, vandalism, drugs, truancy, and other forms of delinquency.

5. Since children can hardly have a positive self-image if their parents do not, educating parents is essential for effective education of children.

6. The tendency of teachers to blame the home for many of the children's deficiencies is reduced by the feeling of partnership between teachers and parents in the education of the young.

7. Economy is effected through the elimination of needless duplication of facilities, administration, and services.

8. Interest, significance, and purpose are brought into the lives of aging citizens.

9. Business and industry benefit from more competent, stable, and satisfied personnel.

10. A sense of personal responsibility and self-reliance strengthens government at the local level.

11. Citizens are given the opportunity to meet the continuous demands of change and discover new skills.

12. All ages working together on problems significant to all bridges the gap between youth and their elders.

13. Adults learn to read and write; new mothers learn to care for their families.

14. People of all racial and social groups learn to understand and respect one another by working and playing together.

15. Community projects develop leadership and followership.

16. The traditional verbalism of the classroom is impugned.

17. Community schools help alleviate the impersonal ills of urbanization by integrating and unifying the neighborhood.

18. A vehicle is provided for attacking illiteracy, poverty, disease, and unemployment.

19. The survival and strength of democracy are assured by the fullest development of all human resources.

Criticisms and Difficulties to Be Anticipated   *Do you agree?*

1. A good community-school program is excessively costly.

2. Few teachers have the orientation, dedication or skills needed to conduct an effective program.

3. It is difficult to involve low-income people and others to whom community-school participation could be of great benefit.

4. It is also difficult to secure the support of community leaders and organizations.

5. Most of the services included in the program are not the legitimate function of the school.

6. Education and services for adults are sure to decrease the funds available for educating children and youth.
7. The community-school concept implies a planned society, inimical to our heritage of freedom.
8. Involvement in many different activities will cause the schools to lose sight of their responsibility for intellectual excellence.
9. A community school presents too many diverse problems to be handled expertly by one agency.
10. Adults are difficult to involve in constructive programs and quickly lose interest.
11. Project planning by lay people frequently results in squabbling and dissension with the community, and the activities that are so planned usually degenerate into trivia.
12. Use of school facilities by teachers during off-school hours is likely to result in conflict with teachers and administrators in the day school.
13. Transportation and liability are real problems.
14. The community school takes support away from clubs, churches, and other organizations in the community.
15. Socialistic ventures of this kind destroy private initiative and create wasteful bureaucracies.

Summary Assessment

The community-school concept embraces two aspects: One relates to a life-centered educational program for pupils in the elementary and secondary schools; the other places major emphasis on continuing education for all citizens and providing services for enriching the life of the individual and the community.

The former seems to be a natural extension of educational opportunity for youth, consistent with the school's responsibility for making its program vital and relevant and for discharging its obligation to the society that supports it. The need to add realism and motivational power to conventional school experiences by moving out of the walls of the classrooms into the challenging laboratories of life has long been recognized. However, little more than lip service has been given to the idea.

At the present time, citizens are dissatisfied with the inability of many youth to move smoothly into the social, political, and economic life of the community. They question new values of youth and their apparent lack of readiness to contribute constructively to the progress of the nation. The current restlessness of young people may be an expression of their dissatisfaction with existing educational programs. They may not see a relationship between what and how they are being taught and the life which they envision. The pressure of parents and their children forces educators to reflect on possibilities for change. The demand for accountability and efforts to meet it may indicate a need for the schools to go out into their communities to provide motivation and experiences which can revitalize existing programs and to discover new approaches which can make education important to children and their parents.

The need for extending education and other services to all citizens is re-emphasized by the rapidly increasing complexity of urban problems. Population mobility, demands for new skills, and the breakdown in family and community life add urgency to the search for new solutions. Poverty, drug addiction, pollution, and crime cry out for help. There are those who insist that the time is past due for the school to become a truly social institution. They believe that only through active participation in decision-making can adults as well as youth build a positive self-concept and escape alienation.

Those who have thought of education as a need only for young people are beginning to wonder if we should invest all our educational resources in one age group between the ages of five and 22. During the past few years great stress has been placed on the need for compensatory education for preschool children. It is evident that in a world that changes as rapidly as ours, education for employment, leisure-time pursuits, economic readjustments, and interpersonal relationships can never be terminal. To neglect the growing needs of increasing millions of aging citizens would indeed be a travesty of their dignity.

The community school holds great promise for both the schools and the community. It requires a rethinking of the roles of both. If the program is soundly conceived, carefully planned, and adequately supported, it can avoid the pitfalls and overcome the objections that confront it. It could bring new excitement to education and to living by making the education of youth more productive and by making citizens of all ages and socioeconomic groups lifelong learners. Schools could become truly public and genuinely educational.

In the community school there is no "before school" or "after school," there is no "new school year," there is no age limit for attendance. Basic tools of learning, home membership, citizenship, vocational skills, recreational and social experiences for all segments of the population contribute to enhancing the life of each individual and to improving the total community. New goals, ideals, values, and hopes are fostered. Educators give their professional know-how and leadership to making the school the catalytic agent for building cohesiveness and unity of purpose throughout the community.

In the final analysis, the solution to most of our problems lies in more and better education. Deciding to continue study, seek help, or simply engage in play in a community school program opens a new door to help the participant solve many of his problems. He is provided with an opportunity to grow in responsibility and self-direction. Self-improvement and success in solving problems are likely to breed satisfaction and stimulate higher aspirations.

Opportunities are provided for high school dropouts to get a new start, for returning veterans, for the unemployed, and for those who because of modern technology have more time than before to engage in activities of their own choice. By becoming a center of community life and by providing education for all, schools are likely to generate greater public support. There are those who believe that education in a free society should exercise strong leadership in extending opportunities for self-improvement to all citizens.

It appears that the time has come when schools must go to the streets to help people help themselves. This can be accomplished if school people have the necessary imagination, and if citizens are ready to provide the resources for schools and community to join forces and march forward to a brighter future.

A Few Leaders in the Movement

Clyde M. Campbell
  Michigan State Univ.
Peter Clancy
  Flint (Mich.) Community Schools
Israel C. Heaton
  Brigham Young Univ.
Vasil Kerensky
  Florida Atlantic Univ.
Daniel Levine
  Univ. of Missouri at Kansas City

Harold McCluskey
  Univ. of Michigan
Ernest Melby
  Florida Atlantic Univ.
Jack Minzey
  Eastern Michigan Univ.
Harding Mott
  Mott Foundation
Edward G. Olson
  California State College
  at Hayward

Nick Pappadikis
Nat'l. Center for Community
  Education
Robert G. Pickering
  Reading (Ohio) Schools
Maurice Seay
  Western Michigan Univ.
Harold G. Shane
  Univ. of Indiana

Mark Shedd
  Harvard Univ.
James Showkeir
  Miami Univ.
W. Fred Totten
  Flint, Mich.
Curtis Van Vorhees
  Univ. of Michigan

A Few Places Where the Innovation Is Used

Alpena, Mich.	Flint, Mich.	Phoenix, Ariz.
Atlanta, Ga.	Florida Atlantic Univ.	Reading, Ohio
Aurora, Colo.	Lakewood, N. Y.	St. Louis, Mo.
Baltimore, Md.	Milwaukee, Wis.	San Jose State College
Chattanooga, Tenn.	Minneapolis, Minn.	Springfield, Ohio
Clark, Nev.	Monroe, Mich.	Tipp City, Ohio
Corning, N. Y.	Monterey, Calif.	Toledo, Ohio
Dade County, Fla.	Muskegon, Mich.	Western Mighigan Univ.
E. Baton Rouge, La.	New Haven, Conn.	Wilmington, Del.

Annotated References

Anthony, John, Esther Kemp, and Barbara Jackson, "Challenge of a Community-Controlled School," *Instructor,* LXXX, No. 1 (1970), 62-63. Cites the workings of the Morgan Community School in Washington, D. C. Reports conversation between the principal and two teachers about the advantages of the community school. Teachers suggested they are held accountable to the parents and feel more in touch with educational needs of the community.

Campbell, Clyde M., *Toward Perfection In Learning.* Midland, Mich.: Pendell, 1969. Presents in case history form the success of the Mott program at Flint, Michigan. Explains the special success of the community school with disadvantaged urban students. Stresses the desirability of starting a program and making improvements as it moves ahead.

Carmichael, Benjamin E. and Nita Nardo, "Emerging Patterns in Community-Centered Schools," *Childhood Education,* XLIII, No. 6 (1967), 319-323. Stresses the need for complete collaboration between school and community in order to produce a citizenry capable of sustaining the life of the nation. The profession of teaching has an inherent obligation for leadership in bringing school and community together.

Cordasco, Francesco, "Urban Education—Leonard Covello and the Community School," *School and Society,* XCVIII, No. 2326 (1970), 298-299. Stresses need for allaying distrust and for fostering friendliness and intelligent cooperation through community involvement. As principal of the Benjamin Franklin High School in East Harlem from 1934 to 1957, Leonard Covello was a pioneer in the community-school concept.

Cox, Donald W. and Liza Lazorko, "A School Without Walls: A City for a Classroom," *Nation's Schools,* LXXXIV, No. 3 (1969), 51-54. Explains briefly the Parkway Plan in operation in Philadelphia. The authors tell how it works and present some of the questions raised by community and educational leaders about the effectiveness of the program.

Douglas, Leonard, "The Community School Philosophy and the Inner-City School," *Urban Education,* V, No. 4 (1971), 328-335. Describes the community school philosophy. A model is proposed which includes a citizen's advisory council and committees. Advocates the mobilization of community, home, and school to help inner-city youth.

Greenberg, James and Robert E. Roush, "A Visit to the School Without Walls: Two Impressions," *Phi Delta Kappan,* LI, No. 9 (1970), 480-484. A summary of impressions gained by two men when they visited the Parkway Program in Philadelphia. One of the authors was very impressed with the way the school integrated with the community, but the other had several reservations and suggestions for altering the program.

Henry, Nelson B., *Community Education, Principles and Practices from World-Wide Experience.* Chicago: National Society for the Study of Education, 1959. Presents articles concerning the nature and purpose, history, cultural and psychological factors, representative programs throughout the world, and leadership training related to community schools. Advocates a world-wide program of community education to progress toward a world community.

Herman, Barry E., "Winchester Community School: A Laboratory of Ideas," *Educational Leadership,* XXV, No. 4 (1968), 341-343. Describes the community school concept as it is carried out in an inner-city elementary school. Constructed expressly for this purpose, the Winchester Community School is one of seven New Haven schools serving as an educational center, a community center, a center for services, and a center of neighborhood life.

Hickey, Howard W. and Curtis Van Vorhees, eds., *The Role of the School In Community Education.* Midland, Mich.: Pendell, 1969. Presents articles by 12 authorities on community education. A broad range of topics is covered including purposes, organization, administration, staffing, financing, facilities, operation, and evaluation. Theory is integrated with practical suggestions.

Irwin, Martha and Wilma Russell, *The Community Is The Classroom.* Midland, Mich.: Pendell, 1971. Argues that the open-classroom concept, as exemplified through the use of community resources, adds meaning and reality to the learning of young people. Guidelines are supplied for the development of a community-centered curriculum and community-classroom learning activities.

Jackson, Ronald B., "Schools and Communities: A Necessary Relevance," *The Clearing House,* XLIV, No. 8 (1970), 488-490. Asserts that teaching staffs are as underused as buildings in most school systems. In order to be relevant teachers and the educational program must become involved in community affairs.

_____, "Student Community Halls: A New Relevance for High Schools," *Journal of Secondary Education,* XLV, No. 4 (1970), 163-166. Advocates a student community hall as a part of a school designed for the complete user.

A new approach is presented to collaboration among schools, field experiences, academics, home, in-school employment, and post school development.

Kerensky, V. M. and Ernest O. Melby, *Education II The Social Imperative.* Midland, Mich.: Pendell, 1971. Advocates a meaningful education to lead the individual and society out of the morass of traditional education. Urban communities demand that attention be given to the self-concept and the utilization of community resources for all.

Lanning, Frank and Wesley A. Many, eds., *Basic Education for the Disadvantaged Adult: Theory and Practice.* Boston: Houghton Mifflin, 1966. A book of readings stressing the urgent need for adult education and ways of coping with the problems of illiteracy and other aspects of undereducation. Attention is given to social and psychological implications and to methods and materials of instruction.

Levine, Daniel U., "The Community School in Historical Perspective," *Elementary School Journal,* LXVII, No. 4 (1967), 192-195. Emphasizes the vital role of the community school in serving the needs of low-income citizens in the inner-city. Education, mental and physical health services, employment training, community development, and social services are attacking poverty.

————, "The Community School in Contemporary Perspective," *Elementary School Journal,* LXIX, No. 7 (1968), 109-117. Proposes that schools must become sponsors of many new social functions including the development of political and social skills in low-income citizens. Only by being accessible and responsive can schools avert apathy and hostility toward education and government.

Malone, J. E., "The School the Community Built," *The Bulletin of the National Association of Secondary School Principals,* LIV, No. 348 (1970), 39-49. Reports the community school innovations in the education-conscious community of Yellow Springs, Ohio. The local high school is part of the NASSP Model School Projects School and has become community-centered. The school and community work together in a comprehensive educational program.

Melby, Ernest O., "The Community-Centered School," *Childhood Education,* XLIII, No. 6 (1967), 316-318. Expresses urgency for educating people of all ages through a community-centered school. Inner-city children can be educated only if both school and home provide a climate conducive to learning. The attitude of the teacher is crucial.

Moore, Donald R., Frederick V. Mulhauser, Barbara S. Powell, et al., *Community and the Schools.* Cambridge, Mass.: Harvard Educational Review, 1969. Includes articles that examine the relationships between school, community, and political structure. Describes community as it is related to teacher training, experimental community schooling, and black curriculum. Two articles discuss the community school's relationship with the ideal community and the future of community schools.

Olsen, Edward G., ed., *The School and Community Reader.* New York: Macmillan, 1963. Discusses various aspects of school and community interaction. The section on developing the community school contains numerous articles covering definition, rationale, objectives, characteristics, criteria, and development, and gives a comparison of traditional schools, progressive schools, and community schools.

Rich, Leslie, "Instead of Molotov Cocktails," *American Education,* VI, No. 5 (1970), 11-15. Reports experiences of inner-city schools in Harlem, where children are learning to be aware of the needs of the community. Advocates the use of community schools by commending the fact that children are learning to improve their community and are motivated to try to improve their environment.

Rippey, Robert M., "The Researcher in the Community," *School Review,* LXXIX, No. 1 (1970), 133-144. Cites research and evaluation of the Wood-lawn Experimental Schools Project in Chicago. The research team generally concluded that change is difficult but the benefits include involvement of parents and effective classes set up for all ages. Suggested are ways to better research the community school and issues involving time and space.

Stebbins, Marion, "How to Use a Community School Director," *Nation's Schools,* LXXVIII, No. 4 (1966), 116-117. Discusses the roles of the community director at the elementary, junior high, and senior high school levels. At the junior high school level he serves on a regional counsel team, at the senior high level he develops a school useful to the total city. Personal contact is the key to his effectiveness.

Totten, W. Fred, "Community Education: Best Hope for Society," *School and Society,* XCVIII, No. 2328 (1970), 410-412. Advocates a community school which is concerned with all aspects of life in the community. Suggests the community school concept is the best hope for a society to become healthy. Cites statistics and supports argument by referring to Flint, Michigan, where a community school has existed since 1935.

_____, *The Power of Community Education.* Midland, Mich.: Pendell, 1970. Discusses carefully the theory, purposes, and potential of the community school concept. Development of the individual citizen and community improvement are blended through involvement and group action. Experiences related by the author should be important for those contemplating a community school program.

Totten, W. Fred and Frank J. Manley, *The Community School: Basic Concepts, Function, and Organization.* Galien, Mich.: Allied Educational Council, 1969. A practical resource explaining, in detail, aspects of the community-school concept, such as objectives, impact on community, organization, resources, staffing, financing, facilities, initiation of the program, and impact on curriculum.

Witt, Robert L., *A Handbook for the Community School Director.* Midland, Mich.: Pendell, 1971. Presents significant help for the community school director. Attention is directed to community involvement and support, program development, interest groups, and fiscal problems. Attitudes of teachers toward the program and especially toward disadvantaged children are discussed.

Audiovisual and Other Resources

To Touch a Child (16mm film, loan or purchase). Flint Community Schools, 923 E. Kearsley St., Flint, Mich. 48502.

Middle School   13

Definition

The middle school is not an organizational pattern for administrative convenience. It is an idea, a philosophy, to provide a unique educational program to shape the learning pattern of a unique age group. Typically it encompasses the work of the traditional sixth, seventh, and eighth grades. Often the fifth grade is included; infrequently the ninth grade is part of the school.

Three main forces contributed to establishing the middle school. In many school districts capacities of old and newly constructed buildings were a significant factor. When pressure for additional space existed in the junior high school, relief could be found by reorganizing and shifting the ninth grade to the senior high school. In other instances, excessive enrollment in several elementary schools could be avoided by combining the sixth grade with the seventh and eighth to form a middle school. A new building was often built to relieve overcrowding in a number of existing buildings by bringing some junior high school students and some elementary pupils together in a new middle school. Decisions to include the fifth or ninth grade in the middle school were frequently based on similar considerations.

A second incentive to the development of the middle school was the realization that the conventional junior high school was

150

no longer performing the functions for which it had originally been established. It had drifted away from its objectives of providing a unique program for a special age group. It no longer emphasized guidance, broad exploratory experiences, and smooth transition from elementary to secondary education. Through the years it had drifted into being a miniature high school.

The third and perhaps most justifiable reason for developing a new type of school was the feeling of need for a unique program for a unique group of young people. The extended influence of mass media, particularly television, increased mobility of population, and improved educational opportunities had produced fundamental changes in pupils and created a need for new approaches to their education. Reorganization of the traditional structure of the schools seemed to be a step toward meeting the new demands. The middle school proposed to provide smoother transition from elementary education to high school by regrouping the students, shifting its emphasis, realigning its objectives, and incorporating many innovative changes in methodology and curriculum content.

As it emerges, the middle school attempts to establish its own special identity as a school for pupils between elementary and high school and specifically strives to serve the needs of older children, preadolescents, and early adolescents, between 10 and 14. It is usually housed in a separate building, ideally in facilities specially designed for its purposes. The program emphasizes continuous progress, individualization of instruction, and team teaching. The development of self-reliance by placing increased responsibility for learning upon the student is a significant feature. The teacher's role is that of stimulator, guide, and director of learning. Ann Grooms emphasizes this role when she says:

> The middle school teacher is not teaching math; he is not teaching Mary; he is not teaching math to Mary. He is providing support so that she can learn math.*

Significant Components   *Which ones are essential?*

1. The reasons for establishing a middle school must be educationally sound, and its goals and objectives clearly stated.
2. Teachers who are committed to the philosophy and purposes of the middle school must be selected and developed.

---

*M. Ann Grooms, *Perspectives on the Middle School* (Columbus, Ohio: Charles E. Merrill Publishing Company, 1967), p. 51.

3. Teachers must have competence in counseling as well as in specific subject areas.
4. The resource center must contain varied and appropriate materials for use in individualized study programs.
5. Activities normally considered extracurricular should be meaningfully integrated into the regular program.
6. Educators should grasp the opportunity that a new middle school provides for introducing innovative practices.
7. If a new building is being constructed, it must reflect the philosophy, goals, and program that will determine its use.
8. Decisions to include certain age groups in the middle school should be made upon the basis of distinctive needs and qualities of the pupils rather than for the sake of relieving overcrowding in certain buildings.
9. Sufficient space must be available to allow for freedom of movement, large and small group instruction, and independent study.
10. The school should avoid letting emphasis on subject matter interfere with close personal relations among teachers and pupils.
11. Balance must be established between stability and flexibility.
12. Special effort must be made to avoid simply transferring a traditional junior high school program to the middle school.
13. The total program should be a functional entity, capable of providing a unique program for pupils of this age.
14. The desirability and feasibility of team teaching should be given careful consideration.
15. The psychological, physical, and social needs of the pupils must be a basic factor in deciding upon the program.
16. The school should incorporate the concept of continuous progress.
17. The program should emphasize self-motivation, independent study, and individual responsibility through personal involvement.
18. Flexible scheduling should be utilized to provide for variations in activities.
19. The middle school must give special emphasis to providing a cohesive, but still flexible, link between the primary education and the high school.

Proposed Advantages   *With which ones do you agree?*

1. The middle school provides for an integrated program to meet the physical, emotional, and intellectual needs of a unique age group.

2. The philosophy of the middle school avoids miniature high school courses, replacing them with a varied program of its own.
3. A variety of integrated experiences is substituted for such isolated activities as interschool athletics.
4. The program promotes individualization for a student group characterized by great variability.
5. Smooth articulation is provided between the educational experience of childhood and adolescence.
6. The best features of the self-contained program of the primary school and the departmentalized structure of the secondary school are incorporated into the program.
7. The middle school capitalizes on the special talent of teachers to meet the varied needs of individuals and groups.
8. The program emphasizes self-direction and pupil involvement.
9. A good middle school program reduces undesirable emotional pressures on youth and stresses humaneness.
10. Flexibility in time schedule, freedom of movement, and variation in learning activities are provided for.
11. Interdisciplinary approaches in all subjects are encouraged.
12. A new approach generates increased interest and motivation on the part of pupils, teachers, administrators, and parents.

Criticisms and Difficulties to Be Anticipated *Do you agree?*

1. Teachers, pupils, and parents may be oriented to a more traditional approach to the extent that they misunderstand and even reject the philosophy of the middle school.
2. The pattern of the junior high school is likely to persist and thus hinder the development of distinctly new purposes and approaches.
3. The distinct nature and problems of the 10- to 14-year-old may continue to be neglected.
4. Administrative and organizational factors often become the dominant considerations.
5. Lack of adequate space, equipment, and materials are likely to be an obstacle.
6. To some observers, flexibility and freedom may seem like disorganization and confusion.
7. Fragmentation interferes with unity of learning.
8. Existing buildings may require extensive alteration.
9. Excessive attention given to the new unit will be resented by primary and high school staffs.
10. Changes in program and methodology are likely to be introduced too abruptly.

11. Teachers and administrators will not give the time necessary to enable the middle school to realize its high purposes.
12. In some states legislation pertaining to teacher certification, subject requirements, and promotion standards may have to be revised.

Summary Assessment

The middle school seems to be gradually overcoming one of its early handicaps resulting from misinterpretation of its purposes. In many places, it was instituted merely as a means of accommodating rapidly increasing enrollments by shifting them from one building to another. The new school is good only as it emerges as a distinct institution with its own objectives and programs designed to serve a segment of the school population that possesses unique characteristics. The failure of the traditional junior high school to serve the needs of its students has been a stimulus and an advantage in shaping the new school, although remnants of the previous structure and program persist and occasionally appear to endanger the continued vitality of the middle school.

The middle school must not be a miniature high school or an advanced elementary school, but must establish its own identity as an institution capable of meeting the intellectual, personal, social, aesthetic, emotional, and physical problems that confront pre-teen and early teen-age youth. It is a good beginning toward creation of a climate in which each child is able to wrestle with the incongruities of life facing him as a result of the pressures, needs, potentialities, and opportunities that confront him on every hand.

To date very little systematic research has been directed toward assessing the success of the new school in achieving its proposed objectives or toward comparing its effectiveness with that of conventional elementary and junior high programs. Distinct strengths of the middle school lie in its commitment to placing children's needs ahead of organized subject matter and to tailoring content and method to the unique characteristics of each learner. In theory the new emphasis is on humaneness and personal and social adjustment. However, some signs indicate that excessive use of subject specialists is turning the program away from its well-intended concern for affective learnings. In some schools, team teaching is degenerating into departmentalization with members of the teams vying for isolated success in their individual subjects.

If the middle school is to contribute maximally to the development of the values, attitudes, and personal qualities of each learner, it will have to increase its efforts to spell out its objectives in precise, behavioral terms. Only if outcomes in the affective areas of learning can be assessed with reasonable specificity, will teachers be stimulated to strive for observable results. Caution must be exercised to prevent the changes of the middle school from being changes in form and organization only. The underlying philosophy and thinking upon which the concept of the new school is based must not yield to complacency, with superficial changes in structure or with impressive observance of instructional rituals. New strategies must be accompanied by new, more relevant content and produce new and better results. Only by continuous review of its objectives and rigorous evaluation of results as they relate to the objectives, can the middle school attain the high goals that it has set for itself.

Currently, a distinct handicap to realizing the fullest potential of the middle school is the failure of teacher-education institutions to prepare teachers for the new school. Advantages and disadvantages continue. Whether the advantages in a particular school outweigh the disadvantages depends in large measure upon the support given to the developing ideas and programs, the quality of administrative and supervisory leadership, and the commitment of the teachers. Vision, creativeness, continuous assessment, and readjustment are essential to continued progress.

A Few Leaders in the Movement

William M. Alexander
  Univ. of Florida
Donald H. Eichhorn
  Institute for Development of
  Educational Activities
Robert Finley
  Glen Cove (N. Y.) Schools
Nicholas Georgiady
  Miami Univ.
M. Ann Grooms
  Educational Services Institute
Alvin Howard
  Univ. of New Mexico
Leslie W. Kindred
  Temple Univ.
Jon Rye Kinghorn
  Institute for Development of
  Educational Activities

Theodore Moss
  State Univ. of New York
  at Oswego
Donald Overly
  Centerville (Ohio) Schools
Samuel H. Popper
  Univ. of Minnesota
Richard Preston
  Defiance (Ohio) Schools
Louis Romano
  Michigan State Univ.
Cyril G. Sargent
  Harvard Univ.
Emmett L. Williams
  Univ. of Florida

A Few Places Where the Innovation Is Used

Amory, Miss.	Eagle Grove, Iowa	New Haven, Conn.
Barrington, Ill.	East Lansing, Mich.	Philadelphia, Pa.
Bellingham, Wash.	Glen Cove, N. Y.	Pleasant Hills, Pa.
Beloit, Wis.	Glencoe, Ill.	Reading, Ohio
Boulder, Colo.	Goshen, N. Y.	Saginaw, Mich.
Centerville, Ohio	High Springs, Fla.	St. Clair, Pa.
Cleveland, Ohio	Highland Park, Ill.	Sarasota County, Fla.
Del Mar, Calif.	Midland, Mich.	Sunbury, Ohio
Des Moines, Iowa	Mt. Kisco, N. Y.	Tiburon, Calif.

Annotated References

Alexander, William, Emmett L. Williams, Mary Compton, Vynce A. Hines, and Dan Prescott, *The Emergent Middle School.* New York: Holt, 1968. Covers the purposes and rationale of the middle school movement and gives reasons why such an idea will meet the needs of young people in our complex society. Practical suggestions for operating procedures are provided.

Alexander, William and Emmett L. Williams, "Schools for the Middle School Years," *Educational Leadership,* XXIII, No. 3 (1965), 217-223. Suggests that traditional junior high schools are places where children must hurry and get ready for high school. Guidelines are presented stressing proper use of staff talent and a program geared to the special needs of preadolescents.

Association for Supervision and Curriculum Development, *Developing Programs for Young Adolescents.* Washington, D. C.: National Education Association, 1954. In spite of the fact that this booklet is not recent, the concepts presented in terms of curricular programs designed for the needs of this age learner are still sound.

Batezel, George W., "The Middle School: Philosophy, Program, Organization," *The Clearing House,* XLII, No. 8 (1968), 487-490. An ideal middle school provides a gradual transition from the elementary school to the high school, allows each student to be well-known to at least one teacher, sees that the child is considered above the program, and adapts its program to his special needs.

Blair, Glenn Myers and R. Stewart Jones, *Psychology of Adolescence for Teachers.* New York: Macmillan, 1964. Although written with the adolescent learner as the focal point, some of the concepts are adaptable to the later childhood and early adolescent learner. Clearly written, the book is easily understood by persons other than students of psychology.

Bondi, J., "Middle School Requires Some Direction," *The Clearing House,* XLV, No. 9 (1971), 568. Gives some guidelines for developing middle schools emphasizing the need for planning in terms of purposes and philosophy. Educators must become actively involved in the movement rather than just arguing.

Bough, Max, "Theoretical and Practical Aspects of the Middle School," *The Bulletin of the National Association of Secondary School Principals,* March, 1969. Insists that one must justify a middle school on the basis of both population and finance. Theoretical and practical factors must be considered. Three points from Alexander and Williams's guidelines are listed which should be weighed carefully before "jumping on the bandwagon."

Brinkman, Arthur R., "We Call It the Middle School," *The PTA Magazine,* LXII, No. 10 (1968), 12-14. Stresses the point that the middle school is not a building or a plan for grouping children. It is rather an opportunity to develop a much-needed program for a special age group. Additional teachers are not essential; old buildings can be adapted.

Brod, Pearl, "Middle School in Practice," *The Clearing House,* XLIII, No. 9 (1969), 530-532. Suggests the need for developing special training and certification for teachers and counselors in the middle school.

———, "The Middle School: Trends Toward Its Adoption," *The Clearing House,* XL, No. 6 (1966), 331-333. Lists and discusses 16 advantages claimed for the middle school organization. Most of them deal with enriched opportunities for development of children of this age level.

Buell, Clayton, "An Educational Rationale for the Middle School," *The Clearing House,* XLII, No. 4 (1967), 242-244. Presents a good list of characteristics of preadolescents which indicate that youth during this stage differ sharply from children in grades 1-5 and just as distinctly from those of high school age.

Cass, J., "School Designed for Kids: Beloit-Turner Middle School," *Saturday Review,* LIII, No. 12 (1970), 65-71. Gives a profile of the Beloit-Turner middle school in Wisconsin where "teachers like kids." Individual and personalized learning experiences characterize the school.

Compton, M. F., "Middle School," *Education Digest,* XXXIV, No. 8 (1969), 22-24. Discusses many areas in which the traditional junior high school program has failed to meet the needs of the children it serves. The article points up 10 important elements common to most middle schools.

Conant, James Bryant, *Recommendations for Education in the Junior High School Years.* Princeton, N. J.: Educational Testing Service, 1960. Based on a study of 237 junior high schools, Conant makes recommendations to school boards for reorganizing the program in light of new needs.

Cuff, William A., "Middle Schools on the March," *National Association of Secondary School Principals Bulletin,* LI, No. 316 (1967), 82-86. Report of a nationwide survey on middle schools for the 1965-1966 school year. Poses some questions unique to this pattern of organization.

Curtis, Thomas E., ed., *The Middle School.* Albany, N. Y.: Center for Curriculum Research and Services, State University, 1968. Collection of presentations on middle school from a curriculum conference. Provides different viewpoints (pro and con) toward middle schools.

Curtis, Thomas and Wilma Bidwell, "Rationale for Instruction in the Middle School," *Educational Leadership,* XXVII, No. 6 (1970), 578-581. A well-thought out rationale, giving reasons, characteristics, and three basic areas around which a middle school should be built. Purposes of the middle school and suggested changes in methods are described.

DeVita, Joseph C., Philip Pumerantz and Leighton B. Wicklow, *The Effective Middle School.* West Nyack, N. Y.: Parker, 1970. Presents practical and successful strategies and approaches to aid the teacher and administrator in developing middle school programs.

DiVirgilio, James, "Administrative Role in Developing a Middle School," *The Clearing House,* XLIII, No. 2 (1968), 103-105. Explains that in middle schools, "the exciting part is the freedom to attempt new ideas free from the controls that operated in the junior high."

―――――, "Our Middle Schools Give the Kids a Break," *Today's Education,* LX, No. 1 (1971), 30-32. Goes over the activity programs of three middle schools in Howard County, Maryland. The author discusses many interesting things the students and teachers have suggested such as pie-eating contests and knitting hours.

―――――, "Switching from Junior High to Middle School," *The Clearing House,* XLIV, No. 4 (1969), 224-226. Discusses points to be considered by a school system before it changes to middle schools. The article points up good suggestions which might be implemented in effective middle school programs.

Eichhorn, Donald H., "Nongraded Middle School—Supporting Theory and Conceptualized Functional Model," *Dissertation Abstracts,* XXVII-A (July-September, 1966), 627. Offers support for the hypothesis that students possess varying personal characteristics and educational needs which suggest a restructuring of the present organization to include a middle school composed of students presently found in grades six, seven, and eight.

―――――, *The Middle School.* New York: The Center for Applied Research, 1966. A small, well-researched book about the middle school concept. An examination of the appropriate, philosophical, social, and psychological foundations of the middle-school age child is followed by a presentation of a model middle school.

Elkind, J., "Middle School Muddle," *The Clearing House,* XLIV, No. 7 (1970), 400. Urges that educators not "make a muddle of this concept (the middle school) as was done with the junior high."

Gastwirth, Paul, "Questions Facing the Middle School," *The Clearing House,* XLI, No. 8 (1967), 472-475. Cautions educators to evaluate carefully and define a "middle school" before joining the bandwagon. Suggests that a good junior high school can achieve the same purposes that proponents of middle schools claim can best be achieved through this new organizational pattern.

Grooms, M. Ann, *Perspectives on the Middle School.* Columbus, Ohio: Merrill, 1967. Examines closely the physical and behavioral characteristics of a changing and restless group. Many suggestions are given for getting parental support and understanding. A parents' day plan is outlined.

Hamm, R. L., "Middle School vs. Junior High School," *The Clearing House,* XLIV, No. 5 (1970), 267. Points up the characteristics of a good middle school. Ways that the middle school differs from the junior high school are discussed.

Hansen, John H. and Arthur C. Hearn, *The Middle School Program.* Chicago: Rand McNally, 1971. Traces the history and defines the nature and function of the middle school. The instructional program is treated in overview and by individual subjects. Discussion of the institutional support programs considers student activities, guidance, organization and administration, and evaluation.

Hillson, Maurie and Ramona Karlson, *Change and Innovation in Elementary School Organization.* New York: Holt, 1965. A collection of readings, several of which are apropos to middle school or junior high school education: ability grouping, ungraded, semi-departmental and departmental, team teaching, and evaluation.

Howard, Alvin, *Teaching in Middle Schools.* Scranton, Pa.: International, 1968. A valuable reference for teachers. There are many suggestions of specific techniques to use for teaching students ages 10-14. If a teacher is having a problem, he will probably find the suggestions helpful.

———, "Which Years in Junior High?" *The Clearing House,* XLI, No. 4 (1966), 227-230. Expresses a real need for an intermediate school specifically designed to deal with the problems of early adolescent learners. "But what grade groupings are best?" is the question posed by the author.

Howard, Alvin W. and George C. Stoumbis, *The Junior High and Middle School: Issues and Practices.* Scranton: Intext Educational, 1970. Considers controversies and problems, changing patterns of instruction and the newer grade organizational patterns and curricula of the middle schools.

Howell, Bruce, "The Middle School—Is It Really Any Better?" *North Central Association Quarterly,* XL, 281-287. Deals with one school's self-appraisal, and what it did to help correct and improve its program. Ideas could be adapted to help other schools check their goals and results.

Hunt, John J. and Lyle L. Berg, "The Continuing Trend Toward Middle School Organizational Patterns," *Journal of Secondary Education,* XLV, No. 4 (1970), 170-173. A report of the number of middle schools in the individual states and the grade organizational patterns. Texas ranks first in number with 6-7, 6-7-8, and 5-6-7-8 reported as the most common patterns.

Jennings, Wayne, "The Middle School? No!" *Minnesota Journal of Education,* XLVII (January, 1967), 73-74. Merely changing the name and/or grades included will not effect a better program for early adolescents. Altering the present junior high school classroom practices, developing a curriculum significant for life, and preparing competent staff will effect a desirable change.

Kindred, Leslie W., *The Intermediate Schools.* Englewood Cliffs, N. J.: Prentice-Hall, 1968. Explores the movement to replace the junior high school with the middle school.

Lounsbury, John H., Gordon F. Vars, and William Van Til, *Modern Education for the Junior High School Years,* Second Edition. Indianapolis: Bobbs-Merrill, 1967. A comprehensive volume emphasizing curriculum and curricular organization for the junior high school.

Madon, Constant A., "The Middle School: Its Philosophy and Purpose," *The Clearing House,* XL, No. 6 (1966), 329-330. States reasons why the middle school is replacing the junior high school.

Maynard, Glenn, "The Junior High School—Education's Step-Child," *Education in Ohio,* January 17, 1965. As the title suggests, the junior high school often is made up of hand-me-down curricula, teachers, and buildings. A new school with new purposes and fresh approaches is indicated.

McCarthy, Robert J., "A Nongraded Middle School," *National Elementary Principal,* XLVII, No. 3 (1968), 15-21. An accounting of what prompted one school system, Liverpool, New York, to reorganize the traditional K-12 program into an elementary, middle school (6-8), and high school. Particular emphasis is placed on the nongraded concept.

————, *How to Organize and Operate an Ungraded Middle School.* Engle-wood Cliffs, N. J.: Prentice-Hall, 1967. Gives a description of the author's experiences in setting up a nongraded middle school. The book contains helpful hints and tells of the problems of the first year. Interdisciplinary teaming and independent study are given a good deal of consideration.

Mellinger, Morris and John A. Rackauskas, *Quest for Identity.* Chicago: Chicago State College, 1970. Reports findings of a survey of middle schools including numbers by geographic region, enrollment size, counseling service, and instructional program. There are 1,689 middle schools, with the greatest number in the Midwest.

Moss, Theodore C., *Middle School.* Boston: Houghton Mifflin, 1969. Gives careful attention to the way programs can be geared to middle school youngsters. Contains a good section describing characteristics of children ages 10-14. Attention is given to administrative and organizational problems and facilities.

Murphy, Judith, *Middle Schools.* New York: Educational Facilities Labora-tories, 1965. Presents profiles of significant schools. The booklet gives excel-lent background on the middle schools in operation in the United States. Representative programs illustrating new concepts are described.

National Association of Secondary School Principals, *Guidelines for Junior High and Middle School Education.* Washington: NASSP, 1966. A filmstrip and record presentation of guidelines prepared by a committee of the Na-tional Association of Secondary School Principals.

Nickerson, Neal C., *Junior High Schools Are on the Way Out.* Danville, Ill.: Interstate Printers and Publishers, 1966. An 18-page booklet suggesting that the middle school is the coming type of school organization.

Oestreich, Arthur H., "Middle School in Transition," *The Clearing House,* XLIV, No. 2 (1969), 91-95. Expresses concern about inability to identify characteristics peculiar to the middle school. Suggests need for planning the organization for instruction, the utilization of teacher talent, and the content of the subject matter.

Overly, Donald, Jon Kinghorn and Richard L. Preston, *The Middle School: Humanizing Education for Youth.* Worthington, Ohio: Charles A. Jones, 1972. Explains the curricular program of a modern middle school including basic subject matter areas, extracurricular activities, scheduling, and school plant planning. Behavioral objectives, staff organization, evaluation, and humanizing experiences are discussed in detail.

Popper, Samuel H., *The American Middle School.* Waltham, Mass.: Blaisdell, 1967. Traces the historical development of the middle school in America, stressing the need for a school geared both in staff and program to the special needs of pre- and early adolescents. Diagrams and discussion of the middle school of the future are included.

Post, R. L., "Middle School: A Questionable Innovation," *The Clearing House,* XLIII, No. 8 (1968), 484-486. Refutes points made in a previous article extolling the merits of the middle school. Simply realigning grades seems ridiculous since the graded school itself may be on the way out. The author feels the middle school does not merit serious consideration.

Pray, H. Edgar and John A. McNamara, "Transition to Middle School," *The Clearing House,* XLI, No. 7 (1967), 407-409. Describes the vertical, departmental organization and the horizontal, team organization of a Schenectady, New York, middle school (5-8) which was formerly the Van Antwerp Junior High School (6-8). Discusses how the new organization attempts to better meet the needs of the youngsters.

Pumerantz, Philip, "Imperatives in the Junior High and Middle School Dialogue," *The Clearing House,* XLIII, No. 4 (1968), 209-212. Advocates a somewhat ambivalent feeling toward middle schools. Calls for re-examination and redefinition of the middle school and the junior high.

Rollins, S. P. and G. W. Ellis, "Are Middle Schools the Answer?" *Senior Scholastic: Scholastic Teacher,* XCIV, No. 11 (1969), 9-11. Presents pros by Rollins and cons by Ellis in a strong argument over middle schools.

Sanders, Stanley G., "Challenge of the Middle School," *Educational Forum,* XXXII (January, 1968), 191-197. Discusses the pitfalls of the junior high school and cautions that should be employed so that the middle school will not experience the same difficulties.

Thornburg, H., "Learning and Maturation in Middle School Age Youth," *The Clearing House,* XLV, No. 3 (1970), 150-155. Points out six tasks which should be accomplished within the framework of the middle school. Emphasis is on humanizing and using innovations of various kinds.

Turnbaugh, R. C., "Middle School: A Different Name or a New Concept?" *The Clearing House,* XLIII, No. 2 (1968), 86-88. Summarizes that many of the new developments in education in the next decade will be associated with middle schools.

"Twenty-Eight Ways to Build Mistakes Out of Your Middle School," *The American School Board Journal,* LVIII, No. 1 (1970), 17-24. A well-illustrated article by the staff and architects and engineers suggesting undesirable aspects of middle school buildings which should be avoided. It should be helpful to those planning a new school.

Vars, Gordon F., "Junior High or Middle School? Which is Best for the Education of Young Adolescents?" *The High School Journal,* L, No. 3 (1966), 109-113. Pros and cons of both types of organizations resulting in a view that either can be successful in meeting the needs of this age learner.

Wattenberg, W. W., "Middle School as one Psychologist Sees It," *Education Digest,* XXXV, No. 7 (1970), 26-29. Discusses phenomena such as self-destructiveness, the generation gap, and delinquency. The article then discusses ways the middle school can help society deal effectively with these phenomena.

Williams, Emmett L., "The Middle-School Movement," *Today's Education,* LVII, No. 9 (1968), 41-42. Discusses ways of serving needs of children 10 through 13 by combining the best features of self-contained programs and of departmentalization. The home-base teacher is a significant element as are student self-direction and responsibility for learning. Team teaching and nongrading are common innovations in middle schools.

_____, "What About the Junior High and Middle School?" *The Bulletin of the National Association of Secondary School Principals,* May, 1968. Ex-

plains what a middle school is, why it is, and how widespread the movement is. Characteristics, variations in emphasis, and contemporary innovative features are discussed.

Wilson, M. T., "What is a Middle School?" *The Clearing House*, XLIV, No. 1
(1969), 9-11. Discusses the program of the Conwell Middle Magnet School
in Philadelphia. Several effective ways are pointed out in which individualization can be effected.

Wilson, Mildred T. and Samuel H. Popper, "What About The Middle School?"
Today's Education, LVIII, No. 2 (1969), 52-54. Expresses the view that
fifth grade is not too early to tailor programs for each child and to allow for
early adolescents to discover for themselves. Dr. Popper calls the middle
school an institutional corruption because significant adolescent change
begins at about the seventh grade level.

Preschool Education

14

Definition

Preschool education is planned learning experience for children from birth to entrance into the first grade. Frequently the term is applied to organized school programs for children between the ages of three and six. Built on the foundations of Jean Jacques Rousseau, Johann Pestalozzi, and Friedrich Froebel, the theoretical concepts of early childhood education were advanced in this country by G. Stanley Hall, William James, and Arnold Gesell. More recently, Jean Piaget's work on intellectual development has stimulated interest in the education of the very young.

Current interest in preschool education grows out of the belief that young children profit from exposure to stimuli and participation in a variety of activities, structured and unstructured. Most people are of the opinion that the benefits of the activities can be increased through planning, utilization of many materials, professional guidance, and opportunity to interact with other children. In the proper setting the young child can greatly improve his self-concept and his ability to relate with satisfaction to others. Sensitivity, observation, and perception are improved, and meaningful concepts are built.

The experiences of early childhood are very important in developing confidence, love, aspiration, and other positive values and attitudes. The early years are more significant than the later ones in building security, curiosity, and creativity. Interaction with other children develops social skills that enable the child to enter smoothly into the primary school. Preschool education provides learning experiences—cognitive, affective and psycho-motor—that will benefit the child in his subsequent school work and enhance his self-realization.

For many years, education of the very young has received at least passing attention here and abroad. The kindergarten for five-year-olds has grown steadily, and many school systems have established nursery schools. During World War II public and private agencies provided day-care centers for children whose mothers went to work to support the family while the father was in military service. After a brief decline following the war, the number of mothers employed outside the home again increased. As public sensitivity to the needs of neglected children grew, sociologists and psychologists expanded their studies of children, the family, and the community. The recent revival of interest in the Montessori method reflects the search for better solutions to the learning problems of millions of children. Mounting costs of welfare and aid to dependent children aroused the interest and concern of taxpayers and government officials.

As attention focused upon the deficiencies of economically and socially disadvantaged children, psychological researchers warned of the danger of permanent retardation as the price to be paid for neglecting preschoolers from disadvantaged environments. Dramatic increases in I.Q. scores were reported for slum-area children whose experiences were enriched. The launching of the Office of Economic Opportunity's Head Start program in 1965 spurred an almost frantic increase in research and program development.

In many intervention programs, a new emphasis on preparation for academic achievement appeared. In contrast to the free, play-oriented programs of conventional kindergartens and nursery schools, the new approach stresses a highly structured plan to remedy the deficiencies that have been identified. It attempts to discover what areas of learning a child lacks and to provide for them. As a result of this emphasis, the new programs are often looked upon as remedial rather than developmental.

Classes for preschoolers are sponsored by a great variety of agencies, ranging from the federal government to women's clubs. Some programs are well financed, many are conducted on a volunteer basis. Classes, tutoring, and counseling for parents pursue a broad range of objectives and include such functions as health services and instruction for reading and number readiness. Most of the programs are directed toward manipulating the environment of children of the poor and of minority groups in such a way that the pupils will be able to compete more effectively with other children in the academic pursuits of the primary school. Broad and varied experiences are provided to improve perception of the environment, enhance self-concept, and develop new knowledge and skills. All of these, it is hoped, will contribute significantly to intellectual, social, emotional, and physical growth in subsequent years.

Significant Components   *Which ones are essential?*

1. Preschool education should be an integral part of the total school program.
2. The purposes of the program must be understood by all those directly involved and by the general public.
3. Good, attractive physical facilities and stimulating learning materials are especially important for very young children.
4. Classes should be kept small.
5. Research findings relating to children, particularly disadvantaged children, should be the basis for establishing objectives and techniques.
6. When the program is focused on the disadvantaged, methods and materials must be appropriate for them.
7. Pupils and parents should be prepared for the preschool experience because parental cooperation and participation are important to the success of the program.
8. Frequent conferences and meetings with parents should be arranged.
9. Special effort must be made to prevent preschool experiences from becoming purely a program for developing reading readiness or preparing for other academic pursuits.
10. Sensitive teachers with warmth, special insights, and positive attitudes are particularly important for dealing with the very young.
11. Preschool programs should begin as early as possible.
12. Safety, joy, freedom, and opportunity for making choices and decisions should characterize the program.
13. Emotional stress that might occur when wide differences occur between the home and school environment should be anticipated and relieved.

14. Preschoolers should be given the opportunity to work with instructors, with other children, and by themselves.
15. Intervention programs for disadvantaged children, in particular, should provide help for parents as well as children.
16. Facilities and personnel must be available for diagnosing a great variety of problems.
17. The relationship between school and home experiences must be clear so that parents and teachers can capitalize on the diversity of these experiences.
18. The program must offer a wide variety of opportunities for exploring, manipulating, interacting, and inquiring.
19. An accepting emotional climate that is conducive to security and discovery should be established.
20. A careful balance should be maintained between freedom and responsibility.
21. More research is needed in the areas of program development and evaluation of results.

Proposed Advantages   *With which ones do you agree?*

1. Early experiences are vital for developing a positive self-concept, wholesome attitudes, and healthy relationships with others.
2. Improving the early environment can increase intelligence substantially.
3. By helping the child during his most formative years, preschool education improves his general educability and prepares him for success in academic areas.
4. During the formative years most progress can be made in all aspects of development—physical, intellectual, social, and emotional.
5. Cultural and intellectual deprivation can be overcome, thus preventing permanent retardation.
6. Many diseases, physical handicaps, neurological disorders, and nutritional deficiences can be discovered early.
7. By providing a background of common experience, preschool education helps to close the gap between disadvantaged and advantaged children.
8. Deviant behavior resulting from poor home environment can be corrected or alleviated.
9. Early education provides a setting for developing tolerance for frustration and for learning to deal with hostility and aggression.

10. Preschool education is a great aid in developing language and communication skills and in furthering reading and number readiness.

11. A foundation is laid for enjoying the subsequent years of school by having the child become accustomed to going to school, free of academic pressures.

12. The child's experiences can be manipulated to sharpen his observation, improve his perception, and extend his ability to internalize his actions.

13. Association with other children teaches the preschooler to be sensitive to the desires of others and respect their rights.

14. Preschool experiences increase attentiveness and ability to listen to and follow directions.

15. Children develop autonomy and learn to care for themselves and their materials.

16. Preschool education eliminates prejudice and fosters accepting behavior.

17. The program provides a happy place for the child, particularly one from an inadequate home, to live with other children and with understanding and helpful teachers.

Criticisms and Difficulties to Be Anticipated   *Do you agree?*

1. Teachers will encounter many disappointments and frustrations.

2. Mothers of young children may be very difficult to work with because of their close attachment to the children, rivalry with the teacher, guilt feelings, and other factors.

3. Children will develop qualities and habits that the parents won't like.

4. The mother may feel that she and child are growing apart, or that she is being rejected.

5. Very young children need the warmth of the home and the tender love of their mothers.

6. Most preschool programs are baby-sitting operations and pervert the function of the schools.

7. Having the schools take care of infants will make parents even more neglectful than they are.

8. The idea of taking care of people from the cradle to the grave is a communistic concept.

9. Having children in school too young causes competition, rivalry, and conflict among them that would otherwise not develop.

10. Qualified teachers and tested programs are not available.
11. Most Head Start teachers do not understand the basic principles of child psychology.
12. Most existing programs are very, very weak.
13. We really do not know how to help very young, disadvantaged children.
14. Having children in school for years before they settle down to work spoils them for real learning.
15. The initial better adjustment which those who attended preschool later exhibit in regular school classes soon fades.
16. Manipulated experiences of school will make children unhappy with their families and homes.

Summary Assessment

A hundred years after Mrs. Carl Schurz opened her home in Watertown, Wisconsin, to the first preschool class of 1856, half the children in America were still without kindergartens. It looks as if preschool education, in the years ahead, will be accepted more readily than kindergartens were. The acute problems of nonmotivated youth in urban communities have caused the federal government to take decisive action. The planning, experimentation, and extension of programs during the past decade have been dramatic.

Many educators have long realized that the formative years of childhood constitute the most vital period of a person's life for shaping attitudes toward himself and others and for planting the seeds of curiosity, initiative, and desire to succeed. Yet, public junior colleges, technical institutes, colleges, and graduate schools have continued to receive the bulk of attention of educational planners. Ever-increasing enrollments at the elementary, secondary, and college levels have exhausted available funds.

The first big thrust for extending education into the earlier years came from the Office of Economic Opportunity and the U. S. Office of Education. Hand in hand with formal classes for children are nonclassroom experiences, visits to the home, and programs to help parents help their children extend interests and skills. For example, "Sesame Street," a television program designed to develop skills with numbers and letters, has reached millions of children between three and five.

During the next few years expansion of preschool programs may be retarded because of general economic uncertainty, increased competition for the tax dollar, reluctance of citizens and legislative bodies to approve additional revenue, and the plight of private and parochial schools. However, interest in education for the very young will continue.

In the meantime more study needs to be given to determine the real needs of young children—emotional, social, intellectual, and physical. The process of growth and development in intelligence and behavior needs to be reviewed. The desirability of having men teachers work with preschoolers is currently being considered. Strategies for generating greater parent involvement and participation need to be developed. The importance of prenatal care for mothers and work with newborn infants is being assessed. In some places educators are going into homes to teach parents how to stimulate and interact with infants. Many deficiencies are being discovered and corrected long before the child would normally come to school. However, those responsible for guiding preschool education must be careful that in their enthusiasm they do not separate the child emotionally from the parent, nor the parent from the child. The self-concept of the child is important, but so is the self-concept of the parent.

A number of questions remain to be answered. What are the most important and attainable objectives? What is the relative significance of personal, social, and academic competencies? How early should instruction begin? What kind of instruction is most beneficial? Who should do the teaching? How much effort should be devoted to helping parents help their children? How productive are preschool programs in the long run? As activities become more structured, will there be a tendency to put too much pressure on the very young? Is there a limit to the extent to which schools should take over traditional responsibilities of the home? As research continues in this important field, it is hoped that answers to some or all of these questions will be found.

A difference of viewpoint has developed between those who believe in the traditional nursery school approach of warmth, free play, and spontaneous activity and those who advocate structured programs designed to overcome specific deficiencies. The former approach stresses social adjustment, the latter emphasizes academic educability. A common ground must be worked out. Ability to get along with others, emotional stability, and healthy physical development must not be lost sight of in a scramble to increase intellectual capacity to cope with cognitive learning.

A Few Leaders in the Movement

Carl Bereiter
University of Toronto
Benjamin S. Bloom
Univ. of Chicago
Bettye M. Caldwell
Univ. of Arkansas
Martin Deutsch
Massachusetts Institute of
Technology
Siegfried Engelmann
Univ. of Illinois
J. McVicker Hunt
Univ. of Illinois, Champaign
James Hymes, Jr.
Carmel Valley, Calif.
Barbel Inhelder
Univ. of Geneva
Lilian G. Katz
Univ. of Illinois

Omar K. Moore
Univ. of Pittsburgh
Maya Pines
Washington, D. C.
Katherine Read
Oregon State Univ.
David Rosenbloom
Twentieth Century Fund
Milton J. E. Senn
Yale Univ.
June Grant Shane
Indiana Univ.
Evelyn Weber
Wheelock College
David Weikart
High/Scope Educational
Research Foundation
Emmy Widmer
Florida Atlantic Univ.

A Few Places Where the Innovation Is Used

Athens, Ga.
Berkeley, Calif.
Biloxi, Miss.
Central Midwest Regional
Educational Laboratory
Cincinnati, Ohio
George Peabody College

Greenwich, Conn.
Jackson, Miss.
Lincoln, Nebr.
Newark, N. J.
Sacramento, Calif.
Shawnee, Okla.
Univ. of Chicago

Univ. of Illinois
Univ. of North Carolina
Urbana, Ill.
Waterloo, Iowa
Winnetka, Ill.
Yale Univ.
Ypsilanti, Mich.

Annotated References

Anderson, Robert H., "Schools for Young Children: Organizational and Administrative Considerations," *Phi Delta Kappan,* L, No. 7 (1969), 381-385. Discusses the means by which the most effective preschool education can take place and the roles that individuals as well as institutions play in the process. Lack of sympathy of administrators for the importance of nursery school and kindergarten is a definite roadblock.

Axline, Virginia. *Dibs, in Search of Self.* New York: Ballantine Books, 1964. Shows the development of an extremely withdrawn, unresponsive child through play therapy. The deep effect of family and school relations on Dibs was resolved through therapy which enabled him to know and accept himself and to acquire satisfying relationships through social interaction.

Bereiter, Carl, "Are Preschool Programs Built the Wrong Way?" *Nation's Schools,* LXXVII, No. 6 (1966), 55-56, 92. Insists that Head Start is a program of child welfare rather than child education. Most of the glib objectives are devoid of educational meaning. Rationalizing failure to achieve and jurisdictional squabbles have impeded progress.

―――, "Instructional Planning in Early Compensatory Education," *Phi Delta Kappan,* XLVIII, No. 7 (1967), 355-356. Stresses the importance of being sure that preschool achievement is real. Necessary learnings should be identified, and experiences should be provided to develop skills and habits to achieve these learnings.

Berson, Minnie, "The All-Day Kindergarten," *Today's Education,* LVII, No. 8 (1968), 27-29. Suggests that all-day kindergarten is beneficial for some children, but detrimental to others. Comprehensive, individualized programs, flexible timetables, and contact with parents are important considerations.

Biemiller, Andrew J., ed., *Problems in the Teaching of Young Children.* Toronto, Canada: The Ontario Institute for Studies in Education, 1968. Includes seven papers presenting different approaches to early childhood education. Emphasis is on direct teaching methods with four of the papers dealing specifically with methods for teaching disadvantaged children. The final chapter summarizes the conference and considers broader problems and issues.

Braun, Samuel J. and Esther P. Edwards, *History and Theory of Early Childhood Education.* Worthington, Ohio: Charles A. Jones, 1972. Traces the development of early childhood education in Europe and America. Treated in depth are the application of competence theory and crisis intervention, stimulation, approaches to learning, and the future role of early childhood education.

Bromwich, Rose M., "Early Education: Current Concepts and Directions," *Elementary English,* XLVI, No. 6 (1969), 741-747. Discusses the factors which have contributed to the increasing interest in early development. Six theoretical propositions relating to the development of thought and language are stated. The author advocates nongraded classrooms which provide for much pupil interaction.

Christianson, Helen, Mary Rogers, and Blanche Ludleem, *The Nursery School —Adventure in Living and Learning.* Boston: Houghton Mifflin, 1961. Describes in detail the purposes, organization, and activities of the nursery school as a vital part of the lives of preschool children.

Densham, William E., "The Children Who Had to be Found," *American Education,* VII, No. 2 (1971), 11-14. Describes a program that was set up to help handicapped preschool children prepare for school. Need for expansion in this area is stressed.

Deutsch, Martin, "Happenings on the Way Back to the Forum: Social Science, IQ, and Race Differences Revisited," *Harvard Educational Review,* XXXIX, No. 3 (1969), 523-557. Responds to commentary and rebuttal of a previous article by Arthur Jensen dealing with increases in I.Q. and scholastic achievement. The article lists 87 references relating to the controversy.

Di Lorenzo, Louis T., "Which Way for Pre-K: Wishes or Reality," *American Education,* VI, No. 1 (1970), 28-32. This article points out how many times the wishes for success in various areas of the preschool program conflict with results of the follow-up studies. It goes on to discuss some of the changes now being made in preschool programs.

Ebel, Robert L., ed., *Encyclopedia of Educational Research,* 4th ed. London: Macmillan, 1969. Gives results of educational research by leaders in the specific educational field. Also provides a history and philosophy background to each specific field.

Elkind, David, "The Case for Academic Preschool: Fact or Fiction," *Young Children,* XXV, No. 3 (1970), 132-139. Argues against the notion that preschools should be more academically oriented, especially for the middle-class child. Preschool programs do have room for improvement, but making them more academically oriented could prove detrimental to mental growth.

Erikson, Erik H., *Childhood and Society,* 2nd ed. New York: W. W. Norton, 1963. Proposes to be a "psychoanalytic book on the relation of the ego to society." The relationships of the mature and the infantile are explored through personal clinical experiences. Childhood in two Indian tribes, the growth of the ego, and the evolution of identity are given detailed consideration.

Ernst, L., "New Minds for Old—Can Chemistry Stimulate Learning?" *Nation's Schools,* LXXXV, No. 2 (1970), 56-57. Discusses brain reactions of animals to drug injections. Positive results are reported, and hope for speeding up learning, improving retention, and inflating I.Q.'s is expressed.

Fisher, Robert, "Project Slow-Down: The Middle Class Answer to Project Head Start," *School and Society,* XCVIII, No. 2327 (1970), 256-257. Advocates forgetting Head Start, which teaches poor children that their way of life is wrong, and setting up a "Slow Down" program for middle-class children to teach them that middle-class values are wrong.

Foster, J. C. and Neith E. Headley, *Education in the Kindergarten.* New York: American Book, 1959. Provides essential background information on the kindergarten and how the contemporary concept of the kindergarten has evolved to its present form. Also, includes research on the importance of kindergarten in today's society.

Frymier, Jack R., "Teaching the Young to Love," *The National Elementary Principal,* XLI, No. 2 (1969), 19-21. Reviews 10 levels of rejective and accepting behavior. Man is the end of education. The development of love is determined by the interaction between child and teacher and the kind of person the teacher is.

Gilstrap, Robert, Eleanor L. Douthat, and Annette Guenther, "Some Questions and Answers," *Today's Education,* LIV, No. 4 (1970), 39-41. Raises questions about the difference between kindergarten and nursery school, who should be in the programs, what should be taught, how should teachers be prepared, what materials and equipment should be used, what activities are appropriate, and what results should be expected. Answers are supplied for these and other questions.

Harms, Thelma, "Evaluating Settings for Learning," *Young Children,* XXV, No. 5 (1970), 304-306. Stresses the importance that environment plays in the learning process of young children. Some suggestions are given for creating an effective setting for learning.

Hartman, Allan S., "How to Improve Preschool Programs," *Nation's Schools,* LXXVII, No. 6 (1966), 57-58. Suggests the possibility that good conventional preschool programs may not be good programs for disadvantaged children.

Contrasts between experimental programs for disadvantaged and child development programs are drawn.

Headley, Neith, *The Kindergarten: Its Place in the Program of Education.* New York: The Center for Applied Research in Education, Inc., 1965. Discusses the place of the kindergarten within the total educational program. Purposes, characteristics of a good kindergarten, program, and evaluating are described. An open climate is emphasized throughout.

Heffernan, Helen, "Influence on the Elementary School," *Today's Education,* LIV, No. 4 (1970), 41-42. Indicates that the kindergarten has finally been accepted as an integral part of the educational program. Seven objectives of kindergarten are outlined, including social adjustment, physical and mental health, expansion of knowledge and concepts, creativity, and improvement in communication skills.

Hess, Robert D., and Roberta Meyer Bear, eds., *Early Childhood.* Chicago: Aldine Publishing Company, 1968. Includes 16 papers and a summary reporting the Social Science Research Council Conference on Preschool Education. The report covers theory, administration, program, methodology, and evaluation. The writers try to point direction for early childhood education.

Hetzel, Donna C., "An Overview of British Infant Schools," *Young Children,* XXV, No. 6 (1970), 336-339. Describes some of the new methods employed in the British Infant Schools such as vertical grouping, gradual reception, open-school planning, and free activity programs.

Hickman, L. C., "'Sesame Street' Asks: Can Television Really Teach?" *Nation's Schools,* LXXXV, No. 2 (1970), 58-59. Describes the impact of educational television on the early development of children, particularly the disadvantaged. "Sesame Street" is an example of programs that combine instruction and entertainment to further intelligence of preschoolers.

Hymes, James L., "Why Programs for Young Children?" *Today's Education,* LIV, No. 4 (1970), 34-36. Raises questions about what preschool programs should be expected to do. Answers often come and are accepted too quickly. The wholeness of the human being must be recognized, and the program must seek to promote the child's maximum total development. Schools must serve both society and the individual.

"If Kids Act Smarter 'Sesame St.' May be the Reason," *Nation's Schools,* LXXXVII, No. 3 (1971), 34-35. Reports on the valuable contributions that the television program "Sesame Street" has made on first-grade children. In addition to teaching the children, it gives them a better attitude toward school and prods the teachers to be more creative.

Jensen, Arthur R., "How Much Can We Boost I.Q. and Scholastic Achievement," *Harvard Educational Review,* XXXIX, No. 2 (1969), 1-123. States that I.Q. is more strongly influenced by genetic than by environmental factors. The chief environmental influences are nourishment of mother and child during the prenatal period and first year of life. The author says that many compensatory preschool programs are misdirected because they fail to recognize this fact.

————, "Reducing the Heredity-Environment Certainty," *Harvard Educational Review,* XXXIX, No. 3 (1969), 449-483. A reply to seven responses to a previous article by the author which generated considerable controversy relative to the role of heredity and environment in the development of intelligence. The points of agreement and disagreement are carefully explained. Certain misunderstandings are discussed.

Katz, Lilian G., "Children and Teachers in Two Types of Head Start Classes," *Young Children,* XXIV, No. 6 (1969), 342-349. Reports the results of a study of two methods of conducting preschool classes. The traditional method involving teacher warmth and spontaneous activity resulted in significant gain in pupil satisfaction. Other outcomes were inconclusive.

Knoll, Erwin, "Will Public Schools Control Head Start?" *Nation's Schools,* LXXVII, No. 6 (1966), 48, 90. Reports that both accomplishments and problems have exceeded expectations. Shortage of funds and consequent difficulty of establishing Head Start on a year-round basis are chief difficulties.

Kodman, Frank, Jr., "Effects of Preschool Enrichment on Intelligence Performance of Appalachian Children," *Exceptional Children,* XXXVI, No. 7 (1970), 503-507. Reports findings of a research study involving an enriched group and a control group of 20 preschool children each. A significant difference was found between the pre- and postintervention I.Q. scores of the enriched group at the end of the first, second, and third year.

Larrabee, Margery M., "Involving Parents in Their Children's Day-Care Experiences," *Children,* XVI, No. 4 (1969), 149-154. Describes problems existing between the home and day-care center that affect the emotional status of the child and the mother. Clarifying roles of teachers, social workers, and parents and involvement of parents in the day-care center are beneficial.

Lavatelli, Celia Stendler, "Contrasting Views of Early Childhood Education," *Childhood Education,* XLVI, No. 5 (1970), 239-246. Discusses the controversy between the free play theory and the academically structured idea in today's preschool programs. The British Infant Schools use play to stimulate cognitive growth.

————, "Early Education for the Thinking Child—A Piaget Program in Action," *Grade Teacher,* LXXXV, No. 2 (1967), 123-127. Outlines a program by Piaget in which the accent is on logical thought process instead of the usual three-R's or the perceptual approach. Emphasizes getting the child to think and draw conclusions from his sense impressions. Pupils are encouraged to invent their own games.

Lay, Margaret, "The Scene Then and Now," *Today's Education,* LIV, No. 4 (1970), 37-38. Discusses the great change that has come over preschool education in the past decade. Emphasis on compensating for deficiencies in the home, structured programs, and stress on diversity have become "traditional" within just a few years.

Lesser, Gerald S., "Learning, Teaching, and Television Production for Children: The Experience of 'Sesame Street,'" *Harvard Educational Review,* XLII, No. 2 (1972), 232-271. Explains the research, cooperative planning between educators and producers, and strategies that are used in developing television programs for children. Specific goals and principles of children's learning join with teaching and production techniques to capture and direct attention and to effect learning.

Miller, Wilma H., "When Mothers Teach Their Children," *The Elementary School Journal*, LXX, No. 1 (1969), 38-42. Analyzes teaching style of mothers from three socioeconomic levels. Active and passive styles are correlated with reading readiness of children. Social level of mothers is not significantly related to their teaching styles.

Moscrip, Ruth, "Classroom Tips from Trips," *Today's Education*, LVIII, No. 6 (1969), 20-24. Reports the benefits that a kindergarten teacher derived from traveling abroad. New toys and games and a wealth of new material were found to be available in the school and community. Family-life education was introduced through a new approach to mathematics.

Neill, A. S., *Summerhill—A Radical Approach to Child-Rearing*. New York: Hart, 1960. Shows a mode of education based on the concept of the goodness of the child. Summerhill proved that children do learn when they are ready, at their own pace, and in areas of most interest to them.

The Nursery School—A Human Relations Laboratory. New York: Macmillan, 1964. A broadened view of the nursery school and how it has evolved. This book provides an outline to many aspects of the nursery school child, readiness, physical development, and the goals of the nursery school.

Read, Katherine H., *The Nursery School*. Philadelphia and London: Saunders, 1966. Relates experiences of college students in the nursery school laboratory. Building security, curbing hostility, and promoting social relationships through dramatic play, creative expression, and intellectual development are the core of the nursery school program.

———, *The Nursery School*. Philadelphia: Saunders, 1971. Stresses the importance of early childhood education and explains recent developments in preschool programs. Different types of programs are explained and compared in regard to their philosophies, organization, activities, and results.

Rice, Arthur H., "Let's Not Force Preschool Programs on Everybody," *Nation's Schools*, LXXVIII, No. 3 (1966), 10, 12. Discusses who can benefit from preschool programs and emphasizes the need for the programs to point toward the disadvantaged.

Ross, Dorthea and Sheila Ross, "Leniency toward Cheating in Preschool Children," *Journal of Educational Psychology*, LX, No. 6 (1969), 483-487. Reports an experiment employing incomplete picture stories with two groups of preschool children, rule breakers and conformers. Rule breakers became more lenient toward misbehavior and conformers more severe.

Schaefer, Earl S., "A Home Tutoring Program," *Children*, XVI, No. 2 (1969), 59-61. Reports positive results of a tutoring program for children of 36 months of age. Improvement in adjustment, intelligence test scores, and task-oriented behavior is indicated. Uninvolvement, neglect, and maladjustment correlate.

Scott, Byron, "Turning on Tots With Educational T.V.," *Today's Health*, XXXVI, No. 11 (1969), 28-32. Discusses reactions of children to "Sesame Street." Attention span, repetition, growth of intelligence, and the moral of a story is touched upon.

Senn, Milton J. E., "Early Childhood Education—For What Goals?" *Children*, XVI, No. 1 (1969), 8-13. Recognizes dangers in highly structured programs that are directed primarily toward improving I.Q. scores. Initiative, creativity, happiness, positive feelings, and sentiment are essential for developing the whole man. Intellect and intelligence are not synonymous.

Shane, Harold G., "The Renaissance of Early Childhood Education," *Phi Delta Kappan*, L, No. 7 (1969), 369, 412-413. Traces the history of preschool education and examines some of the factors that are again making it popular. Environmental mediation, creating intelligence, "psychoneurobiochem-education," experiments in early learning, improved understanding of subcultures and group membership, and other topics are discussed briefly.

Shuster, Albert H. and Milton E. Ploghoft, *The Emerging Elementary Curriculum*, pp. 169-199. Columbus, Ohio: Merrill, 1970. Traces the development of preschool education indicating that only about 50 per cent of children attend kindergarten. Values of early education are reviewed. Investigations raise questions concerning the permanence of improvement in such programs as Head Start.

Smith, Marshall S. and Joan S. Bissell, "Report Analysis: Impact of Head Start," *Harvard Educational Review*, XL, No. 1 (1970), 51-103. Discusses at great length the effectiveness of various Head Start programs. The article goes into a history of the program and points to areas where it has been successful.

Spitze, Glennys S., "Fantasizing and Poetry Construction in Preschoolers," *Childhood Education*, XLVI, No. 5 (1970), 283-286. Reports the results of a study which demonstrated the unique creative ability of preschool children by having them make up stories and poems. It stresses the idea that encouraging creativity is more important than the subjects that are taught.

Spodek, Bernard, "Early Learning for What?" *Phi Delta Kappan*, L, No. 7 (1969), 394-396. Examines various traditional instructional models and goals for early learning and suggests improvements in the form of three models: The School as an Accumulator, An Agency for Vocational Preparation, a Preparer for College Entrance.

Stabenau, Joan C., Myra Sklarew and Sophie Shakow, "Infant Education: A Community Project," *Young Children*, XXIV, No. 6 (1969), 358-363. Describes experiences of home study volunteers with children from the age of one to three. Verbal and non-verbal language are emphasized through the use of books and imaginative play. Many positive results are reported.

Stearns, Marion Sherman, "Early Education: Still in its Infancy," *American Education*, VI, No. 7 (1970), 3-5. An account of the successes of intervention programs and questions about objectives and techniques that need research. Numerous agencies sponsoring early childhood education are mentioned.

Stine, Oscar C., et al, "Selected Neurologic and Behavioral Findings of Children Entering an Early School Admissions Project from Culturally Deprived Neighborhoods," *The Journal of School Health*, XXXIX, No. 7 (1969), 470-477. Describes major needs identified in culturally deprived children entering an Early School Admissions Program. Efforts to help disadvantaged children to learn through a multidiscipline evaluative approach are productive.

Strickland, Stephen P., "Can Slum Children Learn?" *American Education*, VII, No. 6 (1971), 3-7. Reports the impressive results of a program to educate preschool children from slum areas. Through the efforts of this program many potentially mentally retarded children are able to function normally.

Taylor, Katarine Whitside, *Parents and Children Learn Together.* New York: Teachers College Press, 1967. Discusses parent cooperative nursery schools. The volume proposes to help parents better understand their children and to assist teachers in working with parents. Emphasis is on parent as well as child development.

Taylor, Katherine, "Who Benefits from Nursery School?" *The PTA Magazine,* LXII, No. 8 (1968), 24-26. Points out benefits for children of widely diversified needs from a diversified preschool program. Parents are relieved from being with their children constantly, and volunteer workers benefit significantly.

Thomson, Peggy, "Preschoolers Pose Some Tough Questions," *American Education,* VI, No. 8 (1970), 16-19. Stresses the importance of helping preschoolers develop a healthy attitude towards sex. It is important to do this at this stage because this is when children begin to develop their ideas of sexuality.

Todd, Vivian and Helen Heffernan, *The Years Before School.* New York: Macmillan, 1964. Encompasses the social, developmental and intellectual stages of the preschool child. Includes a background history of preschool education and all aspects involved in the nursery school.

Weber, Evelyn, *Early Childhood Education: Perspectives on Change.* Worthington, Ohio: Charles A. Jones, 1970. Presents innovative practices in the education of children from age two through the primary years. Philosophical, psychological, and sociological bases are related to new directions. Numerous successful programs throughout the country are described.

Weber, Lin, "Learning Readiness for Migrant Children," *Grade Teacher,* LXXXVIII, No. 4 (1970), 36-39. Describes a new program designed to help migrant children get ready for first-grade reading. It stresses the development of social awareness as well as language skills.

Widmer, Emmy Louise, *The Critical Years: Early Childhood Education at the Crossroads.* Scranton, Pa.: International, 1970. Warns against dangers of telescoping the years of childhood in a rush toward adulthood. Characteristics and needs of the child, objectives, and program are presented. The kindergarten is given special attention.

Wolff, Max and Annie Stein, "Head Start Six Months Later," *Phi Delta Kappan,* XLVIII, No. 7 (1967), 349-350. Reports test results and reactions of parents and teachers relative to the values of Head Start. Initial adjustment to school is improved, but other children catch up. The importance of the Head Start teacher is stressed.

Audiovisual and Other Resources

Frustrating Fours and Fascinating Fives (16mm film, 22 min., color $275, rental $15, b&w $160, rental $12). Shows what may be expected of the child in a modern nursery school. McGraw-Hill Films, 330 W. 42nd St., New York, N. Y. 10036.

The Time of Their Lives (16mm film, b&w, 29 min., $35). One morning in the lives of 24 kindergarten children. Narrated by Alexander Scourby. NEA, 1201 16th St., N. W., Washington, D. C. 20036.

Flexible Scheduling

15

Definition

Flexible scheduling is a procedure for organizing the school day to provide varied lengths of time for different classes and other activities. The term is most commonly applied to schedules in the secondary school. Units of time, usually of 15, 20, 25, or 30 minutes and referred to as *modules,* are used in various multiples. A school employing a 15-minute module may put two together to constitute a 30-minute period, three to make a 45-minute period, five to build a class period of 75 minutes, or any other combination involving multiples of 15.

Whereas traditional high school schedules employed cycles of one day, repeating the same timetable each day, the typical flexible schedule is constructed to repeat itself each wᵣ ᵏk. Some schools have considered a longer cycle. A given class may meet for two long periods and two shorter periods during the week and omit a class session on one of the days or utilize any combination of modules to make up the week's total time allotted for a particular subject.

Flexible scheduling is frequently used with team teaching, in which case the responsibilities of the teachers vary from day to day. Provision is usually made for large-group presentations, small discussion or inquiry sessions, and individual work. The terms *flexible, modular,* and *variable* are usually used inter-changeably.

Flexible scheduling should not be looked upon merely as a rearrangement in the time schedule allowing longer periods for one subject than for another, or for more time during the week to be devoted to one course than to another. Basic to it is the effort to improve learning through increased individualiza-tion, greater recognition of individual differences, more effective teaching methods, and more adequate provision for developing the student's decision-making and responsibility for organizing his own time and energy. In practice, high school students are commonly assigned to independent study for as much as 40 per cent of their time.

The amount and arrangement of time is determined by the objectives, activities to be carried out, and facilities available.

20-Minute Module	Mon.	Tues.	Wed.	Thurs.	Fri.
1					
2					
3					
4					
5					
6					
7					
8					
18					

Flexible Modular Schedule: Provision for Variations in Length of Periods from Day to Day in a Five-Day Cycle

Planning together, teachers tell the schedule-maker the number and varying lengths of the periods, the days and time when the periods should come, and the size of the groups. Where team teaching is operating, all members of the team work together in making these decisions.

The size of groups is varied to serve specific purposes and functions. Large groups and longer periods are commonly scheduled for showing films, presentations with other visual aids, and testing. Small groups clarify the presentations through discussion, inquiry, and interaction. Independent study allows for enrichment, remediation, and in-depth investigation of individual subjects.

Combining a varying number of modules to build the instructional period recognizes the fact that some subjects are best learned through distributed study, others through effort concentrated over longer periods. If, for example, typing and social problems are both to be allowed 270 minutes in the week's schedule, it could be advantageous to schedule social problems for three 75-minute blocks and one period of 45 minutes. Typing students and their teachers may find that distributing their work over nine 30-minute periods produces better results. These time arrangements are feasible if a 15-minute module is being used. Modules of other lengths allow for different time allotments.

Subjects involving laboratories or field experiences are usually scheduled for long periods. Although the vast majority of modular schedules currently in operation repeat each week, attention is being given to the feasibility of schedules that would build a whole day or even more into the regular schedule to allow for class study trips without interfering with work in other courses.

Under such a schedule, a government class, for example, could have two days scheduled in the spring to observe the state legislature in session. The students would miss no work in their other classes, and the teacher would not be scheduled to meet other classes on these two days. Naturally a sophisticated schedule with provisions of this kind requires much long-term planning and is complicated to construct. Reference to it is made here only to call attention to the possibilities for program revision that lie in flexible scheduling.

Significant Components   *Which ones are essential?*

1. Before adopting flexible scheduling, administrators and teachers must be sure that they are committed to the idea that learning opportunities are more important than ease of schedule development or convenience of operation.

2. The principal should work directly with the teachers in developing a flexible schedule since it, more than a traditional schedule, reflects the philosophy of the school and affects the priorities, procedures, and outcomes of instruction.

3. Roles and responsibilities of the principal, teachers, guidance counselors, department heads, team leaders, and others involved should be carefully delineated.

4. Planning time for individuals and teams should be provided.

5. To achieve maximum success, flexible schedule-making should be a year-round activity.

6. No school can institute a successful flexible schedule without much careful, cooperative preparation. If the principal or faculty is not willing to work hard on it, forget about it.

7. Students must understand the reason for flexible scheduling, what opportunities exist for them, and what they must do to make it effective.

8. Grouping and regrouping should be done on the basis of student needs.

9. Going hand in hand with developing the schedule is study of needs; evaluation of program; and planning improvements in content, strategies, techniques, and facilities.

10. Instructional practices must change with the introduction of the new schedule.

11. Inservice training should be planned to develop new ways of teaching small groups and of motivating and directing independent study.

12. Everybody must realize that it takes months of patient and responsible effort to become accustomed to a new approach as fundamental as flexible scheduling involving large and small groups and independent study.

13. Schools should not revert to a traditional schedule unless they have diagnosed problems carefully and made every effort to make the new schedule work.

14. The schedule should be based on sound principles of learning and curriculum development and built to achieve established objectives. Preconceived notions or personal desires of administrators and teachers should receive secondary consideration.

15. Lack of adequate facilities should be recognized in advance so that raising unachievable expectations can be avoided.

16. Involvement of administrators, teachers, students, and the public contributes significantly to acceptance and to hastening the time when the program will operate smoothly and effectively.

17. Those considering flexible scheduling should also consider team teaching.
18. Space is a vital consideration. More space is not always required, but better utilization of space should be effected.
19. An instructional materials center is very important.
20. At the outset of planning, an inventory of space and other facilities should be prepared.
21. Provision should be made to identify and help students who cannot manage open time, and performance criteria should be developed to guide them.
22. Although the goal is to provide a high degree of freedom in planning and using time, the plan must be carefully organized to assure orderly operation.

Proposed Advantages   *With which ones do you agree?*

1. Flexible scheduling moves a big step forward toward individualizing instruction.
2. The varying time demands of different subjects are taken into account.
3. A fuller utilization of community resources through study trips that require extended periods of time is made possible.
4. New approaches to learning and innovative ways of teaching are encouraged.
5. Flexible scheduling makes possible more effective and efficient utilization of staff.
6. The variety and challenge which flexible schedules offer sustain interest and decrease boredom.
7. Flexible scheduling allows slow as well as gifted students to proceed at their own rates; they are not paced by rigid class grouping.
8. The opportunity for students to work with teachers on a one-to-one basis is made possible.
9. Teachers conceive of their roles as that of helping students learn rather than that of presenting information.
10. The size of the group can be varied according to the purpose of the instruction, the nature of the content, and the methods to be employed.
11. Flexible scheduling encourages students to experiment with different ways of learning and solving problems.
12. Relief is provided from massive movement of students through the corridors every hour on the hour.

13. More intimate contact with students and their performance enables teachers to assign more reliable grades and makes them more secure about grading.
14. Meetings of department heads, councils, and teaching teams can be scheduled within the regular program.
15. Teacher talents are matched with tasks that they can perform well.
16. Students are encouraged to assume responsibility for organizing their time and energy.
17. Teachers organize their material better when they are preparing for large-group presentations.
18. Since courses can be tried out by allotting only limited time to them, expanding course offerings is made easier.
19. A freer, more enjoyable climate is provided for developing flexible social relations and positive emotional qualities.

Criticisms and Difficulties to Be Anticipated   *Do you agree?*

1. Flexible scheduling requires too much time and effort. Computerizing it is very costly.
2. Varying time allocations will create conflict among teachers who will insist upon more time for their particular subjects.
3. Adequate space and other facilities are not available.
4. If the school becomes involved, it cannot back out if flexible scheduling does not work.
5. A school operating under a flexible schedule falls into confusion and disorder since it is difficult to keep track of students.
6. Teachers may be unwilling or find it impossible to change their methods to make the new program work or may become insecure and frustrated.
7. Because of the many variables involved, teachers will not be able to assign fair grades.
8. Unscheduled periods cause much waste of time as well as behavior problems.
9. Unavoidable cancellation of a field trip, for example, might upset the plan for several weeks.
10. The Carnegie Unit, specifying minimum numbers of periods and minutes per week, presents a real problem; and accrediting agencies, state departments, and colleges are uncooperative.
11. A flexible schedule reduces the teacher's time with students.
12. Some teachers in a team do not do their share.

13. Teachers will experience difficulty in handling the inquiry groups effectively.
14. Students and teachers are likely to be confused.
15. Once the flexible schedule is set, it too becomes rigid; and everybody must adhere to the established plan.

Summary Assessment

In the elementary school, the classroom teacher has a great deal of control over his schedule. In team-teaching programs at the elementary level, teams are relatively free to adapt time to program. However, uniformity and rigidity have characterized traditional schedules in the high school. Each subject is commonly studied for the same length of time each day and for the same number of days and weeks. With few exceptions, the schedule for each day is like that for the other days. Many believe that the practice of instructing high school students as groups is one of the chief roadblocks to individualization. Slowly, but forcefully, the six- or eight-period day is being challenged in urban and rural communities alike.

It appears that the number of high schools on some kind of flexible schedule will soon exceed 10 per cent of the total. Some that adopted flexible schedules have reverted to traditional ones because of the confusion that resulted. In some instances, perhaps, this could have been avoided by more thoughtful planning, greater understanding of individualization and commitment to it, and the additional time and work needed to develop conditions essential to success. Differences of opinion continue between those who insist that in converting to a variable schedule one should do the whole job or nothing at all and those who would move gradually, making additional revisions as they are indicated. In many instances lack of readiness on the part of some teachers or absence of needed space and equipment makes the latter approach the more feasible one.

There are those who hold that the schedule reveals whether a high school is learning-centered or teaching-centered—whether it exists for students or for the principal and teachers. Traditionally, teachers and administrators have clung to a rigid timetable because they feared the difficulties involved in developing a program better adapted to effective learning. The daily program has, in the main, been a principal's and teachers' schedule. After the teachers, rooms, and periods were determined, students in sufficient numbers to fill the classes were assigned to them. Then teaching plans and classroom activities were developed to accommodate the conditions and built-in constraints.

Many principals still fear that utter confusion will result from trying to make the schedule the servant of the learner. However, computer programs have been developed to receive all relevant data from principals, counselors, teachers, and students; build the master schedule; and assign students, teachers, places, and times. This advance should relieve some of the principals' anxieties about becoming lost in the details and conflicts involved in making variable schedules. The fact remains, however, that a school can be only as good as its schedule. The philosophical, psychological, and instructional premises that underlie flexible scheduling are sound. Present evidence seems to indicate that the advantages of flexible scheduling more than justify the additional planning and work which is required. Arranging time, facilities, and personnel to make it work presents a formidable challenge to those who search for better ways to help students learn.

A Few Leaders in the Movement

David W. Beggs
  Indiana Univ.
Lloyd K. Bishop
  Univ. of Georgia
B. Frank Brown
  Institute for Development of
  Educational Activities
Donald T. Campbell
  Northwestern Univ.
Robert R. Gard
  Univ. of Missouri, St. Louis
Eugene R. Howard
  Ridgewood (N. J.) High Schools
John Jenkins
  Univ. of Miami
Jon Rye Kinghorn
  Institute for Development of
  Educational Activities

Donald Manlove
  Indiana Univ.
Robert V. Oakford
  Stanford Univ.
James Olivero
  Southwestern Cooperative
  Education Laboratory
Gerald P. Speckard
  Valparaiso Univ.
Theodore R. Storlie
  Institute for Educational Research
J. Lloyd Trump
  Nat'l. Association of
  Secondary School Principals
W. Deane Wiley
  New York Univ.

A Few Places Where the Innovation Is Used

Alliance, Nebr.	Holland, Mich.	Melbourne, Fla.
Cohasset, Mass.	Honolulu, Hawaii	Memphis, Tenn.
Eugene, Oreg.	Lincoln, Calif.	Montvale, N. J.
Flossmoor, Ill.	Livonia, Mich.	Norridge, Ill.
Greenville, Del.	Meeker, Colo.	North Haven, Conn.

Phoenix, Ariz.   Princeton, Ohio   Skokie, Ill.
Portland, Oreg.   Racine, Wis.   Troy, Mich.
Poway, Calif.   Sacramento, Calif.   Wayland, Mass.

Annotated References

Beggs, David W. III and Edward G. Buffie, *Independent Study—Bold New Ventures.* Bloomington: Indiana University Press, 1965. Presents a number of "sacred cows" relating to high school schedules. New needs demand new approaches to utilization of pupil and teacher time. Several models are included.

Braddock, Clayton, "Changing Times Are Changing Schools," *The Education Digest,* XXXIII, No. 6 (1968), 7-10. Stresses the need for abundant resource materials, good guidance programs, and adequate staff. It is costing $50,000 additional at this large high school, but the concensus is that the increased cost is justified by the benefits.

Burril, William, "The Modular System at Work," *The Balance Sheet,* L, No. 5 (1969), 214-215, 237. Describes a flexible modular schedule in operation. Students use the resource center, laboratories, library, and regular classrooms to which they are not scheduled as facilities for independent study or for pursuing interests and individual projects.

Bush, Robert N. and Dwight W. Allen, *A New Design for High School Education—Assuming a Flexible Schedule.* New York: McGraw-Hill, 1964. Suggests a number of possibilities for innovation in high school schedules. New freedoms without controls to implement them cannot be realized. Examples of the new design in program and facilities are included.

———, "Can British Reforms Work Here?" Condensed from *Nations Schools, Education Digest,* XXXVII, No. 1 (1971), 5-8. Points out importance of freer, more informal, and highly individualized learning experiences, with flexible interdisciplinary curriculum. Need for careful planning focused on definite objectives for skills is stressed.

Carmichael, Dennis, and Warren Kallenback, "The California Teacher Development Project: An Individualized Approach to In-Service Education," *Journal of Secondary Education,* XLVI, No. 1 (1971), 16-20. Lists goals and objectives of the CTDP, with emphasis placed on individualized learning programs providing greater flexibility in terms of student interaction, teacher relationships, and curriculum materials and methods.

Doherty, James E., ed., "Are You Afraid of Flexible Scheduling?" *School Management,* XI, No. 5 (1967), 97-102, 104-105, 108. Describes a plan with 25-minute modules in which some departments run with periods of varying lengths and others with 50-minute periods five times per week. Another plan is suggested. It provides for offering each subject area in a separate school building and for having students move to a new school every six weeks.

Dressel, Paul L., and Mary M. Thompson, "A Survey of Independent Study Practices," *Educational Record,* LI, No. 4 (1970), 392-395. Considers goals of independent work programs to develop self-reliance, self-direction, and curiosity. Because of selective limitations and inflexible faculty autonomy, further development of the program is unfortunately not encouraging.

Drumheller, Sidney, "Using Group Work in Developing Functional Concepts in an Individualized Instruction Setting," *Journal of Secondary Education,* XLV, No. 5 (1970), 230-237. Notes importance of motivation, reinforcement, open-ended responses, and self-concept on student performance. Suggests need to improve flexible group interactions through planned formats.

Ferguson, Hugh, "Modular Scheduling and Social Atmosphere," *The Clearing House,* XLII, No. 9 (1968), 529-530. Insists that flexible scheduling is merely a vehicle for promoting responsible freedom through enjoyable learning. It must produce a better climate for learning and freer emotional qualities in students and teachers.

Flanigan, John C., "Project PLAN: Basic Assumptions, Implementation and Significance," *Journal of Secondary Education,* XLVI, No. 4 (1971), 173-178. Reports on major points providing basis for design of PLAN. Modules as segments of instruction provide for flexibility in individualized instruction.

Gard, Robert T., "A Realistic Look At the Flexible Schedule," *The Clearing House,* XLIV, No. 7 (1970), 425-429. Cites difficult problems that confront the computer if faculties planning a flexible schedule are not aware of the demands, particularly on space. Changes in a student's schedule after the schedule is set cause real problems.

Georgiades, William, and J. Lloyd Trump, "NASSP Model Schools Project," *Journal of Secondary Education,* XLVI, No. 4 (1971), 168-171. Reviews purposes of NASSP project with emphasis on "self-help approach to change." Change in teacher role, allowing for independent study, informal learning environments, and vast changes in scheduling are required.

Graham, M. Robert, "Free School or Chalk Talk Time," *English Journal,* LX, No. 6 (1971), 754-759. Refers to rigidity of lecture, traditional literature study, and specified material teaching as "chalk talk" syndrome. Active student involvement is proposed by fostering free school traditions of flexible scheduling in a student-oriented approach.

Hoffman, Orrin, "Flexible Schedule," *Journal of Secondary Education,* XLIII, No. 6 (1968), 278-282. Expresses enthusiasm about the success of flexible days in the schedule of a small high school. Increased interest of faculty, innovations in teaching methods, and improvement in the attitudes and behavior of students are reported.

Howard, James, "Independent Study for Today's Schools," *Journal of Secondary Education,* XLVI, No. 1 (1971), 25-31. Advocates value of independent study in the learning process. Change in school schedules, appropriate attendance and reporting procedures, and new evaluation techniques are needed.

Jones, Richard, "Getting Started Into a Package Program," *Journal of Secondary Education,* XLVI, No. 5 (1971), 218-226. Emphasizes need for systematic planning on the part of administrators and teachers for individualized instruction. Goals in utilization of materials, media, time, and space are discussed.

Lamb, Gene, "A New Design in Professional Development: The San Jose State Administrative Extern Program," *Journal of Secondary Education,* XLVI, No. 3 (1971), 137-141. Explores major problems of secondary education administrators. Program guidelines for San Jose Extern Program are discussed. They are built around objectives based on flexibility, interdisciplinary programs, and integrated seminars.

Leigh, Thomas G., "Big Opportunities in Small Schools Through Flexible-Modular Scheduling," *Journal of Secondary Education,* XLII, No. 4 (1967), 175-187. A high school with an enrollment of 130 uses modular scheduling to cope with restricted curricular offerings. The importance of course objectives stated in terms of performance criteria is stressed.

Leondar, Barbara, "English in Experimental Schools," *English Journal,* LX, No. 6 (1971), 748-753. Argues that rigid English curriculums treat world in neutral, objective, and public manner. Open labs, responsive to students' concerns, provide personal experiences, flexibility, and availability of help if desired. Importance of informal, critical learning is stressed.

Manlove, Donald C. and David W. Beggs, *Flexible Scheduling—Bold New Ventures.* Bloomington: Indiana University Press, 1965. Explains what flexible scheduling is, the purposes it can serve, and the need for adapting teaching procedures to take advantage of new opportunities. Steps in developing a schedule are outlined in detail including considerations in dealing with pupils, teachers, space, facilities, and time.

Mitchell, Joy, and Richard Zoffness, "Multi-Age Classroom," *Grade Teacher,* LXXXVIII, No. 7 (1971), 55-61. Recommends a flexibly scheduled program based on a philosophy that children possessing varied interests can have meaningful relationships with friends in other age groups. A multiaged classroom provides effective individual or group learning.

Morris, Van Cleve, *Existentialism in Education.* New York: Harper, 1966. Refers to the three constituent awarenesses which make up the "self," as *choosing, free,* and *responsible* agents. Learning situations should be arranged to stress these in every individual.

Petrequin, Gaynor, *Individualizing Learning Through Modular-Flexible Programming.* New York: McGraw-Hill, 1968. Describes a new organization of space and time aimed at individualization of instruction in a high school of 2,200. Large and small group instruction, independent study, and utilization of resources centers are enhanced through a computerized flexible schedule.

Storlie, Theodore, "Evaluating Flexible Scheduling," *Educational Leadership,* XXV, No. 2 (1967), 177, 179, 181, 183. Suggests ways of evaluating the effectiveness of flexible scheduling. Time series experimentation, sampling tests, base-line data, student instruments, and teacher instruments applied in several schools are discussed as research techniques for evaluating innovations.

Swenson, Garner S., Donald Keys, and J. Lloyd Trump, *Providing for Flexibility in Scheduling and Instruction.* Englewood Cliffs, N. J.: Prentice-Hall, 1966. Explains that removing the rigid schedules imposed on teachers and providing for instruction for various group sizes were the two purposes for adopting a flexible schedule at Brookhurst Junior High School at Anaheim, California. Developing the schedule, using a flow chart, providing for large and small groups, and evaluating the effectiveness of the flexible schedule are topics which are considered.

Trump, J. Lloyd, "Flexible Scheduling—Fad or Fundamental," *Phi Delta Kappan,* XLIV, No. 8 (1963), 367-371. Considers several types of flexible schedules using modular approaches and points out that each can become almost as rigid as a conventional schedule. Flexibility is fundamental in the search for better use of numbers, space, and content for educating students.

Trump, J. Lloyd and Delmas F. Miller, *Secondary Curriculum Improvement,* pp. 307-316. Boston: Allyn and Bacon, 1968. Lists the objectives of flexible scheduling. Among them are: meeting teacher requests, providing choice for pupils, reducing schedule conflicts, and increasing individualization. Examples are provided.

Waack, William, "Symposium III: Flexible Modular Scheduling at Evanston, Illinois," *The Speech Teacher,* XVIII, No. 1 (1969), 105-108. Advocates student-centered flexibly scheduled modular system, allowing for self-discovery and self-improvement. Uses theater class to illustrate the importance of independent study programs, mini courses, workshops, and conferences.

Wiley, Deane and Lloyd K. Bishop, *The Flexibly Scheduled High School.* West Nyack, N. Y.: Parker, 1968. Defines conventional, flexible, and variable schedules and builds a case for variable class scheduling. The book includes forms, procedures, and techniques used to develop a computerized program for Claremont High School in California.

Wilmoth, Juanita and Willard Ehn, "The Inflexibility of Flexible Modular Scheduling," *Educational Leadership,* XXVII, No. 7 (1970), 727-731. Presents problems arising from cancellation of a large group program and the inability of teachers to work effectively with small inquiry groups. Division of labor among team members is also a concern.

Wood, Charles L., "Modular Scheduling? Yes But—," *Journal of Secondary Education,* XLV, No. 1 (1970), 40-42. Lists 10 factors that are essential for success of flexible scheduling. The idea is sound, but failure to plan carefully and to avoid formidable pitfalls can prevent the program from operating effectively.

Year-Round School

16

Definition

The year-round school year is an educational program that offers instruction on the same basis during the summer as during the traditional nine months. Frequently it is called the extended school year or the rescheduled school year. The term does not necessarily mean that students will attend school all year, or that teachers will work for 11 or 12 months. These considerations depend upon the plan and policies which a district adopts. By adopting any one of a variety of plans, the schools would be seeking to improve the efficiency of school operation through fuller utilization of buildings, personnel, and other facilities and at the same time to enhance opportunities for students.

Most common among the plans are the rotating term, the year-round acceleration approach, the multiple trails continuous learning program, and the expanded summer school. Both the rotating term plan and the student acceleration approach have several variations in calendar. Chief among these are the quadrimester or quarter system and the trimester system. The quarter plan usually calls for 12-week quarters with a month free in the summer or for four 12-week periods with one week between each. The most common trimester arrangement is that of three periods of 16 weeks with a month off in the summer. The 45-15 rotating calendar calls for a student being in school for 45 days followed by 15 days off. Three-fourths of the students are in school at the same time. Expanded summer school provides for a summer program up to eight or nine weeks added to the conventional 180 days.

The concept of the extended school year is not a new idea, but for the first time in many years it seems to be "catching fire." Currently more schools are exploring its possibilities and adopting one plan or another than has been the case for a generation.

Pressure for reorganization of the school calendar comes principally from two sources: people stressing economical use of resources and those seeking to extend educational opportunities. The economy-minded are concerned about having expensive school plants idle for a quarter of a year. On the other hand, there are those who believe that the expansion of knowledge and the increased demands of our complex business-industrial life require more and better education for all. Others who are interested in acceleration want to provide for having the student in school throughout the year to enable him to complete his requirements more rapidly or to extend his education by taking additional courses.

This type of program increases costs. The rotating quarter or trimester aims primarily at greater utilization of physical and human resources with more limited modifications in offerings. Costs are not necessarily increased or decreased although experience reveals that they are usually not decreased as the proponents of the year-round school had hoped they would be.

Reduction in the number of dropouts, elimination of the necessity of repeating a whole year, providing a more comprehensive program, and giving the student more options loom large in the thinking of those who are concerned primarily with advantages for learning. To them the opportunity to provide compensatory education for disadvantaged pupils is very significant as are enrichment programs for the gifted.

The year-round calendar may be divided into trimesters, quarters, or even sixths. If it wants to move to the year-round school, the district should adopt that plan which best takes into account the peculiar needs and conditions of the community and appears to possess the greatest potential for expanding curriculum and reshaping methodology to make them more relevant and responsive to changing times and more beneficial to students of varied interests and abilities.

Significant Components   *Which ones are essential?*

1. All segments of the community, students at all levels, and all employees of the board of education must be represented in planning.

2. Increase in educational opportunity, rather than financial saving, should be the foremost consideration.

3. Financial support for the extended portion must be the same as for the rest of the program.

4. Valuable experience which students usually gain from work out of school, vacationing, and other summer activities should not be sacrificed.

5. Time must be allowed for teachers to replenish themselves, build their professional competencies, and plan their work for the next term.

6. Provision should be made for acceleration, but it should not be required.

7. Short courses, complete in themselves, are very helpful for providing more options for students and their counselors.

8. At the same time that calendar revision is being studied, possibilities for installing other changes such as team teaching, differentiated staffing, inquiry groups, nongrading, and flexible scheduling should be explored.

9. Courses of study should be thoroughly overhauled.

10. The plan should be carefully coordinated with all other programs and services offered in the community during the various seasons of the year.

11. Enrichment, new experiences, and new dimensions of joy, excitement, and satisfaction should be injected into the program.

12. A climate conducive to flexibility and change should be built and maintained.

13. Scheduling and registration should be done by computer.

14. Sympathetic consideration should be accorded parents and pupils who experience hardships as a result of their calendar and schedule assignments.

15. Programs in the summer must incorporate a broad offering of those activities that can be carried on best during the summer.

16. That plan should be selected which is best suited for a particular community and can be most effectively integrated with existing programs.

17. The best plans serve the entire community, are nongraded, and operate for more hours per day and more months per year.

18. The program must provide dynamic curriculum change to gear the schools to the dynamics of societal change.
19. A sound rationale should be worked out for the reasons for the change and for the goals which it seeks. Special attention should be given to the orientation of teachers and to their continuous inservice improvement.
20. Extensive planning should consider both experimental and long-term aspects.
21. Legal requirements and constraints must be given careful consideration.
22. Much study and effort must be devoted to assuring orderly transition from the existing program to the new plan.
23. It may be necessary to do away with the Carnegie Unit, specifying minimum minutes of instruction per week; the concept of four years of English or three years of mathematics may have to be discarded.
24. Changes in curriculum to include camping, outdoor education, and work experience are more fundamental and more promising than rearrangements in the calendar.
25. Funds and additional personnel should be provided to plan, explain, make adjustments, and keep the program running smoothly.
26. Effective communication with the public, students, board of education, and teachers must be established at the outset of planning, stressed during the time the program is being put into operation, and maintained long after administrators think everybody understands it.
27. Acceptable personnel policies and practices must be worked out between school management and the organizations representing the teachers and other employees.
28. An early decision should be made relative to what is mandatory and what is voluntary.
29. Continuous evaluation should be a built-in feature of the plan.

Proposed Advantages   *With which ones do you agree?*

1. The year-round school provides for greater use of buildings and facilities, fuller utilization of staff, and financial savings.
2. Students can cover more subject matter, accelerate progress, and take courses for enrichment and pleasure.
3. Teachers have an opportunity to earn much-needed money if they want to teach more than nine months.
4. Children like to be busy in the summer.

5. The need for new plant is reduced by about 20 per cent, and less equipment and fewer books are needed.

6. Greater opportunities are provided for disadvantaged learners as well as for the gifted.

7. Delinquency problems, which usually peak in the hot summer when students are out of school, are reduced.

8. Pupils are allowed to enter school at many different times instead of once in a calendar year; thus the problem of having a child wait a whole year because he was a few days too young at the annual admission time is eliminated.

9. Students who are retained do not have to repeat a whole year, and the number of dropouts is decreased.

10. The required number of teachers is reduced, making possible greater teacher selectivity and relieving pressure on the facilities and resources of teacher-education institutions.

11. The extended school year provides a springboard for developing a more flexible curriculum and for introducing innovative practices.

12. Students can get into colleges at different times during the year, as openings become available.

13. Staggered vacations are a convenience to many families since there is a growing tendency on the part of business and industry to set up rotating vacation schedules.

14. The rescheduled school year is particularly beneficial to culturally disadvantaged, physically and mentally handicapped, and emotionally disturbed children.

15. The status and prestige of teachers is enhanced because they are not looked upon as part-time workers.

16. The value of Head Start, summer recreation, and camping might be enhanced if such activities were placed under the administration and operation of the schools.

Criticisms and Difficulties to Be Anticipated   *Do you agree?*

1. The year-round school puts excessive pressure on children.

2. Parents do not want their children out of school in the winter because their vacation plans are disrupted, and many teachers would have to resign if their open terms did not correspond with those of their small children.

3. Having several children from one family enrolled in school makes staggered scheduling very difficult.

4. The cost of air conditioning is substantial, and without it pupils and teachers are unhappy and nonproductive.

5. In many states, schools with extended programs run into conflict with statutory requirements.

6. Plans involving rotation can work only in large cities or large districts without causing unduly small classes in some subjects.

7. For many students, necessary sequence in some subjects, such as foreign languages, is broken.

8. Preparing very complex schedules increases work and costs.

9. In many areas summers are too hot for effective study, and winters are too cold for enjoyable vacations.

10. Some students would miss participation in athletics and other seasonal extracurricular activities.

11. Most teachers want to be free in the summer; and for others the year-round school prevents adequate planning, curriculum development, and continuing education.

12. Under a rotating plan, daytime recreation in the community would have to operate on a year-round basis.

13. During the summer, teachers should work in businesses, laboratories, banks, offices, governmental agencies, or parks learning what they should be teaching in a vital and relevant program.

14. Students will be cut off from camping, scouting, working, loafing, planning their own activities, and other experiences that add significantly to their wholesome maturation.

15. When all factors are considered, the proposed savings disappear rapidly leaving only problems and frustration.

Summary Assessment

Over the years, the basis of interest in the year-round school has shifted significantly. The original advocates of rescheduling stressed the economy resulting from the decrease in demands for more classrooms. Male teachers, particularly, welcomed the possibility of longer employment; but women frequently preferred more vacation time. Administrators appeared to fear additional complexities in scheduling, registering, and staffing. They were also sensitive to adverse reaction of parents who did not want a rotating plan to turn their children out of school in the winter and complicate their vacation plans.

The idea of extending the school year has suddenly come to life after lying practically dormant for a quarter century. It is somewhat surprising to see its popularity surge at this particular time. In most school districts the decline in the national birthrate has to a degree relieved much of the pressure for additional buildings that harassed school planners a few years ago. For the first time in two decades the supply of teachers is coming into balance with the demand. It seems reasonable, then, to suspect that the current increased interest in the year-round school arises more out of financial than educational concerns. Whatever the cause may be, study and adoption of plans are increasing at a rapid rate. Educators are joining laymen to point out that the traditional nine-month schedule was established when 90 per cent of the population of the country lived in rural areas, and now 90 per cent lives in cities.

Most school districts are proceeding cautiously, doing more thinking and talking than acting; but a breakthrough in rescheduling appears imminent. Currently study of year-round programs is being carried on in all parts of the country. Most of the school districts reorganizing their calendars are adopting plans that have only a portion of the student population in school at the same time, with a given percentage on vacation at all times. In these instances it seems that the demand for more efficient use of buildings, personnel, and other facilities is overriding proposed educational advantages.

The 45-15 rotation plan appears to be gaining steadily in its appeal to school people and parents. It contributes significantly to relieving the need for more space but does little to enrich offerings, provide for acceleration, or help pupils with learning difficulties. Moderate success is reported for the program. It is usually better accepted than the rotating quarter or trimester calendar. Frequently study of the year-round school is seized upon as an opportunity to consider other innovations such as differentiated staffing, team teaching, nongrading, independent study, and flexible scheduling.

Just a few years ago businessmen and board members frequently favored the year-round school, and teachers and school administrators stressed the problems and difficulties associated with it. Now when administrators are becoming more willing to give serious consideration to the year-round school, psychologists and curriculum leaders are raising questions. They fear that teachers are too steeped in the traditional stereotype of schooling to launch successfully into a new era of enrichment through individualization for meeting personal interests and needs. They are particularly apprehensive about programs that would confine pupils to the classroom for the entire year. They fear that the bookishness of the schools might rob children of many of the significant opportunities for social, emotional, and aesthetic development in the world beyond the classroom during the summer vacations.

Thoughtful reflection on how the formal and informal educational forces of our times can be integrated for more complete development of youth will enable teachers and their leaders to seize the opportunities and yet avoid the pitfalls of the year-round school.

A Few Leaders in the Movement

Andrew Adams
  Univ. of Virginia
Raymond Arverson
  Hayward (Calif.) Schools
W. Scott Bauman
  Univ. of Oregon
David Bjork
  Univ. of South Alabama
Cyril B. Busbee
  Columbia (S. C.) Schools
Evelyn Carswell
  National Education Association
Kenneth Hermansen
  Valley View Schools,
  Lockport, Ill.

George Jensen
  Univ. of California at Los Angeles
John Letson
  Atlanta (Ga.) Schools
John D. McLain
  Univ. of Akron
Donald H. Morris
  Butler County (Ohio) Schools
James Nickerson
  Mankato State College
George I. Thomas
  State Univ. of New York at Albany
Herman Torge
  Twin Valley Schools
  W. Alexandria, Ohio
C. Taylor Whittier
  Kansas Dept. of Education

A Few Places Where the Innovation Is Used

Aliquippa, Pa.
Ann Arbor, Mich.
Atlanta, Ga.
East Lansing, Mich.
Elida, Ohio
Enfield, Conn.
Fairfield, Ohio
Forest Hills, Ohio
Ft. Lauderdale, Fla.

Freeland, Mich.
Hayward, Calif.
Hazlett, Mich.
Hornell, N. Y.
Jefferson Co., Ky.
Langshore, Pa.
Lockport, Ill.
Mankato State College
Molalla, Oreg.

Newark, N. J.
Northville, Mich.
Port Huron, Mich.
Rochester, Minn.
Romeoville, Ill.
St. Charles, Mo.
Syosset, N. Y.
Utica, Mich.
W. Carrollton, Ohio

Annotated References

Adams, Andrew, "Look Hard at This Year-Round School Plan," *American School Board Journal,* CLVI, No. 1 (1968), 11-15, 31. Presents a "sliding" plan for a four-quarter year with schools closed for one week between the quarters, designed to relieve the objection to winter vacations. Twenty per cent of the students have winter vacations once every five years.

Adams, Velma A., "The Extended School Year: A Status Report," *School Management,* XIV, No. 6 (1970), 13-19. Emphasizes need for greater efficiency in use of buildings, staff, and equipment, but says savings are not easy to effect. Cites schools that have abandoned year-round programs and describes several that are currently operating various forms of extended programs.

Alam, Sami J., *The 4 Quarter Plan and Its Feasibility for the Port Huron Area School District, A Research Study.* 1970. Available from ERIC Document Reproduction Services; order no. ED 046 105. Examines the economic, educational, and physical feasibility of the four-quarter plan with unassigned vacation and describes the results of a survey conducted to assess the attitudes of the community, business, and industry.

An Appraisal of the Extended School Year. New York: New York State Department of Education Report, 1968. Makes recommendations for enabling legislation relating to program design, support, teaching techniques, and collaboration with colleges and universities. Seven basic designs are described. Program objectives, results, and attitudes of students, parents, and teachers in three districts are studied in detail.

Bauman, W. Scott, "Four-Quarter Plan Uses Schools All Year Long," *Nation's Schools,* LXXX, No. 5 (1967), 69-70. Argues for a 48-week year of four quarters on the basis of increased salaries for teachers and savings to taxpayers. Answers eight common criticisms of the year-round school.

Beavan, Keith, "Age of the Year-Round School," *The Times Educational Supplement,* No. 2885 (1970), 13. Points out that in America serious consideration is being given to year-round schools. The almost universal practice of leaving school plants and personnel idle at a time in our history when every available resource is needed is being carefully re-examined.

————, "Eliminating the Long, Hot Summers," *The Times Educational Supplement,* No. 2833 (1969), 15. Explains programs of several cities in the United States, which are instituting programs for a longer than normal school year. It indicates ways in which such a program is advantageous to the students and to the community.

Beckwith, R. M., "Valley View 45-15 Continuous School Year Plan," *American School and University,* XLIII, No. 3 (1970), 19-24. Describes Valley View, Illinois, plan in some detail. Considers educational and social advantages and problems that had to be solved. Concludes that no plan is necessarily the answer to every community's needs and problems.

Cammorota, Gloria, John A. Stoops and Frank R. Johnson, *Extending the School Year.* Washington, D. C.: National Education Association, Association for Supervision and Curriculum Development, 1961. Overview of summer programs including their purposes, development, and administration. Programs in two cities are presented in detail, and trends are discussed.

Childress, Jack R. and Harlan A. Philippi, "Administrative Problems Related to the 11- or 12-month School Year," *The High School Journal,* XLVII, No. 6 (1964), 230-237. Examines measures which must be taken to avoid problems in instituting a year-round school program. Pupils, parents, staff, and program are major factors considered.

Cuddy, Edward H., *The Year-Round School or the Rescheduled School Year, 1969.* Available from ERIC Document Reproduction Services; order no.

ED 041 364. Reviews literature on the concept of the year-round school, the experience of those who have tried this approach to education, and the recent trends in this direction.

Dell, Alan M., "Becky-David the Year-Round School," *School and Community*, LVI, No. 5 (1970), 13. Reports a good beginning for a year-round school, where the district is divided into four rotating areas. Nine-week sessions are followed by three-week vacations. Bus schedules and room assignments are rotated.

Driscoll, T. F., "School Around the Calendar," *American Education*, VII, No. 3 (1971), 21-23. Explains that under Valley View Plan (Illinois), report cards are issued every 45 days. The pupil slow to learn needs not fail an entire year—loses only 45 days. Teachers get a new class every 45 days.

Ellena, William J., "Extending the School Year," *Today's Education*, LVIII, No. 5 (1969), 48-49. Reviews various plans that have been used to extend the school year. Comments and criticism are made about various proposals. A list of questions is included which should be considered before a school system launches an extended program.

Englert, L., "New Lesson Plan, Year-Round Schools Win Increased Support of Parents, Teachers," *Wall Street Journal*, CLXXVIII, No. 52 (1970), 1. Reports progress at St. Charles's Frances Howell School District in its 45-15 year-round program begun July 1969. Cited economies and increased curricula choice that are by-products of this "the wave of the future."

Glines, Don E., "12-Month School," *Instructor*, LXXX, No. 1 (1970), 72-73. Takes the position that the year-round school is economically desirable, but more significant are its provisions for human needs. The year-round concept is the key to 62 other different approaches used at the Campus School.

Jensen, George M., "Year-Round School: Can Boards Sidestep It Much Longer?" *American School Board Journal*, CLVII, No. 1 (1969), 8-12. A former school board member calls present school calendars "outrageously wasteful and whimsically anachronistic." He cites progress toward year-round programs and 15 advantages, mostly relating to financial savings.

Letson, J. W., "Atlanta Schoolman Discusses His Year-Round School Program," *Nation's Schools*, LXXXVI, No. 6 (1970), 12. Describes teacher, student, and public reaction, after two years of operation, to Atlanta's Grades 8-12 four-quarter school schedule. Cautions against selling year-round program solely on basis of utilizing empty buildings.

McLain, John D., "Developing Flexible All-year Schools," *Education Digest*, XXXVI, No. 9 (1971), 12-14. Reports on a position paper adopted at the close of the Second National Seminar on Year-Round Education. The programs which seem most acceptable are those providing flexibility or optional attendance.

———, *The Flexible All-Year School.* Clarion, Pennsylvania: Research Learning Center, 1969. Stresses the point that the flexible all-year schedule allows pupils to come to school when they don't have anything better to do. Programs are completely individualized and automatically nongraded. Computers, paraprofessionals, and multimedia learning centers facilitate learning in a school which has no opening or end to any year.

Mallory, S. R., "Year-Round School, Coming, Coming, Here," *School Management*, XV, No. 8 (1971), 24-25. Reports how another district, Chula Vista

Elementary School District, California, with 4,000 students in four schools (K through 6) joined the ranks of the 45-15 plan in July, 1971.

National Education Association, Association of Classroom Teachers, "Rescheduling the School Year," *Today's Education,* LIX, No. 9 (1970), 37. Recognizes that each school district should vary the design of its school year to fit its own needs—the best interest of the students and the community. All concerned must be involved in exploring possibilities and in arriving at decisions.

New York State Department of Education, *The Impact of Rescheduled School Year: A Special Report Prepared for the Governor and the Legislature of the State of New York,* 1970. Describes findings relating to the feasibility of extended school year plans and outlines several approaches which can be recommended for their economical and educational implementation.

New York State Department of Education, Bureau of Occupational Training Program, *Application of the Extended School Year Concept to a Board of Cooperative Educational Services Occupational Training Program,* 1969. Concludes that a quality program can be made available to all students, and that total use of equipment and facility for 12 months allows a greater number of students to use the equipment for a longer period of time.

Research Division of the National Education Association, *The Rescheduled School Year.* Washington, D. C.: National Education Association, 1968. Reviews 10 plans for rescheduling the school year. Their advantages and disadvantages are weighed in respect to cost, time, improved opportunities for students, and effect on curriculum revision.

Scala, Anthony W., "Year-Round School," *Bulletin of the National Association of Secondary School Principals,* LIV, No. 344 (1970), 79-89. Sets forth obstacles that are likely to be encountered including natural resistance to change, cost, and reluctance of teachers and teacher organizations. Acceleration seems to be frowned upon. An experiment carried on at Syosset, New York, is explained in some detail.

Schoenfeld, Clarence A. and Neil Schmitz, *Year-Round Education.* Madison: Dembar Educational Research Services, Inc., 1964. Reviews the history of calendar revision. The proposed advantages of year-round programs in elementary and secondary schools and in colleges are considered together with problems and prospects.

Scott, P., "Row Threatens Over Length of College Year," *The Times Educational Supplement,* No. 2878 (1970), 8. Reports technical college teachers in England are angry about attempts to force colleges to stay open for more weeks in the year in the absence of a national agreement.

Setting the Stage for Lengthening School Year Programs, Report for the Governor and the Legislature of the State of New York. Albany: The State Education Department, 1968. The state commissioner reports results of research and experimental programs dealing with the lengthened school year. Recommendations are made to the legislature for effecting improved education and economy.

Stefanich, G. P., "Year-Round School Plan With Summer Vacation For Everyone," *School and Community,* LVII, No. 4 (1971), 14-15. Suggests seven-session plan which gives every student at least seven weeks of summer vacation. Each child would attend five of seven sessions offered, thus insuring approval of year-round school by dissenting parents.

Stickler, Hugh and Milton W. Carothers, *The Year-Round Calendar in Operation.* Atlanta: Southern Regional Education Board, 1963. A study by the Southern Regional Education Board of year-round programs for colleges. Need for a longer period of study, increased enrollments, and financial pressures are discussed, and several case studies are presented.

Szuberla, Charles A., "Year-Round School Evolution," *American School Board Journal,* CLV, No. 7 (1968), 13. Describes a tuition-free summer program for grades 1-12 enrolling more than 25 per cent of the pupils in Enfield, Connecticut. The growth from one to 25 per cent occurred in five years.

Thomas, Steven C., "Valley View's 45-15 Year-Round School," *Today's Education,* LX, No. 8 (1971), 42-43. Presents reasons for the movement and effects on space utilization, on student learning, on teacher salaries, and on services. Other problems experienced in carrying out the 45-15 plan and changes being made are discussed.

Torge, Herman, "The Year-Round School," Unpublished Master's Thesis, Miami University, Oxford, Ohio, 1968. A master's thesis describing and giving illustrations of a normal quarter schedule, a quarter schedule with rotating quarters, a flexible quarter schedule, and a two-semester schedule. Calendars and plans for efficient transition are presented.

West, Paul D. and Douglas G. MacRae, *Fulton County Schools Four Quarter Plan.* Atlanta, Ga.: Fulton County Board of Education, 1969. A detailed outline of the curriculum of the school system in 12 areas. Course descriptions, scheduling, and graduation requirements are reported.

White, Richard E., "A Board Member Looks at the Extended School Year," *Education,* LXXXVIII, No. 3 (1968), 245-248. Explains Rochester, Minnesota, plan of enriched and expanded summer school. Continuous and trimester plans are considered. That plan should be adopted that best fits local needs.

Year-Round Education, Mt. Sequoyah National Seminar on Year-Round Education. Fayetteville, Ark.: Arkansas School Study Council, 1969. Papers by 14 leaders in the field are presented. Purposes, plans, and results are reviewed. Improvement of educational opportunity is stressed over economy through fuller utilization of facilities.

Year-Round School. Washington, D. C.: American Association of School Administrators, 1970. Presents four plans: staggered quarter, full 48-week year for all, voluntary summer school, and summer for faculty. Merits and disadvantages of the four plans are discussed.

Audiovisual and Other Resources

Consider a Year-Round School (pkg. of 30 leaflets, $1.50). Discusses factors parents and others should consider before deciding to adopt year-round plan. NEA, 1201 16th St., N. W., Washington, D. C. 20036.

Free Schools

17

Definition

The free school is an alternative to the public school and is established on the philosophy that a child learns best when he is curious and feels a need to learn. It is an attempt by communities of people to replace the conventional school with a free school—free from authoritarian control of students and their learning, free from courses of study, school regulations, bells, texts, and administrators. Students are allowed to come and go as they please. By placing planning, execution, and evaluation of learning in the hands of the students, the advocates of alternative schools propose to develop enough confidence and responsibility in the students to enable them to handle their own affairs.

The schools may be housed in basements, warehouses, or vacant stores. The curriculum depends upon the curiosity, interests, and needs of the students. Teachers are available to serve as resource persons and to help pupils as they pursue their objectives. The openness of the school is conducive to experimentation and introduction of innovations in purposes, content, and methodology. Multiage grouping, nongrading, individualized learning, and team teaching are among the common practices used in the programs.

The free school is often looked upon as a revolt against the practices of conventional education. Many of the schools were begun because frustrated parents with deep dissatisfactions and sincere commitments decided to start their own schools. Desires for moral and religious training, for better preparation for college, for humane treatment, and for greater emphasis on vocational training have caused parents to band together to start their own schools. One of the most common reasons for starting new schools is a determination to break away from restrictions and pressures for conformity placed upon children by traditional schools. All this adds up to dissatisfaction and a search for alternatives.

Underlying the free school movement are the ideas of the British Infant Schools, A. S. Neill's Summerhill, and Jean Piaget. Parents observe millions of nonmotivated pupils, particularly among the disadvantaged in urban centers of population. They are concerned about the apparent inhumanity of many schools and the lack of interest and progress of too many children. Students are bored and humiliated and feel that their education is useless. Some teachers too are dissatisfied and frustrated because they cannot break out of the lockstep of the traditional system to provide humane individual help for children who desperately need it. To them many faculties, administrators, and school communities appear to be adamant in their resistance to change. Caught up in what they consider a web of hopeless frustration, some teachers are eager to try out their ideas in a freer setting with fewer restrictions and less domination from above.

The chief value of the free school movement may lie in its success in convincing public schools that deep dissatisfaction with some aspects of traditional education does in reality exist, and that something needs to be done. Alternative schools may shake the complacency of some public schools and stimulate beneficial reform. But the reformers should bear in mind that thousands of teachers and administrators have been working diligently for years to achieve the same ends that they propose. These educators have thought about many of the proposed approaches to improving learning and have been frustrated by slow progress, but they have chosen to work within the framework of the established system and resent attempts to replace the conventional system with new, untried ideas.

Free schools are located in black ghettos, upper class suburbs, and rural towns. Their orientation may be reflected in such names as "The Mind Restaurant," "New Morning," "Stone

Soup," "All Together Now," "Play Mountain Place," "The Elizabeth Cleaners," "Rough Rock," and "World of Inquiry."

Most free schools subsist on sheer determination. They are plagued with financial problems and harassed by governmental and community pressures. A few of the schools including six in Berkeley, California, receive community support. The Other Ways school has a contract with the Berkeley Board of Education to carry out its unique program and to train teachers. The voucher system, proposed by the Office of Economic Opportunity, is being given consideration in several quarters as a way to bolster the sagging financial structure of parochial and private schools. Its acceptance would be a big boost for alternative schools and give parents the opportunity to make decisions and choices about the education of their children.

Educators in conventional schools have for years recognized the value of many of the ideas which free schoolers emphasize. Humaneness, intrinsic motivation, freedom, and self-direction have long been important goals for many teachers, administrators, and boards of education. Traditional expectations and established requirements have too often prevented these educators from doing what they knew should be done for children. The safe way always seemed to be to stress knowledge and skills that would be measured by standardized tests and college entrance examinations. The interference and constraints suggested by public harassment of the free schools is not entirely new to those who have been working in the public schools. Some of the proposed new ideas were thought of long ago, tried out, found ineffective, and discarded.

Significant Components   *Which ones are essential?*

1. Free schools should be looked upon as communities of people committed to providing a better education for themselves and their children.
2. Self-direction enables the student to plan his own curriculum and ways of achieving his objectives.
3. Close cooperation with parents is necessary.
4. The program must be built on the child's natural curiosity and his felt need for learning.
5. The child decides when he wants to attend school and what he wants to learn when he is there.
6. Freedom and humaneness are the two dominant considerations in the free school.

7. Many opportunities must be provided to pursue creative activities and self-initiated enrichment experiences.

8. The curriculum is multistructured, relying heavily upon spontaneous learning experiences.

9. Close personal relations and affection should prevail between teachers and pupils.

10. The community replaces the classroom as the main source of learning experiences.

11. Courses of study, textbooks, and lectures are replaced with student-initiated activities.

12. Teachers, like students, must have a high degree of autonomy and freedom.

13. Grades, competition, and comparisons between individuals are discarded because they are injurious to the student's self-concept.

14. Interested and knowledgeable people from all walks of life are welcomed as teachers.

15. Students should be allowed to pursue many areas of learning not included in traditional school programs.

16. Alternative schools do not have bells, class schedules, school regulations, school boards, or principals and supervisors.

17. Freedom and informality should be tempered with individual responsibility.

Proposed Advantages   *With which ones do you agree?*

1. Free schools provide an effective alternative to expensive public schools that have lost their effectiveness.

2. Designing their own curriculum and working independently foster initiative, self-reliance, and responsibility in the pupils.

3. Alternative schools do what traditional schools talk about.

4. Citizens with great talent are utilized to stimulate and help students learn.

5. Boredom and behavior problems are reduced.

6. Alternative schools enable students to study problems that are important to them and the solutions of which will help them in the future.

7. Free schools foster creativity and independent thinking.

8. The program frees students from rigid requirements and individualizes both content and learning method.

9. The inner resources of human nature are released and nourished.

10. Teachers can personalize education by working on a one-to-one basis.

11. Close relationships with teachers and peers permit the student to respond to the humaneness of his education.

12. Alternative schools provide freedom for parents and students to select a school that benefits them most.

13. Parents become more interested and more involved in the education of their children.

14. Force and extrinsic motivation through imposed regulations are replaced by natural curiosity and genuine desire to learn.

15. The community is used as a very valuable, yet inexpensive, laboratory for a multitude of learning experiences.

Criticisms and Difficulties to Be Anticipated   *Do you agree?*

1. Free schools usually lack purpose that is well enough defined to allow for meaningful evaluation of results.

2. Students experience great difficulty when they transfer to a regular school because they lack fundamental skills and are unable to adjust to a planned program.

3. Lack of building facilities, material, and equipment often makes effective learning impossible.

4. Alternative schools are handicapped by continuous lack of funds.

5. It is most difficult to secure the necessary clearances, enrollment, and facilities to start a good free school.

6. Students released from reasonable restraints and guidelines often run wild.

7. Parents are misled by false hopes and promises.

8. Students must learn that they cannot always plan their own programs and evaluate their own efforts.

9. Except in a few isolated instances, alternative schools cannot hire competent, well-trained personnel.

10. Even the most willing teachers find it impossible to respond to the excessive demands on their time and energy.

11. Most alternative schools do not meet state and local standards.

12. Free schools are often operated by idealistic people who cannot compete in the real world or adjust to it.

13. Very few teachers can function effectively in a situation in which the student plans his own program and pursues his own interests as the spirit moves.

14. Children come to believe that they can do exactly what they want to do in and out of school.

15. Many of the teachers in free schools teach children attitudes and values that run counter to those of society.

Summary Assessment

The free school movement seems to be more than a fad that is sweeping the country. It is a complete reversal of the trend toward bigness through consolidation of small school districts and toward the establishment of larger and larger administrative units. It is an attempt to eliminate compulsory attendance and other governmental controls and to place education back under the control of the people and learning back into the hands of the learners. The movement possesses many characteristics of the hippie or communal living culture and the practices of such groups as the Amish and other religious sects. In another sense, it is a return from the bureaucratic socialism of state education to the freedom and self-reliance of rugged individualism.

The alternative schools are small and are run by people of varied persuasions and commitments including intellectuals, members of the hip culture, idealists, frustrated educators, and just concerned people who are trying to improve education for children who, to them, appear to be floundering hopelessly in the bureaucracy of conventional education. Their professed goal is to make education more open and to place the control of it in the hands of parents and pupils. They propose to re-establish the personal worth and dignity of children who have lost hope because of repeated failure and rejection.

Free schools actually advocate many of the things that educators have espoused for years. However, if they are to make a significant contribution to improving education, they will have to generate far greater financial support. Most of them will have to secure stronger leadership and a more stable supply of teachers.

They will have to convince the public that they are not a passing fad. In many cases, thoughtful long-term effort will have to replace unstudied accusations and flamboyant assertions. The goals and objectives of the new movement must be spelled out in understandable terms so that the results of the programs can be reliably assessed. In some instances, attention will have to be given to aligning the objectives and outcomes with the purposes and needs of society as well as with those of the individual. A balance may have to be worked out between individual freedom and the welfare of society—between rights and responsibilities. Utopian ideas and ideals may have to be tempered by the hard realities of an imperfect world as it exists.

In this effort, those in the public schools as well as those in the alternative schools must guard against developing one-sided students who are too inflexible to adjust to a freer or to a more structured environment. Advocates of public education as well as champions of free schools would do well to refrain from denunciation of the others until they have taken time to study and understand the purposes to which they aspire, their commitments, and the reasons that underlie their actions.

The new schools have the advantage that their philosophy lends itself well to innovations of many kinds. The competition of the free schools will cause conventional schools to re-evaluate their programs in the light of the criticisms that they are receiving. To maintain support of parents and communities, schools everywhere may be forced to humanize their instruction and make their curricula more responsive to the wishes of parents and the needs of children.

The full impact of the alternative schools has not been felt yet because of the short period that they have been in operation and because of the limited funds that have been at their disposal. However, the proposal for a voucher system and other suggestions that funds be given to children and their parents rather than to publicly supported schools may encourage the spread of free schools. If the voucher system gains support, alternative schools will be able to provide more adequate buildings, equipment, and learning materials. They will be able to attract better teachers and provide the special personnel which they now lack. They will very likely become a greater threat to public education because they promise new challenges and opportunities for individual students.

In the process, however, their programs are likely to become more structured, and they will lose some of the appeal which characterized their fresh and open approach in the beginning. As they come to grips with many of the problems that have plagued conventional schools through the years, free schools may become less critical of the public schools. Conventional education has already begun to experiment with many of the ideas on which the free school movement is based. As they find some of the practices helpful in promoting better learning, public schools are likely to become less critical of the free schools. As both groups learn to work together, share their successes and admit their failures, a better educational program may evolve. Through cooperative effort free schools and conventional schools might accomplish what both believe is good for children.

Charles H. Rathbone expresses the conviction of many free-schoolers when he says,

> Alternatives come and alternatives go, but until the teacher is willing to risk himself—to put his own beliefs on the line—no significant classroom change is possible. Choosing to change means more than taking on the system. It means taking on full responsibility for one's own professional actions. And that is about the most difficult, most mature, action a teacher can ever demand responsibility for.*

Impatient with the slowness of change in public education, many of the leaders of the alternative school movement are putting their beliefs on the line. They are involved in a difficult struggle. It will be interesting to see what happens.

A Few Leaders in the Movement

Donald Cox
  Univ. of Missouri
William Glasser
  Williams College
Paul Goodman
  State Univ. of New York
  at Oswego
Nat Hentoff
  New York, N. Y.
Carl Hoffman
  Colorado State Univ.
John Holt
  Univ. of California at Berkeley

Herbert Kohl
  Teachers and Writers
  Collaborative
Jonathan Kozol
  Boston, Mass.
Charles H. Rathbone
  Syracuse Univ.
Harvey B. Scribner
  New York City Schools
Charles Silberman
  Columbia Univ.
Alvin Toffler
  Cornell Univ.

A Few Places Where the Innovation Is Used

Berkeley, Calif.
Boston, Mass.
Burlington, Vt.
Celina, Ohio
Chicago, Ill.
Cincinnati, Ohio
Cleveland, Ohio

Decatur, Ga.
Detroit, Mich.
El Cajon, Calif.
Longwood, Fla.
Manhattan, N. Y.
Minneapolis, Minn.
Philadelphia, Pa.

Phoenix, Ariz.
San Francisco, Calif.
Santa Barbara, Calif.
Santa Cruz, Calif.
Santa Fe, N. M.
Venice, Fla.
Washington, D. C.

---

*Charles H. Rathbone, "Assessing the Alternatives," *Childhood Education*, XLVII, No. 5 (1971), 238.

Annotated References

Bruner, Jerome S., *The Process of Education*. Cambridge, Mass.: Harvard University Press, 1969. Concerned with a renewal of interest in the quality and intellectual aims of education, emphasizes curriculum planning. The importance of structure, readiness for learning, intuitive and analytic thinking, motives for learning, and aids to teaching are discussed.

"Chaos and Learning: The Free Schools," *Time*, XCVII, No. 17 (1971), 81-82. Gives a brief sketch of the free school movement—the different types, names and reasons for the movement—and examines a free school, Exploring Family School in El Cajon, California.

Cooper, Baynard, "An Experiment: Philadelphia's School Without Walls," *Life*, LXVI, No. 19 (1969), 40-42. Presents a skeleton outline of the Parkway Program in Philadelphia and photographs of the program in action.

Cox, Donald W., "Learning on the Road," *Saturday Review*, LII, No. 20 (1969), 71. Discusses the progress that Philadelphia's Parkway Program has made. It also discusses the curriculum of this radically different school.

Cox, Donald W. and Lisa Lazorko, "A School Without Walls: A City for a Classroom," *Nation's Schools*, LXXXIV, No. 3 (1969), 51-54. Describes Philadelphia's Parkway Program of no formal school building, utilization of community resources, and students' aid in curriculum planning. Student-faculty management groups run the program without formal discipline or code. The authors indicate approval of the program.

Fantini, Mario, "Options for Students, Parents, and Teachers: Public Schools of Choice," *Phi Delta Kappan*, LII, No. 9 (1971), 541-543. Suggests a system under which the student and his family are offered several options in schooling to improve the prospects for learning. Seven different options are discussed.

Fischer, John H., "Who Needs Schools?" *Saturday Review*, LIII, No. 38 (1970), 78-79. Provides an overview of the alternative schools program and its implications for the public schools. He discusses the possible use of the voucher system and possible reasons for dissatisfaction with the public schools. The author does take a stand that the public schools should be reformed, strengthened and preserved.

Greenberg, James and Robert Roush, "A Visit to the 'School Without Walls': Two Impressions," *Phi Delta Kappan*, LI, No. 9 (1970), 480-484. Provides an overview of the Parkway Program, an impression of an exciting alternative, and some reservations concerning the program.

Guernsey, John, "Portland's Unconventional Adams High," *American Education*, VI, No. 4 (1970), 3-8. Explains the philosophy and operation behind the school. Special emphasis is placed on the curriculum, student and teacher attitudes, and community reaction.

Holt, John, *The Underachieving School*. New York: Pitman, 1969. Describes the inadequacies of present-day public schools and concludes that they are prisons for children. He urges that every child be the planner and director of his own education and use as much or as little as he wishes.

Howard, Jane, "We Can Too Start Our Own Schools," *Life*, LXX, No. 1 (1971), 45-51, 54. Relates the establishment of a free school in Decatur, Georgia, called the New School of Decatur, the purpose, program, and problems in setting up a free school. It also includes information about the free school movement such as leaders, the beginnings, and examples of what types of facilities these free schools are housed in.

Morse, David, "The Alternative," *Media and Methods,* VII, No. 9 (1971), 29-34. Gives a history of the free school movement along with a discussion of its problems and merits. Mr. Morse also discusses the "alternate media" that is being used by the free schools. It contains a page of resources on the free school movement, alternate video, and alternative culture information.

"The Parkway Experiment," *Time,* XCV, No. 12 (1970), 55. Discusses the establishing of the Parkway Program in Philadelphia. It gives a present rating of satisfactory to the experiment. It also mentions other cities that plan to imitate the program, as Chicago already has done.

"Philadelphia Free School," *Saturday Review,* LII, No. 46 (1969), 98-99. Presents an explanation of Philadelphia's Parkway Program and how it originated. It also mentions some of the problems it has encountered and its plans for solving them.

Rasmussen, Victor, "Toward a Freer School," *The Education Digest,* XXXVI, No. 9 (1970), 22-25. Emphasizes the fact that when pupils are happy in school, they can make full use of the school's offerings. Gladsaxe, director of education in Copenhagen, cites the Verebro School as an example of the objectives and environment essential to a free school.

Rathbone, Charles H., "Assessing the Alternatives," *Childhood Education,* XLIV, No. 5 (1971), 234-238. Provides an excellent assessment and includes history, names of schools, locations, and discussions of curriculum, teachers, student rights, affective conditions, sources of authority, and the challenge to the public schools.

"Should Schools Be Abolished?" *Time,* XCVII, No. 23 (1971), 33-35. Ivan Illich, an ex-priest now involved in a free university in Mexico called The Center for Intercultural Documentation, is convinced that faith in formal schooling is misplaced and that only a radical re-evaluation of education can enlarge human freedom of mind, spirit, and talent. His program for change is outlined in this article.

Silber, Ken, "Students and Their Rights and Responsibilities in a Learning Environment," *Audiovisual Instruction,* XVI, No. 6 (1971), 47. Contrasts a regular school program with the Parkway Program, concluding that the learning environment at Parkway gives not only students the right to learn but also the desire to learn. Several factors for this conclusion are mentioned.

Smith, Joshua L., "Free Schools: Pandora's Box?" *Educational Leadership,* XXVIII, No. 5 (1971), 464-468. Provides a description, brief history and assessment of the impact of the free school movement.

Stevens, William K., "A School Without Walls," *The Times Educational Supplement,* No. 2858 (1970), 4. Emphasizes the work of John Bremer, an Englishman, who is the director of Parkway, and his thoughts about the project. The author is favorably impressed with Parkway at the end of one year in operation.

"Storefront Schools," *Grade Teacher,* LXXXVIII, No. 6 (1971), 41-48. Herbert Kohl, "Options," *Grade Teacher,* LXXXVIII, No. 6 (1971), 50-52. The first of these articles is descriptions of three alternative schools: Hilltop Center, in Dorchester, Massachusetts; Morgan Community Nature Center in Washington, D. C.; and The Teachers, Inc., a federation of storefront training organizations. The descriptions are objective and good. The latter article is a description of the six options available to students in the Berkeley, California, Public School System. Described in detail is Other Ways Corporation which was formerly directed by Herbert Kohl. It contracts directly with the public school system. The author maintains that public schools ought to have options, and these should not be separate from the public schools. Cooperation is needed.

Sullivan, Ruth, "We'll Start Our Own School," *Instructor,* LXXX, No. 10 (1971), 64-68, 71. Schools in Boston, Washington, D. C., and Santa Cruz are cited as examples of the free school movement. The learning atmosphere in all three schools is discussed.

Toffler, Alvin, *Future Shock.* New York: Random House, 1970. Indicates that competing schools will help create the diversity that education desperately needs and that in time technology will make them effective, efficient, and unavoidable.

Audiovisual and Other Resources

Alternative High Schools: Some Pioneer Programs (booklet, 56 pp., 1972, $3). Describes schools-without-walls, mini-schools and other experimental schools. Educational Research Service, NEA, 1201 16th St., N. W., Washington, D. C. 20036.

The Curriculum (tape, part of the Discussion-Starter Tape Library, reel or cassette, $9, includes leader's guide and worksheet). Discusses the Parkway Program and other innovations. NEA, 1201 16th St., N. W., Washington, D. C. 20036.

Busing

18

Definition

In the present context, busing refers to the practice of transporting children from one attendance area or administrative district to another for the purpose of achieving racial balance.

Four approaches are encompassed in the concept of interracial busing. Following the landmark 1954 decision of the Supreme Court striking down the principle of equal but separate schools, attention focused on busing black children from segregated schools in the South and the inner-city schools of the North to schools with entirely or predominantly white enrollments. This practice was limited to transfers within the same city or school district. The second stage, involving busing white children into predominantly black schools, encountered much greater parental and community resistance.

Because many city school districts were made up of a preponderance of black students, and many suburban districts were entirely white, a reasonable balance could not be achieved without crossing district lines. The idea of intercommunity desegregation was explored. This involved transporting black children across district lines from the inner city to the suburbs and white children from the suburbs into the schools of the central city. A great furor of opposition was aroused. Emotional excitement, disorder, school boycotts, violence, administrative orders, and court rulings only added to the anxieties and heated opposition to busing. Transporting from one district to another created many jurisdictional disputes and legal problems relating to planning, finance, taxation, policy development, and school operation and management. Local school boards and administrators thought they were being stripped of their autonomy and authority by the courts and by state and federal legislation.

Then in January 1972 the United States District Court of Virginia rendered another monumental decision. Judge Robert R. Merhige, Jr. ordered the schools of the city of Richmond, Virginia, Henrico County, and Chesterfield County to consolidate into one school district in order to make it possible to achieve racial balance in the schools of the area.

Although the seven-judge Circuit Court of Appeals subsequently granted a temporary stay of the consolidation order, school desegregation and busing had entered a new era. The Richmond decision marked the first instance in which a federal court ordered consolidation across school district, city, and county lines to achieve desegregation by requiring a racial balance in school attendance.

Quickly the anti-busing movement generated new fervor and support and moved in new directions. For citizens everywhere the idea of metropolitan school districts took on new meaning and aroused new anxieties.

The opposition to forced busing sought support from three sources: from the courts, from congressional legislation, and from a constitutional amendment prohibiting mandatory busing.

Between two and three dozen constitutional amendments, numerous bills, and a variety of amendments to pending legislation were submitted to Congress. School boards and state legislatures passed resolutions opposing busing. Sensing widespread opposition to mandatory busing merely for desegregation, almost all the serious candidates for the 1972 presidential nominations expressed their opposition to it. Legal and political confusion added to the emotional unrest throughout the country. Many senators and congressmen as well as other citizens in all parts of the country were relieved by President Nixon's assurance that he too questioned the efficacy of mandatory busing for achieving equality of educational opportunity. He also pledged the support of his office in finding alternatives to busing to improve education for all children.

Those who think that working for the solution of such problems as segregation is not properly the responsibility of education might profit from the words of Theodore M. Hesburgh, who says,

> Education must serve a broader function than providing children with the technical tools necessary to compete in the technical society of modern-day America. It is a function which should prepare people not just to earn a living, but also to live a life—a creative, humane, and sensitive life.*

While the courts seem to be pushing for busing as a means of desegregation, the legislative and administrative branches of government appear to be concerned about using school busing purely for racial desegregation without having major attention focused on improved educational outcomes. Those who advocate freedom of choice in busing may be engaging in a delaying action to prevent change. They could, however, be right in suggesting that mandatory busing is not the only way—perhaps not even a good way—of achieving greater understanding, fair treatment, improved education, and better quality of life for all Americans.

Significant Components   *Which ones are essential?*

1. Compliance with legal requirements are of special significance.
2. Schools must recognize their responsibility for leadership in improving life in the community and nation.
3. It must be recognized that busing is only a tool for achieving desegregation.
4. Since busing is a very emotional issue, special effort must be devoted to developing understanding of its purposes and to involving the community in planning and implementing the program.
5. The cooperation and support of all those concerned with education is vital.
6. The educational benefits should be kept in the forefront of deliberations.
7. The purposes and values of education must be considered in broad perspective as they relate to the present and future well-being of the individual and society.

*Theodore M. Hesburgh, "The Challenge of Education," *Journal of Negro Education*, XL, No. 3 (1971), p. 291.

8. Equality of educational opportunity for all children should be paramount.

9. The rights, feelings, and opinions of families on both sides of the busing issue should be respected and taken into account.

10. The value of local autonomy should not be overlooked.

11. The achievement of long-range goals must not be jeopardized by needless and fruitless conflict.

12. Persistence and patience are likely to be more productive than executive orders, confrontation, and force.

13. Busing must not be accepted as a substitute for other necessary improvements in schools and community life.

14. Improvement in attitudes and creative changes in instructional programs and procedures must accompany busing if it is to be an instrument for effective desegregation.

15. Curricula must capitalize on the variety of cultures and past experiences of the pupils and meet the needs of all students.

16. Schools must enlist the cooperation of the homes, churches, housing authorities, employers, public and private services, and governmental agencies in achieving the goals which busing tries to attain.

17. Improvement in the quality of education for all children must be the primary objective.

18. The effectiveness of the program must be objectively evaluated so that desirable changes can be effected.

19. Help should be provided to enable teachers to understand their new roles and to improve their competence in meeting new challenges.

20. When their effectiveness is indicated, alternatives to busing should be dispassionately explored.

21. Although busing may not be able to achieve all its objectives, its potentialities for success should be thoughtfully considered.

22. Concerns and fears should not be ignored; unwarranted hopes should not be raised; sincere suggestions should not be ignored.

Proposed Advantages   *With which ones do you agree?*

1. Providing a balance of white and black students makes all schools better.

2. School integration relieves restrictions in housing and zoning, employment practices, and other related areas.

3. Learning to live and work with one another is a valuable experience for children on both sides of the integration question.

4. The best possible educational opportunities must be open to all children.
5. It is unconstitutional to tie support of schools to real estate values in slum areas.
6. As children grow up, they must learn to consider both sides of issues and to work together to resolve them.
7. Real understanding and tolerance can be developed only if children of different cultures go to school with one another.
8. Life in the central cities can be improved only if education in these areas is improved.
9. Integrated education provides new hope for the disadvantaged.
10. Unrest, turmoil, and riots are prevented.
11. Better education increases employability and reduces welfare costs.
12. Desegregation of schools is a promising approach to solving other problems in race relations.
13. Only racists and bigots try to deny black children their constitutional rights.
14. Sooner or later all children will have to adjust to the differences among various social and economic groups.
15. The nation cannot afford to overlook the many advantages inherent in desegregating its schools.
16. Busing is a tool for helping the schools discharge their responsibility for planning and supporting desirable economic and social change.

Criticisms and Difficulties to Be Anticipated   *Do you agree?*

1. The schools are the victims of "harebrained" thinking and scheming of well-meaning social reformers.
2. Although the goal is good, busing is a ridiculous way to achieve the goal.
3. The schools must respond to the desires of the people including the anti-busing forces.
4. The advocates of busing employ more emotion than reason.
5. Districts are often broken up and schools destroyed merely to achieve an irrelevant objective.
6. If present districts are retained, children will have to be shuttled back and forth from one area to another.
7. Suburbs have everything to lose and nothing to gain.
8. Nobody is willing to make a sensible decision because it will immediately be challenged in the courts.

9. The courts should not be writing laws.
10. If the laws were clearly written in the first place, the interpretations of the courts could be kept within reasonable bounds.
11. Forced busing violates the civil rights of those who oppose the idea.
12. Schools are for education, not integration.
13. The real fault of racial inequality lies with governmental agencies, real estate interests, financial institutions, unions, employers, colleges, and churches.
14. Schools should not be expected to solve the problems which other agencies create.
15. As long as society itself is segregated, the schools will be segregated.

Summary Assessment

Busing has perhaps caused more discussion, emotional involvement, serious concerns, and conflict than any other educational problem in many decades. Strong public reaction may be a natural outgrowth of the fact that the issues involved go deep into the value system, hopes, fears, aspirations, and anxieties of the human being.

Citizens in all parts of the country find themselves torn between honoring a commitment to equal opportunity for all people and defending what they look upon as the best interests of their own families. They are particularly disturbed about having their children taken from their neighborhoods into alien environments. Many people who are deeply dedicated to better education for all children of all races believe busing will benefit children of others only at the expense of their own. As they see the problems involved, they are determined not to pay the price of sacrificing their own children.

Many people are accused of racism to whom the label does not apply. Parents on both sides of the argument have many valid, though often exaggerated, concerns that have nothing to do with race. It is unfair to accuse all opponents of busing of being racists or bigots. Such over-simplifications stand in the way of resolving the busing issue.

Opposition to busing exists among black as well as among white parents. In September 1971, a Gallup poll reported that only 45 per cent of Negroes were in favor of busing. Chinese citizens in San Francisco went to the streets and the courts when they sensed that busing threatened their culture and the welfare of their children. Reasons for the opposition vary from one situation to another, but it is naive to assume that differences in race lie at the bottom of all objections. Many people are opposed to busing, but in favor of integrated schools.

Many emotional, personal, and educational issues need desperately to be resolved. Legal problems of all kinds persist. Debate continues even about constitutional matters. Opponents of busing point out that the 1954 decision of the Supreme Court declared that segregated schools are in violation of the Constitution, and that children may not be assigned to this school or that one on the basis of race. They insist with considerable logic that subsequent court decisions have often ordered schools to assign black and white children to schools purely on the basis of race, a principle that was declared unconstitutional by the Supreme Court in 1954.

Differences of opinion continue relative to the school's responsibility to the individual and to society. People are often confused about who speaks for society and about how differences between different desires of different individuals should be resolved. The distinction between desires and rights also needs to be clarified, as does the relationship between moral and legal justice.

Brown v. Board of Education of Topeka, Kansas (1954) considered separate schools "inherently unequal" and consequently unconstitutional. *De jure* segregation in schools was declared in violation of the law, and in 1955 the southern and border states were ordered "to proceed with all deliberate speed" to establish single educational systems. During the succeeding years desegregation moved slowly through many disruptions and court battles.

After 15 years of *deliberate speed* the Supreme Court in *Alexander v. Holmes* (1969) ordered immediate desegregation of schools throughout the South. *De jure* segregation was declared intolerable under the law, and school districts turned to busing as a means of effecting the necessary changes. In April 1971, the Burger court confirmed the constitutionality of busing for desegregation.

The present furor about busing grew out of recent efforts to cope with *de facto* segregation in schools, resulting from housing restrictions and housing patterns rather than from legislative intent to prevent desegregation. Most of the communities drastically affected were in the North. The Richmond, Virginia, court decision was aimed at correcting racial imbalances in adjacent school districts in an effort to eliminate *de facto* segregation.

In these instances, strongest opposition comes from suburban families who have often selected their places of residence because of the high quality of the schools in the district.

It seems that preparing for and supporting desirable social and economic change are not inconsistent with the purposes of education. However, it may be unwise to use the schools as the chief agent for instituting such changes as desegregation when other approaches may be more basic and provide a more effective way of achieving the objective with less danger.

Busing alone will not bring about productive integration. It could serve as a vehicle for enabling the schools to accept the challenges presented by a multiracial society. The task is not easy or pleasant and will require fundamental changes in the content and methods of education, which should be implemented whether or not busing continues. Having black and white children bused to a single school or classroom does not insure successful integration any more than having their parents live in the same county, city, or ward insures integration.

Schools that adopt busing programs must not relax under the assumption that they have done their share in achieving desegregation. When the children arrive at the racially desegregated school, the opportunity for effective learning is only beginning.

Dedicated and understanding teachers and administrators must increase their efforts to expand humaneness, individualized and personalized instruction, and other changes that search for better ways of correcting the basic inequalities in society. Busing could contribute significantly to achieving effective integration by bringing students of varied backgrounds and cultures together to work for common goals in a climate of understanding and respect. Busing could help narrow the gulf between the races. The multiracial and multicultural classroom is a valuable laboratory for enriching the learning and improving human relations for both children from the slums and those from the suburbs. Better economic conditions, health services, recreation, housing, and employment practices are but a few of the other opportunities in the total social structure that must move forward with better education to effect successful racial desegregation. Responsibility for improvements in all these areas should be shared by all individuals and all racial groups.

It is often argued that parents resist busing more than pupils do. To those who stress this point, it seems appropriate to point out that the attitudes and behavior of parents are vital factors in determining the climate in which the child lives and learns and grows to mature or immature adulthood. The attitudes of parents have an important bearing on what the child achieves. These attitudes should not be ignored.

Those who take the position that schools should be exempt from contributing significantly to solving racial problems must not overlook the fact that the child's contacts and experiences during his formative years are of vital importance in shaping his attitudes and behavior in subsequent years.

In dealing with busing, what is good for parents, for children, for schools, and for society as a whole must all be weighed and handled in such a way that the desires, rights, and well-being of all can be best served. Patience, compromise, clear thinking, understanding, cooperation, and humaneness seem like trite and overworked generalities. But they must all be heeded and exercised by whites and blacks if the issues surrounding busing are to be successfully resolved. To reconcile the differences between those who insist on moving rapidly now and those who want to move slowly or not at all is obviously a difficult task. But the issue must be resolved. Compassion for both sides can be achieved through a careful blending of patience and action.

Progress demands change, but change is not always good. Perhaps harmonizing rights and responsibilities is more urgent in the case of busing than in the case of almost any other problem facing the schools. Agreement on goals and objectives is essential to success. The nation appears to be closer to agreement on its long-range goals than on ways of attaining the goals. Perhaps those on both sides of the busing issue are not trying hard enough to understand the feelings and opinions of those on the other side.

Working out a solution to the problem of integration will take time, but it appears that the nation is determined to honor its commitment to better education and a better life for all its citizens, young and old. The busing issue seems to center around differences regarding ways and means rather than differences concerning goals and objectives.

A Few Leaders in the Movement

Reubin Askew
  Governor of Florida
Alexander Bickel
  Yale Univ.

Warren E. Burger
  Chief Justice, U. S. Supreme Court
Wayne Carle
  Dayton (Ohio) Schools

Congress on Racial Equality (CORE)
Gerald R. Ford
   U. S. House of Representatives
Gordon Foster
   Univ. of Miami
Jacob K. Javits
   U. S. Senate
Norman Lent
   Rockville Center, N. Y.
John N. Mitchell
   Gorham State College
Walter F. Mondale
   U. S. Senate
National Association for Advance-
   ment of Colored People

Elliot L. Richardson
   U. S. Attorney General
Neil Sullivan
   Massachusetts Dept. of Education
William L. Taylor
   Yankton College
U. S. Dept. of Health, Education,
   and Welfare
Urban League
   New York City
David E. Wagoner
   Seattle, Wash.

A Few Places Where the Innovation Is Used

Atlanta, Ga.	Grand Rapids, Mich.	Pontiac, Mich.
Augusta, Ga.	Hartford, Conn.	Portland, Oreg.
Berkeley, Calif.	Indianapolis, Ind.	Richmond, Va.
Charlotte, N. C.	Jacksonville, Fla.	St. Louis, Mo.
Corpus Christi, Texas	Lansing, Mich.	San Francisco, Calif.
Dallas, Texas	Louisville, Ky.	Springfield, Mass.
Dayton, Ohio	Minneapolis, Minn.	Tampa, Fla.
Denver, Colo.	Nashville, Tenn.	Washington, D. C.
Detroit, Mich.	New York, N. Y.	Wilmington, Del.

Annotated References

Batten, James K., "Desegregation, a View from Washington," *Integrated Education*, VIII (1970), 36-41. Describes and elaborates on the Nixon Administration's policies and attitudes towards desegregation, with emphasis on Title VI of the 1964 Civil Rights Act.

"Bus to Integration Bogs Down," *Life*, LXVIII, No. 9 (1970), 22-29. Reports various incidents of violence and stories of human interest that have resulted because of busing.

"Busing: The North Reports," *Saturday Review*, LIV, No. 25 (1971), 52. Explains ways in which busing has been used effectively to combat Northern *de facto* segregation and cites two reports released by the Center for Urban Education on the programs in Berkeley and Hartford, Connecticut.

"Busing: U. S. Civil Rights Commission 1970," *Negro History Bulletin*, XXXIV, No. 3 (1971), 68. Supports the philosophy behind busing in a short editorial and gives reason for this support.

Clift, E., "Progress in Jackson," *Newsweek*, LXXVIII, No. 12 (1971), 34. Relates the Jackson, Mississippi, plan to achieve racial balance after eight years of defiance to federal and court-ordered plans.

Cooper, Charles R., "An Educator Looks at Busing," *The National Elementary Principal*, L, No. 5 (1971), 26-31. Supports integrated education and discusses many of its controversial components including busing. This is an enlightening and comprehensive article which weighs the pros and cons of integrated education.

Cory, Christopher, "The Agony of Busing Moves North," *Time,* XCVIII, No. 20 (1971), 57-60, 63-64. Explains the busing problem as it applies to the North's *de facto* segregation, elaborating on the issues involved and giving many and various examples and case studies.

"Desegregation Now—Court Cracks Down," *Senior Scholastic,* XCV, No. 10 (1969), 21-22, 24. Describes the situation in desegregation of schools from 1954 to 1969. An informative article.

"Desegregation—To Bus or Not To Bus," *Newsweek,* LXXVIII, No. 10 (1971), 16-17. Reviews President Nixon's stand on busing and the effects of his position on school integration; it also reviews the latest developments in the South.

"Green Light for Busing," *Saturday Review,* LIV, No. 21 (1971), 68. "Desegregation plans cannot be limited to the walk-in school," wrote Justice Burger in ruling on Charlotte-Mecklenburg case. Amendments are presented in Congress following Supreme Court decision to end *de jure* and *de facto* segregation.

Hesburgh, Theodore M., "The Challenge to Education," *Journal of Negro Education,* XL, No. 3 (1971), 290-296. Philosophically supports racial integration as a means of educating children to the larger world and stresses the immediacy to do so.

Mahan, Thomas, "The Busing of Students for Equal Opportunities," *Journal of Negro Education,* XXXVII, No. 3 (1968), 291-300. Reports on the results of busing and integration in four communities. Also deals with what is considered effective educational programs in the area of integration.

Morsell, J. A., "Racial Desegregation and Integration in Public Education," *Journal of Negro Education,* XXXVIII, No. 3 (1969), 276-284. Reviews the major court decisions regarding the desegregation of schools and delineates the numerical developments from 1964-1969. Stresses the harmful effects of segregated education on Negro children.

Noon, Elizabeth F., "Is Busing the Answer?" *Instructor,* LXXIX, No. 2 (1969), 123-124. Surveys and discusses how inner-city parents feel about their children being bused to suburban schools.

Osborne, J., "Busing and Politics," *The New Republic,* CLXIV, No. 22 (1971), 19-20. Reports the Nixon stand on busing and the recent incidents which occurred between the Department of Justice and the Supreme Court.

Panetta, Leon, "The Law, Says the Man Who Was Fired for Enforcing It, Is the Law," *Life,* LXVIII, No. 9 (1970), 30. The former chief of the Office for Civil Rights at HEW states strongly his reasons for immediately ending segregated schools; he also relates the efforts of his department and the Administration's position.

"Pyrrhic Victory?" *Newsweek,* LXXVIII, No. 20 (1971), 83. Elaborates on a recent education bill before the Senate which contains a clause forbidding the use of federal education funds to aid busing.

Render, Edwin R., "High Court's Desegregation Ruling Needs Explanation," *Nation's Schools,* LXXXVIII, No. 1 (1971), 40. Explains Supreme Court ruling of May, 1971, on Charlotte-Mecklenburg busing case. High Court said that busing is one of several legal ways to achieve integration, but the court didn't define the limits on busing with any precision.

Rice, Arthur H., "Rigid Integration Policy Ignores Community Values," *Nation's Schools,* LXXXV, No. 3 (1970), 6, 8. Points up the need for maintaining the neighborhood school and supports strongly integrated parental involvement.

Ross, Richard S., "ABC's of Busing Furor," *U. S. News and World Report,* LXXI, No. 20 (1971), 82-85. Answers basic legal and political questions pertaining to the controversies surrounding busing as a technique to desegregate schools.

Scudder, Bonnie Todd and Stephen G. Jurs, "Do Bused Negro Children Affect Achievement of Non-Negro Children?" *Integrated Education,* IX (1971), 30-34. Describes a study involving six elementary schools to determine the effects on the academic achievement of non-Negro children attending the same schools and classes. The results showed that there was no evidence of any general effect of the presence of Negro students on the achievement of non-Negro pupils.

"Trouble in Pontiac," *Newsweek,* LXXVIII, No. 12 (1971), 33-34. Reports the findings and practice of *de jure* segregation in Pontiac, Michigan, and relates the violence that resulted from the implementation of busing.

"Turn Around on Integration," *Time,* XCV, No. 10 (1970), 9-16. Explores the 1970 retreat from integration relying on the political events of the early 70's and the Administration's role in creating a climate of uncertainty and indecisiveness. Relates historically events from 1954 to 1970 and describes the issues at hand.

"Unpopular but Crucial Goal," *Life,* LXVIII, No. 9 (1970), 32. Considers the issues and efforts of integration in the schools with special attention given to the separatist philosophy which is against integration.

Wagoner, David E., "The North, Not the South is Where School Desegregation Isn't Happening," *American School Board Journal,* CLIX, No. 3 (1971), 31-34. States that busing is too controversial and costly to be funded locally. Busing isn't the issue, but rather at issue is tenor and tone of life in urban environment.

Audiovisual and Other Resources

Busing: Some Voices from the South (16mm film, 50 min., $550, also available in 3 filmstrips/cassettes or records, $29.50). Comprehensive report on Southern efforts to achieve racial desegregation. Westinghouse Learning Press, Film Div., 100 Park Ave., New York, N. Y. 10017.

Parochiaid   19

Definition

Parochiaid is the provision of public funds for the support of private and parochial schools. Although the word itself is more closely related to church-affiliated education than to other forms of private schooling, the term has recently been applied in a generic sense to refer to tax aid for all nonpublic schools. Because of the large proportion of elementary and secondary schools that are church-related, the issue of providing tax funds for the support of nonpublic schools focuses primarily upon parochial schools.

The issue and the differences surrounding it are not new. Many of the pressures for and against public support for church schools grew out of practices and problems of education in Western Europe. There operations of government, churches, and schools have been closely interwoven since medieval days. In the Middle Ages learning and organized schools survived chiefly through the efforts of the church.

In the ensuing centuries, ecclesiastical influence waned and waxed as political and social conditions varied. Dramatic changes resulted from such events as the Reformation, the French Revolution, major wars, reorganization of national boundaries, establishment of new governments, and landmark legislative acts. In most western countries of Europe, however, the church has always played a very important role in education, ranging from moderate support to complete domination.

Similarly, public financial support of church schools varied but always has been and still is much more extensive than in the United States. In many countries—notably Germany, France, the Scandinavian countries, Austria, and Italy—revenue for church schools is very substantial or comes almost entirely from state sources.

Schools in colonial America reflected their European backgrounds in financial support as well as in organization and curriculum. When the First Amendment to the Constitution was passed in 1789, the founding fathers thought they had settled the issue of "establishment of religion, or prohibiting the free exercise thereof." But subsequent, often conflicting, laws and court decisions testify to the fact that the issues involved are not yet clarified nor resolved.

Thomas Jefferson took the position that the First Amendment built "a wall of separation between Church and State." Differences persisted. In 1925 the Supreme Court ruled that an Oregon law requiring all children to attend public schools was unconstitutional, and private and parochial schools were allowed to operate in Oregon.

In 1947 the Supreme Court again rendered a decision regarding the relationship between church and state, this time denying the right of the state to interfere with the church by passing laws that "force or influence a person to go to or remain away from a church against his will. . . ." The decision also says:

> No tax in any amount, large or small, can be levied to support any religious activities or institutions, whatever they may be called, or whatever form they may adopt to teach or practice religion. Neither a state nor the Federal Government can, openly or secretly, participate in the affairs of any religious organizations or groups and vice versa. In the words of Jefferson, the clause against establishment of religion by law was intended to erect "a wall of separation between Church and State."*

In 1948 the Supreme Court ruled against religious instruction in public schools and subsequently against prescribed prayers and devotional Bible reading. In 1968 it approved public subsidy for secular textbooks in nonpublic schools.

Basic Documents Relating to the Religious Clauses of the First Amendment (Silver Spring, Md.: Americans United for Separation of Church and State, 1970), p. 5.

The Court's ruling of June 1971 appears to be a landmark decision. A Rhode Island law providing state money to pay 15 per cent of teachers' salaries in nonpublic schools was declared unconstitutional. A similar law in Pennsylvania providing salary aid and state funds for secular textbooks and instructional materials was likewise found to be in violation of the Constitution. The ruling pointed to the difficulty of making distinctions between secular and religious aspects of parochial education without becoming involved in excessive entanglement between church and state.

Less than a month later, in July 1971, the same court approved the use of federal funds in constructing buildings for nonreligious uses at church-related colleges. These and other decisions of the Supreme Court and lower courts indicate that many questions relating to parochiaid remain to be answered before the issues involved can be resolved.

Most of the court decisions deal with public support for parochial schools. In the meantime, pressures increase as Catholic schools continue to bear the heaviest burden. They have by far the largest nonpublic enrollment and find their supply of religious teachers declining. A quarter century ago Francis Cardinal Spellman called for assistance with busing, nonreligious textbooks, health facilities, and other auxiliary services. Today as financial resources lag, the need extends to buildings, equipment, and salaries.

Church leaders, laymen within the church, and citizens affiliated with other churches or no churches at all recognize the plight of parochial schools. Educators in public schools, school boards, and state and federal government realize more keenly than ever that the problems of financing public and nonpublic education are closely interwoven.

Legislators are receptive to the idea that it is cheaper to provide a little aid to private and parochial schools than to face the possibility of their collapse, which would force public education to assume the cost of educating about 10 per cent more children. A complicating factor is that some school districts which are already in dire financial straits would be very drastically affected because of the large number of students in their districts presently attending parochial schools. In the minds of many people, a conflict is developing between the economic realities of our time and the doctrine of separation of church and state.

Recently attention has been directed toward exploring the possible constitutionality of making tuition grants to parents and their children rather than giving funds directly to the schools. The opponents of parochiaid have labeled this approach a ruse for circumventing the law. But pressed by critical financial need, the proponents of parochiaid are redoubling their efforts to secure greater tax support.

More and more state executives and legislators are responding to the needs of private and parochial schools and colleges by passing laws, facing challenges in the courts, and awaiting final decisions. Arguments about parochiaid continue with as much heat on the street corner as in the courts and legislative halls.

Significant Components   *Which ones are essential?*

1. Unusually careful attention must be given to constitutional requirements, legislation, and court decisions.
2. Implementation of an effective program of parochiaid must take into account the views and feelings of all groups and individuals.
3. Safeguards must be established to prevent using public financial support for narrow, sectarian purposes or for private financial gain.
4. Opponents of parochiaid must try to understand the views of those who believe that children are young only once; and that if they miss vital learning experiences in their early years, they may never recover.
5. Careful consideration must be given to the argument that children cannot reasonably be expected to supplement their public school education with religious instruction during out-of-school hours.
6. The importance of separation of church and state must not be treated lightly.
7. Scars resulting from unnecessary conflict should be avoided through patient consideration of the differences between the proponents and opponents.
8. Private and parochial schools that request or accept public funds must expect to forfeit some of their autonomy.
9. Schools that receive public financial support should open their records for public review.
10. Ways must be devised to insure acceptable standards of facilities, services, and results.
11. Provision must be made for coordinating planning among all schools receiving public funds.
12. A plan must be developed for dealing with alleged violations of regulations or requirements.

13. Representation of the general public on boards of nonpublic schools should be considered.
14. Admission and employment practices as well as curricular offerings of all schools should be under continuous review.
15. Restrictions that stand in the way of desirable diversity should be avoided.
16. Experiences relating to state support for private and parochial schools in foreign lands deserve thoughtful study.
17. Care should be exercised to prevent forcing parochial schools to secularize, thus destroying their fundamental purpose for many parents who choose these schools for their children.
18. Consideration must be given to citizens who believe they are being forced to support programs that are contrary to their beliefs.
19. Aid to private and parochial schools should not be at the expense and to the detriment of public schools.
20. The danger of the support gradually creeping from minor forms of aid to complete financing of private and parochial education should not be overlooked.

Proposed Advantages   *With which ones do you agree?*

1. All children need and deserve quality education.
2. The nation cannot afford to be unconcerned about the education of any of its citizens.
3. Pluralism in the educational system improves opportunities for all students.
4. Public, private, and parochial schools learn much from one another.
5. People who pay school taxes should benefit from them even if they choose to have their children attend private or parochial schools.
6. Sharing tax money with nonpublic schools generates greater interest in and support of education on the part of all citizens.
7. Parents and pupils have the right to choose among alternatives.
8. Monopolistic control of education breeds complacency and leads to mediocrity.
9. Because of their philosophy and special emphases private and parochial schools often can provide better programs for students with special needs.
10. Most of the money spent for education in private as well as public schools is expended for the development of competencies and qualities essential for effective citizenship.

11. Resistance to aid to nonpublic schools is usually the result of bias and prejudice.
12. In a pluralistic educational system teachers have greater freedom to engage in creative teaching and in experimentation with innovative materials and procedures.
13. Varied goals and objectives among public, private, and parochial schools complement one another to the benefit of the total society.
14. Children should not be discriminated against because of their religion.
15. Public schools often overlook the spiritual, moral, and religious aspects of human development.

Criticisms and Difficulties to Be Anticipated   *Do you agree?*

1. Separation of church and state is one of the basic principles on which our nation was built.
2. Schools should not tell children what they should believe.
3. Diverting tax funds to private and parochial education is against the federal Constitution and the constitutions of most states and is forbidden by many laws.
4. Giving parents vouchers to pay tuition is an obvious attempt to circumvent the Constitution and the law.
5. Tax money should not be used to pay for private and parochial enterprises of any kind.
6. The argument that tuition benefits the child rather than the school is a hollow one.
7. Splintering our system of free public education destroys the effectiveness of most schools.
8. If carried to extremes, pluralism results in chaos.
9. The government already provides public educational opportunity for all children.
10. Parents who don't want to take advantage of public education should be free to choose alternatives, but should not expect others to help pay for their choices.
11. If support is given to nonpublic schools, taxes that are already too high will skyrocket.
12. It is impossible to keep denominationalism out of nonreligious aspects of a parochial school program.
13. Private and parochial schools resent and resist governmental insistence on establishing standards and exercising reasonable control of curriculum and school operations.

14. When nonpublic schools accept tax money, they forfeit much of their freedom and character.
15. Forcing citizens to support two systems of education is double taxation.

Summary Assessment

Through the years, proposals for providing tax support for private and parochial education have always generated heated debate. This condition still exists, but the differences are not as bitter and divisive as they once were.

The financial distress in which schools of all kinds and levels find themselves has produced a less emotional climate. Discussions are more rational. Ecumenical relations have dulled the edge of sharp religious conflict. Those on both sides of the issue seem increasingly to appreciate the complementary contributions made by schools with different goals and varied emphases.

As teachers from private, parochial, and public schools work and study together, they grow in understanding of their common problems and goals. Federal and state appropriations have tended toward relieving the anxieties of taxpayers at the local level and toward making the problems associated with parochiaid more impersonal. Indirect aid for special instruction and auxiliary services has reduced the conflict over sectarian considerations.

Problems of the ghetto and the need for compensatory education have called for cooperation among all educational systems. In recent years the reluctance of taxpayers to provide adequate support for public schools has aroused serious concern about the ability of parochial schools to survive. Many of those who send their children to public schools think that having the millions of children attending church-supported schools thrown upon the already distressed public system would be calamitous.

The proponents of parochiaid stress the importance and desirability of freedom of choice in selecting schools for children of different interests, needs, and temperaments. They believe that some of their tax money should be made available to the schools which their children attend. If such appropriations are not legally possible, parents of parochial children believe they should be exempt from paying taxes for public education.

These parents see no reason for making education a public monopoly, when a more satisfactory alternative is already available if it can be adequately supported. To many of them the separation of church and state does not seem to be a genuinely significant consideration. In fact, many of them believe that education should integrate the academic, social, spiritual, political, and economic life of students.

Efforts to prevent public support of educational opportunities for all children appear to those who advocate parochiaid as unjustifiable discrimination against the free exercise of religion, which places undue financial strain upon those least able to pay for the kind of education in which they believe. The opponents of public aid for private and parochial schools fear the possibility of weakening the public schools, of governmental establishment of religion, and of dangers to religious freedom.

Providing adequate schools and freedom of choice in education may well be problems which can be solved by additional money, but using that money to support private and parochial schools is perhaps not a problem that can be solved. It should be looked upon as an issue, which at best can be resolved through clear thinking, establishing agreed-upon goals, and working out acceptable compromises to achieve these goals. Laws and tricks to circumvent them are not likely to resolve the basic differences between the proponents and opponents of parochiaid.

A Few Leaders in the Movement

American Civil Liberties Union
  New York City
American Jewish Council
  New York City
Americans United for Separation of
  Church and State
  Washington, D. C.
Association of Catholic Teachers
  Washington, D. C.
William Ball
  Monticello, Ark.
Paul Blanshard
  Thetford Center
Virgil Blum
  Marquette Univ.
Daniel Callahan
  Institute of Social Ethics
  and the Life Sciences

Edd Doerr
  Univ. of Michigan
Donald A. Erickson
  University of Chicago
Richard Gabel
  Univ. of Southern California
George R. LaNoue
  Columbia Univ.
Neil McCluskey
  Univ. of Notre Dame
Leo Pfeffer
  New York City
Mary Perkins Ryan
  Penn State Univ.
Anson P. Stokes
  Brookline, Mass.
V. T. Thayer
  Nalcrest, Fla.

A Few Places Where the Innovation Is Used

When public financial support has been provided for private and parochial schools, it has usually been done by the federal government or individual states. Among the states are:

Illinois	Minnesota	Ohio
Maryland	New Hampshire	Pennsylvania
Massachusetts	New York	Rhode Island

Annotated References

"Aid to Parochial Schools? School Board Members Just Don't Bless the Idea," *American School Board Journal*, CLVII, No. 7 (1970), 24-28. Polls school board members on their views of parochiaid. Most favor no form of state aid to parochial schools and give their reasons. Those who favor aid indicate what types of aid they accept and cite conditions necessary to receive aid.

Arons, Stephen, "The Joker in Private School Aid," *Saturday Review*, LIV, No. 3 (1971), 45-47. Discusses public funding of nonpublic schools and points out the possibility of low- and middle-class children being slighted if it came to pass.

"Await High Court Ruling on De segregation, Parochial Aid," *Nation's Schools*, LXXXVI, No. 6 (1970), 27. Summarizes some cases before the Supreme Court in 1970 which were related to education, including a case involving public funding of nonpublic schools.

Ball, William, "An Examination of the Church-State Issues," *Wilson Library Bulletin*, XLI, No. 7 (1967), 694-700. Examines the separation of church and state with the two extreme viewpoints, and the Elementary and Secondary Education Act. Much will be lost educationally if the religious issue distracts from the great issue of solving the education crisis.

_____, "Church and State: The Absolutist Crusade," *Saturday Review*, L, No. 3 (1967), 58-59. Argues that the opponents of parochiaid have stirred the worst of fears in the public and will drive a wedge between groups at a time when there is a need for unity. There is not and never was an absolute wall of separation.

Basic Documents Relating to the Religious Clauses of the First Amendment. Silver Spring, Md.: Americans United for Separation of Church and State, 1970. Summarizes some of the history of the First Amendment. Discussions of James Madison's and Thomas Jefferson's writings and ideas concerning the First Amendment are included.

Blum, Virgil C., *Freedom in Education: Federal Aid for All Children*. Garden City, N. Y.: Doubleday, 1965. Discusses the relationship between church and state in education, focusing on the freedom of the individual pupil. The financial problem, freedom in education, constitutionality of equal benefits, diversity in a free society, precedents, freedom in education in other democracies, and progress in America are discussed.

"Can Parochial Schools Survive," *U. S. News and World Report,* LXXI, No. 2 (1971), 26-28. Recognizes that the recent Court rulings against "excessive entanglement" were a blow to parochiaid, but that it isn't the end of Catholic education. Other approaches to getting aid are looked at.

Christenson, Reo, *Challenge and Decision: Political Issues of Our Times,* pp. 128-163. New York: Harper and Row, 1967. Develops two logical, but different, sides of the constitutionality of parochiaid. Only federal funds to parochial schools are treated. The church-state relationship is stressed more than other facets of the issue.

Clayton, A. Stafford, "Church, State, and School," *Encyclopedia of Educational Research,* pp. 199-205. New York: Macmillan, 1960. Describes the historical background of the issue and the focal issues today in terms of separation of church and state. Concerns itself with the problem of religion in education.

Cogdell, Gaston D., *What Price Parochiaid?* Silver Spring, Md.: Americans United for Separation of Church and State, 1971. Argues that public money should not be used to fund nonpublic schools. In addition to the many reasons for not funding nonpublic schools, there is a summary of the U. S. Supreme Court decisions on the subject.

Congressional Research Service, *Public and Non-public Schools.* Washington, D. C.: National School Public Relations Association, Library of Congress, May 25, 1971. Describes the Catholic school crisis, the battle on the federal front, as a national debate, state programs for support of parochial schools, and viewpoints of different lobbyist groups, pro and con.

"Crisis of Confidence," *Newsweek,* LXXV, No. 5 (1970), 75-76. Describes the financial aspect of the parochiaid issue in terms of school closings and the added burden to the public school system. Different and existing solutions are described.

Deedy, John, "Trouble for the Catholic Schools," *New York Times,* CXX, July 4, 1971, Section 4, 7. Suggests that the financial aspect is but one of the problems confronting parochial schools. A lack of priorities and a general dissatisfaction with the parochial school presents a graver problem, one which must be solved or there will be no need for parochiaid.

Doerr, Edd, *The Parochiaid Bomb.* Silver Spring, Md.: Americans United for Separation of Church and State, 1970. Discusses the issue of parochiaid with an emphasis on the reasons why parochiaid is not a good idea. The pamphlet states that the parochiaid blitzkrieg must be stopped.

————, "Public Schools Publicly Supported," *Compact,* IV, No. 2 (1970), 32-34. States that public funds should go to public schools only, for parochial schools are different, selective, and operated for religious purposes. Several reasons are given why parochiaid is unnecessary, inefficient, and means disaster for public education.

"Federal and State Aid To Nonpublic Education: Selected References, 1966-1970," *Congressional Research Service,* June 18, 1970. Lists sources of further information on the topic of public funding of nonpublic schools. Sources are annotated and listed by Library of Congress call numbers.

Friedman, Murray and Peter Binzen, "Politics and Parochiaid," *New Republic,* CLXIV, No. 4 (1971), 12-15. Recognizes that parochiaid is as much a political as a constitutional issue. Catholics should not be discriminated against and the perils of extending public funds to parochial schools are recognized. In our pluralistic society, there is room for both public and private schools.

Huff, Russell, "Parochiaid: The Cry for Help Gets Louder," *Nation's Schools,* LXXXIV, No. 3 (1969), 16-24. States that the separation of church and state aspect seems to be giving way in many states and the more pragmatic economical problem—that it may be cheaper to aid parochial students where they are—is becoming more important in deciding this issue.

Karpatkin, Martin, "Public Assistance to Parochial Schools," *America,* CXIV, No. 15 (1966), 506-513. States the position of the American Civil Liberties Union that there is no constitutional provision for any public funds for church schools and that taxpayers are denied their First Amendment rights in aiding a religion of another belief.

Koob, Albert, "Public Aid for Nonpublic Schools: the Real Issue," *Nation's Schools,* LXXXVII, No. 5 (1971), 75-77. Argues that use of public funds for nonpublic schools should be determined not on church-state grounds, but on whether schools make a contribution to society that is worth supporting.

LaNoue, George, *Public Funds for Parochial Schools.* New York: National Council of Churches, 1963. Opposes funding on the grounds that it violates the constitutional requirement of separation of church and state, and also because it would undermine the public school system.

McCluskey, Neil, *Catholic Viewpoint on Education.* Garden City, N. Y.: Hanover House, 1959. Presents his view on public support for parochial schools, noting that practice outruns theory in this area. It appears to him that parochial school children will be included more and more in public education benefits.

"Michigan Voters Turn Down Parochial Aid," *Nation's Schools,* LXXXVI, No. 6 (1970), 86. Describes the predicament of nonpublic schools in Michigan. Voters' refusal to approve funds has impeded development of program.

Miller, James, "Should Parochial Schools Get Public Funds?" *Reader's Digest,* XCVI, No. 2 (1970), 113-116. Describes the financial problem, the constitutional issue, what some states have done concerning parochiaid, and its constitutionality. He says the issue is difficult to resolve because both sides are sincerely convinced that they are right.

"No State Funds for Private Schools," *NEA Research Bulletin,* XLVIII, No. 4 (1970), 114-115. Summarizes the feelings of the 1969 Representative Assembly of the NEA which rejected public funds for private schools. Several reasons for this rejection are included.

"Parochiaid in the States," *Church and State,* XXIV, No. 10 (1971), 10-13. Summarizes the present situation regarding parochiaid in the 50 states, including programs present and underway. Transportation is the most common form of state aid to parochial schools followed by shared-time plans and aid for handicapped children.

"Parochiaid: More Legal Turmoil Ahead," *Nation's Schools,* LXXXVIII, No. 2 (1971), 9-13. Summarizes the implications of the U. S. Supreme Court decision that public money used for nonpublic schools is unconstitutional. Parochiaid is discussed as a national issue in years to come.

"Parochial Opinion," *Newsweek,* LXXVIII, No. 2 (1971), 55. States the views of the U. S. Supreme Court ruling on public funding of nonpublic schools. The plans of action of various groups concerned with parochiaid are also included.

"The Parochial School Tangle," *Saturday Review,* LIV, No. 34 (1971), 48-49. Reviews some of the possibilities that may result from the Supreme Court decision that public funding of nonpublic schools is unconstitutional. The issue is still not resolved.

Pfeffer, Leo, "The Parochiaid Decision," *Today's Education,* LX, No. 6 (1971), 63-64, 79. Summarizes some of the history leading up to the Supreme Court decision that public funding of nonpublic schools is unconstitutional. A separation between church and state is indicated.

"Public Funds for Parochial Schools," *Scholastic Teacher,* XCVI, No. 5 (1970), 3. Indicates that the economic issue is taking precedence over the constitutional issue. Opponents of parochiaid are still fighting hard to make state laws unconstitutional and may succeed.

Robison, Joseph, "In Congress, the Legislatures, and Parochiaid," *Compact,* IV, No. 2 (1970), 8-11. Discusses legislative developments, constitutional considerations, the balance of forces, the battle in the courts, and saving the public schools. The principle of parochiaid is permissible in many cases, except in providing money.

Series of articles on parochiaid, *Christian Science Monitor,* LXIII, Feb. 1-5, 1971. Provides a comprehensive description of the problems and viewpoints involved, including the financial and constitutional aspects, and takes a look at different solutions. No matter how it is resolved, the parochial school will change.

Sonkup, Sister Ann, "Twilight Years of Nonpublic Education?" *National Elementary Principal,* L, No. 6 (1971), 82-84. Stresses that a vigorous, improved, independent private school system is necessary in order for public schools to be strong and efficient. A school which is publicly supported is better than one which is closed down. Competition between private parochial schools and public schools yields better education.

"Untangling Parochial Schools," *Time,* XCVIII, No. 2 (1971), 32-37. Considers the parochiaid issue in terms of the constitutionality of public aid to church-state separation, previous rulings, and current resolutions, including the voucher plan and shared-time. It indicates that whatever happens, parochial schools are in for a hard time.

"Voucher Parochiaid Plan Still Alive," *Church and State,* XXIV, No. 9 (1971), 12-13. Lists the latest developments in promoting the voucher plan for providing full public funding for parochial schools. The voucher plan is treated as a hoax being sold to the public through dubious means.

Woodring, Paul, "Education in America," *Saturday Review,* LIV, No. 3 (1971), 44. Describes the sorry financial state of affairs in education today, and in particular, that of parochial schools, saying that parochiaid will benefit both public and private schools.

Audiovisual and Other Resources

Parochiaid—Issue of the 70's (filmstrip, $4). Examines the arguments for and against government aid to parochial schools. Visual Education Consultants, Inc., Box 52, Madison, Wis. 53701.

Multiage Grouping and Pupil-Team Learning

20

Definition

Multiage grouping and pupil-team learning are here treated together because they are both inherently part of the single concept of having children learn from one another by working together for common ends. Both provide for individual interests and abilities, for mutual support and aid among the members of the group, for allowing students to progress at their own rates, for flexible use of teacher time, and for having students evaluate one another's efforts and achievement. Both emphasize shared planning, thinking, and working leading to a single product of the group or different products for each individual.

Multiage grouping includes students of various ages while pupil-team learning may involve children of the same age or of quite different ages. Commonly team teaching is used with multiage grouping, and the total number in the group is usually larger than in programs in which the students are of about the same age.

Briefly defined, multiage grouping is the practice of grouping pupils of different ages in the same work groups so that the older ones can profit from helping the younger ones, and the younger ones can be stimulated by the older ones and learn from them. It is often referred to as *interage grouping* or *family grouping*. The latter term reflects the similarity between the grouping in school and life in the home, where children of widely different ages help one another grow in knowledge, skills, and social and emotional maturity.

An interage plan may operate within a graded framework or on a nongraded basis. In a graded system, the group includes children who consider themselves in specific grades. Nongraded interage programs eliminate grade labels. Both approaches incorporate the concept of continuous progress for each member of the group.

The age range within a group commonly is about three years, but in a few instances primary children and high school students have been put together in working groups. In a multigraded program, a primary class usually has approximately an equal number of first-, second-, and third-grade pupils. The pupils in a multigraded intermediate group are distributed about equally among fourth-, fifth-, and sixth-graders.

Grouping within the classroom disregards grade levels and allows children of similar interests and abilities to work as a team. A pupil moves from one grade level to another as his skill and ability in different subjects indicate. He advances at a different rate in each subject. In one area of study he may be working with pupils who are considerably older than he is. In another, the members of his group may be distinctly younger than he. If the unit consists of three grade levels, a pupil usually starts as one of the youngest in the group and spends his last year as one of the oldest. Flexibility within the group avoids having him held back or pushed ahead because he is in a particular grade or has reached a certain age. He can progress at a rate appropriate to his needs.

In a nongraded school, children work together according to their interests, abilities, and needs regardless of age or conventional grade level. Here grouping is very flexible and temporary and is readily changed when the need for shifts appears. Older children gain self-confidence from helping younger ones, and younger ones receive academic help and social and emotional support from the older ones.

This type of organization resembles more closely than conventional programs the real world of the child outside the school, in which people of all ages work and play and learn together. Multiage grouping provides an opportunity for integrating classroom experiences with learning beyond the school and for developing positive attitudes toward continuous learning throughout life. In a sense interage grouping is an attempt to capitalize on some of the academic, psychological, and social advantages of the one-room school.

Although pupil-team learning is generally an accepted part of multiage grouping, it is frequently practiced in classrooms in which the children are all of approximately the same age or at the same grade level. Defined briefly, it is the practice of grouping students in teams of two or more, usually not more than six, with the intention of providing mutual support and help in learning from all members of the team.

Team learning has been found to contribute significantly to furthering individualization of instruction by capitalizing on diversity as well as on commonality of interests and abilities. It can be used in many different learning situations and in all subject areas. It can be employed effectively in developing skills in such specific subjects as spelling and arithmetic, but it may prove even more useful in development of attitudes and clarification of values.

The size of the team, its membership, the duration of its working together depend upon its purposes. Team planning, discussion of materials previously studied, learning of specific information and skills, clarification of thinking, investigation of special topics, or developing a group product require different organization and operational procedures. Some teams may work for an entire year with the same membership. Others may change from day to day.

Significant Components   *Which ones are essential?*

1. Sufficient time should be taken to develop readiness in the students—understanding of the purposes, possible advantages, potential pitfalls, expected results, and willingness to accept responsibility.
2. Provision should be made for avoiding overdependence of some students on other members of the group.
3. Understanding on the part of the community, school administration, teachers, and students is vital.
4. A wide range of materials is needed.
5. The value of differences as well as similarities among members of the groups should be recognized and used to advantage.
6. Opportunity should be provided for independent and individual study by members of the groups.
7. Flexibility in time, space, and staffing enhances the likelihood of success.

8. Evaluation should be in terms of individual as well as group learning. Assignments should be clear and specific.

9. Continuous progress should be an inherent part of the program.

10. Team learning should be looked upon as a method to be altered or discontinued when other approaches seem to be more effective.

11. The program should capitalize on its opportunity for promoting group processes as a means of working together on problems of common concern.

12. Team learning should not neglect activities by the entire class nor individual instruction.

13. Membership and size of groups should be changed whenever such change promises better results.

14. Team members must be brought to the realization that they can and must contribute to the group process if it is to be productive.

15. The roles, objectives, and norms must be agreed upon and understood by all those involved.

16. Tests and examinations should be taken individually and graded by the teacher.

17. The teacher must be comfortable serving as an adviser, guide, and facilitator who lets the teams proceed according to plans.

18. The emphasis must be on learning rather than on teaching.

19. Special training and inservice work for teachers contribute greatly to success.

20. Safeguards should be established to avoid having older students dominate multiage teams.

21. Democratic procedures should be encouraged and demonstrated.

22. The contributions of all should be respected and recognized.

23. Provision should be made for special difficulties that require intensive instruction.

24. Teams should be selected with care, taking into consideration such factors as common interests, diversity, and compatibility.

25. It should be recognized that multiage grouping and team learning are not effective for all students or all topics.

26. Although it may be difficult, careful evaluation of results is essential.

27. The activities of the groups should be relevant to the curriculum and the goals and objectives of the school.

Proposed Advantages   *With which ones do you agree?*

1. Individualized learning is promoted through team learning.
2. Multiage grouping provides models for the younger members of the group.
3. Children can learn from one another with little fear of appearing to be stupid.
4. Inattention, boredom, and disciplinary problems are reduced.
5. The group activities are similar to experiences that students will encounter in life out of school.
6. The teacher is given time to work with small groups and individuals.
7. Each student has more opportunity to express his ideas than in a classroom using another method.
8. Children learn to criticize without offending and to be criticized without being offended.
9. Students learn to understand one another and to appreciate one another's ideas and views.
10. Working in pairs or with a few classmates encourages a student to attempt more difficult tasks than he would undertake before the entire class.
11. Students gain experience in planning, studying, thinking, and critical evaluating.
12. Pupil-team learning fosters the joy of giving and appreciation for help received.
13. Pupils receive immediate feedback from other members of the group and can redirect their efforts if they have made a mistake.
14. Students learn self-discipline and personal responsibility.
15. Tensions are relieved when pupils receive immediate help with problems that they cannot solve by themselves.
16. Interage grouping fosters worthy home membership.

Criticisms and Difficulties to Be Anticipated   *Do you agree?*

1. Pupil-team learning usually degenerates into a situation in which the most vocal rather than the most able take over.
2. The result of this approach is that the blind are leading the blind.
3. The programs require more time and work on the part of teachers.

4. Teachers usually have more students to work with.
5. Teachers are not prepared to work in these programs.
6. In multiage grouping, older children and high achievers resent being assigned to work with younger or slower ones.
7. Many problems resulting from differences in physical and social maturity arise in multiage groups.
8. It is almost impossible to evaluate the progress of each individual and to grade him fairly when he is a member of a team.
9. Adjusting to constantly changing groups is very upsetting to many children.
10. Moving team members from one group to another becomes very complicated.
11. Satisfactory criteria are not available for assigning pupils to groups or for moving them from one group to another.
12. It is almost impossible to hold intelligent parent-teacher conferences.
13. Parents want to have objective evidence of their child's progress, not of a team's achievement.
14. Students waste time finding material that could be presented to them more efficiently by the teacher.
15. The academic progress of superior students is impeded by their having to help the slower students in the group.

Summary Assessment

Multiage grouping and pupil-team learning have emerged as popular new organizational patterns because of their apparent initial success in arousing student interest and cooperation and in developing self-discipline. Many teachers have realized for some time that lecturing to large groups and other conventional teaching strategies were not producing the results that were expected of them.

Both of the new approaches appear to be well accepted by students and seem to generate mutual aid and cooperative effort toward achieving common goals. Besides teaching pupils to live and work together in respect for one another, the methods seem to supply in-group support for individualized learning. They assist in breaking down barriers to individualization that result from rigid grade standards and lock-step progress and encourage planning vital experiences that are uniquely appropriate for each learner.

The advantages of working together in teams may be more social and emotional than academic. Some children develop confidence in leadership roles. Others profit from the emotional support of their group. By helping and being helped all of them develop values and attitudes that should benefit them in life beyond the classroom.

Warren Hamilton and Walter Rehwoldt report that data from a controlled experiment conducted in Torrance, California, reveal higher academic achievement as well as superior personal development and social adjustment for students in multiage classes in comparison with the progress of single-grade classes.

Like any other organizational plans, these two approaches cannot be used equally well for all types of learning nor with all kinds of children. Early reports attest to their effectiveness for learning specific skills and information such as those involved in mathematics and spelling and for developing attitudes and clarifying values.

It appears that neither pupil-team learning nor multiage grouping will lighten the teacher's load as some critics imply. Neither will they solve many of the persistent problems of motivation and instruction.

Although it must not be overworked, there are many indications that small-group activity is a productive classroom technique for developing leadership and creative learning. Caution must be exercised to prevent abuses in grouping and to avoid pitfalls inherent in extensive involvement of students in planning, decision-making, and classroom management.

Dorothy Westby-Gibson places grouping in proper perspective by pointing out:

> Whatever grouping practices we choose, however, cannot solve all our teaching-learning problems. For grouping, let us emphasize once more, is not a method—it is only a means of classroom management. What remains most important is the nature and quality of the instructional program.*

These patterns for organizing students for learning do not determine the curriculum content nor the goals and objectives of the school. Whether or not they should be introduced as a significant part of an instructional program will depend upon the

---

*Dorothy Westby-Gibson, *Grouping Students for Improved Instruction* (Englewood Cliffs, N. J.: Prentice-Hall, 1966), p. 32.

contribution they can make to achieving the program objectives. They will not fulfill all the high hopes of their advocates. They cannot be as bad as their critics suggest.

Many of the benefits that the proponents of the two plans ascribe to them might properly be called concomitant or incidental learnings, that result from direct student involvement in planning and implementing common experiences. In a democratic society, these outcomes may seem to be self-evident benefits.

Although they may appear to be obvious, positive outcomes must not be taken for granted. The activities must be carefully evaluated to determine the degree to which agreed-upon goals and objectives have been realized.

In balance, the probable benefits of interage grouping and pupil-team learning bode well for their continued growth and improvement. It presently appears that they hold promise for contributing significantly to the education of young people, and that they deserve objective consideration as useful tools for promoting learning.

A Few Leaders in the Movement

Robert H. Anderson
   Harvard Univ.
John M. Bahner
   Institute for Development
   of Educational Activities
Robert B. Borcheratt
   Rossford (Ohio) School Dist.
B. Frank Brown
   Institute for Development
   of Education Activities
Robert DeLozier
   Univ. of Tennessee
Donald D. Durrell
   Boston Univ.
J. Carl Fleming
   Fernwood Schools, Portland, Oreg.
John I. Goodlad
   Univ. of California at Los Angeles
Warren W. Hamilton
   U. S. International Univ.
Richard Hawk
   Univ. of Chicago

J. H. Hull
   California Educational Research
   Commission
Gerald T. Kowitz
   Univ. of Oklahoma
Walter J. McHugh
   Boston Univ.
Pauline McKeon
   Johnson Ave. School
   Cajon, Calif.
John C. Manning
   Univ. of Minnesota
Walter Rehwoldt
   U. S. International Univ.
George B. Rockfort, Jr.
   Northeastern Univ.
Richard P. Runyon
   Long Island Univ.
Samuel G. Sava
   Institute for Development of
   Educational Activities

Harvey B. Scribner
  New York City Schools
John L. Tewksbury
  Ohio State Univ.
Herbert A. Thelen
  Univ. of Chicago

Lydia Welborn
  Johnson Ave. School
  Cajon, Calif.
Lorne H. Woolatt
  New York State Education Dept.

A Few Places Where the Innovation Is Used

Abington, Mass.	Denver, Colo.	Rock Island, Ill.
Alachua County, Fla.	Des Moines, Iowa	Rossford, Ohio
Auburn, Ala.	El Cajon, Calif.	Sarasota County, Fla.
Bethpage, N. Y.	Honeoye Falls, N. Y.	Seattle, Wash.
Boston, Mass.	Janesville, Wis.	Tampa, Fla.
Boston University	Johnson City, Tenn.	Toledo, Ohio
Centerville, Ohio	Larchmont, N. Y.	Tonawanda, N. Y.
Chelmsford, Mass.	Madison, Wis.	Torrance, Calif.
Chicago, Ill.	Madison Hts., Mich.	University City, Mo.
Columbia, S. C.	Marshall, Minn.	Univ. of Tennessee
Dayton, Ohio	Portland, Oreg.	Wooster, Ohio
Dedham, Mass.	Racine, Wis.	Youngstown, Ohio

Annotated References

"All Pupils Aided by Team Learning," *The New York Times,* CVIII, No. 37, 031 (June 14, 1959), 156. Summarizes the team-learning study at Dedham, Massachusetts. Discusses observations in the classroom and many advantages found by allowing students to progress at their own rate through team learning.

Borcheratt, Robert B., "A Self-Designed Science Curriculum," *Science Teacher,* XXXVII, No. 8 (1970), 21. Illustrates self-contained science units designed by a junior high school science teacher. Groupings were both homogeneous and heterogenous. Cooperation of group members and logical organization of thoughts were results.

Cohn, Maxine D., "Pairing of Remedial Students," *Journal of Reading,* XIV, No. 1 (1970), 109-112. Advocates pairing remedial students in order to relieve anger and hostility; ease tensions, elevate the self-image, and stimulate learning through competition. Fulfilling these emotional needs then leads to more essential learning tasks.

Del Giorno, Bette J. and Millicent E. Tissair, "The Research Team Approach to Learning: Part II," *School Science and Mathematics,* LXX, No. 623 (1970), 833-844. Discusses studies conducted at various grade levels involving students, in teams of three, who were individually assigned to a specific responsibility for investigating a research problem. Students showed enthusiasm and great knowledge gain in their field.

Dembro, Myron H. and Thomas L. Good, "Team Learning: Implications for the Classroom Teacher and School Psychologist," *Journal of School Psychology*, VIII, No. 1 (1970), 57-59. Deals with the methods, procedures, and implications involved in team learning. The article illustrates the roles played by both the teacher and learner in the pupil-team learning situation.

Durrell, Donald D., "Pupil Team Learning," *Instructor*, LXXIV, No. 6 (1965), 5, 130. Advocates pupil-team learning because of its primary concern for increased efficiency and effectiveness in the classroom. The article discusses grouping, activities, and techniques in suggesting that educators should explore this method.

Elder, Glen H., *The Student Group in Formal Education*. Washington D. C.: American Education Research Association, 1970. Recognizes that individual differences and opinions in a heterogeneous group can themselves be resources of exchange. This will lead to intellectual growth and to interdependence of students.

Fleming, J. C., "Pupil Tutors and Tutees Learn Together," *Today's Education*, LVIII, No. 7 (1969), 22-24. Example of pupil teams used for tutoring. A student tutors other students in a lower grade in a pupil-team situation. The article stresses the student role in both teaching and learning.

Franklin, Marian Pope, "Multigrading in Elementary Education," *Childhood Education*, XLII, No. 9 (1967), 513-515. Discusses the similarities and differences between multigraded and nongraded classes and reviews the research done at Torrance, California. Also mentions places using multigraded classes.

Frazier, A., "Learning in Pairs," *Grade Teacher*, LXXXVII, No. 7 (1970), 95-100. Discusses the factors involved in setting up a learning by pair situation or program. Goals and objectives are outlined as well as criteria for grouping. Examples of programs are listed along with organization and results.

Glotthorn, Alan A., *Learning in a Small Group*. Dayton, Ohio: Institute for Development of Educational Activities, 1971. Discusses the effectiveness of pupil-team learning in education today. Brings to light some of the problems and how to cope with these problems. Various techniques and the values that can be derived are explained.

Graffam, Donald T., "Why Not Team Learning?" *Journal of Teacher Education*, XV, No. 3 (1964), 289-292. Relates the experiences of the author in advocating team teaching. The factors involved, principles, and objectives are listed and explained. The goals of team learning, to make a better citizen who can work in groups and the improvement of learning, are concluded as the basis for team learning.

Hamilton, Warren and Walter Rehwoldt, "By Their Differences They Learn," *National Elementary Principal*, XXXVII, No. 4 (1971), 27-29. Proposes that the essential quality in a learning environment is its internal differences rather than its similarities. The greater the diversity among children in a group, the more the children will be able to learn from each other.

Hawk, Richard L., "Individualized Instruction in the School Setting," *Educational Horizons*, IL, No. 3 (1971), 71-83. Looks at the school of tomorrow, characterized by a new level of humanistic emphasis. A balanced adaptation must occur between learner and teacher.

Heathers, Glenn, "Grouping," *Encyclopedia of Educational Research,* 4th ed., pp. 559-570. London: Macmillan, 1969. Provides an over-all description of various types of groupings. Many research projects are cited and a very adequate bibliography is included.

Hull, J. H., "Multigrade Teaching," *The Nation's Schools,* LXII, No. 1 (1958), 33-36. Summary of a three-year study on the multigrade system at Torrance, California. The results of their research findings (all favoring multiage grouping) are given.

Hunter, Madeline, "Individualized Instruction," *Instructor,* LXXIX, No. 7 (1970), 53-63. Explains the various meanings of individualized instruction in which pupil-team learning is included. Several dimensions of learning are discussed along with problems involved and results obtained.

Jeep, H., and J. W. Hollis, "Group Dynamics in Action," *The Clearing House,* XLI, No. 4 (1966), 203-209. Advocates group dynamics in learning for individual to grow toward independence and self-security. Listed are four significant elements that characterize a good learning situation, some factors involved in establishing group dynamics, and 46 principles of group dynamics.

Job, Kenneth A., "Helping Small Groups Teach Themselves," *Instructor,* LXXX, No. 2 (1970), 138-140. Objects to giving self-instruction assignments to small groups before the group has had an opportunity to practice specific skills for group activities. Steps for introducing group skills are listed.

Klausmeier, Herbert J., Chester W. Hanis, and William Wiersma, *Strategies of Learning and Efficiency of Concept Attainment by Individuals and Groups.* Madison, Wis.: University of Wisconsin, 1964. Relates research done in efficiency of strategies with three types of stimuli material. This research was done on groups of various sizes and various ages and discusses the effects and conclusions.

Lewis, James, *Administering the Individualized Instruction Program.* West Nyack, N. Y.: Parker, 1971. Describes the particular atmosphere of the ghetto which tends to miseducate children. The author's personal experiences with individualized study units are presented.

McNamara, Helen, Margaret Carroll, and Marvin Powell, *Individual Progression.* New York: Bobbs-Merrill, 1970. Presents teachers and administrators with the theoretical and applied aspects of individual progression. The book also includes the results of two research studies of individualized instructional programs.

Mauer, David, "Team Learning: 'How Did You Work Number Five?'" *Today's Education,* LVII, No. 9 (1968), 63-64. Advocates team learning for creating incentive and motivation. Describes a school which has incorporated team learning into its program and lists the advantages, including a description of the components of the teaching kit used.

Mitchell, Joy and Richard Zoffness, "Multi-age Classroom," *Grade Teacher,* LXXVIII, No. 7 (1971), 55-61. Discusses multiage classroom at Central School in Larchmont, New York. Philosophy behind program, basic organization, academic achievement of children, and social growth are presented.

Nelson, Pearl A. and Martha A. John, "Suggestions for Group Presentation Techniques in Social Studies and Science," *Journal of Education,* CLII,

No. 4 (1970), 28-30. Advocates methods for use because most students are not aware of the different techniques they can use to produce a group presentation more effectively. Suggestions are offered for more effective techniques and comments from students are listed in response to the effectiveness of techniques.

N. T. L. Institute for Applied Behavioral Science, "Team Learning," *Today's Education,* LVIII, No. 9 (1969), 59. Suggests experimenting with team learning and lists ideas about forming groups. An example is related to explain how team learning works and gives a model for use in a team-learning situation.

Parachini, Sister M. Rose Elaine, "An Experiment in Team Learning," *Catholic School Journal,* LXVIII, No. 1 (1968), 49-50. Describes an experimental program in team learning at the Academy of Holy Names, Tampa, Florida. The program was begun to utilize each student's full potential. Advantages and disadvantages are listed and concludes that a favorable attitude on the student's part is the most advantageous factor.
Advantages and disadvantages are listed and concludes that a favorable attitude on the student's part is the most advantageous factor.

Pearl, Arthur, "Are You Sure Pupils are Better Off at School?" *Nation's Schools,* LXXVIII, No. 2 (1966), 46-48. Advocates the use of cooperative team learning instead of individual competition because there is evidence that students aren't learning positively. Older pupils may be used to teach younger students in the team-learning situation.

Phillips, Gerald M. and Eugene C. Erickson, *Interpersonal Dynamics in the Small Group.* New York: Random House, 1970. Considers the interaction of individuals within a group. Regards their responsibilities of sharing ideas and communicating with each other, their conformity, rank, and influence in the group.

Poirer, Gerard, "Isn't it Time to Change From Linear Teaching to Team Learning?" *Journal of Secondary Education,* XLIV, No. 6 (1969), 243-251. Proposes a sequential outline of a team-learning program. Structure and advantages are stressed for individualized learning. Steps in group dynamics and the method involved are discussed.

Rehwoldt, Walter and Warren W. Hamilton, "An Analysis of Some Effects of Interage and Intergrade Grouping in an Elementary School," Doctoral Dissertation, University of Southern California, January 1957. Points out that in the 1957 Torrance, California, study, the academic achievement of students in wide-range classes was superior to that of students in single-grade classes. The favorable effects of multiage grouping were found on the students' social adjustment and on their personality development.

Runyon, Richard P., "Early Identification of the Gifted through Interage Grouping," Educational Resources Center Information Center, Department of Health, Education, and Welfare, U. S. Office of Education, Part I, July 1962. Explains the formation, rationale, hypotheses, and evaluation of the experiment. Scores of the Metropolitan Achievement Test are interpreted.

――――, "Early Identification of the Gifted through Interage Grouping," Educational Resources Center Information Center, Department of Health, Education and Welfare, U. S. Office of Education, Part II, July 1963. Evaluates the experiment from a behavioral objective point of view. Explains the type of test given to determine the evaluations. Points out areas of further research and evaluation.

Shepherd, Clovis R., *Small Groups: Some Sociological Perspectives.* Scranton, Pa.: Chandler, 1964. Points out the sociological features of a successful small group. Describes the roles of individual members and their responsibilities in participation and interaction within the group.

Smith, Lee L., *Teaching in a Nongraded School.* West Nyack, N. Y.: Parker, 1970. Considers all the aspects of the nongraded school situation. The entire school's program is enhanced by encouraging diversity and creativity in the students.

Stone, Thomas, "Effects of Mode of Organization and Feedback Level on Creative Task Groups," *Journal of Applied Psychology,* LV, No. 4 (1971), 324-330. Records experiment that tested mode of organization on performance and satisfaction of creative task groups. Groups organized in project teams completed the trials faster and had a higher level of task satisfaction than did groups organized according to specialization.

Stott, D. H., "Chemistry by Group Learning," *The Times Educational Supplement,* No. 2668, 2670 (July 8 and 22, 1966), 113, 221. Describes an experiment in group learning and argues that it solves problems that are encountered in repetitive programed learning. Included is a description of how group learning can be utilized in teaching chemistry.

Thelen, Herbert A., "Tutoring by Students," *The School Review,* LXXVII, Nos. 3-4 (1969), 229-244. Advocates and gives reasons for conducting a pupil-team learning program. Stresses the advantage of the pupil overcoming prejudices. The author feels learning through helping each other is advantageous.

Torrance, E. Paul, "Dyadic Interaction as a Facilitator of Gifted Performance," *The Gifted Child Quarterly,* XIV, No. 3 (1970), 139-143. Shows that dyadic interaction of gifted children will facilitate the production of original ideas, stimulate longer persistence in a task, and motivate attempts of more difficult tasks. Explains studies conducted in relation to this suggestion.

Trow, William Clark, "Group Processes," *Encyclopedia of Educational Research,* 3rd ed. New York: Macmillan, 1960. Stresses the role of the individual in a group. Relates how an individual personality can be changed by the influence of a group and how one attains personal satisfactions through group interaction.

Welborn, Lydia and Pauline McKeon, "Team Reading," *Grade Teacher,* LXXXVIII, No. 3 (1970), 96-98. Cites how new life was put into a fifth-grade reading program by pairing students for discussions after individual reading and seatwork assignments. Students learned that "reading is more fun when you share."

Westby-Gibson, Dorothy, *Grouping Students for Improved Instruction.* Englewood Cliffs, N. J.: Prentice-Hall, 1966. Discusses many different ways of grouping students for instruction, briefly mentioning multiage grouping. Has an excellent statement on grouping in general, its purposes and limitations.

Wilken, Robert A., "Team Learning Launched," *The Christian Science Monitor,* LI, No. 45 (1959), 2. Reports on advantages to students and teachers found in the first months of the team-learning study in Dedham, Massachusetts. Learning was based on sharing rather than competition.

Witty, Paul, "Individualized Reading—A Summary and Evaluation," *Elementary English,* XXXVI, No. 6 (1959), 401-412, 450. Presents grouping as a method of individualization. Enumerates types of groups that can be used in a good reading program: achievement groups, special needs, skill teams, tutorial, research, and interest groups.

Wolfson, Bernice J., "The Promise of Multiage Grouping for Individualizing Instruction," *Elementary School Journal,* LXVII (1967), 354-362. Discusses an application of multiage grouping to the University of Chicago nongraded programs. Advantages, adaptability and practical problems of assessment are enumerated. Advantages and problems that may be encountered are presented.

Audiovisual and Other Resources

Multi-Age Grouping: Enriching the Learning Environment (booklet, 40 pp., $1). American Association of Elementary-Kindergarten-Nursery Educators, NEA, 1201 16th St., N. W., Washington, D. C. 20036.

Multi-Grade Plan (film, no charge). Emphasizes individualization and small group study. Saugus Union School District, 26590 Bouquet Canyon Road, Saugus, California 91350.

The Tutors of Fernald (film, 30 min., $185, rental $25). The use of students to tutor other students, mixing children from low- and high-income groups who are underachievers. Special Purpose Films, 26740 Latigo Shore Dr., Malibu, Calif. 90265.

What's New At School (16mm film, sound, 45 min., $250, color $525). CBS News Special contrasts lock-step traditional classroom in New York State with North Dakota classroom which is being converted to open classroom. Carousel Films, Inc., 1501 Broadway, Suite 1503, New York, N. Y. 10036.

Part Four
Newly Emphasized Curriculum Content

Drug Abuse Education 21

Definition

Drug abuse education is an instructional program designed to help students of all ages deal with the drug culture. It usually consists of three elements: 1) information and understandings of drugs and their use for the benefit of man; 2) development of insights, attitudes, and values that sensitize young people to the dangers of drug misuse and prevent their falling prey to the ravages of drug abuse and addiction; and 3) rehabilitation of those who have been damaged by wrong decisions. Dangers involved in the use of tobacco, alcohol, and marijuana are commonly included with the problems of heavier drugs.

Drug misuse and abuse has always been a serious social and health problem. In America it assumed special significance during the 1960's. Society as a whole, particularly youth, searched for new ways of coping with frustrations, re-explored the meaning of life, revolted against old values, challenged long-accepted customs and practices, and groped frenziedly for self-fulfillment amid contradictions of poverty and affluence and national and international tensions and conflicts that made little sense.

The explosion in drug use and abuse was part of an accelerated press for personal rights and freedom of self-expression. It was abetted by the weakening influence of the home and church, anonymity resulting from urbanization and technology, mobility of population, adult use of tranquilizers and stimulants for the relief of a variety of tensions, and advertising by mass media. Youth's inherent desire for new experiences and its tendency to follow the crowd in its search for social acceptance were exploited.

By the middle 1960's the misuse of drugs had become a serious problem on college campuses throughout the country. From there it moved into the high schools, junior high schools, and elementary schools. Simultaneously drug abuse increased on the streets, in business and industry, and in the armed forces.

Federal, state, and local governments turned their attention to the mounting problem. Crash programs of legal restriction and law enforcement were instituted. Churches, clubs, and community agencies recognized the need for immediate action. Public debate sprang up concerning the effects of such drugs as marijuana and their prohibition or legalization.

Much of the controversy concerning drugs centers around the distinction between legal and illegal drugs. There are those who contend strongly that some legal drugs are harmful, and that some illegal ones are harmless. A point at issue in the debate about legalizing certain drugs is whether or not they are habit-forming and whether or not they are beneficial when used in moderation.

A sound drug abuse education program starts in the home and early grades, moving from an understanding of the differences among various drugs and their uses to increased emphasis on the dangers of drug misuse and abuse. In the middle school years, attention is directed to the importance of drugs for good health—mental, emotional, and physical. The high school student studies ways of protecting himself and society against unwise and illegal use of drugs. Throughout the total program emphasis is on the person, not on drugs. Developing attitudes and values that will enable the student to make wise choices when he is confronted with the need to make them is the paramount objective of the program.

The difficulty of the challenge and the controversies that are likely to arise in implementing a drug abuse program should not deter schools from discharging their responsibility for helping youth face the realities that are sure to confront them. The problem demands the support and cooperation of the home, government, and all community and social agencies. Unless schools address themselves seriously to solving the problems associated with drug abuse, these problems will continue to be seedbeds for delinquency, crime, and misery.

Significant Components   *Which ones are essential?*

1. To avoid having instruction come too early for some and too late for others, special attention must be given to individualization.
2. The goals and objectives must be carefully developed and clearly stated.
3. A balance should be maintained between providing information, prevention, and rehabilitation.
4. Drug abuse education should extend from the primary grades through the college years.
5. An interdisciplinary approach is advantageous. Drug abuse education should be a natural outgrowth of study in many subject areas.
6. Distinctions should be made among drug use, drug misuse, and drug abuse.
7. Public support and cooperation are necessary.
8. Openness, honesty, and objectivity are of particular significance.
9. Provision should be made for working closely with private and public agencies in the community.
10. Research findings and reliable information are needed.
11. Only teachers with competence in the development of attitudes and values and special skill in dealing with difficult situations should be involved in the program.
12. The main concern of the program is with people, not with drugs.
13. The role of the teacher should be that of helping students clarify their values and attitudes and make wise choices for which they can be responsible.
14. Teachers must engage in careful, intense, and continuous planning.
15. Commitment should be made to providing the time needed to achieve the objectives.
16. Programs should be tailored to fit each school and to meet the needs of each student.
17. Student participation in planning, implementation, and evaluation is vital.

18. Moving the program out into the community and brining the community into the school are highly beneficial.
19. Whenever possible, moralizing and preaching should be avoided.
20. Continuous evaluation and program revision are very important.
21. A strong counseling program should be integrated with the instructional program.
22. An effective program strikes a balance and helps children differentiate between the benefits of drugs to the life of modern man and the dangers of their misuse.

Proposed Advantages   *With which ones do you agree?*

1. Drug abuse education prepares a student for one of the difficult decisions that is likely to confront him very soon.
2. Young people are helped to find ways to deal with reality other than by using drugs as an escape.
3. Both teachers and students expand their insights concerning personal beliefs and attitudes.
4. Internalizing information about drugs and their use clarifies the learner's values.
5. The school replaces the street as a source of information and as the leading agent for shaping attitudes and directing behavior relating to drugs.
6. Drug abuse education makes it possible to avoid damage to the chromosomes that might cause congenital damage for generations.
7. Youth learns to treat persons with drug problems with compassionate understanding.
8. Students learn to deal intelligently with problems and to accept responsibility for wrong decisions.
9. Drug addiction is reduced.
10. Schools cannot stand idly by ignoring such a serious problem of individuals and of society as a whole.
11. The probability of a successful and satisfying life is increased.
12. The students assume responsibility for ordering their lives and establishing guidelines for exercising their freedom.
13. Family life is improved in the present and for the future.
14. Attacking and solving real life problems enhances respect for the schools and increases public support of education.
15. Unemployability is prevented.

Criticisms and Difficulties to Be Anticipated   *Do you agree?*

1. Controlling the use of drugs is not the proper responsibility of the school.

2. Although schools can't handle the responsibilities that they now are charged with, they are always reaching out to take on more jobs.

3. Taking a stand for the use of drugs is terrible.

4. Taking a stand against the use of drugs is an invasion of the privacy of young people and a violation of their civil rights.

5. Young people should be allowed to make up their own minds about using or not using drugs.

6. Drug education makes children curious and encourages experimentation.

7. Many drug education programs teach students where they can secure drugs, how they can use them, and how they can escape legal consequences.

8. Drugs defy description. Many household sprays, spices, and foods are drugs.

9. Research has produced few facts about drugs that can be safely taught in the schools. Both fact and fiction masquerade as truth in drug abuse education.

10. There are many better ways to cope with drug misuse than through school programs.

11. The dangers of drugs are grossly exaggerated.

12. Very few teachers are available who can handle instruction in such a way that more benefit than harm results.

13. Drug education programs teach the morality and values of middle-class America.

14. Everyone uses drugs—for health or sickness, for pain or pleasure, to stay asleep or awake, to pep up or relax.

15. There is very little material available that can be accepted as honest and objective enough for instructional purposes.

Summary Assessment

It appears that the views of the proponents and opponents of drug controls and drug abuse education have polarized to the point where people have retreated into two camps, each group accusing the other of having closed their minds to the views of the other. They both seem unwilling to explore the possibility that they have overlooked significant facts.

Perhaps certain drugs are considered harmful when they aren't. Perhaps some people consider some harmful drugs harmless. Perhaps certain laws should be relaxed or repealed. Others should perhaps be strengthened, and additional legislation may be needed. Some people may be placing their personal rights and freedom above societal needs. Some may be trying to impose unnecessary restrictions on others.

It can be hoped that truth will come out of the differences and conflict. But finding a better way in drug abuse demands open-mindedness and responsibility. All those engaged in this urgent search for a better way must be prepared to make some personal sacrifices for the general welfare and to comply with individual personal desires.

The way of education has many advantages over the way of legal prescription and restriction. Reducing all human behavior to compliance with legal requirements seems to be shirking the exercise of moral responsibility. It seems to be a sure way of destroying individual freedom, for under such conditions self-direction and freedom of choice are replaced by enforcement of law. The line between what is legally permissible and what is morally right often becomes blurred. Living to the limit of the law usually results in stricter laws that further curtail freedom of choice.

Every year hundreds of new chemicals are developed and hundreds of new drugs are marketed. Old ones by the dozens are declared unsafe. Yet the youngest people are exposed to more and more drug users and little drug education. In the meantime increasing numbers are experimenting with the use of drugs not knowing what they are doing. It is likely that the schools will increase their attention to drug abuse education, sex education, child and adolescent psychology, and counseling in order to prepare students for their roles in the social structure. Education will help students to use beneficial drugs and to avoid abuse by using harmful ones.

The effectiveness of drug abuse programs will come under close scrutiny. Goals and objectives need to be clarified. Decisions must be made to determine whether the prime focus should be on providing information, preventing drug abuse, building positive attitudes, or rehabilitating drug addicts. Reliable information needs to be prepared. Productive methods and appropriate activities need to be developed that will involve students in making choices and responsible decisions.

The schools cannot long stand aloof from fighting drug abuse. As public pressure for the schools to develop programs of instruction mounts, educators realize that the problem is critical, and that the need for drug abuse education is great. But their lack of experience in the field and the absence of tested programs arouse uncertainty and apprehension.

Gradually it has been recognized that drug abuse is often the symptom of other related problems such as poor health, unwanted pregnancy, venereal disease, social inadequacies, and personal failures. Because of the interrelatedness of these many problems, society and education will have to view drug abuse education in its total perspective. Attacking the underlying causes will require a massive effort. If the results are to be permanent, it seems reasonable to proceed on the assumption that they will have to be achieved through education. To many educators the magnitude of the problem is baffling.

A Few Leaders in the Movement

American School Health Association
Kent, Ohio
Harold Cornacchia
San Francisco State College
Gerald Edwards
Agricultural and Technical College,
Greensboro, S. C.
Robert Elliott
Univ. of Colorado
J. F. Jekell
Yale Univ.
Barbara B. Johnson
City Community College, Brooklyn

Walter Modell
Cornell Univ. Medical College
National Clearinghouse for Drug
Abuse Information
Chevy Chase, Md.
National Institute of Mental Health
Rockville, Md.
Carmen Ness
Western Illinois Univ.
Stanley F. Yolles
State Univ. of New York at
Stonybrook

A Few Places Where the Innovation Is Used

Butler Univ.
Copiaque, Long Island,
N. Y.
Coronado, Calif.
Fort Bragg, Calif.
Glen Cove, N. Y.

Livonia, Mich.
Lower Merion Twp., Pa.
Seymour, Conn.
Smithtown, Long Island,
N. Y.

South San Francisco,
Calif.
Univ. of Arizona
Univ. of Cincinnati
Westfield, Conn.

Annotated References

American School Health Association and Pharmaceutical Manufacturers Associations, "Teaching About Drugs—A Curriculum Guide K-12." Kent, Ohio: American School Health Association, 1970. In addition to a curriculum outline for grades K-12, this volume also contains works on specific topics (depressants, drugs in our society, etc.) by different authors.

Aubrey, Roger F., "Drug Education: Can Teachers Really Do the Job?" *Teachers College Record,* LXXII, No. 3 (1971), 417-422. Sets forth the premise that the prevention of drug abuse has been thrust on schools, the least likely institution to dissuade youngsters. This procedure is understandable, and therefore schools cannot shirk the responsibility. The author moves on to raise questions about the schools' competency for the job, not being able or willing to give drug education top priority, and methods of attempting to "teach" this matter.

Barrins, Phyllis C., "Drug Abuse: the Newest and Most Dangerous Challenge to School Boards," *American School Board Journal,* CLVII, No. 4 (1969), 14-18. Describes many freak incidents of drug abuse and states "The African Black variety of marijuana is now finding its way into the United States. It is an addictive strain of the plant . . . that can cause withdrawal symptoms similar to . . . heroin." Also cites several programs including one school's mandatory physical test for drug abuse. (American Civil Liberties Union promised to bring suit.)

————, "How to Face Up to Drug Abuse in Your Schools and in Your Community," *American School Board Journal,* CLVIII, No. 1 (1970), 17-20, 26. Uses scare tactics ("I don't think there's any question that within a year or two, from 40 to 60 per cent of elementary students will be frequent users, not only of marijuana, but of harder, addictive drugs") and moral persuasion ("Nothing fortifies children against possible drug abuse better than the respect for others"). It outlines a program which includes "Ask school authorities to document every case of drug-taking" and "Notify local disk jockeys that lyrics pushing drug use are OUT."

Blavat, Herbert and William Flocco, "A Survey of a Workable Drug Abuse Program," *Phi Delta Kappan,* LII, No. 9 (1971), 523-533. Discusses a brief program aimed at drugs, drug abuse, alcohol and smoking. Its effectiveness over a short-term period was positive. The effects of classes, counseling, and parental influence were appraised.

Deardon, M. H. and J. F. Jekel, "A Pilot Program in High School Drug Education Utilizing Nondirective Techniques and Sensitivity Training," *Journal of School Health,* XLI, No. 3 (1971), 118-124. Discusses a program which tends to sensitivity training and evaluates it in terms of changes in behavior and attitude. Short-term accomplishments were positive.

Dreier Educational Systems, *Drug Education for Elementary Teachers.* Highland Park, Ill.: Dreier Education Systems, 1970. Plans a program for elementary teachers including background information and techniques. Lesson plans, resources material, and suggested approaches and activities are presented.

"Drug Hearings Produce Agreement on One Point: Starting Drug Education Early, Even in Preschool," *Education Summary,* XXIV, No. 8 (1971). Results of hearings by National Commission on Marijuana and Drug Abuse produced conflicting and confusing testimony which included the recommendation indicated by the title above. Alarming trend for younger children to begin use of pot and failure of school programs in nine Washington, D. C., area schools are reported.

Elliott, Robert, "Narcotics: A New Area of Secondary School Responsibility," *North Central Association Quarterly,* XLIV, No. 4 (1970), 325-334. Discusses a five-point program emphasizing people rather than drugs, desirability of teaching the subject in the schools, open discussion by students, provision of alternatives, and a varied approach. The examination of the total drug problem presents the causes, defines drugs, and stresses the failure of many traditional programs.

Federal Source Book: "Answers to the most frequently asked questions about drug abuse," Chevy Chase, Md.: National Clearinghouse for Drug Abuse Information, 1970. Includes answers to questions from "What is a drug?" to "What is known about belladonna and jimson weed abuse?" The fact book was produced jointly by the departments of Defense, HEW, Justice, Labor and the Office of Economic Opportunity.

Gelinas, M. V., "Classroom Drug Scene," *American Education,* VI, No. 9 (1970), 3-5. Reports on SFSC workshop where sensitivity training was used in drug education (inservice training for professionals). It urges schools to become more people-oriented for effective drug education programs.

Johnson, Barbara B., "A Junior High School Seminar on Dangerous Drugs and Narcotics," *Journal of School Health,* XXXVIII, No. 1 (1968), 84-87. Reports on a discussion-panel-film program designed to convince students not to use "dangerous drugs." They felt successful. "We feel that we really 'reached' most of these young people. . . ."

Jordan, Clifford W., "A Drug Abuse Project," *Journal of School Health,* XXXVIII, No. 10 (1968), 692-695. Claims that if students were furnished with facts and a basic knowledge of the dangers of drug misuse, they would refrain from using drugs. The program has not yet been assessed in practice. The development of the three-phase program in the Coronado Schools is explained.

Ketterman, Clark S., "A Drug Abuse Workshop," *School Counselor,* XVII, No. 2 (1969), 99-101. Presents a case study of the Metropolitan School District. Sources of pharmaceutical materials and information are included.

Leach, Glenn, "Drug Abuse Is Hitting Younger Children," *Instructor,* LXXIX, No. 1 (1969), 60-61. Identifies the problem with drugs and lists elementary drug facts. It continues with a survey of pointers: "school is legally obligated to notify local or county enforcement," "program for parents," "positive programs are needed based on fact."

Marx, Sanford H., "How a Health Council Developed a Narcotics Education Program," *Journal of School Health,* XXXVIII, No. 4 (1968), 243-246. Lays out three-phase narcotics education program. The article covers the medical side of the drug problem; moral, social, and legal implications; and a film-panel discussion.

Mikeal, Robert L. and Mickey C. Smith, "A Positive Approach to Drug Education," *Journal of School Health,* XL, No. 8 (1970), 450-452. Restates facts and definitions of drugs and other terminology. "Values" have no importance; drug education must be restructured around "objectively empirical" knowledge.

Miller, Theodore J., "Drug Abuse: Schools Find Some Answers," *School Management,* XIV, No. 4 (1970), 22-31. A lucid presentation of what prompted one school system, Westfield, New Jersey, to develop a comprehensive program of drug education (drug over-dose deaths of six teenagers) through corollary programs of district attorneys' offices.

Modell, Walter and Alfred Lansing, *Drugs.* New York: Time, 1967. An historical survey of drugs, concluding with forms of abuse and use. It reveals the story of drugs from its beginnings in homeopathic medicine to the assembly line of pills and capsules.

Moskowitz, R., "Leaving the Drug World Behind; Awareness House," *American Education,* VI, No. 1 (1970), 3-6. Develops the theory of a community-school clinic (outside school grounds) where students can receive drug information and sensitivity training—"truth-rap sessions."

Otto, James H., Lloyd J. Julian, and J. Edward Tether, *Modern Health,* pp. 136-141. New York: Holt, 1959. Exemplifies the point of view and means of persuasion typical of traditional instruction. It covers alcohol and tobacco as well as narcotics.

Petrillo, Robert F., "A Comprehensive Action Model to Combat Drug Abuse in High School," *Journal of School Psychology,* VIII, No. 3 (1970), 226-230. Adopts a program policy for dealing with the drug problem. The crash program included essential drug information, parental education, increased supervision in priority areas, peer group counseling, creation of community acceptance and participation.

Pinkerton, Peter B., "A Crash Program On Drug Abuse," *Journal of Secondary Education,* XLIII, No. 5 (1968), 228-232. Reports on program at Buena High School, Ventura Unified District, California. The students' questions were studied to find the areas of conflict, interest, and importance.

"A Preventative Package Kids can Relate to," *School Management,* XIV, No. 4 (1970), 25. The Do-It-Now Foundation offers a packet, described in this article, that includes a rock recording, anti-drug "spots" for local media, a drug "I.Q. test," a counselor training program, a description of the drug education program of Paramount, California. There are also materials for parents, and questionnaires and other materials for students.

"Principal's Problem: Helping a Possible Drug User," *Instructor,* LXXX, No. 5 (1971), 37. Panel discussion about measures to be taken by school staff with a drug user. Panel members show insight into drug use problem. "Education based on facts must be presented to children before opinions based on misconceptions are established."

"The Student Drug User May Make a Teacher His only Confidant," *Education Summary,* XXIII, No. 24 (1971), 3-4. Art Linkletter says teachers themselves may be a menace, and children deserve confidentiality. H. Bryce Brooks, whose programs at Awareness House in Tucson are being adopted by other schools, says we are not facing a drug problem but a human problem and should be looking for teachers who are "not experts in drugs, but experts in human relations. Confidentiality between students and teachers or counselors is vital."

Tate, Constance P., "Inservice Education for Teachers," *Science Teacher,* XXXVII, No. 6 (1970), 49-50. Delineates a student-centered program of drug education. It defines the problem as social and the individual must decide whether to use or abuse.

U. S. Department of Health, Education and Welfare, *Resource Book for Drug Abuse Education.* Washington, D. C.: PHS publication No. 1964, 1969. Collective works of different authors on subjects from marijuana to the drug problems. Various drugs and problems are described objectively, and guidelines are suggested for policies and programs of education.

Weinswig, M. H., D. W. Doerr, and S. E. Weinswig, "Drug Abuse Education," *Phi Delta Kappan,* L, No. 4 (1968), 222-223. Enumerates conclusions of a conference on drugs by three schools of pharmacy and the Smith, Kline and

French Laboratories. It was also conceded that materials were "outdated, incomplete, misleading, one-sided, or—even worse—inaccurate."

Winston, Sheldon L., "The Drug Counseling Workshop: A New Resource for Schools," *Journal of Secondary Education,* XLIV, No. 8 (1969), 352-353. Surveys briefly a mandatory program for drug abusers and their parents. It explores "the pharmacological aspects of illegal drugs, the meanings and dangers of drug abuse and personal observations of relevant guest speakers."

Wolk, Donald J., "Youth and Drugs, Guidelines for Teachers," *Social Education,* XXXIII, No. 6 (1969), 667-674. Contains a discussion about the drugs in use. Presents a fair summary of important considerations for a drug program. Suggests that the drugs themselves may not be our major concern.

Yolles, Stanley F., "Managing the Mood Changers," *New York University Education Quarterly,* II, No. 3 (1971), 2-8. Discusses drug problem, the need for drug education, and the education of professionals. Comments on the "untenable position" of teachers in terms of student drug abuse.

Audiovisual and Other Resources

Drug Talk — Some Current Programs (16mm film, sound, color, 30 min., $63.75, rental $12.50). Compares several programs for the secondary level. National Audiovisual Center, Washington, D. C. 20409.

Jordan Paul—One Teacher's Approach (16mm film, sound, b&w, 30 min., $33.23, rental $10). National Audiovisual Center, Washington, D. C. 20409.

Mr. Edler's Class—Drug Education at the Elementary Level (16mm film, sound, color, 30 min., $70.25, rental $12.50). National Audiovisual Center, Washington, D. C. 20409.

Environmental Education and Ecology

22

Definition

Environmental education is the study of man's interaction with his environment. It involves fostering sensitivity to the forces that act upon an ecological community, promoting knowledge and understanding of them, and developing skill in dealing with the conditions that surround the life of man. Above all, however, environmental education seeks to build attitudes and commitment that will preserve and improve the environment.

During the past few years, public attention has been focused upon the reservoirs of disease, poverty, crime, and misery in the centers of large cities. Litter, congestion, unsanitary housing, malnutrition, and a host of anxieties have undermined the mental and physical health of millions of people. It has become clear that air and water pollution, wanton depletion of natural resources, and overpopulation lie at the bottom of the dilemma that man now faces.

Strip mining, soil erosion, mismanaged technology, and toxic materials of many kinds have aroused widespread concern. Expressways and their massive interchanges have ripped through the nation's heartland in utter disregard for the beauty of the natural surroundings or food production. Clear lakes and streams have been turned into cesspools. Smog clouds darken the bright sun and hide the clear blue sky. News media, legislative bodies, and community planners have sounded the alarm about the ecological crisis caused by exploitation of the environment. They have convinced the nation of the need for immediate action if man is going to survive.

Ecology is the branch of biological science which deals with the relationships of living organisms, plants and animals, with one another and with their total environment. Human ecology, environmental control, ecology of population, and ecology of nutrition are some of the subdivisions of the general field. Nature can maintain a favorable balance among its various factors, but man's ruthless interference with the processes of nature has upset the balance and has created grave dangers. Suddenly man has become concerned about controlling the factors in his environment and has begun to recognize his responsibility for preventing further deterioration and for correcting imbalances in such a way that life can be advanced.

Realization that no life exists on the moon and perhaps not on planets other than earth has stirred in many people a subconscious feeling of awesome responsibility for preserving and improving life on this planet. The need for enhancing the quality of living in our time and to save our earth for future generations has taken on new meaning and greater urgency.

Survival, the quality of life, and the stability of the economy rest upon what John Thompson refers to as the conservation equation and its corollaries:

$$\text{Supply of Resources} = \text{Demand for Resources} \; \overset{+}{-} \; \text{Undetermined Variables}$$

$$\text{Demand} = \text{Population} \times \text{Level of Living}$$

$$\text{Supply of Resources} = \text{Natural Resources} + \text{Technology}$$

Technology has advanced to the point where it can maintain and utilize the supply of resources to support even an increasing population if the level of living does not create unreasonable demands involving misuse and waste. Ecological science has the basic knowledge and will move forward with the expansion of insights necessary to improve the supply of natural resources.

The most fundamental and difficult problem lies in the attitude of the consumer. The responsibility for conservation of resources and for their prudent use rests upon the consumer if survival and a higher quality of life is to be achieved. Intricate economic problems remain to be solved, but it seems quite certain that the demand for goods will be there if they can be supplied.

Ecology and environmental education present new challenges to teachers and administrators, involving new objectives, new content, and new methods. A fundamental change in societal values is needed to generate commitment to environmental control and improvement. Advances in technology will help greatly in solving the grave dilemma in which society finds itself, but it is generally accepted that lasting results can be achieved only through education. People will have to change their view of nature from an attitude of wanting to subdue and exploit it to one of living with it and caring for it. They must come to understand that they do not in reality own their land and other property. They are the trustees of the earth, preserving and improving it for future generations of man.

Significant Components   *Which ones are essential?*

1.   An effective program of environmental improvement is built on the realization that permanent results can be effected only through education.
2.   The desire of people to improve their environment is even more important than knowledge of how to do it.
3.   Inservice training for teachers, supervisors, and administrators is essential for developing a philosophy for an ecology program and commitment to it.
4.   Interest on the part of students, the board of education, and the public must be developed.
5.   The instructional program must be taken into the community, and the human and material resources of the community must be brought into the school.
6.   A variety of equipment and materials is necessary for experimentation and multisensory learning.
7.   The purposes of the entire program and of specific activities in the school and in the community must be clear to the students.
8.   Ecology should be considered a vital part of learning in such areas as language arts, mathematics, art, and social studies, as well as in science.

9. The relation between a good physical environment and the quality of life should be stressed in all aspects of the program.
10. Flexible time schedules and freedom in utilization of space are important.
11. The psychological effects of noise pollution, for example, should receive careful study.
12. The program should help students understand the political and societal problems involved in environmental improvement and enable them to make intelligent decisions about the various issues.
13. The welfare of the individual and of society as a whole should receive balanced consideration and concern.
14. Imagination and careful study is necessary for successful utilization of field experiences in classroom instruction.
15. The urgency of the need for improving the balance of nature cannot be overemphasized.
16. The relationship between natural resources and the national economy should receive due consideration.
17. Conservation programs available from national, state and local sources should be utilized.
18. The responsibility of individuals as well as of industry, business, agriculture, and government should be emphasized.
19. Scientific information should be studied to develop ability to redress and maintain the balance of nature.
20. The program should be systematically evaluated in terms of changes produced in attitudes and behavior.

Proposed Advantages   *With which ones do you agree?*

1. Environmental control and improvement is necessary for survival on this planet.
2. First-hand experience with natural phenomena enables a person to relate his life to them and understand himself better.
3. Understanding ecology will reverse the deterioration in nature and improve the quality of life.
4. Conservation of natural resources provides opportunities for leisure-time activities for a growing population.
5. Knowledge of ecology encourages citizens to support government in promoting the general welfare through conservation programs.
6. The beauties of open spaces enable people to live in dignity.

7. Increased sensitivity to environmental problems makes young and old more willing to care for their immediate surroundings.
8. More than in most fields of study, learning in ecology is likely to carry over into adult life.
9. The relationship of natural resources to economic progress is clearly demonstrated.
10. Understanding the world about him and the differences that set him apart from other creatures gives unity, significance, and purpose to the life of a young person.
11. Excellent inexpensive laboratories for environmental studies are available near almost every school.
12. Study of ecology provides unusual opportunities for furthering self-directed study, scientific investigation, and creativity.
13. Study of natural environment enables the student to predict changes in advance and avoid harmful results.
14. Environmental education stimulates interest and opens up vistas for enrichment in all areas of the school curriculum.
15. Plant and animal life that would otherwise become extinct are preserved.

Criticisms and Difficulties to Be Anticipated   *Do you agree?*

1. Ecology is one field that the schools can stay out of because everybody else is working on the problem.
2. Forcing environmental controls on individuals violates their rights and freedom.
3. Improving the environment involves problems so large and so costly that they are far beyond the capabilities of schools.
4. Teachers lack the technical knowledge to carry on effective programs in environmental education.
5. Teaching ecology causes conflict between pupils and their parents, who have ideas that are distinctly different from those taught in the schools.
6. Environmental education is nothing more than the old courses in conservation that were found useless long ago.
7. At this time the country cannot afford to handcuff industry in its struggle with foreign competition.
8. Schools have had a sorry record in solving community and national problems like pollution.
9. Promoting environmental improvement may arouse the disfavor of business and industry toward education in general.

10. Too much public effort destroys the initiative of individual citizens to improve their own living conditions.

11. Education is too slow a process to cope with many of the environmental problems that must be solved immediately.

12. Ecology is just one of those bandwagons that frequently comes along, makes a lot of noise, and then rapidly disappears.

13. When the current frenzied interest in the field subsides, schools will be left with established programs that they cannot support.

14. Much more must be known about the problems of ecology before the schools can take positions relating to them.

15. Marxists are trying to destroy the productivity of competitive capitalism.

Summary Assessment

The Environmental Quality Education Act of 1970 aroused much interest and stimulated action for environmental education in elementary schools, high schools, and colleges. State departments of education are moving ahead with the development of materials and instructional programs. Special courses are being introduced; but more importantly, emphasis is being placed upon the conservation of natural resources in many subject matter areas through active participation in outdoor experiences. Teachers are being encouraged to couple environmental control and improvement with learning whenever it is possible to do so. The danger still exists, however, that ecology will become just another science course.

Young people have responded to the call with special enthusiasm. Throughout the country, school youth and college students have led campaigns to alert the public to the environmental impasse, to clean up litter, and to combat pollution. In some instances, perhaps, more sound than substance accompanied their efforts to charge industry with full responsibility for solving the problems. Too frequently the young people themselves continue to wear ugly paths across green lawns and litter the landscape with cans and cartons. In many more instances, however, they exhibit praiseworthy sensitivity to their environment and real understanding of many of the problems. Whether their present interest is nothing more than a fad or passing fancy will depend in large measure upon the leadership and example they receive from their parents, neighbors, and teachers.

The need for changing the values and attitudes of present and future generations is urgent. The responsibility for doing it rests upon society as a whole, but particularly upon the schools and colleges. Mastery and conquest of nature have too often aroused man's most destructive instincts. The high value placed upon economic growth and financial gain has caused him to tear up the soil and destroy forests with wild abandon to build motels, casinos, and curio shops. Clear streams, fertile agricultural lands, and the forest primeval have been laid waste when speed, production, and profits required the construction of new superhighways or factories. All this must change quickly if man wants to live in dignity with good physical and emotional health. It is incumbent upon responsible educators to plan and develop programs of environmental education immediately if they are going to be accountable for meeting one of today's most pressing needs. The problem is real, the solution is possible. The challenge is to education.

A Few Leaders in the Movement

Dan Alpert
Univ. of Illinois at Urbana
G. N. Arnstein
National Education Association
Chris Barthel
Miami Univ.
Lynton K. Caldwell
Indiana Univ.
Barry Commoner
Washington Univ.
Raymond F. Dasmann
Conservation Foundation
Garrett De Bell
Stanford Univ.
Joseph L. Fisher
U. S. Dept. of Agriculture
Walter W. Heller
Univ. of Minnesota

Cecil E. Johnson
Riverside College
Grant S. McClellan
New York City
Ian L. McHarg
Univ. of Pennsylvania
Margaret Mead
American Museum of Natural History
Harvey S. Perloff
Univ. of California at Los Angeles
Arthur C. Stern
Univ. of North Carolina
Mark Terry
Univ. of Washington
John L. Thompson
Miami Univ.
Richard H. Wagner
Penn State Univ.

A Few Places Where the Innovation Is Used

Ann Arbor, Mich.
Atlanta, Ga.
Boulder, Colo.
Cincinnati, Ohio

Dartmouth College
Evergreen State College
State of Florida
Lowell, Mass.

Miami Univ.
State of Michigan
Middletown, Ohio
State of New York

Oak Ridge, Tenn.	Univ. of California	Univ. of Wisconsin,
Orange Co., Calif.	at Riverside	Green Bay
Penn State Univ.	Univ. of North Carolina	Washington Univ.
	Univ. of Washington	Wittenberg Univ.

Annotated References

Abramson, Paul, ed., "Ecology," *Grade Teacher,* LXXXVI, No. 5 (1969), 93-127. Discusses these areas of ecology: Why you must teach it, issues behind the science, how it can be taught, four important concepts, lessons to make it come alive, programs, and books and audiovisual materials.

Boughey, Arthur S., *Ecology of Populations.* New York: Macmillan, 1968. Presents the fundamentals of species, populations, interactions with the environment, food supply, and evolution. These topics are related to man's survival in an overcrowding world.

Calder, Nigel, *Eden was No Garden.* New York: Holt, 1967. Attempts to relate man, environment, and technology. The question asked is, will this relationship preserve or destroy humanity and the world?

Caldwell, Lynton K., *Environment, A Challenge to Modern Society.* Garden City, N. Y.: Natural History Press, 1970. Presents the relationship between man and his environment. Social, political, and individual needs are stressed as being most important to the future of our society.

Dasmann, Raymond F., *Environmental Conservation.* New York: Wiley, 1968. Presents the view that man must learn to preserve wild land and wild creatures. This is necessary if man's life is to have real meaning now and in the future.

Ehrlich, Paul R. and Anna H., *Population, Resources, Environment.* San Francisco: Freedman, 1970. Stresses population as it affects man's ability to satisfy basic needs. Education in these three topic areas is proposed as being vital to our future well-being.

Ellis, Helene M., "Build a Nature Trail," *Instructor,* LXXIX, No. 9 (1970), 97. Describes how to build a nature trail by using student committees and local experts. Securing the land, mapping it, deciding the kind of path, and producing guidebooks are described.

Humphrey, Hubert H., chmn., *From Sea to Shining Sea.* Washington, D. C.: Government Printing Office, 1968. Reviews the state of our environment. The committee's recommendations to the President are presented. Lists of public and private agencies which are working on beautification programs are included.

Jensen, Pennfield, "A Student Manifesto on the Environment," *Natural History,* LXXIX, No. 4 (1970), 20-22. Summarizes the need for concern with ecology and lists the demands drawn up by young people at a conference attempting to lay the framework for action. Urgency and commitment are stressed.

Knapp, Clifford, "Noise Pollution," *Instructor,* LXXX, No. 9 (1971), 52-53. Defines noise and discusses the following areas: measuring sound, sound makes noise, noise problems, increasing noise, and noise controls. Suggests six activities in this area.

———, "Particles and Noxious Gases," *Instructor,* LXXX, No. 6 (1971), 76-77. Defines "pure air" and relates the topic to these areas: air pollutants, pollution, sources of air pollution, and solutions. Five classroom activities on this topic are suggested.

———, "Urban Sprawl and Blight," *Instructor,* LXXX, No. 4 (1970), 56-58. Discusses the problems and causes of intercity sprawl and blight. Offers concrete suggestions for an outdoor program in urban areas including purposes, program, and procedures.

McClellan, Grant S., *Protecting Our Environment.* New York: H. W. Wilson, 1970. Reviews the major aspects of pollution: air, water, land, and noise. Some solutions for the pollution problem are proposed.

McHarg, Ian L., *Design with Nature.* Philadelphia: Falcon, 1969. Contrasts the glorious beauty of the outdoors with the plight of our grim cities. Dangers to survival are related to anti-ecological views. Three chapters are devoted to values, their processes and responses.

Marine, Gene, *America the Raped.* New York: Simon and Schuster, 1969. Reviews the basic circumstances which apparently are leading man to his death through the destruction of his world—overpopulation; water, air, and noise pollution; and urban problems. A plea is made for immediate concern.

Marland, S. P., Jr., "Environmental Education Cannot Wait," *American Education,* VII, No. 4 (1971), 6-10. Discusses the apparent decision of the American people and their government to make the 1970's the Environmental Decade. From Capitol Hill to the remote countryside, people are looking to their schools and colleges to provide leadership for solving this most critical problem. Commitment and concern for the environment must be brought into every aspect of learning.

May, Jacques M., *The Ecology of Malnutrition in North Africa.* New York: Haftner, 1967. Concludes that man's feeding systems do not respect international boundaries. The type of information presented is useful when providing foreign aid in the form of food.

Mead, Margaret, "The Island Earth," *Natural History,* LXXIX, No. 1 (1970), 22, 102, 103. Advocates educating children so they will become concerned adults and will be prepared for their task of saving the earth for future generations. Positive attitudes on the part of youth will insure success.

Means, Richard L., "The New Conservation," *Natural History,* LXXVIII, No. 7 (1969), 16, 18-25. Explains why the new conservation movement grew out of the old and how it is being encouraged through books, magazines, and even television. National concern has been aroused.

Perloff, Harvey S., ed., *The Quality of Urban Environment.* Baltimore: Resources for the Future, 1969. Depicts through a series of essays the problems of the present-day urban environment. Some important questions about the quality of modern life are asked.

Perloff, Harvey S. and Richard P. Nathan, eds., *Revenue Sharing and the City.* Baltimore: Johns Hopkins, 1968. Reviews plans for revenue sharing and discusses the advantages of each plan. Walter H. Heller presents a case for revenue sharing, Richard Ruggles disputes the Heller plan, and Lyle Fitch and Carl Shoup comment on both proposals.

Rockefeller, Nelson A., *Our Environment Can Be Saved.* Garden City, N. Y.: Doubleday, 1970. Presents a practical guide to saving our environment. This book is based upon experiences of the Governor, rather than on theory, and is of practical significance as well as of general interest.

Williamson, Robert E., ed., "Ecology: The New Great Chain of Being," *Natural History,* LXXVII, No. 10 (1968), 8-16, 60-69. Discusses the balance which exists in nature and how man has upset that balance. Education can point the way to restoring balance and insuring opportunity for wholesome living in the future.

"The Young Eco-Activists," *Time,* XCIV, No. 8 (1969), 43. Concerns students from the campuses and public schools who have become involved in the ecology movement. Great interest is developing among young people.

Audiovisual and Other Resources

Environmental Crisis: What the Individual Can Do (filmstrip, record, script, $15). Prepared in cooperation with the Association of Classroom Teachers, Association for Supervision and Curriculum Development, Future Teachers of America, National Council for the Social Studies and National Science Teachers Association. NEA, 1201 16th St., N. W., Washington, D. C. 20036.

Environmental Education for the 70's (leaflet, 4 pp. 25¢). American Association of Elementary-Kindergarten-Nursery Educators, NEA, 1201 16th St., N. W., Washington, D. C. 20036.

Man and His Environment: A New Approach to Environmental Education (color filmstrip, record, script, 14 min., $17). To orient teachers and others to new approaches to environmental education. NEA, 1201 16th St., N. W., Washington, D. C. 20036.

Programs in Environmental Education (booklet, 50 pp., $1.50). Describes more than 50 programs that can respond to inquiries from other schools. National Science Teachers Assn., 1201 16th St., N. W., Washington, D. C. 20036.

Occupational and Career Education

23

Definition

Occupational education is that aspect of the school program that is directed toward meeting the employment needs of the individual and the manpower demands of society. Programs of various titles and purposes have existed since the early days of the American schools. Trade schools, manual training, continuation schools, mechanics institutes, job training, industrial arts, community colleges, and industrial, vocational, and technical programs have employed various approaches and emphases. Career planning, occupational information, exploration of new fields of interest, consumer education, specialized skills, interpretation of the nature of industrial society, updating and upgrading of competencies, and the safe use of tools and machinery have all received attention.

In recent years a new dimension of the total field, commonly referred to as *career education,* has come into focus. Beginning in the primary school, the program emphasizes self-awareness, the importance of productive effort, the dignity of all types of work, and the great variety of vocations which offer gainful employment and self-fulfillment.

Growing out of the realization that too many young people feel that they are failures unless they aspire to the traditional professions or management positions, career education emphasizes broad exploration and the importance and respectability of excellent performance in all vocational areas. Career education adds meaning to academic studies and to the development of personal qualities that are important for earning a living and contributing significantly to societal needs.

Occupational education is not new. It is included among the innovative practices of recent years only because of the renewed interest in it on the part of government, education, the general public, business, industry, and the professions. Urgency has been added to the movement by problems of welfare, unemployment, technology, dislocated groups, and school-alienated youth. If their interests and talents can be identified and developed, many of these alienated young people can make significant contributions to society. New perspectives, goals, and innovative programs and procedures have been spearheaded by the Vocational Education Act of 1963 and the Vocational Education Amendments of 1968.

The three most common occupational programs of the secondary schools have been industrial arts, vocational education, and technical education. Industrial arts education stresses the need for general education—an understanding of the nature of industry and technology, their relationship to society and the individual, and the knowledge necessary to be an intelligent producer and consumer of goods. Industrial arts educators take the position that the more than 20,000 listed occupations and the rapid changes occurring in industry and society make it unwise for education to focus on specific skills for specific jobs. Like science teachers, they believe that the learning of significant concepts and principles can stand on its own, regardless of its vocational implications. They prefer to stress exploration of occupational and avocational interests and development of attitudes, concepts, generalizations, and principles.

Vocational education emphasizes the development of knowledge, attitudes, interpersonal relations, and specific skills needed for a particular job. It commonly includes four areas: vocational-industrial education, vocational-agricultural education, vocational-homemaking education, and vocational-business and office education. Most programs are geared to the upper years of the secondary school and the years after high school.

Technical education is designed to develop technicians to perform many of the functions formerly carried out by professional personnel. Students are selected on the basis of their interests and aptitudes. Industrial technicians, for example, are provided with sound knowledge of communications, science, and mathematics and are prepared for high-level positions in design, production, maintenance, planning, and supervision. Well-trained technicians are in increasing demand in medicine, transportation, education, and many other fields. Technical training programs are usually post-secondary and include two or more years of intensive study.

Among the new approaches stressed by recent legislation, particularly the Vocational Education Amendments of 1968, are cooperative training programs and cooperative work experience programs. Under a carefully developed partnership between the employer and the school, the student in a cooperative training program works with a sponsoring supervisor, a teacher-coordinator, and other teachers at the school in part-time vocational training and part-time employment. Cooperative training is an extension of conventional programs of distributive education, office occupations, and diversified occupations. It is enriched by more systematic organization, greater financial support, and deeper commitment on the part of education, business, and industry.

Cooperative work experience education is focused on developing positive attitudes, wholesome interests, and good work habits among disadvantaged youth who are alienated from conventional school programs. These work experiences are the core around which the total school program of the student is built. Job supervision and classroom instruction are tied together inseparably.

Attitudes, work habits, and social relationships with supervisors, co-workers, and teachers are given primary attention. Experiences on the job and in the school are developed in an order of increasing difficulty and complexity, but the emphasis is not on specialized skill performance. Opportunity for success provides satisfaction, enhances self-image, and reinforces learning. The experiences of the classroom are integrated with outside work and thus given new relevance and meaning. Counseling in appropriate behavior is made more effective.

Cooperative work education generally selects students upon the basis of their proficiency for specific stations and is limited to the upper two years of high schools. Students in the program for behavioral improvement are from those who need the experiences most, regardless of competence. Effort is made to assign them at a young age, as soon as arrangements can be made for beneficial experiences. Providing an opportunity for developing a positive attitude toward physical work is one of the promising challenges of Public Law 90-576, known also as the Vocational Education Amendments.

Occupational education recognizes that technological changes demand flexibility and new competencies for entry into the first job after school. Orientation to the world of work and experiences with manual, as well as intellectual, effort are essential for helping youth establish their self-identity, develop respect for working people, and assume a constructive role in society. The dignity of work is especially important in our time.

Significant Components   *Which ones are essential?*

1. Programs of occupational training should be relevant and accountable, based on manpower needs, and kept abreast of changes in jobs and skill requirements.
2. Vocational programs should provide the options of continuing post-secondary training, taking a job, going to college, or a combination of these.
3. Students should be selected with care, but all students should be selected for something.
4. The student should have a definite career objective, high motivation, and aptitude consistent with his objective.
5. Every effort should be made to prevent vocational programs from becoming dumping grounds for nonmotivated students, or those who cause trouble in academic classrooms.
6. Special provision should be made for the academically and socially disadvantaged and the physically handicapped.
7. Prevocational education for occupational orientation should be provided for children from their initial school experience until a career choice has been made, and continuing education should extend beyond the regular school years.
8. Councils of business and industrial leaders are necessary for advising and planning, but the educational program should basically rest with educators.
9. The cognitive, affective, and psychomotor proficiency of the student should all receive attention.
10. The purposes and programs of vocational, technical, and work experience for behavioral improvement should be clearly differentiated.
11. In cooperative work education, a competent teacher-coordinator and a positive sponsor are essential.
12. The activities of the work station and the classroom must be carefully integrated.

13. Small school systems must join together in order to provide a variety of quality programs.
14. Jobs must be carefully analyzed in order to determine desirable exploratory experiences and to define in behavioral terms the proficiency level necessary for successful entry into them.
15. In order to insure high quality, sound financial support and strong personnel must be provided.
16. Flexibility must be an inherent part of all programs so that classroom procedures can rapidly adjust to the changing nature of jobs, job specifications, and skill requirements.
17. Programs should provide for a careful blend among general education, technical education, skill training, and career development.
18. Necessary changes should be effected in training programs for teachers and requirements for certification in vocational and technical fields.
19. Agreements among employers, students, and the school must be carefully developed and clearly understood.
20. A favorable attitude on the part of labor organizations is a distinct advantage.
21. To a greater degree than in many other phases of education, all those involved must be deeply committed to the program and thoroughly prepared for their roles and responsibilities.
22. Although the employer is interested in production even during the training period, learning and training, rather than production, should be the prime objective.
23. All programs should stress the dignity of work, the worth of people, and the creative aspects of learning.

Proposed Advantages   *With which ones do you agree?*

1. Occupational education develops marketable skills and reduces waste of human resources.
2. Certain subjects such as auto mechanics, typewriting, homemaking, or electricity have great value for personal use and can be correlated with other subjects to provide greater motivation for learning and fuller understanding in these areas.
3. Good cooperative work education generates support of business and industry for the entire educational program.
4. The program provides an opportunity for youth and their elders to work side by side in a joint enterprise.
5. Occupational education enhances the ability of the consumer to assess and select products of industry and services of business intelligently.

6. The satisfaction of getting a job, succeeding, and receiving a paycheck adds zest to a young person's life.

7. By providing opportunities for success, occupational education builds self-assurance in many who do not excel in academic areas.

8. The number of school dropouts is significantly reduced.

9. Through face-to-face encounters and close supervision of work, opportunity is provided for individualization of instruction, guidance, and counseling.

10. Particularly to disadvantaged youth, achievement in vocational and technical work gives tangible evidence of progress.

11. Business and industry provide relevant, costly laboratories that would otherwise be unavailable for instruction.

12. Occupational education offers opportunity for creative expression and enhances ability in solving problems.

13. The value of proficiency and excellence is more convincingly demonstrated than in many other subject fields.

14. Cooperative work education makes schools aware of changes and stimulates them to keep the curriculum up-to-date.

15. Students can discover that they are not suited for some vocations before they become permanently committed to them.

16. Occupational education offers hope for coping with problems of disadvantaged youth by helping them become contributing members of society.

17. Earning even a little money provides some feeling of financial independence.

Criticisms and Difficulties to Be Anticipated *Do you agree?*

1. Industry does not understand the problems of schools or the purposes of their programs, and schools do not understand the needs and programs of industry and business.

2. Overprotective social taboos and legal obstacles stand in the way of providing significant work experience at an early age, when it would be a genuinely valuable learning opportunity.

3. Restrictive educational requirements of state departments, colleges, and local schools obstruct progress.

4. Many teachers seem to believe that real learning cannot take place unless the student is sitting at a desk with a book listening to the teacher.

5. One of the distinct difficulties in cooperative work experience is that of preventing the urge for performance and production from overshadowing learning and the learner.

6. The mobility of our population and the danger of obsolescence make preparation for specific jobs unrealistic.

7. Vocational education neglects social, intellectual, and emotional development.

8. Occupational education contents itself with isolated bits of knowledge and routine skills to the neglect of concepts, generalizations, and principles.

9. Many of the facilities needed for adequate vocational-technical education are excessively costly.

10. Lack of desire, initiative, and responsibility, rather than of specific skills, are the ingredients of unemployability.

11. Defensiveness and insecurity of public school teachers, including industrial arts teachers, are a real obstacle to imaginative programs of occupational education.

12. Cooperative work education focuses attention on earning rather than on learning.

13. Occupational programs will be the dumping ground for non-motivated students and behavior problems.

14. Most businesses and industries will not make the commitment necessary for effective occupational education.

Summary Assessment

The problems that face people shape the direction of their energy and efforts as a society and as individuals. At times these demands are long-term, at others they are focused on temporary emergencies. From the time of the Pilgrims through the years of the frontier, physical survival was the most urgent problem. Production of food, clothing, and shelter required top priority in the job market. Clearing land, logging, building roads, making and distributing agricultural equipment, constructing houses and farm buildings, growing food, and caring for domestic animals constituted the chief vocations.

The advent of electricity, the railroad, the telephone, the automobile, and the farm tractor caused occupational changes in their time similar to those occasioned by the introduction of the computer. Time and human energy were released to refocus on new ventures. The building of the railroads required efforts similar to those directed toward construction of airports and expressways. Occasionally employment was diverted to temporary disruptions such as the California gold rush or a major war.

The occupational requirements of the years ahead will likewise be determined by the kind of society that evolves and by the priorities that it establishes. It appears that growth in population, depletion of natural resources, increase in the number of old people, pollution, and congestion in urban centers will receive increasing attention. Health, law enforcement, education, and recreation will make continuing demands. Domestic and international tensions are likely to require intensive planning and effort. Continuing foreign competition for markets both at home and in other countries will force a searching re-examination of our productivity.

Accelerated change will quicken the demand for new competencies and for their continuous upgrading. The idea that occupational education equips the young for occupations and professions will rapidly disappear as schools realize that they can prepare youth only for entry into an occupation. Technological sophistication, knotty social problems, and an ever-accelerating rate of change demand education from the cradle to the grave. Preservice, inservice, and postservice education will all assume greater significance. How much of it is to be provided by private enterprise and by public agencies is yet to be determined.

Too many academic programs have failed to capture the imagination of youth. The home and the school have left too many high school graduates floundering on college campuses, in the world of work, on the street, and in their homes. The colleges and universities have too often turned them out ill-prepared for many responsibilities of adulthood. Recently, colleges have been engaged in an almost frantic re-examination of their goals, practices, and results. Special effort has been directed toward greater involvement of students and citizens in planning and decision-making. Curricula and methods have come under scrutiny.

Career education for elementary children holds great promise for changing attitudes toward the dignity of work and productivity. Its objectives need to be sharpened, and its effectiveness must be carefully evaluated.

With encouragement, often bordering on prodding, from all levels of government, secondary and elementary schools are similarly reassessing their accountability for results consistent with the desires and needs of society. The demand for improved occupational education has clearly asserted itself.

Beyond the metropolitan areas, the trend toward larger administrative and attendance units holds promise for curricular expansion and improvement in vocational and technical education. The practice of developing programs jointly supported by several school districts and often housed in a building outside the local district gives rise to several concerns. In many instances, an excessive amount of the student's time is being spent in getting to and from the vocational or technical school. More significant, perhaps, is the danger that the high school may tend to become even more academically oriented than it has been in the past. Many of the students who remain there may find the curricular offerings less inviting than those of the comprehensive high school of a former era.

Students must be equipped to take their place in the workaday world to produce and distribute the goods and services essential to the good life. But education for a technological age must not neglect the humane aspects of learning if man is to retain mastery of the machine and control of his own destiny. Only through combining careful study of values with vocational-technical skills can society determine the desirable quality of life and give direction to scientific and technological change.

A Few Leaders in the Movement

David Allen
  Univ. of California at Los Angeles
Melvin L. Barlow
  Univ. of California at Los Angeles
Carl Barthel
  Arizona State Univ.
John A. Beaumont
  Penn State Univ.
George L. Brandon
  Penn State Univ.
Lowell A. Burkett
  American Vocational Association
Leslie H. Cochran
  Central Michigan Univ.
Celia Denues
  San Jose City College
Rupert N. Evans
  Univ. of Illinois

C. Nelson Grote
  Schoolcraft College
Norman Gysbers
  Univ. of Missouri
Silvius G. Harold
  Wayne State Univ.
E. W. Kavanagh
  Great Oaks Joint Vocational School
  Cincinnati, Ohio
Gordon McMahon
  State Univ. of New York at Oswego
A. J. Miller
  Ohio State Univ.
Carl J. Schaefer
  Rutgers Univ.
Robert Taylor
  Ohio State Univ.
Robert Worthington
  U. S. Office of Education

A Few Places Where the Innovation Is Used

Bucks County, Pa.	Detroit, Mich.	Kenosha, Wis.
Cleveland, Ohio	Fort Wayne, Inc.	Las Vegas, Nev.
Dayton, Ohio	Hamilton County, Ohio	Miami-Dade Jr. College

Milwaukee Technical
College
New York, N. Y.
North Haven, Conn.
Oswego, N. Y.
Owens Technical
College, Ohio

Penn State Univ.
Penta County (Ohio) Joint
Vocational School
Portland, Oreg.
Quincy, Mass.

Stout State Univ.
Univ. of California at
Los Angeles
Univ. of Minnesota
Univ. of Missouri

Annotated References

Arnold, Walter M., "Washington Report," *Industrial Arts and Vocational Education*, LX, No. 4 (1971), 6. Surveys the newer teacher job requirements in vocational education and the failure of the traditional credits and degrees to do the job. Suggests new approaches.

Baer, Max F. and Edward C. Roeber, *Occupational Information*. Chicago: Science Research Associates, 1964. Offers valuable help for teachers and counselors in helping students understand the world of work, manpower needs, job requirements, and training opportunities. Many sources of information are provided. The occupations curriculum is described.

Barlow, Melvin L., *History of Industrial Education in the United States*. Peoria, Ill.: Charles A. Bennett, 1967. Traces the development of vocational and industrial education in America. The volume presents valuable information about alterations in organization, approach, and emphasis as they are adapted to social and occupational changes.

Beaumont, John A., "The Broadening Scope of Vocational Education," *American Vocational Journal*, XLIV, No. 4 (1969), 19-20, 54-55. Considers possible new directions that programs may take in light of the Vocational Education Amendments of 1968. New purposes are indicated by Congress, disadvantaged youth are given special considerations, and state councils are mandated.

Bottoms, Gene and Kenneth Reynolds, "Work Experience Programs for Behavior Modification," *American Vocational Journal*, XLIV, No. 5 (1969), 24-26. Presents the need for work experience for the development of attitudes, self-concepts, and behavioral patterns essential for successful employment. The purpose is the development of personal qualities rather than of specific skills.

Bradley, John G., "Teaching Industrial Arts in a Workaday World," *School Shop*, XXX, No. 10, 19. Warns against forgetting the practical. The pursuit of knowledge *per se* is commendable but most students will have to work to eat.

Burkett, Lowell A., ed., "Research Visibility," *American Vocational Journal*, XLIV, No. 7 (1969), 33-48. Reports research and development dealing with exemplary projects and residential schools for vocational education. Guidance in secondary and area vocational-technical schools is reported. Includes list of criteria for a good cooperative education program.

————, ed., "Research Visibility," *American Vocational Journal*, XLIV, No. 4 (1969), 33-48. Presents four reports synthesizing the literature relating to research and development through seminars and workshops, leadership training, teacher education, and study of professional personnel. A bibliography for each area is provided.

_____, ed., "Research Visibility," *American Vocational Journal,* XLV, No. 1 (1970), 45-60. Develops six topics: curriculum development, agricultural education, business and office education, distributive education, health occupations, and home economics education. Bibliography is included for each of the topics.

Burt, Samuel M., *Industry and Vocational-Technical Education.* New York: McGraw-Hill, 1967. Presents case-study reports of cooperative efforts between industry and education designed to further understanding of purposes and problems of both agencies. Procedures for encouraging and facilitating increased cooperative effort are developed.

Cochran, Leslie H., *Innovative Programs in Industrial Education.* Blooming-ton, Ill.: McKnight and McKnight, 1970. Describes programs developed during the past ten years. The background, purposes, and results of manufacturing and construction, occupational and technical programs, industrial education in elementary schools, family education, and other areas are discussed.

_____, "Innovation: A New Direction for Industrial Education," *Industrial Arts and Vocational Education,* LVIII, No. 2 (1969), 22-24. Reports a doctoral dissertation comparing seven innovative programs. Objectives, content, and methods are analyzed; agreement in positions taken by leaders in the seven projects is reviewed.

Crawford, Bryant, Jr., *Scope and Sequence of Content.* Bloomington, Ill.: McKnight and McKnight, 1971. Argues that little has been written about the subject within industrial arts collegiate undergraduate programs and proposes a pattern based on greatly increasing both breadth and depth of content starting at the elementary school level.

Cunningham, J. W., "The Job Cluster Concept and its Curricular Implications: A Symposium." Center Monograph N.4. 1969. Center for Occupational Education, North Carolina University, Raleigh. ED 042897. Proposes clustering jobs by developing a conceptual framework (based on concepts and principles of learning transfer, psychometrics, and systems theory) for defining and interrelating classes of variables which might prove useful in establishing job similarities for educational purposes.

Denues, Celia, *Career Perspective: Your Choice of Work.* Worthington, Ohio: Charles A. Jones, 1972. Discusses the world of work in a changing world, the basis of career choices, and the process of making initial choices and changing jobs. Requirements and possibilities for young and older workers are considered.

Drier, Harry N., Jr., *Career Resources Handbook.* Worthington, Ohio: Charles A. Jones, 1973. A resource sourcebook for those seeking specific help in career education curriculum development or planning to incorporate career education into their programs. Draws together the best material available in the field. Contains lists of printed material, films/filmstrips, kits/games, and other resources available.

Drier, Harry N. and Associates, *K-12 Guide for Integrating Career Development into Local Curriculum.* Worthington, Ohio: Charles A. Jones, 1972. Presents a coordinated career development program, field-tested in the elementary schools of Wisconsin. Stresses the development of self through career planning and preparation. Appropriate films, tapes, filmstrips, slides, and printed materials together with their sources are provided.

Duffy, Joseph W., "From Tinker Toys to Robots," *Industrial Arts and Vocational Education,* LX, No. 2 (1971), 28. Presents an innovative four-year industrial arts curriculum leading to a B. S. in education. New courses were prepared using contempory teaching methods presenting present concepts of industry with its rapid changes in technology.

Evans, Rupert N., "Advantages, Disadvantages, and Factors in Development," *American Vocational Journal,* XLIV, No. 5 (1969), 19-22, 58. Stresses the significance of recent congressional action for cooperative education. Able coordinators are the backbone of the program. Inherent advantages, disadvantages, and problems are discussed.

———, *Foundations of Vocational Education.* Columbus, Ohio: Merrill, 1971. Claims elimination of the general curriculum will result in higher rates of college attendance, since it has by far the highest dropout rate of the present three high school curricula and has by far the lowest rate of college attendance by its graduates.

———, "How Do They Exit From Your Program?" *School Shop,* XXIX, No. 10 (1970), 23-25. Stresses the failure of the high school to provide for many of its students. The general curriculum produces two-thirds of the dropouts and many of the unemployed graduates. Better college-preparatory and vocational-educational programs are suggested for killing the general curriculum.

Giachino, J. W. and Ralph O. Gallington, *Course Construction in Industrial Arts, Vocational and Technical Education.* Chicago: American Technical Society, 1968. Sets forth procedures for developing objectives, curriculum plans, and courses of study. Distinction is made between the purposes and procedures of technical and vocational education, and the benefits for secondary students, dropouts, and adults are presented.

Gysbers, Norman C., Harry N. Drier, and Earl J. Moore, *Career Guidance: Practice and Perspectives.* Worthington, Ohio: Charles A. Jones, 1973. Presents new ideas on both present practices and future planning for more individualized counseling results. Gives direction toward needed objectives and goals in school counseling programs.

Huffman, Harry, "Cooperative Vocational Education," *American Vocational Journal,* XLIV, No. 5 (1969), 16-18. Lists the seven types of cooperative programs and common factors among them. The importance of the teacher-coordinator and the local advisory committee is underlined. Cooperative education is the key to the success of vocational programs.

Isaacson, L. E., *Career Information in Counseling and Teaching.* Boston: Allyn and Bacon, 1966. Suggests that during the junior high school period, as the awareness of self is becoming more pronounced, the student inevitably moves towards a view of himself as seen against a background of the world of work.

Kimbrell, Grady and Marilyn Pilgeram, "Work Experience Education—An Answer to the Question, 'Who am I?'" *Journal of Secondary Education,* XLV, No. 5 (1970), 205-208. Suggests that, as work occupies the major portion of one's waking hours for most of adulthood, we should select our work rather than fall into it, and that work experience education helps assure that a career choice is appropriate.

Lifton, W. M., *Introducing the World of Work to Children. What Could I Be?* Chicago: Science Research Associates, 1960. Insists that final vocational choice is not the primary goal of occupational exploration in junior high school but rather to provide the experiences that will help the student in making choices when he has to.

Maley, Donald, "How Industrial Arts Relates to Occupational Education," *Industrial Arts and Vocational Education,* LIX, No. 2 (1970), 30-32. Contrasts and compares the role of industrial arts with that of occupational education. Industrial arts has the opportunity to work with people as individuals. The multitude of occupations and rapid change present real problems.

Marland, Sidney P., Jr., "Career Education Now," *Vital Speeches,* XXXVII, No. 11 (1971), 334-337. Suggests that we get rid of general education as it is neither truly vocational nor truly academic, then eliminate the term vocational education and adopt the term career education. Everyone should receive career education.

Matheny, Kenneth B., "The Role of the Middle School in Career Development," *American Vocational Journal,* XLIV, No. 9 (1969), 18-21. Describes the role of the middle school in career development through improving attitudes toward self, decision-making, exploration, and finding appropriate class and work experience. This age group seems too young to make vocational decisions, but is motivated by relating work in the community to classroom activities.

Milsted, Louis E., "A Trade and Industrial Cooperative Program," *Industrial Arts and Vocational Education,* LVIII, No. 2 (1969), 25-27. Outlines steps for successful program operation. Criteria for selecting students and training stations are listed. Student check lists for evaluating themselves and their training stations are included.

Morton, Luis M., Jr., "It's Time to Paint or Get Off the Ladder," *American Vocational Journal,* XLVI, No. 3 (1971), 18-20. Stresses that the outlook of vocational education must be re-examined and redirected so that motivation and competition are prime factors based on measureable performance, job generation, and availability to everyone.

National Committee on Employment of Youth, *A Guide to the Development of Vocational Education Programs and Services for the Disadvantaged.* New York: National Child Labor Committee, 1969. ED 035742. Contends that this type of training will enable the individual to move back and forth over several occupational categories as well as vertically within the occupation.

Neel, Elsie O., "Preparing Students for Employment," *The School Counselor,* XVIII, No. 4 (1971), 294. Describes an occupational workshop for senior high school students to help them choose a job, locate a job, apply for a job, keep the job, and change jobs.

Norwich, Anthony L., "A Career Development Program in the Chicago Public Schools," *Elementary School Journal,* LXXI (1971), 391-399. Summarizes a current program in career development. The program does not prepare a child for a specific career, but it makes him aware of his interests and incorporates the traditional curriculum into these interests.

Olsen, Jerry C., "Forces and Factors Producing Change In Industrial-Education Facilities," *School Shop,* XXVIII, No. 8 (1969), 86-90. Indicates the necessity for aligning the needs and expectations of students, employers, and the public. Effective program planning for new facilities, courses of study, methods and techniques, and better utilization of space and time schedules are indicated.

Pautler, Albert J., "Occupational Education," *Educational Leadership,* XXIX, No. 2 (1971), 174-177. Argues that the philosophy and objectives of a school are basic to all curriculum planning. An occupation program should operate at all levels of the school system with changing emphasis. It must be a planned program—either a separate subject or an interdisciplinary offering—which provides for consistency and articulation.

Raybourn, James W., "Industrial Arts for Educable Mentally Retarded Students," *Journal of Secondary Education,* XLV, No. 1 (1970), 24-26. Objects to courtesy promotion or denying of helpful training for these students. Proposes a special industrial arts program based on homogeneous grouping with a low pupil-teacher ratio and cued to pupil needs and capabilities.

Reed, Donald R., "The Nature and Function of Continuation Education," *Journal of Secondary Education,* XLIV, No. 7 (1969), 292-297. Takes the position that divergent youth cannot benefit maximally from the program of the comprehensive high school. The continuation high school offers more effective guidance orientation, individualized attention, short-term goals, and meaningful relationships with adults.

Ressler, Ralph, *Career Education: The New Frontier.* Worthington, Ohio: Charles A. Jones, 1973. Offers principles and guidelines to assist teachers, administrators, and counselors in integrating quality career development programs within existing curricula. Emphasizes the elementary school program.

Riendeau, Albert J., "Expectations in Community-College Vocational Education," *School Shop,* XXIX, No. 4 (1969), 33-35. Presents the two-year college as an answer to the demands of a technically oriented society. Conditions of employment demanding attention are listed together with provisions of P. L. 90-576 designed to meet them. Nine trends for the future are developed.

Roe, Anne, "Early Determinants of Vocational Choice," *Journal of Counseling Psychology,* IV, No. 3 (1957), 212-217. Takes the position that occupational choice is not a matter of a few decisions but is a lifetime development. Interests must be subject to the same developmental principles as any other aspects of personality.

Rumpf, Edwin L., "The Planning Job Ahead," *American Vocational Journal,* XLIV, No. 4 (1969), 24-26. Proposes nine guidelines for councils, boards, and committees. New emphases, new purposes, and organization of the educational agency for planning are stressed for local, state, and federal levels. The function of planning is second only to program operation.

Ruskin, Arnold P., "Industry Cooperation: A Guide For Effective Involvement," *Industrial Arts and Vocational Education,* LVIII, No. 9 (1969), 88-94. Emphasizes the point that industrial people should act only as advisors in planning and evaluating. Professional educators must determine methods of implementation. Six difficulties in working with advisory committees are discussed.

Ryan, Charles W., "Innovations in Career Development," *Vocational Education,* XLIV, No. 3 (1969), 63-65. Suggests an integrated interdisciplinary approach, a broad view of the curriculum, and reassessment of the role of the counselor as basic to the revision program. Career development should employ gaming techniques, computer technology, video techniques, and vocational tryout courses.

Schaffer, George M., "Gearing the Area Vo-Tech School for Service in the 70's," *School Shop,* XXIX, No. 8 (1970), 126-130. Reports the placement record of graduates of a technical school and insists that the success of the graduate evaluates the school. Pretraining for cooperative education, education of the disadvantaged and handicapped, and opportunities for senior citizens are considered.

Siegel, Herb and Harry Krane, "Curbside Shops for New York City," *Industrial Arts and Vocational Education,* LX, No. 3 (1971), 37. "Hopefully, there will be kids whose elementary industrial arts experience serves to acquaint them with the world of work around them; give them occupational orientation, information, pride in accomplishment, and not the least important, hands-on-experience and an appreciation of tools."

Stevenson, John B., *Career Education Handbook.* Worthington, Ohio: Charles A. Jones, 1973. Provides a complete survey of the major components for an effective K-12 career development school program. Presents an approach for teachers, administrators, and counselors for individualizing career-oriented instructional programs.

Teeple, John B., "Planning Vocational Programs to Meet National Goals," *American Vocational Journal,* XLIV, No. 8 (1969), 31-33. Examines the relationship between vocational education and national goals. The priorities which the nation establishes will influence occupational trends. Indications are that demand for technicians and service personnel in paraprofessional jobs will increase.

Trump, J. Lloyd and Delmas F. Miller, *Secondary Curriculum Improvement,* pp. 208-222. Boston: Allyn and Bacon, 1968. Considers poverty in the midst of affluence the impetus for the Vocational Education Act of 1963. New types of vocational and technical schools are sure to develop, but the types of programs are less certain.

Wernick, Walter, *Teaching for Career Development in the Elementary School.* Worthington, Ohio: Charles A. Jones, 1973. Explains the importance of career education for young children and outlines a continuous program through the elementary and secondary years. Program planning, resources, and learning activities are included.

Wood, Walter, "A Cargo of Career Education," *American Education,* VII, No. 8 (1971), 16. Illustrates how a jobmobile (a truckvan filled with desks, typewriters, adding machines, automobile systems, film projectors) takes five-week, 50-hour occupational courses to the disadvantaged rural migrants, both children and adults, on a year-round basis.

Perceptual-Motor Learning **24**

Definition

Perceptual-motor learning is the process of developing improved efficiency in body movement through a carefully organized program of learning activities. It is based upon the principle that people develop their native potential through many experiences, one of which is perceptual-motor learning. There are those who believe that body control, body image, self-concept, social adjustment, academic learning, emotional stability, and general personality can be improved through perceptual-motor training. How the child assesses his abilities within the total context of self and environment is considered a significant aspect of his self-concept and his interaction with other people, objects, and experiences.

Although perceptual-motor learning is recognized as valuable for all children, it seems to be particularly beneficial for the neurologically impaired, physically handicapped, hyperactive, mentally retarded, and emotionally disturbed. Children with these deficiencies constitute about 10 to 15 per cent of the school population. The instructional program is designed to enhance body-image, awareness of time, spatial judgment, and movement control.

Differentiation of body parts and functions, laterality, reaction time, balance, locomotion, manual dexterity, strength and endurance, agility, visual fixation and mobility, and auditory skills are among the functions included in the program. Among the learning activities are crawling, walking lines or balance beams, metronomic pacing, relaxation exercises, rhythmic games, skipping, chalkboard exercises, hopping into squares or circles, throwing, catching, grasping, drawing, and writing. The work is done in classrooms, gymnasiums, and clinics.

Incorporated in the program are activities for improvement in general performance and those designed for development of specific skills. The relationship between motor development and intellectual learning is frequently emphasized. Perceptual manipulation of real things is considered essential for building a foundation for meaningful symbolic perception needed in classroom learning. The perceptual relationships are extracted from the various motor experiences and serve as a basis for perceiving new relationships in such areas as reading, writing, arithmetic, spelling, and handwork.

Many functions of perceptual-motor programs are not yet understood. Strong differences exist between those who believe that improvement in motor coordination and reaction is likely to have positive effects upon growth in intellectual processes and improved performance in cognitive areas, and those who insist that no relationship between the two has been discovered. Others are inclined to think that general positive effects result from improvement in body movement. The child's attitude and the general climate for many kinds of learning are improved. Those who take this position believe, for example, that a pupil who displays improved physical coordination is better accepted by his peers, parents, and teachers. As a consequence he develops an improved self-concept and greater confidence.

The success that the learner has experienced with perceptual-motor tasks encourages him to attack other school work with increased enthusiasm and satisfaction. In this way, many believe, improvement in motor control contributes significantly to the child's ability to learn in many other areas. How significant this incentive really is needs further study, but there is considerable evidence to indicate that self-acceptance and social-acceptance are important factors in learning as is the effective interaction between the individual and his environment.

Perceptual-motor training can be useful for normal as well as for atypical children. In the early years of life, intellectual and physical activities are closely related. Vision, hearing, and movement, for example, provide much of the basis for the child's mental processes. They must be considered together and integrated so as to prevent overdependence of one on the other. The child needs to know his body, what it can do, and how it relates to things around him. This knowledge is basic for receiving perceptual data and for relating them to one another. Likewise this knowledge is necessary for maintaining order among perceptions. Understanding the relationship of the parts of the body to one another and to the total environment assists the child in overcoming many obstacles that interfere with effective learning.

Significant Components   *Which ones are essential?*

1. Perceptual-motor programs should be based on sound principles of child development and of learning.

2. In order to prevent raising unwarranted hopes on the part of parents, claims for the program should, whenever possible, be based on scientific research.

3. Early identification and treatment is very important.

4. All those concerned must realize that deficiencies are not of the child's making and are subject to remediation, especially if recognized and dealt with early.

5. Instruction should start at a low level and move forward in a developmental progression.

6. Because deep feelings relating to self-concept are commonly associated with motor disabilities, readiness for training must be given even greater consideration than in most other learning situations.

7. At the outset comprehensive examination of the pupil's physical, mental, and emotional functioning is indispensable.

8. Motor-perception should be treated as part of a total instructional program.

9. Competent teachers with some special training, who understand many aspects of learning, are needed.

10. Teachers should work closely with doctors, psychologists, and other specialists.

11. To insure maximum success, a well-qualified team should be used wherever possible.

12. Some special equipment is necessary.

13. The program must not be looked upon as a panacea for all motor, academic, and behavioral problems.

14. Learning activities should be selected and so arranged that children are encouraged to develop confidence through participation in decision making.

15. Special effort must be made to place parents of children with disabilities at ease, to develop their understanding of the problem, and to foster cooperation and a positive attitude on their part.

16. More than in most areas of learning, special attention should be given to transfer of training.

17. Basic in the program is a wide variety of learning activities designed to improve differentiation and integration of the movements of the different body parts.

18. Pupils must be free from social pressure, criticism, and threat.

19. Special training should be provided in relaxation and impulse control to relieve tensions and alleviate disruptive behavior.

20. Observations and suggestions of parents and the regular classroom teacher should be invited and carefully considered.

21. Provision must be made for careful, continuous evaluation.

Proposed Advantages   *With which ones do you agree?*

1. Relieving problems of movement allows the pupil to concentrate on the experience or task itself, rather than on the locomotor obstacles.

2. Early motor learning improves total development as well as movement efficiency.

3. Cognitive learning, such as perceiving printed symbols, benefits from improvement in perception.

4. The attention span is lengthened, especially in the case of the hyperactive pupil.

5. Functioning of the central nervous system is improved if appropriate motor activities are practiced.

6. Perceptual-motor learning is important for emotional development and effective emotional functioning.

7. Ability to participate in games and other physical activities improves the self-concept of the child.

8. The child is assisted in building those readiness skills that help him to achieve in academic areas such as reading, writing, arithmetic, and spelling.

9. Motor improvement develops independence, self-confidence, and willingness to try.

10. Improving visual-manual skills relieves tensions and anxieties resulting from inability to perform many tasks.

11. Improvement in a child's motor functions improves his social relations with his peers.

12. Children are taught to see relationships and arrange components of a situation in a specific order.

13. In the overactive child, motor training develops self-control and poise.
14. Improved movement is significant because others readily observe the child's movement and judge him by it.
15. Tensions are relieved through vigorous movements.
16. Relief of emotional problems facilitates greater success in the classroom.
17. Unity and wholeness of the child's life is enhanced by his awareness of his relationship with objects around him.
18. Individual movements are combined into patterns, many of which become automatic.
19. Ability to handle himself more efficiently is significant for the child's safety.
20. The child's capabilities for exploring, manipulating, and securing different kinds of information are increased.

Criticisms and Difficulties to Be Anticipated   *Do you agree?*

1. Concern and anxiety of parents and teachers may present problems different from those encountered when working with normal children and may compound the child's problem.
2. Facilities for diagnosis and help in special areas may be inadequate.
3. Teachers may try various approaches without having sound, verified reasons for using them.
4. Concerned parents may be misled and disillusioned by those who hold out false hopes.
5. Unscrupulous individuals take advantage of families that have children with marked deficiencies.
6. Some people imply that motor activities affect the central nervous system directly.
7. Requiring pupils to engage in motor activities in which they have marked deficiency frustrates them and destroys self-confidence.
8. Competent personnel for conducting the work is not available.
9. There is a lack of tested knowledge to determine the activities that are appropriate for particular deficiencies.
10. The fact that the child who is atypical in body movement is usually deficient in other areas complicates diagnosis and treatment.
11. Teachers, parents, and administrators often do not understand the purpose and nature of the program.

12. Progress requires patience and hard work over a long period of time, and results are often difficult to identify.
13. If pupils are threatened or punished for lack of effort or deficient performance, their feelings of failure are accentuated.
14. It is untrue that improvement in body movement improves the likelihood of better learning in academic areas.

Summary Assessment

Interest in perceptual-motor learning has spread rapidly during the past decade as educators have become increasingly aware of the significance of instruction in motor efficiency. They have come to recognize its potential for furthering perceptual awareness and its possibilities for helping deficient children with reading, writing, spelling, arithmetic, and other classroom pursuits. There is considerable evidence indicating that perception improved through motor training releases latent capabilities and enhances intellectual performance. The conflict between those who believe in specificity of perceptual-motor skills and those who stress generality and transfer in performance seems to be subsiding.

The value of carefully planned motor activities for hyperactive and emotionally disturbed children is receiving increased attention. There is also evidence of the usefulness of movement training in helping normal children with a variety of learning difficulties. Significant, too, is the recent emphasis on enhancing the self-concept and improving social adjustment of the handicapped. Although perceptual-motor training consists primarily of activities for improving motor, auditory, and visual abilities, its significance for helping the child to understand himself better and to gain social acceptance is increasingly being recognized.

The nervous system of the perceptually handicapped child receives, organizes, and transmits information differently from that of the normal child. His relationship with all those with whom he comes in contact is also quite different. Such functions as eye-hand coordination, laterality, directionality, and spatial exploration can be improved unless there is permanent organic damage. School systems, colleges, and many other agencies concerned about children are sponsoring programs to help special instructors and regular classroom teachers work more effectively with pupils with perceptual-motor deficiencies. More and more, teachers and school administrators are realizing that they have a responsibility for identifying and helping children with movement disabilities at the earliest possible age.

Many aspects of the functioning of motor systems as well as the operation of perceptual processes are not yet understood. However, researchers in neurology, physiology, psychology, optometry, medicine, and physical education are engaged in serious and productive study. Additional research is needed concerning the nature and causes of deficiencies and the kinds of motor and other experiences that are needed to relieve specific motor disabilities and to improve performance in other areas of classroom learning. Increasingly, the outcomes of systematic investigations report positive results. Progress to date and the growing interest in the field give promise of increasing help from perceptual-motor learning for both teachers and pupils. If the number of children needing help are to receive it, the schools must make the necessary curricular provisions because private practitioners and clinics cannot handle the large load.

A Few Leaders in the Movement

Ray H. Barsch
  Seattle, Wash.
Arthur Benton
  Univ. of Iowa
H. J. Birch
  Albert Einstein Medical Center
Robert Boger
  Michigan State Univ.
Clara Chaney
  Glen Haven (Colo.)
  Achievement Center
Bryant Cratty
  Univ. of California at Los Angeles
R. M. N. Crosby
  Univ. of Maryland
Carl H. Delacato
  Institute for the Achievement
  of Human Potential

Glenn Doman
  World Organization of
  Human Potential
Marianne Frostig
  Marianne Frostig Center for
  Educational Therapy
G. N. Getman
  Wayne, Pa.
Newell C. Kephart
  Glen Haven (Colo.)
  Achievement Center
James J. McCarthy
  Univ. of Wisconsin, Madison
Margaret Martin
  Alverno College
Douglas Wiseman
  St. Paul (Minn.) Schools

A Few Places Where the Innovation Is Used

Colorado State Univ.
Columbus, Ohio
Dayton, Ohio
Evanston, Ill.

Glen Haven, Colo.
Madison, Wis.
Miami Univ.
New Haven, Conn.

Philadelphia, Pa.
Providence, R. I.
Purdue Univ.
Racine, Wis.

St. Paul, Minn.   Somerset, Ky.   Univ. of Wisconsin
Seattle, Wash.   Tucson, Ariz.   Winter Haven, Fla.

Annotated References

Auxter, D., "Perceptual-Motor Characteristics of Preschool Children with Suspected Learning Disabilities," *Psychology in the Schools,* VIII, No. 2 (1971), 148-151. Proposes that a child's inability to perform simple perceptual-motor tasks may result from a learning impairment. Surveys two kindergarten classes. Takes the position that poor locomotive development hinders further intellectual growth.

Axline, Virginia, *Dibs in Search of Self.* New York: Ballantine, 1964. Shows the development of an extremely withdrawn, unresponsive child through play therapy. The deep effect of family and school relations on Dibs was resolved through therapy which enabled him to know and accept himself and to acquire satisfying relationships through social interaction.

Barlow, Bruce, "Perceptual-Motor Activities in the Treatment of Severe Reading Disability," *Reading Teacher,* XXIV, No. 6 (1971), 513-525. Emphasizes that perceptual-motor programs are additions to, not replacements for, careful diagnosis and teaching of basic skills. Argues that current programs aim at mass correction when individualized programs are needed.

Barsch, Ray H., *Achieving Perceptual-Motor Efficiency: A Space-Oriented Approach to Learning,* Volume 1 of a *Perceptual-Motor Curriculum.* Seattle: Special Child Publications, 1967. Discusses in depth research findings and theoretical considerations underlying motor development in the context of education. Function and relationship of different aspects of motor efficiency and of the various senses are considered in detail.

_____, *Enriching Perception and Cognition: Techniques for Teachers,* Volume 2 of a *Perceptual-Motor Curriculum.* Seattle: Special Child Publications, 1968. Stresses the points that the need for education in perceptual-motor learning is urgent, the time is now, and the school is the place. Perception is considered the dynamic force in learning. Activities and experiences are explained in detail.

Bell, Richard J., et al., "Perceptual-Motor Program Produces Positive Results," *School and Community,* LVI, No. 3 (1969), 17, 79. Reports improvement in emotional stability, social relationships, following directions, posture, balance, locomotion, and oral reading. It is recommended that physical activities and classroom experiences be correlated.

Chaney, Clara M. and Newell C. Kephart, *Motoric Aids to Perceptual Training.* Columbus, Ohio: Merrill, 1968. Practical volume explaining the relationship between motor, perceptual, and cognitive learning. Teacher behavior with the learner is treated in detail as well as procedures for instruction and evaluation in specific psychomotor areas.

Christiansen, Ted, "Visual Imagery as a Factor in Teaching Elaborate Language to Mentally Retarded Children," *Exceptional Children,* XXV, No. 7 (1969), 539-541. Explains that visual imagery is a factor in improving the elaborative language performances in mentally retarded children. Images operate as associational aids and mediate the easy recall of learned verbal symbols.

Cleland, Charles C., "Intra-Institutional Administrative Problems: Employee Communications," *Training School Bulletin,* LXIV, No. 3 (1967), 81-91. Results of an investigation of paired groups show some gains in young educable in bilateral balance, attention span, perceiving printed symbols, reading readiness, and beginning reading. Coordination training is effective for low level retardates as well as educable retardates.

Clifton, Marguerite, "A Developmental Approach to Perceptual-Motor Experiences," *Journal of Health, Physical Education, Recreation,* XLI, No. 4 (1970), 34-37. Describes program for improving mastery and use of ones body for children two to five. Objectives and organization of aquatic, perceptual-motor, and gymnasium areas are outlined. Records, personnel, and inservice education of staff are explained.

Cratty, Bryant J., *Perceptual-Motor Behavior and Educational Processes.* Springfield, Ill.: Charles C. Thomas, 1969. Reprints of the author's articles and speeches presented to physical educators about motor activities, behavior and intelligence, the interaction of movement behavior, and other aspects of classroom programs. Suggestions are made for developing motor activities for children with learning difficulties.

Cratty, Bryant J., Namiko Ikeda, Sister Margaret Mary Martin, Clair Jennett, and Margaret Morris, *Movement Activities, Motor Ability and the Education of Children.* Springfield, Ill.: Charles C. Thomas, 1970. Reports four experiments which give insight into the self-concept of a deficient child and explores the problems that he will encounter. Some essays are also included which discuss the role of perceptual-motor training of the intellect.

Cratty, Bryant J. and Sister Margaret Mary Martin, *Perceptual-Motor Efficiency in Children.* Philadelphia: Lea and Febiger, 1969. Stresses the importance of movement activities as tools for many aspects of education. The literature on perception, motion, and thought is reviewed. Principles of perceptual-motor education and procedures and activities for learning are presented.

Cratty, Bryant J. and Leon Whisell, *Perceptual-Motor Behavior and Educational Processes.* Springfield, Ill.: Charles C. Thomas, 1969. Discusses the importance of movement in all the aspects of learning and personality development. In addition to stressing its place in general education, special attention is given to the blind, clumsy, mentally retarded, and orthopedically handicapped.

Dillon, Edward J., Earl J. Heath, and Carroll W. Biggs, *Comprehensive Programming For Success In Learning.* Columbus, Ohio: Merrill, 1970. Outlines a program to prevent academic failure. Programming for the whole child through developmentally oriented experiences is explained. Project CHILD is described and evaluated.

Frierson, Edward C. and Walter B. Barbe, eds., *Educating Children With Learning Disabilities.* New York: Appleton-Century-Crofts, 1967. Authorities in various areas of learning disorders discuss their nature, specialized approaches to them, diagnosis, educational rationale, instructional procedures, and remediation in classroom skills. A glossary of terms associated with learning disabilities is included.

Frostig, Marianne and David Horne, *The Frostig Program for the Development of Visual Perception.* Chicago: Follett, 1964. The program described in this manual is intended for use not only by specialists in the field of visual perception training, but also by regular primary-grade classroom teachers and teachers of special classes for young children with learning difficulties. Exercises are also given for perceptual development.

Getman, G. N. and Elmer R. Kane, "The Physiology of Readiness (An action program for the development of perception for children)." Minneapolis: Programs to Accelerate School Success, 1964. A program for developing perceptual readiness through practice in general coordination, balance, eye-hand coordination, eye movements, and visual memory. Program is based on the premise that perceptual skills, which affect academic learning, can be learned.

Gruber, Joseph J. and A. H. Ismail, "Recent Developments in Mind-Body Relationships," *Education*, LXXXIX, No. 1 (1968), 57-63. Stresses the interdependence of physical and intellectual activity. Research indicates coordination, balance, and kinesthetic factors are related to intelligence and academic achievement. Organized physical education program improves readiness for reading and arithmetic, but not I.Q.

Herkowitz, Jacqueline, "A Perceptual-Motor Training Program to Improve the Gross Motor Abilities of Preschoolers," *Journal of Health, Physical Education, Recreation*, XLI, No. 4 (1970), 38-42. Discusses a university perceptual-motor program for teachers of preschool children. Two objectives are pursued: to develop a more realistic concept of one's own body and to utilize varied modalities to improve motor performance. Apparatus and activities are described.

International Approach to Learning Disabilities of Children and Youth. Third Annual International Conference, Tulsa, Oklahoma, 1966. Tulsa: The Association for Children with Learning Disabilities, 1967. Papers and speeches presented by participants at the international conference. Identification, diagnosis, and treatment of many disabilities together with implications for living are discussed by leaders from a number of disciplines.

Johnson, Doris J. and Helmer R. Myklebust, *Learning Disabilities.* New York: Grune and Stratton, 1967. Discusses types of learning disabilities, verbal and nonverbal. Principles and procedures for remediation are presented for reading, auditory and visual language, arithmetic, and nonverbal learning.

Kephart, Newell, *Aids to Motoric and Perceptual Training.* West Lafayette, Ind.: Purdue University, 1964. Presents suggestions for parents and teachers to use in approaching the learning and training of perceptual-motor deficient children. Through the understanding of sequential motor development, parents and teachers are better able to remediate these learning difficulties.

———, *Slow Learner in the Classroom.* Columbus, Ohio: Merrill, 1960. Explains the many areas of perceptual-motor learning. Problems and procedures for coping with them are explained for the classroom teacher.

Kephart, Newell C. and D. H. Radler, *Success Through Play.* Minneapolis: Harper, 1964. Dr. Kephart shows that the initial step in learning must be proceeded by the basic steps of readiness in order for a child to achieve success in school. Physical and perceptual training are essential in helping the child reach his potential.

298 Newly Emphasized Curriculum Content

McCarthy, James J. and Joan F., *Learning Disabilities.* Boston: Allyn and Bacon, 1969. A concise volume defining disabilities, examining their causes, describing their symptoms, and outlining procedures for dealing with them. Historical background, legislation, and research findings are briefly covered.

McCormick, Clarence C., and Janice N. Schnolrich, "Perceptual-Motor Training and Improvement in Concentration in a Montessori Preschool," *Perceptual and Motor Skills,* XXXII, No. 1 (1971), 71-77. Proposes that a Montessori program when coupled with perceptual-motor training will help to increase auditory and visual attention spans. Reviews the clinical experiment. Concludes that the hypothesis is true and points out that ego development is present.

Otto, Wayne and Richard A. McMenemy, *Corrective and Remedial Teaching.* Boston: Houghton Mifflin, 1966. Discusses correlates of learning disabilities and fundamentals of remedial instruction. Help for teaching underachievers is provided in the form of tested techniques and materials. Among the skill areas, reading is given special emphasis.

Otto, Wayne and Karl Koenke, eds., *Remedial Teaching.* Boston: Houghton Mifflin, 1969. Includes general discussion and research reports relating to disabilities. Problems of remedial teaching in general are discussed as well as those relating specifically to reading, handwriting, arithmetic, spelling, and written expression.

"Perceptual-Motor Development: Action with Interaction; a Report of an AAHPER Conference," *Journal of Health, Physical Education, Recreation,* XLII, No. 1 (1971), 36-39. Presents summary of a report by Margaret Fox and another by Paul Smith. All the senses need to be involved in perceptual-motor training. Schools must administer to the perceptual-motor needs of children. Many programs are presently in use, and some are successful.

Poindexter, Hally B. W., "Programs for Handicapped," *Journal of Health, Physical Education, Recreation,* XL, No. 6 (1969), 69-71. Takes the position that inability to perceive is related to emotional disturbance, and that both are related to motor proficiency. Vigorous physical activity increases tensions and hostility. Many motor activities improve perceptual development.

Portland Public Schools, *Improving Motor-Perceptual Skills.* Portland, Oreg.: Northwest Regional Education Laboratory, 1970. Activities suggested for use with kindergarten and first-grade children. Activities deal with developing general coordination, body image, balance, eye-hand coordination, eye movements, and sensory perception.

Rosner, J., "Perceptual Skills: A Concern of the Classroom Teacher?" *Reading Teacher,* XXIV, No. 6 (1971), 543-549. Discusses standard and substandard visual and auditory perception. Stresses that substandard perception results in a physical and/or psychological adaptation or in intellectual failure. Suggests some motor activities to improve perceptual problems.

Roth, J., "Intervention Strategy for Children with Developmental Problems," *Journal of School Psychology,* VIII, No. 4 (1970), 311-314. Describes the program set up by Newark State College to aid children with perceptual-motor difficulties. Emphasizes the sense of self-worth the children gained from the program.

Seiderman, A. S., and H. A. Solan, "Case Report on a Grade One Child before and after Perceptual-Motor Training," *Journal of Learning Disabilities,* III, No. 12 (1970), 635-639. Urges perceptual-motor training during primary school years. Illustrates the success of this program by describing the growth of a perceptual-motor deficient girl in training. Warns that neglect may result in a low classroom operational level.

Simpson, Dorothy M., *Learning to Learn.* Columbus, Ohio: Merrill, 1968. Considers the relationship between motor development and academic achievement. The author describes her personal experiences in arriving at deeper understanding of learning disabilities and procedures for working with them.

Smith, Hope M., "Implications for Movement Education Experiences Drawn from Perceptual-Motor Research," *Journal of Health, Physical Education, Recreation,* XLI, No. 4 (1970), 30-33. Reports perceptual-motor research under five classifications. Findings are discussed for vision, audition, tactile perception, and proprioception. In each area, implications are extracted for teachers of physical education.

———, "Motor Activity and Perceptual Development," *Education Digest,* XXXIII, No. 8 (1968), 41-44. Suggests that motor experiences found effective with children with learning disabilities be provided for all pupils in elementary education. We need to know more about the nature of perception and of the kind of motor experiences that improve perceptual-motor performance.

Smith, Paul, "Perceptual-Motor Skills and Reading Readiness of Kindergarten Children," *Journal of Health, Physical Education, Recreation,* XLI, No. 4 (1970), 43-44. Explains the use of multisensory approaches in developing movement skills utilizing two methods, directed and problem solving. No significant difference is found between the two methods in developing reading readiness in kindergarten children.

Sutphin, Florence E. and Charles W. McQuarrie, *A Perceptual Testing-Training Handbook for First Grade Teachers.* Winter Haven: Boyd, 1967. A detailed guidebook for first-grade teachers emphasizing the value of perceptual training for learning to learn. Testing procedures and learning activities stressing motor development and concept building are outlined in detail.

Audiovisual and Other Resources

Movement Exploration (16mm film, color, 22 min., $220, rental $20). Shows techniques of movement exploration with K-Sixth Grade students. Documentary Films, 3217 Trout Gulch Rd., Aptos, Calif. 95003.

Sex Education and Family Living

25

Definition

Sex education and family living is that component of the instructional program that attempts to enable the child to develop understanding of the physical, emotional, social, and spiritual nature of sexuality. It recognizes that sex is the basis of reproduction and continuity for all life, and that males and females have equally important roles in the home and community. These roles complement one another. They provide for the richest fulfillment of the individual, the family, and society as a whole. Love, respect, security, and happiness in general are built upon an understanding of these roles and the attitudes that prevail relative to persons of the opposite sex.

These attitudes are vastly more important than factual information. An understanding of the role of boy and girl and man and woman, the interrelationship between them, and the joys and satisfactions of successful family life are the significant aspects of sex education and family living. Programs of sex education are most effective when they consider total sexuality in a sound scientific and moral perspective as it relates to the totality of the family and of social values and everyday relationships. Personal responsibility of all involved must be a dominant characteristic.

In one form or another instruction in sex education and family living has been carried on since the beginning of recorded history. In the home, however, too often it has been absent entirely, incomplete, or too late. In the school it frequently has been limited to reproduction, menstruation, and disease. On the street it usually has been sordid—arousing curiosity, experimentation, and anxiety. During recent years, reports indicating an increase in sex relations among adolescents, sex assaults, illegitimate births, and venereal disease have raised concerns and spurred efforts to find ways of combating the problems.

Proposals suggest that, starting in the home and early grades, programs deal primarily with general concerns of children such as the origin of life, differences in male and female appearances, and social roles. With the approach of adolescence, physiological changes and functions receive increased attention. How emotions are aroused and controlled is given more thoughtful consideration. Respect for others and limits of social relationships become significant and legitimate concerns. Family relationships and love of parents and children become matters of continuing importance.

Study of family and sexuality lends itself better to such subjects as social studies, health and physical education, homemaking, and biological science than to most other areas. However, even if he wishes to, no teacher can avoid teaching sex. Just as sex is indispensable for life, it is an integral part of life for boys and girls in the school as well as in the home. The school program should start in the kindergarten and continue through college, developing gradually as need demands.

A sensitive, understanding, discreet teacher is the most important single factor in carrying out a successful program. In-service education can enable teachers in the lower grades to handle problems of sex education and family relations indirectly as they arise and as need becomes evident. Prudence, tact, skill in communicating, discretion, and effectiveness in dealing with basic considerations of sexuality are within the reach of every teacher. Occasionally more formal approaches through planned programs are beneficial at the intermediate school level. The middle school and secondary years are likely to require a more sophisticated approach and more organized instruction, best achieved through multidisciplinary efforts involving teachers from many fields, counselors, doctors, nurses, clergymen, social workers, and other members of the community.

It is essential to devote a great deal of time to determining the emphasis that will prevail and the objectives for which teachers and pupils are striving. Healthy attitudes, scientific answers to questions, knowledge concerning natural physiological changes, understanding of differences in roles, respect for persons of the opposite sex, and appreciation of the characteristics and importance of a good home and family are all worthwhile goals. Unless time is taken, however, to clarify the objectives and develop understanding of them among all those concerned, the program will not realize its maximum potential. More than in any other aspect of the curriculum perhaps, careful cooperative planning with parents and other responsible people in the community who have interest and expertise in the field is necessary to avoid unnecessary suspicion, criticism, and fear.

Significant Components   *Which ones are essential?*

1. Sex education should extend from infancy through adulthood, the nursery school through college.
2. The purposes of the program must be clearly established before it is begun.
3. Instruction should be individualized to provide for the varying interests and capabilities of pupils.
4. Particularly in the elementary school, sex education is best integrated with other subjects.
5. Attention must be directed toward strengthening positive attitudes that the child brings from home and changing negative ones.
6. An open climate and understanding teachers are all-important.
7. Answers should be honest and direct, not going beyond what the child wants or needs to know.
8. Counseling should be provided to assist parents in dealing effectively with the problems of their children.
9. Special provision must be made for children from different socioeconomic and ethnic backgrounds.
10. Dignified and precise vocabulary should be developed.
11. Materials should be carefully pre-studied by the teacher, who must exercise prudence and good sense.
12. Sex education must not be equated with "giving them the facts of life."
13. A sex education program must not be allowed to deteriorate into a consideration only of menstruation, intercourse, pregnancy, and venereal disease.

14. Many resource people including counselors, doctors, nurses, clergymen, social workers, and other members of the community should be utilized in planning and carrying out a program.

15. Careful and continuing evaluation of the program and its results is essential.

16. The school must recognize that it is an important instrumentality for developing wholesome attitudes toward sex, but that there are also several other very important ones.

17. Parental education and cooperation aimed at improving preschool guidance is important.

18. Mass instruction often presents concepts that are too early for some, too late for others, and poorly presented in any case.

19. Skilled teachers who are understanding and comfortable when facing pupils' questions and problems are essential.

20. Teachers must be alert to opportunities for indirect teaching since this is often more effective than direct instruction.

21. Every teacher must realize that, although he perhaps cannot be a specialist in sex education, he cannot escape questions and problem situations.

22. Study of emotions—how they are aroused and controlled—is as important as considerations of physiological function.

23. Sex must be recognized and accepted as a natural, normal part of life.

24. It must be recognized that the misuse of sex can be extremely detrimental to emotional and physical health.

25. New concepts should be introduced only as warranted by the maturity level and social problems that confront or are likely to confront the child.

Proposed Advantages   *With which ones do you agree?*

1. Sex education helps children find their way through happy adolescence to satisfying and effective adulthood.

2. Insights for formulating sound values are developed.

3. Sex education extends the cooperative efforts of the home and the school and de-emphasizes the influences of the street in providing information and shaping attitudes.

4. Future parents will be better equipped to deal with the problems of their children.

5. Sex education assists in bridging the generation gap by helping youth to identify with and understand adults.

6. Youth are encouraged to treat one another with love, respect, and consideration.

7. If emotional pressures and physiological changes are understood as normal functions, unwarranted fears and anxieties are reduced.
8. The probability of success and dignity in adult life is increased.
9. Sex education decreases promiscuity and illegitimacy.
10. The incidence of venereal disease is reduced.
11. Guidelines and limits of conduct are established for thoughtful use of increasing independence.
12. Sex education helps married couples to avoid and resolve conflict through increased understanding of physical, emotional, and psychological differences.
13. Although physical attraction is recognized and accepted as a real factor in love, deeper and more comprehensive meanings of self and of sexuality are discovered through an adequate educational program.
14. The child sees the process of human reproduction as it relates to that of plants and other animals and to the perpetuation of life.

Criticisms and Difficulties to Be Anticipated   *Do you agree?*

1. Sex education and family living is a very personal matter and belongs in the home and the church.
2. The schools are continually assuming roles inconsistent with, and in neglect of, their primary responsibilities.
3. Mass education is ineffective in dealing with matters as personal as sex education and family living.
4. Bringing sex relations to the attention of children arouses unnecessary curiosity and anxiety.
5. Sexuality and sex should not be reduced to a science.
6. Sex education promotes experimentation and promiscuity.
7. Much of the text material used is produced primarily for its sensational appeal and is very "raw."
8. The stability and maturity of teachers who are constantly dwelling on sex are open to serious question.
9. Teaching attitudes and values is not education; it is indoctrination.
10. Students may take the discussions far afield and pervert the purpose of the instruction.
11. Mass media and producers of pornographic material capitalize on the interest and curiosity generated in children by the schools.

12. Lasting attitudes toward sex and family living are established long before children come to school.
13. Prudishness of teachers, their own uncertain attitudes, and their insurmountable prejudices create frustration, anxieties, and fears.
14. Children can learn all they need to know about sex in a very short time.
15. Sex education "demoralizes" young people and violates every principle of decency and good taste.
16. Advocates of sex education are really Marxists in disguise.
17. The money that is spent on sex education should be put to better use.

Summary Assessment

Instruction in sex education and family living is not new. It has long been a concern in the junior and senior high schools, but the realization that it must receive continuous attention at all levels is of more recent origin. Increase in the number of working mothers, decline in the cohesiveness within the family and in the positive influence of the neighborhood, changing emphasis in many churches, and easy transportation have contributed to quickening the search for new solutions to the ever-present problems of young people.

There appears to be general agreement that teaching sex education and family living is important, even crucial, for the individual, the home, and society. If love, concern, and emotional stability are not developed in the home, other agencies must share the responsibility. Community education for premarriage couples and for parents holds promise. There appears to be an increasing realization that the marriage ceremony may be the beginning of a happy and satisfying married life or a prelude to misery.

Who should teach sex education and family living, how it should be taught, and what aspects should be stressed, have been matters of heated controversy. The public flare-ups of the last few years have perhaps been the result of poorly conceived programs, misplaced emphases, ineptness and indiscretion on the part of some teachers, unduly sensational materials, misunderstandings, and unwillingness on the part of certain individuals and groups to face the needs of youth and society squarely and realistically.

Despite agreement on high-sounding objectives, too many programs have emphasized only negative approaches. Copulation, masturbation, menstruation, contraception, reproductive organs, illegitimacy, and venereal diseases constitute the entire content of some programs. Little wonder, then, that they arouse vehement objections. Educators must stop looking at sex education as a way of teaching "the facts of life" and address themselves to all the emotional, psychological, physical, and spiritual factors that contribute to vital and successful living.

Those who make extravagant claims for the benefits of instruction in sex education must concede that even in districts where programs have been in operation for years, the results are not above challenge. Those who would repudiate all efforts of the schools to move into this controversial field must realize the difficulty of producing significant results with programs isolated in individual school districts or buildings. The proponents may be right in insisting that the time has come to launch a massive nationwide attack upon the problem. This dilemma of youth may well become worse if school people and the public do not address themselves vigorously to it.

In a positive sense, sex education is character education; and that must be a vital concern of all groups, not of a single agency. Some states and communities are moving forward with standards and strategies while other states and citizen groups clamor for elimination of all programs. Healthy attitudes, sound values, positive interpersonal relations, and better understanding of ourselves and our masculine and feminine roles are common aspirations of all groups. Serious mistakes make the concerns of parents legitimate, but people of good intentions must not obstruct progress through emotional controversy.

As Carl Fehrle puts it, "Sex created the family. Proper sex education can preserve the family."*

A Few Leaders in the Movement

American Medical Association
  Chicago, Ill.
Mary S. Calderone
  Sex Information and Education
  Council of the U. S.
Paul Cook
  Wabash College

Gordon Drake
  Shelton College
Stanley Fowler
  Oklahoma State Univ.
Alan Guttmacher
  New York City

---

*Carl C. Fehrle, "The Natural Birth of Sex Education," *Educational Leadership,* XXVII, No. 6 (1970), 577.

Elizabeth Jackson
  Longwood College
Lester Kirkendall
  Oregon State Univ.
Carl Knutson
  Minnesota Dept. of Education
Adeline Levin
  Mankato State College
James L. McCary
  Univ. of Houston

Thomas McGinnis
  Morris Harvey College
Frederick Margolis
  Harvard Univ.
Patricia Schiller
  Marjorie Webster Jr. College
Sex Information and Education
  Council of the U. S.
  New York City

A Few Places Where the Innovation Is Used

Anaheim, Calif.	Flint, Mich.	St. Louis, Mo.
Atlanta, Ga.	Indianapolis, Ind.	San Mateo Co., Calif.
Buffalo, N. Y.	Kalamazoo, Mich.	Selah, Wash.
Dallas, Texas	Kansas City, Mo.	Trottwood, Ohio
Evanston, Ill.	Mamaroneck, N. Y.	Washington, D. C.

Annotated References

Abramson, Paul, ed., "Sex Education: Eight Teachable Moments," *Grade Teacher,* LXXXVI, No. 3 (1968), 65, 121, 122, 128. Gives three basic principles for handling teachable moments: 1) find out what the child wants, 2) answer on his age level, 3) use proper terminology. The principles are then applied to eight teachable moments.

———, ed., "Sex Education: A Sixth Grade Teaching Program," *Grade Teacher,* LXXXVI, No. 3 (1968), 123-127. Presents five units for the sixth grade, listing for each: philosophy, objectives, approach, method, content, summary, teaching tips, and materials. The units are: 1) Knowing Yourself, 2) The Cell, 3) Plants, 4) Animal Life, 5) You.

———, ed., "Sex Education: Here's How We Did It," *Grade Teacher,* LXXXVI, No. 3 (1968), 64-65, 122. Describes a sex education program started by a sixth-grade teacher and a nurse. Questions are answered about how far to go in discussions, how to construct a curriculum, and how to relate the social and biological aspects of sex.

———, ed., "Sex Education: Teachers Believe Sex Education Should Be Taught in Elementary Schools," *Grade Teacher,* LXXXVI, No. 3 (1968), 60-63. A survey blames superintendents, principals, and supervisors for obstructing progress in sex education in the elementary school. Teachers, pupils, and parents want it, but few vital programs exist. Topics and teachers to teach them are discussed.

Baker, Richard J., "New Trouble for Sex Education," *Ohio Schools,* XLVII, No. 8 (1969), 13-15. Cites numerous instances of vehement reaction from the public and from a broad range of organized groups. Amid unprecedented opposition, states and school systems proceed with development of new programs and restructuring existing ones.

Breasted, Mary, *Oh! Sex Education!* New York: Praeger, 1970. Reports violent differences between proponents and opponents at Anaheim and among antagonists like Mary Calderone and Gordon Drake. The book castigates both those who oppose all sex education and those who insist on an out-dated moralistic approach.

Bruess, Clint, "A Comparison of Biblical Views of Sexuality," *Journal of School Health,* XL, No. 10 (1970), 531-532. Refutes those who oppose sex education because of religious objectivity. The success of the program becomes dependent on the people, methods, and materials involved rather than on the theological arguments in favor of the program.

Calderone, Mary S., "Goodbye to the Birds and the Bees," *American Education,* II, No. 10 (1969), 16-22. Portrays the teaching of sex as vital and insists it is a must to educate the young. Contrary to popular belief, the author does not here display an extreme point of view.

———, "Sex—Healthy or Disease," *Journal of School Health,* XXXV, No. 6 (1965), 253-257. Attempts to relieve the minds of those who doubt the validity of such an important program. Stresses that children should know the facts about sex and should learn them in an environment conducive to building a healthy attitude.

———, "Shameful Neglect of Sex Education," *P. T. A. Magazine,* LXI, No. 9 (1967), 4-7. Straight-forward discussion by a leader in the field of the need for sex education in schools. Regrettably slow progress is being made despite the increased urgency of student needs.

Dale, Gayle and George C. Chamis, *Sex Education Guide for Teachers.* Flint, Mich.: Flint Public Schools, 1968. A guide presenting three concepts of sex education: (1) Family Life Education, (2) Sex Education, (3) Reproduction Education. Objectives and programs for different age levels are included with resource agencies, films, and suggested book list.

Dunbar, Ernest, "Sex in School," *Look,* XXXIII, No. 16 (1969), 15-17. Lists some of the advantages of implementing a program, and gives the attitudes of students toward such a program.

Ellis, Albert and Albert Abarbanel, *The Encyclopedia of Sexual Behavior,* 2 vols. New York: Hawthorne, 1961. Comprehensive two volumes presenting the physical, emotional, psychological, and sociological impact of sexuality on the life of the individual and the family. Love, marriage, and parenthood are treated in considerable detail.

Ellis, Effie O., "The Challenge of Sex Education," *Ohio's Health,* XIX, No. 3 (1967), 1-8. A doctor considers sex education from kindergarten through high school as a necessity and unavoidable responsibility. Benefits that will accrue, need for planning, and approaches to implementation are discussed.

Fehrle, Carl C., "The Natural Birth of Sex Education," *Educational Leadership,* XXVII, No. 6 (1970), 573-577. Recognizes that sex education is charged with dynamite, and that only through careful work with parents and community can it be effective. Parents must be educated to cope with the all-important preschool years and to join with the school later.

Fulton, Gere B., "Sex Education: Some Issues and Answers," *Journal of School Health,* XL, No. 5 (1970), 263-268. Addresses itself to the irrationality of those who oppose sex education in our schools. There is an awareness of the importance of distinguishing between the voices of concern and those of malice. Cooperation between the two factions is very important.

Gendel, Evalyn and Pauline Greer, "Sex Education Controversy—A Boost to New and Better Programs," *Journal of School Health,* XLI, No. 1 (1971), 24-28. Indicates that despite the controversy, increasing numbers of schools are initiating, developing, or expanding programs of human growth and development, with the majority of administrators, teachers, and students supporting it.

Goodheart, Barbara, "Sex in the Schools: Education or Titillation?" *Today's Health,* XLVIII, No. 2 (1970), 28-30, 76, 79-80, 83-85. Presents views of proponents and opponents. An excellent question and answer section with Dr. Merle Musselman, a parent, a physician, a medical-educator, and a public school teacher is reported.

Greenberg, Herbert M., *Teaching with Feeling,* pp. 177-186. Toronto: Macmillan, 1969. Sexuality is unavoidable in any classroom, and questions arise whether or not the school has a formal program of sex education. The masculinity and femininity of teachers and pupils and student-teacher relationships are part of the school climate.

Hamburg, Marian V., "Sex Education in the Elementary School-Teacher Preparation," *National Elementary Principal,* XLVIII, No. 2 (1968), 52-56. Points out the growing demand for elementary sex education and why few elementary teachers are trained to teach it adequately and comfortably. Describes a new graduate program for the elementary school offered by N. Y. U. School of Education.

Hoch, Loren L., "Current Views on Sex Education," *Science Teacher,* XXXVII, No. 8 (1970), 41-44. Recognizes the problems in sex education—implementation, communication, and planning—and suggests alternate approaches and their outcomes to help students accept the need for certain social rules concerning sexual behavior.

Inlow, Gail M., *The Emergent in Curriculum,* pp. 212-234. New York: Wiley, 1966. Considers the roles of teachers and parents in sex education. It is necessary for a culture to make known its standards of propriety. A natural climate, sequence, consideration of emotions, positive emphasis, scholarship, and broad cooperation are the essentials.

Jennings, Robert E., "Sex Education and Politics," *The Educational Forum,* XXXIV, No. 3 (1970), 347-352. Exposes the danger of educators' yielding to pressures and allowing political leaders to become makers of educational policy. Presents details of a successful struggle to preserve a program in a large city.

Juhasz, Anne McCreary, "Background Factors, Extent of Sex Knowledge and Source of Information," *The Journal of School Health,* XXXIX, No. 1 (1969), 32-39. Reports findings from a sex knowledge inventory relating to sources of information, background, and timing. Printed matter is indicated as the chief source of information for more than half of the respondents. Positive and negative influences are identified.

———, "Characteristics Essential to Teachers in Sex Education," *The Journal of Health Education,* XL, No. 1 (1970), 17-19. A study of opinions of administrators and researchers relating to the characteristics of teachers in sex education. Acceptance of human sexuality, respect for youth, empathy, and knowledge are considered essential.

Karmel, Louis J., "Sex Education No! Sex Information Yes!" *Phi Delta Kappan,* LII, No. 2 (1970), 95-96. Argues for providing sex information woven into appropriate courses and for avoiding any attempt to shape attitudes, values, and moral concepts. Ten dangers of sex education are listed.

Kesling, Linda, "Sex Education: A County-Wide Approach," *Journal of School Health,* XL, No. 10 (1970), 544-545. Recognizes that small communities may lack the necessary resources for implementing a sex education program in their schools and provides an answer to those who want an effective program.

Kilander, Holger F., *Sex Education in the Schools.* Toronto: Macmillan, 1970. A very readable book for teachers. Part I includes broad goals of sex education, objectives, curriculum planning, methods, evaluation, and unit planning. Part II contains basic content material for sex education.

Kirkendall, Lester A., "Sex Education Blunt Answers for Tough Questions," *Reader's Digest,* XCII, No. 554 (1968), 80-84. Deals with answering questions most frequently raised by parents, teachers, and students. Who is qualified to teach? What type of material will be used? What about morality?

Kleinerman, Gerald and Michael Grossman, "Sex Education in a Ghetto School," *Journal of School Health,* XLI, No. 1 (1971), 29-33. Describes the purposeful solicitation of questions on sex from students by the teacher as an effective approach. The report documents student concern in sexual matters and the success of the program.

Knowles, Lawrence W., "Schools Upheld in Two Sex Education Cases," *Nation's Schools,* LXXXVII, No. 5 (1971), 80. Cites two arguments raised by opponents of sex education: the invasion of privacy and violation of religious freedom. The good of the state is looked upon as of prime importance.

Laganke, Anne Falther, "Sex Education in the Elementary Schools," *Ohio's Health,* XIX, No. 3 (1967), 19-25. Explains the need for sex education in the home and the elementary school. The importance of the indirect approach and the attitude of the teacher is illustrated through instances that arise naturally in the kindergarten and at each grade level.

Leach, Glenn, "Sex Education in a Permissive Society," *Educational Product Report,* III, No. 6 (1970), 2-4. Takes the position that sex education should be taught through careful planning in the school. In this permissive society, there is a great need for the child to be properly equipped to cope with all problems that he will encounter.

Luckey, Eleanore B., "Sex Education: Develop an Attitude Before You Develop a Program," *American School Board Journal,* CLVI, No. 10 (1969), 20-23. Stresses the importance of establishing the purposes of the program before the content and organization are developed. The influence on children must be considered in the context of the home and community and evaluation must take all of these into account.

Neff, Neal, "Sex Education in the Public Schools," *School and Community,* LVI, No. 9 (1970), 20. Insists that teaching sex education is a difficult assignment. The teacher must possess unusual poise. Parents and students should be involved in selecting materials.

Schuel, Doris, "The School Nurse—Her Role in Sex Education," *Journal of School Health,* XXXVI, No. 5 (1966), 200-206. Presents the idea that the school nurse is perhaps the logical one to take responsibility for setting up programs involving sex education. Certain requirements for those who are to be involved in such a program are given, including proper knowledge and a positive philosophy.

"Sex Education: How It Is Being Taught In Elementary Classrooms," *Grade Teacher,* LXXXIV, No. 9 (1967), 122-125, 172-173. Emphasizes the advantages of early teaching. Four basic concepts for elementary pupils are self-awareness, physiological concepts, reproduction, and family concepts. A successful program depends on the teacher, resource people, and community support.

Szasz, George, "Sex Education and the Teacher," *Journal of School Health,* XL, No. 3 (1970), 150-155. Indicates skills needed by the teacher for effective instruction in sex education, amount and type of information needed, special educational techniques, and guidelines for problem moments. A sex education program is evaluated on these bases.

Uslander, Arlene, "Study of People in Skokie," *Instructor,* LXXX, No. 3 (1970), 78. Presents a successful elementary sex education program which considered the "how" of sex education more important than the "what." This approach resulted in a harmonious relationship between the child and his teacher.

Weinstock, Henry R., "Issues in Sex Education," *The Educational Forum,* XXXIV, No. 2 (1970), 189-196. A carefully documented article reports different prevailing viewpoints concerning the proper place for sex education. Six reasons are given for viewing the public schools as the most appropriate agency to take initiative in coordinating the efforts of school, home, church, library, and medical profession.

Audiovisual and Other Resources

Prepare to Decide: Teachers Look at Human Sexuality (4 taped lessons and leader guide, reel $26.50, cassette $24.50). An introduction to sex education for teachers. Association for Productive Teaching, 5408 Chicago Ave., S., Minneapolis, Minn. 55417.

Sex Education in the Schools: Philosophy and Implementation (16mm film, color, 25 min., $250, rental $25). Two national authorities describe elements of an outstanding sex education program. Also *Sex Education: Organizing for Community Action* (16mm film, color, 23 min., $225, rental $22.50). Basic guidance for communities considering sex education programs. Perennial Education, Inc., 1825 Willow Rd., Northfield, Ill. 60093.

What Parents Should Know About Sex Education in the Schools (pkg. of 30 leaflets, $1.50). NEA, 1201 16th St., N. W., Washington, D. C. 20036.

Value and Attitude Clarification

26

Definition

Teaching values and attitudes is an educational process which uses a planned program to help students clarify the ideals which they hold dear and the principles and standards around which they build their lives. Included also are emotion-laden positions that people take toward problems and issues which arise in the course of living. Many thoughtful people insist that values and attitudes cannot be taught. At best, teachers can only assist students in clarifying their own values. Others believe that helping students clarify different points of view is precisely what *teaching* is, and that the two terms are synonymous. Teaching values and attitudes is often referred to as character education, moral education, and affective learning.

Values may be defined as deep-seated beliefs or moral convictions which constitute the core of the inner self. They are the basic feelings and commitments from which interests, appreciations, attitudes, and, eventually, action spring. They supply unity and consistency to behavior and are not easily shaken. They constitute the psyche of the individual, and their continuation without fundamental or marked change determines the person's life style. Deep commitment to friendships, family, beauty, justice, compassion, reason, wealth, power, service to others, equality, or getting ahead are among the values that direct the

lives of people. One's generalized values constitute his philosophy of life.

Attitudes are ways of viewing problems and issues that arise
in the course of living. Although they may be based on facts and
reason, they commonly are rooted in emotion. They grow out of
the person's values, lie closer to the surface than values, and
can be changed without altering the basic nature of the inner
man. Although attitudes develop within the framework of values,
they are less generalized in that they are usually directed toward
specific problems or situations. As a consequence attitudes are
characterized by more variations than are values. A person may
have a favorable attitude toward sports, but dislike football. He
may be deeply dedicated to community improvement and have
a very positive attitude toward flouridation of the water supply,
but a very negative attitude toward zoning. Friendships may be
among his highest values, but he may have a very unfavorable
attitude toward some individuals.

Attitudes frequently are more important than knowledge or
reason in determining an individual's conduct as it relates to a
specific situation at a given time. His values influence his attitudes and usually indicate the position he is likely to take regarding specific problems or incidents.

Throughout history the goals and emphases of education have
changed in response to cultures, problems, and perceived needs
of individuals and groups. In his *Republic* Plato stressed the importance of developing virtuous citizens who could live in harmony with one another. As education developed in western Europe, the authority of the church made moral and religious education a dominant concern.

The influence of the culture of the old world was obvious in
the schools of colonial America as well as in the public and
private colleges and universities, whose charters, well into the
nineteenth century, commonly mandated instruction in religion
and morality. The popularity of the McGuffey readers with their
emphasis on generally accepted values of the time testify to the
public concern for character education and moral training that
characterized the lower schools well into the twentieth century.
Courses in ethics continued as part of the general and professional curricula of secondary schools and colleges.

As time went on, growing secularism and pluralism insisted on
more distinct separation of church and state and caused a decline
in the emphasis on religious and moral instruction in public

schools. The area of values and attitudes received less attention as knowledge, skills, and thinking processes became the prime considerations.

Four of the Seven Cardinal Principles, released in 1918 for the guidance of American secondary schools, were worthy use of leisure time, good citizenship, worthy home membership, and ethical character. The 1951 report of the Educational Policies Commission, which included such members as Dwight D. Eisenhower and James B. Conant, urged the teaching of values in the schools and explored the values that should be taught.

In 1948, the annual conference of the Association of College and University Examiners directed its attention to course objectives. Among those deeply involved with the problem was Benjamin Bloom. He was joined by Max Englehart, Edward Furst, Walker Hill, David Krathwohl, and Bertram Masia in developing taxonomies of educational objectives in three domains: cognitive, affective, and psychomotor. The affective domain concerns itself with attitudes, interests, emotions, and appreciations. The five hierarchial levels of objectives in ascending order are receiving or attending, responding, valuing, organization, and characterization by a value or a value complex.

THE COGNITIVE DOMAIN	THE AFFECTIVE DOMAIN	THE PSYCHOMOTOR DOMAIN
(Thinking)	(Feeling)	(Acting)
Knowledge of	Receiving	Reflex Movements
Specifics	Responding	Basic—Fundamental
Ways and Means	Valuing	Movements
of Dealing with Specifics	Organization into	Perceptual Abilities
Universals and	a System	Physical Abilities
Abstractions	Characterization	Skilled Movements
Intellectual skills	by a Value or	Non–Discursive
and Abilities	Value Complex	Communication
Comprehension		
Application		
Analysis		
Synthesis		
Evaluation		

Taxonomy of Educational Objectives

Taxonomy of Educational Objectives, Handbook II: Affective Domain, published in 1964, revived the interest of educators who long had been concerned about the emotions and feelings of students. They sensed an opportunity to restore what they considered a vital ingredient into educational programs and to respond to what they considered a very urgent need of the individual and of society.

The social sciences and humanities began to receive attention, which they had lost in the post-sputnik era, when educators everywhere joined the hectic scramble for more science and mathematics. Informational knowledge, random facts, and skills dominated the concerns of the schools, and government seemed to be encouraging the movement by providing funding for special institutes, equipment, and program development in technical and scientific areas.

During the past decade, problems in international relations and domestic affairs renewed a deep concern about such areas as war and peace, civil rights, industrial operations, the home, life in the great cities, established institutions, and the place of the individual in a democratic-industrial society. Old values were challenged and deeply shaken, new ones were championed. The whole area of individual rights and social responsibilities came under careful scrutiny. Long-established ideas, customs, and practices became matters of serious concern, debate, and conflict. Some wondered if a democratic society could survive without common values, goals, and objectives. Others believed that self-fulfillment of the individual required diversification, independence of thought and action, and freedom to pursue life as he chooses. A conflict became evident between the desires and choices of the individual and the apparent desires and needs of society. The necessity to reassess the values and attitudes of individuals and groups seemed urgent.

As this reassessment focuses upon the schools, accountability for results looms large in the minds of all those concerned with education. Educators refer to the attitudes of students, and students advocate more freedom and humaneness. Parents are confused by rapidly changing values, and the public wants to hold the schools accountable for the conduct of youth that seems not to meet societal expectations. In one way or another, concerns seem to have shifted to the affective domain.

Significant Components   *Which ones are essential?*

1. The affective domain must be looked upon and treated as an essential part of curriculum planning.
2. The statement of the philosophy, beliefs, and functions of the school should set forth the affective goals clearly and as precisely as is appropriate.

3. All those involved must recognize the importance of affective learning and accept the position that it can be developed through appropriate learning experiences.

4. Emphasis should be on helping students clarify their values and attitudes and arrive at choices that take into account personal needs and social responsibilities.

5. In creating an environment for personal development of ethical reasoning and value formation, the school should avoid trying to impose the values of others upon students.

6. A climate of respect for the dignity of each student and mutual trust must be maintained.

7. The beliefs and views of all students must be given thoughtful consideration.

8. The teacher should be flexible in accepting change and should encourage analysis and adaptation of attitudes that are affecting the lives of students.

9. Meaningful recognition and rewards for effort and accomplishment enhance the likelihood of success in achieving goals.

10. Differences among the impact of the school, the home, mass media, and peer groups must be recognized and taken into account.

11. The affective domain must not be separated from the cognitive because it is impossible to divorce knowing from valuing.

12. Hypocrisy must be avoided.

13. Teachers must be sensitive to the value content of the subject matter which they are presenting.

14. The program must provide for diversity and pluralism.

15. Insisting on "right" answers should be avoided, but it should be recognized that some answers are better than others.

16. The program must recognize that humaneness in education cannot exist without sound values and positive attitudes.

17. Although it is usually desirable for the teacher to declare where he stands on most value issues, it should be clear to the students that other positions may be desirable for them.

18. Special qualities of teachers and special preparation are important.

19. Sensitivity on the part of the teacher and considerateness toward others are basic.

20. Consideration of affective learnings must take place in a climate free from the threat of punishment or reprisal.

21. Schools must recognize that they teach values and attitudes whether they want to or not.

22. The process of developing attitudes and values must be considered as important as the attitudes and values themselves.
23. Affective development should give the students the tools to cope with changes in their own value system and in that of the world around them.
24. It is important that teachers and students plan together in setting explicit goals, specific strategies for achieving them, and definite ways of assessing results.
25. It should be recognized that healthy values and attitudes can be developed without eliminating diversity.
26. The child's cultural background and experiences and the environment in which he lives must receive special consideration.
27. Freedom and openness should not be interpreted as license.
28. The effective teacher should strive to demonstrate through his own actions the values which he considers important.
29. Emphasis should be placed upon developing the habit of examining one's attitudes and values in order to find the most intelligent relationship between the life of the individual and his world.
30. Students should be encouraged to consider thoughtfully and to utilize the values that are established and accepted by the majority.
31. Through rational processes, affective development should integrate the rights and dignity of the individual and the welfare of society.
32. Precise, understandable objectives are essential to rational assessment of results.
33. It is essential that teachers, students, parents, and policy makers agree that teaching values and attitudes is the responsibility of the school.

Proposed Advantages   *With which ones do you agree?*

1. Teaching sound values and healthy attitudes promotes devotion to truth and reason.
2. Students are protected against propaganda and false points of view.
3. A yardstick is provided against which future problems can be assessed and solved. The life of the family and home is strengthened.
4. The relationship between individuals and institutions and their mutual obligations are clarified.

5. The student is assisted in discovering truth and in building peace and unity within himself and his world.

6. Good citizenship is promoted by providing public intelligence for evaluating social institutions and shaping them in directions consistent with moral values and human needs.

7. A sound basis is built for social and political leadership.

8. Provision is made to further the wishes and desires of the majority of the citizens.

9. All other learning is aided and reinforced.

10. A basis is provided for critical analysis and evaluation of problems and situations that confront the student.

11. Instruction in the school insures greater objectivity, balance, and stability than leaving the instruction to family, peers, or other individuals and agencies.

12. A sound set of values and constructive attitudes add direction and dignity to life.

13. Well-clarified values and healthy attitudes are essential for occupational success.

14. Teaching values develops a strong sense of responsibility and a willingness on the part of the individual to devote his efforts to furthering the well-being of the community.

15. Understanding and recognition of differences in attitudes and values avoids undesirable and often unnecessary conflict.

16. Society cannot prosper unless its members have clarified their attitudes, values, and goals.

Criticisms and Difficulties to Be Anticipated   Do you agree?

1. Everybody has the right and should be allowed to have different feelings, values, and attitudes.

2. The teaching of personal feelings belongs in the home and church, not in the school.

3. Molding the thinking of students smacks of demagoguery and totalitarianism.

4. Values and attitudes cannot be taught.

5. Teachers often set a bad example for youth.

6. Continuous friction within the school detracts from effective student learning and public support.

7. Clinging to outmoded values prevents change and progress.

8. Focusing on affective areas detracts from the real purpose of education, and more important areas of learning are neglected.

9. Individuality and creative thinking are destroyed.

10. Students rebel against having older people tell them what to value and how to think.
11. Schools do not know what values and attitudes should be taught.
12. Teachers do not know how to deal effectively with value issues.
13. Materials and guidelines for courses of study are not available.
14. Teachers and students are confused because there is no way to measure the success of their efforts.
15. Conflict between the values taught in the school and those manifest in society beyond the school causes confusion and disenchantment in youth.
16. Teaching moral values leads to religious indoctrination.

Summary Assessment

Today an increasing number of educators and other citizens believe the schools have gone too far in stressing the cognitive domain to the neglect of humane values, feelings, and moral and ethical qualities. They are reassessing the practices of education, particularly of public education. Humaneness and personalized procedures are being proposed. There seems to be a long-neglected need for education to give increased attention to helping students clarify their values and attitudes so that they can live in peace with their value systems and with the desires of society.

Most educators believe this need demands a thoughtful review on the part of the entire nation of its goals, aspirations, commitments, and obligations. We need to decide what we consider the good life to be, and what we are willing to do to achieve it. The schools must determine how they can contribute maximally to these ends through changes in their objectives, subject content, and instructional practices.

More and more, an increasing number of people believe values and attitudes are important in the lives of children and adults, and that these areas must be taught if students are to learn to live happily in today's complex world. But three questions seem to remain unanswered. Is value teaching the proper responsibility of the schools? Which values should be taught? Who should decide which ones should be taught?

Those who seem to think that teaching values in the school is a new idea which has sprung up during the past few years are often surprised to discover that concern for the affective domain has been an integral part of education from the beginning of organized school programs, particularly in the early schools of America. Even a glance at the history of education may add some perspective.

The emphasis of colonial education on moral and religious values is strikingly presented in the 1647 law of the Massachusetts Bay Colony requiring the establishments of schools in all townships with fifty or more householders. Because of the needs and objectives expressed in the act, it has become known as the Old Deluder Law which says:

> It being one chief project of the old deluder, Satan, to keep men from the knowledge of the Scriptures, as in former times by keeping them in an unknown tongue, so in these latter times by persuading them from the use of tongues that so at least the true sense and meaning of the original might be clouded by false glosses of saint-seeming deceivers, that learning may not be buried in the grave of our fathers in the church and commonwealth, the Lord assisting our endeavors,
> It is therefore ordered,—*

In a world far more complex than that of colonial days, it seems that the school should carry some responsibility for developing the child as a worthy person, sensitive to the well-being of others. Examining the purposes of value instruction may help answer the questions about which values should be taught and who should decide on them.

In a rapidly changing social structure, the processes which are learned are often more important than the material itself. To be able to order their own lives and to contribute to building a better world, students must learn to examine their purposes. They must acquire tools for clarifying their values and attitudes. Developing skills in working out intelligent and satisfying relationships to their world may be the most important benefit of value education. Accepting the learning of this important process as a prime objective tends to lead to the conclusion that the students should decide which of their values need clarification and which ones should be studied.

If this position is accepted, teachers will not be tempted to impose their values upon the students. They will find challenging and satisfying roles in helping students wrestle with conflicts

---

*Edward A. Krug, *Salient Dates in American Education 1635-1964* (New York: Harper and Row, 1964), pp. 9-10.

and threats, identify alternatives, and make intelligent decisions. If learning the process of doing this is the important consideration, questions of what values should be clarified and who should decide on them become less baffling. Teachers will not be dictating to students. They will be helping students with their problems and uncertainties. They will be helping students develop models that they can use in building their lives. They will be helping students choose among alternatives, know why they have chosen, and be prepared to accept the consequences of having made good or bad decisions. Several investigators report that the use of value clarifying methods makes a difference in students. Their behavior becomes more self-directed and purposeful.

Much has already been done in the affective areas of teaching and learning, but much more needs to be done. Stanley Casson points to the urgency of working out solutions when he says, "Whenever his practical inventiveness ran ahead of his moral consciousness . . . then man has faced . . . destruction. Perhaps we are today at this stage."*

In the total reassessment and realignment that education is going through in these years, the teaching of values and attitudes is likely to take on greater significance; for such instruction seems to be essential to establishing and maintaining a viable balance between rights and responsibilities that will at the same time insure self-fulfillment for the individual and safeguard the well-being and improvement of society.

A Few Leaders in the Movement

Clive Beck
   Univ. of Toronto
Paul Brandwein
   Columbia Univ.
George Brown
   Univ. of California
   at Santa Barbara
Arthur W. Combs
   Univ. of Florida
George Dennison
   Univ. of Arkansas
Mario D. Fantini
   Ford Foundation

Merrill Harmin
   Southern Illinois Univ.
Howard Kirschenbaum
   Adirondack Mts. Humanistic
   Education Center
Lawrence E. Metcalf
   Univ. of Illinois
Louis Raths
   Newark State College
Carl R. Rogers
   Western Behavioral Sciences
   Institute

---

*A. P. Mattaliano, "Materialism and Youth: How Can Schools Induce Better Values?" *The Clearing House*, January 1964, 93.

Milton Rokeach   Gerald Weinstein
  Michigan State Univ.   Univ. of Massachusetts
Sidney B. Simon
  Univ. of Massachusetts

A Few Places Where the Innovation Is Used

Anaheim, Calif.	Greeley, Colo.	Philadelphia, Pa.
Atlanta, Ga.	Miami Univ.	Univ. of Florida
Cleveland, Ohio	Notre Dame Univ.	Univ. of Massachusetts
Ford Foundation	Pensacola, Fla.	

Annotated References

Archambault, Reginald D., ed., *Dewey on Education: Appraisals.* New York: Random House, 1966. Discusses moral development in Dewey's philosophy of pragmatism. One of the articles by Jerome Bruner suggests that education is the fundamental method of social change. Bruner contends that education transmits to students the values a culture holds which makes that culture unique.

Armstrong, Robert J., et al., *The Development and Evaluation of Behavioral Objectives.* Worthington, Ohio: Charles A. Jones, 1970. Presents valuable help in defining learning outcomes and developing the skills necessary to write and use specific objectives for the attainment of improved results in learning. Behavioral objectives are developed for the cognitive, affective, and psychomotor domains.

Bauer, Nancy W., "Can You Teach Values?" *Instructor,* LXXX, No. 1 (1970), 37-38. Summarizes that the only way to teach values is through open-end questioning that will not force children to accept the viewpoints of teachers, society, or classmates. The teacher must protect the freedom of the child to seek values of his own.

Beatty, Walcott H., "The Feelings of Learning," *Childhood Education,* XLV, No. 7 (1969), 363-366. Maintains that education has neglected the feelings of children and actively attempted to suppress emotions. Crippled learning and stunted growth of the child to maturity is the result.

Belok, Michael, O. R. Bontrager, Howard C. Oswalt, Mary S. Morris, and E. A. Erickson, *Approaches to Values in Education.* Dubuque, Iowa: Wm. C. Brown, 1966. Outlines the teacher's role in facilitating the formulation and redirection of value generalizations—of guidelines of conduct—that will move future generations in survival directions. An approach to the building of positive values is indicated.

Bettelheim, Bruno, "Autonomy and Inner Freedom: Skills of Emotional Management," In *Life Skills in School and Society,* ASCD Yearbook. Washington, D. C.: Association for Supervision and Curriculum Development, 1969, pp. 73-94. Stresses that it is the educative process and the everyday human interactions characteristic of school life that determine what kind of individual is being shaped. Human behavior may be the result of present and not past experiences and perceptions.

Bloom, Benjamin S., Max D. Engelhart, Edward Furst, Walker H. Hill, and David R. Krathwohl, *Taxonomy of Educational Objectives, The Classification of Education Goals, Handbook I: Cognitive Domain.* New York: David McKay, 1956. Explains the development of the taxonomy. The cognitive domain is arranged in six ascending levels: knowledge, comprehension, application, analysis, synthesis, and evaluation.

Bono, J. D., "Languages, Humanities and the Teaching of Values," *Modern Language Journal,* LIV, No. 5 (1970), 335-347. Disagrees strongly that values can or should be taught in the public schools. The author says that concern for values is a "red herring" that prevents excellence in curriculum development.

Borton, Terry, *Reach, Touch, and Teach.* New York: McGraw-Hill, 1970. Emphasizes the concerns of students rather than knowledge as the chief focus of education. Habits, concerns, and processes are the valuable and lasting outcomes of learning.

Botkin, Robert, "Can We Teach Values?" *Educational Record,* XLIX, No. 2 (1968), 189-196. Argues that for most Americans the education goals are to prepare a person for a vocation, to help him cope with all aspects of his environment, and to guarantee as much as possible that he will be an asset to society. When teachers believe that education should reach these goals, then there is no reason to fear teaching values.

Brandwein, Paul F., "Skills of Compassion and Competence," In *Life Skills in School and Society,* ASCD Yearbook. Washington, D. C.: Association for Supervision and Curriculum Development, 1969. Insists that values—and the skills which enable the child to acquire beliefs—can be taught and that they are taught. This can be a positive contribution to the development of our society.

————, *Toward a Discipline of Responsible Consent.* New York: Harcourt, 1969. Takes the position that building values begins with a conflict of values between society and the individual. This conflict makes the student's search for clarifying his personal values relevant and important for himself and society.

Counts, G. S., "Should the Teacher Always Be Neutral?" *Phi Delta Kappan,* LI, No. 4 (1969), 186-189. Supports the teaching of values in the schools. The author expresses the view that some measure of "indoctrination" is inevitable, but rejects the notion that anything, including values, should be taught as "absolutely fixed and final."

Cross, G. I., "Moral Values or Higher Education?" *School and Society,* LXXXIV, No. 2098 (1956), 168. Provides excerpts from a commencement speech at the University of Oklahoma. States that the control of the emotions and the development of the proper attitudes in the use of modern knowledge and power are the principal educational problems of the future. Stresses that the barrier that may prevent wise use of our possessed power and knowledge is the great difference between our ethical and moral development as compared with that of science and economics.

DeGeorge, Richard T., ed., *Ethics and Society.* Garden City, N. Y.: Doubleday, 1966. Presents a series of essays centering on contemporary moral questions. A unity with respect to specific moral judgments is the result.

Dennison, George, *The Lives of Children.* New York: Random House, 1969. Relates how, as parents, if we were to take as our concern not the instruction of our children but the lives of our children, we would find that our schools could be used in a powerfully regenerative way.

Drummond, T. Darrell, "To Make a Difference in the Lives of Children," *National Elementary Principal,* XLIX, No. 4 (1970), 31-36. Concludes that if the school is to be a more humane place for children, administration must inform the staff and set up behavioral objectives to reach the goal. In this way schools may become more responsive and efficient institutions in the teaching of children.

Dunkel, Harold B., "What is at Stake: Value Conflicts and Crisis," *A Curriculum for Children.* Washington, D. C.: ASCD-NEA Publication, 1969. Contends that if we are going to be an urban society, we need to rediscover the actual values of urban living, or if they no longer exist, to invent and perfect new ones. Once we are clear about them, these values are likely candidates for emphasis in our educational programs.

Ellison, Mildred, "Classroom Opportunities to Express Feelings," *Childhood Education,* XLV, No. 7 (1969), 373-377. Observes that the task of the teacher is to develop and encourage an environment that spawns spontaniety, freedom of expression, creativity, and individuality. Strategies for the development of this kind of environment are presented.

Engretson, William E., "Values of Children and How They Are Developed," *Childhood Education,* XXXV, No. 6 (1959), 259-264. Defines a value as a directive factor in human behavior. The article explains that this experience includes imitating and eventually internalizing the values of those with whom the children are in daily contact.

Fox, Robert, Margaret Brown Luszki, and Richard Schmuch, *Diagnosing Classroom Learning Environments.* Chicago: Science Research Associates, 1966. Deals with diagnostic tools helpful in identifying forces in classroom interaction which influence the student's whole environment. Methods and procedures are included in this descriptive work.

Harbeck, Mary B., "Instructional Objectives in the Affective Domain," *Educational Technology,* X, No. 1 (1970), 49-52. Urges that if we are to guarantee quality in education, we can no longer afford to assume that people will develop a value complex as they continue to learn. Values which society agree with must be taught.

Harmin, Merrill, Howard Kirschenbaum, and Sidney B. Simon, "Teaching History with a Focus on Values," *Social Education,* XXXIII, No. 5 (1969), 568-570. Warns against moralizing and tendency to foist values on the students, but emphasizes knowing the subject matter well enough to suggest reading and areas to explore in search of value clarity.

Harrow, Anita J. *A Taxonomy of the Psychomotor Domain.* New York: David McKay, 1972. Offers a guide for developing behavioral objectives in the psychomotor domain. Six levels of achievement are broken down and discussed for the beginning, intermediate, advanced, and highly skilled learner.

Hayter, Jean, "Self-Fulfillment as an Educational Objective," *School and Society,* XC, No. 2204 (1962), 50-52. Pleads for the development of personal values by education as a bulwark against the pressures of mass conformity. It considers the teaching of values in schools necessary to maintain individuality, initiative, and creativity—ingredients necessary in a democracy.

Teachers must understand social changes and the interrelationship between social change and education.

Hitt, William D., *Education as a Human Enterprise*. Worthington, Ohio: Charles A. Jones, 1973. Shows how humanists and technologists can work together to help youngsters become effective human beings. Provides guidelines for developing educational objectives that lead to the realization of each pupil's potentiality for self-fulfillment.

Holt, John, "The Values We Teach in School," *Grade Teacher*, LXXXVII, No. 1 (1969), 72-80. Warns against a growing dissonance in our schools, that of continually causing our children to have to compete for approval of the school and the teacher when at the same time, we preach sharing, kindness, making choices.

Imperatives in Education, A Report. Washington, D. C.: American Association of School Administrators, 1966. Identifies nine imperatives in education. These include "To strengthen the moral fabric of society" and "To keep democracy working." All the nine imply that the teaching of values is implicit in education.

Junell, Joseph S., "Can Our Schools Teach Moral Commitment?" *Phi Delta Kappan*, L, No. 8 (1969), 446-451. Points out the need to pass on to future generations a body of fixed values, but the new teacher of the "emergent values" philosophy asks, "Whose values? Yours or mine?"

_____, "Do Teachers Have the Right to Indoctrinate?" *Phi Delta Kappan*, LI, No. 4 (1969), 182-185. Supports the idea that schools should teach socially acceptable morals; or rather that the schools should continue teaching (indoctrinating, as the author points out) values in the classroom.

Kaltsounis, Theodore, "Decision Making and Values," *Instructor*, LXXX, No. 8 (1971), 51-53. Reports the emphasis is on teaching the valuing process (value free process) and not on specific values. Children need skill in clarifying and making choices.

Keller, Irvin A., "The Morality Gap," *School and Community*, LVI, No. 3 (1969), 42. Suggests six steps to more effective teaching of attitudes, ideals, morals, integrity, and other emotional patterns basic to good citizenship.

Kelly, Earl C., "The Place of Affective Learning," *Educational Leadership*, XXII, No. 7 (1965), 455-460. Stresses that no matter what we do affective learning goes on anyway. We must make sure the affective learning is positive, thus causing constructive behavior.

Kline, Lloyd W., *Education and the Personal Quest*. Columbus, Ohio: Merrill, 1971. Calls for appreciation by the humanist and the scientist of the contributions of each other and of their differences as positive influences for educational improvement.

Krathwohl, David R., Benjamin S. Bloom, and Bertram B. Masia, *Taxonomy of Educational Objectives, The Classification of Educational Goals, Handbook II: Affective Domain*. New York: David McKay, 1964. Defines, describes, and lists educational objectives in the affective domain in the five categories: 1) receiving or attending, 2) responding, 3) valuing, 4) organization, 5) characterization by a value or value complex.

Labenne, Wallace D. and Bert I. Greene, *Educational Implications of Self-Concept Theory*. Pacific Palisades, Calif.: Goodyear, 1969. Emphasizes the impact of education upon the personalities of students and the importance of implementing sound theory in transmitting values and attitudes.

Ability grouping, promotion and failure, grading, discipline, and problems associated with the measurement of self-concept are discussed.

Llewellyn, Ardelle and David Cahoon, "Teaching for Affective Learning," *Educational Leadership,* XXII, No. 7 (1965), 469-472. Identifies as principles that nurture affective learning those that support openness, uniqueness of person, atmosphere of trust, and personal significance to learner.

Lowe, Alberta, *The Value Approach to Student Teaching.* Cedar Falls, Iowa: The Association for Student Teaching, 1960. Presents her material in the form of a diary of a student teacher. The author believes that values are the guides to teachers' action, and that each teacher must set her important values ahead of herself in order to be effective. A careful look at each entry in the diary reveals that it contains a hidden reference to some value.

Mager, Robert F., *Developing Attitude Toward Learning.* Palo Alto, Calif.: Fearon, 1968. Points out the importance of attitudes in the learning process. One of the most significant outcomes of teaching and learning is the development of a favorable attitude toward the materials learned and toward continuous learning.

Mathis, Lois Reno, "Responsibility for Teaching Moral Values," *Educational Forum,* XXXI, No. 1 (1966), 91-93. Concludes from results of questionnaires sent to parents of 1,912 children in Franklin City, Ohio, in 1965 that 80 per cent believe the primary responsibility for teaching moral values to the child lies in the home. A consistent set of values is essential for a healthy society.

Mattaliano, A. P., "Materialism and Youth: How Can Schools Induce Better Values?" *The Clearing House,* XXXVIII, No. 5 (1964), 292-293. Concludes that our way of life is sorely lacking if our teenagers view material gain as their primary goal. Since materialism is perhaps a reflection of home ideals, educators must accept the responsibility for teaching "correct" values.

Maurice, Sister Mary, "Awakening to Human Values in Children's Literature," *Catholic School Journal,* LXVIII, No. 3 (1968), 41-43. Lists values to be found in children's literature as those which implant an empathy for all others, values which stimulate imagination, and values that give the child a sense of the dignity of just being.

Meadows, Milo M., "Attitudes and Values: Ingredients of Good Teaching," *The Clearing House,* XLV, No. 6 (1971), 377-379. Visualizes the teaching of values as the hypothesizing and forming of viewpoints, but not conclusions. Values and attitudes as interpretations of subjective viewpoints are presented.

Metcalf, Lawrence E., ed., *Values Education: Rationale, Strategies, and Procedures.* Washington, D. C.: National Council for the Social Studies, 1971. Expresses concern about the lack of progress in values education and stresses the importance of instilling sound values in youth. Three chapters deal with the objectives, teaching strategies, and procedures for value analysis. A fourth is devoted to resolving value conflicts.

Mowry, Carolyn I., "Teaching Values Through Today's News," *Instructor,* LXXVII, No. 7 (1968), 62-66. Proposes daily newspaper for each child in fifth-grade class to operate as a catalyst for increasing students' sensitivity to people, their environment, and their values.

Muessig, Raymond H., ed., *Youth Education*. Washington, D. C.: Association for Supervision and Curriculum Development, NEA, 1968. Stresses the need for wholeness in the education of adolescents going beyond cognitive development. Problems, perspectives, and promises for the future in the education of youth are thoughtfully presented.

"Patriotism," *NEA Journal*, LVI, No. 1 (1967), 8-11, 76. Fifteen famous Americans in different fields agree that patriotism should, in some way, be nurtured in the classroom. It is important for social survival and improvement.

Punke, Harold H., "Value Change and Education," *High School Journal*, LIV, No. 3 (1970), 167-171. Describes the practical origins of value conflicts, intelligence as a value, the value conflict between the individual and society, the free mind as a conflict area, and the educational implications.

Raths, James, "Mutuality of Effective Functioning and School Experiences," *Learning and Mental Health in the School*, ASCD Yearbook. Washington, D. C.: Association for Supervision and Curriculum Development, 1966. Discusses growing agreement among educators that the cognitive and affective areas of learning cannot be treated as effectively separated as they can together.

Raths, Louis E., "Values Are Fundamental," *Childhood Education*, XXXV, No. 6 (1959), 246-247. Indicates that there is a need for the process of serious interchange for children to become proficient and discriminating in the face of choices. The process is as important as the choices made.

Raths, Louis E., Merrill Harmin, and Sidney B. Simon, *Values and Teaching*. Columbus, Ohio: Merrill, 1966. Presents a clear definition and breakdown of a value. A student must form values for himself, but a teacher can help light the way by clarifying issues and the student's personal thoughts on issues. The book gives step-by-step instructions to teachers with examples of classroom applications.

Rich, John Martin, *Education and Human Values*. Reading, Mass.: Addison-Wesley, 1968. Discusses values and education in four areas: cultural values, organizational values, moral values, and aesthetic values. Each area is defined, and approaches to the development of these values are considered. Concerns of both the individual and society are indicated.

_____, *Humanistic Foundations of Education*. Worthington, Ohio: Charles A. Jones, 1971. Develops the theme that the basis for personal autonomy lies in the ability of the individual to choose intelligently for himself the essential direction of his life.

Ripple, Richard E., "Affective Factors Influence Classroom Learning," *Educational Leadership*, XXII, No. 7 (1965), 476-480. Considers attainment of classroom goals will be facilitated if the affective qualities of teachers and classrooms are characterized by tolerance of moderate expressions of emotions by all.

Rogers, Carl R., *Freedom to Learn*, pp. 239-257. Columbus, Ohio: Merrill, 1969. Includes a chapter explaining a modern approach to the valuing process. Because of their desire for love and approval, infants and adults cling to the values of those who are important in their lives. Becoming open leads to psychological maturity.

Rubin, Louis J., ed., *Life Skills in School and Society*. Washington, D. C.: Association for Supervision and Curriculum Development, NEA, 1969. Points out that for the future, we must have education which concerns itself with skills that enable the individual to know, to think, to feel, to value, and to act.

Sizer, Nancy F. and Theodore R., *Moral Education*. Cambridge, Mass.: Harvard University, 1970. Supports the position that values can and should be taught in schools. Articles by James M. Gustafson, Richard S. Peters, Lawrence Kohlberg, Bruno Bettelheim and Kenneth Keniston emphasize the moral responsibilities schools have to teach values, within what context they could be taught, and toward what end they should be taught.

Stewart, Charles E., "Human Interaction: A Source of Affective Learning," *Educational Leadership*, XXII, No. 7 (1965), 487-491. Recommends another potential for pupil-pupil interaction—the interschool pupil exchange including public and parochial schools.

Trusty, Kay, "Principles of Learning and Individualized Reading," *Reading Teacher*, XXIV, No. 8 (1971), 730-736. Points out that the flexibility of the individualized program allows opportunity for self-expression and teaching the affective area of learning.

West, Earle H., "The Affective Domain," *Journal of Negro Education*, XXXVIII, No. 2 (1969), 91-93. Insists that we need to set specific goals in the affective area of learning and the explicit development of ways to achieve and evaluate them.

Audiovisual and Other Resources

Values in Early Childhood Education (booklet, 96 pp., $1.50). American Association of Elementary-Kindergarten-Nursery Educators, NEA, 1201 16th St., N. W., Washington, D. C. 20036.

Outdoor Education 27

Definition

Outdoor education involves using the out of doors with all its vast resources to help the learner better know and understand the world about him and his place in that world. Through direct learning experiences, involving participation, actual use of skills, and enjoyment, the student comes to appreciate natural phenomena, his relationship to them, his dependence upon them, and their dependence upon him. Insights and skills in dealing with natural resources and problems involving the out of doors are developed. With an arousal of interest in nature the basis for meaningful academic study is developed.

Emphasis might be placed upon conservation, ecology, and appreciation of beauty; or perhaps on socialization, group action, democratic living, economic insights, or man's interrelationship to man. In addition to creating environmental awareness and social sensitivity, an adequate approach offers almost limitless possibilities for enriching all phases of the school program. As a supplement to the activities of the classroom, outdoor education usually includes study of plant and animal life, conservation, rock and land formations, astronomy, and ecology. It is carried out by means of camping, school farms, hiking, construction of various facilities, garden projects, art activities, and recreational pursuits.

In reviewing the successes and failures of schools, it is perhaps important to note that most of the changes that educators consider as innovative deal with the *how* rather than the *what* and the *why* of the learning process. Many of the approaches to individualization, improvement in school management, assessment of outcomes, shifts of different grades to different schools, space alterations, and provisions for varied time allotments are devoted mainly to doing better what is already being done. Nongrading, the middle school, programed instruction, simulations, and inquiry learning all focus on methodology, not on content. These manipulations of time, things, and persons often overlook the importance of giving more time to the study of what children are learning and what they should be learning.

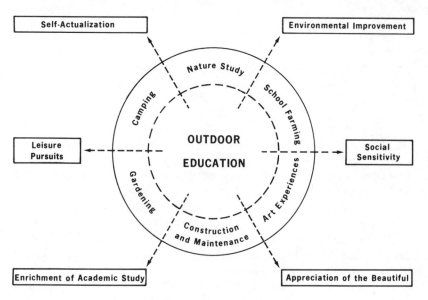

Values of Outdoor Education

Frequently new information such as outdoor education is fed into the operation with little thought of what it should do in affecting the way children conduct the affairs of their lives. In the main, what the college refers to as disciplines struggle to remain individually distinct, and the subjects offered in elementary and secondary schools are categorized in discrete departments.

Attempts to reorganize content into more functional unities such as survival, the beautiful, man and his environment, economic efficiency, or self-realization are usually sporadic and short-lived. Only when such acute problems as a long and unpopular war, pollution, crime, high taxes, or riots disrupt their complacency, do the public and the schools give even transient attention to whether children are learning what they should be learning, or whether they should be learning something else.

Only in such areas as sex education and family living, vocational and technical education, and outdoor education are new content, new objectives, and new methodology introduced at the same time. Since educators could not decide whether to assign responsibility for sex education to the department of biological science, literature, physical education, social studies, or home economics, it has become rather generally accepted that sex education is the responsibility of all teachers.

Similarly, it is yet to be determined whether teaching outdoor education is more appropriate for biological science, art, physical education, social studies, homemaking, or industrial arts. This indecision demonstrates the integrated and integrating nature of outdoor education, stimulates productive thinking, and gives a promising indication of the innumerable ways in which outdoor education can benefit children. Perhaps the broad scope of its content and the general nature of many of its objectives and outcomes constitute one of its strong qualities, which allows it to serve the learner in many areas of living. This strength enables it to contribute significantly to the expansion of knowledge, acquisition of skills, improvement of social relationships, deepening of aesthetic values, integration of human personality, and broadening of recreational interests.

Significant Components   *Which ones are essential?*

1. To be vital, an outdoor education program should be carried on out of doors.
2. Teachers should guard against the danger of thinking that sitting within the confines of the four walls of a classroom reading and talking about the out of doors is an adequate outdoor education program.
3. The activities should have definite purpose and well-defined objectives.

4. The aims and program activities should be coordinated with the work of most classrooms, not treated as a separate subject.

5. Minimal facilities and transportation are prerequisites, but elaborate and expensive buildings and equipment are not essential.

6. A balance should be maintained among expansion of knowledge and understanding, development of skills, furtherance of wholesome social relationships, deepening of aesthetic appreciations, and promotion of recreational outlets.

7. Only teachers with imagination and awareness of the multifold learning opportunities in the world beyond the classroom can pursue the program with enthusiasm.

8. Direct experience and personal involvement on the part of pupils should be used whenever possible.

9. It should be recognized that outdoor education is especially important for urban children who have little opportunity to learn to understand and appreciate natural phenomena.

10. Precaution should be taken to assure the safety of the children.

11. Careful preplanning and preparation on the part of students and teachers are necessary to secure good results.

12. Observation, discovery, involvement, experimentation, work, and play become the prime bases for learning experiences.

13. Teachers must have basic knowledge of natural phenomena and skill in directing social interaction.

14. A free and open climate should be maintained to foster creativity and to encourage capitalizing on learning opportunities that go beyond those specifically planned.

15. Emphasis should be on excitement, appreciation, and new experience.

16. In order to guard against creating the impression that the out of doors is purely recreational, the purposes of the program should be made clear and the learning outcomes emphasized.

17. As the program progresses systematic evaluation should be made of what the students actually are learning.

18. The community, board of education, administration, teachers, and pupils must all understand the program and support it.

19. A significant part of the program is the development of abilities in outdoor living, safety, and leisure-time activities.

20. Teachers of all children and all subjects should understand the potentialities of the out of doors for generating interest in learning and for making it meaningful.

Proposed Advantages   *With which ones do you agree?*

1. Outdoor education provides an inexpensive laboratory for demonstrating the advantages of real experiences utilizing problems and objects to promote learning.
2. Involvement in the out of doors provides students and teachers with relief from the noise, bustle, and tension of everyday living.
3. Students are aided in understanding their relationships to their natural environment.
4. Vast resources for outdoor learning are near many school buildings, often on the school grounds.
5. The out of doors can be used to motivate and support the work of almost any classroom or subject.
6. Physical involvement provides relief from the sedentary pursuits and continuous verbalization of the typical classroom.
7. Many motor skills can be effectively developed in the out of doors.
8. Students develop a close relationship with one another and with their teacher, which carries over into their work in the school.
9. Urban children are provided with a basis for assessing their own environment through comparison with another.
10. Self-reliance, keen observation, careful analysis and synthesis, and application of understandings to the solution of practical problems are reinforced.
11. Outdoor education opens new vistas for leisure-time activities.
12. Firsthand, direct experiences are more readily retained than those learned through indirect means.
13. The program presents an opportunity to discover new possibilities for careers.
14. An appreciation of nature, a positive attitude toward the conservation of natural resources, and increased knowledge and skill for making a personal contribution toward the improvement of the environment are fostered.
15. The rudiments of economics are best learned in the out of doors.
16. Work and play in the out of doors give unity and completeness to human personality.
17. The study of natural phenomena provides a solid base for sex education and family living.

18. Outdoor education gives enriched meaning to our historical origins and cultural heritage.

19. A basis is provided for understanding and appreciating the values of the American frontier.

20. Working in the out of doors develops many valuable vocational skills.

21. Observation of natural phenomena fosters humility and reverence in the student and assists him in establishing his self-identity.

22. Contact with the forces of nature develops a sense of personal responsibility and the realization that blame cannot be shifted to someone else when things do not turn out well.

23. Natural beauty deepens patriotism by developing in the young person appreciation of his country and his legacy.

Criticisms and Difficulties to Be Anticipated   *Do you agree?*

1. The cost of adequate facilities, particularly for school camps, is excessive.

2. Transportation is expensive and often difficult to obtain.

3. Children are apt to be exposed to undue physical danger, and facilities for meeting emergencies are usually unavailable.

4. In many areas, state school legislation presents a formidable obstacle to outdoor education programs.

5. Children in the inner city, who need outdoor education most, are farthest removed from opportunities for it.

6. Teachers already in service lack the knowledge and skill necessary to perform effectively, and few new teachers are being prepared for the work.

7. Especially in the case of pupils who need remedial work in skills, time is diverted from these more important areas of learning.

8. Land and camping facilities are difficult to find and costly to acquire and use if they can be found.

9. Teachers use outdoor education to further their own interests.

10. Many teachers are reluctant to accept the added responsibility and the additional effort required for an effective program.

11. The community may consider outdoor education a frill, a waste of time and money.

12. Although the benefits that may accrue from the program sound good, the danger exists that the results will not match the hopes.

Summary Assessment

For a number of reasons, perhaps, the growth of programs in outdoor education has been slow. School and community leaders have not comprehended its goals and recognized its possibilities. Similarly, teachers have not quickly seen the potentialities of this direct contact with various aspects of the environment. Many have had an exaggerated impression of the cost of an effective program. Continuous shortage of funds in most school districts has prevented school leaders from making even a modest beginning. Absence of trained and interested personnel, coupled with the reluctance of many teachers to put forth the additional time and energy necessary to plan and implement a workable program, has added to the problem.

Recently, however, recognition of the seriousness of pollution, congestion in the large cities and its related problems, non-motivated children, increased demand for recreational outlets, and desire for environmental improvement have again brought the possibilities of outdoor education to the attention of those who are looking for solutions for community and school problems.

It would appear that vital and well-planned experiences with nature and its influences hold significant promise for improving both educational programs and the environment. Additionally, many social problems might be relieved through direct contact with the out of doors. Perhaps a dramatic change from the concrete walls and asphalt playgrounds of the schools in our teeming urban centers is imperative to enable millions of children to value and respond to a world unknown to them.

Failure to capitalize on the potentialities of education in the out of doors may overlook a promising approach to assisting young people in establishing their identity and in building their life values. Youth seem eager to turn from present-day social, educational, business, and industrial superficialities to the realities of the natural world. Certainly the problems of pollution will not be solved without greater appreciation and understanding on the part of the leaders and followers of tomorrow. Only through education relating to their natural environment can people learn to live in satisfaction and dignity.

Outdoor education is not the kind of innovation that deals only with changes in classroom organization, scheduling, and management. It moves to the heart of purposes, content, and outcomes. It takes into account changing needs of individuals and society and embraces change in content as well as in method. It provides varied experiences in many areas of learning without the need for elaborate equipment. It offers children a chance for wholesome growth in their physical, emotional, social, and intellectual development. It emphasizes fresh objectives, varied activities, and new results.

A Few Leaders in the Movement

Floyd Anderson
  Northwestern Univ.
Reynold Carlson
  Bloomington, Ind.
Orval Conner
  Miami Univ.
Jack Davidson
  Montana State Univ.
George W. Donaldson
  Northern Illinois Univ.
W. R. Evans
  Trenton State College
George Gibbens
  Florence State College
John W. Gilliland
  Univ. of Tennessee
Oswald Goering
  Northern Illinois Univ.

John Kirk
  Newark State College
Larry McKown
  Denver, Colo.
H. B. Masters
  Helen, Ga.
Jack K. Mawdsley
  Battle Creek (Mich.) Public Schools
W. G. Metcalf
  Cortland, N. Y.
Peggy L. Miller
  Michigan Dept. of Education
Edwin Pumala
  San Diego, Calif.
Julian W. Smith
  Michigan State Univ.

A Few Places Where the Innovation Is Used

Antioch College
Battle Creek, Mich.
Frederick Co., Md.
Harrison, Ohio
Hillsborough Co., Fla.
Indianapolis, Ind.
Jefferson County, Colo.
Long Beach, Calif.

McPherson, Kans.
Mansfield, Ohio
Michigan State Univ.
Milwaukie, Oreg.
Monmouth County, N. J.
Nassau County, N. Y.
New Paltz, N. Y.
Northern Illinois Univ.

Oregon, Ill.
Pacific Grove, Calif.
Seattle, Wash.
Toledo, Ohio
Traverse City, Mich.
Tyler, Texas
Univ. of Indiana
Webster Groves, Mo.

Annotated References

Brehm, Shirley A., *A Teachers Handbook for Study Outside the Classroom.* Columbus, Ohio: Merrill, 1969. A how-to-do-it guide of practical and detailed outlines for planning visits in the community. Purposes, personnel, transportation, the visit itself, and follow-up are carefully developed. An invaluable aid for teachers and administrators.

Callison, Charles H., *America's Natural Resources*. New York: Ronald, 1967. Provides essential background of information for soil, water, grasslands, forests, wildlife, fish, and parks and wilderness. Land-use principles are presented.

Ewald, William R., Jr., ed., *Environment and Change*. Bloomington: Indiana University Press, 1968. Looks ahead to the next 50 years of change in an urban society. Planning is needed to cope with the impact of technology upon the individual and a complex metropolitan society.

Finlay, Robert, "Schools Without Doors," *Ohio Schools*, XLIII, No. 6 (1965), 15-19. Suggests that many Americans do not have sufficient knowledge of the out of doors to appreciate its many wonders. Effective use of school camps and land labs can help students come to know and appreciate nature.

Gabrielson, M. A. and C. Holtzer, *The Role of Outdoor Education*. New York: The Center for Applied Research in Education, 1965. Discusses curriculum, resources, leadership, activities, and projects in outdoor education. Stresses how to establish leadership in developing an outdoor education program.

Gilfillan, Warren C. and Robert Burgess, *The Counselors' Handbook for the Outdoor School*. Portland, Oreg.: Multnomah Outdoor Education, 1970. A guide explaining the organization of the outdoor school and the relationship of the counselor to the other personnel. Specific information for junior counselors is presented.

_____, *Students' Handbook for the Outdoor School*. Portland, Oreg.: Multnomah Outdoor Education, 1970. Guidebook to orient pupils and parents to experiences of the outdoor school. Pictures, diagrams, and cartoons illustrate activities and regulations and prepare for the learning experiences.

Gillenwater, Mack H., "Outdoor Education—A Coat of Many Colors," *Peabody Journal of Education*, XLVI, No. 5 (1969), 311-315. Defines terms and establishes boundaries of outdoor education. Areas needing research are indicated.

Herbert, Clarke L., "Outdoors With Title III," *National Elementary Principal*, XLVI, No. 2 (1966), 71-75. Discusses the programs of a number of school districts using Title III funds to develop outdoor education projects and the way the funds are used. A listing is made of schools which have projects in the planning stage.

Homan, Paul B., "Rugged Path to Outdoor Education," *American School Board Journal*, CLIV, No. 6 (1967), 10-14. Considers characteristics of a good outdoor education camp site, specifically water facilities, master plan facilities, people involved and other things that are of vital importance.

Hug, John W. and Phyllis J. Wilson, *Curriculum Enrichment Outdoors*. Evanston: Harper and Row, 1965. A practical guide for implementing outdoor education in the regular classrooms in such subjects as language arts and social studies. Activities and aids for teachers at various grade levels are included.

Isenberg, Robert M., "Education Comes Alive Outdoors," *Today's Education*, LIV, No. 4 (1967), 34-35. Gives a resume of a number of outdoor education projects in various parts of the country. Ideas are developed for broadening objectives and enhancing the benefits. Children deal with real things and retain longer what they learn.

Kogan, Deen, "This is Street Theater," *Parks and Recreation,* V, No. 1 (1970), 44-46. Describes the activities of the Society Hill Playhouse and its project "Street Theatre." The group of actors travels throughout Philadelphia putting on free dramatic performances.

Kraus, Richard, *Recreation Today.* New York: Meredith, 1966. Provides background material for giving perspective and direction to planning outdoor recreational and learning facilities for students. A chapter is devoted to outdoor recreation and nature activities.

Lewis, Charles, "Integrating Outdoor Education into the Curriculum," *Journal of Health, Physical Education, and Recreation,* XL, No. 6 (1969), 63-64. Discusses reasons for making outdoor education a definite part of all curricula at all levels rather than a program by itself. Working out of doors provides a laboratory for all subject areas and for learners of varied interests and abilities.

Marsh, Norman, *Outdoor Education on Your School Grounds.* Sacramento: The Resources Agency, State of California, 1968. Stresses the importance of having an outdoor learning laboratory on the school grounds. Planning the facility, suggested learning areas, and integrating the work of the laboratory with that of the classroom are clearly and meaningfully presented.

Outdoor Education—Elementary Social Studies. Title III Project. Unpublished Guide—The Rose Tree Media School District, Media, Pa., 1966. An instructional materials guide for intermediate social studies. The discovery approach is used in the outdoor classroom to develop understanding of the values of natural resources in studying man's relationship to his environment.

Outdoor School Handbook. Unpublished Curriculum Guide. Milwaukie School District No. 1, Milwaukie, Oreg., 1969. Covers responsibilities of outdoor school personnel, activities, and living procedures. Specific outlines for all instructional and noninstructional programs are included.

Outdoors U. S. A. Washington, D. C.: The United States Government Printing Office, 1967. Replete with colored photographs, black-and-whites, and diagrams, this comprehensive volume contains over a hundred articles under four headings: The Big Woods, Water, Beautification, and The Countryside.

Revelle, Roger and Hans H. Landsberg, *America's Changing Environment.* Boston: Houghton Mifflin, 1970. Nineteen essays treat environment under five headings: ecology as an ethical science; water, air, and land; economics and politics; the human city; playgrounds for people. The role of education in improving the environment is emphasized.

Reyburn, Jerry H., "Wilderness Program for One-Week Campers," *Camping Magazine,* XLIII, No. 6 (1971), 14. Stresses activities such as first-aid, math, biology. Presents views on ecology, wild life, self-sufficiency and survival under difficult conditions, and cooperative nature of group living.

Schramm, Wilbur, "Classroom Out of Doors—Part 2," *National Elementary Principal,* XLVIII, No. 6 (1969), 80-96. Explains the present camping program of the San Diego schools and some of the plans for new building projects. After describing a full day's routine, the article presents comments from the camp staff about the value of the program of the three camps.

Shomon, Joseph J., *A Nature Center For Your Community* (Information Education Bulletin No. 1). New York: National Audubon Society, 1962. Illustrated book explaining what a nature center is, its value, its objectives, and costs. Questions about planning and establishing a center are answered.

Smith, Julian, "AAHPER Outdoor Education Project 1955-1970," *Journal of Health, Physical Education, and Recreation,* XLI, No. 2 (1970), 44-45. Report of major accomplishments of outdoor education in general and outdoor education projects, specifically of the AAHPER. Includes information on teacher training, publications, growth figures, and future trends.

Smith, Julian W., et al., *Outdoor Education.* Englewood Cliffs, N. J.: Prentice-Hall, 1963. A guide for developing learning experiences incorporating outdoor skills into the classroom. Importance, content, facilities, and strategies are covered in detail.

Wagner, Guy, "What Schools are Doing—Promoting Outdoor Education," *Education,* LXXXVI, No. 4 (1965), 248-252. Considers reasons for moving children into the out of doors. Opportunities for developing new interests, greater motivation, provision for varied ability levels, and adding meaning and realism to in-school learning are among the benefits.

Wagner, Nancy M., "160-Acre Kindergarten," *Today's Education,* LVI, No. 2 (1967), 41-42. Kindergarten children make repeated trips to same farm and observe the cyclical nature of growing corn and other processes in nature.

Williams, Robert J. and Norman G. Rodgers, "Classroom in the Out-of-Doors," *The Bulletin of the National Association of Secondary School Principals,* LIV, No. 344 (1970), 42-47. A farm, summer gardens, a science laboratory, and a Christmas tree plot are all part of a 76-acre land laboratory near Warren, Ohio. The land laboratory is an especially valuable learning aid.

Newly Emphasized
Strategies and Methods

Community Resources

28

Definition

Community resources for education are precisely what the term implies—the opportunities in the community that can be used to expand and enrich learning experiences for children. These resources may be natural, human, material, or institutional. A wooded canyon, a soldier just returned from war, an industrial plant, a family relations court all are rich in their potential for helping teachers and pupils. Social studies, art, science, industrial arts, foreign languages, business education, and essentially all other areas of learning can discover rich resources that lie ready to be tapped.

Among the most common approaches are surveys and studies of community problems, interviews, resource persons, study trips, displays of products, audiovisual and printed materials, and service projects. Activities involved in a study trip may range from studying the habits of a beaver family to observing the operation of a blast furnace. Visits may be made to a farmyard or to a cathedral. Equally significant as a resource for teaching and learning are the less tangible resources present in all communities, large or small. They include individual or group relations; historical or cultural development of the community; and business, social, economic, or political problems and processes.

Too frequently human resources within the community have been overlooked. Often volunteers with many varied interests and competencies are able to provide valuable services to schools. Much talent is untapped among retired teachers, legislators, labor leaders, scientists, and other professional men and women. Retired business and industrial leaders, government officials, college professors, farmers, journalists, and zookeepers often enjoy sharing their knowledge and experience with youth. Many high schools have instituted a wide range of community services and study projects. Thousands of secondary students are going far beyond the immediate community to participate in foreign exchange programs during the school year. Many more are traveling and studying abroad during the summer.

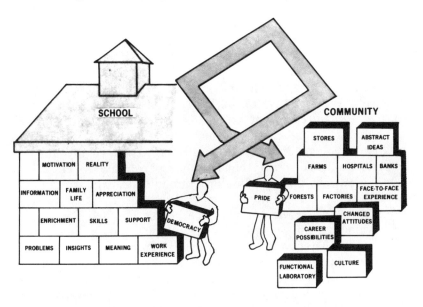

Community Resources: Two-Way Benefits for School and Community

One of the most frequent criticisms of the school is that classroom instruction is separated from real life and consequently holds little interest or significance for many students. By involving the school in the life of the community and the community in the education of youth, a partnership is welded to the benefit of all. Bigness both in schools and communities tends to diminish personal involvement and willingness to contribute to the improvement of the conditions of life. Full utilization of community resources reverses that trend. Like the community school, the use of community resources goes far beyond observing and analyzing things, people, and processes beyond the school or bringing new subject matter into the classroom. It makes students partners with adults in attacking and solving problems of common concern. Teachers and students become important contributors to improving the life of the entire community.

The National Community Workshop Association sponsors summer workshops for teachers, with academic credit awarded by cooperating universities. The workshops give participants an opportunity to study area resources, visit establishments in the community, and prepare curriculum materials. The oldest of the workshops has operated continuously for two decades.

These inservice training programs are supported in various ways including financing by business and industry, school district funds, state and federal grants, and student tuition. As one of their common activities, participants in the workshop prepare or update a directory of physical and human resources within the community and environs which they distribute to all teachers in the school system. Frequently they prepare an inventory of school resources which the community can use to enrich the lives of citizens not in school. Community leaders are involved in raising funds, planning the workshops, providing facilities for study trips, serving as resource people and seminar leaders, and evaluating the results. By working and studying in the community, teachers learn to understand its operations, appreciate its opportunities, and equip themselves to contribute to its improvement. Community leaders who work with the workshops broaden their understanding of schools and develop a strong desire to help them strengthen their programs.

Significant Components   *Which ones are essential?*

1. Study trips or bringing resource persons to the school requires careful planning.
2. Only knowledgeable resource people who speak effectively and relate well to young people can be of great value.
3. To be justified, study trips should give information or provide motivation not otherwise obtainable.

4. Students should understand clearly what the purpose of the trip is and know what to look for.

5. Those being visited and resource people invited to the school should know what the purpose is.

6. The value of utilizing community resources is increased by incorporating provision for them in the course of study.

7. The effectiveness of each experience should be evaluated in regard to both the learning outcomes and the administrative planning and organization.

8. An inventory of all material and human resources in the school community should be made and kept up to date.

9. Groups making study trips should be kept small enough for effective instruction.

10. It is important that teachers study in advance the resources to be brought into the classroom or those to be visited outside the school.

11. Previous study by the class and follow-up, after a trip has been taken or a special resource has been brought into the school, add significantly to the value of community resources.

12. Arrangements should be made carefully to insure safety when pupils are away from school.

13. Necessary permission should be secured, and students should be instructed in proper conduct.

14. Utilization of community resources should go far beyond observing and studying to active and meaningful participation in the solution of community problems.

15. Many simple resources that are passed by daily by teachers and students have great possibilities for providing significant help for learning.

16. The community can contribute many valuable things for building a functional learning resource center.

17. The teacher has the obligation to understand the people and the community in which he works.

18. Community service projects should help solve problems, not create them.

19. Effort must be made to have pupils and their parents understand the relationship between utilization of community resources and significant learning.

20. Allowance should be made for both structured and unstructured study trips since some dimensions of unplanned experience in the community may be of more interest and value to some pupils than many of the planned activities.

21. Imagination of teachers and encouragement and help from administrators are essential.

Proposed Advantages   *With which ones do you agree?*

1. Study trips give students direct experience with their environment and make them sensitive to it.
2. Contacts with reality give meaning to abstract ideas and theories.
3. Visits in the community or presentations at school open doors to career possibilities.
4. Pleasurable experiences with the concrete increase motivation for further study and increased retention.
5. A community is a large and functional laboratory of human interaction, production and consumption, services, and natural and man-made phenomena of all kinds—a laboratory unreproducible even at a fantastic cost.
6. Contacts between school and community improve public support of education.
7. Field trips bring country children to the city and city children to the country.
8. Valuable and inexpensive specimens can be secured right in the community.
9. Some nonschool agencies can teach many things more effectively than the school.
10. Teachers are benefited by gaining a better understanding of the culture of the community, the people with whom they work, and new sources of teaching aids.
11. Study of the community promotes understanding and cooperation among individuals and groups of different interests and backgrounds, including the pupil's peers.
12. Appreciation is developed for the contribution made by all groups in the community.
13. The problems and needs of different agencies and officials are brought to light.
14. Attitudes are more readily changed and prejudices more easily broken down by face-to-face experience.
15. Work in the community provides opportunity to study democracy at work—its values, needs, and processes.
16. Experience in cooperative planning, cooperative work, and cooperative evaluation is made possible.
17. Pride in one's community and neighbors develops.
18. Often people have not seen things in their own community which visitors travel long distances to see.

19. Study trips teach children how to explore, observe, investigate, and share direct personal experiences with others.
20. Every community has retired people of unique talent who can bring valuable benefits to school children. They may range from retired legislators to artists and entertainers.
21. Actually study trips can be undertaken with little expense; they may be as simple as taking a walk to study the trees or rocks on the school grounds.
22. Parents often benefit from being involved in study trips or panel discussions at the school.

Criticisms and Difficulties to Be Anticipated   *Do you agree?*

1. Some phases of community life are too sensitive to welcome close scrutiny and study by students. Social, labor, racial, political, and business segments of the community may not want to be subjects of investigation and analysis.
2. Most field trips are a waste of time because they accomplish little that could not be achieved in another way.
3. Teachers are conditioned to think that significant learning takes place only within the four walls of the classroom.
4. Teachers are committed to the idea that studying textbooks and learning are synonymous.
5. A successful program in utilization of community resources is very difficult to implement if the administration of the school is skeptical or fails to provide leadership.
6. If experience with the concrete is stressed, ideas and generalizations are neglected.
7. Students who enjoy study trips and using objects in solving problems lose interest in reading.
8. Study trips often expose children to conditions and experiences which they should not see.
9. Responsibility and liability of teachers for the safety of the children on study trips is too great.
10. Taking care of a myriad of necessary details involved in utilizing community resources becomes extremely burdensome for the teacher.
11. By taking students out of the classes of teachers other than the one taking the trip, study trips in departmentalized schools are a source of conflict among teachers.
12. The results obtained do not justify the cost and time involved.

Summary Assessment

The relevance of education to the lives of individuals and the problems and needs of society has come under serious question in the past few years. Perhaps the schools have lost touch with the real world beyond their walls. Only by moving out into the vast laboratories of our complex social and industrial life can education give increased meaning and purpose to classroom instruction.

In an era of small schools and rural communities, the home, church, school, and community understood one another's roles and were able to integrate their functions and responsibilities. Change to a technological-urban culture has left the influence of various groups and agencies upon the education of youth disjointed and uncoordinated. Media like the television have made many people more conversant with and often more interested in distant places than in their immediate surroundings. Particularly in urban centers, citizens are often little involved in solving their own problems or in improving the life of their community. Improvement in books, programs, and technological aids has until recently enabled teachers to feel increasingly more self-sufficient within the confines of their classrooms.

Bringing community resources into the schools is limited somewhat in value because it is better adapted to presenting products than to demonstrating processes. Taking the resource out of its setting also destroys some of its fidelity. Resource persons who come to the classroom usually work under the same constraints under which teachers operate. They frequently confine their teaching to telling and showing, thereby limiting discovery, inquiry, and individualization of learning. But the fears and concerns of administrators are a far greater obstacle to extensive use of community resources. Planning and arranging for trips and utilizing the community as a laboratory for meaningful, individualized learning usually place greater demands upon teachers than presenting lessons in a classroom.

A little discouragement from the principal or supervisor is often sufficient to make an enthusiastic teacher abandon his plans for involving students in learning in the community. Too often the first and only contribution of the principal to a study trip is a well-meant, but utterly devastating, warning about the teacher's liability. If it frightens teachers and discourages use of community resources, the statement that liability cannot be stressed too much may not be as true as it usually has been thought to be. Teachers must at all times be seriously concerned about the safety of children, make reasonable provisions for it, and constantly exercise professional prudence. However, repeated warning and rewarning on the part of the educational leader does not contribute significantly to fostering creative teaching and to supporting innovative efforts to make learning more productive.

In assessing the accountability of administrators and supervisors, a distinction may have to be made between efficient management and stimulating leadership. As schools are held accountable for developing citizens who can contribute significantly to building a better community and a better life, they will reach out for every aid to achieve this goal. Use of community resources seems to be a promising approach to improving society by making education more relevant and vital.

The community is a boundless multimedia center—an unreproducible laboratory of human interaction; a huge storehouse of enjoyment, problems, challenges, and opportunities. To the people who live there, work there, play there, and rear their families there, it should be a source of concern, security, hope, and pride. Youth, too, should find it so.

Fuller understanding of the problems of society and involvement in their solution will help students in shaping their values, building their loyalties, and developing perspective. Young people will be able to vote intelligently only if they have had many opportunities to observe and work with real life problems. To this end, the full utilization of community resources is not only an aid; it is an urgent necessity.

A Few Leaders in the Movement

Albert L. Ayars
  Spokane (Wash.) Schools
John Bremer
  Univ. of Hartford
Bertis Capehart
  American Iron and Steel Institute
Charles DuVall
  Georgetown Univ.
Morris Gall
  Educational Associates
  Consulting Agency
W. J. Giddes
  Hope College
Kenneth Glass
  Miami Univ.

Lyal E. Holder
  Brigham Young Univ.
Ronald B. Jackson
  Mass. Advisory Council
  on Education
Herbert Otto
  National Center for the Exploration of Human Potential
Conrad Toepfer, Jr.
  State Univ. of New York at Buffalo
Thomas Webb
  Middletown (Ohio) Board
  of Education

A Few Places Where the Innovation Is Used

Arlington County, Va.	Hickory, N. C.	Philadelphia, Pa.
Bay City, Mich.	Kokomo, Ind.	San Francisco, Calif.
Buffalo, N. Y.	Middletown, Ohio	Spokane, Wash.
Butler, Pa.	Norwalk, Conn.	Tacoma, Wash.
Chicago, Ill.	Oak Creek, Wis.	Wyandotte, Mich.
Fall River, Mass.	Oceanside, N. Y.	Youngstown, Ohio

Annotated References

Bailey, Stephen K., "City as Classroom," *Bulletin of the National Association of Secondary School Principals,* LV, No. 351 (1970), 163-172. Argues that the city is teeming with opportunities for educational enrichment. The author compares the diversity of activities of the people in a city with the diversity of interests among the students. These diverse interests must be taken into account in teaching.

Bennett, Dean B., "Environmental Education: A Regional Approach," *Bulletin of the National Association of Secondary School Principals,* LIV, No. 348 (1970), 56-60. Describes a current project in Maine where several small schools have purchased land to set up a program in environmental education. Children learn about nature, wildlife, ecology, and recreation.

Burgdorf, Lucille P. and Irene F. Harney, "Children Experience Community Action," *The Instructor,* LXXIX, No. 9 (1970), 70-72. Suggests a study of the goals, methods, and effects of action groups on both the local and national level through class discussion and student research in the community. A list of possible topics is included.

Clancy, Peter M. and Milton A. Gabrielson, eds., "A Report of First National Community School Clinic," *The Journal of Educational Sociology,* XXIII, No. 4 (1959), Complete issue. Report of the First National Community School Clinic, sponsored by the Mott Foundation and the Flint Board of Education. Included are a description of the Mott Foundation Program, proposed benefits, and evaluation of its effectiveness.

Cleary, Maryell, "Wingspread: Where People are People; Development of an Urban Studies Program," *American Education,* VII, No. 3 (1971), 21-24. Points out the excellent educational opportunities of school exchange programs exercised between inner-city and suburban schools. The success of Project Wingspread in Chicago is reported in detail.

Cory, Kenneth E., "Using Local Resources in Developing Geography Concepts and Understandings," *Social Education,* XXX, No. 12 (1966), 617-620. Explains how to use community resources in a geography class. A great variety of valuable instructional materials exist in almost every community. Identifying them and places to look for them are discussed.

Cultice, Wendell W., *Field Trips, and How to Make Sure Your School Gets the Most Out of Them.* Englewood Cliffs, N. J.: Prentice-Hall, 1967. Discusses values, procedures, and problems of field trips. The importance of planning, interpreting, and following up is emphasized. Sample checklists and forms are provided.

Draper, Brown, "Research Persons Aid in Teaching," *Agricultural Education Magazine*, XLIII, No. 4 (1970), 100. Advocates resource persons in agricultural studies. An important point applicable to all areas of study is that with the rapid improvements and changes being made, it would be difficult for any one teacher to keep up with all developments.

Dyer, J. Pope, "Modernizing Social Studies Instruction," *Social Studies*, LXII, No. 1 (1971), 23, 26. Highly recommends a modernization of social studies programs. Textbooks can be dull and must be supplemented by conferences and seminars with community personnel and by field study trips to stimulate interest and assure relevance.

Helvey, T. C., "Educational Facilities in the Urban Environment," *Educational Technology*, X, No. 9 (1970), 33-35. Stresses the importance of the "school in reverse"—where students are brought to the subject matter rather than creating poor replicas in the classroom of nature and life in the outside world.

Hirsch, Bennett, "Living Laboratories Aid Science," *The Instructor*, LXXV, No. 10 (1966), 32-33. Explains how the community is used in science courses. Many valuable and inexpensive resources are available to the school at a minimal cost.

Jackson, Ronald B., "Schools and Communities: A Necessary Relevance," *The Clearing House*, XLIV, No. 8 (1970), 488-490. Points up that using the community as a laboratory for learning adds needed relevance to classroom experiences. Life in the school must be related to that in the community in order to have meaning.

Kenough, Jean, "Updating Community Helper Projects," *The Instructor*, LXXV, No. 9 (1966), 54, 102. Explains a project in economic and social ideas and how the community was used to present these ideas to the students. The project added realism and motivation.

Lacattiva, Claire A., "Selected Supervisory Practices in the Use of Community Resources," *Journal of Educational Research*, LX, No. 3 (1966), 139-141. A summary of a doctoral dissertation evaluating 46 practices in the supervision of community resources in 136 New York City schools. Prevalence of the practices in different type schools, the persons administering the program, and the value of various practices were studied.

Leith, D. Malcolm, "Morgan Community Nature Center," *Grade Teacher*, LXXXVIII, No. 6 (1971), 43-45. Presents a fascinating story of how elementary school students with aid from the community built their own nature center. The center has become an integral part of the school's science and ecology programs.

Levinson, Eliot and Saul Yanofsky, "After the Water Is Clean (or Not), Then What? How? and Why?" *Social Education*, XXXV, No. 1 (1971), 67-73. Urges an urban environmental curriculum which will enable the student to understand and cope with his city home, and to change it to meet his needs.

Marcus, Robert, Edward Bispo, and Irving Catuna, "Cultural Profiles for All. . . . ," *National Association of Secondary School Principals*, LI, No. 316 (1967), 91-99. Explains how the Benjamin Franklin School in San Francisco uses citizens of the community to present people with whom students can identify. Many hours are spent in the preparation and discussion of the people, both with them present and in their absence.

Olsen, Edward G., ed., *The School and Community Reader.* New York: Macmillan, 1963. Points up the necessity of closer and more harmonious relationships between school and community. The section entitled "Using Community" contains statements of rationale and practical suggestions for using the community as a vital part of the educational program.

Rodwin, Lloyd and Michael Southworth, "Needed: A National Urban Service," *Educational Technology,* X, No. 10 (1970), 54-57. Proposes a National Urban Service. Working along the lines of the National Park Service, this agency would set aside "living museums," portions of industry, cities, or nature, which would inform students about local activities and history.

Rolser, Thomas, "How Industry Can Aid Inner-City Education," *Catholic School Journal,* LXIX, No. 6 (1969), 21-22. Explains how the Quaker Oats Company has been helping educate the children in the ghetto areas of Chicago. People from the company assist with remedial reading programs and in other areas in which they feel qualified.

Roth, Marjorie L., "Resource File," *The Instructor,* LXXVIII, No. 1 (1968), 41. Presents ideas on the types of questions to ask on a questionnaire for developing a resource file. Careful preparation of the instrument will uncover many valuable aids, both material and personal.

Staley, Frederick A., "Community Resources, the Forgotten World of Knowledge," *Educational Screen and Audiovisual Guide,* XLIV, No. 3 (1965), 27. Presents a brief discussion of the value of community resources, four roadblocks that stand in the way of utilization, and ways of dealing with them.

Street, David, ed., *Innovation in Mass Education,* pp. 145-176. New York: Wiley, 1969. Discusses community action programs and specific details of their organization. Such programs ". . . are testimony to the increased prominence of schools as agents of social change and the emergence of education as a community process."

Taylor, George R., "The Effects of Using Non-Teaching Professionals in a Selected Senior High School," *Journal of Secondary Education,* XLVI, No. 2 (1971), 63-68. Reports the favorable effects of using a nonteaching professional on a "regular semester assignment basis." The professional taught with the regular instructor. Achievement levels of students were raised, and interest was stimulated.

Weatherford, I. W., "Using Community Resources," *Business Education Forum,* XXI, No. 7 (1967), 11-13. Suggests the use of guest speakers and field trips in a distributive education program. The need for careful planning, establishing objectives, evaluation, and followup is stressed.

Wright, Elizabeth Atwell, *Educating for Diversity.* New York: The John Day Co., 1965. Suggests several ways to educate the students of today for the complex responsibilities of tomorrow. One of the most effective approaches is through involvement in the life of the community.

Zubkoff, Myrtle, "All Aboard for Broader Horizons," *The Instructor,* LXXX, No. 4 (1970), 70-71. Reports on fifteen different study trips taken by a kindergarten class and the reactions of the children. Basic concern was the enrichment of the socially deprived child's contacts with the community.

Creativity Development   **29**

Definition

E. Paul Torrance defines creativity as "the process of sensing problems or gaps in information, forming ideas or hypotheses, testing and modifying these hypotheses, and communicating the results. Creativity has also been defined," he says "as a successful step into the unknown, getting away from the main track, breaking out of the mold, being open to experience and permitting one thing to lead to another, recombining ideas or seeing new relationships among ideas, and so on."* He also accepts defining creativity in terms of an original product.

Many people take the position that testing ideas, revising them, and retesting them is more a process of problem-solving than of creativity. They conceive of creativity as being a process that is different, distinct, and unusual. Feasibility and productivity assume significance subordinate to originality of the idea, new perspective, and expansion of personality.

Creativity development encourages the student to be curious, resourceful, and inventive. Most important is his thinking. His desires and his efforts are directed toward producing or stimulating something that is uniquely his. He must feel the urge to go

---

*E. Paul Torrance, *Creativity* (Washington, D. C.: The National Education Association, 1963), p. 4.

beyond learning from others by accepting their ideas to learning from personal, innovative discovery and invention. This can come about only through building individual confidence. Creativity is a growth process that encourages the child to discover and invent and at the same time leads him to recognize his mistakes and inadequacies. It is self-perpetuating in that new discoveries rekindle curiosity. The old idea that there is only one correct answer is discarded. However, thought must still be given to consideration of what is ethically and morally right.

Creativity can be nurtured most effectively in young children since they are less conditioned to conformity than older ones. Repeated experience with success or failure has not yet stereotyped their approach to the solution of many problems. But all students must be led to go beyond rote learning and routine assimilation of ideas and urged to inquire, seek, and invent their own approaches to learning.

At the heart of creativity are people and their unique ideas. As in the case of other human qualities, the degree of creativity varies greatly from one person to another. Recognition of its importance and realization that it is not a purely hereditary trait have stimulated great interest in discovering ways of furthering its development. The climate of the classroom must foster a feeling of creativity on the part of students and teacher. Self-expression and freedom from fear of making mistakes must be encouraged. Insistence on correctness must give way to rewards for originality. Freedom to experiment and create demands freedom from stifling constraints of time, space, limited materials, and uniform requirements and assignments.

Creativity fosters divergent, rather than convergent, thinking. When feasible, the teacher's inclination to demand conformity should be restrained. In this way new avenues are opened for viewing life and attacking its problems. To avoid emotional disintegration, however, resistance to facing the realities of life by escaping into fantasy must be guarded against. Self-actualization must be achieved within a framework of responsible freedom in order to avoid the student's infringing on the freedom of others and to enable him to function satisfactorily in his social setting. The line between what is a creative person and an abnormal one is sometimes blurred.

The relationship between the self-realization of the creative individual and his responsibility to the rights and feelings of those around him is receiving increased attention. The value of freedom and responsibility is being re-examined as they affect the needs of the individual and society. Some consider creativity indispensable for the development and survival of the qualities essential for man to be a human being. Others believe that excessive emphasis on it is likely to destroy the basic cohesiveness needed for society to provide an opportunity for its members to achieve self-fulfillment.

Significant Components   *Which ones are essential?*

1. Only the creative teacher can truly develop creativity.
2. An open, relaxed atmosphere is necessary to foster the development of creativity.
3. Children must be encouraged and stimulated to experiment and discover for themselves.
4. Limitations and mistakes should be accepted as normal.
5. Teachers and pupils must feel free to fail in their search for answers; they must realize that even when they "fail," they are likely to have learned something valuable.
6. Students should be rewarded for exploring strange approaches and coming out with unique relationships.
7. Activities initiated by the students should be pursued whenever possible.
8. Rigid conformity and creativity are incompatible.
9. Insisting on arriving at a "right" solution to problems should be minimized.
10. Guessing, questioning, speculating, challenging, and contradicting should be accepted and rewarded.
11. Sensitivity to environmental stimuli is a prerequisite to creative activity.
12. Flexible schedules and unstructured periods are helpful for promoting imagination and discovery.
13. Teachers must plan for teaching creativity as they plan for achieving other objectives.
14. Inservice experiences to probe factors that stifle creativity development are worthwhile.
15. Detailed directions often prevent spontaneous and original approaches to the solution of problems.
16. Critical evaluation by peers and teacher should be controlled.
17. A stimulating environment with many varied materials and experiences contributes to the program.
18. Open-endedness enhances the potential for fostering creativity.

19. New experiences, new problems, new challenges stimulate growth in creativity.
20. Teachers must believe in the discovery method.
21. Opportunity should be provided for meditation, reflective thought, and even daydreaming.
22. Grades, competition, and comparisons between individuals should be minimized.
23. Individual and small group activities are conducive to the development of creative thinking.

Proposed Advantages   *With which ones do you agree?*

1. New ideas and approaches to solving problems are likely to occur when the possible answers to a problem are unlimited.
2. Today's society places a high premium on originality and has a great need for it.
3. Imaginative people are more successful than less imaginative ones in school work and later as adults.
4. In this day of machines which store and retrieve information better than people, people are needed who relate data in novel ways.
5. Creative students usually are flexible in shifting their behavior to meet new problems. They can tolerate or respond to events or situations that they do not fully understand, disagree with, or cannot control.
6. Creative students discover new areas of interest and pursue them with enthusiasm and vigor.
7. Self-expression contributes to self-realization and the development of an integrated personality.
8. Originality encourages persistent search for alternative answers when success is not immediately apparent.
9. Creativity leads students to higher levels of thinking and problem solving.
10. Most of the significant discoveries of man have sprung from creative impulses.
11. The creative person can better cope with the dehumanizing pressures of conformity in our society.
12. Creativity adds meaning and significance to whatever the child is learning.

Criticisms and Difficulties to Be Anticipated   *Do you agree?*

1. Many teachers are uncomfortable and insecure when a free and open climate exists in the classroom.

2. Insistence on creativity destroys conformity.
3. Creativity development is often thought to be limited to certain kinds of subject areas.
4. People tend to distrust what is new, different, and potentially upsetting.
5. An informal classroom may appear to lack planning, organization, and control on the part of the teacher.
6. Unique responses are frequently not "correct" responses.
7. Creativity disrupts logical and orderly pursuit of learning and lowers achievement.
8. Many administrators do not understand the conditions that are conducive to creativity development and therefore misinterpret or resent them.
9. Parents often condemn creative behavior and look upon divergent behavior as an abnormality.
10. Creativity is sometimes considered inimical to systematic problem solving and maximum accomplishment.
11. Teachers often do not know that creative thinking can be stimulated nor how to stimulate it.
12. There is a lack of evidence concerning the effects of various instructional approaches.
13. Teachers may expect all bright children to be creative and the less gifted to be incapable of creative thinking and expression.
14. Creative pupils are frequently scorned by their classmates.
15. Many students feel repressed and lack the courage to launch out into the unknown and face the possibility of failure.
16. It is often difficult to distinguish between creative thinking and careless thinking.
17. Many teachers do not realize that creativity can be defined and has different stages of growth.
18. Unless divergent thinking takes place within a relatively stable setting, it may destroy whatever exists.
19. Creative people are born, not developed.

Summary Assessment

Dissidence, lack of self-identity, and abandonment of age-old values by youth are frequently ascribed to too much permissiveness on the part of parents and teachers. Quite the opposite could be true. Insistence on conformity may cause extreme frustration in students with high creative potential, driving them to resistance, nonconformity, and even anger. Self-discovery can be achieved through the release of the creative energy of the inner self, but individuality must be balanced with concern for the rights and well-being of others. Equally important is a willingness to accept the degree of conformity necessary to safeguard those rights. Truly creative students are perhaps best equipped to cope with necessary conformity because their minds are busy creating new ideas, acceptable diversions, and adequate adjustments. An integrated personality requires confidence built upon the student's pride in his unique contributions. Spontaneity and initiative depend upon freedom to explore and to express oneself through ideas and behavior that are genuinely one's own.

Growth in creativeness does not occur simply because the teacher says he believes in creativity, is creative himself, and wants his pupils to be creative any more than learning in mathematics occurs because the teacher believes in mathematics, is himself competent in it, and wants his students to excel in it. As in every other area of learning, the teacher must carefully set objectives, plan strategies, and develop learning activities. Often overlooked is the need for continuous evaluation of the progress demonstrated by the learners. Goals must be realigned, methods revised, and deficiencies diagnosed. In teaching creativity, planning and individualization are perhaps more important than in many less complex areas of learning.

Demonstrated recognition of the value of creative responses, involvement in varied experiences and with many materials, freedom and security to be different in attacking problems, and encouragement of self-initiated activities are essential elements in creativity development. Activity coupled with time for reflection is important. Self-criticism contributes to the development of responsibility and ability to cope with problems which arise from deviating from a normal course or standard. The world in which students live and will live is characterized by activity, pressures, and change. Discovering new ways of viewing his complex environment and solving the problems which arise out of it are vitally important for every child. Schools should grasp every opportunity to help children develop originality and ingenuity in coping with the multitude of challenges that confront them.

Adaptability is essential for effective functioning in a mobile and rapidly changing society. Within their lifetimes, school children of today will be called upon to come to grips with problems that neither they nor their teachers can even visualize at this time. They are likely to live in many parts of the world and be required to adjust to different cultures, ideas, and customs. The vocational pursuits to which they will devote a major portion of their lives may yet be unheard of. Values relating to all areas of living may be radically different from those which they are learning. Capability to think freely and creatively will be needed to attack their new problems. Only one thing is certain. The world of their adult lives will be different from that of their school years. To equip them to live in their world in their time, the schools must teach adaptability by promoting flexibility and fostering creativity. To do otherwise would leave the schools unaccountable.

There seems to be consensus that creativity can be developed, and that the schools should address themselves to developing it. Many of the really significant contributions to society have been made by those who think imaginatively and discover new approaches to the solution of important problems. Hence, serious study should be directed toward discovering new and more effective ways of fostering creativity that lead to self-realization without infringing on the well-being of others.

A Few Leaders in the Movement

W. Lambert Brittain
  Cornell Univ.
Alexander Frazier
  Ohio State Univ.
Donald MacKinnon
  Univ. of California at Berkeley
J. H. McPherson
  Saginaw Valley College
George E. Monroe
  Univ. of Illinois, Chicago
Walter T. Petty
  State Univ. of New York at Buffalo

Hanns Sachs
  Louisiana Poly. Institute
Geraldine Siks
  Univ. of Washington
James A. Smith
  Univ. of Wisconsin, Sheboygan
Harriet Talmage
  Univ. of Illinois, Chicago
Calvin Taylor
  Univ. of Utah
E. Paul Torrance
  Univ. of Georgia

A Few Places Where the Innovation Is Used

Athens, Ga.	Eastern Washington	Pensacola, Fla.
Attelboro, Mass.	State College	Univ. of Connecticut
Baltimore, Md.	Goucher College	Univ. of Georgia
Centerville, Ohio	Lansing, Mich.	Univ. of Oregon
Columbia Univ.	New Haven, Conn.	Univ. of Utah
Dayton, Ohio	New York, N. Y.	Warwick, R. I.
		Wayne, Nebr.

Annotated References

Ashton-Warner, Sylvia, *Teacher.* New York: Bantam, 1963. Stresses the author's belief in creative teaching and describes the methods which she developed and utilized to help students cope with the pressures which tend to destroy human personality.

Brown, George J., "Teaching Creativity to Teachers and Others," *The Journal of Teacher Education,* XXI, No. 2 (1970), 210-216. Describes structuring experiences of a workshop designed to increase the participant's awareness and creativity. The procedure moves from cognitive and verbal content to nonverbal and affective behavior. Advantages of the method are explained.

Bruner, Jerome S., "The Act of Discovery," *Harvard Educational Review,* XXXI, No. 1 (1961), 21-32. An excellent discussion of the discovery method of education and the elements that compose it.

Coggins, Dessie-Ellen, "Five Steps to Creativity," *Parents Magazine,* XLV, No. 3 (1970), 52-53, 87-88. Addresses itself to both parents and teachers. The author cites ways in which the child is most likely to create and develops situations that will help foster creativity.

Demarko, Sharon K., "A Place Where Learning Happens," *American Education,* VII, No. 4 (1971), 21-23. Describes the "humanized education" at the Escarosa Humanities Center in Pensacola, Florida, where the students are treated as creative individuals who are eager to learn.

Eisner, Elliot W., *Think with Me About Creativity.* Dansville, N. Y.: Owen, 1964. A collection of 10 essays from *The Instructor* magazine which consider creativity and intelligence, creativity in the classroom, and creativity as it relates to mental health.

Frazier, Alexander, "A Tougher Look at Skills/A Closer Look at Children," *Grade Teacher,* LXXXVII, No. 5 (1970), 95-97. Pinpoints the two demands which seem uppermost among the nation's current social goals, mastery and demand for growth, and shows how they may influence what goes on in our classrooms. Problems of growth are discussed and suggests some things we must give attention to in the curriculum of the 1970's.

Goodlad, John I., M. Frances Klein, and Associates, *Behind the Classroom Door,* 2nd ed. Worthington, Ohio: Charles A. Jones, 1973. Explores improved approaches to unlocking human potential. Classroom observations are used to analyze 10 expectations for childhood schooling, curricular provisions, and instructional practices. Reconstruction of schooling is indicated to accomplish what needs to be done.

Haefele, John W., *Creativity and Innovation.* New York: Reinhold, 1962. Discusses the anatomy of creativity—the creative process, the creative stages, and the creative personality.

Inslow, Gail M., *The Emergent In Curriculum,* pp. 69-89. New York: Wiley, 1966. Offers six definitions of creativity and indicates its relationship to mental health. Permissiveness, divergence, and a creative teacher are important. The creative child and the intelligent one are not necessarily the same.

Jameison, Frances H., "Children Need to Create," *Parents Magazine,* XXXIV, No. 6 (1959), 52-53, 109, 110. Involves a discussion of why children need to create and the importance of learning by doing.

Kagan, Jerome, ed., *Creativity and Learning*. Boston: Houghton Mifflin, 1967. Contains 16 articles by various authorities in the field considering issues which have relationship to the development of creativity. The articles consider various opinions about creativity and stress that its development must be cultivated.

Kohl, Herbert, "Earth, Air, Fire, and Water," *Grade Teacher*, LXXXVIII, No. 7 (1971), 5-6. Describes several techniques for creating an open classroom in which the teacher is not at the center, and which employs full pupil involvement and greater self-awareness.

———, "Making Physical Contact," *Grade Teacher*, LXXXVIII, No. 4 (1970), 16-22. Describes some ways to bring children into nonhostile physical contact with each other and to be able to feel at ease in each other's presence; e.g. through such games as the squeeze message, the Amoeba, and through Improvisation.

Kravetz, Nathan, "The Creative Child in the Un-Creative School," *The Educational Forum*, XXXIV, No. 2 (1970), 219-222. Makes an interesting, but rather sad, appraisal of the way creative growth is often stunted in the classroom when the teacher fails to make provision for or give reward for creative thinking. Specific ways are cited to guide and encourage creativity by shifting curriculum patterns to serve best the unique needs of the student.

Lowenfeld, Viktor, *Creative and Mental Growth*. New York: Macmillan, 1959. Explores creative growth with an emphasis on art. Creative products provide a foundation for developing creativity and for assessing growth.

Maccoby, Michael, "The Three C's and Discipline for Freedom," *School Review*, LXXIX, No. 2 (1971), 227-242. Proposes the teaching of the three basic C's, Concentration, a Critical Attitude, and Communication, along with the teaching of the Three R's to encourage in children an interest in knowing and creating, and to develop individual powers to become active, productive people, not passive consumers in a highly technological society.

McHale, John F., "A Definition of the Creative Process," *Educational Technology*, X, No. 12 (1970), 56-57. Proposes a definition of the creative process based on self-creation through ideation and work.

MacKinnon, Donald W., "The Courage to Be: Realizing Creative Potential," *Life Skills in School and Society*, ASCD Yearbook, Washington, D. C.: Association for Supervision and Curriculum Development, 1969. Discusses characteristics of the creative person. Otto Rank's theory of development of the creative person is considered at length, and the various stages of growth are described.

Madsen, Edna, "Children of All Ages Create in a Variety of Media," *School Arts*, LXII, No. 9 (1963), 8-11. Stresses the need for the availability of all types of materials in the classroom for the maximum use of creative processes.

Miller, Peggy L., "Innovation and Change in Education," *Educational Leadership*, X, No. 1 (1970), 334-340. Considers humans both obstacles to and facilitators of educational change. The greatest facilitating factors are community support, cooperation of administration and faculty, and involvement of teachers in planning projects. The human obstacles are lack of communication with the staff and criticism from non-project teachers.

Mock, Ruth, *Education and the Imagination*. London: Chatto and Windus, 1970. Of particular relevance are the last two chapters, "Imaginative Teaching" and "The Education of Imagination," in which the author gives insight into these topics from her own personal experiences and beliefs.

Neperud, Ronald W., "Artists at Work: A Key to Understanding," *Art Education*, XXIII, No. 2 (1970), 33-35. Explains creativity as a process of "searching, discovering, exploring, decision-making, evaluating, revising, and re-evaluating." A creative artist recommends creative teachers and opportunities for seeing creative people at work as an aid to teaching creativity.

Newman, Roberta, "Music Education: The Need for Change," *School Review*, LXXIX, No. 3 (1971), 441-448. Stresses the necessity of teaching music in a subjective manner and in a manner relevant to individual needs and society's needs. Also advocates allowing students to make value judgments about music, creating personal, individual experiences with music, and helping students understand their own musical likes and dislikes.

Parnes, Sidney J., "Creativity, Developing Human Potential," *Journal of Creative Behavior*, V, No. 1 (1971), 19-36. Describes and explores the make-up of the creative person and supports curricula that nurture creative development to foster the living of fuller lives—both in school and in the future.

Piltz, Albert and Robert Sund, *Creative Teaching of Science in the Elementary School*. Boston: Allyn and Bacon, 1968. Gives practical suggestions to teachers for improving creativeness in their performance. Teachers can stimulate creative ways of learning if they use creative approaches and encourage them in students.

Rich, L., "Creativity Takes Over," *American Education*, VI, No. 10 (1970), 16-22. Enthusiastically supports and describes the "creativity take-over" in the Attleboro School System where "disciplines are being related to one another in an organized effort to get children to view the world around them in a fresh, creative, integrated way," and where the emphasis is placed on collaborative teaching and learning and on making subjects come alive.

Scott, Robert, "Why Johnny Can't THINK," *School and Community*, LVI, No. 4 (1969), 8-9, 46-47. Schools tend to thwart creativity by considering creative children as troublemakers. Creative teachers who can accept mistakes are essential.

Shumsky, Abraham, *Creative Teaching in the Elementary School*. New York: Appleton-Century-Crofts, 1965. Discusses the importance of the teacher in educational change and the "repetitive-creative conflict." Creative teaching is considered as it applies to each of the subject areas of the elementary school. Attention is given to the education of the creative teacher.

Siks, Geraldine Brain, *Creative Dramatics: An Art for Children*. New York: Harper and Row, 1958. Discusses the art of releasing the creative processes children possess. Dramatic activities are emphasized as functional factors while principles apply to any creative process. Activities and guidelines are given for various age levels.

Smith, James A., *Creative Teaching of the Creative Arts*. Boston: Allyn and Bacon, 1967. Relates how teachers can be more effective in areas such as music, art, and drama. Teachers must strive to present children with situations which will lead to creative responses.

————, *Creative Teaching of the Language Arts in the Elementary School.* Boston: Allyn and Bacon, 1967. Deals with such topics as creative teaching, creative communication, creative listening, and creative writing. The book is designed to help teachers aid students in developing their creative potentials and offers practical aids.

————, *Creative Teaching of Social Studies.* Boston: Allyn and Bacon, 1967. Gives many ideas for fostering creativity in learners by using creative teaching methods. Many excellent pictures, charts, and other graphic material are provided.

————, *Setting Conditions for Creative Teaching in the Elementary School.* Boston: Allyn and Bacon, 1966. The first in a series of books devoted to the discussion of how the precious resource of creativity can be developed through careful teaching. Examples of unimaginative as well as creative teaching methods are presented.

Stephens, Ada D., *Providing Developmental Experiences for Young Children.* New York: Bureau of Publications, 1952. Stresses the need for active, involved teachers in order to foster creativity in the classroom.

Swyers, Betty J., "Must They Conform," *Grade Teacher,* LXXXVIII, No. 6 (1971), 16-22. Stresses the need for helping students become creative, independent thinkers and delineates the teaching practices which retard and suppress creative thinkers.

Taylor, Calvin W., ed., *Creativity: Progress and Potential.* New York: McGraw-Hill, 1964. Summarizes current knowledge about creativity and discusses some of the programs now being developed to foster it. A list of several hundred references is included.

Thomas, George I. and Joseph Crescimbeni, *Individualizing Instruction in the Elementary School,* pp. 161-184. New York: Random House, 1967. Describes the characteristics of the creative person and indicates ways of developing them in the classroom. The climate of the classroom and opportunity to share creative experiences are important.

Torrance, E. Paul, "Comparative Studies of Creativity in Children," *Educational Leadership,* XXVII, No. 2 (1969), 146-148. Explains administration of the Torrance Test of Creative Thinking and the Minnesota Test of Creative Thinking, both the verbal and nonverbal forms. Children from different cultures show great variations in gain and loss in creative functioning.

————, *Creativity.* Washington, D. C.: National Education Association, 1963. A pamphlet in the series "What Research Says to the Teacher." It discusses evidence, measurements, development patterns of creativity and what teachers can do to stimulate creative behavior.

————, *Education and the Creative Potential.* Minneapolis: University of Minnesota Press, 1963. Excellent source on the definition of creativity, the child as the potential creator, and the creative process as a whole.

————, *Encouraging Creativity in the Classroom.* Dubuque, Iowa: Wm. C. Brown, 1970. Moves rapidly from a theoretical discussion of needs for creativity to practical aspects of instruction in the classroom. Sequences for building creative skills are developed for reading and heightening anticipation. Discovering unrecognized potential and hidden talents is given special attention.

———, *Guiding Creative Talent.* Englewood Cliffs, N. J.: Prentice-Hall, 1964. Emphasizes the problems of highly creative children and discusses varying age and ability levels. Two chapters deal specifically with qualifications of counselors, teachers, and administrators who can effectively develop creative talent.

———, *Rewarding Creative Behavior.* Englewood Cliffs: Prentice-Hall, 1965. A thorough discussion of creative behavior and ways of encouraging it. The appendix contains descriptions of instruments used to measure creative ability and suggests ways to foster creative thinking.

———, "Uniqueness and Creativeness: The School's Role," *Educational Leadership,* XXIV, No. 6 (1967), 493-496. Points out that research has demonstrated that creativity can be fostered by planned methods. Creativity involves awareness of novel problems, searching for solutions, and communicating the results of the search.

Torrance, E. Paul and R. E. Myers, *Creative Learning and Teaching.* New York: Dodd Mead, 1970. Explains the way a teacher should conduct her classroom in order to foster creativity. The book gives many practical suggestions which can be used by the teacher to help students learn more creativity.

Vernon, P. E., ed., "Creativity" in *Selected Readings in Creativity.* Baltimore: Penguin, 1970. Of benefit to the teacher who desires to know about creativity, some pioneer studies in creativity, and conditions which can be set for the stimulation of creativity. The book also includes "Introspective Materials" (source readings from Mozart, Tchaikovsky, Poincare, et al.), "Theoretical Contributions" (source readings from Freud, C. Rofers, Sinnott, Bartlett, et al.), as well as chapters on "Psychometric Approaches" and "Personality Studies." The book's merit lies in its comprehensive quality—in dealing with many different though related aspects of creativity.

Audiovisual and Other Resources

Creative Education Bibliography (leaflet, 8 pp., 25¢) and *Creative Teaching Tips* (leaflet, 4 pp., 25¢). American Association of Elementary-Kindergarten-Nursery Educators, NEA, 1201 16th St., N. W., Washington, D. C. 20036.

Creativity (booklet, 35 pp., 35¢). Describes patterns of development and how to stimulate creativity. NEA, 1201 16th St., N. W., Washington, D. C. 20036.

Creativity and Learning (16mm film, color, sound, 22 min., $200, rental $11). Features Dr. E. Paul Torrance, one of the leading figures in the development of ways to increase creativity in teaching and learning. /I/D/E/A/, P. O. Box 628, Far Hills Branch, Dayton, Ohio 45419.

Design for Growing (16mm film, color, sound, 34 min., $137.25, rental $15). Cleveland, Ohio, program for stimulating imaginative approach to problems of living in modern world. National Audiovisual Center, Washington, D. C. 20409.

Is Your Child Creative? (leaflet, pkg. of 30, $1.50). Describes how parents can recognize and nurture creative spirit. NEA, 1201 16th St., N. W., Washington, D. C. 20036.

Humaneness

30

Definition

Education which focuses on the development of humaneness sees nothing in the learning process more important than the individual and the development of his unique human qualities. This philosophy insists that each person must be allowed to grow in his own way and at his own rate if he is to have a chance to develop fully. No two people are exactly alike, no two develop in the same way, and no two reach the same level of their potential. Therefore, education which hopes to nurture humaneness must allow for freedom, personal choice, and expression of emotions so that human characteristics such as individuality, sensitivity to the needs and feelings of others, concern, and empathy can be properly nurtured. There must be chances for mistakes, and the learning situations must allow students to feel free to take risks. It is only through trying different alternatives that young people will be able to arrive at answers and values which are truly meaningful for their lives. The road to becoming a fully functioning human being is not an easy one; and there are many attitudes, new concepts, and values which each person must glean from the bumps along the road of experience.

The question of how to develop the quality of humaneness in youth has become a popular one in educational circles in the last few years. In the late 1950's and during the 1960's great concern was focused on developing the minds of young people. Society seemed to lose sight of the fact that man is not merely the sum total of his intellectual capacity. The emphasis in learning was placed on the accumulation of knowledge almost to the exclusion of the development of the child's values and humane qualities. Some critics of education contend that this misfocusing of effort may have led to an emotionally undernourished society surrounded by a complex technology which it cannot understand or utilize for effective living.

After years of concentration on the cognitive development of young people, society saw that it could put men on the moon, build intricate computers, and make great strides in other areas of science. But it discovered that many of the young people who had been so carefully molded by our educational system neither make society happy nor are happy themselves. A shift has begun which may see humaneness move to the fore in educational thought and planning, and the primary goal of education may become that of helping each person become fully humane.

There now seems to be an emphasis on the development of the whole child, his mind, heart, and soul, and those qualities which make him uniquely human. Arthur Combs describes the situation this way:

> What makes people human are matters of feeling, belief, values, attitudes, understandings. Without these things a man is nothing. These are the qualities which make people human. They are also the qualities which, in our zeal to be objective, we have carefully eliminated from much of what goes on in our public schools. The problem of dehumanization is no accident. We brought it on ourselves. We have created a Frankenstein's monster which has broken loose to run amok among us.
>
> Everyone starts life with the capacity to become a good human being. People are not born bad or inhuman. The qualities we describe as human are "warm" qualities of compassion, understanding, fulfillment, love, caring, justice, and the like, while the qualities we describe as inhuman, on the other hand, are "cold" ones, generally the reverse of these. We speak of a man as "a good human being." By that we refer to his uniqueness and value as a person, his sensitivity and compassion for others, and his capacity to interact effectively in his world. Elsewhere in this book, these traits have been called

"humane." They are also the characteristics of self-actualizing persons as they are described by psychologists who have studied such people.*

Education seems to be shifting toward a total concern on the part of educators and the public for all that a child has the potential to become. Learning experiences which aim at developing fully each person's potential for humane living must allow students to follow roads of inquiry which appeal and are relevant to them. Students must be allowed to seek answers to such questions as: Who am I? How can I best fulfill my destiny? What values should I accept as guiding lights in my life? How can I best get along with other people? How can I function most effectively as a part of the universe? What is the purpose of my existence? The answers to such questions will be different for each person, and each individual must discover his own answers to these questions.

Education which is centered around the development of humaneness must include a rich and varied learning environment. Teachers need to be extremely humane themselves and must look upon each child as unique and of great value. They must realize that all young people need an equal opportunity to develop fully as people embodying the most human qualities. Classrooms must provide many and varied ways of learning, and doors should be passed through often as the child seeks experiences outside the school. It is only through broad experiences that the child will get a true picture of the world.

Education for humaneness encourages the development of those things within each person which are valued most in terms of helping people develop into fully functioning and complete human beings. Such education recognizes the true uniqueness and worth of each person and works toward the maximum development of each person's most human qualities. It promises to improve his own self-realization, enhance his contribution to the self-fulfillment of those with whom he comes in contact, and add new dimensions to the quality of life of civilized human beings.

---

*Arthur W. Combs, "An Educational Imperative: The Human Dimension," in *To Nurture Humaneness,* 1970 Yearbook, Association for Supervision and Curriculum Development, NEA. (Washington, D. C., 1970), p. 174.

Significant Components   *Which ones are essential?*

1. Teachers must be more concerned with the personal and human development of each child than with learning material, organizing information, and acquiring bodies of knowledge.

2. A nonpunitive evaluation system, which allows students to experiment and to make mistakes in their quest for meaningful answers, must be established.

3. Teachers must remember constantly to comment favorably on students' efforts, provide encouragement, and offer frequent opportunities for success.

4. Sensitivity training can be used to advantage by those who have had careful training in the use of this technique.

5. Flexible schedules and nonrigid curriculum guidelines must allow students to pursue the learning experiences which are most meaningful to them.

6. Students must assume a greater share of the responsibility for their own learning.

7. Small classes are important to give students more freedom and a greater chance for spontaneous interaction with teachers and with one another.

8. Students must become so completely involved in the learning process that the learning which takes place becomes internalized.

9. There must be a reassessment of the basic purposes of education and the desired outcomes of the educational process.

10. Commitment must be made to putting humanistic goals first and to pursuing them above other objectives.

11. Equal opportunities must be given to all people if there is to be a development of a society of truly humane individuals.

12. Community resources and learning experiences outside the classroom must be fully utilized.

13. Society as a whole must work to reduce problems such as pain and hunger, for a person cannot concentrate on establishing a value system or improving interaction skills when he is starving.

14. There must be less emphasis on schools as a preparation for specific skills and more stress on developing each individual's capacity for humaneness.

15. Basic in the program are materials which allow the humaneness of the teacher to be brought out and the humaneness of the student to be developed.

16. The intricate nature of each person's personality must be recognized and appreciated.

17. Individualized instruction is essential.
18. There must be ample time in the school program for non-structured socializing experiences, which greatly facilitate the humanizing process.
19. Each student must initiate many of his own learning experiences.
20. Inservice programs are necessary to help change the thinking of the teachers who are oriented primarily to the development of the cognitive areas of learning.
21. Students must be given chances to experiment with interacting with all people around them so that they can develop good interpersonal relationships.
22. Students must be given the opportunity to study their relationship to the machine and technology.
23. Teachers must treat all students in a humane way and not tolerate inhumaneness among those in their classes.
24. Society must be deeply concerned with the development of each child into a warm, compassionate, and understanding individual.
25. The inquiry method is often very effective in the affective areas of learning.
26. Children must have early experiences which foster curiosity and allow them to develop as fully functioning individuals, who interact totally with life.
27. Emphasis must be placed on truly educating as opposed to training or indoctrinating.
28. Superior and varied learning environments are essential.
29. Time must be provided for reflection and introspection.
30. Pupils should be deeply involved in planning their learning activities.

Proposed Advantages   *With which ones do you agree?*

1. As a child assumes more responsibility for his learning, he assumes more responsibility for other aspects of his life.
2. Self-expression, thought processes, and creative thinking improve as the child is given more freedom in his learning activities.
3. Individuals do not blindly accept old virtues, but test and revamp traditional values to fit their own lives.
4. Young people develop a sincere respect for the meaning and worth of their lives.
5. Interpersonal relationships improve.

6. Principles and values are integrated with knowledge and skills.
7. Great emphasis is placed on "how to learn."
8. People come to the conclusion that the life they lead does make a difference in the ultimate scheme of things.
9. Constant change and growth of the total human personality result.
10. Warm qualities such as love and kindness are valued and nurtured in the learning experiences.
11. Use of community resources and learning activities which take place outside the classroom make learning more vital.
12. Students enjoy taking a real part in the planning of their own learning experiences.
13. Flexible scheduling allows each child to pursue in depth those experiences having most meaning for him.
14. Children become eager questioners and energetic seekers for important answers.
15. Pupils are not inhibited by the threat of constant and immediate evaluation.

Criticisms and Difficulties to Be Anticipated   *Do you agree?*

1. There are always those who feel that education should have, as its primary function, preparing a person for a career.
2. Advances in the development of humane behavior are difficult to measure and to report to parents.
3. Emphasis on humaneness in education necessitates changes in the structure of society as a whole, not only of the schools.
4. Reassessment may lead to discarding some values which have stood for centuries.
5. The spirit of competition in many instances will be eliminated to the disadvantage of progress in an industrial society.
6. Young people are sometimes slow in assuming responsibility for their own learning.
7. Changes in curriculum priorities take time.
8. Humaneness in any aspect of education springs from broad and often abstract goals which can be interpreted and carried out in an infinite variety of ways.
9. Teachers may get so involved in humane learning activities that they neglect skills areas.
10. People may feel that too much freedom results from letting each child do what is meaningful to him.
11. Many basic concepts involved in the development of humaneness are difficult to agree upon and are extremely complex.

12. Teaching for humaneness may be rather hit or miss.
13. Many great changes and even more minor adjustments must be made in our schools if education for humaneness is to become a primary goal of education.
14. It is extremely difficult at times to determine what will best help a child to develop to his fullest.
15. Overemphasis on cognitive learning may continue even though basic goals of education change.
16. Precise objectives are extremely difficult to state.

Summary Assessment

As our population increases and people are pressed constantly closer, the need for human beings to be able to get along well with one another and to respect the rights and values of others is becoming more important. The fostering of such attitudes and feelings should come at an early age, and people are realizing that schools are the natural learning laboratories where young folks must have a good chance to test and develop their total personalities. To survive in an overpopulated environment will take more than a grasp of knowledge. Relevant values and proper attitudes and humane actions are increasingly essential.

A new concern with humaneness in education has come into being in the last few years. Man in the last third of the twentieth century finds that he has educated himself and developed his mind to the point where he is able to make scientific advances undreamed of only a few decades ago. But with the satisfaction of his strictly intellectual achievements has come the realization that the development of certain very important facets of his being has been neglected or at best often left to chance. It seems now that all those involved in education are looking for teachers, scheduling plans, curriculum ideas, and learning experiences which will develop the heart of man as well as his mind. Development of the heart and mind should not be considered incompatible, for in truth a true deepening of the experiences of the heart may facilitate the functioning of the mind. A relaxed child with meaningful values, who is able to get along well, is usually extremely receptive to new ideas, and easily acquires new knowledge and skills.

Exceptional teachers must be sought if the nurturing of humaneness in the schools is to be effective. Those who seek to guide students toward truly humane development must of necessity be humane individuals themselves. They must be loving and understanding and must send out powerful invitations to young people to seek the answers that will have truth and meaning in their lives. The teachers must be consistently supportive of each child in his earnest endeavors to seek the things which will hold meaning for his life. Teachers must also be certain to help each child develop positive concepts about his ability to achieve academically, form good social relationships, and develop emotionally.

Humaneness in education will spread significantly as educators realize that each child must be respected as a unique human being who is capable of developing his ultimate potential in a way which will differ from that of anyone else. To truly develop humaneness a child must be involved in experiences which make learning very meaningful and relevant to him. He must have a chance to develop at his own rate and in his own way. He should be given ample opportunities to explore life in the world outside the classroom and to interact with others.

Flexible scheduling, individualized instruction, nongradedness, use of community resources, and outside educational experiences will greatly facilitate the development of humane learning. Each child needs to seek, test, and establish for himself a meaningful value base for his life. Those who are interested in humaneness in education must respect the strictly intellectual, but they must be extremely careful also to bring attitudes, interaction skills, and values into the spotlight. The focus in developing humaneness is the whole child. The focus is not so much shifted as it is broadened to allow values, feelings, and attitudes into the educational picture, which has all too often been dominated by a quest for knowledge and a development of skills.

In order to nurture humaneness in young people, it is extremely important that schools be concerned with fostering curiosity and helping sustain and cultivate the wonder and sincere desire to seek with which young people are blessed. Schools that are focusing on developing humane qualities such as empathy, compassion, and sympathy must help students in their search for self-identity and true understanding of themselves and their relationship to other people and the rest of the universe.

President Nixon, in his acceptance speech to the Republican National Convention in 1968, stated that he felt that it should be a definite goal of our society that each child develop to the fullest of his potential. Our society must allow each of its members to develop in his own way and develop fully if all are to make contributions to the world community. Those involved with the education of young people must give their best efforts to help nurture and release the full potential of those whom they guide in the learning process. The full development of the youth that will guide the future of our world is at stake. The heart as well as the mind must have a chance to develop if our future world citizens are to be humane.

One of the chief values of humanely centered education is that it necessitates having an ample chance for young people to practice getting along with others. Being humane implies being kind, considerate, compassionate, and having a very real concern for others. Each child must have many opportunities to work and play with others and eventually to realize his need for others. The quest for humaneness must be something which is constantly building and changing because the ultimate meaning of every person's life is constantly in flux. The fully developed qualities of humaneness would be of little value without other human beings.

Speaking of higher education, John Millett sees both the difficulty and the extreme importance of fully implementing humane learning experiences. He states, "But if humane learning as subject matter content is difficult to define, imagine the complications when we turn to the affective characteristics of learning. Contrary to the prevailing academic beliefs of 40 and even 20 years ago, I think there is a general realization today within our academic communities that emotions, attitudes, and value judgments are an integral part of higher education. The intellectual life cannot be neatly separated from the affective life of an individual."*

The importance of nurturing humaneness is definitely coming to the fore. The next decade may well see it making its presence more strongly felt at all levels of education.

A Few Leaders in the Movement

Francis S. Chase	Donald E. Glines
Univ. of Chicago	South Dakota State Univ.
Arthur W. Combs	Edmund W. Gordon
Univ. of Florida	Columbia Univ.

---

*John D. Millett, *Value Change and Power Conflict* (Boulder, Colo.: Center for Research and Development in Higher Education and Western Interstate Commission for Higher Education, 1970), p. 9.

Leland B. Jacobs
Columbia Univ.
Sidney M. Jourard
Univ. of Florida
James B. MacDonald
Univ. of Wisconsin

William W. Purkey
Univ. of Florida
Carl R. Rogers
Western Behavioral Sciences
Institute
Herbert A. Thelen
Univ. of Chicago

A Few Places Where the Innovation Is Used

Anaheim, Calif.
Atlanta, Ga.
Burnt Hills, N. Y.
Concord, Mass.
Fountain Valley, Calif.
Gainesville, Fla.

Harmony Hill, S. D.
Hillside, Ill.
Kansas City, Mo.
Las Vegas, Nev.
Mankato, Minn.
Miami, Fla.

New Orleans, La.
Pierre, S. D.
Portland, Oreg.
Rockville, Md.
Tulsa, Okla.
Ypsilanti, Mich.

Annotated References

Adler, Richard, ed., *Humanities Programs Today.* New York: Citation Press, 1970. Gives an overview of the humanities programs in 35 schools across the nation. A chapter is devoted to an explanation of how to organize a good humanities program.

Borton, Terry, *Reach, Touch, and Teach.* New York: McGraw-Hill, 1970. Stresses the importance of giving children freedom in their educational experiences. Examples are included of how teachers and children who had much freedom developed responsibility while finding the learning experiences relevant and fun.

Cohodes, Aaron, "Technology May Produce A New Kind of Humanism," *Nation's Schools,* LXXXVII, No. 6 (1971), 16. Opposes the belief that advances such as computers have a dehumanizing effect on education. The author points out that electronic teaching aids are never prejudiced, don't play favorites, and do free teachers to interact with students in small group situations in a very humane way.

Combs, Arthur W., "An Educational Imperative: The Human Dimension," in *To Nurture Humaneness,* 1970 Yearbook, Association for Supervision and Curriculum Development, NEA. Washington, D. C., 1970, pp. 173-188. One of 22 chapters dealing with humaneness in schools. The author stresses the importance of humane relationships for effective learning as well as for healthy personal development.

Glines, Don E., *Creating Humane Schools.* Mankato, Minn.: Campus Publishers, 1971. Discusses many practical suggestions for building humaneness into school programs. The author explains attempts to create more humane schools and gives a list of guidelines for implementing more humane educational procedures.

Harvey, Robert C. and Robert V. Denby, "NCTE/ERIC Report: On Humanizing Teacher-Pupil Relations," *Elementary English,* XLVII, No. 8 (1970), 1121-1134. Indicates the need for teachers to be more sensitive to the ways they unconsciously direct learning experiences. The article summarizes several articles and books which give ideas for working with disadvantaged children.

Hitt, William D., *Education as a Human Enterprise.* Worthington, Ohio: Charles A. Jones, 1973. Shows how humanists and technologists can work together to help youngsters become effective human beings. Provides guidelines for developing educational objectives that lead to the realization of each pupil's potentiality for self-fulfillment.

Jacobs, Leland B., "Humanism in Teaching Reading," *Phi Delta Kappan,* LII, No. 8 (1971), 464-467. Emphasizes the great importance of having every part of the curriculum help each child develop a feeling of worth. The necessity for successful reading experiences is brought out along with the importance of making reading truly meaningful to each child.

Kopp, O. W. and David L. Zufelt, *Personalized Curriculum: Method and Design.* Columbus, Ohio: Merrill, 1971. Traces a century of change in elementary education. Curricular development, roles of the teacher, leadership functions, evaluation, and guidance of learning experiences are discussed. The emphasis throughout is on personalized instruction.

Manning, Duane, *Toward A Humanistic Curriculum.* New York: Harper, 1971. Presents many excellent ideas and suggestions for creating more humanistic programs in schools. How innovations can help students and teachers move toward more humane learning is explained.

Marshall, Bernice, ed., *Experiences in Being.* Belmont, Calif.: Brooks/Cole, 1971. Seeks to give aid to those who desire to apply humanistic principles to the educational experiences of youngsters. Many facets of life are discussed, and humane ways of dealing with various situations are suggested.

Minter, W. John and Patricia O. Snyder, eds., *Value Change and Power Conflict.* Boulder, Colo.: Western Interstate Commission for Higher Education, 1970. Discusses the unrest in education today and the newly emerging value system which is causing conflict among educators and the students they intend to serve. Several outstanding men give suggestions on how the crisis can and must be handled.

Murphy, Gardner and Lois Barclay Murphy, "Nurturing Humaneness in the Elementary School," *The National Elementary Principal,* L, No. 3 (1971), 15-17. Stresses the need for those involved in educating young people to consider the total child rather than just his academic abilities. The authors present the importance of the development of the humane qualities such as empathy and cooperation.

Nyquist, Ewald, "Making Education More Humanistic," *New York State Education,* LVIII, No. 1 (1970), 21-22. Proposes that in order to be an effective teacher, a person must be well-trained, compassionate, and understanding. The author feels that the emphasis in education must be shifted to developing values and to seeking appreciation of the worth of mankind.

Ojemann, Ralph H. "Humanizing the School," *The National Elementary Principal,* L, No. 5 (1971), 62-65. Stresses the need for teachers to develop a great sensitivity to the feelings, needs, and actions of young people. The author describes five basic personal tasks and points out various ways different people have of attempting to work out these tasks.

Overly, Donald E., Jon Rye Kinghorn, and Richard L. Preston, *The Middle School: Humanizing Education for Youth.* Worthington, Ohio: Charles A. Jones, 1972. Provides practical suggestions for developing a humanistic program, significant extraclass activities, and functional facilities for youth. Emphasis is placed on development of objectives and evaluation in terms of humanizing outcomes.

Patterson, C. H., *Humanistic Education.* Englewood Cliffs, N. J.: Prentice-Hall, 1973. Emphasizes the importance of humanistic education, traces its early background and recent developments. The roles of teachers and students in affective learning are explained. Special attention is given to the preparation of humanistic teachers.

Primack, Robert, "Accountability for the Humanists," *Phi Delta Kappan,* LII, No. 10 (1971), 620-621. Presents ten major suggestions for humanists to consider when they are attempting realistically to implement programs. The author feels that those stressing humaneness in the schools have made great contributions to education but that they must analyze their thinking carefully.

Purkey, William W., *Self Concept and School Achievement.* Englewood Cliffs, N. J.: Prentice-Hall, 1970. Emphasizes the important part self-concept plays in the achievement of each child. The author goes into detail about how self-concept is developed, and how teachers can and must make a diligent effort to enhance the self-concepts of all students.

Rich, John Martin, *Humanistic Foundations of Education.* Worthington, Ohio: Charles A. Jones, 1971. Explores the meaning of humanistic education. The three parts deal with educators and learners, the content of instruction, and the role of education in society.

Roberts, Dayton, *A Humanistic Approach to Curriculum and Instruction.* Gainesville, Fla.: Institute for Higher Education, University of Florida, 1971. Discusses the use of the systems approach and points up the humanizing elements of it. The four parts considered necessary for a humanistic approach appear under these headings: environment for learning, provision for realization of self-concept, calendar for learning, and nonpunitive philosophy for learning.

Rowe, Eleanor, "Humanistic Dimension in Academic Achievement," Doctoral Dissertation, University of Florida, Gainesville, Florida, 1970. Explains the testing the author did and the conclusion she came to that humanistic dimensions are measurable. This would be interesting reading for those who feel that accountability and education for humaneness are incompatible.

Saylor, J. Galen and Joshua L. Smith, eds., *Removing Barriers to Humaneness in the High School.* Washington, D. C.: Association for Supervision and Curriculum Development, 1971. Includes nine articles on curriculum design and humane learning. The two main parts of this volume are "The Barriers— and the Way Out" and "Identification and Assessment of the Barriers: Reports from the Study Groups."

Scobey, Mary-Margaret and Grace Graham, eds., *To Nurture Humaneness: Commitment for the '70's.* Washington, D. C.: Association for Supervision and Curriculum Development, 1970. Presents the views of many outstanding educators. The four main parts of this yearbook are: Perceptions of Humanness and Humaneness, Revolutions Affecting the Nurturing of Humaneness, Inhibiting and Facilitating Forces in Nurturing Humaneness, and Educational Imperatives in Nurturing Humaneness.

The Elementary School: Humanizing? Dehumanizing? Washington, D. C.: National Association of Elementary School Principals, 1971. Presents the views of teachers, school administrators, and laymen as to how the schools can become more humane. Several of the authors look into facets of the school program which tend to have a dehumanizing effect on students.

Weinstein, Gerald and Mario D. Fantini, eds., *Toward Humanistic Education: A Curriculum of Affect.* New York: Praeger, 1970. Turns away from cognitively oriented materials and learning to the affective domain, "the realm of emotion and feeling." The report of two-and-a-half years of curriculum work in this field reveals significantly positive results in the growth and learning of children that transcend social and economic bounds.

Audiovisual and Other Resources

Humanizing the Teaching-Learning Climate in the Classroom (audiotape, reel $7.50, cassette $6.80). Dr. David Cahoon discusses criteria for humanizing the teaching-learning climate. Association for Productive Teaching, 5408 Chicago Ave., S., Minneapolis, Minn. 55417.

Inquiry Learning

31

Definition

Inquiry or discovery is a method of learning which stresses self-discovery through identifying a problem, gathering information relating to it, analyzing the data, and arriving at a defensible conclusion. Through active involvement and investigation, the students are led to formulate hypotheses, test them, and weigh diverse points of view. Possible solutions or answers are proposed by the students and are submitted to group discussion and analysis. Decisions to accept or reject conclusions are arrived at on the basis of the amount of pertinent data that can be discovered and mobilized to support them.

The inquiry approach is less structured than most other learning methods, employs multisensory techniques, and encourages independent and creative thinking. Conclusions that contradict other generalizations are deliberately injected for analysis and comparison. Skill in arriving at intelligent decisions is developed by letting students examine conflicting observations and opinions. Valid information and thoughtful weighing of alternatives are a vital part of the process. The answer that is finally selected must be strongly supported by accumulating evidence and submitting it to rigorous testing.

Discovery learning follows ideas about the learner and the learning process developed by such educational leaders as John

Dewey, Jean Piaget, and Jerome Bruner. The main emphasis is upon problem-solving and the process of acquiring knowledge rather than upon the material itself. New understandings and concepts are acquired through broad exploration, manipulation of materials, challenging, and testing. No suggestion is rejected without examination. Having individual students, the teacher, and groups weigh alternatives, raise questions, and demand proof is an integral part of the process. The method contributes significantly to furthering the student's ability to form judgments, develop attitudes, and make decisions upon the basis of valid information.

Using the Socratic approach, the teacher plays the role of questioner, challenging the data, methods used, and conclusions arrived at by the students. Thus the students are forced to clarify inconsistencies and resolve discrepancies. The teacher avoids giving information or posing as an authority on material or method. He is a mediator of the learning process. As a fellow investigator, he provides input of data, suggests sources of information, offers ideas for attacking problems, and participates in evaluating findings and arriving at decisions. He is careful not to discourage free and active participation of students by dominating the learning situation or by insisting on predetermined answers.

Through exercising self-direction, students learn to differentiate between questions or problems that have definite answers and solutions and those for which conclusions rely upon judgment based on the best available data. The teacher is especially helpful in suggesting sources of information and in securing resource material without implying what is to be found in the material. He plays an important role in posing significant problems for the students to consider and in helping them refine and delimit their own proposals. Like other members of the study group, he suggests alternative routes for searching for solutions and answers.

Significant Components   *Which ones are essential?*

1. An open classroom climate is necessary to encourage new ideas and foster unique approaches to solving problems.
2. The teacher should raise questions that help the child clarify problems and discover approaches to their solution.
3. Adequate resources for carrying on the inquiry must be available to the students.

4. Safeguards must be considered to prevent decisions from being made upon the basis of unsubstantiated opinions of the majority.
5. The introduction of new topics should be carefully timed.
6. Essential skills for attacking and pursuing the problem must be present or developed before the pupil can proceed profitably.
7. Conclusions should be considered tentative and subject to modification when new evidence is discovered.
8. The process of evaluating information and of accepting significant information and discarding irrelevant data should be given priority over the importance of the information itself.
9. Divergent views, different methods, and varied interests must be expected and encouraged.
10. Teachers should have training in the use of the discovery method.
11. Teachers must not be disturbed by having their opinions and views challenged or rejected by the students.
12. Teachers must be reasonably sure that the problems they propose are of interest and concern to the pupils.
13. Competition and comparison with peers should be avoided.
14. The teacher does not insist on final and absolute answers.
15. The opinions, values, and attitudes of each child should be respected and given consideration.
16. The role of the teacher is changed from that of dispenser of information and a maker of assignments to that of a resource person, who helps students solve their problems.
17. The role of the student is that of an active inquirer rather than a passive listener.
18. Careful planning and execution of the inquiry experience is important for maximum learning.
19. Improvement in forming judgments, developing attitudes, and making decisions should be among the main objectives.
20. Creative thinking and imaginative results should be encouraged and rewarded.
21. The teacher must have faith in the inquiry method and confidence in her ability to teach it.
22. Systematic evaluation should be made to determine whether or not the discovery method is producing positive results.

Proposed Advantages   *With which ones do you agree?*

1. The inquiry method provides strong motivation for learning.

2. Effective methods are developed for solving problems and arriving at decisions.
3. Students learn to take an active and responsible part in pursuing their interests and evaluating them.
4. Pupils become sensitive to many problems and become willing and even eager to attack them.
5. Freedom of thought and creative approaches to learning are fostered.
6. Inquiry learning results in long-range learning habits superior to those produced by other methods.
7. Using the discovery method is likely to make classroom work important to students.
8. Ability is developed in locating material, assessing its pertinence, and organizing it for a specific purpose.
9. Pupils are prepared to deal with strange and unexpected situations.
10. Emphasizing the use of significant data and careful thinking reduces the likelihood of resorting to emotion in making decisions.
11. Inquiry learning is actually a process of learning how to learn.
12. Considering one another's problems develops social sensitivity, mutual respect, and compassion among pupils.
13. Ability to use information is considered more important than its accumulation.
14. Initiative, self-direction, and self-evaluation are encouraged.
15. Children learn that value judgments require much reflection, and that some are much sounder than others.
16. The discovery approach provides an excellent opportunity for self-expression and self-actualization.

Criticisms and Difficulties to Be Anticipated   *Do you agree?*

1. Inquiry learning stresses method at the expense of content.
2. The procedure is apt to degenerate into activity for interest and activity sake.
3. Inquiry is inappropriate for many teaching fields and for many students.
4. Many teachers find it very difficult, sometimes impossible, to take on their new roles.
5. The most aggressive students usually monopolize the group sessions.
6. The teacher must seize the exact moment to open up a new topic.

7. Openness in the classroom often results in disorder detrimental to good learning.
8. Students are poorly prepared for work in subsequent years, especially if they go on to college.
9. Inquiry learning consumes time disproportionate to its benefits.
10. Students are misled by having incorrect answers and solutions accepted.
11. If free inquiry is used, there is no need to have a competent, well-informed teacher.
12. Many students cannot discipline themselves and accept the responsibility necessary to make the discovery method work.
13. Many students are led to believe that unstructured courses have no essential content, objectives, or real purpose.
14. Many teachers and students talk about the inquiry approach, but few actually use it.
15. Children become disrespectful of their teachers, parents, and everybody except themselves.

Summary Assessment

Since the beginning of formal instruction, teachers have used different ways of teaching, and learners have approached their experiences in diverse ways. Great teachers appear to stand out more because of their personal impact upon students than because of the specific method they use. Socrates is one of the few teachers whose method carries his name. The Socratic method is one of challenge, questioning, and dialogue. All teaching methods contain common elements, but some of them, like inquiry learning, are designated by a special name because they emphasize a particular approach to motivating students, organizing material, or involving students in interacting with the material. Basically only two things are essential for learning to occur—a learner and an environment.

Inquiry learning seems to be more talked about than used in its pure form. Most teachers employ many elements of this approach, but few follow the model in its entirety. Undoubtedly this is good, for no method of teaching and learning is equally effective for all people in all situations. The great differences that exist among individuals and the dynamic nature of the learning process make the factor of appropriateness a most significant consideration. The skilled teacher selects from many approaches to promoting learning those elements that, under a given set of circumstances, seem to him to be most appropriate to meet the needs of the learners, the objectives of the work, and the nature of the material being studied.

The discovery method has been used most frequently and with greatest success in the fields of science and social studies. In science, laboratory experimentation and field testing lend themselves well to verifying conclusions. Observation of specimens, scientific phenomena, and processes readily can be used in testing hypotheses and giving meaning to principles and theories. Learning and scientific method is usually more important than mastering the material or information used in the process. The discovery approach is equally effective in the study of contemporary political, social, or economic problems. Exploring the development of issues and analyzing possible resolutions of them develop sensitivity to problems and skill in working out solutions or accommodations to them. Here the exercise of judgment based on careful analysis of experience and data is brought into play.

Inquiry is appealing because it involves the student in identifying problems, gathering and organizing information, analyzing and synthesizing, weighing decisions, and evaluating outcomes. The method can be used by one teacher or by an entire school system. It can be used continuously or intermittently and with relatively minor changes in space utilization or time schedules. Any teacher can make a beginning in any classroom. Creative thinking on the part of teachers and students, the teacher's willingness to trust students with becoming deeply involved in their own learning, and some training for the students in the process are the basic prerequisites to success.

To be effective, inquiry learning requires a change in the teacher's perception of his role. His chief functions are to help students discover problems and methods and materials appropriate for solving them. He mediates the learning process. His main concern shifts from presenting information to planning, guiding, and examining its impact. He is child-centered rather than subject-centered.

Discovery does not solve many of the problems of teaching and learning, but it moves the child into the center of the process. It involves him deeply in planning his learning activities and relating closely with them. It gives him valuable experience in weighing evidence, making decisions, and solving problems.

Teachers owe it to themselves and their students to examine the possibilities of inquiry by trying and testing it in their classrooms.

A Few Leaders in the Movement

Jerome Bruner	Theodore Kaltsounis
Harvard Univ.	Univ. of Washington
Helen M. Carpenter	Byron Massialas
Trenton State College	Florida State Univ.
C. Benjamin Cox	John U. Michaelis
Univ. of Illinois	Univ. of California at Berkeley
John F. Davidson	J. Richard Suchman
Univ. of Nebraska	Ortega Park Teachers Laboratory
Owen A. Hagen	E. Paul Torrance
St. Cloud State College	Univ. of Georgia
Bruce Joice	Jack Zevin
Columbia Univ.	Queens College

A Few Places Where the Innovation Is Used

Bothell, Wash.	Los Angeles, Calif.	St. Louis, Mo.
Cypress, Texas	Miami Springs, Fla.	Univ. of Nebraska

Annotated References

Allender, Jerome S., "Some Determinants of Inquiry Activity in Elementary School Children," *Journal of Educational Psychology,* LXI, No. 3 (1970), 220-225. Reports the findings of the author in relation to whether children have higher inquiry as they get older. The author found that age is generally linked positively to higher scores.

Brakken, Earl, "Inquiry Involves Individualizing," *The Instructor,* LXXVIII, No. 2 (1968), 95, 98, 113. States some of the problems involved in inquiry learning and gives some of the advantages of the method. The basic advantage stressed in the method is the individual interest that is developed in relation to the student.

Crabtree, Charlotte A., "Inquiry Approaches: How New and How Valuable?" *Social Education,* XXX, No. 7 (1966), 523-25, 531. Examines some assumptions, practices and support for inquiry in relation to concept learning and reflective thinking skills. Recognized are the drawbacks of inquiry learning to impulsive children but that it is advantageous to motivated children.

Demchik, Michael J. and Virginia C., "How Inquiry May Set the Structure for Learning," *Science Education,* LIV, No. 1 (1970), 1-3. Stresses inquiry learning's relation with learning from experience as the major aspect. Gives excellent examples of how traditional laboratory experiments can be changed to the inquiry approach. These examples utilize pupil team learning.

Esler, William K., "Structuring Inquiry for Classroom Use," *School Science and Mathematics,* LXX, No. 5 (1970), 454-458. Describes some factors related to the lack of success of the inquiry method on all levels of the classroom. Discussed also are the purposes of inquiry, techniques, and methods involved, and good planning which is the main factor.

Hagen, Owen A. and Steven T. Stansberry, "Why Inquiry," *Social Education,* XXXIII, No. 5 (1969), 534-537. Advocates the use of inquiry learning and reports personal perceptions of students that took part in an inquiry process. The purpose of the article is to restate in a new way what the author feels is a strong case for inquiry.

Kaltsounis, Theodore, "Swing Toward Decision Making," *Instructor,* LXXX, No. 8 (1971), 45-56. Describes the use of decision-making in social studies by the use of inquiry to prepare children for society and life. Inquiry learning can be the basis for later problem-solving and decision-making.

_____, "What About Inquiry," *Instructor,* LXXX, No. 5 (1971), 49-51. Advocates inquiry since it is a necessary part of decision-making and since it resembles the natural way of learning. Also includes an inquiry test for teachers and two sample inquiry situations.

Kuslan, Louis I. and A. Harris Stone, *Teaching Children Science: An Inquiry Approach.* Belmont, Calif.: Wadsworth, 1968. Explains the inquiry approach to the teaching of science and contrasts it with book-centered instruction. A broad range of topics and problems involved in the elementary science program are effectively treated.

Laforse, Martin, "Why Inquiry Fails in the Classroom," *Social Education,* XXXIV, No. 1 (1970), 66, 81. Relates the history of inquiry, concluding that it is nothing new. Listed are components of which the inquiry teacher must be aware. These components are related to the philosophy and concerns of society, sensitivity to children, and a perception of values. Skepticism toward inquiry may help.

Manson, Gary A. and Elmer D. Williams, "Inquiry: Does It Teach How or What to Think?" *Social Education,* XXXIV, No. 1 (1970), 78-81. Suggests points of agreement and disagreement between advocates and critics of inquiry. Different models of inquiry are considered and discussed. Questions are posed in the article about the models of inquiry learning which are related to the goals the teacher wants from each method.

Massialas, Byron, "Evaluating Social Inquiry in the Classroom," *High School Journal,* LIII, No. 2 (1969), 75-86. Discusses the inquiry-centered classroom in relation to the emerging role of educational evaluation. Examination and evaluation have not kept pace with educational changes. The validity of current standardized instruments for evaluating inquiry learning are questioned.

Massialas, Byron G. and C. Benjamin Cox, *Inquiry in the Social Studies.* New York: McGraw-Hill, 1966. Discusses social studies curriculum; reflective thinking; the classroom and inquiry, creativity, and discovery; systematic analysis of values; textbooks and materials; evaluation of inquiry; and the role of the teacher in inquiry.

Massialas, Byron G. and Jack Zevin, *Creative Encounters in the Classroom.* New York: Wiley, 1967. Explains the process of inquiry and its relation to the classroom. Analytical episodes and discovery episodes are compared and contrasted. Special attention is given to clarifying values through creative encounters.

Massialas, Byron G., Jack Zevin, Mary Sugrue, and Jo A. Sweeney, "Teaching and Learning Through Inquiry," *Today's Education,* LVIII, No. 5 (1969), 40-44. Examines the roles of the teacher and techniques in an effective inquiry-learning situation. Emphasizes those elements vital to the inquiry situation and outlines the need for planning and management as the critical duty of the classroom teacher.

Michaelis, John U., "An Inquiry-Conceptual Theory of Social Studies Curriculum Planning," *Social Education,* XXXIV, No. 1 (1970), 68-71. Proposes a social studies curriculum based on development of concepts in the use of inquiry. Discussed are modes and processes of inquiry, concepts as tools, a curriculum design with charts including processes and concepts, and a design for planning at classroom level.

Miller, George L., "The Teacher and Inquiry," *Educational Leadership,* XXIII, No. 7 (1966), 523-525, 531. Advocates the use of the inquiry method and gives prerequisites which the teacher must use for effective inquiry to take place. Cited is research that upholds the use of inquiry in the classroom.

Nelson, Albert L. and Lisso R. Simmons, "Using Learning Resources for Inquiry," *Social Education,* XXXIII, No. 5 (1969), 543-546. Describes the important parts and steps in the inquiry process, the use of resources as necessary ingredients, and the application of inquiry techniques. Discussed is the use of existing materials for inquiry, rather than materials prepared specifically for inquiry.

Newton, David E., "The Dishonesty of Inquiry Teaching," *School Science and Mathematics,* LXVIII, No. 9 (1968), 807-810. Argues that traditional ways of teaching, such as the lecture method, are being abused and neglected because of the new "fad" of inquiry learning especially in the science fields. Contends that inquiry is not an adequate preparation for college or any real aid to learning.

Sagl, Helen, "Problem Solving, Inquiry, Discovery?" *Childhood Education,* XLIII, No. 3 (1966), 137-141. Discusses the differences she sees in the methods and what she considers the same in them. Concludes that the answer to the meaning of the terms is not in the definition but in exploring the relationships between them.

Scott, Norval, "Strategy of Inquiry and Styles of Categorization: A Three Year Exploratory Study," *Journal of Research in Science Teaching,* VII, No. 2 (1970), 95-102. Reports results of a three-year study comparing learning of students taught by inquiry and those instructed by more traditional methods. Concludes that inquiry had a measurable and continuing effect on behavior in relation to traditional methods.

Shulman, Lee S., and Evan R. Keislar, eds., *Learning by Discovery; A Critical Approach.* Chicago: Rand McNally, 1966. Compiles various experiences in the area of inquiry learning situations. Criticizes discovery methods when they are employed without proper rationale or planning. Weighs the positive and negative points of view and discourages the implementation of inquiry learning in the classroom.

Skeel, Dorothy J. and Joseph G. Decaroli, "The Role of the Teacher in an Inquiry-Centered Classroom," *Social Education*, XXXIII, No. 5 (1969), 547-550. Addresses itself to the teacher as a motivator and diagnostician in the inquiry-centered classroom. Discussed are methods for motivation, goals, preparation and planning, and evaluating both the teacher and pupil behavior.

Smith, Frederick R. and James A. Mackey, "Creating an Appropriate Social Setting for Inquiry," *Phi Delta Kappan*, L, No. 8 (1969), 462-466. Discusses society as related to inquiry learning. Listed are social obstacles against inquiry, community pressures, bureaucratic atmosphere, role conflict of the teacher, and the need of an appropriate reference group. More effort needs to be expended on definition, retraining and communication.

Suchman, J. Richard, "The Child and the Inquiry Process," *Intellectual Development; Another Look*. Washington, D. C.: Association for Supervision and Curriculum Development, 1964. Analyzes the process of inquiry, what it is, how to develop it, the motivation of inquiry, how it is related to cognitive style and conceptual growth, and its implications for curriculum.

———, "The Conditions for Inquiry," *The Instructor*, LXXV, No. 3 (1965), 30, 137-138. Stresses a framework of inquiry in which it has the greatest opportunity to succeed. Proposed conditions are the freedom to seek understanding, assurance of open-mindedness to ideas, and the focusing in on available data.

———, *The Elementary School Training Program in Scientific Inquiry*. Urbana: University of Illinois, 1962. Investigates the development of materials and procedures for teaching skills in scientific inquiry in the elementary school.

———, "Inquiry in the Curriculum," *The Instructor*, LXXV, No. 5 (1965), 24, 64. Recognizes the limitations of inquiry but also its usefulness in curriculum. Lists the outcomes of an inquiry-centered curriculum and advocates the use of the general theme of inquiry in the classroom.

———, "Inquiry—The Role of the Teacher," *The Instructor*, LXXV, No. 4 (1965), 26, 64. Discusses the specific functions of teachers to effectively promote inquiry and the characteristics the teacher must possess. The teacher must have an understanding of the process, know subject, know how to introduce focal stimuli, and know sources to suggest.

———, "The Motivation to Inquire," *The Instructor*, LXXV, No. 2 (1965), 26, 122, 125. Discusses whether inquiry is solely due to curiosity, to which the author objects. Cites other factors which he feels motivate the inquirer, such as a need to understand something.

Torrance, E. Paul, *Creativity, What Research Says to the Teacher*. Washington, D. C.: Department of Classroom Teachers, American Educational Research Association of the National Education Association, 1968. Explains techniques and factors involved in encouraging genuine inquiry learning. Discusses some possible problems which are encountered and suggests some methods for evaluation of inquiry and creativity.

Turner, Thomas N., "Individualization Through Inquiry," *Social Education*, XXXIV, No. 1 (1970), 72-73. Advocates inquiry to answer dilemmas caused by indictments of the educational system. Listed are beliefs that are a prerequisite to successful inquiry, the setting or environment that is necessary in the classroom, and postulates for individualizing instruction.

Wehlage, Gary, "Inquiry and Explanations," *High School Journal,* LIII, No. 2 (1969), 87-98. Argues that a single model of inquiry is inappropriate and all inquiry does not have scientific explanation as a goal.

Young, Darrell D., "Enquiry—A Critique," *Science Education,* LII, No. 2 (1968), 138-142. Presents the viewpoints of those who have written on inquiry, especially as related to science. Discusses the definition of inquiry, the kind of inquiry, the need for it, the limitations, and its future.

Audiovisual and Other Resources

Independent Study Bibliography (booklet, $1.20). Educational Research Council of America, Rockefeller Bldg., Cleveland, Ohio 44113.

Learning Through Inquiry (16mm film, color, sound, 22 min., $200, rental $11). Training film illustrates teacher's role. /I/D/E/A/, P. O. Box 628, Far Hills Branch, Dayton, Ohio 45419.

My Name is Children (film, b&w, 60 min., $200, rental $12). Shows how Nova Elementary School at Fort Lauderdale, Florida, uses inquiry approach. Produced by National Educational Television. Indiana A-V Center, Bloomington, Indiana 47401.

Montessori Method   32

Definition

The Montessori method is an approach to educating preschool children, usually between the ages of three and six, through the performance of simple tasks and the utilization of specially prepared materials and equipment. These materials stress sensory-motor learning and provide for pupils working independently in self-initiated activities. Thus each child progresses at his own rate. The role of the teacher is to diagnose learning difficulties and to provide each individual child with materials appropriate for overcoming his problems. Although the program is rather precise in structure, its application proceeds on an individualized basis.

The frequency with which it is discussed and the unfamilarity of the term often leave the impression that the Montessori method is new. In reality, however, it is a revival of a program prepared by Dr. Maria Montessori in Italy at the beginning of the century. Her medical studies convinced her that an educational program should be developed to prevent permanent retardation among poor, deaf, and disadvantaged children. She developed special material and equipment for specifically planned purposes.

Today the Montessori revival in the United States has two branches: the Association Montessori Internationale, which uses

389

only orthodox methods and materials; and the American Montessori Society, which uses the original Montessori methods and materials, but also incorporates new equipment and activities such as tape recorders and modern math. Mario Montessori, Maria's son, produces the authentic equipment in Holland. Nancy McCormick Rambusch, who founded the Whitey School in Greenwich, Connecticut, in 1958, is head of the American Montessori Society. Its program incorporates painting, clay modeling, electronic devices, and additional toys.

The discovery method is followed in carrying out many adult life activities with small-scale equipment. Planned freedom is combined with personal responsibility for choosing tasks and setting work schedules to develop self-direction and self-reliance. The pupil finds it necessary to evaluate his own progress and correct his own mistakes. While most conventional schools rely heavily on hearing and seeing for developing learning, the Montessori method stresses a multisensory approach. Manipulation of a great variety of objects places special emphasis on sensory training through tactile, kinesthetic experience. Blocks, movable numbers, and sandpaper letters are among the materials used to improve observation, discrimination, sensory reactions, and understanding.

The program and materials move the activities forward. The teacher typically remains in the background arranging the learning environment, analyzing problems, and planning experiences appropriate for overcoming the various difficulties. He deliberately avoids excessive direction or domination in order to encourage the child to choose and plan his own tasks by becoming directly involved and personally responsible. The advocates of the Montessori method believe the child must explore and conquer his environment himself. His teacher cannot do this for him. Through self-discipline the pupil becomes master of his own will and conduct. Decision-making, concentration, and responsibility are fostered. Those who view the Montessori approach skeptically point out what they consider neglect of free play and excessive isolation of each pupil. They believe these procedures hamper the development of good interpersonal relations among children.

Parents are impressed by the speed with which many children learn to count, read, and write at a very early age. The Montessori teacher insists that the pupil is not forced to read or write.

The system breaks these skills down into small tasks, and the child is allowed to choose and perform them as he does all other tasks. Pacing themselves and moving forward under their own initiative, children learn complex skills at a surprisingly early age. They learn by being involved themselves, rather than from the teacher. They take great pride in their accomplishments. The Montessori school believes that if a child is stimulated and given an opportunity, he will take advantage of his natural desire to be active and to learn.

Significant Components   *Which ones are essential?*

1. Tactile and other materials specially designed for the Montessori method are a basic part of the program.
2. Teachers trained in the Montessori method are essential for guiding activities.
3. The child is allowed to construct and follow his own time schedule.
4. Within broad limits, children are permitted to stay with a given task as long as they want to or to turn to another as soon as they want to.
5. The teacher devotes the major portion of his efforts to diagnosing difficulties and providing for their correction.
6. Having the child ask for help is a significant part of the method.
7. Space and facilities are necessary for freedom of movement and performance of a wide variety of physical tasks.
8. Manners and courtesy toward other children are stressed.
9. The school must ignore the graded concept.
10. Many everyday life situations such as dressing, washing, eating, and looking after his surroundings are incorporated in the child's learning experiences.
11. Responsibility is placed upon the learner to take care of his material and equipment and return it to its proper place when he has finished the task.
12. In the main, children work by themselves and do not interfere with the activities of others.
13. Tasks for which the child assumes responsibility play a central role in the Montessori method.
14. Careful study should be directed toward determining the relationship between the objectives, activities, and outcomes of the system.

Proposed Advantages   *With which ones do you agree?*

1. Children are freed from the constant supervision of adults, which they experience in kindergartens and nursery schools and in middle- and upper-class homes.
2. Pupils are allowed to progress at their own learning rates.
3. Transfer of experiences from the child's school activities to those which he encounters in the home is facilitated.
4. Working on specific, individual tasks develops the capacity for problem-solving.
5. Valuable training in sensory-motor perception is provided.
6. Abundance of material provides for experimentation and for stimulating curiosity and interest.
7. Originally planned for physically and neurologically handicapped children from homes of the poor, the program now provides value for all types of children.
8. Brighter children may pursue their own interests and tasks appropriate to their maturation levels.
9. Taking care of his own equipment and materials fosters in the pupil a sense of responsibility.
10. Meaning and significance are added to the child's experience by substituting directed activities for free play.
11. Allowing pupils to proceed to reading and writing when they are ready enables many to learn to read and write at a very early age.
12. His contact with physical objects and tasks provides the child with a sense of reality.
13. Having children assume responsibility for their own tasks and schedules reduces the number of personnel needed.
14. Planned physical experiences provide for the development of coordination, grace, and poise.
15. The Montessori method teaches the child to explore and try out new approaches to solving problems.
16. Required responsibilities introduce children to work and the dignity of it.
17. His success in completing observable tasks supplies the pupil with satisfaction and builds confidence.

Criticisms and Difficulties to Be Anticipated   *Do you agree?*

1. Rigid structure in materials and their use stifles the development of imagination.

2. A conventional kindergarten program can produce better results and does not require special equipment and specially trained teachers.

3. Children are given too little opportunity to express their feelings freely.

4. High tuition rates in most existing schools limit the clientele to types of children for whom the program was not planned and developed.

5. Emphasis on working on one's own task and on rejecting interaction with others neglects social adjustment.

6. Children are not brought into close relationship with others except by their own choosing.

7. The materials are unduly expensive.

8. Having to work continuously with prescribed materials and in strictly specified ways frustrates children.

9. It is very difficult to find properly trained teachers.

10. Heavy reliance on things and manipulation of them dominate the child's experience to the neglect of imaginative ideas and the development of concepts and principles.

11. The Montessori movement is divided within itself so that it cannot agree on objectives or methods.

12. The method is static, resisting new theories, methods, and teaching aids.

13. Teachers remain too neutral.

14. The pupil's natural instinct for free, unrestricted play is suppressed.

15. Music and art are neglected.

16. The permissiveness of the schedule is a handicap for children when they enter a more structured school.

17. The whole program promotes self-centeredness.

Summary Assessment

Today the Montessori method is most popular in upper middle-class families, many of whom consider it a badge of distinction to have their children enrolled in a Montessori school. The research that stimulated increased interest in early childhood education gave rise to Head Start, growth of nursery schools, and the impressive revival of Montessori. Many of the materials have been reproduced in modified form. Proponents of the movement have perhaps exaggerated its successes, and the opponents seem unwilling to give it reasoned consideration. Thus it has become a matter of considerable controversy. Those who are critical of the generally unstructured programs of nursery schools and kindergartens welcome the planned tasks of Montessori.

The limited research on the subject gives some indication that Montessori children address themselves more directly to tasks than other children of the same age. They also seem to be more oriented to concrete objects and daily life tasks. Children from nursery schools and kindergartens appear to be somewhat more creative and to exhibit greater social orientation. The Montessori program seems to contribute to achievement in sensory-motor skills. Success is reported in preparing brain-injured children for conventional programs. Additionally, the program proposes to build the child's self-concept through successful experiences. Specifically designed to present the pupil with materials and tasks that he alone works with, the program is reported to produce positive results in helping the child improve his concentration and organize and order his learning.

With the passage of time, the American Montessori Society is likely to move farther away from the orthodoxy of the European Association Montessori Internationale, and the nursery schools and kindergartens are apt to continue to explore the use of Montessori methods and materials. Despite its popularity among upper middle-class families, the hope exists that the Montessori method will continue to be used with disadvantaged children in America as it has been in Italy and other parts of the world since its beginning.

A Few Leaders in the Movement

John Blessington
  Greenwich, Conn.
Martha Gartrell
  Covington, Ky.
Lena Gitter
  Washington, D. C.
Douglas Gravel
  New York, N. Y.
Shahbaz K. Mallick
  Xavier Univ.
Cleo H. Monson
  American Montessori Society
Robert Morris
  St. Louis, Mo.
R. C. Orem
  College Park, Md.

Mary Pabst
  St. Paul, Minn.
Yvonne Plamback
  Montessori Education Center,
  Omaha, Nebr.
Nancy McCormick Rambusch
  American Montessori Society
Hilda Rothchild
  Xavier Univ.
Jeannine Schmid
  Purdue Univ.
Edward Wakin
  Fordham Univ.
Effi Weinberg
  Michigan Montessori Training
  Center, Drayton Plains, Mich.

A Few Places Where the Innovation Is Used

Atlanta, Ga.	Danbury, Conn.	Oak Park, Ill.
Baltimore, Md.	Detroit, Mich.	Oklahoma City, Okla.
Bel Air, Md.	Germantown, Pa.	Philadelphia, Pa.
Blue Springs, Mo.	Greenwich, Conn.	St. Paul, Minn.
Chicago, Ill.	Mt. Vernon, N. Y.	Santa Monica, Calif.
Cincinnati, Ohio	New Rochelle, N. Y.	Seattle, Wash.
Corpus Christi, Texas	New York, N. Y.	Xavier Univ.

Annotated References

Adams, Anne H., "Selected Principles and Methodology of Maria Montessori," *Educational Horizons*, XLVIII, No. 4 (1970), 124-128. Presents the major points of Maria Montessori's work. It gives criticisms of her methods and her reactions to these criticisms.

———, "Maria Montessori: A Vignette," *Education*, XC, No. 1 (1969), 49-50, 78. Gives Maria Montessori's biographical background. Explains why and how she began her study of the "inhumane treatment of mentally defective children." Concludes with a brief discussion of the movement and her various lectures.

Ahlfeld, Kathy, "The Montessori Revival: How Far Will It Go?" *The Nation's Schools*, LXXXV, No. 1 (1970), 75-80. Describes the rebirth of the Montessori method in the United States. The author regrets that high tuition often makes it impossible for children from lower-income homes to take advantage of the program.

Bellak, Richard, "Montessori In Guatemala," *Saturday Review*, LII, No. 33 (1969), 47-49. Tells of missionaries and Guatemalans building a Montessori school in Guatemala.

Besch, Grace and Lana G. Hilliard, "Montessori: Mania or Mainstay?" *Instructor*, LXXVI, No. 4 (1966), 16-17. Divided into a section of criticism of the Montessori method and a section defending the methods. The discussion, particularly on the defense, is quite general.

Braun, Samuel J. and Esther P. Edwards, *History and Theory of Early Childhood Education*, pp. 110-127. Worthington, Ohio: Charles A. Jones, 1972. Traces the development of early childhood education in Europe and America. Treated in depth are the application of competence theory and crisis intervention, stimulation, approaches to learning, and the future role of early childhood education. Includes a section on Montessori education.

Brock, Linda, "A Montessori School in Missouri," *School and Community*, LVI, No. 4 (1969), 17-19. Answers 18 questions about a Montessori school. The school uses Montessori materials but deviates from strict adherence to the program. The pupil-teacher ratio is one to 12, and the cost is $47.50 per month.

Chuchel, Suzanne, "The Montessori Method: Helping a Child 'Create Himself,'" *Minnesota Journal of Education*, XLVIII, No. 7 (1968), 16-17. Discusses activities of a Montessori school and how these activities contribute to the child's progress.

Denny, Terry, "Once Upon a Montessori," *Education Forum,* XXXIV, No. 4 (1966), 513-516. Reviews two books on the Montessori method by Dorothy Canfield Fisher. Most of the article is devoted to reviewing the books and only part of it gives some general information on the method itself.

Dreyer, Albert and David Rigler, "Cognitive Performance in Montessori and Nursery School Children," *Journal of Educational Research,* LXII, No. 9 (1969), 411-416. Compares the cognitive approach of the Montessori schools with the social adjustment-centered program of conventional preschools. Montessori children are more interested in the physical world and work while the traditionally educated preschoolers are more spontaneous in expressing feeling.

Fisher, Dorothy Canfield, *Montessori for Parents.* Cambridge, Mass.: Bentley, 1965. Instructions for parents who wish to use Montessori methods in training their children. Apparatus and theory underlying Montessori, adaptation to the United States, discipline and moral training, difficulties of universal adoption, and differences between Montessori system and kindergarten are discussed.

_____, *The Montessori Manual for Teachers and Parents.* Cambridge, Mass.: Bentley, 1964. Points up the important ideas which are basic to the method. A major part of the book discusses the use of the various pieces of equipment.

Gardner, Riley W., "A Psychologist Looks at Montessori," *Elementary School Journal,* LXVII, No. 2 (1966), 72-83. Presents psychological foundations for the Montessori method. The article explains why the activities or tasks are structured, and why considerable emphasis is placed on sensory-motor activities.

Gitter, Lena A., *The Montessori Way.* Seattle, Wash.: Special Child Publications, 1970. Explains the essentials of Montessori to parents and teachers without extensive formal training who want to use the method. Various chapters describe in detail the role of the teacher and the actual activities in which children become involved.

_____, *A Strategy for Fighting the War on Poverty* (The Montessori Method as Applied to the Brookhaven Project). Washington, D. C.: Homer Fagan, 1965. Explains how many of the basic Montessori principles were used in setting up programs in a poor section of New York. The various materials and procedures used with the children in the project are presented.

Hertzberger, Herman, "Montessori Primary School in Delft, Holland," *Harvard Educational Review,* XXXIX, No. 4 (1969), 58-67. Very interesting article on the entire set-up of a Montessori school in Holland. Seems to refute many of the disadvantages that one can anticipate in consideration of a Montessori school.

Hess, Robert D. and Roberta Meyer Bear, *Early Education,* Chapter 9, "Montessori with the Culturally Disadvantaged: A Cognitive-Developmental Interpretation and Some Research Findings." Chicago: Aldine, 1968. In the use of Montessori methods with culturally disadvantaged children, pilot research suggests promise for the method in stimulating cognitive advance, and suggests that the Montessori emphasis on attention and on operations of classification and ordering are at least partially in line with current theory and findings on children's cognitive functioning.

Josephina, Sister, "Research Findings Related to the Montessori Method," *Education,* LXXXVIII, No. 2 (1967), 139-144. Delves into the history of the Montessori method.

Littledale, Harold, ed., "Montessori Method," *Grade Teacher,* LXXXVII, No. 4 (1969), 58-59. A brief account of the Montessori classroom in Danbury, Connecticut. It follows the activities of the children from the moment they enter until they leave. Montessori materials are used only about a third of the time leaving other time for French, music, art, and nature study.

Montessori, Maria, Dr. *Montessori's Own Handbook.* New York: Schocken, 1967. An introduction by Nancy McCormick Rambusch describes what role the teacher is to play when guiding children. The various materials used are presented with an explanation of how and why they are used.

―――, *The Montessori Elementary Material.* Cambridge, Mass.: Bentley, 1964. Is the second volume of the Advanced Montessori Method. The book is divided into several parts: grammar, reading, arithmetic, geometry, drawing, music, and metrics.

―――, *The Montessori Method.* New York: Stokes, 1912. The foundation from which the present day revival sprang. This is the English translation of the famous *Il Metodo della Pedagogia Scientifica* and is concerned with the education of children three to six years of age.

―――, *Spontaneous Activity in Education.* Cambridge, Mass.: Bentley, 1964. The first volume of the Advanced Montessori Method. This theoretical volume is devoted to the education of children between the ages of seven and eleven.

Orem, R. C., *Montessori and the Special Child.* New York: Capricorn, 1970. Shows that many of the techniques and principles advocated by Montessori are basically the same as many modern approaches. Use of Montessori methods and adherence to Montessori philosophy can help slow learners and other handicapped children.

Pines, Maya, *Revolution in Learning,* Chapter 6, "The Americanization of Montessori." New York: Harper & Row, 1967. An excellent chapter explaining American enthusiasm for the original method, how it faded away, and how it was revived 50 years later.

Prendergast, Raymond, "Pre-Reading Skills Developed in Montessori and Conventional Nursery Schools," *Elementary School Journal,* LXX, No. 3 (1969), 135-141. Cites a test comparing Montessori children, nursery school children, and children who had never attended nursery school. In all areas tested, the Montessori-trained children had higher scores than any others.

Selman, Elsie and Ruth Selman, "Montessori/68," *Instructor,* LXXVII, No. 5 (1968), 20-22. Discusses the advantages and disadvantages as seen by the writers. Such points as structured activity and social development are presented from differing points of view.

―――, "No! Not for My Child, Yes! for Mine," *Instructor,* LXXVII, No. 5 (1968), 20-22. Divided into two parts, one discussing the advantages and the other the disadvantages. Specific points are debated and the article adds valuable understanding of the existing controversy.

Smaridge, Norah, *The Light Within.* New York: Hawthorne, 1965. The story of a woman who had courage and determination to become the first woman doctor in Italy and left medicine to teach handicapped children. Maria Montessori's spectacular achievements with all types of children attracted wide interest, and schools were founded all over the world.

Standing, E. M., *The Montessori Revolution in Education.* Fresno, Calif.: Sierra Printing and Lithograph, 1962. Explains the foundations and under-lying principles of the Montessori theory of learning. The second part presents actual learning activities and pictures of children engrossed in learning.

––––––, "The Montessori Method," *Grade Teacher,* LXXXVII, No. 4 (1969), 58. Gives a description of materials, room, and the daily schedule of activ-ity. The only real constant is the materials used. Most of the material in-volves the tactile sense.

Wakin, Edward, "The Return of Montessori," *Saturday Review,* XLVII, No. 47 (1964), 61-63. Takes a look at the origins of the Montessori revival in the United States. The method has many good features, but it must not be con-sidered a panacea.

Compensatory Education 33

Definition

Compensatory education refers to planned programs and activities designed to overcome or compensate for inadequacies resulting from deficiencies in the economic, cultural, or educational backgrounds of children. It provides "catch-up" training to enable the underprivileged to proceed on a more equal footing with their peers who, because of broader experiences, are better prepared to move ahead in school.

Programs to provide equality of opportunity are developing primarily in the core areas of large cities and in remote rural districts. They recognize that culturally and economically deprived children often are so handicapped by their deficient backgrounds that they cannot function adequately in and out of school. The interest in compensatory education grows out of the fact that many children of the poor and of minority groups do not respond satisfactorily to typical school programs. Conventional education is not geared to the needs and ability of these children. *Underprivileged, disadvantaged, children of the poor, culturally deprived, economically deprived, culturally different,* and *socially disadvantaged* are terms that are often used interchangeably.

In recent years, concern has increased as research in human growth and development pointed out the danger of permanent retardation unless the problem is attacked at an early age. Expanding the experiences of deprived children seems to be essential for normal intellectual, social, emotional, physical, and educational development.

There are many facets of educational deprivation. Normal development of perceptual, conceptual, and language skills is often retarded and results in distinct cognitive handicaps. Early expectation of inevitable failure discourages curiosity and destroys motivation for trying and achieving. Often opportunity is absent for the development of sensory experiences necessary for the child's meaningful interpretation of his environment. The deficiencies that are most commonly manifest are low self-concept, lack of experiences common to most children, disabilities in language and communication skills, and negative attitudes toward others.

The general goal of compensatory programs is to improve the social, economic, psychological, and educational status of disadvantaged children and their parents. More specifically, compensatory education aims at 1) raising the child's aspirations by improving his self-image, 2) making him successful in school, 3) enabling him to become a contributing member of society, and 4) developing interests, insights, and skills that will allow him to live in harmony and satisfaction with himself and others.

Impetus was given to the compensatory education movement during the early 1960's by the growing national concern about civil rights, equal opportunity for all children, and the War on Poverty. Michael Harrington's book, *The Other America,* was influential in helping the country realize that the invisible poor were victims of an affluent, industrial society, and that they had few resources to improve their lives. J. B. Conant's *Slums and Suburbs* compared slum schools with those in the suburbs and warned that poor schools were producing "social dynamite." In *Education and Income,* P. B. Sexton pointed out that the poor, blacks, and other minority groups were receiving inferior schooling. These and many other writers brought to public attention the need for equality of educational opportunity for all people regardless of neighborhood, income, race, or social status.

Compensatory education leaves to special education primary responsibility for such deficiencies as brain damage, physical handicaps, and genetic limitations. Its chief concern is to provide "catch-up" experiences for a group of special children who have special difficulties because they have missed many of the ex-

periences that come to most other children in the normal course
of living.

Many different approaches are being used to compensate for
deficiences resulting from deprivation. Common among these
are reading readiness and remediation programs, health services,
field trips, extracurricular activities, emphasis on developing a
positive self-concept, expanded guidance services, and curriculum enrichment in many areas. Tutorial programs, social adjustment experiences, and career development are receiving increased emphasis. Frequently the length of the school day and
school year is extended to provide compensatory experiences.

Significant Components   *Which ones are essential?*

1. To be effective, compensatory programs must be specially
   planned for culturally disadvantaged children.
2. Adequate financial support must be provided.
3. Special attention must be directed toward generating broad
   community commitment to the program.
4. Teachers are needed who are particularly sensitive to the
   needs of socially and educationally deprived children and have
   special competence in working with them.
5. Such factors as malnutrition, inadequate health services, and
   asocial behavior must be given even greater consideration than
   in the case of children who have greater advantages and
   broader experiences.
6. Teachers and program planners must take into account the
   lack of parental reinforcement of socially appropriate behavior.
7. Classes should be kept small, and opportunity must be provided for instruction on a one-to-one basis.
8. Compensatory education requires a climate that is vastly different from the formal, rigid, and often strained environment
   of many conventional schools.
9. Program objectives must be clearly defined in terms of the
   special needs of the pupils and behavioral outcomes.
10. Integration of children of varied social, racial, and economic
    backgrounds is important.
11. Reaching them at a very early age is particularly important
    in the case of disadvantaged children.
12. Teachers must be creative and willing to experiment with new
    and different methods and materials.

13. Additional time in school is important for offsetting the negative effects of an impoverished home environment.
14. Every effort should be made to improve the pupil's self-image.
15. Increased guidance and counseling is necessary.
16. The program should recognize the different life styles of the pupils and emphasize the positive aspects of their culture.
17. Humaneness and personalized instruction are vital.
18. Teachers must start where the children are and accept their deficiencies.
19. Provision must be made for coping with the mobility and transience of the students.
20. A much broader range of real and vicarious experiences must be provided than is usually offered in schools.
21. All the significant factors in the child's environment, the family, school, and neighborhood should work together to offset cultural deprivation.
22. All those involved must be convinced that disadvantaged children can learn and want to learn.
23. The focus of instruction should be on helping the student to discover himself, the world around him, and his place in it.
24. Extensive use of real and audiovisual materials and a broad range of supportive services are important.
25. In compensatory programs it is especially important that teachers have an accepting attitude toward unusual vocabulary and language patterns of pupils and parents.
26. Although developing intrinsic motivation may be unusually difficult, it is vital for success.
27. Planning and implementing an effective compensatory program require competent administrative leadership, sensitive to new demands and imaginative in discovering improved approaches to instruction.
28. Flexibility in requirements, time schedules, materials, staff utilization, curriculum, and methods is essential.

Proposed Advantages   *With which ones do you agree?*

1. Schools better serve the needs and desires of their people.
2. Shifting blame to others ceases as the school accepts the responsibility for producing results rather than just offering programs.
3. As parents see that the needs of their children are being met, they become more supportive of the schools and the community.

4. The involvement of parents in compensatory education offers valuable experiences in adult education.
5. Supporting compensatory efforts develops understanding and cooperation among all segments of the community.
6. The program forces the school to rethink its objectives and reassess its role in the total social structure.
7. All citizens are enabled to contribute significantly to society, and society can benefit from these contributions.
8. The effectiveness of high intensity treatment of special learning difficulties is demonstrated.
9. Improved communication skills benefit the student throughout his life.
10. Delinquency and crime are reduced.
11. Teachers are shown the need for individualized instruction and are encouraged to develop ways of implementing it.
12. The number of people who have to depend on others for subsistence is reduced.
13. Improvement of the self-concept fosters initiative and ambition.
14. Assuming responsibility for producing results for disadvantaged children improves the quality of education for all.
15. The self-fulfilling prophecy of failure is destroyed.
16. Compensatory education in such areas as language arts enables children to function more effectively in other academic fields.

Criticisms and Difficulties to Be Anticipated   *Do you agree?*

1. Devoting disproportionate resources to the education of disadvantaged children tends to detract from the education of those who could benefit most and should be groomed for leadership roles.
2. Problems of deprivation must be attacked in the home and neighborhoods.
3. Most teachers are not qualified to deal with many of the problems of the disadvantaged, and it is impossible for them to acquire all the necessary competencies.
4. The best a school can do is to provide equality of opportunity. In the final analysis, the learner decides whether the results among different students are equal or unequal.
5. Schools always overreach their capabilities by proposing to take on responsibilities that should be left to other agencies.

6. The school should not be expected to solve problems such as deprivation, racism, unemployment, and crime which are really problems of society at large.

7. Trying to solve all personal and community problems through the schools makes parents even more irresponsible and neglectful than they have been.

8. Claims that compensatory education increases the intelligence quotient are inaccurate since it has been demonstrated that apparent initial improvement soon fades out as the child progresses in school.

9. The nature of man and society makes it impossible to eliminate inequality, competition, prejudice, disadvantages, and deprivation.

10. The present programs of the schools persist in teaching for academic subjects, not for the needs of children.

11. Conventional middle-class curricula are irrelevant and useless in the ghettos.

12. Enthusiasm for compensatory education is too often generated by emotion than by scientific facts.

13. Nothing can improve until teachers change their expectations of inner-city children.

14. Most disadvantaged people have little desire or commitment to better themselves.

15. Trying to make disadvantaged children like other children denies them the right to their own life style.

16. Disadvantaged children are usually concentrated in areas that cannot provide the financial resources needed for successful programs.

17. Many people want to produce middle-class results but condemn middle-class approaches and middle-class schools for the inner-cities.

Summary Assessment

Compensatory education is based on the assumptions that:

1) Differences between disadvantaged and other children are differences in degree rather than in kind.

2) Culturally deprived children lack experiences that are necessary as a background for successful pursuit of conventional school programs because the designers of these programs assume that pupils have had these experiences.

3) Differences among children are to a major degree dependent upon cultural differences among different social and economic classes.

4) Schools are failing to motivate many of their students and are achieving unsatisfactory results because they are not giving adequate attention to the needs of the disadvantaged.

5) Providing appropriate experiences will enable culturally deprived children to benefit more fully from their school work and increase the likelihood of success in the classroom and in the years after they leave school.

Few educators or other citizens disagree basically with any of the assumptions. They recognize that schools have not achieved what they should achieve, nor what they want to achieve. The main differences arise concerning the wisdom of singling out a special group for special consideration. This reluctance may be the result of a desire to procrastinate in coming to grips with a difficult problem.

Although citizens recognize the urgent need for better education for underprivileged children, they often object to proposals for achieving this objective. Busing seems unacceptable to many. Others are disturbed by the demand for increased taxes. Many teachers have grown weary working with nonmotivated students who often appear not to care. Some doubt that new programs and new approaches will really make a difference. Many of the tensions and conflicts of recent years may have been the product of inadequate education, but their emergence appears to have created anxieties and doubts that contribute significantly to hesitation and disagreement about the root causes and the efficacy of attacking the causes through programs of compensatory education.

Arguments to the effect that schools should not assume responsibility for contributing to the solution of social and economic problems seem to overlook many of the purposes and values of education. On the other hand, insistence that schools should carry primary responsibility for solving persistent social and cultural problems without the leadership and help of the total society appear to be equally indefensible.

The results of various programs that have been in operation appear to range from highly successful to totally ineffective. Since compensatory education deals only with knotty problems that have plagued education and society through the years, successful results should perhaps receive more attention than failures.

Among the various compensatory ideas that have been implemented throughout the country, the preschool programs seem to be the most promising ones. Dramatic increases in I. Q.

scores have been reported, but some follow-up studies have indicated that these increases soon disappear as the pupils move into the elementary school. Increased readiness for school work is commonly reported.

More study is needed to determine the effectiveness or ineffectiveness of various programs and methods. More significant perhaps is the need for continued research relating to the psychological and sociological factors that affect learning and the implications of these factors for program planning and implementation.

Education for the culturally deprived can be improved only as the total educational program improves. If education in general is upgraded, much of today's remedial instruction may be unnecessary. Improvement in the homes and neighborhoods in which children grow up, expansion of diagnostic procedures for identifying needs and deficiencies, individualization of teaching and learning, and extension of humaneness through personalized instruction may hasten the day when compensatory programs are no longer needed.

Until that time arrives, the urgent needs of underprivileged people deserve the serious attention of all those who believe in education as a means of improving the quality of life. Progress is likely to be slow, but something needs to be done. The needed resources must be made available. If they are, there is no defensible reason for schools to resist planning and implementing a viable program focused on the special needs of disadvantaged people. Ways must be found to improve the education of all without lessening opportunities for any. Compensatory education seems to be one of those ways.

A Few Leaders in the Movement

Carl Bereiter
  University of Toronto
John B. Bergeson
  Western Michigan Univ.
Martin Deutsch
  Massachusetts Institute of Technology
Michael Doyle
  Univ. of California at Los Angeles
Edmund W. Gordon
  Columbia Univ.
Ira J. Gordon
  Univ. of Florida

Robert Havighurst
  Univ. of Chicago
Adelaide Jablonsky
  Yeshiva Univ.
Arthur Jensen
  Univ. of California at Berkeley
H. A. Johnson
  Virginia State College
Frank Kodman
  Murray State Univ.
Edward L. McDill
  Johns Hopkins Univ.

George S. Miller
Western Michigan Univ.
Allen C. Ornstein
Chicago, Ill.

Paul Street
Texas State Univ.

A Few Places Where the Innovation Is Used

Auburn, Ala.	Hartford, Conn.	Pittsburgh, Pa.
Baltimore, Md.	Howard Univ.	St. Louis, Mo.
Bloomington, Ind.	Indianapolis, Ind.	San Diego, Calif.
Boston, Mass.	Jacksonville, Fla.	San Jose, Calif.
Boston Univ.	Joliet, Ill.	Temple Univ.
Buffalo, N. Y.	Los Angeles, Calif.	Terre Haute, Ind.
Champaign, Ill.	Milwaukee, Wis.	United States Army
Detroit, Mich.	New Haven, Conn.	Univ. of Florida
Flint, Mich.	New Rochelle, N. Y.	Univ. of Illinois
Fresno, Calif.	New York, N. Y.	Washington, D. C.
George Peabody College	Oakland, Calif.	Ypsilanti, Mich.

Annotated References

Allen, LeRoy B., "Replications of the Educational Park Concept for the Disadvantaged," *The Journal of Negro Education*, XL, No. 3 (1971), 225-232. Discusses the educational park, or multiunit campus, as a means of providing equal educational opportunity for inner-city black children. The article provides background and cites two examples.

Anastasiow, Nicholas, "Educational Relevance and Jensen's Conclusions," *Phi Delta Kappan*, LI, No. 1 (1969), 32-35. Disputes the conclusions of the Jensen study of the relationship between intelligence and race. Developmental environment is seen as more important than inherited abilities.

Apple, Joe A., ed., *Readings in Educating the Disadvantaged*. New York: Selected Academic Readings, 1970. This book compiles 25 articles in a rather unrelated fashion. They cover such topics as teaching strategies, adolescent subcultures, lower-class language, self-attitude, values, and some 17 other topics.

Bergeson, John B. and George S. Miller, eds., *Learning Activities for Disadvantaged Children*. New York: Macmillan, 1971. This compilation of essays presents teaching methods and learning materials that are effective with disadvantaged children. Areas covered are language arts, social studies, science, mathematics, fine arts, and behavior modification.

Buckley, James J., "The Determination to Pioneer: Six Ways of Improving the Process of Selecting Urban School Administrators," *Phi Delta Kappan*, LII, No. 6 (1971), 361-362. Emphasizes the need for aggressive, forward-looking and inventive educators to improve the school situation. To this end six criteria are set forth to help select this type of administrator.

Campbell, Clyde M., ed., *Toward Perfection in Learning*. Midland, Mich.: Pendell, 1969. Presents the Mott Institute activities related to improving inner-city education. Discusses the causes and problems of these schools' plight. Examples of teacher education, educational programs and designs are explained.

Clothier, Grant, *Innovation in the Inner-City*. Kansas City: Mid-Continent Regional Education Laboratory, 1969. Describes the cooperation of local school systems and a variety of higher education institutions. Ideas and programs for inner-city education are formulated and proposed.

Cuban, Larry, *To Make a Difference: Teaching in the Inner City*. New York: Free Press, 1970. Shows the ways of the inner-city school—the children, the teachers, and the system. Explains how these schools could be with new materials, improved instruction, teacher-community understanding, and well-trained teachers.

Doyle, Michael, "A Review of Three Significant Compensatory Education Language Programs for the Culturally Disadvantaged," *Elementary English*, XLVIII, No. 2 (1971), 193-197. Presents the basic philosophic ideas of three different programs and four developmental objectives of any such program. The goals are positive self-image, senses and perception, problem-solving and concept formation, and language skills.

_____, "What is Compensatory Education?" *Contemporary Education*, XLII, No. 1 (1970), 39-43. Defines compensatory education and describes three categories of such programs. Cites several examples of these programs and discusses their successes and failures.

Draper, Imogene H., "The Slum Child. To Have Any Value Learning Must Be on a Personal Basis," *The Clearing House*, XL, No. 1 (1970), 48-50. The author contends that all inner-city teaching must be related to the child's needs, wants, and goals. The student should set his own objectives, evaluate his progress, and be responsible for meeting his goals.

Falik, Louis H. and Sandra Wexler, "The Tutorial Program," *Urban Education*, V, No. 4 (1971), 357-377. Concludes that tutoring has no decisive effect on academic achievement, self-image, or attitudes toward education. The findings, however, may not be relevant to other situations.

Faunce, R. W., "Attitudes and Characteristics of Effective and Not Effective Teachers of Culturally Disadvantaged Children," ERIC reference EDO 39-289. Analyzes a questionnaire of 186 items sent to inner-city teachers and administrators. Effective teachers seem to display empathy and commitment to these children.

Fliegel, Seymour, "Practices that Improved Academic Performance in an Inner-city School," *Phi Delta Kappan*, LII, No. 6 (1971), 341-343. Cites commitment in the form of money and effective building leadership as the first two steps in inner-city success. Several other vital elements are also pointed out.

Gant, Jack, "Preparing Teachers for Inner-City Schools," *Contemporary Education*, XLI, No. 4 (1970), 420-424. Offers a model program for the preparation of inner-city teachers. The basic premise is that teacher education is a continuing process.

Gordon, Edmund W. and Adelaide Jablonsky, "Compensatory Education in the Equalization of Educational Opportunity, I," *Journal of Negro Education*, XXXVII, No. 3 (1968), 268-279. Provides a good summarization of the main compensatory programs in effect. Also states which criteria may be effective in determining the success of any program.

_____, "Compensatory Education in the Equalization of Educational Opportunity, II," *Journal of Negro Education*, XXXVII, No. 3 (1968), 280-290.

Provides models for compensatory programs. The areas discussed are early child care; primary, elementary, and secondary schools; and camping. The article speaks to the cost factor and the question, "Is compensatory education the answer?"

Gordon, Ira J., *Parent Involvement in Compensatory Education.* Champaign, Ill.: University of Illinois Press, 1968. Addresses itself to such questions as: What are we proposing to compensate for? Do we have a right to do this? Who should do it? What should the objectives be? The importance of the family and of its involvement is brought out. A number of university and school and community programs are described.

Havighurst, Robert J., "The Reorganization of Education in Metropolitan Areas," *Phi Delta Kappan,* LII, No. 6 (1971), 354-358. Proposes the need for wisely administered power and authority at the central office. This could balance the need for effective power and autonomy at the local school level.

Hopkins, Lee B., *Let Them Be Themselves.* New York: Clifton, 1969. Compiles suggestions to make the teaching-learning act more exciting, significant, and rewarding. All have been successfully used, but must be varied to suit each teacher and class.

Janowitz, Morris, *Institution Building in Urban Education.* New York: Russell Sage Foundation, 1969. Explains the basic characteristics of the school as a social institution to determine how to transform and adapt it to meet contemporary requirements. Models and theories are effectively presented.

Johnson, H. A., "Educational Needs of Economically Deprived Children," *Education Digest,* XXXV, No. 7 (1970), 45-48. Provides a good review of the deficiencies of these children. The necessary ingredients for a good program for them are listed.

Johnson, Kenneth R., "Teacher's Attitude Toward the Nonstandard Negro Dialect—Let's Change It," *Elementary English,* XLVIII, No. 2 (1971), 176-184. States that teachers must discard their negative attitudes toward nonstandard Negro dialect. Until this is done, failure will continue in attempting to teach standard English to disadvantaged children.

Kodman, Frank, Jr., "Effects of Preschool Education on Intellectual Performance for Appalachian Children," *Exceptional Children,* XXXVI, No. 7 (1970), 503-507. Reveals marked improvement in the intellectual performance of Appalachian children subjected to an enriched day-care program. This is contrasted with a loss in intellectual development in a control group.

Lanoff, Richard, "Supervisory Practices that Promote Academic Achievement in a New York City School," *Phi Delta Kappan,* LII, No. 6 (1971), 338-340. Proposes "effectiveness of supervisory practices" as the cause of high levels of achievement in P. S. 20, New York City. The supervisors' job is to introduce new ideas and provide leadership.

Levin, Henry M., "Why Ghetto Schools Fail," *Saturday Review,* LIII, No. 12 (1970), 68-69, 81-82. Deals with ideas for reform in inner-city schools. Educational effectiveness must be improved possibly by the use of the market approach (vouchers) and a political approach (decentralization). Without real reform, increased expenditures will make little difference.

Levine, Daniel U., "Concepts of Bureaucracy in Urban School Reform," *Phi Delta Kappan,* LII, No. 6 (1971), 344-347. Cites institutional complexity and overload, goal displacement, deficiencies in communications and decision-making processes, and social and psychological distance between client and institution as the cause of urban school failure. Suggestions for overcoming these difficulties are presented.

Newby, Robert G. and David B. Tyack, "Victims Without 'Crimes': Some Historical Perspectives on Black Education," *The Journal of Negro Education*, XL, No. 3 (1971), 192-206. Views compensatory education as a means of overcoming cultural deprivation. Cultural deprivation, however, is seen as a cop-out term to explain the failure of the schools and society to educate black children.

Ornstein, Allan C., "Recent Historical Perspectives in Educating the Disadvantaged," *Urban Education*, V, No. 4 (1971), 378-399. Summarizes the historical factors influencing the education of disadvantaged persons. Provides a superb bibliography on this subject.

Research and Policy Committee of the Committee for Economic Development, *Education for the Urban Disadvantaged: from Preschool to Employment*. New York: Committee for Economic Development, 1971. Determines seven imperatives of a successful school's mission: Environment, Preschooling, Functional Education, Teachers and Instructional Systems, Accountability and Control, School Expenditures, and, Research, Development and Application. These topics are examined in depth.

Shankman, Florence V., "Innovations in Teacher Training for Inner-City Schools," *The Reading Teacher*, XXIV, No. 8 (1971), 744-747. Explains how Temple University is trying to make its educational coursework more relevant and practical for the future inner-city teacher. The University has become actively involved in an inner-city program.

Street, Paul, "Compensatory Education by Community Action," *Phi Delta Kappan*, LI, No. 5 (1970), 320-323. Looks to community action as a possible means of involving those served by the school. Interested citizens plan and implement a program to overcome the handicaps and deficiencies that they possess.

Summaries of Selected Compensatory Education Projects. Washington, D. C.: U. S. Department of Health, Education, and Welfare, 1970. Describes numerous projects dealing with preschool and compensatory education under the sponsorship of the federal government. The purposes of the programs, activities, results, and sources of additional information are supplied.

Audiovisual and Other Resources

Children Without (16mm film, b&w, 29 min., $35). Documents inner-city conditions and efforts of schools to help children. NEA, 1201 16th St., N. W., Washington, D. C. 20036.

Portrait of a Disadvantaged Child (16mm film, b&w, 16 min., $135, rental $12). Illustrates factors affecting a slum child's ability to learn. McGraw-Hill Films, 330 W. 42nd St., New York, N. Y. 10036.

Teaching the Disadvantaged (color filmstrip, narration, script, 12 min., $10). The world and education as seen by the disadvantaged child. And *Teaching the Disadvantaged* (booklet, 32 pp., 50¢). NEA, 1201 16th St., N. W., Washington, D. C. 20036.

Simulation

34

Definition

Simulation is a teaching procedure which uses a model of a real system to provide a lifelike representation to stimulate and aid learning. The representations of the real world may be physical or symbolic and are designed to introduce realism into the learning environment. Symbolic models are usually verbal or mathematical. The mathematical ones are often used to express qualitative relationships in quantitative terms.

The most common forms of simulation are simulation games, dramatization, sociodrama, role playing, case studies, and computerized models. The crucial components of the real situation are incorporated into the constructed model and are presented as verbal descriptions, diagrams, pictures and other symbolic representations. The real environment is limited and simplified so that it can be more readily manipulated. Time and space are usually compressed, and significant aspects of reality are selected.

Gaming refers to a contest between individuals or groups of individuals operating under definite rules and competing for a victory or reward. The game represents life situations for which the players in the game are learning to develop competencies. As the game progresses, the participants play the role of decision-makers and try to achieve established objectives. The reactions of the adversaries provide immediate feedback and redirect the action of the players.

War games have existed for hundreds of years. Chess is often referred to as the oldest of the war games. During the eighteenth century more realistic and complex war games were designed. Engineering early developed physical scale models for constructing machines, buildings, dams, and other projects. For about 15 years, business and industry have used simulated models, particularly for training workers and executives. Dramatization, role playing, and other reproductions of reality have been used in schools since their beginning; but sophisticated models for education have appeared only during the past decade. Much of the early work has been done in the field of social studies with attention being focused on group interaction.

Simulation usually stimulates a high level of interest and vigorous activity. Because of the deep mental and emotional involvement and the opportunity to use alternate solutions to problems, students gain insights into themselves and their strengths and weaknesses in facing up to problems and attacking them. They learn to put themselves into the other person's place and to assume responsibility for their actions in solving the problem. This is particularly true in the social sciences, where models are representations of real social or psychological processes and behavioral relationships. In the face-to-face encounters involved in gaming, the responses of the opponents are important and demand reaction to the various countermoves. The consequences of the different responses are observed and later analyzed.

Significant Components   *Which ones are essential?*

1. In order to produce transferable results, the model must possess fidelity in its representation of reality.
2. Purpose and major focus must be clearly understood.
3. Rules for simulation games must be established.
4. The sophistication of the game usually increases its instructional potential.
5. Game designs must result from rigorous experimentation.
6. Simulation of all types should be evaluated in terms of the established objectives.
7. In games, learners must be free to carry out their own decisions, even when making mistakes.
8. Opportunity and space must be provided for free, uninhibited movement and for flexibility of grouping.
9. An open climate should be maintained, free from leader domination.

10. A variety of resource material and equipment is needed.
11. Clear and immediate feedback must be provided to let the learner perceive the consequences of what he does.
12. The scope of the simulation should be limited to selected critical aspects of actions or processes.
13. Creativity on the part of leaders and students is required.
14. Accurate information and facts are essential.
15. Reasonable assurance for intelligent use can be increased by setting significant goals and by previous testing.
16. Interpersonal action and reaction are essential.
17. Simulation should provide for teaching both the cognitive and the affective areas.
18. In the main, decisions must be sufficiently satisfying and rewarding to provide adequate motivation.
19. Provision must be made for developing generalizations.
20. The situation should be repeatable in its original form so that follow-up can be provided.

Proposed Advantages   *With which ones do you agree?*

1. Simulation is appealing, motivates intense effort, and increases learning.
2. Success or failure is rapidly and readily recognizable.
3. Vividness, meaning, and potential for greater retention are added.
4. Simulation has demonstrated its power to generate deep emotional involvement.
5. Learning to act by acting, learning to make decisions by making decisions, and learning to solve problems by solving problems are developed.
6. The technique is particularly effective with under-motivated children.
7. Simulation allows for manipulation by simplifying the complexity of what it represents, thus providing for control of extraneous factors that exist in the real situation.
8. The procedure can be used for the acquisition of information, improvement of new processes, and identification of alternatives in decision-making.
9. A part of life can be selected, and specific experiences can be designed relating to that part.
10. Games lengthen the attention span and develop persistent application to work.
11. Students with a wide range of ability can benefit from playing the same game.
12. Optional starting and stopping are distinct advantages.

13. Factors can be changed if the process indicates need for doing so, and alternate strategies are emphasized.
14. Pupils learn to cope with unpredictable circumstances.
15. Games provide an immediate opportunity to apply learning to the solution of a problem or the attainment of a goal.
16. Games illustrate vividly the relationship between decision-making and its consequences.
17. The need for constant communication between players teaches social interaction.
18. A background of experience essential for developing concepts and principles is given.
19. Simulation can be an aid to all levels of education, with specific value for the education of teachers and administrators.
20. Games are particularly effective in teaching values and attitudes.
21. Simulation provides for critiques of solutions, successes, mistakes, and decisions made.
22. Simulation prevents alienation by involving learners in the environment and by having them accept the responsibility for controlling it.
23. The cost and time necessary for involvement in the real world are reduced.

Criticisms and Difficulties to Be Anticipated   *Do you agree?*

1. At best, simulation is very artificial and oversimplified.
2. Games place too much emphasis on competition.
3. Models are too rigid and narrow in their applicability.
4. Simulation takes too long to get to the heart of a lesson.
5. Loss of fidelity may prevent transferability to life problems and processes.
6. The cost is higher than that of other forms of instruction.
7. The process and its analysis are unreasonably complex.
8. Teachers employing simulation may be looked upon as allowing too much freedom and disorder.
9. There is a dearth of personnel qualified to implement programs and evaluate their effects.
10. Games cannot be readily adapted to the peculiar needs of an individual or a particular class.
11. Simulation is not likely to arrive at generalizations necessary for application to different situations.
12. Games are more appropriate for clinical or laboratory use than for the classroom.
13. Situations are often over-simplified.

14. Gaming and role-playing often become activities for activity's sake and fail to provide for transfer.
15. Games are available in only a few areas.
16. Students who have minor roles lose interest.
17. A complex model confuses; if it is simple, it bores.
18. Limitations of time, machinery, and proper setting may be handicaps.
19. Because of the absence of dangerous consequences of mistakes, simulation may develop a tendency toward irresponsibility in decision-making.
20. The features represented and the outcomes to be achieved are predetermined by the designer, who builds in his own biases.

Summary Assessment

Paralleling the growth in systems analysis, simulation techniques of all kinds are in a stage of rapid experimentation and utilization. In schools, simulations are becoming alternative methods of instruction to the lecture, discussion group, and case study. Research evidence concerning the effectiveness of the techniques is limited. Thus far there is little claim that factual learning is increased, but some evidence indicates that the learning of processes is enhanced. Students become quickly and deeply involved in simulation, enjoy it, and are stimulated to persistent application to work. Although simulation appears to be well adapted to the teaching of values and attitudes, there are mixed reactions concerning its effectiveness for changing behavior.

As the construction and use of models move forward, increased attention is being given to what the learner is to achieve through use of the model. Using physical, verbal, and mathematical media, the models are employed in the teaching of information, skills, attitudes, values, and behavioral change.

When simulations are used effectively, students learn to generalize to the extent that they see the analogous relationships between the activities in which they are involved and situations that confront them in real life. There are indications that they develop the habit of relating events to principles and of applying principles to the solution of problems. Hence learning acquired through simulation seems to be more functional and more readily retained than that developed through reading, listening, and discussing.

In the development of simulations there is no substitute for systematic planning and testing. Goals must be carefully developed and clearly understood by both teacher and students. They must be spelled out in precise objectives, which lead naturally into the evaluation procedures. Both the simulation and the assessment of results should be field-tested to secure feedback for desirable changes.

Although careful adherence to established rules is important, adaptation to local conditions, as indicated by field testing, is likely to enhance learning. Failure to proceed with care and to give close attention to details will not prevent the development of an activity, but it may render the simulation quite worthless or even cause it to produce results opposite to those that were intended at the outset.

During the ensuing years, the use of simulations of various kinds is likely to grow rapidly as the computer is used more widely as an instructional tool. Contrary to the opinion of some, however, many of the most effective simulations will continue to be prepared by classroom teachers who understand local conditions and local needs.

Simulation techniques show evidence of being effective for working with undermotivated students. They will perhaps expand more rapidly in colleges and high schools than at the elementary level. They will probably enjoy broader acceptance in occupational education and in social studies and other behavioral sciences, where they have been heralded as promising tools for developing skills in interpersonal and intergroup relations. They are also likely to be used more extensively in the training of prospective teachers, administrators, and supervisors.

A Few Leaders in the Movement

John Andes
  West Virginia Univ.
Clark C. Apt
  Cambridge, Mass.
H. O. Belden
  Western Washington State College
James S. Coleman
  Johns Hopkins Univ.
Donald R. Cruickshank
  Ohio State Univ.
Harold Guetzkow
  Northwestern Univ.

B. Y. Kersh
  Oregon College of Education
James A. Robinson
  Mt. St. Mary's College
Fannie R. Shaftel
  Stanford Univ.
Gary Shirts
  La Jolla, Calif.
Paul A. Twelker
  Oregon State Univ.
C. J. Wallen
  Univ. of Oregon

A Few Places Where the Innovation Is Used

Baltimore, Md.
Boston, Mass.

Fort Lauderdale, Fla.
Johns Hopkins Univ.

Massachusetts Institute
  of Technology

Michigan State Univ.	Philadelphia, Pa.	Univ. of Michigan
New York, N. Y.	Pittsburgh, Pa.	Univ. of Oregon
Northwestern Univ.	San Francisco, Calif.	Univ. of Wisconsin
Ohio State Univ.	South Bend, Ind.	West Virginia Univ.

Annotated References

Adams, Dennis M. *Simulation Games.* Worthington, Ohio: Charles A. Jones, 1973. Explains the value of learning through carefully developed simulation games. Available games are presented. Designing and using games are clearly explained.

Anderson, Lee F. and Margaret G. Hermann, *A Comparison of Simulation, Case Studies and Problem Papers in Teaching Decision-Making.* Research Project, Northwestern University, 1964. An experimental study comparing three approaches to teaching decision-making. Three behavioral measures of interest reflect superiority of simulation over case studies in stimulating interest. The results in achievement are mixed.

Apt, Clark C., *Serious Games.* New York: Viking Press, 1970. Urges the use of simulation, or role-playing, as "excellent preparation" for real life. Discussed are how education is improved by the use of games, how they are advantageous to disadvantaged groups, certain selected games, how to evaluate cost-effectiveness, and the use of games.

Barton, Richard F., *A Primer on Simulation and Gaming.* Englewood Cliffs, N. J.: Prentice-Hall, 1970. Surveys simulations for the purpose of introducing techniques so the readers can organize and execute simulations themselves. The book discusses some techniques, certain models, computer simulations and survey applications, and includes a bibliography of literature on simulation application.

Bennon, Barbara and Annette Cianfrini, "Superhighway—A Simulation Game," *Instructor,* LXXX, No. 6 (1971), 94-95. Presents a game to be used as part of a transportation unit for fifth or sixth graders. Seven objectives are outlined. Roles for 35 students are identified. Steps in playing the game, character cards, decision cards, and final result cards are explained.

Carlson, Elliott, *Learning Through Games.* Washington, D. C.: Public Affairs Press, 1969. Reviews the use of games in schools, government, and business to supplement other methods of instruction. Principles are meaningfully developed through having the learner discover them for himself. Utilization in schools is growing rapidly.

Christine, Charles and Dorothy, "Simulation, a Teaching Tool," *Elementary School Journal,* LXVII, No. 8 (1967), 396-398. Points out positive effects of simulation such as increased motivation, learner involvement, and rapid understanding. Details are given for using it in teaching international trade relations in intermediate social studies.

Coleman, James S., "Academic Games and Learning," *National Association of Secondary School Principals Bulletin,* LII, No. 325 (1968), 62-67. Advances the idea that a student in a simulation basically learns to be motivated. Simulations are valuable for stimulating learning and for assimilating content material and developing attitudes.

Cruickshank, Donald R., "The Use of Simulation in Teacher Education: A Developing Phenomenon," *The Journal of Teacher Education,* XX, No. 1 (1969), 23-26. Points out that simulation can provide a variety of planned experiences in a brief period of time and in a threat-free environment. Although further research is needed, simulation provides motivation for relating theory and practice.

Dumas, Wayne, "Role Playing: Effective Technique in the Teaching of History," *The Clearing House,* XLIV, No. 8 (1970), 468-470. Illustrates how role-playing adds reality and personal meaning to the academic abstractions of history. Eight examples of opportunities for role-playing in American history are given together with six suggestions for making it effective.

Guetzkow, Harold, et al., *Simulation in Interval Relations.* Englewood Cliffs, N. J.: Prentice-Hall, 1963. Five authors contribute essays on research in simulation of international relations at Northwestern University. Progress is reported in developing simulation for purposes of research and teaching.

Guetzkow, Harold, ed., *Simulation in Social Science: Readings.* Englewood Cliffs, N. J.: Prentice-Hall, 1962. A book of 14 readings explaining in technical terms simulation in teaching the behavioral sciences. Use of the technique in business management and the military is discussed. Simulation is useful for research as well as for training.

Heinkel, Otto A., "Evaluation of Simulation as a Teaching Device," *The Journal of Experimental Education,* XXXVIII, No. 3 (1970), 32-36. Evaluates statistically the difference in students' cognitive learning between simulation and "lecture-question-answer" method and reports that there is no significant difference, refuting those who criticize simulation.

Henderson, Robert G. and W. George Gaines, "Assessment of Selected Simulations and Games for the Social Studies," *Social Education,* XXXV, No. 5 (1971), 508-510, 512-513. Proposes the use of their "Simulation and Game Assessment Form" in choosing a simulation and gives examples of the types of questions asked on this form. The article then illustrates the findings of several supervisory teachers discussing the strong and weak points of six simulations.

Hirsch, Werner Z., et al., *Inventing Education for the Future.* San Francisco: Chandler, 1967. Devotes three chapters of the volume specifically to games and simulations for instruction. Value for stimulating interest, developing meaning, and transmitting concepts is illustrated. A game for planning education is explained.

Hyman, Ronald T., *Ways of Teaching,* pp. 186-198. Philadelphia: Lippincott, 1970. Distinguishes between gaming, sociodrama, and dramatization. Better motivation, thinking, learning, values, environmental control, and social relationships are promoted through the use of simulation. Each is explained and justified.

Kelly, William H., "Are Educational Games Effective in Teaching?" *Agricultural Education Magazine,* XLIII, No. 5 (1970), 117-119. Recommends the development of games by teachers. Author bases findings on an experimental situation used for his recent dissertation and suggests guidelines and procedures helpful to the teacher in the use of simulations.

Kysilba, M. L. and V. M. Rogers, "Simulation Games—What and Why?" *The Instructor,* LXXIV, No. 7 (1970), 94-95. Defines and explains the nature and use of simulations in the classroom. Their real value must be assessed in terms of their effectiveness in producing worthwhile learning.

London, Herbert I., "The Futility of Testing: Simulations as a 'Test' Case," *Educational Leadership,* XXVIII, No. 1 (1970), 93-95. Warns against becoming obsessed with scientific testing in relation to simulation techniques because of the limitations of tests and certain untestable qualities. Tests on simulations have been inconclusive, states the author, and have ignored their real value.

Montgomery, L., J. Towler and J. Waid, "Simulation Games . . . How To Use," *The Instructor,* LXXIX, No. 7 (1970), 96-97. Gives the teacher who is contemplating the use of simulation a guide for effective operation. A basic simulation model can be adapted to fit different situations. The value of teacher-developed simulations and a few possible drawbacks are discussed.

Ochoa, Anna, "Simulation and Gaming: Simile or Synonym?" *Peabody Journal of Education,* XLVII, No. 2 (1969), 104-107. Emphasizes the importance of accurateness of the representation. The author argues with those who say that all games are simulations. Simulations are much closer to reality than games are and are better adapted to abstract relationships and imagination.

Pulliam, Cameron, "Boom Town," *School and Community,* LVI, No. 7 (1970), 30-31. Explains a week of role-playing by a seventh-grade class integrating work in mathematics and social studies. Informality encouraged students to discuss their problems freely in studying the complexities of community living.

Raser, John, *Simulation and Society.* Boston: Allyn and Bacon, 1969. Covers many phases of simulation from historical war games to computer simulations. The chapter entitled "Games for Teaching" is of special interest to those in education.

Rogens, Virginia M., "Simulation in Preparing Social Studies Teachers," *Social Education,* XXXIV, No. 3 (1970), 337-340. Discusses purposes and values of different simulation approaches such as video-tapes, films, and teaching laboratories in the preparation of social studies teachers. Describes a number of games that have been used successfully in methods courses in the social studies.

Sachs, Stephen M., "The Uses and Limits of Simulation Models in Teaching Social Science and History," *The Social Studies,* LXI, No. 4 (1970), 163-167. Warns against over-expectation in the use of simulation. Questions are raised about its discouraging creative thinking, poor choice of models, inappropriateness of objectives, and the problem of timing.

Shaftel, Fannie R., "Role Playing: An Approach to Meaningful Social Learning," *Social Education,* XXXIV, No. 5 (1970), 556-559. Illustrates the value of role-playing for considering delicate human problems without the danger of hurting the other person's feelings. Nine steps are suggested for teaching content as well as process.

————, *Role-Playing for Social Values: Decision-Making in the Social Studies.* Englewood Cliffs, N. J.: Prentice-Hall, 1967. One part devoted to theory and methodology and a second to materials. Purposes of role-playing in the classroom and for guidance are detailed. Problem stories are provided in the areas of integrity, group responsibility, self-acceptance, and managing one's feelings.

Shirts, Gary R., "Simulations, Games, and Related Activities for Elementary Classrooms," *Social Education,* XXXV, No. 3 (1971), 300-304. Advocates the use of simulations and discusses at length examples related to the building of a teacher's own simulation. Urges teachers to be creative in developing their own simulation.

Stoll, Clarice, "Games Students Play," *Media and Methods,* VII, No. 2 (1970), 37-41. Presents an explanation of simulation games and points out how games may be utilized in the classroom. The author suggests how to choose and begin a game, how to play, and provides a list of selected games.

Tansey, P. J. and Derick Unwin, *Simulation and Gaming in Education.* London: Methuen and Company, Ltd., 1969. Discusses the advantages of simulation and games. Models and varieties of simulation, academic gaming, games in the classroom, simulation in the classroom and in teacher training, and computers in simulation are treated.

Thorpe, Gerald L., "A Brief Survey of Research in Learning Through the Use of Simulation Games," *The High School Journal,* LIV, No. 7 (1971), 454-469. Extensively considers the various claims made for the use of games in the classroom and discusses the problems involved in researching the use of games. Concludes that present research does not support the fact that simulation is a superior teaching technique.

Twelker, Paul A., "Designing Simulation Systems," *Educational Technology,* IX, No. 10 (1969), 64-70. Explains how an instruction simulation system determines what shall be taught, how it may be best taught, and how it can be validated. Thirteen steps are suggested for designing systems.

Audiovisual and Other Resources

Introduction to Simulation (tape, $30). McGraw-Hill Book Co., 330 W. 42nd St., New York, N. Y. 10036.

Simulation as an Educational Tool (6 tapes and leader's guide plus two simulation models, reel $42.50, cassette $38.50). An introduction to simulation as an educational tool, designed for use in teacher education. Association for Productive Teaching, 5408 Chicago Ave., S., Minneapolis, Minn. 55417.

Simulation as an Instructional Alternative in Teacher Preparation (research bulletin, 27 pp., $1.25). Published in collaboration with the ERIC Clearinghouse on Teacher Education. Association of Teacher Educators, NEA, 1201 16th St., N. W., Washington, D. C. 20036.

Part Six

Personnel Utilization and Improvement

Collective Negotiations   35

35

Definition

In the context of public education, collective negotiations are formalized procedures by which representatives of a teacher group and of a board of education attempt to work out an agreement setting forth the terms and conditions of employment for teachers and of other matters that have been determined by the two parties. Although boards often negotiate with other groups of employees, the present discussion is limited to negotiations with certificated personnel.

The process includes identifying concerns, resolving differences, arriving at a mutually-acceptable position, and writing a master contract that will govern the operations of a school district for a specified period of time. Contracts usually contain grievance procedures for resolving disputes over alleged violation of contracts.

In case of an impasse, negotiation agreements often provide for mediation, fact-finding, and arbitration. The mediator tries to achieve agreement through persuasion, suggestion, and advice. The fact-finder reviews data relating to the impasse and makes a report and recommendations for resolving differences. His recommendations may be accepted or rejected by the negotiators. Similarly, the arbitrator considers the differences and makes decisions resolving them; but they are usually binding.

Where strikes are prohibited by law, the services of a fact-finder or arbitrator frequently takes the place of a strike.

"Good faith" bargaining is basic to collective negotiations. It is commonly accepted to mean that the negotiators refrain from making irresponsible proposals, seriously consider the proposals of both parties, and reject none without good reason. Most commonly negotiated issues are differences relating to salary schedules, extra pay, calendar, grievance procedures, provisions for coping with impasse, work load, released time, class size, fringe benefits, no strike provisions, and nonprofessional duties.

There is little substantive difference between the terms *collective bargaining, collective negotiations,* and *professional negotiations.* Similarly, it is difficult to identify differences between the approaches of professional organizations and of teacher unions. In larger cities, the American Federation of Teachers (AFT) is frequently the recognized bargaining unit. In other large cities and in most smaller communities the local branch of the National Education Association (NEA) selects the representatives for the teachers.

Much of the early legislation relating to collective negotiations was developed in Connecticut during the 1950's. After 1960, Connecticut, Massachusetts, Michigan, New Jersey, New York, and other states enacted legislation requiring boards of education to bargain with certificated personnel. Other state statutes permit boards to negotiate, but the laws of many states still prohibit boards from entering into formal agreements for collective bargaining. Teacher organizations usually support proposed legislation providing for compulsory negotiations, and school boards frequently oppose it.

The number of districts with formal procedures for conducting negotiations and with contractual agreements is increasing. Although items pertaining to the welfare of teachers continue as the major issues to be resolved, participation in policy development and decision-making relating to budgets and other matters are receiving more and more consideration. Boards are giving increased attention to counterproposals. The pressure for accountability points in the direction of incorporating criteria of teacher performance and pupil achievement into the negotiated contracts. Increasingly, board members and superintendents are playing less active roles in the actual bargaining; and assistant superintendents, other administrators, and special consultants are assuming more of the responsibility.

The rapid spread of negotiation procedures has been furthered by some extreme and selfish positions of militant teachers and by some cases of authoritarian indifference of boards and administrators toward the legitimate concerns of their employees.

Significant Components   *Which ones are essential?*

1. A negotiating instrument must be developed, setting forth well-defined conditions and procedures for initiating negotiations, for conducting them, and for writing the master contract.
2. One bargaining unit should be recognized and should negotiate for all teachers.
3. Negotiations should be looked upon as cooperative efforts to solve problems of mutual concern to employer and employee.
4. Proposals and objections to them must be assessed in light of the degree to which they serve the best interests of pupils and the public.
5. The teachers and the board should select their representatives without influence from the other group.
6. In most instances, it is not considered good practice for board members to be part of the negotiating team since such participation does not leave them in a position later to reverse stands taken in the heat of negotiating.
7. Before negotiations start, there should be agreement on the items to be considered; new ones should not be introduced as negotiations proceed.
8. Patience and willingness to devote the time necessary to reach mutually acceptable solutions are essential.
9. The superintendent should be the chief adviser to the management team.
10. The board should maintain close contact with the substance of the negotiations, playing a role similar to that of a corporate board.
11. Items of minor disagreement should be considered first, and major differences left until last.
12. Both parties must feel accountable for the results.
13. The board should avoid being in a position to make only a residual share of the total budget available to the negotiators.
14. Similarly, the board should not commit unavailable funds.
15. Guidelines should be established for determining what is and what is not negotiable.
16. The roles of all those involved should be clearly delineated.
17. Supervisory personnel should be placed on the employers' negotiating team only after careful deliberation.

18. Provisions must be made for impasse, and these provisions should be clearly understood by both parties.

19. Negotiators must be given enough flexibility to respond effectively to unanticipated attitudes or possibilities that develop at the table.

20. It must be recognized that flexibility and responsiveness are not the same as capitulation. Good faith on the part of both parties is essential.

21. Teacher-representatives should be assured freedom from reprisals, and the rights and welfare of teachers who are not members of the bargaining unit must be safeguarded.

22. Honesty, frankness, and common sense should govern the actions of both parties at all times.

23. To avoid having agreements rejected, negotiation teams must remain in close contact with their constituencies.

24. Outbursts of temper, hostility, threats, inflammatory language, and personality conflicts should be avoided.

25. Respect for the integrity, responsibility, and prerogatives of teachers and board members should prevail.

26. Both teams must try hard to understand the feelings and positions of the other group and to assume that proposals and objections to them are serious and sincere.

27. The master contract must include carefully developed grievance procedures for orderly and peaceful resolution of difficulties encountered after the contract has gone into effect.

Proposed Advantages   *With which ones do you agree?*

1. Improving salaries, fringe benefits, and other conditions of employment creates a better educational climate and enhances educational opportunities for children.

2. Failure to negotiate causes greater division between management and employees than do actual negotiations.

3. Teachers are professional people who should have reasonable autonomy and should participate in decision-making.

4. Improved salaries and other benefits make teachers more willing to accept increased hours of work, growing demands for additional training, and expanding problems of teaching more difficult children.

5. Negotiations provide a safety valve for preventing sanctions, strikes, and other work stoppages.

6. Sharing decision-making, although commonly resisted by management, is much better than the loss of morale resulting from unilateral decisions.

7. Negotiations enable the teachers and boards to bring their concerns out into the open.

8. Teachers need an outlet for consideration of constructive suggestions that are otherwise ignored.

9. Collective negotiation agreements establish orderly procedures for resolving conflicts and provide stability and continuity of operation during periods of unrest.

10. Festering irritations that detract from effective performance are diminished.

11. Collective negotiations help make teachers' salaries comparable to those of other professional groups and raise the general level of the profession.

12. The public is more likely to be convinced of the needs of the schools agreed upon through the combined judgment of management and teachers than of those forced upon the citizens through coercion in the form of threats or strikes.

13. Only teachers who enjoy the rights of all citizens and participate in democratic decision-making can teach children an appreciation of democracy.

14. Since the great majority of teachers are teaching because of their commitment to better education of youth, their proposals are a valuable contribution for improving the educational program.

15. Traditional intimidation of teachers and subservient acceptance of undesirable conditions are detrimental to the best interests of children.

16. By being allowed to participate in improving their working conditions and rewards, teachers are encouraged to improve their competence.

17. Improved educational climate encourages able young people to prepare for teaching careers.

18. Negotiations allow for some degree of academic freedom for elementary and secondary teachers, who have long been the victims of public whims and arbitrary board judgments.

Criticisms and Difficulties to Be Anticipated   *Do you agree?*

1. Negotiations and grievance procedures generate a search for dissatisfactions where none would otherwise emerge.

2. The sudden demand for collective negotiations has sprung from the rivalry between the American Federation of Teachers and the National Education Association.

3. The public views collective bargaining, sanctions, and strikes as activities unbecoming a professional teacher.

4. Teacher militancy generates unrest among students and deterioration in discipline.

5. Public employees should not be allowed to engage in collective bargaining or work stoppages because such practices are not in the public interest or consistent with the public will.
6. Negotiations often lead to increased costs and less service.
7. Invariably, the need for more supplies, maintenance, and equipment is neglected by pressure to divert money to teacher benefits.
8. The labor-management model does not fit professionals.
9. Tensions and conflicts are increased because negotiations assume that the parties are antagonists, and ugly scars remain after negotiations are completed.
10. Contracts violate the principle of individual differences and individualization of treatment.
11. Negotiations alienate taxpayers who vote on appropriations.
12. Continuous wrangling and confrontation detract significantly from the joy and satisfaction of teaching.
13. A definite conflict of interest exists when teachers establish priorities for the allocation of public funds.
14. Boards of education do not understand the feelings, commitments, and concerns of teachers; and teachers do not appreciate the responsibility, pressures, and constraints under which the board must operate.
15. Collective negotiations destroy administrative authority and leave nobody responsible to the public.
16. Frequently, both parties make unrealistic demands.
17. Often association leaders do not present the views of their membership, and boards do not represent the citizens.
18. Teacher organizations are unyielding, self-seeking bureaucracies, which allow teachers little freedom of thought and by their militancy actually intimidate teachers who as professionals are deeply dedicated to the welfare of children.
19. Spelling out in detail duties, uniform class size, and time commitments discourages experimentation and innovation.

Summary Assessment

The spread of collective negotiations has been one of the most dramatic, controversial, and perhaps fundamental educational developments of recent years. Many educators as well as lay citizens are deeply disturbed by the movement. Others view it as a breakthrough for long overdue educational reform.

Although the proponents insist that collective negotiations are designed to establish an orderly means of resolving differences and providing stability through contractual agreement, negotiations often develop into a bitter power struggle.

Insistence upon rights, sometimes with disregard for commensurate responsibilities, has sharpened differences among all groups in our social structure. In education, the competition between the NEA and the AFT for achieving economic concessions for their members, sanctions, and teacher strikes have confounded boards and administrators and bewildered pupils and parents. Arbitrary and unreasonable boards, few as they may be, too often have been insensitive to sincere and legitimate requests of teachers. They have contributed to the pressure for collective negotiations. Competing teacher organizations probably will move in the direction of mergers. Negotiations will become more sophisticated and responsible. As educators and the public demand greater state support for schools, it is probable that teachers will turn more and more to the states to negotiate their requests, and that harassed and weary boards will welcome such a turn.

The well-being of the total educational program and the will and interests of the citizens have too often been neglected. The welfare of children is not negotiable. Their educational opportunities and progress must be placed above the wishes of boards to keep down costs and above the desires of teachers for personal gain. If low costs and teacher benefits are pitted against one another, conflict is sure to increase. Both management and employees must recognize their common interests and responsibilities as well as their common problems. If the welfare of pupils is kept in clear focus, collective negotiations can serve as a common ground for teachers and school management to work together in mutual respect and to discharge their accountability to students and taxpayers.

The roles of the superintendent and other administrators in negotiations need to be clarified. All groups must appreciate the need for determining and responding to public interests in order to achieve support for better education. Unless rigid contracts which spell out in minute detail size of classes, time limits, and other conditions of employment are avoided, progress through experimentation and innovation may be hindered. The mobility of teachers and equal protection under the Fourteenth Amendment may warrant exploration of federal legislation covering collective negotiations.

Public demand for accountability is likely to shift the emphasis from considerations of work load and economic welfare to provisions that will give specific promise for improved performance and productivity. Working together as equals, boards, administrators, and teachers must jointly develop policies to improve the quality of education and see to it that their policies work.

As negotiations continue to spread and mature, many of the procedural problems of the early years of collective bargaining will be relieved. Likewise the early suspicions and fears both on the part of teachers and boards will fade. All those responsible for education are likely to find common cause in discharging their accountability to children and parents. Instructional performance and learning results will increasingly become joint concerns and eventually receive cooperative attention.

Problems inherent in the relationship of productivity to continuous demands for more money, more services, and increased salaries will generate searching reappraisal of many factors involved in negotiations. Boards of education and school administrators will come to understand that the whole structure of education does not collapse when teachers are allowed to participate meaningfully in planning and policy development. Teacher organizations will realize that militancy is not a cure-all for their concerns nor an adequate substitute for sensitivity to pupil needs or responsiveness to the desires of school patrons.

Involvement may well increase sympathetic understanding on the part of teachers and their organizations of the problems of boards of education and the constraints under which management is forced to operate. Working together with teacher groups is likely to make boards more sensitive to and more sympathetic toward legitimate concerns of teachers. Better understanding of each other's problems should foster new perspective and greater harmony as board members, administrators, and teachers work together seeking answers to the questions that trouble a society which suddenly finds itself in a world demanding to share in the good things of life and able, in many instances, to compete for them.

If properly directed and skillfully executed, collective negotiations add excitement and satisfaction to all those involved in education. It appears that negotiations are here to stay. Whether they are a boon or a plague rests with all those involved.

A Few Leaders in the Movement

Robert Baker
  Ohio School Boards Association
Stanley Elam
  Phi Delta Kappan

John H. Fisher
  Columbia Univ.
Myron Lieberman
  City Univ. of New York

Michael Moskow   George W. Taylor
  City Univ. of New York   Univ. of Pennsylvania
Charles R. Perry   Wesley A. Wildman
  Univ. of Pennsylvania   Univ. of Chicago
Reynolds C. Seitz
  Marquette Univ.

A Few Places Where the Innovation Is Used

State of Connecticut   National School Board   State of New Jersey
State of Michigan   Association   State of New York
National Education
  Association

Annotated References

Bowers, Raymond W., ed., *Studies on Behavior in Organizations,* pp. 101-134. Athens, Ga.: University of Georgia, 1966. Discusses theoretical aspects of the negotiation process. Processes, behavioral phenomena, and effects are studied experimentally. Interaction patterns and mediator behavior are significantly related to outcomes.

Brown, K. R., "Instructional Change May Be Negotiated," *CTA Journal,* LXV, No. 2 (1969), 39-40, 47. Argues that teachers, as well as administrators, since they have daily contact with the operations of the schools, must have a part in negotiating procedures for making changes in school systems.

Carlton, Patrick W. and Harold I. Goodwin, eds., *The Collective Dilemma: Negotiations in Education.* Worthington, Ohio: Charles A. Jones, 1969. Groups essays by recognized authorities under three headings: the Organized Teacher, the Practitioners, and the Academicians. Historical backgrounds and sociological factors, cases, techniques, and theoretical considerations are effectively blended.

Critical Incidents in Negotiation. Washington, D. C.: American Association of School Administrators, 1971. Presents incidents from the negotiation table grouped in five categories: procedural decisions, preliminary resolutions, substantive determinations, culminating actions, and final settlements. The book presents records from video-tapes of simulations enacted by personnel of the Montgomery County, Maryland, Schools.

Elam, Stanley, Myron Lieberman and Michael H. Moskow, *Collective Negotiations in Public Education.* Chicago: Rand McNally, 1967. A comprehensive volume of selections covering the background, issues, and potentialities of collective negotiations. The broader context of private and public employment, legal aspects, organizational issues, and strategy and tactics are considered.

Elkin, Sol M., "Another Look at Collective Negotiations," *School and Society,* XCVIII, No. 2324 (1970), 173-175. Argues that comparing teaching with law and medicine is using the wrong yardstick. Convincing reasons are mustered for accepting vigorous collective negotiations without compromising principles and standards applicable to a true profession.

Grieder, C., "NEA Is Off Base on Campaign for Federal Negotiations Law," *Nation's Schools,* LXXXIV, No. 1 (1969), 6. This article argues against passage of a federal law for teachers comparable to the NLRA. The author contends that such an act would subvert the states' authority over education.

Heald, James E. and Samuel A. Moore, II, *The Teacher and Administrative Relationships in School Systems,* pp. 247-263. New York: Macmillan, 1968. Discusses reasons for the rise of the negotiations movement, different patterns, and procedures for starting bargaining. Teachers should choose their representatives, the board should not sit at the table, the superintendent's proper role is yet unclear.

Hertling, James E. and Howard G. Getz, "Negotiations: Cure or Cause of Teacher Strikes?" *School and Community,* LVI, No. 8 (1970), 23, 41-42. Takes the position that lack of understanding of negotiations has promoted teacher strikes. The confrontation model needs to be replaced by one which considers complementary interests and mutual problems.

Hottleman, Girard D., "Curriculum Through Negotiation? A Reply," *Educational Leadership,* XXVII, No. 3 (1969), 297-298. Responds to an editorial by Wendell M. Hough. Objections to including curriculum revision among the items for collective negotiations are unpragmatic, erroneous, and anachronistic.

Jozwiak, Robert L., "Professional Negotiation: Some Questions and Comments," *National Elementary Principal,* XLIX, No. 1 (1969), 38-42. Provides answers to questions of concern to administrators, particularly supervisory personnel, who may wish to negotiate with school boards for changes in the educational system. Such negotiations are quite appropriate.

Kafka, Emanuel, "Negotiate for What?" *New York State Education,* LVII, No. 6 (1970), 3. Enumerates the things teachers should be seeking through negotiations. The ultimate goal of negotiations is to reinforce the teacher's professional status and to improve learning.

King, James C., "Principals', Supervisors' Position In Negotiations Need Examination," *Ohio School Boards Journal,* XIV, No. 8 (1970), 12-13. Recommends that boards organize administrators and supervisors into teams and provide inservice training in negotiations. The relationship of principal with teacher should be given thoughtful consideration.

Koerner, T. F., and C. Parker, "Bargaining for Beginners," *American School Board Journal,* CLVI, No. 10 (1969), 11-15; No. 11 (1969), 28-30; No. 12 (1969), 21-23; CLVII, No. 1 (1969), 22-24; No. 2 (1969), 21-22. This series of articles discusses the preparation needed by the school board and administrators to negotiate effectively and successfully with teacher associations, the selection of the negotiating team, the writing of a precise contract, and the development of a grievance clause.

Law, Kenneth L., "The Real Heart of a Negotiated Agreement," *Today's Education,* LXIX, No. 2 (1970), 36-38. Advocates clearly outlined grievance procedures as an orderly approach to resolving problems and improving teacher effectiveness. Associations must be alert to narrow definition of grievances, excessive number of steps, and objection to arbitration.

Lieberman, Myron, "Get Ready to Negotiate with Nonteaching Employees," *School Management,* LIII, No. 11 (1969), 32-38. Suggests as much preparation for negotiating with nonteaching personnel as with teachers. Negotiating with a single group including all nonteachers has distinct advantages. Benefits achieved by one group are expected by the others.

———, "Negotiating with Pressure Groups," *School Management,* XIII, No. 9 (1969), 22-26. Urges caution in sharing decision-making with student, parent, or community groups that cannot be held accountable for results.

Flexibility and responsiveness must not be confused with capitulation. Responsibility and constraints are essential for negotiations.

————, "Negotiating with Teachers," *School Management,* XIII, No. 3 (1969), 38-40, 42, 44. Points out the grave danger of making crippling concessions in lieu of salary. The board is not obligated to make a counterproposal to every teacher proposal. Giving good reason for rejection constitutes good faith.

————, "Negotiations," *School Management,* XIV, No. 6 (1970), 10-11; No. 9 (1970), 28-29; No. 10 (1970), 11; No. 12 (1970), 8-9. This series of four articles suggests how top management should negotiate with middle management and discusses statutory and contractual agreements, submission of grievances to arbitration, and the amount of consideration seniority should be given in deciding teachers' benefits.

Lieberman, Myron and Michael H. Moskow, *Collective Negotiations for Teachers: An Approach to School Administration.* Chicago: Rand McNally, 1966. Includes a comprehensive analysis of the nature and process of negotiations and goes into details of procedures. A complete glossary, extensive bibliography, and helpful appendices are included. Positions of the NEA and AFT are compared.

Perry, Charles R. and Wesley A. Wildman, *The Impact of Negotiations in Public Education: The Evidence from the Schools.* Worthington, Ohio: Charles A. Jones, 1970. Considers both theoretical and practical aspects of negotiations in relation to results achieved in salaries, working conditions, and other policies. Strategies are developed for bargaining and for resolving impasse.

Perry, Richard, "Achieving a Meeting of Minds," *Today's Education,* LXIX, No. 2 (1970), 34-35. Emphasizes the necessity for giving the negotiators for both parties enough authority to provide flexibility. An attitude of serious inquiry, time for clarifying misunderstandings, and avoiding personality conflicts are essential.

Perry, Richard, Kenneth Law, Roy Van Delinder, Jr., and Robert St. Germain, "Professional Negotiation: Symposium," *Today's Education,* LIX, No. 2 (1970), 33-40. An informative article which presents an overview of professional negotiation from the NEA point of view. The meeting of the negotiating parties, the negotiated agreement, and a model grievance procedure are considered.

Roumell, George T., "Fact Finding Can Unblock Bargaining Impasse," *Nation's Schools,* LXXXV, No. 3 (1970), 77-79. Considers the fact finder a valuable agent for resolving differences. Need for narrowing the issues, careful preparation of briefs, criteria for consideration by the fact finder, and typical issues are presented.

Shannon, Thomas A., "The Principal's Management Role in Collective Negotiations, Grievances and Strikes," *Journal of Secondary Education,* XLV, No. 2 (1970), 51-56. Indicates the tendency of negotiations to drive the principal closer to the management team and the board of education. Principals' negotiating for themselves should be accepted and will not destroy effectiveness of the management team if the superintendent heads the team.

Stinnett, T. M., Jack H. Kleinmann, and Martha L. Ware, *Professional Negotiations in Public Education.* New York: Macmillan, 1966. Discusses the background and legal status as well as methods for developing agreements and conducting negotiations. Major issues and ways of enhancing potentialities for success are presented. The appendix includes various sample documents.

Swihart, Roy L., "Teacher Negotiations and the Role of the Superintendent," *The Clearing House,* XLIII, No. 9 (1969), 533-535. Points out that the recency of negotiations leaves little research, precedent, or experience relating to the role of the superintendent. He can hardly negotiate against the teachers, maintain staff morale, and provide effective leadership.

Taylor, George W., "The Public Interest in Collective Negotiations in Education," *Phi Delta Kappan,* XLVIII, No. 1 (1966), 16-22. Points out differences between concepts of public and teachers. If teacher power is balanced with public interest, collective negotiations can serve to improve education, but at increased cost.

Urich, Ted R., "A Q-Sort Analysis of Attitudes of School Personnel in Iowa Toward Collective Negotiations," *Journal of Educational Research,* LXIII, No. 2 (1969), 74-77. Reports agreement between teachers, board members, and superintendents from city and rural districts relative to the educational leadership role of the superintendent. Important differences appear between city and rural groups in regard to the scope of negotiations and the superintendent's role.

Van Delinder, Roy, Jr., and Robert H. St. Germain, "A Model Four-Stage Grievance Procedure," *Today's Education,* LXIX, No. 2 (1970), 38-40. Stresses the importance of the grievance procedure for making the contract enforceable. Outlines a four-stage approach involving the supervisor, chief executive, board of education, and arbitrator.

Vander Werf, Lester S., "Militancy and the Profession of Teaching," *School and Society,* XCVIII, No. 2324 (1970), 171-173. Takes the position that hard bargaining and strikes are distasteful to many professional teachers. Sound preparation, careful admission criteria, and elimination of incompetents are needed for teachers to achieve professional status.

Von Haden, H. I., "Principles for Salary Schedules," *The American School Board Journal,* CXXXVII, No. 4 (1958), 26-28. Provides a checklist of sample items to identify differences between boards and teachers relative to salary schedules. Basic principles developed from statements of "this we believe" should assist in resolving differences and in avoiding impasse.

Weinstock, Henry R. and Paul L. Van Horn, "Impact of Negotiations Upon Public Education," *The Clearing House,* XLIII, No. 6 (1969), 358-363. Examines many of the assumptions made by teachers and board members relative to the advantages and dangers of negotiations. Involvement of employees in decision-making is important, but conflict and impasse may have detrimental effects.

"What's Negotiable," *NEA Research Bulletin,* XLVI, No. 2 (1968), 42-43. Reports results of analysis of 1,540 agreements in 13 states. Frequency of inclusion is listed for items in such areas as negotiation procedures, scope of agreement, instructional program, fringe benefits, and absence.

Audiovisual and Other Resources

A Whisper of Dissent—Collective Negotiations in Education (16mm film, color, sound, 30 min., $275, rental $15). The issues of collective negotiations presented for communities considering making contracts with organized groups. /I/D/E/A/, P. O. Box 628, Far Hills Branch, Dayton, Ohio 45419.

Differentiated Staffing 36

Definition

Differentiated staffing is a plan providing for differentiated student needs, interests, and abilities through more effective deployment and utilization of differentiated teacher interests, talents, ambitions, and skills. Basically, it is a process of matching teaching with learning and of eliminating inefficiency resulting from mismatches. It is based on the premise that redeployment of teaching personnel and more effective use of special talents will provide greater opportunity for individualization of instruction and clinical teaching. The learning experiences of pupils are likely to be enriched, and teachers and paraprofessionals can benefit from the interaction within the team.

Inherent in the program is increased professional autonomy and involvement of professional personnel in planning and decision-making. Subprofessionals perform technical, clerical, and routine functions, thus making the varied competencies of professionals available for higher-level instructional responsibilities.

In practice the danger exists that differentiated staffing may be looked upon as an opportunity to cut costs by having a paraprofessional attempt to do the work of a fully-qualified teacher. The idea behind differentiation is not to save money. The concept is viable only if it aims to produce better learning through better use of available funds. Team teaching and differentiated staffing go together. More opportunities are provided to permit individual teachers to devote more of their time and energy to doing what they do best and to be relieved of many of those duties which they dislike or for which they have limited ability. Concentrated study of more effective utilization of teaching personnel was begun by J. Lloyd Trump in the early 1960's. Such men as Dwight Allen developed paper models, converted them to operational plans, and subjected them to practical application. Temple City, California, was perhaps the earliest system to test a hierarchical model of differentiated staffing. The program includes four levels of teachers: master teachers, senior teachers, staff teachers, and associate teachers. Teacher aides, resource center assistants, and laboratory assistants are included among the subprofessionals. Beaverton, Oregon, and several county systems in Florida are representative of other schools that have given intensive study to staff deployment and utilization.

Although different names are applied to the various staff positions and variations in organization, roles, and relationships with the administrative structure are used, almost all of the models follow the hierarchical pattern. They usually have one teacher in the top leadership role. Most of the instructional personnel is designated by senior, staff, associate, assistant, or some comparable title. The leader or leaders are referred to as master teachers, executive teachers, curriculum specialists, subject specialists, directors of learning, research teachers, and by other designations. In all instances, roles and duties of each

Temple City, California, Model of Differentiated Staffing*

*L. C. Hickman, ed., "Differentiated Staffing," *Nation's Schools,* 85, No. 6 (June 1970): 45.

staff member are defined in detail, and a different salary range is established for each classification.

Clear delineation of roles, however, must not stand in the way of functional flexibility that will encourage each member of the team to pitch in and do what needs to be done even if it is outside his area of special competence. Any one model will not fit all situations. The philosophy and objectives of the school, special needs of students, talent among the teachers, amount and arrangement of space, and materials and equipment available, determine, to a great extent, the program and the best deployment of teaching personnel.

Tenure status	Position	Degree	SALARY RANGE
NON-TENURE	Teaching Research Specialist	Doctorate degree	$17,500–19,000
NON-TENURE	Teacher Curriculum Specialist	Master's degree	$15,000–16,500
TENURE	Senior Teacher	MS, MA, or M Ed	$12,500–14,000
TENURE	Staff Teacher	BA, BS, or B Ed	$10,000–11,500
NON-TENURE	Associate Teacher	BA, BS or B Ed	$7,500–9,000
NON-TENURE	Assistant Teacher	Associate degree (2 years)	$5,500–6,500
NON-TENURE	Educational Technician		$4,500–5,500
NON-TENURE	Teacher Aide		$3,500–4,500

Florida Model of Differentiated Staffing*

In contrast with the hierarchical plans, synergetic or cooperative team teaching considers all qualified teachers as equals. In constituting these teams, special attention must be given to including staff members whose talents complement those of the other members of the group. One teacher may, for example, have special ability in diagnosis of learning difficulties,

*L. C. Hickman, ed., "Differentiated Staffing," *Nation's Schools,* 85, No. 6 (June 1970): 45.

while another is particularly effective in large-group instruction. Another member of the team may be especially strong in human relations and make an outstanding contribution in dealing with alienated pupils or disturbed parents. Still another teacher may have unusual ability in keeping things organized, in balance, and moving toward specified objectives.

Under this plan all certificated teachers are master teachers in their own right. Here there is no hierarchy, no top teacher. Each is recognized by the other members of the team as the leader in the area of his special talent. Under this arrangement special attention must be given to providing for planning and coordinating the group effort. If special talent among individual members of the team is not blended, it may actually stand in the way of effective results. Careful planning is the key to success in differentiated staffing.

Significant Components   *Which ones are essential?*

1. Learning needs of students should determine the organizational plan for staffing; and better instruction, rather than economy, must be its goal.
2. Ideally, the plan should be initiated by the teachers, and they must have leadership roles in developing the model.
3. Community understanding and support must be developed.
4. Flexibility in schedules is indispensible for utilization of various staff talents at different points and in varying amounts of time and degrees of intensity.
5. Those concerned must feel that the staffing plan is fair and can be justified by its contribution to learning.
6. Objective and detailed job descriptions are essential.
7. Greater autonomy must be given to the staff of an individual building than is usually the case.
8. Flexible space and a good learning center are necessary.
9. Adequate time must be provided for group planning.
10. Administrators must be willing to become partners with teachers in decision-making.
11. To expect promotions and salaries above those of their colleagues, teachers must understand what leadership and additional responsibility on their part mean.
12. All members of the hierarchy should teach for at least part of the day.
13. The higher levels of the hierarchy must be seen as positions of service rather than of authority.

14. Persons from outside the school system should be brought in, especially for the evaluation of program and personnel.
15. A program of differentiated staffing will stand or fall upon its ability to improve learning.
16. It is particularly important in differentiated staffing that all members of the group clearly understand the objectives in order to provide for meaningful evaluation.
17. Whenever possible, the program should be built on research-tested information.
18. All members of the hierarchy must be willing to be held accountable for their decisions and performance.
19. Associate and staff teachers must realize that having the master teacher provide service does not mean that the leaders should do all the unpleasant chores that the team members at the lower levels dislike.
20. It must be recognized that there is often a significant difference between a paper model and an operating program.
21. The responsibilities of such groups as "planning councils" or "steering committees" and their relationship with the administration and board of education should be carefully defined and clearly understood.
22. Experimentation with models appropriate for each school as well as with evaluation of teaching and learning should be an integral part of the program.

Proposed Advantages   *With which ones do you agree?*

1. Differentiated staffing increases the opportunity for greater individualization of instruction and more diversified and beneficial group activities.
2. Pupils have contact with a greater variety of talents and skills.
3. Differentiated staffing enables competent personnel whose first love is teaching to attain prestige, satisfaction, and financial reward without leaving the classroom to go into administration.
4. Accompanying new authority and decision-making will be new responsibility for teachers.
5. Beginning teachers are placed in continuous contact with leaders of outstanding ability and given the opportunity to work into the profession gradually.
6. Associate and staff teachers are relieved of the insecurity and anxiety resulting from having to carry responsibilities they feel they are not qualified to discharge.
7. The plan gives teachers a part in establishing standards, determining direction and goals, and enjoying career incentives.

8. Teachers are given a choice in the roles they feel best qualified to play, the responsibilities they want to assume, and the number of months they want to work.
9. Differentiation of roles throws out the traditional false assumption that all teachers are equal.
10. Making provision for teachers to move up as classroom teachers promises to improve the quality of administrators because only those who are genuinely interested in administrative work will aspire to it.
11. The employment of part-time personnel is facilitated, and provision is made for variation in the number of months of service.
12. The plan taps unused resources and puts special teacher talents and skills to work for pupils.
13. Having the opportunity to function in one's area of interest and at his level of competence increases job satisfaction.
14. Teaching part of the time enhances the senior teachers' understanding of the problems of staff teachers and associates.
15. Subjects are correlated, and learning experiences of children are enriched and integrated.
16. Especially at the secondary level, the multidisciplinary approach to learning is enhanced.
17. New interest, focus, meaning, and significance will be given to inservice education.

Criticisms and Difficulties to Be Anticipated   *Do you agree?*

1. At present there is no valid way of deciding the comparative value of different tasks in the totality of teaching.
2. Although the hierarchical model proposes to produce teamwork, it will in reality have a splintering effect.
3. The plan is a surreptitious way of putting in a merit pay plan and exploiting teachers.
4. Merit pay is better than differentiated staffing because it is based on quality of performance, which is more valid than roles assumed, number of hours or weeks put in, or degrees held.
5. To put differentiated staffing into operation, many of the salaries of associate and staff teachers will have to be cut; and they will leave.
6. The prestige and self-image of all teachers except the master will be lowered.
7. Differentiated staffing will move the cleavage that now exists between administrators and teachers right into the classroom, where the youngsters will be caught up in the dissension and conflict.

8. In many schools, teachers are reluctant to accept criticism and direction from their peers.

9. The whole idea is based on the false assumption that there are hundreds of thousands of teachers available who are willing to assume leadership roles and possess the competence that, in the eyes of their co-workers and the public, justifies high salaries.

10. The process of securing enough top-level personnel will start a chain reaction, robbing poorer districts of their best teachers.

11. The competent teacher is not necessarily the competent co-ordinator of the efforts of others, the perceptive developer of curriculum, or the skillful supervisor.

12. Teachers, who have always considered themselves coequals, resent the idea of a hierarchy.

13. By fostering specialization, the system moves the school away from being child-centered to being subject-centered.

14. Many of the most competent prospective leaders do not want to work on a 12-month schedule.

15. Conflict between the planning council of teachers and the administration is unavoidable.

16. Shared decision-making makes everybody's business nobody's responsibility.

17. By failing to discharge their responsibility, staff teachers will force those at the higher levels to perform routine tasks required to keep the operation going.

18. Differentiated staffing is a plan to introduce a cheap Lancastrian system, which was common in the first half of the nineteenth century.

Summary Assessment

Although the idea of differentiated staffing is relatively new, the interest that it has generated indicates that it will receive continued attention. Occasional reference is still made to reduced costs, but the mainstream of current thinking is directed toward improvement of learning through better planning and better utilization of talent. In fact, it is quite generally agreed that, except where unusual volunteer resources are available, costs will not be reduced.

The program is more than a redeployment of teaching personnel. It constitutes a basic change in philosophy relative to what teaching and learning are and how they relate. The structure of school organization, planning, and decision-making is intricately involved. It is commonly agreed that there is a place for both administrators and instructional leaders. How their roles can complement one another to achieve more effectively the purpose of the schools needs intensive study and analysis.

Teachers should consider carefully what they should be doing and what should be turned over to paraprofessionals. In selecting what he will do himself and what he will ask those lower in the hierarchy to do, a teacher too often chooses what he likes or what seems least burdensome to him. In establishing priorities, the importance of the task is not given adequate consideration. A teacher may busy himself with dictating spelling words or reading a story to a class while paraprofessionals are assigned to what appear to be routine functions, but actually are difficult and important teaching assignments.

For example, "supervision" of study halls, cafeterias, and corridors is usually among the first duties assigned to aides. These areas of the schools are busy laboratories of human inter-action, full of potential for important learning and difficult to manage in such a way that maximum learning results. Teaching children in these areas of the school should not be dismissed with the custodial indifference implied by the word "supervision" when it is used in this context. Teaching attitudes, values, human relations, responsibility, and respect for one another and for orderly procedures requires special attention in corridors, cafeterias, and study halls. It demands the deepest insights and finest skills of the superprofessional if the positive behavioral outcomes are to be achieved which society so desperately needs. Here paraprofessionals cannot teach. They can only patrol.

As one reflects on the proposed advantages of differentiated staffing and its criticisms, problems, and pitfalls, he is struck by the great number of arguments that can be presented both for and against it. One of the more baffling problems is that of determining the different levels of responsibility, assigning duties to the respective levels, and assessing the competencies required. Many teachers fear that the plan is a scheme to exploit them. Conservative administrators are reluctant to involve teachers in policy development and decision-making. Others see better staff utilization as another significant move toward providing an education appropriate to each child. The advocates of the plan insist that it will put teaching on the broad, though bumpy, road to becoming a true profession.

A Few Leaders in the Movement

Dwight W. Allen
  Univ. of Massachusetts
Donald Barbee
  National Education Association
Lloyd K. Bishop
  Univ. of Georgia
Roy E. Edelfelt
  National Education Association
Fenwick English
  Arizona State Univ.
Larry Frase
  Bell Telephone Laboratories
Robert Gourley
  Northern Illinois Univ.
Myron Lieberman
  City Univ. of New York
Bernard McKenna
  San Francisco State College

Robert B. Moore
  Dade County (Fla.) Junior College
Jerry Novotny
  Univ. of California at Los Angeles
M. John Rand
  Temple City (Calif.) Schools
Alexander Shapiro
  DeKalb (Ill.) Schools
Donald M. Sharpe
  Indiana State Univ.
Donald K. Sharpes
  U. S. Office of Education
Rodney P. Smith
  Florida Dept. of Education
Richard Tirpak
  Parma (Ohio) School System
J. Lloyd Trump
  Nat'l. Association of Secondary
  School Principals

A Few Places Where the Innovation Is Used

Amherst, Mass.
Beaverton, Oreg.
Cherry Creek, Colo.
Dade County, Fla.
Fountain Valley, Calif.
Granite Schools, Utah
Greenwich, Conn.
Kansas City, Mo.

Lakewood, Ohio
Leon County, Fla.
Lexington, Mass.
Los Angeles, Calif.
Mankato State College
Mesa, Ariz.
Newtonville, Mass.
Parma, Ohio

Pittsburgh, Pa.
Sarasota, Fla.
Shaker Heights, Ohio
Snake River, Idaho
Temple City, Calif.
Urbana, Ill.
Warren, Ohio
Williamsville, N. Y.

Annotated References

Backstrom, Doris, "Trying New Patterns—Differentiated Staffing and Modular Scheduling," *The Science Teacher,* XXXVIII, No. 3 (1971), 50-51. Promotes differentiated staffing as a means to permit teachers to concentrate on their specialty in a certain area and to allow students to hear two or more points of view in the same subject area.

Barbee, Don, *Differentiated Staffing: Expectations and Pitfalls,* Write-in Papers No. 1. Washington, D. C.: National Commission on Teacher Education and Professional Standards, National Education Association, 1969. Explains the purposes for which differentiated staffing is commonly established and the dangers that should be anticipated in planning a program. The pitfalls include fadism, emphasis on economizing, replacing teachers with auxiliary personnel, excessive hierarchical distinctions, personality conflicts, and overspecialization.

Beubier, Edward W., "Experiences with Differentiated Staffing," *Today's Education,* LVIII, No. 3 (1969), 56-58. Describes a program in which a co-ordinating teacher works with six to eight classroom teachers as a team. A learning analyst, one paid teacher aide, community volunteers, and college students are a vital part of the program.

Bishop, Lloyd K. and Patrick W. Carlton, "Staff Differentiation: A Model for Developing Professional Behavior," *High School Journal,* LIV, No. 7 (1971), 422-431. Addresses itself to two primary influences in striving for teacher professionalism: control of time and differentiation of job responsibilities. Differentiated staffing is seen as a step toward this professionalism. A model for staffing is presented.

Caldwell, Bruce G., "Differentiated Staffing, A Probe or a Plunge?" *Educational Technology,* XI, No. 4 (1971), 6. Stresses that comprehensiveness is a necessary criterion for the success of educational innovations. Differentiated staffing meets this criterion if it is carefully planned.

_____, "Differentiated Staffing and Collegial Evaluation," *Educational Technology,* XI, No. 6 (1971), 7. Describes and commends the collegial evaluation aspect of differentiated staffing. The classroom is no longer able to remain a self-contained entity, and differentiation is the best way to increase teacher accountability.

_____, "Differentiated Staffing and the Process of Decision Making," *Educational Technology,* XI, No. 5 (1971), 63. Proposes differentiated staffing as a way to place power and leadership in the hands of creative and competent teachers thus leading to improved teaching and learning. Teachers respond to increased responsibility.

_____, "Differentiated Staffing, Who is Labor and Who is Management?" *Educational Technology,* X, No. 12 (1970), 59-60. Recommends differentiated staffing to bring together administrators and teachers so as to diffuse political power of both groups and to better equalize pay schedules for both sides. Individualism and leadership among teachers is recognized.

Conte, Joseph M., and Fenwick English, "The Impact of Technology on Staff Differentiation," *Audiovisual Instruction,* XIV, No. 5 (1969), 108. Suggests that the introduction of teaching aids and machines stimulated a reexamination of the teacher's role. Lack of performance criteria and resistance to organizational change are obstacles to differentiated staffing. Differentiated goals and the teacher's ability to use human and nonhuman resources are the key.

Cooper, James A., *Differentiated Staffing.* Philadelphia: W. B. Saunders, 1972. Discusses differentiated staffing for both teaching and administrative personnel. Background, advantages, and problems involved are considered. Among the significant concerns are professional and political considerations of differentiation in staff utilization. Insights and implications are brought out through a review of reorganization of staffing in Florida.

Darton, Edythe, "Differentiated Staffing According to Needs," *School and Community,* LVIII, No. 2 (1971), 12-13. Describes a differentiated staffing plan in an elementary school. The importance of building design to function and personnel utilization is brought out. A model is presented relating staff position, responsibilities, selection, and training.

Differentiated Staffing in Schools, Education U. S. A. Special Report, Washington, D. C.: National School Public Relations Association, 1970. A comprehensive review of current policies and programs relating to differentiated staffing. Purposes, principles, and practices are discussed. Profiles of three plans and a list of operating programs are included.

Edelfelt, Roy A., "Differentiated Staffing: Is It Worth the Risk?" *New York State Education*, LVII, No. 6 (1970), 22-24. Concludes that more effective deployment of teaching talent, improvement of the professional status of teachers, and benefits to students justify the risks involved. Manpower for educating children is enhanced through better utilization and greater retention in the profession.

Engel, Ross A., "The Teacher Evaluates Teacher for Pay Differentials," *The Clearing House*, XLV, No. 7 (1971), 407-409. Advises collegial evaluation for pay differentials in a differentiated staffing situation as a big step toward professionalizing teaching. Interest and accountability are promoted through participation in making decisions.

English, Fenwick, *Et Tu, Educator, Differentiated Staffing?* Write-in Papers No. 4. Washington, D. C.: National Commission on Teacher Education and Professional Standards, National Education Association, 1969. Emphasizes the importance of differentiated staffing for effective learning. The goals and possibilities of the program are explained and compared with conventional staffing patterns. The Temple City, California, model is presented together with a chart setting forth role responsibilities of different staff members.

————, "Teacher May I? Take Three Giant Steps! The Differentiated Staff," *Phi Delta Kappan*, LI, No. 4 (1969), 211-214. Explains necessity for establishing a research base. Four types of models are mentioned. Risk cannot be avoided, but can be minimized by following a sequence of ten steps.

————, "The Differentiated Staff: Education's Technostructure," *Educational Technology*, X, No. 2 (1970), 24-27. Recommends differentiation in staffing as a way of improving the effectiveness of instruction through better utilization of talent, encouragement of change, and diffused decision-making. Dissatisfaction with schools battles 150 years of traditionalism and bureaucracy.

Firester, Lee and Joan, "Differentiated Staffing," *New York State Education*, LVII, No. 6 (1970), 27-28. Raises the question of whether differentiation should be made on a vertical or horizontal basis. The desirability of specialization of personnel and of moving subject matter down into lower grades is challenged.

Hair, Donald and Eugene Wolkey, "Differentiated Staffing and Salary Pattern Underway in Kansas City," *School and Community*, LV, No. 8 (1969), 8-14. Reports a new pattern of staff deployment in an elementary and junior high school. Diagrams staff organization, lists objectives of the program, describes functions of the different classifications, and presents time and salary schedules.

Hickman, L. C., ed., "Differentiated Staffing," *Nation's Schools*, LXXXV, No. 6 (1970), 43-49. Reports specific models where differentiated staffing is used, the theory behind it, and teacher reaction. A chart is included to relate staffing and salaries as well as a round-table interview with three administrators reporting their view of differentiated staffing problems.

————, ed., "Differentiated Staffing OK but More Research Wanted," *Nation's Schools*, LXXXVI, No. 3 (1970), 37. Reports results of a poll of sampling of school administrators in 50 states concerning differentiated staffing.

Administrators respond positively to form questions, considering the pattern of differentiated staffing as beneficial, understandable, and workable. They do not look upon it as a disguise for merit pay.

Joyce, Bruce R., "Staff Utilization," *Review of Educational Research,* XXXVII, No. 3 (1967), 323-336. Reviews research on staff utilization 1963-1966. Studies here reported investigate innovations in staff utilization patterns. Team teaching, man-machine systems and computer-assisted instruction are covered. Studies of teacher role are summarized.

Keefe, J. W.,"Differentiated Staffing—Its Rewards and Pitfalls," *The Bulletin of the National Association of Secondary School Principals,* LV, No. 355 (1971), 112-118. Details the primary pros and cons of differentiated staffing. The author concludes that differentiated staffing will succeed only when an effective systems approach based on current management design is utilized.

Krull, R. Pratt, ed., "What is Differentiated Staffing?" *Instructor,* LXXX, No. 9 (1971), 19. Reports the meaning of differentiated staffing to a random sample of *Instructor* subscribers. Questions are asked concerning ability and discrimination in regard to teachers or other members of the professional staff.

Krumbein, Gerald, "How to Tell Exactly What Differentiated Staffing Will Cost Your District," *The American School Board Journal,* CLVII, No. 11 (1970), 19-24. Presents formulae for determining the number of teachers needed, the cost of their salaries, the dollars saved, the cost of other employees, and the cost of the personnel for a differentiated staff.

Lown, Donald E., "Proceed with Deliberation on Differentiated Staffing," *New York State Education,* LVII, No. 6 (1970), 25-26. Suggests that defining and clarifying roles that can be placed in a hierarchical model may be so difficult as to make it impossible successfully to implement differentiated staffing as presently conceived. Teachers may be reluctant to accept supervision from their peers.

McKenna, Bernard H., "Patterns of School Staffing," *California Teachers Association Journal,* LXIV, No. 2 (1968), 34-38. Calls team teaching a structural change which has not made basic alterations in purposes and program. A warning is sounded against the danger of intensifying specialization in team teaching to the neglect of interrelatedness.

————, *Staffing the Schools.* New York: Bureau of Publications, Teachers College, Columbia, 1965. Focuses upon the quality and number of professional staff members. Research procedures and findings are presented relating to teacher qualifications, the number and deployment of professionals, and the kind of professionals that are needed in a school system.

Olivero, James L., "The Meaning and Application of Differentiated Staffing in Teaching," *Phi Delta Kappan,* LII, No. 1 (1970), 36-40. Advocates differentiated staffing as one alternative to improving education especially since the challenge of accountability is presently squarely on the shoulders of educators. Better utilization of personnel should produce better results.

Olivero, James L., and Edward C. Buffie, eds., *Educational Manpower: From Aides to Differentiated Staff Patterns.* Bloomington: Indiana University Press, 1970. A comprehensive volume including the use of auxiliary personnel and differentiated staffing as part of better utilization of educational manpower. Discussions by authorities in the field present valuable information relative to models, operations, and evaluation.

Rand, M. John, "Case for Differentiated Staffing," *California Teachers Association Journal,* LXV, No. 2 (1969), 29-33. Indicates the need for promotional opportunity as a teacher. The Temple City model shifts decision-making power to teachers together with autonomy for self-regulation. The competent professional is not afraid of being replaced.

Rand, M. John and Fenwick English, "Towards a Differentiated Teaching Staff," *Phi Delta Kappan,* XLIX, No. 5 (1968), 264-268. Provides job descriptions for the original Temple City model, which includes the teaching research associate and the teaching curriculum associate above the senior teacher in the hierarchy. The functions of the academic senate and the school manager are explained.

Staropoli, Charles J. and George W. Rumsey, "A Career-Ladder Approach to Differentiated Staffing: Program and Implications," *Contemporary Education,* XLII, No. 6 (1971), 307-308. Favors differentiated staffing as a means to full utilization of personnel. Differentiated staffing is projected as a statewide reality in Delaware in the future.

Stocker, Joseph, *Differentiated Staffing in Schools.* Washington: National School Public Relations Association, 1970. Defines and describes differentiated staffing in action. Advantages, problems, and organizational patterns are presented. Three case studies and a number of differentiated staffing schools are included.

Storm, George, "Differentiated Staffing—A New Approach to Classification and Assignment," *Industrial Arts and Vocational Education,* LIX, No. 1 (1970), TE6, TE10. Views differentiated staffing as a way of increasing teaching effectiveness and of rewarding dedicated, conscientious instructors. It is an outgrowth of increased technology and the resultant trend toward team teaching.

Teacher Education Issues and Innovations, pp. 78-104. Washington, D. C.: The American Association of Colleges for Teacher Education Yearbook, 1968. Papers by Roy Edelfelt, Dwight Allen, Arthur Pearl, and E. Brooks Smith discussing staff differentiation and the preparation of educational personnel in relation to the Education Professions Development Act.

Trump, J. Lloyd, *Images of the Future,* pp. 13-14. Washington, D. C.: Commission on the Experimental Study of the Utilization of the Staff in the Secondary School, Library of Congress, 1959. Considers the instructional staff of the school of the future, which will include teacher specialists, general teachers, instruction assistants, clerks, general aides, community consultants, and staff specialists. Their roles and functions are explained.

Audiovisual and Other Resources

Differentiated Teaching Assignments (booklet, 32 pp., 25¢). NEA, 1201 16th St., N. W., Washington, D. C. 20036.

The Teacher and His Staff: Differentiating Teaching Roles (conference report, 120 pp., $3.50 cloth, $2.50 paper). NEA, 1201 16th St., N. W., Washington, D. C. 20036.

Team Teaching

37

Definition

Team teaching is a process involving two or more teachers who work together closely in planning, carrying out, and evaluating the learning experiences of a group of students usually the size of two to five conventional classes. The students may work as one large group, in small groups, or as individuals. The size of the assembly group may be as small as 50. Occasionally the total number taught by the team is as large as 180. Rarely are there more than six teachers on the team.

Teams may be organized in a number of ways. Some teams are made up of teachers from the same or closely related fields who work on a vertical basis with students in all grades. In the secondary school, teachers of one subject who teach the same course frequently constitute a team. Other teams are composed of several teachers who work on a horizontal level with students of the same grade or a limited number of grades. In the elementary and middle schools teams are frequently organized for different blocks of students. In these instances, the team is made up of teachers of several different disciplines who serve a common group of pupils. When teams for blocks of pupils are organized, focus is usually upon selecting teachers of special competence in subject areas. More recently attention has been directed to selecting persons whose special talents complement one another in such areas as large-group instruction, diagnosis of learning difficulties, use of audiovisual materials, or counseling. In addition to teachers certificated with special competence in various aspects of the instructional program, most teams include clerical aides, technical assistants, and other paraprofessionals. These aides perform many vital functions and make it possible for the regular teachers to work more closely with their students.

Differentiated staffing is, however, not a prerequisite for team teaching. Some teams consist entirely of co-equals. Others follow a hierarchical model with several levels of certificated teachers and paraprofessionals. In either case a leader is essential to arrange staff meetings, develop schedules for instruction, and coordinate other aspects of the team effort. When teams are organized in one subject area, the teacher who makes the presentation to the assembly group often serves as team leader. A leader with special skill in group dynamics, knowledge of curriculum development, and ability to organize activities is particularly important for effective operation of the team. Members of the team should have an important role in selecting their leader.

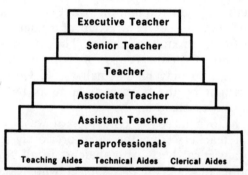

Hierarchical Staffing with Various Levels of Responsibility, Competence and Prestige

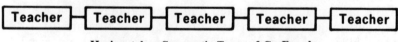

Horizontal or Synergetic Team of Co-Equals

It must be clearly recognized that having one teacher teach all the reading, mathematics, social studies, or science for a block of students is not team teaching. At best, such division of responsibility constitutes departmentalization. Joint planning, closely correlated teaching, and shared responsibility are distinguishing characteristics of team teaching. Cooperative teaching demands common purposes, harmonious teamwork, and coordinated evaluation.

Team teaching is more than an organizational pattern developed to make efficient use of staff, space, and equipment. Basically it is a philosophy of learning designed to vitalize the curriculum, develop more confident and competent teachers, and individualize instruction. There is no common pattern for setting up the teams or for carrying out the instruction. The size and composition of the team is determined by the objectives to be achieved, number of students, available facilities, activities to be pursued, and other factors that vary from school to school.

Although a hierarchical structure is quite generally followed, some schools prefer the synergetic plan, in which all teachers have equal status. Flexibility which allows staff members to function in the roles in which they can contribute significantly is more important than a particular organizational pattern. Provision for individualized help and variation in groupings to accommodate various learning styles of pupils are among the chief advantages of the program. A broad range of activities and a variety of appropriate materials are important. Freedom in utilization of space and time is essential.

More important than materials, space, and schedule arrangements, however, are the attitudes, understandings and working relationships that exist among the members of the team. Mutual agreement on objectives, mutual trust, and mutual support must prevail. The leader must manage human differences in such a way that commonality of purpose is achieved without suppression of individuality. Personal identification of each team member with common objectives and group commitment to agreed-upon results allow for resolving differences without creating conflict.

Significant Components   *Which ones are essential?*

1. Before launching on a team teaching program, the staff should engage in extensive planning and visit other schools.
2. The teachers must be committed to working as a team, sensitive to one another's views, and ready for new roles.
3. The leader should possess strong leadership qualities, sound knowledge, and skill in curriculum development.
4. Supporting personnel, clerical and technical, are needed to free regular teachers from routine duties.
5. Space for large and small group instruction and for individual study is necessary.

6. Every member of the team should be involved in the planning from the beginning and should have regular time for continuous planning.
7. Definite assignments of responsibilities should be made for the different members of the team.
8. Time must be taken to insure that all members of the team agree upon the goals and objectives.
9. Schedules with maximum flexibility add significantly to success.
10. In setting up teams, special attention should be given to seeing to it that teachers complement one another in temperament, background, interests, experience, and special talents.
11. A generous supply of well-selected instructional supplies and equipment is important.
12. Space and time for teacher planning, developing materials, and organizing activities are essential.
13. Cooperation among teachers and ability to communicate are very important.
14. The administration must be prepared for other innovations that invariably grow out of team teaching.
15. Since it is unlikely that the program will run smoothly from the beginning, need for changes must be anticipated and welcomed.
16. Effective communication is needed within the team and with all other segments of the school and community.
17. Provision for independent study, experimentation, and a wide range of projects and activities is invaluable.
18. Administrators, particularly building principals, must understand the purposes and processes and participate actively.
19. Orientation and provision for continuing inservice development is needed, particularly for inexperienced teachers.
20. Students must be prepared for team teaching.
21. Evaluation should include not only pupil learning, but also the assessment of the team operation, with emphasis on intragroup relations.
22. It is usually better to move into team teaching on a limited basis than to try to reorganize the entire school at one time.

Proposed Advantages   *With which ones do you agree?*

1. Team teaching provides an opportunity to utilize the strengths and discard the weaknesses of both the self-contained and departmentalized programs.
2. The differences in personalities of team members enables each child to find one teacher with whom he relates exceptionally well.

3. Presentation, followed by student-led discussion groups, develops leadership and improves communication skills.

4. Team teaching provides a laboratory for planning and testing other innovations.

5. Special teachers can be meaningfully involved in an integrated learning program.

6. Working together develops teamwork and high morale in the staff.

7. Flexible schedules and provision for one-to-one instruction contribute to individualization.

8. Having one or more teams operating in a building provides an opportunity for other teachers not directly involved to observe the advantages of team teaching.

9. Teachers develop increased respect for one another.

10. Joint evaluation provides valuable feedback for each team worker and is an incentive for self-improvement.

11. Teachers prepare more carefully and put forth greater effort when they are being observed by their colleagues.

12. Unity of purpose is fostered by having teachers plan together and an awareness of what others are doing.

13. Evaluation of students is more objective and fair because the viewpoints and insights of several teachers are taken into account.

14. Allowing learners to participate in large and small groups and in independent study provides for differences in learning styles.

15. Judgments of various teachers add balance to the curriculum.

16. Several teachers are better able than one to diagnose learning problems and reach nonmotivated children.

17. Opportunity to communicate with their adult colleagues relieves teachers from constant exchange of ideas with children.

18. Contact with a number of teachers develops the pupil's ability to adjust to change.

Criticisms and Difficulties to Be Anticipated   *Do you agree?*

1. Effective team teachers are hard to find; few colleges are turning them out.

2. Competent team leaders are extremely scarce.

3. In a hierarchical structure the master or executive teacher is likely to be resented by the other teachers.

4. Some competent teachers prefer to work alone.

5. In the elementary school, team teaching tends to destroy the values of the self-contained classroom by introducing excessive departmentalization.

6. Some students and teachers experience difficulty in adjusting to large groups or to flexible schedules.
7. Failure to provide orientation, preparation, and planning time will render the effort ineffective.
8. Very able teachers who prefer to work alone are often over-critical of their colleagues.
9. Confusion often arises concerning whether the team leader's responsibility is to instruct children or to teach the other teachers.
10. Increase in salary and other costs will result.
11. Unless guarded against, rivalry and strife may spring up within the team.
12. In a team situation, it may be difficult to allocate responsibility to one teacher for lack of achievement or undesirable conduct on the part of an individual student.
13. Lack of rigid structure and definite time schedules creates disorder and wastes a lot of time.
14. Students take advantage of different expectancies among teachers and pit one teacher against the other.
15. Much additional time is required to develop schedules for team teaching.
16. No teacher is likely to know the individual children well enough to be able to confer effectively with parents.
17. Sharp differences often develop in deciding on grades to be assigned.
18. Team teaching requires more time and effort on the part of teachers than is needed in operating self-contained classrooms.

Summary Assessment

There is little disagreement with the philosophy, purpose, and even most of the proposed advantages of team teaching. More argument arises over the possibilities for its successful implementation. Few of the objections or reservations expressed are insurmountable; but several of them—including lack of committed teachers, adequate space, and necessary facilities—should receive serious consideration in planning for the program.

The chief value of team teaching lies in its potential for enabling students to pursue learning activities appropriate to their needs and learning styles. Large group experiences, inquiry groups, and independent study provide varied advantages. The careful planning and cooperative effort demonstrated in a good team teaching situation can encourage teamwork and improve morale among teachers and students. Independent study should foster self-reliance and responsibility on the part of the students.

Working together, teachers develop confidence in the essential worthwhileness of their efforts. They share their disappointments and satisfactions. They gain new insights from joint planning. Balance is added to the instructional program, and methods are refined through observing one another at work. Increased professional satisfaction frequently results from sharing success in bringing varied talents to bear on the solution of difficult and frustrating problems.

The danger of conflict developing among members of the team must not be ignored. Variations in time and space requirements are likely to present problems in building schedules. The difficulty that some children experience in adjusting to different teachers, schedules, and activities are often exaggerated, but should not be overlooked. More important than the obstacles commonly cited, perhaps, is the unwillingness of many educators to cut loose from their traditional moorings. In order to approach its promise and potential, team teaching must be grounded upon a philosophy of creativity, mutual support, thoughtful planning, flexibility, and individualization. Those who hold with rigid standards, neat organization, and conformity find little comfort or challenge in teaming. Even more disturbing to them may be the realization that team teaching, more than most innovations, provides a seedbed for other changes. Yet, the enthusiasm generated by having groups of teachers thinking, planning, and working together might easily set off chain reactions that could lead far beyond the bounds of traditional thinking.

In team teaching there is no substitute for joint planning. All personnel must be involved from the beginning, must take time for continuous planning, and must share in evaluation. If this can be insured, it appears that the advantages of teaming outweigh the problems that are likely to be encountered. Cooperative effort among individuals, groups, and nations is essential to the solution of the pressing problems of the world. Children must learn to work together harmoniously and productively in facing the many challenges which they are constantly meeting, and which they will be called upon to solve in the years ahead. It would seem reasonable to assume that cooperative effort among teachers on a team would set an impressive example for youth, demonstrating the value and effective techniques for achieving results through working together.

The keys to success in team teaching are cooperation, preplanning, flexibility in scheduling, variety of materials, and individualization. Pooling the professional and personal strengths of each of the team members offers richer opportunities to the pupils and stimulates professional growth of the teachers. Having begun at the high school level, teaming is currently popular in middle schools and is gaining acceptance at the elementary level, particularly in nongraded programs.

A Few Leaders in the Movement

E. J. Anderson
  Anne Arundel County (Md.)
  Schools
Robert H. Anderson
  Harvard Univ.
John M. Bahner
  Institute for Development of
  Educational Activities
Medill Bair
  Hartford (Conn.) Schools
David Beggs
  Indiana Univ.
B. Frank Brown
  Institute for Development
  of Educational Activities
Harold S. Davis
  Educational Research Council of
  Greater Cleveland

John I. Goodlad
  Univ. of California at Los Angeles
Robert W. Jones
  Georgia State Univ.
Philip Lambert
  Univ. of Wisconsin
Henry F. Olds
  Harvard Univ.
Judson T. Shaplin
  Washington Univ.
Harold Spears
  Univ. of Indiana
J. Lloyd Trump
  Nat'l. Association of Secondary
  School Principals
Helen Wagner
  Lake Erie College
Richard G. Woodward
  Hartford (Conn.) Schools

A Few Places Where the Innovation Is Used

Auburn, Me.
Carmel, Calif.
Claremont, Calif.
Concord, Mass.
Denver, Colo.
Easton, Pa.
El Dorado, Ark.
Evanston, Ill.
Fort Lauderdale, Fla.
Fort Wayne, Ind.

High Springs, Fla.
Idaho Falls, Idaho
Jefferson Co., Colo.
Las Vegas, Nev.
Lexington, Mass.
Melbourne, Fla.
Muskegon, Mich.
Norridge, Ill.
Northbrook, Ill.
Norwalk, Conn.

Palo Alto, Calif.
Plainview, N. Y.
Racine, Wis.
Salina, Kans.
San Antonio, Texas
San Diego, Calif.
Snyder, Texas
Staton, Oreg.
Univ. of Chicago
Univ. of Wisconsin

Annotated References

Altman, Burton E., "Micro Team Teaching with Student Teachers," *Instructor*, LXXIX, No. 2 (1969), 88-89. Wisconsin State University coordinated a program to include student teachers in team teaching. It not only prepared student teachers for team teaching but was decidedly an effective plan for La Crosse Schools.

Anderson, Robert H., *Teaching in a World of Change*, pp. 71-108. New York: Harcourt, 1966. Outlines the development of team teaching since the nineteenth century. Definition, characteristics, and advantages are delineated.

Effect on teacher morale and attitudes and on pupil achievement and adjustment are examined.

Arone, Frank T., "Toward Greater Success in Team Teaching," *The Clearing House*, XLV, No. 8 (1971), 501-502. Lists 11 points on team teaching. For example, "Students and teachers need an understanding about how people work in groups."

Atwood, Ronald K., "Team Teaching: New Models Are Needed," *The Science Teacher*, XXXVII, No. 1 (1970), 59-60. Claims that team teaching suggests pooling students of two classrooms into one or switching instructors on a rotating basis. It adds hopefully that a new model—two or more instructors jointly planning and conducting a program of instruction—can be practiced.

Bair, Medill and Richard G. Woodward, *Team Teaching in Action*. Boston: Houghton Mifflin, 1964. A comprehensive book describing early experiments in the field and analyzing the characteristics of the plan. Advantages of flexible space and time schedules are assessed, and methods of evaluation are considered.

Beggs, David W., ed., *Team Teaching: Bold New Venture*. Bloomington: Indiana University Press, 1964. Takes a practical look at team teaching and how it can be implemented most effectively in schools. Procedures are considered for evaluating the program. Qualities which make good or poor team members are described.

Behrendt, David, "Away with Tradition," *American Education*, VI, No. 1 (1970), 18-22. Describes new scheduling and teaching strategies employed in multiunit schools in Racine and other Wisconsin cities. A unit leader, five unit teachers, an intern, and an aide comprise a typical staff.

Biggs, Stanley F. and Linwood E. Gilbert, "The Team Approach Helps Beginning Teachers," *Educational Forum*, XXIV, No. 2 (1969), 29-30. A joint effort at teaching has benefits for both teachers and students. The team approach shortens the work load in determining course content, developing objectives, and determining teaching procedures.

Butler, Walter and Joe D. Cornett, "Effect of a Team Approach in Achieving the Objectives of an Introductory Course in Education," *Journal of Educational Research*, LXIII, No. 5 (1970), 222-224. A case study, involving experimental and control groups, reported the effects of team teaching. It concludes that team teaching was effective in student achievement but not effective in swaying them to become a teacher in that particular subject.

Davison, John, "Team Teaching with an Accent on Science," *Science Education*, LIV, No. 2 (1970), 136-171. The objectives and organization of team teaching are defined, advantages and disadvantages are discussed, well-known team teaching plans are reviewed, and the innovation is assessed briefly in the conclusion.

Gamsky, Neal R., "Team Teaching, Student Achievement and Attitudes," *The Journal of Experimental Education*, XXXIX, No. 1 (1970), 42-45. Outlines a case study in World History and in English, with "experimental" and "conventional" groups. No change in achievement. Team-taught students displayed greater growth in their feelings of self-reliance and personal freedom.

Goldstein, William, "Problems in Team Teaching," *The Clearing House*, XLII, No. 1 (1967), 83-86. Discusses horizontal and vertical organization and variations of these. The close working relationship of team members presents many intricacies. Team teaching indicates differentiated staffing.

Hanslousky, Glenda, Sue Moyer, and Helen Wagner, *Why Team Teaching?* Columbus, Ohio: Merrill, 1969. Considers how a school should go about establishing a team teaching program and points out the diverse opportunities such a plan affords. The appendix contains examples of an interdisciplinary lesson plan, interdisciplinary assignments, and different schedule plans.

Hug, William E., "Teamwork in Biology," *Science Education,* LIII, No. 5 (1969), 385-388. Comments on the team teaching plan in a high school. It assesses the pupil's achievement and attitudes about the plan.

Hynes, Sister Nancy, "Learning to Read Short Stories," *Journal of Reading,* XIII, No. 6 (1970), 429-432, 473. Reviews a team teaching experiment with large group instruction, small group discussion, and independent study.

Inlow, Gail M., *The Emergent in Curriculum,* pp. 287-306. New York: Wiley, 1966. Stresses the need for flexibility and careful planning. Disadvantages and unresolved issues are discussed. Most assessments of the values of team teaching are cautious, but see advantages in providing greater opportunity for individualization.

Jackson, Ann M., "Two Teachers in the Classroom," *New York State Education,* LVIII, No. 6 (1971), 30, 39. Emphasizes the disaster of the "two-headed monster" of team teaching. A teacher and a student aide, not two teachers, "can do the best kind of a job."

Oliva, Peter F., *The Secondary School Today.* Scranton, Pa.: International Textbook, 1968. Explains the composition of the team, strengths and weaknesses of teaming, and common misunderstandings. The key to success is the ability of team members to work together harmoniously and to plan cooperatively.

Peterson, Carl H., *Effective Team Teaching: The Easton Area High School Programs.* West Nyack, N. Y.: Parker, 1966. Explains why a high school changed to team teaching and how the teacher team was developed. Scheduling, facilities, and techniques for large group instruction and independent study are included.

Pike, Kenneth V., Leon Jordan, Norbert J. Konzal, "Biology Methods—A Team-Teaching Approach," *Science Teacher,* XXXVII, No. 2 (1970), 63-64. Discusses Arizona State University's experimental approach with student team-teaching. It was designed to create teaching behavior to make the transition from student to teacher easier.

Polos, Nicholas C., *The Dynamics of Team Teaching.* Dubuque: William C. Brown, 1965. Goes to great lengths discussing the strengths and weaknesses of team teaching. An extensive bibliography of 21 pages lists articles under specific headings.

Rhodes, Fen, "Team Teaching Compared with Traditional Instruction in Grades Kindergarten Through Six," *Journal of Educational Psychology,* LXII, No. 2 (1971), 110-116. Former evaluations concurred on three points: there was no change in the achievement and attitude of pupils, and teacher attitude was more positive. The data of this experiment drew up the conclusion that the traditional methods were better.

Schmitt, John, John Montean, and Paul Joslin, "An Objective Look at Team Teaching in High School Biology," *Science Education,* LIII, No. 3 (1969), 273-276. Makes observations on an "experimental" group and "conventional" group. It remarks that the two biggest obstacles were time (planning) and expense (budgetary funds).

Shaplin, Judson and Henry F. Olds, *Team Teaching.* New York: Harper and Row, 1964. A comprehensive volume which begins with a definition and history of the movement and moves through suggestions for organization and implementation. An extensive bibliography and appendix listing team teaching projects are included.

Shawver, David E., "Team Teaching: How Successful Is It?" *The Clearing House,* XLIII, No. 1 (1968), 21-26. Goes into a detailed explanation of the Trump Plan. Attention is given to the importance of careful planning, effective use of time and talents, and the deep commitment needed to make team teaching successful.

Sybouts, Ward, "Supervision and Team Teaching," *Educational Leadership,* XXV, No. 2 (1967), 158-165. Concludes that one of the main advantages of team membership is that new teachers receive comments, help, and encouragement from more experienced team members. Suggestions are directed to principals relating to their supervisory responsibilities in team situations.

Trump, J. Lloyd and Delmas F. Miller, *Secondary Curriculum Improvement,* pp. 317-325. Boston: Allyn and Bacon, 1968. Distinguishes between "team teaching" and "cooperative teaching," "rotation of teaching," or "utilization of teacher aides." Planning, instructing, and evaluating together are the essential ingredients of team teaching.

Wey, Herbert W., *Handbook for Principals,* pp. 35-38. New York: Schaum, 1966. Cites as one of the major advantages of the plan the effective use of teachers' strengths. Things to be considered when planning for team teaching are outlined step by step.

York, L. Jean, *Team Teaching.* Dallas: Leslie Press, 1971. Includes a series of seven instructional units using an individualized multimedia approach to the study of team teaching. Each of the seven "modules" treats a different topic relating to team teaching beginning with background, philosophy, and purposes, and finishing with prerequisites for good planning sessions.

Audiovisual and Other Resources

High School Team Teaching: The Ferris Story (16mm film, color, 26 min., $290, rental $15). Explains the planning and experimental stages preceding the initiation of team teaching at a new high school in Spokane, Wash. BFA Educational Media, 2211 Michigan Ave., Santa Monica, Calif. 90404.

The Quiet Revolution (16mm film, color, 28 min., $150, rental $10). An unconventional dialogue between Dante and Virgil on staffing modern schools. NEA, 1201 16th St., N. W., Washington, D. C. 20036.

Team Teaching on the Elementary Level (16mm film, color, 14 min., $150, rental $8). Describes the motivation, plans, workshops involved in introducing team teaching in Cashmere, Wash. BFA Educational Media, 2211 Michigan Ave., Santa Monica, Calif. 90404.

Why Team Teach? (booklet, 60¢). Educational Research Council of America, Rockefeller Bldg., Cleveland, Ohio 44113.

Teacher Aides

38

Definition

Teacher aides are volunteers or paid employees of the school who perform many nonprofessional duties and thus free the teacher for the professional responsibilities of teaching. Except for rare instances, the terms *teacher aides, paraprofessionals, auxiliary school personnel, teacher assistants, nonprofessionals,* and *subprofessionals* are used interchangeably. The duties of aides vary according to the demands of the individual school and the qualifications of the aide. However, a distinction is generally made between the instructional and noninstructional duties. Assisting the teacher with large-group instruction, working with small groups or individual pupils, reading stories, dictating spelling words, and helping a student who has been absent from school are referred to as "instructional duties." Among the "noninstructional services" are clerical work, counting money, running errands, preparing materials, arranging field trips, grading objective tests, and many other routine functions.

Among the first extensive programs involving teacher aides were those started in Bay City, Michigan, and Fairfield, Connecticut, in the early fifties. The movement spread slowly for a decade. The Economic Opportunity Act of 1964, the Elementary and Secondary Education Act of 1965, and the Educations Professions Act of 1967 brought about an explosive increase in the use of paraprofessionals. Currently, about 30 per cent of the classrooms of the country have teacher aides, usually shared by two or more teachers. Paraprofessionals are more frequently used in the elementary school than in secondary schools. In the high schools they play supportive roles, most commonly those of grading papers, assisting with extracurricular activities, and chaperoning social events. Direct contact with pupils in learning activities is more frequent in the elementary school. Clerical and technical aides are very common in schools that engage in team teaching.

Other professions, particularly medicine, have long utilized supportive personnel of many kinds and at various levels. Technicians perform many functions formerly done by trained engineers. During the past 20 years, educators have come to the realization that routine detail work often dampens the professional teacher's enthusiasm for teaching. Trivial duties rob him of the opportunities for creative planning and decision-making that are satisfying to the professional. His skills are often diverted to performing what he considers clerical and technical chores. The public, too, is demanding that the teacher devote his time, energy, and professional competence to diagnosing the problems of children and inspiring and guiding them to excellence.

The movements toward individualization of instruction and differentiated staffing have added impetus to the use of paraprofessionals. Well-trained teachers realize that they can help only a limited number of pupils at one time. They see opportunities for better application of their talent than that involved in performing many of the routine tasks that continually press upon them. They can spend more time planning, diagnosing learning difficulties, and prescribing appropriate activities for individual children. Competent, imaginative teachers usually welcome the help of aides, but many of their less secure colleagues feel threatened by the presence of other workers.

Increasing attention is being directed to identifying the appropriate roles of paraprofessionals. Alert to the possibility that shortage of funds might tempt boards of education to employ cheap help, teacher organizations and unions have sometimes made a strained effort to distinguish between professional and nonprofessional duties. Establishing guidelines to guard against the misuse of unqualified personnel confronts the danger of destroying the flexibility essential for effective and efficient utilization of the talents of both teachers and aides. It is difficult to determine whether teaching certain drill exercises, listening to pupils read, reading stories to groups, conferring with individuals, and many other classroom activities are in reality instructional or noninstructional. Many of these decisions have to be made for each classroom, where the strengths of teachers and aides can be taken into account, and the needs of a particular group of students can be assessed. A French immigrant, for example, working as an aide might be able to teach many aspects of French better than the certificated teacher.

Available space, time, materials, and other facilities that vary from school to school and even from classroom to classroom must be taken into consideration if the employment of paraprofessionals is to produce its maximum advantages. Accountability for learning seems to indicate that individual schools must devote more time to organizing their programs and utilizing their personnel in such a way that maximum benefits accrue to pupils. This is perhaps a valid principle which should direct the determination of the proper roles of teacher aides and their relationship with teachers and students.

Significant Components   *Which ones are essential?*

1. Careful planning is necessary to assure effective utilization of teacher aides.
2. The roles and duties of the professionals and paraprofessionals must be clarified.
3. Inservice training is needed to teach teachers how to use aides to best advantage.
4. Aides should be carefully screened and trained.
5. Aides must possess ability to relate well to people and take a personal interest in children.
6. Flexibility must allow aides to assume increased responsibility as they grow in confidence and competence.
7. Aides must comprehend the philosophy of the school, the objectives, the characteristics of the pupils, their own limitations, and what is expected of them.
8. Provision must be made for teachers and aides to plan together.
9. Regular attendance of the aides should be assured, and wherever possible their schedules should avoid short, intermittent periods of time.
10. Parents must be assured that aides are not performing professional tasks beyond their level of competence.
11. Aides must not be expected to perform mainly those chores that nobody else wants to do.

12. A sound administrative organization and an effective supervisory plan should be established for directing and improving the aide program.
13. Pupils, aides, administrators, and teachers must understand their respective responsibilities and functions.
14. The teacher must be glad to have an aide and to work with her.
15. Aides must be made to feel that they are important people, and that they are making a significant contribution.
16. Paraprofessionals should be treated with consideration and must not be overburdened with work.
17. Recruitment of aides should take into account the unique needs that prevail in a particular situation.
18. Parents and students should be involved from the beginning in planning, implementing, and evaluating a teacher aide program.
19. There are advantages to assign aides to buildings other than the ones which their children or those of their neighbors attend.
20. Teachers must take into account the skills of the aides, their background, and their special talents.
21. The unique talents of the teacher and the aide should be matched so that they can complement each other.
22. The need for the aides must be justifiable, and the public should be informed of the reasons for employing them.
23. Employment of aides must not be an economy measure.

Proposed Advantages   *With which ones do you agree?*

1. The teacher is relieved of trivia and can direct time and energy to professional services for children.
2. More and better instructional materials can be produced.
3. Students can be given more personal and individual instruction.
4. Aides bring special talents, such as proficiency in a foreign language or music, to the classroom.
5. More multimedia materials are likely to be utilized.
6. Aides sometimes uncover information about students that the teacher might not.
7. Additional opportunity for drill and practice reinforces what the teacher has taught.
8. Individual attention gives the pupil a feeling of importance and security.

9. Aides help to bridge the gap between home and school and are important in establishing and maintaining good relations between school and community.
10. The presence of an adult in the room stimulates the teacher to consistently better performance.
11. Change of pace in the routine of the classroom provides an opportunity for reflection and creativity for both teachers and pupils.
12. Some aides from lower-class backgrounds communicate better with some pupils than do middle-class teachers.
13. Aides are particularly helpful with handicapped, emotionally disturbed, or mentally retarded children.
14. Paraprofessionals can help pupils who have been absent from school.
15. Auxiliary personnel provide help with remedial work; they also offer challenges to gifted pupils.
16. Often aides are more proficient and comfortable in clerical and technical areas than teachers.
17. Money is better spent because, although aides are paid less than teachers, they perform many duties as effectively.
18. The paraprofessional program utilizes untapped human resources of the community.
19. Using auxiliary personnel helps provide time for planning and curriculum revision.
20. Some aides go on to professional careers.

Criticisms and Difficulties to Be Anticipated　　　*Do you agree?*

1. Utilizing teacher aides distorts the image of the teaching profession in the eyes of the public by making it appear that anybody can be an adequate teacher.
2. Good paraprofessionals are difficult to recruit and train.
3. The constant presence of adults tends to make children overdependent.
4. Aides from the community cannot be trusted with confidential information and records.
5. Parents are concerned about having their children under the tutelage of a noncertificated person.
6. Some teachers are uneasy with another adult in the classroom, and insecure teachers are threatened by competent paraprofessionals.
7. Many teachers are basically technicians and clerks, enjoy such work, and are reluctant to give it up.
8. If aides can do a satisfactory job, administrators and boards of education may employ them as an economy measure.

9. A teacher-aide program is likely to have a depressing effect on teacher salaries.

10. Some teachers may use aides to avoid necessary work and waste time while the aides are working with the children.

11. Teachers become jealous if they all don't have equal help from paraprofessionals.

12. Standards and the line of demarcation between instructional and noninstructional tasks have not been defined clearly.

13. Volunteer aides usually are available only a few hours per week, are undependable, and cause rapid turnover.

14. There are very few good training programs for paraprofessionals.

15. Aides become unhappy if they have too little responsibility and equally dissatisfied if they have too much.

16. If paraprofessionals become proficient, clashes between them and the teacher are likely to result.

17. Since aides are frequently established members of the community, it is difficult to get rid of them if they are troublesome.

Summary Assessment

The rationale for employing teacher aides usually uses the model of the medical profession, which has changed drastically from a half century ago when many general practitioners ran their own tests, cleaned their own utensils, and kept their own books. Today junior practitioners, interns, nurses, dieticians, and other supportive personnel provide many services formerly performed by expert diagnosticians and surgeons, freeing them to provide better services for patients. Similarly the use of teacher aides and other forms of differentiated staffing aspire to improved services for pupils.

It usually is recommended that the top-level personnel spend a very substantial part of their time working directly with children. If education is to follow the course charted by medicine, it may be necessary to re-examine the long-standing view that the most important part of teaching and learning lies in face-to-face work with pupils. Those who repeatedly return to the model of medicine might point out that the diagnostician, the doctor who prescribes, or even the surgeon who performs his significant service often does it with little bedside contact with the patient. He actually may spend only a single hour or two of the hundreds of hours that a patient is in the hospital or convalescing from an illness in direct contact with the patient. In teaching, however, it usually is looked upon as heresy to suggest that the best professional teachers, those who are contributing most to the pupils' learning, may have little direct contact with them. Perhaps the teacher who has unusual skill in diagnosing difficult problems, outstanding competence in leading his colleagues, or superior creativity in developing new strategies should forego the pleasure of spending much of his time in direct teaching if the school and pupils are to benefit maximally from his talents.

It appears that educators and the lay public have become convinced that supportive personnel are a good investment because they enable teachers to direct their talents to analyzing pupil needs and prescribing appropriate learning experiences. Emphasis on individualizing instruction is perhaps the most promising educational development of our time. Currently, accountability seems to dominate the thinking and concerns of those responsible for managing the schools. More effective and efficient utilization of instructional personnel appears to be essential to achieving either individualization or accountability.

The value of auxiliary personnel in multiunit schools and in team teaching situations has been demonstrated convincingly although their effectiveness varies with the different attitudes of teachers and the commitment of the school system. Some differences of opinion persist regarding assignment of paraprofessionals to duties that bring them into close contact with actual instruction. More study needs to be directed toward defining the respective roles of instructional and noninstructional personnel, assessing the effectiveness of various strategies, establishing minimum standards and criteria for selection of aides, and developing improved programs of preparation and inservice training of paraprofessionals.

The movement toward teacher aides has a brief history. However, the extent of its acceptance by an originally reluctant teaching profession and lay public and its adoption by school districts leave little doubt that it is here to stay. Teacher aides will permit the professional teacher to apply greater imagination to his work and to derive increased satisfaction from it. The program will move teaching a big step closer to achieving its hopes and potential.

A Few Leaders in the Movement

Donald C. Clark
  Industry-Education Council
Sally N. Clark
  California State College,
  Los Angeles

Wendell Eaton
  Bangor (Me.) Schools
Frances P. Friedman
  Univ. of Saskatchewan

John Gardner
Common Cause
Harold Howe
Ford Foundation
Wayne R. McElroy
Southeast Missouri State College
James Olivero
Southwestern Cooperative
Education Laboratory

Bryce Perkins
Univ. of North Carolina
Mel H. Robb
Educational Research Council
of Greater Cleveland
Paul C. Shank
Southeast Missouri State College
J. Lloyd Trump
Nat'l. Association of Secondary
School Principals

A Few Places Where the Innovation Is Used

Bay City, Mich.	Huntington Beach, Calif.	Richmond, Va.
Cincinnati, Ohio	Kansas City, Kans.	San Antonio, Texas
Cleveland, Ohio	Minneapolis, Minn.	San Diego, Calif.
Duluth, Minn.	New Haven, Conn.	Shaker Heights, Ohio
Fairfield, Conn.	Newton, Mass.	Snyder, Texas
Gary, Ind.	Norwalk, Conn.	Trenton, N. J.
Hamilton Co., Ohio	Providence, R. I.	Washington, D. C.

Annotated References

Arcement, Sr. Genevieve, D. C., "A Teacher Aide Program That Really Works," *Catholic School Journal,* LXIX, No. 10 (1969), 26-27. Reports successful use of aides in an elementary school resulting from gradual introduction of aides into their responsibilities and continued growth through inservice training.

Bernstein, Margery R., "Volunteers to Help Individuals," *Instructor,* LXXX, No. 1 (1970), 136-137. Emphasizes the recruitment, supervision, orientation, and training of volunteers, and the selection of pupils. Careful attention in providing adequate supervision and control in recruitment enhances the teacher's efforts to individualize instruction.

Borstad, Rodney M. and John A. Dewar, "The Paraprofessional and the States," *The National Elementary School Principal,* XLIX, No. 5 (1970), 63-67. Reports state by state the results of a questionnaire study of state policies and practices relating to paraprofessionals. Qualifications, duties, legal status, and employment practices are included.

Bosley, Howard E., *Teacher Education In Transition,* pp. 321-331. Baltimore: Multi-State Teacher Education Project, 1969. Lists duties and functions of aides in child care, assisting with materials, and in clerical and teaching activities. Sources of auxiliary personnel are detailed, and 14 unanswered questions are presented.

Brighton, Howard, *Handbook for Teacher Aides.* Midland, Mich.: Pendell, 1971. Gives guidance to teacher aides in approaching, carrying out, and evaluating their work. Purposes of the aide program, procedures of selection, training, working conditions, roles, expectations, and responsibilities are explained.

———, "Thoughts on the Teacher Aide Program," *Adult Leadership,* XIX, No. 4 (1970), 117-119. Defines the purpose of an aide, procedures in the selection and use of the aide, and the requirements for a meaningful functional teacher aide program. Eight proposed aide categories follow.

————, *Utilizing Teacher Aides*. Midland, Mich.: Pendell, 1971. Provides valuable suggestions for using teacher aides. Goals, selection, training, utilization, and legal problems involved are considered. Helpful suggestions and examples of using aides effectively are given.

Briscoe, Cecil D., "A Reading Program With Lay Aides and Programmed Material," *The Clearing House,* XLIII, No. 6 (1969), 373-377. Explains how aides are oriented to a participation in a program of reading instruction. Special preparation and planning for involvement of the aides are recommended. Cooperative planning effects improvement in reading.

Caplin, Morris D., "An Invaluable Resource: The School Volunteer," *The Clearing House,* XLIV, No. 1 (1970), 10-14. Traces the development of the volunteer movement, which includes business executives, housewives, retired citizens, and college students. They provide a wide variety of service and foster good school-community relations.

Clark, Donald C., and Sally N. Clark, "An Effective Instructional Aide Program: Training For Both Teachers and Aides," *Journal of Secondary Education,* XLV, No. 6 (1970), 250-255. Discusses the rationale of instructional aide programs and the orientation and training procedures for teachers and instructional aides for careful and systematic training to increase the effectiveness and efficiency of a classroom teacher.

Clayton, Dean, "Let's Make More Use of Paraprofessionals," *Business Education World,* XLVIII, No. 8 (1969), 12-13. Lists in detail duties that can be performed effectively by paraprofessionals and students in business education classes. Consideration is given to regular and irregular duties.

Densham, A. Davis, "Children Who Had to Be Found," *American Education,* VII, No. 2 (1971), 11-14. Reports on the efforts of one county's school system to minister to the educational needs of the handicapped preschoolers. Gives several illustrations of how high school students have been used effectively as teacher aides.

Fenner, Mildred Sandison, ed., "How Teacher Aides Feel About Their Jobs," *National Education Association Journal,* LVI, No. 8 (1967), 17-19. Report of a national survey giving data on the frequency of teacher aides, functions performed, and teachers' evaluation of their value. Elementary teachers use and value aides more than do secondary.

Friedman, Frances P., "Teacher Aides: Their Role in the School," *Education Canada,* IX, No. 2 (1969), 2-9. Traces the historical development of teacher aides in the United States and Canada. The need for determining the role of the teacher and the aide is brought out, and areas needing further study are indicated.

Hanson, Fred M., "Aides for the Trainable Mentally Retarded," *Journal California Teachers Association,* LXV, No. 3 (1969), 23-26. Outlines a training program for aides to work with trainable mentally-retarded pupils. Lists qualifications of aides and special types of services offered in special classes.

Heppner, Harry L., "Aides . . . -A Boon - A Blessing - An (Open Sesame)," *Journal California Teachers Association,* LXV, No. 2 (1969), 39-43. Describes the use of aides in pre-kindergarten and elementary teams in a ghetto school. Spanish-speaking aides provide warmth and special assistance in the language program.

Johnson, William H., "Utilizing Teacher Aides," *The Clearing House,* XLIII, No. 4 (1967), 229-233. Explains use of teacher aides for providing increased opportunities for disadvantaged pupils. Need for role definition and for orientation prior to introduction of the aide is presented. Skillful administrative decision-making and staff involvement are essential.

Olivero, James L., "Do Teacher Aides Really Aid?" *Journal California Teachers Association,* LXV, No. 2 (1969), 34-36. Differentiated staffing may do much to encourage teachers to stay in the profession. Roles of teachers and aides must be defined and understood by all concerned.

Olivero, James L. and Edward G. Buffie, *Educational Manpower.* Bloomington: Indiana University Press, 1970. A comprehensive volume including the use of auxiliary personnel and differentiated staffing as part of better utilization of educational manpower. Discussions by authorities in the field present valuable information relative to models, operations, and evaluation.

Perkins, Bryce, *Getting Better Results from Substitutes, Teacher Aides, and Volunteers.* Englewood Cliffs, N. J.: Prentice-Hall, 1966. Discusses how to use teacher aides effectively by looking at different schools which use them and their recruitment and screening. Duties and guidelines are provided to build a successful teacher aide program in any school.

Provus, Malcolm M., *Staffing for Better Schools.* Washington, D. C.: Office of Education, U. S. Department of Health, Education, and Welfare, 1967. Proposes many types and sources of aides. The point is made that most communities have a great variety of human resources that need to be discovered, recruited, and trained. Examples of varied services are presented.

Robb, Mel H., *Teacher Assistants.* Columbus, Ohio: Merrill, 1969. A handbook of practical suggestions for securing, orienting, utilizing, and developing teacher aides. The roles, values, and appropriate duties of both paid and volunteer workers are discussed.

Seyforth, J. T., and R. L. Canady, "Paraprofessionals: in Search of Identity," *The Clearing House,* XLV, No. 4 (1970), 221-225. Reports findings of a study on duties of the paraprofessional. Teachers and principals were asked what duties they believed paraprofessionals would be most effective in. The study determined that the functions of the paraprofessional should be performance of clerical tasks and assistance with preparation of instructional materials.

Shank, Paul and Wayne R. McElroy, *The Paraprofessionals or Teacher Aides.* Midland, Mich.: Pendell, 1970. Gives a broad view of the selection, training, and assignment of teacher aides. Material is presented for aides themselves, for teachers with whom the aides work, and for administrative organization and supervision of the program. Joint responsibility is emphasized.

Street, David, ed., *Innovations In Mass Education,* pp. 177-200. New York: Wiley, 1969. Reviews introduction of subprofessionals into five large cities between 1959 and 1966. Professionalism of teachers is improved, and valuable supplementary services are provided. A model of administrative management, one of competitive enterprise, and a composite are identified.

Sullivan, Alice A. and Orlando L. Savastano, "Teacher Aides in Physical Education," *Journal of Health, Physical Education, Recreation,* XL, No. 5 (1969), 26-29. Classifies aides as educational materials assistant, clerical worker, and instructional assistant. Proposed duties are listed in these three areas together with restrictions of functions and qualifications and duties performed in seven representative schools.

Talbot, Virginia, "Teacher Aides," *Grade Teacher,* LXXXVIII, No. 3 (1970), 109-111. Lists some pointers on selecting and training a teacher's aide to make sure that she does the best job possible for maximum benefit to fulfill student needs and to help the teacher.

Tanner, Laurel N. and Daniel, "The Teacher Aide: A National Study of Confusion," *Educational Leadership,* XXVI, No. 8 (1969), 765-769. Reports findings of a national survey covering the role and function, guidelines, and legal status of aides. Problems in differentiating between teaching and nonteaching roles are raised. Marked differences in qualifications are revealed.

"Teacher Aides in the Public Schools," *N. E. A. Research Bulletin,* XLVIII, No. 1 (1970), 11-12. Survey reports that about 25 per cent of teachers have service of aides. Secretarial assistance, 72 per cent, is the most frequent help among 11 kinds studied.

U. S. Department of Health, Education, and Welfare, *Staffing For Better Schools,* pp. 13-26. Superintendent of Documents, Catalog No. FS 5.223:23049, Washington, D. C.: Government Printing Office, 1967. Reports that aides relieve teachers of routine tasks, and that the time gained is spent on lesson and homework preparation and on recitation. Services of home-visiting aides, child-care aides, and lay readers are presented. Volunteers are considered.

Wright, Betty Atwell, *Teacher Aides to the Rescue.* New York: Day, 1969. Advocates the use of program guidelines for better home-school-community partnerships through the use of teacher aides. The various uses, duties, and types of teacher aides are discussed.

Audiovisual and Other Resources

Aides to Teachers and Children (bulletin, 64 pp., $1.50). Identifies aides and their activities. Association for Childhood Education International, 3615 Wisconsin Avenue, N.W., Washington, D. C. 20016.

Teacher Aides At Work (booklet, 32 pp., $1). NEA, 1201 16th St., N. W., Washington D. C. 20036.

Teams for Learning (series of eight 16mm films, sound, b&w, $220.75). Illustrates issues and methods of teacher or teacher aide teams. National Audiovisual Center, Washington, D. C. 20036.

Interaction Analysis 39

Definition

Applied to education, interaction analysis is a system for observing, recording, and analyzing in quantitative terms the behavior of teachers and pupils as they interact in the classroom. Because of the way in which the technique developed, the term "interaction analysis" is commonly associated almost exclusively with verbal behavior.

There are several systems for analyzing the interaction of students and teacher, but the one best known and most frequently used is that developed by Ned A. Flanders in 1963. It provides for studying seven classifications of "teacher talk," two categories of "student talk," and a tenth factor referred to as "silence or confusion." The teacher's verbal expression that is accepting and tends to encourage or clarify is considered "indirect." Communication which expresses the teacher's opinion, gives directions, or criticizes is classified as "direct." A summary of Flanders's categories is presented on page 470. In the process, the qualitative aspects of the verbal communication are quantified in order to facilitate analysis. The purpose for which interaction analysis is used is based on the assumption that the verbal behavior patterns of teachers and pupils in the classroom are significantly related to the effectiveness of teaching and learning.

Verbal behavior of the teacher is tallied according to the appropriate categories and then recorded on a grid, which more easily permits interpretation. Influence which tends to limit the pupil's choice of response is classified as "direct," and that which tends to increase the student's freedom of response as "indirect."

Summary of
Categories For Interaction Analysis*

1. *ACCEPTS FEELING:* accepts and clarifies the feeling tone of the students in a nonthreatening manner. Feelings may be positive or negative. Predicting or recalling feelings is included.

2. *PRAISES OR ENCOURAGES:* praises or encourages student action or behavior. Jokes that release tension, but not at the expense of another individual; nodding head, or saying "um hm?" or "go on" are included.

3. *ACCEPTS OR USES IDEAS OF STUDENTS:* clarifying, building, or developing ideas suggested by a student. As teacher brings more of his own ideas into play, shift to Category 5.

4. *ASKS QUESTIONS:* asking a question about content or procedure with the intent that a student answer.

5. *LECTURING:* giving facts or opinions about content or procedures; expressing his own ideas, asking rhetorical questions.

6. *GIVING DIRECTIONS:* directions, commands, or orders with which a student is expected to comply.

7. *CRITICIZING OR JUSTIFYING AUTHORITY:* statements intended to change student behavior from nonacceptable to acceptable pattern; bawling someone out; stating why the teacher is doing what he is doing; extreme self-reference.

8. *STUDENT TALK-RESPONSE:* talk by students in response to teacher. Teacher initiates the contact or solicits student statement.

9. *STUDENT TALK-INITIATION:* talk by students, which they initiate. If "calling on" student is only to indicate who may talk next, observer must decide whether student wanted to talk. If he did, use this category.

*Edmund J. Amidon and Ned A. Flanders, "Interaction Analysis and Inservice Training," *Journal of Experimental Education* XXXVII, No. 1 (1968): 128.

10.* *SILENCE OR CONFUSION:* pauses, short periods of silence, and periods of confusion in which communication cannot be understood by the observer.

In the Flanders system, verbal behavior is coded at three-second intervals. The coding may be done by a trained observer either in the classroom or from a tape recording at any subsequent time. The purpose of the coding is to quantify the data in terms of its nature and frequency so that it readily can be summarized and analyzed on an objective basis. Its specificity and objectivity provide a common ground for the teacher and the analyst to consider the teacher's directive and nondirective verbal influence. The coding should not be misconstrued as indicating that all direct behavior is bad, nor that all indirect influence is good.

Since the process involves spontaneous verbal behavior and considers only limited aspects of the teaching-learning situation, it is well suited to analysis of both preservice and inservice performance. As in microteaching, its purpose is not evaluation or rating of teachers; it is designed as a tool to provide an objective basis for analysis and subsequent improvement of instruction.

Significant Components   *Which ones are essential?*

1. It must be understood that the purpose of the process is the improvement of teaching and learning.
2. Emphasis is shifted from direct, teacher-initiated response to indirect, student-initiated behavior.
3. The focus is placed upon positive verbal reinforcement.
4. Both cognitive and affective aspects of communication are considered.
5. Rapport and unity of purpose must be established between teacher and analyst.
6. The significance of the relationship between teacher behavior and pupil reaction must be recognized.
7. The process must be objectified so that the outcome is determined by the performance of the teacher rather than by the preconceived notions of the analyst.

*There is NO scale implied by these numbers. Each number is classificatory; it designates a particular kind of communication event. To write these numbers down during observation is to enumerate—not to judge a position on a scale.

8. To increase validity and reliability, provision can be made for a team of coders or a variety of systems.

9. The willingness of the teacher to be analyzed and his desire to improve his performance are essential so that he will volunteer to participate.

10. Recognition of the inherent value of classroom give-and-take is the vital component of the system.

11. To secure observer reliability, teachers should be given training before becoming observers.

12. The administration of the school must understand the system and be supportive of it.

13. To minimize fear and suspicion, data should not be used for administrative purposes.

14. Wherever possible, the teacher should be allowed to select his own analyst.

15. Sufficient time should be provided for follow-up discussion between teacher and analyst.

16. Behavior must be free and spontaneous so that experimentation is encouraged.

17. Evaluator and teacher must feel that they are working together for better teaching and learning.

Proposed Advantages   *With which ones do you agree?*

1. Interaction analysis provides rapid feedback.

2. The system recognizes behavioral goals by indicating specifically the criteria on which performance will be evaluated.

3. The analysis lends itself equally well to preservice and in-service improvement efforts.

4. The system accepts the ideas and performance of students and teachers.

5. Questioning is improved.

6. Teachers are stimulated to adopt creative modes of interaction following unexpected response from students.

7. The process provides a basis for conceptualizing abstract and complex functions and for developing understandable generalizations about them.

8. Students and their ideas are better understood and more readily accepted.

9. Analyzing behavior tends to bridge the gap between theory of instruction, child psychology, and organization of material on the one hand and performance of teachers and pupils on the other.

10. The total climate for learning is improved.
11. Specificity of the variables makes them meaningful and focuses attention on identifiable aspects of specific behavior.
12. Teachers are awakened to new purposes and identification of unique patterns of interaction.
13. The feedback makes teachers aware of different modes and levels of learning.
14. The process reveals discrepancies between what the teacher intends to do and what he actually does.
15. The system is a valuable tool for research because it provides objective data relating to the teaching act.
16. The data serve as a common ground for a supervisory conference, making it objective, meaningful, and relevant.
17. The development of indirect ways of communicating with students and relating to them is promoted.
18. Giving careful attention to detail and technical skill is essential whether teaching is looked upon as an art or a science.
19. Interaction analysis is a strong motivating force for both teachers and pupils.

Criticisms and Difficulties to Be Anticipated *Do you agree?*

1. Teachers mistrust the purposes of interaction analysis because it is new and strange.
2. Judgments may be made after too few visits or too little observation.
3. The analyst may not be skilled enough to insure reliability.
4. The whole process distorts the normalcy of the teaching situation.
5. Statements or questions of teachers are difficult to fit into a classification system.
6. Teachers may try to beat the game.
7. The whole system is too complicated and unwieldy and takes too much time and effort to explain to teachers.
8. The system implies that silence and confusion are the same.
9. The process tells the teacher where he is, but makes no suggestions for improvement.
10. Stressing only verbal behavior denies the importance of teaching style and many other important aspects of instruction.
11. Student teachers particularly may overlook the appropriateness factor and change their performance from one type of behavior to another too soon, too often, or too rapidly.

12. Coding verbal behavior destroys the wholeness of the teaching act.
13. The system tries to make a science out of an art, disregarding the intricate nature of teaching.
14. The system overlooks the unique qualities and strengths of each teacher.
15. Too few trained observers are available.
16. Administrators will insist on using the data for purposes for which they were not intended.
17. Focusing attention on minutiae of a narrow and rigid system like interaction analysis does not serve to improve teaching; it destroys it.

Summary Assessment

The beginnings of the program of interaction analysis can be traced to early research by Kurt Lewin, Ronald Lippett, and Ralph White relating to autocratic, democratic, and laissez-faire leadership qualities. The Flanders method is the best known and most widely used of the verbal analysis systems. Others, however, are being developed. Some of them are merely modifications or adaptations of the Flanders technique and limit themselves to verbal behavior. Others, using the same general approach, propose to incorporate more aspects of the teacher's performance. The OScAR V4 (Observation Schedule and Record 4, Verbal), for example, considers the time a teacher spends in management and instruction. Charles Galloway's work with nonverbal interaction is gaining recognition as a tool for studying another significant aspect of the teaching act.

Although research evidence of its value is not conclusive, interaction analysis has proved itself as a method for gathering one type of objective data and summarizing it. It has established itself as a good tool for diagnosis and improvement. It has also called attention to the relationship between what a teacher does and the influence his performance has upon learners. Those who are concerned about the fact that the Flanders system considers only verbal behavior fail to recognize that that is all it proposes to analyze. Then, too, verbal communication has been, and is likely to continue to be, a very important aspect of almost all teaching and learning. Many methods and instruments are available to examine the areas of teaching and learning that interaction analysis of any type does not attempt to study.

Interaction analysis contributes significantly to identification of verbal behavior patterns that affect learning both positively and negatively. It helps teachers and supervisors in analyzing performance and in planning appropriate behavioral changes.

Although to date it has been used mainly with student teachers, the concept is gaining broader acceptance. The approach is likely to spread to include many aspects of teaching other than verbal interaction. Its use will increase in both the preservice and inservice training of school personnel, and its value will become more significant in research and supervision as teaching continues to mature as a profession.

A Few Leaders in the Movement

Edmund J. Amidon
  Temple Univ.
Joseph C. Bondi
  Univ. of Southern Florida
Merl E. Bonney
  North Texas State Univ.
Ned A. Flanders
  Univ. of Michigan
Charles M. Galloway
  Ohio State Univ.
Norman E. Gronlund
  Univ. of Illinois

John B. Hough
  Syracuse Univ.
Philip Jackson
  Univ. of Chicago
Richard L. Ober
  Univ. of Florida
Bernard Queen
  Marshall Univ.
Phil E. Suiter
  Marshall Univ.
John Withall
  Penn State Univ.

A Few Places Where the Innovation Is Used

Appalachia Educational
  Laboratory
Ball State Univ.
Baltimore County, Md.
Claremont, Calif.
Marywood College
Miami Univ.

Ohio State Univ.
Penn State Univ.
Provo, Utah
St. Martin's College
Temple Univ.
Univ. of Florida
Univ. of Maryland

Univ. of Michigan
Univ. of New Hampshire
Univ. of South Florida
Univ. of Wisconsin
Whitman College

Annotated References

Ager, Merlin, "Dogmatism and the Verbal Behavior of Student Teachers," *The Journal of Teacher Education*, XXI, No. 2 (1970), 179-183. Reports how verbal behavior of student teachers as measured by the Flanders system is used to validate the Rokeach *Dogmatism Scale* of openness or closedness in personality. The relationship between the two instruments is not statistically significant.

Allen, Paul M., et al., *Teacher Self-Appraisal: A Way of Looking Over Your Own Shoulder*. Worthington, Ohio: Charles A. Jones, 1970. Presents procedures for helping teachers in self-evaluation. The qualities approach, changes in students, and teacher performance are reviewed. Ways of observing and recording teacher behavior, stabilizing viewpoints in observation, and techniques of evaluating behavior are explained.

Amidon, Edmund J. and Ned A. Flanders, *The Role of the Teacher in the Classroom.* Minneapolis: Association for Productive Teaching, 1967. A manual for use with teachers for an inservice workshop in Flanders Interaction Analysis. Material is presented simply and clearly.

Amidon, Edmund and John H. Hough, eds., *Interaction Analysis: Theory Research and Application.* Reading, Mass.: Addison-Wesley, 1967. A collection of papers about early and current coding practices. The book is divided into three sections: 1) background and theory, 2) interaction analysis—procedures and research on teaching patterns, and 3) the application of interaction-analysis to problems of teacher education.

Amidon, Edmund and Elizabeth Hunter, *Improving Teaching—The Analysis of Classroom Verbal Interaction.* New York: Holt, 1966. Case studies illustrating how teaching is improved through more effective verbal interaction. The aspects of teaching here discussed are motivating, planning, informing, leading discussion, disciplining, counseling, and evaluating.

Biddle, Bruce J. and William J. Ellena, eds., *Contemporary Research on Teacher Effectiveness,* pp. 196-231. New York: Holt, 1964. A report by Flanders of an investigation of teacher performance and influence on pupil attitude and achievement. Pupils learned more and were more positive and independent when the teacher's approach was indirect. Need for evaluation, new criteria of effectiveness, and improved data-gathering devices is stressed.

Bondi, Joseph C., Jr., "Feedback from Interaction Analysis: Some Implications for the Improvement of Teaching," *The Journal of Teacher Education,* XXI, No. 2 (1970), 189-196. Reports a study of the effects of feedback on the verbal behavior of 40 elementary student teachers as measured by the Flanders system. In 15 to 24 analyses the behavior of the experimental group differed significantly.

————, "The Effects of Interaction Analysis Feedback on the Verbal Behavior of Student Teachers," *Educational Leadership,* XXVI, No. 8 (1969), 794-799. An experimental study involving control and experimental groups, each consisting of 20 student teachers from the University of South Florida. The group receiving feedback from interaction analysis was superior in all 13 categories of a modified Flanders system.

Bosley, Howard E., *Teacher Education in Transition,* pp. 249-261. Baltimore: Multi-State Teacher Education Project, 1962. Explains four ways of providing feedback for the teacher to improve his classroom performance including interaction analysis, microteaching, a generalized planning model, and the concept of teaching strategies. Emphasizes the necessity of privacy and freedom from threat.

Chapline, Elaine B., "A Case Study in Interaction Analysis Matrix Interpretation," in *Teaching,* Ronald T. Hyman, ed. Philadelphia: Lippincott, 1968, pp. 265-271. Presents a matrix interpretation in interaction analysis. A model of a matrix for mathematical interpretation is explained.

Crispin, D. P., "Technology of Interaction," *Educational Technology,* X, No. 7 (1970), 13-17. Defines and describes interaction analysis and explains the quantitative treatment of data. The approaches include analysis by percentages, ratios, and analysis of matrices.

Davidson, Roscoe L., "Teacher Influence and Children's Levels of Thinking," *The Reading Teacher,* XXII, No. 8 (1969), 702-704. Reports research revealing the importance of teacher performance in developing higher levels of thinking in children. Teachers have control over the types of questions posed for directing thinking patterns.

Flanders, Ned A., *Analyzing Teaching Behavior.* Reading, Mass.: Addison-Wesley, 1970. A volume providing both general information on the analysis of the chain of events that constitutes teaching and technical data for developing skill in coding. Search for interaction patterns that improve instruction is the crux of the matter.

————, "Teacher Influence, Pupil Attitudes, and Achievement," in *Teaching,* Ronald T. Hyman, ed., pp. 251-265. Philadelphia: Lippincott, 1968. Summary report of Flanders's system of interaction analysis by its original designer.

French, Russell L. and Charles M. Galloway, "A New Look at Classroom Interactions," *Educational Leadership,* XXVII, No. 6 (1970), 548-552. Suggests a model based on a system to code the personal, institutional, and task events of the classroom. The three types of events and their significance are described.

Galloway, Charles M., "Nonverbal Communication in Teaching," in *Teaching,* Ronald T. Hyman, ed., pp. 70-77. Philadelphia: Lippincott, 1968. Discusses what nonverbal communication is. The author cites examples and postulates categories for their analysis.

Good, T. L. and J. E. Brophy, "Teacher-Child Dyadic Interactions: A New Method of Classroom Observation," *Journal of School Psychology,* VIII, No. 2 (1970), 131-138. Presents a new system for analysis of verbal classroom interaction, referred to as "dyadic." The system is similar to Flanders's, but introduces significant variations.

Hough, John B., Ernest E. Lohman, and Richard Ober, "Shaping and Predicting Verbal Teaching Behavior in a General Methods Course," *The Journal of Teacher Education,* XX, No. 2 (1969), 213-224. An experimental study of the effectiveness of two types of training designs for improving the verbal behavior of students in preservice teacher education. One group used the Flanders 10-category system and microteaching; the other studied verbal teaching behavior without a formal system. Indirect teaching behavior prevailed in the experimental group.

Hughes, Marie M., "What is Teaching: One Viewpoint," in *Teaching,* Ronald T. Hyman, ed., pp. 271-284. Philadelphia: Lippincott, 1968. Condenses an outline of Provo Code. A case study of 41 elementary teachers was examined. Conclusion: different patterns of teaching affect the learning of children.

Lantz, Donald L., "The Relationship of University Supervisors and Supervising Teachers' Ratings to Observed Student Teachers' Behavior," *American Educational Research Journal,* IV, No. 1 (1967), 279-88. An experimental study of the supervisors' perception of student teachers' interpersonal behavior and independent observation of the behavior using interaction analysis. The two were significantly related.

Lewis, Wilbert W., John M. Newell, and John Withall, "An Analysis of Classroom Patterns of Communication," in *Teaching,* Ronald T. Hyman, ed., pp. 48-58. Philadelphia: Lippincott, 1968. Describes and evaluates a new set of observational categories. Teachers were told how to behave in a predetermined way in order to test the sensitivity of the new categories.

Mager, Robert F., *Developing Attitude Toward Learning.* Palo Alto: Fearon, 1968. Discusses the various ways teachers interact with students and the diverse effects differing verbal and behavioral responses can have upon student attitudes. The intricate nature of classroom interaction is detailed.

Medley, Donald M. and Russell A. Hill, "Dimensions of Classroom Behavior Measured by Two Systems of Interaction Analysis," *Educational Leadership,* XXVI, No. 8 (1969), 821-824. Compares the use of Flanders's interaction analysis and OScAR 4V. The strong points of each method are presented with the suggestion that both be used together.

Minnis, Douglas, "Interacting in the Interrogative," *Journal of Teacher Education,* XX, No. 4 (1969), 201-212. Another system of interaction analysis called CLAIM is described and compared with Flanders's interaction analysis. Values of CLAIM are supported by the research reported.

Moriber, George, "Wait Time in College Science Classes," *Science Education,* LV, No. 3 (1971), 321-328. "Wait time is the amount of time after a question is asked that a teacher waits before accepting or supplying an answer." College instructors allow little time for thought, tend to call on the first student who volunteers and cannot be urged to increase the amount of wait time. It was assumed that emphasis on testing and grades forced the instructor to devote as much time as possible to making the testable information clear.

Ober, Richard L., "The Nature of Interaction Analysis," *High School Journal,* LI, No. 1 (1967), 7-16. Explains in detail the operation of the Flanders system, its use, and value in helping teachers to perform six listed operations important for effective teaching. Positive results are reported from three research studies.

Oliver, Donald W. and James P. Shaver, "Teacher Style and the Analysis of Student-Teacher Dialogue," in *Teaching,* Ronald T. Hyman, ed., pp. 404-420. Philadelphia: Lippincott, 1968. An investigation into two styles of teaching: recitation teaching and Socratic teaching. New categories are set up for this analysis.

Papalia, A., "Students' Feedback and Continuance in Spanish," *Hispania,* LIV, No. 1 (1971), 108-109. A case study of verbal interaction and its relationship to continuing with the study of foreign language. A positive correlation is reported between indirect teacher talk and the students' continuing in their study of the language.

Perkins, Hugh V., "A Procedure for Assessing the Classroom Behavior of Students and Teachers," in *Teaching,* Ronald T. Hyman, ed., pp. 285-294. Philadelphia: Lippincott, 1968. Perkins made his own system with a few categories borrowed from Flanders. He collected data and compared the results with data from Hughes's Provo Code and Flanders's system of interaction analysis.

Pickett, Laurel Anne, "Can The Level of Instruction Be Raised Through the Use of Interaction Analysis?" *Educational Leadership,* XXVII, No. 6 (1970), 597-600. Report of a research study attempting to determine the relationship between cognitive level of questioning and indirectness. A small negative correlation is found. Number and level of teacher questions are also unrelated.

Psencik, Leroy F., "Interaction Analysis Improves Classroom Instruction," *The Clearing House,* XLIII, No. 9 (1969), 555-560. Defines interaction analysis, its purposes and procedures, and cites five ground rules for effective analysis. Major considerations are interaction analysis for inservice training and future prospectives.

Queen, Bernarde and Phil E. Suiter, *Interaction Analysis—A Self Instructional Program for Teachers.* Charleston: Appalachia Educational Laboratory, 1968. Detailed analysis of Flanders's interaction analysis. The manual explains technical aspects of the system with specific suggestions and procedures for its use.

Rosenshine, Barak, "Interaction Analysis: A Tardy Comment," *Phi Delta Kappan,* LI, No. 8 (1970), 445-446. Insists that results of 12 studies previously reported as showing relationships between teacher behavior and pupil growth are inconclusive. Limitations of the studies raise a question about applying their findings with confidence.

Shrable, Kenneth and Douglas Minnis, "Interacting in the Interrogative," *Journal of Teacher Education,* XX, No. 2 (1969), 201-211. Establishes a system for objective feedback from interaction resulting from various types of teacher questioning. The report, limited to verbal response only, analyzes three levels of complexity of thinking and of questioning. They are data recall, data processing, and application.

Smith, Othanel, "Recent Research on Teaching and Interpretation," *High School Journal,* LI, No. 2 (1967), 63-74. Interprets recent research studies of teaching behavior in cognitively and affectively oriented systems and in those involving both the affective and cognitive. Analysis of teaching reflects the different conceptual orientation of the researchers.

Stuck, G. B. and M. D. Wyne, "Study of Verbal Behavior in Special and Regular Elementary School Classrooms," *American Journal of Mental Deficiency,* LXXV, No. 4 (1971), 463-469. Draws conclusions from a study of 27 public school classrooms in order to assess the relationship between types of teacher-pupil interaction. The Flanders system was used.

Verduin, John R., Jr., *Conceptual Models in Teacher Education.* Washington, D. C.: The American Association of Colleges for Teacher Education, 1967. A chapter providing detailed information for using the Flanders system. Many meaningful patterns can be ascertained from the matrix that enables the teacher to adjust his behavior.

Audiovisual and Other Resources

Basic Interaction Analysis Training Course (audiotape, reel or cassette $179.50). Self-contained series by Edmund J. Amidon for training teachers and supervisors in verbal interaction analysis. Association for Productive Teaching, 5408 Chicago Ave., S., Minneapolis, Minn. 55417.

Interaction Analysis Training Kits (Level I and Level II training kits, includes tapes and optional transparencies). Level I—28 segments of live classroom interaction (K-12) $13.50; Level II—17 segments of interaction illustrating different teaching patterns, $14.50). Association for Productive Teaching, 5408 Chicago Ave., S., Minneapolis, Minn. 55417.

Skill Development in Teaching (self-instructional, inservice or preservice package in interaction analysis and microteaching, videotapes, manual, guidebooks, exercise books, transparencies, and audiotapes, $200). Association for Productive Teaching, 5408 Chicago Ave., S., Minneapolis, Minn. 55417.

Microteaching   40

Definition

Microteaching is a teacher-training and improvement technique developed at Stanford University in the early sixties. Although video taping is not a requirement, microteaching commonly involves video taping a short lesson, usually of five- to ten-minute duration, playing it back, making a critique of it, and repeating the operation to improve certain components of the microlesson. It is used principally in the preservice education of teachers, for the improvement of teachers in service, and for research involving the study of the teaching and learning process. The number of students involved is small, usually four to six.

For these purposes, microteaching has advantages over regular teaching in that the analysis of the performance is based upon incidents and acts that are specific and can be replayed. Many of the constraints of the normal classroom can be eliminated, and controlled conditions can be developed. The performance can be observed by the teacher himself or by him and his supervisor or colleagues. The feedback is real and rapid. A record is made so that an original teaching performance can be kept for comparison with refinements in subsequent reteaching.

By reducing the usual complexities involved in the classroom, attention can be focused upon a limited number of techniques. Feedback is obtained from the video tape, the reaction of stu-

480

dents, the teacher's own observation and analysis, and the suggestions of other observers such as supervisors. The review makes immediate and individual diagnosis possible and suggests ways of improving. Reteaching can take place immediately after the review and critical analysis of the microlesson or at any subsequent time.

Most of the early work with these scaled-down models was done on college campuses in programs of preservice teacher education. Prime focus was on preparing candidates for student teaching, assisting them in improving their student teaching, and adding meaning to theory in traditional methods courses. The use of taped microlessons was then applied to teaching and learning in such areas as speech and hearing therapy, teaching of the physically handicapped, typewriting, art, handwriting, and perceptual-motor development. The procedure was extended to the training of counselors, clinicians, therapists, and supervisory personnel. Positive results have been reported in many areas, particularly for interns and student teachers. Numerous studies indicate a significant reduction in time required to attain various levels of proficiency in performance. A positive relationship has repeatedly been reported between evaluation of microteaching performance and later assessment of effectiveness in the classroom. Important contributions have been made to breaking down the teaching act into recognizable elements, and some progress has been reported in reaching agreement on criteria of teaching success.

The early popularity of microteaching on college campuses is perhaps the natural result of the climate that prevails among the trainees there. The focus is on improvement. College students in preparation for teaching consider identification of difficulties and efforts to improve performance as the basic purpose of their teacher-training programs. Teachers in service, on the other hand, may feel threatened by attempts to analyze their performance and to evaluate their effectiveness. They associate a move in this direction with renewal of contracts, salaries, promotion, and tenure. It is for that same reason perhaps that microteaching has been used infrequently in studying the effectiveness of college instructors.

One of the promising outcomes of these experiences with microteaching has been the increasing tendency of prospective teachers and teachers in service to use the tapes privately for self-evaluation. More and more teachers are discussing the recordings with supervisors and trusted colleagues. As the strangeness and fear of microteaching wear off, teachers are more frequently volunteering as subjects for experimentation and in-service improvement programs. Taping and analyzing classroom interaction is now moving forward rapidly in elementary and secondary schools. Fortunately current efforts appear to be giving more attention to pupil learning than to teacher performance.

Teachers and supervisors are discovering that operation of the equipment is not as difficult as they once thought. A compact, portable video-tape unit, which can easily be moved from one room to another, can be purchased for under $2,000. Zoom lenses, portable cameras, and film cartridges have simplified the operation and made it more effective. Most teachers feel they can do a reasonably good job with the equipment after an hour's training under an experienced technician. The completion of the first good tape usually marks an important point in the development of the teacher's interest in microteaching and his eagerness to experiment with possible uses of video taping for other purposes.

Significant Components   *Which ones are essential?*

1. The purposes of the microlesson must be clearly understood, and the technique to be analyzed must be identified and defined in behavioral terms.
2. Careful and detailed planning is essential.
3. Only supervisors, teacher-education instructors, and fellow-teachers with positive, helpful attitudes and manners can be effective in microteaching.
4. The trainee must feel free from threat so that he is willing and ready to experiment and risk the possibility of failure.
5. Microteaching should be looked upon as a valuable aid to improving competencies, not as a program complete in itself.
6. Lessons must be considered as bases for diagnosis and refinement rather than as models of perfection.
7. Skilled and experienced supervisors are not always a necessity, but are a distinct advantage.
8. Trust and respect between teacher and evaluator are essential for open and constructive criticism or evaluation sessions.
9. The amount of time devoted to the instruction must depend upon the problems under consideration, the needs of the trainees, and their levels of competence.
10. Adequate space and equipment are essential.

11. Provisions for utilizing microteaching for research should be built into the total program.
12. The entire procedure must be adapted to the needs, purposes, and prevailing conditions peculiar to each trainee or situation.
13. Video taping is not essential, but it is a great advantage in that it displays an objective record of the lesson and allows for immediate or delayed analysis and criticism.
14. Video taping also provides for private self-evaluation by the trainee.
15. Although they are often difficult to secure, groups of students are vital for microteaching.
16. The process should capitalize on its opportunity for immediate feedback.
17. The evaluator should be sensitive to the total climate and be careful not to go faster or further than the trainee wants to go at a given time.
18. The trainee must be able to describe precisely the skill under study, know for what purpose it is to be used, recognize it when he sees it, and know when and under what conditions it is appropriate.

Proposed Advantages   *With which ones do you agree?*

1. Microteaching shifts attention from generalized competencies to specific behavioral acts of the teacher.
2. The process is equally effective for training teachers initially, for improving the skills of experienced teachers of different skill and maturity levels, and for enhancing the performance of supervisors.
3. Analysis of the subject matter, the performance of the teacher, reaction of students, and appropriateness of various activities can be studied by this method.
4. The record that is preserved allows different people to observe the performance and make a critique of it at different times.
5. When desired, alterations readily can be made in the various components.
6. Comments of the supervisor are definite, understandable, and relevant because they pertain to precise acts.
7. The system can be used for improving all aspects of teaching, from grooming to intricate matters of teacher-student interaction.
8. Ideas can be tested in a reasonably realistic setting without great danger to the teacher or his pupils.

9. In the preservice program, microteaching relieves many of the tensions experienced by the neophyte when he confronts a large class in his first experience.

10. By giving a trainee and supervisor a chance to talk alone, the process reduces the embarrassment common in classroom supervision.

11. Microteaching takes less time than traditional student teaching to produce comparable results.

12. The system can be used in any college course, including those designed for the preparation of supervisors and administrators.

13. The teacher can see if his strategies and techniques are doing what he wants them to do.

14. The trainee becomes sensitive to both verbal and nonverbal behavior and to the fact that improvement requires careful reflection and continuous refinement.

15. For research purposes, the microlesson can reduce the range of factors in the teaching-learning situation, readily manipulate variables, and keep factors extraneous to the techniques at a minimum.

16. Involvement in the procedure quickens the preservice student's interest in being a teacher and stimulates the experienced teacher's desire for self-improvement by making the improvement process enjoyable and observable.

17. By comparing subsequent performances with earlier ones, the process vividly portrays growth in skill and develops confidence by displaying observable improvement in performance.

18. The specificity of microteaching enables the teacher to develop concrete ways of implementing such generalizations as "making the lesson more interesting," "demonstrating greater enthusiasm," or "motivating the student."

19. A supervisor who works together with a teacher in analyzing specific performance and making definite suggestions is likely to be fair and helpful and to be recognized as such by the trainee.

20. The supervisor will grow in his skill in identifying and improving important components of teaching.

Criticisms and Difficulties to Be Anticipated   *Do you agree?*

1. Microteaching conveys the impression that the teacher, rather than the student, is the important figure in the lesson.

2. Microteaching is artificial because it eliminates many of the complexities of teaching in the classroom.

3. The short lesson may not fit in naturally, be representative of the activities of a longer period, or be long enough to illustrate many valuable strategies.
4. Supervisors may be overcritical.
5. Continuous concentration on small segments of a lesson and on precise behavior destroys the art of teaching.
6. The small group of students in the class do not put skills and techniques to a real test.
7. The process focuses attention on such factors as grooming, gestures, and voice rather than on more important aspects of teaching, such as pupil-teacher interaction.
8. The outward appearance of skills and techniques may overshadow their appropriateness and inherent value.
9. Equipment is costly, required supervisory time is excessive, and it is difficult to secure students.
10. There are so many things that can go wrong with schedules, persons, and equipment.
11. Trainees, especially teachers in service, may be resistant to participating.
12. Inadequate organization and administration render microteaching ineffective.
13. Little opportunity is provided for experiencing the normal flow of activities that exists in the regular classroom as students move from one learning experience to another.

Summary Assessment

Because of its adaptability, its provision for feedback and reuse, and its focus on specific acts and skills, microteaching has generated great interest on the part of trainees and supervisors. By reducing the complexities of the typical classroom, the teaching-learning environment can be manipulated by the process to direct attention to a limited number of specific techniques. This focus is helpful to both teacher and student.

Because the procedure promotes learning through involvement, reflection, and self-evaluation, it provides unusual opportunity for improvement in teacher competence. Showing him how he has performed is strong motivation for the trainee. Yet the situation is somewhat artificial since few regular classrooms resemble the microteaching model. Criteria of teaching effectiveness are still far from being agreed upon. The appropriateness of different forms of teacher behavior with different children in different situations has not yet been settled. Neither has the precise relationship between the various elements of teacher performance and pupil learning been determined. Study needs to continue to improve ways of changing teacher attitudes and behavior as they relate to children and learning.

Although microteaching has not been without problems, it has had great appeal and promises to become even more popular and valuable as its processes are refined. Students in preparation for teaching, teachers in service, college instructors, supervisory personnel, and researchers are becoming increasingly aware of its motivational power and its potentialities for producing changes in instructional behavior.

At the present time leaders in the movement are satisfied that they have developed an important tool for motivating and effecting significant improvement in the preservice education of teachers. The elementary and secondary schools sense the possibilities that lie in using laboratory conditions to identify and study a few elements of teaching and learning at a time. They propose to use findings made to date to develop better ways of describing, developing, and assessing effective teaching. In so doing they can build feelings of greater accomplishment and the self-assurance needed to meet the challenges of accountability.

Schools and colleges currently are exploring the possible contribution that video taping can make to studying nonverbal behavior, interaction analysis, and differences in children's learning styles. One school is exploring the potential of video taping for discovering and correcting student deficiences in typewriting. Another is experimenting with it in reporting pupil progress to parents. A superintendent is using it to find out whether or not he in reality is providing professional leadership for his board of education. A high school principal is trying to get at the root of some of the problems in the cafeteria and instructional materials center. An elementary principal is using video tape in an effort to improve his teachers' meetings. An elementary teacher is using it to study differences in behavior of individual pupils when they are working on mathematical problems and when they are engaged with language arts exercises. A supervisor is searching for better ways of conducting one-to-one conferences with teachers. A personnel director is using tapes of microlessons to screen candidates applying for teaching positions.

The possible applications of the findings of the past decade relating to the use of microteaching and video taping for improving teaching and learning are practically boundless. They appear to be limited only by the imagination and energy of teachers everywhere and their willingness to continue the search for better ways of doing old and new things.

As they come to realize that microteaching is basically a strategy for improving teaching and learning, not for rating teachers, educators will feel less threatened and be less threatening about participating in recorded performances and in systematic evaluation of them. Innovations in goals, methods, and materials give experienced teachers a feeling of need for lifelong improvement. Microteaching makes continuous growth in proficiency attractive and exciting by providing a vehicle for cooperative effort among all those engaged in the educational enterprise. It is likely to be used more extensively for research, for improvement of college instruction, for training of supervisory personnel, and for enhancing learning opportunities for children. Its future looks bright.

A Few Leaders in the Movement

Keith Acheson
  Univ. of Oregon
Dwight W. Allen
  Univ. of Massachusetts
Horace Aubertine
  Colorado State Univ.
W. R. Borg
  Far West Laboratory for Educational Research and Development
Robert N. Bush
  Stanford Univ.
James M. Cooper
  Univ. of Houston
Jimmie C. Fortune
  Memphis State Univ.
Nathaniel L. Gage
  Stanford Univ.

Warren Kallenbach
  San Jose State College
John Koran
  Univ. of Texas
Frederick McDonald
  Oklahoma State Univ.
James Olivero
  Southwestern Cooperative Education Laboratory
Michael E. J. Orme
  Indiana Univ.
Kevin Ryan
  Univ. of Chicago
David B. Young
  Univ. of Maryland

A Few Places Where the Innovation Is Used

Brigham Young Univ.
Chadron State College
Chicago, Ill.
Detroit, Mich.

Eastern Illinois Univ.
Friends Univ.
Gainesville, Ga.
Howard Co., Md.

Jefferson Co., Colo.
Johns Hopkins Univ.
New Mexico State Univ.

Northeast Louisiana
   College
Pacific Univ.
Providence College
St. Mary's Dominican
   College

San Jose State College
Stanford Univ.
Univ. of Houston
Univ. of Illinois
Univ. of Maryland

Univ. of Massachusetts
Univ. of Texas
Vanderbilt Univ.
West Virginia Univ.

Annotated References

Adams, Raymond S. and Bruce J. Biddle, *Realities of Teaching-Explorations With Video Tape.* New York: Holt, 1970. Explains how microteaching translates learning and teaching theory into practice through the use of video tape. Taking prospective teachers into the classroom by means of television adds reality and meaning to abstractions in teacher preparation.

Allen, Dwight, "Microteaching: A New Framework for In-Service Education," *The High School Journal,* XLIX, No. 8 (1966), 355-362. Explains the purposes and uses of microteaching as a diagnostic and evaluative technique. The author points up the importance of rapid feedback and the opportunity for the teacher to try new approaches for effective teaching styles.

Allen, Dwight and Kevin Ryan, *Microteaching.* Reading, Mass.: Addison-Wesley, 1969. Defines microteaching, its uses, and the video taping approach to studying and improving the component skills of prospective teachers. Detailed plans for operating a program for preservice training of elementary teachers and personnel in other settings are outlined.

Bosley, Howard E., *Teacher Education In Transition, Volume I* pp. 249-261. Baltimore: Multi-State Teacher Education Project, 1969. Examines the effectiveness of microteaching and interaction analysis used in combination for achieving given objectives. Privacy is provided through video tapes, the context of the classroom is preserved, and continuous feedback is provided.

————, *Teacher Education In Transition, Volume II, Emerging Roles and Responsibilities,* pp. 121-150. Baltimore: Multi-State Teacher Education Project, 1969. Devotes two chapters to a report of the use of microteaching in the training of elementary teachers and three examples of selected video applications in teacher education. The studies report very positive results.

Calabro, Hilda, "Microteaching and the Foreign Language Teacher," *Audiovisual Instruction,* XIV, No. 5 (1969), 62-63. Points up the value of this approach to teaching specific techniques for effective foreign language work. The article gives examples of how specific lessons dealing with speaking and reading skills can be used in a microteaching lesson by a foreign language teacher.

Edelfelt, Roy A., ed., *Innovative Programs In Student Teaching.* Baltimore: Maryland State Department of Education, 1969. Reports the Baltimore Conference on Student Teaching (1968). Microteaching, microteam teaching, and minicourses based on the microteaching concept are among the innovations reviewed.

Fortune, Jimmie C., James M. Cooper, and Dwight Allen, "The Stanford Summer Microteaching Clinic, 1965," *Journal of Teacher Education,* XVIII, No. 4 (1967), 389-393. Explains the training program involving 140 trainees in an intensive six-week microteaching experience. Details are given about specific things which were done each week. Significant changes in behavior of the trainees resulted.

Gardner, Marjorie and Rolland Bartholomew, "Microteaching," *Science Teacher,* XXXVI, No. 5 (1969), 45-47. Suggests uses of this technique for analyzing parts of science teaching such as questioning, establishing appropriate frames of reference, setting a model, controlling participation, stimulating involvement, recognizing nonverbal behavior, providing reinforcement, providing feedback, and achieving closure. The advantages are indicated.

Henry, George H., "Style of Teaching and Teacher Evaluation," *English Journal,* LIX, No. 7 (1970), 921-927. Points out that research in education must move out of the laboratory into the classroom. The use of video tape shows what actually happens rather than what theoretically should take place.

Kallenbach, W. Warren, "The Effectiveness of Microteaching in the Preparation of Elementary Intern Teachers," AERA Paper Abstracts. Washington, D. C.: American Educational Research Association, 1968. Compares two groups of students in teacher education, one using microteaching experience on campus, the other observation and actual teaching experience. The study showed no significant difference in effectiveness, but the microteaching experience consumed much less time.

Kallenbach, W. Warren and Meredith D. Gall, "Microteaching Versus Conventional Methods in Training Elementary Intern Teachers," *The Journal of Educational Research,* LXIII, No. 3 (1969), 136-141. Reports research investigating the relative effectiveness of microteaching and student teaching for prospective elementary teachers. Similar results are effected in less time. Economy of time and fewer administrative problems commend microteaching.

Klingstedt, Joe Lars, "Videotape Recorder: Aids Self-Improvement," *The Clearing House,* XLV, No. 6 (1971), 360. Recommends the use of the video tape recorder as a valuable information-gathering tool for teachers who want to become more effective. Cost, ease of operation, and immediate feedback are assets of the recorder.

Langer, Philip, "Minicourse: Theory and Strategy," *Educational Technology,* IX, No. 9 (1969), 54-59. Describes the minicourse which is basic to the idea of microteaching. Input, evaluation, and hoped-for changes in teacher behavior are emphasized.

McCollum, Robert and Donald LaDue, "Microteaching in a Teacher Education Program," *Social Education,* XXXIV, No. 3 (1970), 333-336. Presents exercises for influencing the teacher's role in the social studies classroom through practice and analysis of strategies and techniques. Lessons on drawing inferences and developing problematic situations are considered.

Olivero, James, *Microteaching: Medium for Improving Instruction.* Columbus, Ohio: Merrill, 1970. Gives a concise and easily understood analysis of microteaching. It stresses both the value of this technique in teacher training and as part of an inservice program.

Sandrin, James V. and Bob F. Steere, "Student Involvement in Teacher Education Programs," *School and Community,* LVII, No. 6 (1971, 16. Reports student involvement in teacher education at Missouri Southern College.

Selected students made microteaching episodes to be used as models for future students during the microteaching phase of their training.

Sparks, Rebecca L. and Earl L. McCallon, "Fostering Indirect Teaching Behavior in an Elementary Science Methods Course," *School Science and Mathematics,* LXXI, No. 5 (1971), 381-383. Concludes that preservice elementary school teachers enrolled in a science methods course and participating in a microteaching laboratory experience showed no significant increase in indirect verbal behavior although change in that direction occurred.

"Success With Microteaching," *School and Society,* XCVIII, No. 2325 (1970), 200. Reports that the success of microteaching as an inservice teacher training technique has led to the development of "minicourses"—self-instructional units for teachers.

"Teaching Teachers," *National Elementary Principal,* XLVIII, No. 4 (1969), 30-31. Explains the varied uses of microteaching in helping teachers become more effective in the classroom. Gives interesting reactions of one teacher who was involved in improving her techniques of questioning.

Wood, Robert W. and Roger Wess, "A Program in Microteaching for Prospective Elementary Teachers," *Supervisors Quarterly,* VI, No. 1 (1970), 24-27. Describes a microteaching program at the University of North Dakota developed because of limited student-teaching facilities. Success of the program led to its incorporation as part of a regular planned sequence during the junior year.

Young, David B., "The Modification of Teacher Behavior Using Video-Taped Models in a Microteaching Sequence," *Educational Leadership,* XXVI, No. 4, (1969), 394-403. Reviews the research, 1963-1968, on the effectiveness of perceptual and symbolic models in teacher education. The effect of supervisory guidance and of positive and negative models is described and tested.

Young, David B. and Dorothy A., "The Model in Use," *Theory Into Practice,* VII, (1968), 186-189. Discusses the use of microteaching in pre-training, workshop training, and evaluation. Specific steps used in sessions involving intern teachers are presented.

Audiovisual and Other Resources

Microteaching: Selected Papers (research bulletin, 52 pp., $1.50). Published in collaboration with the ERIC Clearinghouse on Teacher Education. Association of Teacher Educators, NEA, 1201 16th St., N.W., Washington, D. C. 20036.

Index

494   *Index*

The Authors

Herbert I. Von Haden and Jean Marie King are dedicated to improving education, but neither believes in change for the sake of change. This book, their second on innovations, reflects the spirit of open inquiry they advocate. The authors have researched hundreds of current books and articles, interviewed fellow educators, and critically listened at countless conferences and meetings to assess the prevailing thought and practices described here.

Both authors are practicing educators. H. I. Von Haden is chairman of the Department of Curriculum, Miami University in Oxford, Ohio, where he has served in teaching and administrative posts since 1947. He received his master's and doctor's degrees from the university of his native state, Wisconsin.

Throughout his academic career, Dr. Von Haden has been active in educational research and in efforts to encourage citizen participation in school affairs. In the early 1950's he organized a regional association of school boards which later became part of a statewide federation of boards. He continued to serve as a professional adviser to regional and state groups in a comprehensive program of inservice training for school officials and publication development.

He is a frequent contributor to journals and participant in school district survey studies. One of Dr. Von Haden's innovations in teacher training was a long-term practical workshop for educational personnel which has been granted credit status by his university. Dr. Von Haden, who is in demand as a speaker and consultant to numerous groups, recently received the university's distinguished service award.

Jean Marie King's interest in innovative practices is well demonstrated by her special interest in the middle school. She received one of the first certificates for middle school teachers issued by the State of Florida and currently teaches in an Alachua County middle school. Mrs. King has traveled extensively in this country and the Mediterranean, has studied in universities in Florida and Wisconsin, in addition to receiving the bachelor's degree from Wittenberg University and the master's degree from Miami University in Ohio. Mrs. King is the daughter of Dr. Von Haden.

DATE DUE

NOV - 9 75			
APR 1 7 '77			
SEP 25 '79			
DEC 1 1 1981			
JAN 3 0 '83			
NOV 1 0 1997			
GAYLORD			PRINTED IN U.S.A.